Claret & Cabs:

The Story of Cabernet Sauvignon

Also by Benjamin Lewin

In Search of Pinot Noir

Wine Myths and Reality

What Price Bordeaux?

Claret & Cabs:

The Story of Cabernet Sauvignon

Benjamin Lewin MW

Vendange Press
Dover, 2013

Library of Congress Cataloging-in-Publication Data
Lewin, Benjamin
Claret & Cabs: The Story of Cabernet Sauvignon / by
Benjamin Lewin
Includes bibliographical references and index.

ISBN 978-0-9837292-1-1

Library of Congress Control Number: 2012956391

Printed in China
1 2 3 4 5 6 7 8 9 10

Contents

for my constant companion

the anima figure

Preface

"Ripeness is all," runs a famous quotation from King Lear. This is truer for Cabernet Sauvignon than for any other grape variety. The story of Cabernet Sauvignon follows dramatic changes in style that are determined by the pursuit of ripeness, from the herbaceousness of classic Bordeaux to the blackcurrants or even cassis of Bordeaux or Napa today. In reflecting the concern, indeed you might almost say the obsession, with ripeness, and the increasing importance of the New World as a wine producer, Cabernet Sauvignon is a metaphor for the transformation of wine production worldwide over recent decades.

Our view of how Cabernet Sauvignon should taste is enormously colored by decisions on how ripe the grapes should be. In the period when Cabernet Sauvignon came to fame, ripeness was limited by climatic and other viticultural conditions, but today all restraints have been lifted. The historic view that Cabernet Sauvignon is associated with a certain austere herbaceousness reflected conditions (and attitudes) in Bordeaux at a time when few other places grew Cabernet Sauvignon. But today the variety has been disseminated around the world, almost always to places with warmer climates than Bordeaux. Now an international variety, Cabernet Sauvignon is more often associated with black fruits than green peppers. Is Bordeaux still the dominant influence on style or has leadership shifted elsewhere?

The main challenge to Bordeaux comes from Napa, but the relationship goes well beyond mere imitation. Many Napa producers started growing Cabernet Sauvignon, with or without the other Bordeaux varieties, in a conscious attempt to produce wine in a left bank style. After the Judgment of Paris tasting validated their efforts in 1976, Napa slowly developed its own style, giving vent to the richer fruits that are the natural product of its warmer climate. In time, grapes were harvested at greater ripeness, increased extraction occurred during fermentation, more new oak was used, and the controversial "international" style evolved. "Herbaceous" became a term of abuse. Aided by global warming, Bordeaux too has followed this path; we might ask to what extent recent vintages emulate Napa rather than the reverse? So the stakes are much more than whether Napa (or other regions) can produce wines that might be confused with Bordeaux: they are no less than the question of who defines the typicity of Cabernet Sauvignon.

The principal protagonists in this competition are no doubt Bordeaux and Napa, but the spread of Cabernet Sauvignon worldwide opens both up to new challenges. These come largely from the New World, with Chile and Australia at the forefront, but Argentina and South Africa are not to be neglected. Within Europe itself there has been less interest in challenging Bordeaux, but the super-Tuscans provide a formidable essay in Cabernet typicity. Cabernet Sauvignon's spread to new regions raises another question: if you are going to blend Cabernet Sauvignon, are the traditional Bordeaux varieties necessarily those that provide the greatest complementarity and complexity? Not to mention, of course, the question of whether in the era of greater ripeness it is necessary to blend at all.

The story is largely told through the eyes of the producers. For Bordeaux, the question is to what extent they hew to traditional aspirations and how far they want to go by responding in kind to the challenge of the New World. Within the New World, the question is reversed: whether and when they abandoned the initial impetus to imitate Bordeaux, and whether and how they have defined their own character. In Australia, there is a clear view that blended wines are inferior to pure varietals; in South America it is the other way round.

Cabernet Sauvignon also stands out for its domination of the cults and icons of the wine world. From the iconic First Growths of Bordeaux to the more recent cult wines of Napa, it is Cabernet Sauvignon that is most often in the news when price records are broken or very old wines are consumed. Cabernet Sauvignon ages longer than any other variety. Its range of styles is more extreme than any other variety, from generic Bordeaux or an entry-level New World Cabernet assisted by oak chips, to the most prestigious wines in the world. So Cabernet Sauvignon can mean very different things. Beyond defining the range of possibilities for Cabernet Sauvignon, the final question of this book is to ask what it should represent at its best.

What preface in a wine book would be complete without mentioning terroir? For all the vaunted influence of terroir, its effects are less obvious with Cabernet Sauvignon than with some other varieties. But it's a fair question whether Cabernet Sauvignon is best grown on gravel-based soils, as tradition in Bordeaux dictates, and what happens to its character on other soils. And are the new clones improving quality or imposing homogeneity? On top of all this is the age-old question of whether typicity is defined by the intrinsic interaction of variety and site, or whether in the case of Cabernet Sauvignon, winemaking is more responsible for our changing views.

A book like this would be impossible to write without the enthusiastic participation of producers, and I owe enormous thanks to those far too many to name individually for their patience in answering questions, and hospitality in providing tastings. Many producers' organizations were also helpful in making arrangements. Many thanks to all.

Benjamin Lewin

Note about Tastings

This is a book about how the typicity of Cabernet Sauvignon is determined in different regions, so producer profiles and tasting notes are intended to be representative rather than encyclopedic, and to illustrate the themes of the text. With regards to tasting notes, my recommendations for when wines should be drunk are conservative: the suggested window for drinking begins when I believe the tannins will become approachable, but ends with the start of tertiary development. Those accustomed to younger wines may feel able to start earlier; those who like older wines will be able to drink them beyond the indicated range. References in the text to the profiles and tasting notes are indicated by a ⍦ symbol.

Photographs heading chapters

Chapter 1 Grapevine flowering

Chapter 2. Château Grand Puy Lacoste in Pauillac

Chapter 3 The barrel room at Château Lafite

Chapter 4 A view of the Mayacamas Mountains from the To Kalon vineyard

Chapter 5 Over-ripe Cabernet Sauvignon

Chapter 6 Cabernet vineyards in Provence

Chapter 7 Cabernet under the Andes in Aconcagua Valley

Chapter 8 The Leeuwin Ridge in the background at Margaret River

Chapter 9 The famous tower at Château Latour

Front cover

Château Palmer (upper) and Robert Mondavi Winery (lower)

1

Incestuous Relationships

CABERNET SAUVIGNON is by far the world's most important black grape variety. But no one knows when or where it arose and was first used for making wine. My best guess is that this may have been after the Middle Ages on the left bank of Bordeaux.

Cabernet Sauvignon was certainly grown around Bordeaux long before it was grown anywhere else, but we do not know when it first appeared on the scene. It began to be propagated as an identified variety at the start of the eighteenth century. It's impossible to say exactly how long before that it actually originated.

Cabernet Sauvignon is not an ancient variety, but resulted from a chance cross between Cabernet Franc and Sauvignon Blanc.[1] This must have happened at a time and place when the black Cabernet Franc and the white Sauvignon Blanc were growing in close enough proximity for an exceptional cross-pollination event to create a new variety. (Because grapevines are self-fertilizing, cross-pollination is rare.)

Cabernet Sauvignon (left) originated from a cross between Cabernet Franc and Sauvignon Blanc (facing page).

Where was this most likely to happen? Although Cabernet Sauvignon's origins are relatively recent, they are difficult to pin down. On the other side of the river from Bordeaux, the right bank has been growing both black and white varieties, including Cabernet Franc and Sauvignon Blanc, since the twelfth century. But this is not fruitful territory for Cabernet Sauvignon; would that chance progeny have done well enough to be picked out for propagation? Running up from the city on the left bank, the Médoc is dominated by Cabernet Sauvignon and has focused on red wine as long as anyone can remember. "A small area to the northwest of Bordeaux famous for its wines, the Médoc produces excellent red wine under the name of vin de Bordeaux; there are few white wines, and they are not well regarded,"[2] was common wisdom in 1803. So would the Médoc have had enough white grapevines to provide an ancestor for Cabernet Sauvignon? And viticulture did not really develop there until the seventeenth century. Both Cabernet Franc and Sauvignon Blanc have been (and still are) grown in the Graves on the left bank to the south of the city, and Cabernet Sauvignon does well there: so in principle this is a more likely locale—but Cabernet Sauvignon became prominent in the Graves well after the Médoc. We may never know exactly.

When the new variety originated is impossible to say from the DNA mapping that identified its ancestors. Although Cabernet Sauvignon was first identified by name in the eighteenth century, it was not widely grown until near the end of the century. What appears to have been the same variety was previously described by various other names. Between the fourteenth and sev-

enteenth centuries would be a reasonable guess for an origin that would have allowed enough time for the variety to become established.

Six black grape varieties are grown in Bordeaux. All but one originate from crosses among a small group of ancestral varieties, among which Cabernet Franc is central. Merlot, the most important grape of the right bank (and indeed of Bordeaux as a whole), was generated by a cross between Cabernet Franc and a lost cultivar, later rediscovered and now named Magdelaine Noire des Charentes.[3] Magdelaine Noire was also one of the parents of Malbec. Carmenère (no longer grown in Bordeaux[4]) is a progeny of Cabernet Franc with another abandoned variety, Gros Cabernet. Among the black grapes, only Petit Verdot is not connected to the Cabernet group; and the origin of the other white grape, Sémillon, remains unknown. Sauvignon Blanc, important in its own right in Bordeaux and in the Loire, as well as for its parentage of Cabernet Sauvignon, probably originated somewhere in the region of the Loire.

If Bordeaux has an ancestral black grape, it is no doubt Cabernet Franc. Its position at the heart of the parental relationships means that it is the oldest of all the varieties. Cabernet Franc is closely related to two minor cultivars (Txakoli[5] and Morenoa) of the Basque region across the Pyrenees.[6] Mentioned as long ago as the sixteenth century in Rioja,[7] Txakoli Noir is also one of the parents of Gros Cabernet.

This makes it seem likely that Cabernet Franc's origins go back to the Pyrenees. When did it become planted in the Bordeaux region? Indirect evidence suggests it was the predominant grape by the Middle Ages. In 1635, "Cardinal

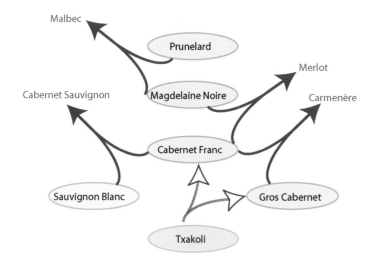

Bordeaux black varieties have incestuous relationships. Parents are shown in pink ovals; progeny varieties are in red.[8] Magdelaine Noire, Gros Cabernet, and Prunelard are minor or lost varieties.

This is the only remaining vine out of six planted in Bordeaux at the end of the eighteenth century by the Duverger family. The trunk has now reached 15 cms in diameter. Originally thought to be one of the Bordeaux varieties, it is in fact a Txakoli Noir (also known as Ondarrabi beltza).[9] It is ceremoniously pruned each year, and the grapes are harvested to make 8-10 bottles of wine that are bottled as AOC Bordeaux as the vine is located in the Place de la Victoire in the city of Bordeaux.

Cabernet Sauvignon has a global distribution.[13]

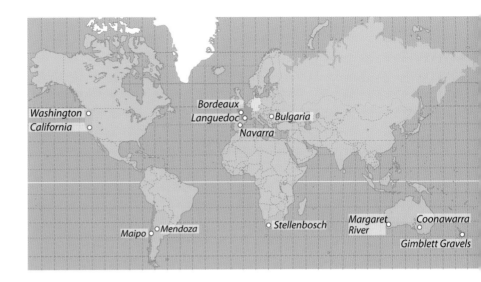

Richelieu sent several thousands of the best vine of Bordeaux to the Abbé Breton in Chinon."[10] Still known as Breton or Petit Breton in the Loire, this is the same grape as Cabernet Franc.[11] The first grapevines were probably brought to Bordeaux by the Bituriges tribe across the Pyrenees during the first century C.E., and maybe this was among them—perhaps it could have been the variety called Biturica that the Roman writer Columella described as "a vine coming from far away."[12] At all events, in the seventeenth century, "the best vine of Bordeaux" was Cabernet Franc!

Since Cabernet Sauvignon became the predominant grape on the left bank of Bordeaux in the second half of the nineteenth century, it has spread throughout the world. Today Cabernet Sauvignon is a true international variety, with a worldwide distribution of plantings. Within Europe, distribution is skewed towards France, which remains the world's largest producer of Cabernet Sauvignon-based wines. In fact, there is relatively little Cabernet Sauvignon of interest elsewhere in Europe. The major exception is Tuscany, where there are some top wines based on blends with Cabernet Sauvignon. Some varietal Cabernet Sauvignon wines are produced in Spain. But with rare exceptions, Cabernet Sauvignon has made little impact in Europe outside of France, and it is grown more as a minor component to use in strengthening the local blend than to make a varietal wine. In the New World it is more widely distributed, with California's Napa Valley at the head of the quality charts, challenged by wines from South or Western Australia, and some cuvées from Chile or Argentina.

Most of the world's Cabernet has been planted in the past twenty to thirty years, and is grafted on to rootstocks. Like all other varieties of Vitis vinifera

A 4 ha plot immediately around the château at Haut-Bailly in Pessac contains a mix of all six black varieties of Bordeaux; the vines are mostly about one hundred years old. Each variety is marked with a colored ribbon to identify when it should be harvested.

(the sole species that produces grapes suitable for making wine), it is sensitive to phylloxera, a louse that was imported inadvertently from the United States to Europe, and which virtually wiped out all the vines in Bordeaux at the end of the nineteenth century. Ever since, it has been necessary to graft the grape-bearing scion on to a rootstock that comes from a different species of Vitis, one that is resistant to phylloxera.

A small patch of ungrafted vines may have survived at Lafite Rothschild until the second half of the twentieth century,[14] but the oldest Cabernet Sauvignon vines still alive today in Bordeaux appear to be in a 4 ha plot at Château Haut-Bailly in Pessac-Léognan, probably planted around 1910, containing a mix of Cabernet Sauvignon, Cabernet Franc, Carmenère, Merlot, Petit Verdot, and Malbec.[15] But the challengers for the title of the world's oldest Cabernet are in the New World. Some vines at the Metala vineyard at Langhorne Creek in Southern Australia, planted on their own roots in 1891, are still producing grapes today. Penfold's Kalimna Block 42 from Barossa Valley also comes from very old Cabernet Sauvignon vines, probably planted in the 1880s. Another source of old vines is at Neyen de Apalta in Chile's Colchagua Valley, apparently planted in 1892. Each of these situations is unique, so none of them casts much light on what Cabernet Sauvignon was like historically.

Cabernet Sauvignon may be the most widely planted black grape in the world. It has been reported that Merlot overtook Cabernet Sauvignon in planted area in the 1990s,[16] but I am not at all sure this is correct (or at least, if

The old Cabernet Sauvignon vines at Château Haut-Bailly are still producing.

it was, I suspect the effect was temporary). Counting up the Cabernet Sauvignon plantings in wine-producing countries, I get about 275,000 hectares—about 3.3% of the world total of grapevine plantings. Merlot comes in just a fraction lower, around 250,000 hectares.[17] Actually, Cabernet Sauvignon and Merlot tend to be planted in the same places, although the relative proportions may be a little different. In France, there is about twice as much Merlot as Cabernet Sauvignon, but in the New World it is the other way round. Worldwide, there may be as many as 6,000 producers who bottle a Cabernet Sauvignon or Cabernet-blend.[18] The key feature about the spread of Cabernet Sauvignon is that almost all the new places where it is now grown are warmer than Bordeaux.[19]

Where does Cabernet Sauvignon grow best? Climate determines which region is most appropriate for any grape variety. The major factor is the temperature during the growing season. (In the northern hemisphere, this is from April through October; in the southern hemisphere it is October through April.) Below a certain temperature range, the variety will not ripen. Above the range, it ripens too fast, typically giving muddy or jammy flavors in the wine. From the average temperatures during the best vintages in regions where Cabernet Sauvignon grows (such as Bordeaux or Napa Valley), we can deduce that its preferred temperature range is a growing season average between 16.5 and 19 °C. (Of course, other factors also influence the success of the vintage, such as the timing of rainfall).

The average is not the only important aspect of temperature: diurnal variation (extremes between high and low temperatures) has a significant effect. Influenced by the Atlantic Ocean, Bordeaux has a maritime climate that evens out extremes. Other regions, where the climate is more Continental or where vineyards are at elevations in mountain sites, can show much wider variation. Extreme diurnal variation can compensate for higher daytime temperatures, because it enables the grapevines to shut down over night and get a respite from the heat of the day. The number of days at very high temperatures also can be a factor. In recent vintages, Napa Valley has experienced an increased number of heat spikes, with high temperatures over 35 °C, a really stressful situation for the vines when the spike continues for more than a couple of days.

In historical terms, Bordeaux only just makes it as a suitable climate for Cabernet Sauvignon. The saving grace is that Cabernet Sauvignon is a late season variety, which is to say that it buds relatively late, enabling it to avoid the problems of Spring frosts in cooler climates. The corollary is that it also ripens late, which leaves it susceptible to problems of low temperature or high rainfall at the end of the season. Wherever it is planted, Cabernet Sauvignon is usually one of the last varieties to be harvested. In the context of the European tradition for growing varieties at their northern limits, Bordeaux has historically achieved only about three vintages in every decade when Cabernet Sauvignon really ripened well—and some decades, such as the 1930s, were truly terrible with no good vintages. This has had a significant impact on our view of the typicity of Cabernet Sauvignon.

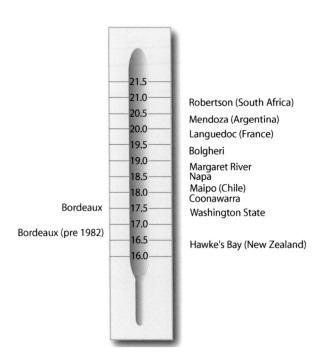

Almost all climates where Cabernet Sauvignon is grown are warmer than Bordeaux.[20]

High temperatures can cause some berries to become dehydrated before others have become ripe. (This is clone 341 Cabernet Sauvignon in Maipo Valley two weeks before harvest in the exceptionally hot 2012 vintage.)

Global warming has changed this in the past two decades, with most vintages coming into the preferred temperature range. The dividing line is the mid 1980s; 1982 was when the style began to change in Bordeaux. Average temperatures have increased more than 1 °C since then, with a significant effect on the style of the wine. Fluctuation between vintages remains high, but few now dip below Cabernet's preferred temperature range. Even so, Bordeaux remains towards the bottom of the climatic range among regions where Cabernet is grown today. Yet the gap has narrowed, for example with Napa Valley, where the temperature increase has been less, and the range of fluctuation is lower. But since Napa started well within Cabernet's preferred range, it now has a problem with average temperatures rising from the middle of the preferred range to the top, and some vintages going over the range.[21] This also has its effects on Cabernet's typicity.

The wines of Bordeaux have certainly changed in the past two or three decades, but when I asked Thomas Duroux at Château Palmer whether Bordeaux had followed the New World in adopting a more "international" style (meaning that the wines are riper, richer, fuller, and more alcoholic) he said that he sees it the other way round. Any apparent convergence is simply due to a common worldwide focus on producing Cabernet-Merlot blends. "Cabernet Sauvignon and Merlot are absolutely not international varieties," he says indignantly,

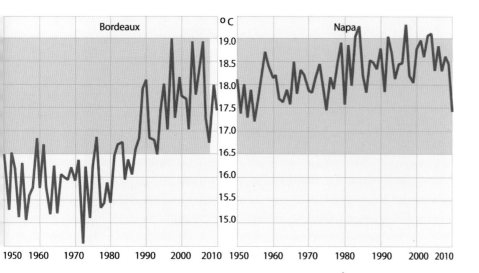

The range of average growing season temperatures is broader in Bordeaux than in Napa. The shaded purple region shows the preferred temperature range for Cabernet Sauvignon.[22]

"they are from Bordeaux but grown elsewhere." Change in Bordeaux, everyone agrees, is due to a variety of effects including warmer vintages, better viticulture, and more precise vinification. All of this reflects, or takes advantage of, Cabernet Sauvignon's sensitivity to heat and sun.

From its origins as a cross between Cabernet Franc and Sauvignon Blanc, Cabernet Sauvignon takes from its white parent the characteristic of extreme variation in flavor profile depending on ripeness. This is why growing season temperature has such a dramatic effect on its character. Volatile compounds called pyrazines accumulate in the berries, giving Sauvignon Blanc a characteristic grassy or asparagus-like flavor, and bringing notes of bell (green) peppers to Cabernet Sauvignon. People are very sensitive to pyrazines because they are an indication of unripeness in fruit.

Pyrazine synthesis is related to vegetative growth; it occurs between fruit set and the period just prior to véraison (when the berries change color). The most important pyrazine is IBMP (3-isobutyl-2-methoxypyrazine). It is very sensitive to sunlight, which causes the level to drop sharply after véraison, when the level of sugar is increasing. When Cabernet Sauvignon grapes used to be harvested early at relatively low sugar levels, there would still typically be quite a significant level of IBMP. This is what gave Bordeaux its characteristic herbaceous taste. But if harvest is delayed until the grapes are riper, IBMP may drop below the threshold for detection. When Cabernet Sauvignon reaches a point of ripeness at which IBMP has been lost, the predominant note in the flavor spectrum is likely to be black fruit, especially blackcurrant. So the aromas and taste of Cabernet Sauvignon are strongly influenced by the typical level of ripeness.

Should Bordeaux's position at the bottom of the temperature league for Cabernet production mean that its style is more restrained than other regions?

IBMP levels fall after véraison.[23] Harvesting at 13% potential alcohol would give an IBMP level just at the detection threshold in this example.

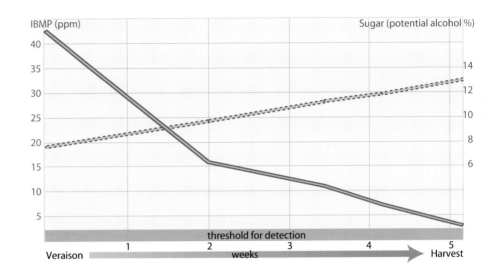

Well, yes and no. Even if the Cabernet Sauvignon is more restrained, Bordeaux is always a blend: the typical blend on the left bank, where the wines are dominated by Cabernet Sauvignon, usually has less than two thirds Cabernet. The rest is mostly Merlot, which brings a fruity mid palate to offset the austerity of the Cabernet Sauvignon. In the New World, wines labeled as Cabernet Sauvignon must have at least 85% of the variety (only 75% in the United States), but they range up to 100%. The argument goes that in Bordeaux you need to blend because the cool climate makes for austerity in the Cabernet, but that in warmer climates, Cabernet Sauvignon achieves sufficient ripeness to make a successful wine by itself. Is this still true in the era of global warming? How does the ability to produce Cabernet Sauvignon without other varieties change our view of its character?

Certainly the dominance of warmer climates has affected perception of typicity. Traditional herbaceous notes have become unfashionable even in Bordeaux; a château proprietor is likely to take it as a criticism if you describe a wine as showing herbaceousness. But have we lost something here? Granted that no one wants to see green, herbaceous wines any more, don't we need variety of aroma and flavor to make a complex wine? Was it not the blend of very faintly herbaceous Cabernet Sauvignon (on the left bank) or Cabernet Franc (on the right bank) with overtly richer and fruity Merlot that gave the wines of top vintages their wonderful elegance and complexity? Can this be achieved, and will the wines age as long, when the flavor spectrum is uniformly ripe?

Herbaceousness (or its absence) is an indication of fashion as much as an intrinsic property of the grape variety. Yes, pyrazines are an indication of unripeness, but they are preserved (up to a point) in Sauvignon Blanc, and avoided in Cabernet Sauvignon. The varieties are not picked to the same crite-

Ripeness

As Cabernet
Sauvignon ripens, its
aroma and flavor
spectrum changes
from bell peppers to
blackcurrant to
cassis to jam.

ria. Herbaceousness is viewed as part of the character of Sauvignon Blanc, and is emphasized by harvesting the grapes at a lower level of ripeness.[24] Now considered undesirable in Cabernet Sauvignon, it is avoided by harvesting the grapes at higher levels of ripeness. By changing criteria, it would be perfectly possible to eliminate herbaceousness in Sauvignon Blanc or to emphasize it in Cabernet Sauvignon. Of course, these options are made possible by warmer vintages, since in cool conditions such as in Bordeaux of the sixties and seventies, high levels of ripeness were not possible. Remember also that IBMP was identified as the source of bell pepper aromas in Cabernet Sauvignon only in 1975 (and in Sauvignon Blanc only in 1982). It wasn't until the end of the 1980s that it was discovered that sunlight degrades pyrazines, so the ability to influence pyrazine level by viticulture is quite recent.

The combination of higher climatic temperatures, plantings in warmer areas, and the fashion for harvesting later, all have driven the recognizable typicity of Cabernet Sauvignon from herbaceousness expressed as bell peppers to black fruits most often dominated by blackcurrants, which can intensify into the more aromatic notes of cassis.[25] The change to the riper style goes along with greater extraction and higher alcohol levels. Just how far the wine goes along this path depends partly on viticulture and vinification. There are old school wines in Bordeaux where herbaceousness is evident, and there are new style wines without a trace of it. There are wines made to optimize freshness in Napa where a herbal touch can be detected, and there are wines made to emphasize the sheer opulence of the fruits, which can turn to jam. Winemaker Michael Silacci at Opus One in Napa Valley, who is conscious of both traditions given his winery's origins in a collaboration between Napa's Robert Mondavi and Bordeaux's Baron Philippe de Rothschild, says, "There absolutely has to be some herbaceous note when you're making Cabernet Sauvignon, it's part of its genetics, whether it shows as black tea or pepper or whatever. It does not show as bell peppers in Napa because it is not cool enough for that here." Perhaps the most fascinating aspect of typicity is the way the wine develops with age, as the primary fruits turn savory. Depending on its character, Cabernet Sauvignon may become savory to the point of sous bois (forest floor), herbaceous, or herbal; sometimes, as tertiary flavors develop, the similarities increase between wines from different regions.

The balance between vegetative growth and berry development is influenced by the character of the plant itself as well as its environment. A variety has a single point of origin—in the case of Cabernet Sauvignon that chance cross between Cabernet Franc and Sauvignon Blanc—but then the progeny begin to diverge. Some develop more desirable properties; others show less desirable traits. How are the best to be chosen for propagation? Alternative ways for planting a vineyard are *selection massale*, when cuttings are simply taken directly from successful vines within the vineyard, or use of *clones*, all guaranteed to be identical because they were propagated from a single plant selected for its desirable character.

A clone is made by taking material from a single grapevine, and putting it through procedures that eliminate viruses or other infective agents that reduce fruit quality. At the end of the day—or rather, at the end of several years—there is a mother clone that can be used to propagate plants that are free of all infections. Most plant viruses reduce yields; some diseases also affect quality of the grapes, such as leaf roll virus, which delays ripening. So using certified clones is considered to have the distinct advantage that the quantity and quality of berries will directly reflect the plant. Part of the recent increase in ripeness in Napa Valley, for example, may be due to replanting with clones that are free of leaf roll virus. This can be a mixed bag. Virus infection has reduced yields of the forty-year-old vines at the Kronos vineyard in Napa valley, but owner Cathy Corison believes that this has also slowed sugar production, so ripeness is achieved at lower levels of potential alcohol. "The University of California has given me a hard time about this," she says ruefully.

Until clones became available, vineyards were usually planted with local selections. When a vineyard is replanted by selecting cuttings from its best plants, the advantage is that there's some assurance of a good match between the plant material and the terroir. Indeed, when this continues over some generations, the plants may begin to diverge from those in other vineyards, and embody the character of the vineyard. There is the disadvantage very often of propagating viruses along with the vines. Certainly it's not black and white: when a vineyard with a low level of viral infection has a history of producing high quality wine, some producers (albeit a dwindling minority) feel it's better to ignore the infection, rather than to risk changing the source material.

Some producers still believe in the value of a selection massale to propagate the heritage of the vineyard, but the modern trend is to replant with clones that are certified to be free of virus infections. (Sometimes this is required by the authorities.) Paul Pontallier at Château Margaux says that, "My experience shows that clonal selection, as long as the selection is accurate, as long as you use several clones, allows us to get rid of viruses, which have been more bad than good. We've never made good wine from virused vineyards. One inconvenience with clones is the simplified use of material, so you need more

Leaf roll virus gives grapevines a very attractive red color in the autumn. You could probably estimate the extent of leaf roll virus in Napa Valley from an aerial photograph in the autumn, with infected plants showing as orange and red, and uninfected plants an ordinary brown.

clones." Some people think that in the long run, the issue becomes irrelevant. "There is a huge debate about selection massale versus clones, but for me it's not a good debate," says Thomas Duroux at Château Palmer, adding that continuing selection massale has the same focusing effect as using clones (in narrowing the genetic heritage), and that terroir is really the important factor. Of course, clones can be a mixed blessing, depending on the criteria used when they were selected. Indeed, it takes 20 years to select a clone—the logic follows the reasoning of generals fighting the last war—so you wonder whether selection massale is more responsive since you can select those plants that have been most successful in the immediate past.

Some grapevine cultivars show a great deal of variation—Pinot Noir is the classic example—and the source of plants can have large effects, both direct and indirect, on its character. One factor that changes significantly with clonal variety in Pinot Noir is the time of ripening, which affects the suitability of each clone for particular climates.[26] This is not such a big issue with Cabernet clones, where the major difference is more with the yield. At Ornellaia in Tuscany, where soils are quite variable, winemaker Axel Heintz says, "We don't attach special importance to the individual clone, the rootstock has more influence," although as a precaution no single clone is ever planted in more than one contiguous hectare.

Quite a lot of damage was done by the first clone of Cabernet Sauvignon to be developed, #15 in 1971. After a series of vintages in the 1960s suffered from rot, with Merlot especially susceptible, the French authorities over-reacted by restricting new plantings to Cabernet Sauvignon, and pushing clone 15 for its reliability. But clone 15 gives high yields with large berries and bunches. This increased the herbaceousness of wines through the 1970s in Bordeaux. Getting the clone wrong has long-term consequences, as vines have an average life-span around 25 years. It took at least another decade before the introduction of higher quality clones started to improve quality. Too productive to give high quality wine in most circumstances, clone 15 is euphemistically described in the official catalog of French varieties as "appreciated in the Midi [the wine lake of southern France] where it gives a good compromise between the level of production and quality if yields are mastered and it reaches sufficient maturity."[27] Could you damn with fainter praise?

New plantings in France focus on about eight clones. Clone 337 is the closest to a cult, known for its small berries and deep color. It has increasing popularity in the New World, but there is some controversy as to whether it is really best suited to cooler sites. Together with clones 169 and 341, it's thought to be best for producing long-lived wines. It seems extraordinary that none of the popular certified clones originated on Bordeaux's left bank, the best area for Cabernet Sauvignon; all came from other areas, which usually have been associated with lower quality for Cabernet Sauvignon. Perhaps for that reason, the clones are not universally used. Many producers continue to replant using selection massale of material from their own vineyards. Jérôme Juhe, the Directeur at Château La Lagune in the Médoc, says flatly, "Today there is no clone that is correct: the clones do not have the typicity of the cépage. The clones are too productive, and it's a risk to have one clone."

The reasons for this apparent retrogression were explained to me by Jean-Philippe Delmas, Directeur at Château Haut Brion. His father, Jean Delmas, the previous Directeur, investigated clones by planting a test plot at Bahans in

Cabernet Sauvignon clones differ in the typical size and weight of their bunches. On the left is clone 7 (the Concannon or Wente clone, one of the first heritage clones of California, widely planted in the 1970s and 1980s). On the right is clone 337, one of the new ENTAV clones (which originated in the Côtes de Blaye of Bordeaux). Both have small tight berries and bunches and are known for good aromatics. Photograph courtesy Bell Wine Cellars.

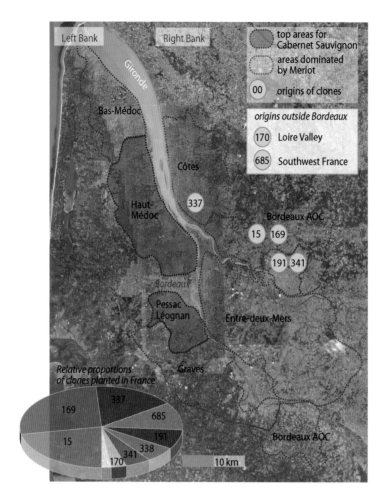

Eight clones are widely used in France. None originated on the left bank of Bordeaux, where all the best Cabernet Sauvignon-dominated wines are made. Most originated on the right bank, where Merlot is the predominant grape variety. Two originated in regions outside Bordeaux. [28]

1978 with the available clones of Cabernet Sauvignon, Cabernet Franc, and Merlot. "The first crop using the government clones was a disaster; there were huge yields. At that time it was impossible for Haut Brion to consider using those clones," Jean-Philippe told me. Together with some plants propagated from Haut Brion's own estate, there are now several hundred vines that are tracked individually for their yield, sugar production, tannins, etc. "Ten percent of the plants always produce poor results, ten percent always produce good results, and 80% depend on the year," Jean-Philippe says. When a vineyard plot is replanted, parent plants are chosen from the ten percent top performers and the eighty percent variable performers. Maintaining diversity is important, but should not go too far. The limit is nine parents for any one plot, as otherwise there is too much variability in harvest dates. "There is a tendency for some producers to use only a single clone," Jean-Philippe says disapprovingly.

An equally skeptical take on the modern evolution of Cabernet Sauvignon comes from Mas de Daumas Gassac in the Languedoc, where Cabernet Sauvignon was planted in the mid seventies with a selection that the nursery claimed had come from Haut Brion early in the twentieth century.[29] "It looks quite different from modern Cabernet Sauvignon; in fact the Bordelais sometimes have difficulty in recognizing the variety," Samuel Guibert told me. It forms long thin bunches with very loose grapes, and a crocodile skin. It's low yielding, giving less than 30 hl/ha in the conditions at Daumas Gassac. It would be interesting to see what would happen if it were planted back in Bordeaux.

The modern French clones are now available in the New World, where there are also "heritage clones" that have been grown in situ for more than a century. For the past fifty years, it has been illegal to import plants into the United States (they have to pass through a very lengthy quarantine period), so growers following the law were restricted to those cultivars that had been imported previously. (Growers who were not prepared to wait sometimes imported "suitcase clones," so called because they were smuggled into the United States.) Of course you have to ask whether it's necessarily true that the clones that do best in Bordeaux's cool, humid climate will necessarily do best in California's warmer, drier climate. "There's a tendency still to copy the French without fully understanding why," says Anthony Bell, who was involved in a major trial of clones in Napa Valley. "The mistake we made was looking at the A list clones from Bordeaux. Their problem is rain, our problem is sun. Conditions are different there," says Michael Silacci of Opus One.

The workhorse clones of Cabernet Sauvignon in California in the 1970s and 1980s were clone 7 (also known as the Concannon or Wente clone) and clone 8, both taken as cuttings from the same vine at the Concannon Vineyard in St. Helena. The first clones to be available in Napa that had been cured of viruses, they are relatively productive, with significantly higher yields than the more recent clones. Two heritage clones that originated with nineteenth century imports into California from Bordeaux are clone 6 (the Jackson clone) and clone 29 (the small-berried clone that Gustave Niebaum imported in 1882 and that was the basis for Inglenook Cabernet Sauvignon from the 1930s through the 1950s; it was rescued in 1991 after years of decay). Another well known clone in California is clone 4, the Mendoza clone, which was imported from Argentina. (It was incorrectly labeled as Merlot clone 11 when it arrived!)

The disadvantage of using clones is loss of diversity; all the plants are genetically identical, so they tend to produce the same flavor profile, and they may or may not adapt well to the particular site. Does using clones have a general homogenizing effect? The extremes of the argument were defined by Bruno Eynard at Château Lagrange, "Clones stop evolution, selection massale preserves it." This tends to be more of an issue for varieties that have more extensive genetic variation, such as Pinot Noir, than for Cabernet Sauvignon. Certainly when I talked with producers about clones, they were often passionate about the effects with Pinot Noir, but rarely about Cabernet Sauvignon. When I asked producers in Bordeaux whether they used clones or selection

Some outlier clones of Cabernet Sauvignon are quite different from most modern clones. California's clone #6 gives small, straggly bunches of small berries (left). The cultivar of Cabernet Sauvignon at Mas de Daumas Gassac has small, very well spaced, berries that form long bunches (right, photograph courtesy Mas de Daumas Gassac).

massale, the answers more often favored clones, but when I asked which clones they used, the response was often a shrug, "I don't remember the number." The clones most planted in Bordeaux are 191, 337, 341, and (more recently) 169, although there is still a good bit of 15 around. A recent trial showed relatively few differences in yields (only 191 was distinguished by distinctly lower yields).[30] There weren't many significant differences in accumulation of sugar, acidity, or tannins. Perhaps that explains the general lack of interest in exactly which clone is used.

There's more interest in clones in Napa Valley, and some wines are even made from specific clones. "Clonal selection has become much more important over here because there were many clones that didn't match well with the soil and climate—we have so much diversity, it's harder to begin with," says winemaker Aron Weinkauf at Spottswoode Winery. A ten year trial of 14 clones at Beaulieu Vineyards in the 1980s revealed a wide range of variation. "We planted a 10 acre vineyard in BV#4, with all 14 clones in 8 different blocks, with never two adjacent clones the same. They were identified by color-coded ribbons. We showed quantitatively that the clones made different wines. There were differences in the time of ripeness, yield, herbal quality," says Anthony Bell, who was in charge of the trial. The variation in yields was extreme, from 40 hl/ha to 90 hl/ha.[31]

The clone that showed the greatest Cabernet typicity—meaning at the time a herbaceous influence—was clone 6. When you compare wine made from clone 6 with wine made from clone 337 side by side, the difference is clear. Clone 6 has more of the traditional character associated with Bordeaux; clone 337 has more of the lush fruits associated with the new international style. "I think 337 lacks varietal typicity in California—it allows winemakers to create the fruit-driven style of Cabernet that tends to be a favorite of the media. If you want to pick late and make very extracted wines, 337 allows you to do this in spades," says Anthony Bell, who makes wine in a traditional style (Υ page 381). Fred Schrader, who makes more powerfully extracted wines in the Napa cult style, sees the relative differences in a similar way. "337 has a bigger berry and higher yield, clone 6 has low yields and is very dense and concentrated, and clone 4 is halfway between with good backbone. Clone 337 doesn't have the steely backbone that 4 and 6 have; the wine is more right bank-ish and ready to go," he says (Υ page 409). Another example of using clones to determine styles comes from Pride Mountain. The Vintner Select, which is intended to be a typical forward Napa wine, comes entirely from clone 337. The Reserve, a more masculine wine intended for aging, is largely based on Pride's own Rock Arch clone, which gives a more massive structure (Υ page 405).

Far away from Bordeaux's indifference to clones and Napa's focus on them, virtually all plantings of Cabernet Sauvignon in Washington State are a single clone (California clone 8). Paradoxically, this illustrates the importance of clones with the indirect consequence that producers are driven to seek diversity by blending Cabernets from different sites. There's a similar effect in Australia, where most of Margaret River was planted with the Houghton heritage selection of Cabernet Sauvignon.

Certainly improvements can be made to Cabernet Sauvignon by planting superior clones or local selections, but the major effect of replanting is probably simply replacing old, overly productive cultivars with lower-yielding plants. Among modern clones, with one or two notable exceptions—such as the extremes of the austerity of clone 6 and the lushness of clone 337—stylistic differences are probably outweighed by factors such as the individual vineyard site or standards of viticulture (especially the decision on when to harvest). Tastings of barrel samples suggest that, if there is any threat of homogenization by clone, it comes from clone 337: it may be more restrained in Bordeaux, but in warmer climates, its tendency towards lushness, its emphasis on black fruits rather than pyrazines, its ripe, rounded tannins, all contribute to a fruit-forward impression that can be more like Merlot or Shiraz than a traditional Bordeaux. But with Cabernet Sauvignon, given the rarity of wines made from single clones, any move to standardization is more likely to come from a common focus on achieving conditions of viticulture and vinification that emphasize uniform ripeness in the grapes, leading to fuller, richer, wines.

Chile is one place where selection massale still rules supreme. Because phylloxera never arrived, most vines are still on their own roots; it is even common to propagate old vines in the traditional way, by sticking a shoot into the ground. This preserves the absolute maximum of the genetic material in the vineyard, the very antithesis of using clones. Some producers draw a distinc-

When a scion is grafted onto a rootstock, it is kept in warm, very humid conditions for a few days to let a callus form around the join. Then it is covered with a protective (green) wax and planted out. After a few weeks, the first shoots begin to push out.

tion between using selection massale for their best vineyards, but using clones for the vineyards for entry-level wines. "Clonal material started to be used a couple of years ago, but we mostly stay with selection massale. When you use the clonal material you standardize. But in the last five years for Casa (the entry-level wine) it's all been clonal because we need more reliable yields; there's a mix of own roots and rootstocks because rootstocks give more consistency. Selection on own roots gives more diversity but we suffer. Clones give more consistency," says Marcelo Papa of Concha y Toro.

Clones (and the rootstocks on which they are planted) provide the basic material, but the major determinants of style are the parameters of viticulture and vinification. Part of the reason for a certain convergence between Bordeaux and the New World over the past decade is due to a common focus on getting the grapes riper by viticulture, and a general agreement on many features of winemaking. The basic objective of viticulture is the same everywhere: to get grapes to ripen as uniformly as possible. The major tool now employed with this aim is canopy management: pruning the grapevine so that it gets the right balance with sufficient leaves to support vegetative growth, and the right amount of exposure of the berries to the sun to ripen but not over-ripen. All sorts of technical issues go into the equation, including the orientation of the grapevine rows (will they run north-south or east-west?), the density of the vines (will they be close together or far apart?), the shape of the canopy (will it be organized horizontally or vertically?), the height of the canopy (close to the ground or well above it?), irrigation (will the vines be irrigated or "dry farmed"?), and so on. The answers are different depending on climatic condi-

Vines grown on their own roots can be propagated in the old way, by sticking a shoot in the earth. When the shoot has rooted, the connection to the mother plant will be cut. This is a common method of propagation in Chile, where there is no phylloxera.

tions and fertility of the soil. At the risk of over simplification, in Bordeaux the challenge is to capture the sun and defy the rain, whereas in much of the New World it is to limit sun exposure and provide enough water.

There is more uniformity of opinion on vinification of Cabernet Sauvignon than there is for other varieties. As a black grape, where color and tannins come from the skin, the level of extraction is a major factor. There's always discussion with Pinot Noir, for example, on whether to include some stems or whether to destem the grapes: Cabernet Sauvignon has quite enough tannin already, thank you, so complete destemming is the norm everywhere. Most often grapes are allowed to sit for a few days before fermentation starts; during this "cold soak," color and tannins are released from the skins into the juice. Once fermentation begins, whether naturally or because yeast are inoculated, it lasts a few days, typically at temperatures in the high twenties Centigrade or high eighties Fahrenheit, as the sugar in the juice is converted into alcohol. (Fermentation temperature is more of an issue for influencing style with white wines.) During fermentation, the skins and seeds rise to the top of the vat, forming a cap; to prevent the cap from drying out, usually the fermenting juice is pumped up and over it from the bottom of the tank. A gentler alternative is to punch-down the cap down into the juice.

Fermentation is generally allowed to continue to dryness, that is, until there is no more sugar. Then the wine may be left in the vat, together with its cap, for a few days, to extract more tannin and color. At the end of this post-fermentation maceration, the juice is drained off, and the cap is pressed, these days most often using one of the new vertical presses, which squeeze the remnants of the grapes very gently. The wine released by pressing is usually more extracted than the free-run wine, and only some of it will be included in the final blend. An alternative that's common in Australia is to drain off the juice just before fermentation is complete; then it's transferred straight to barriques, where it completes fermentation. This "barrel fermentation" gives softer tannins, making the wine more approachable, but less likely to support long ageing.

Like almost all red wines, after Cabernet Sauvignon has passed through its alcoholic fermentation, it needs to undergo malolactic fermentation (MLF). This reduces the level of acidity (by converting malic acid to lactic acid) and introduces softer, creamier, flavors. In the old days, MLF happened spontaneously when the cellars warmed up in the Spring, activating the bacteria that are responsible. Today it's more usual to inoculate the wine with the bacteria. There's still a bit of controversy as to whether the best place to do this is in tank or in oak barrels. The tradition in Burgundy was always to perform the malo (as malolactic fermentation is known) in barrels, but in Bordeaux it was usually done in tanks before the wine was transferred to barrels. There's been a strong impetus in Bordeaux over the past couple of decades to perform MLF in barrique, because this makes the wines seem rounder, softer, and more approachable at an early stage. This is important in Bordeaux because the wines are sold while still in barrique, in the en primeur campaign each April. The counter argument is that performing MLF in barrique adds nothing in the long run, and possibly might mean the wine doesn't age as well. The real answer is that no one knows. In the New World, where wines are not usually sold until they are in bottle, there's a more pragmatic approach; some producers do it one way, some the other, and nobody pays much attention to the issue.

The use of oak is a big issue. Bordeaux started to be held in barriques (225 liter barrels of oak, equivalent to 300 bottles) in order to allow the wine to mature before it was bottled. When the barriques are old, they have little direct effect upon the wine, except to allow it to settle and to have some exposure to oxygen. During the second half of the twentieth century, barriques of new oak became common. New oak adds flavors to the wine, including wood spices such as cloves or cinnamon or nutmeg, and aromas of vanillin or smokiness: and tannins from the oak add to the grape tannins. How much new oak is used in the barrels has a major effect on the wine, as does the length of time the wine stays in the barrels before bottling. Typically the stronger the wine, the more new oak it can handle, indeed may even need, and the longer it can stay there. In Bordeaux, 100% new oak might be used for the very top wines, but most wines have much less. In the New World, there is more of a tendency to use more new oak. (And of course for cheaper wines in the New World there are also other possibilities such as placing oak staves into stainless steel tanks or adding oak chips to wine in vats of stainless steel.)

Traditional fining is still used at Château Palmer; egg whites are whisked up and mixed with a little red wine before being added to the barrique.

Photograph courtesy Château Palmer

With its thick skin, Cabernet Sauvignon gives deeply colored and tannic wines. Tannin management is a major determinant of style, starting with decisions on how much extraction to allow during fermentation and maturation, and ending with deciding whether to fine the wine before it goes into bottle. Fining is a technique for removing, or reducing, unwanted elements, by adding an agent to the wine that interacts with certain components. Its main visible effect is to clarify the wine. Fining with eggs had become common practice by the early eighteenth century. "Take ten fresh eggs, whip them up well with a pint of well water, and add to a tonneau (a wooden barrel of 500 liters)," was the method described in 1721.[32] Because tannins are negatively charged, they interact with the protein of egg whites (albumin), which is positively charged, to form a precipitate that drops to the bottom of the barrique. This is said to give the wine a silkier feel by reducing the level of astringent tannins. Fining is still done traditionally at some Bordeaux châteaux, using 5-6 eggs whites per barrique (225 liter), but in most places the romanticism of egg whites has been replaced by the practicality of powdered albumin (or other agents).

Fining remains the norm in Bordeaux, but is less common elsewhere. It's becoming slightly controversial, like filtration to ensure absolute clarity before bottling, on the grounds that desirable as well as undesirable compounds may be removed. It's a particular issue with Cabernet Sauvignon because of this variety's high level of tannins. "Fining with egg whites helps polish the tannins, and also to clarify and stabilize the wines. But I would like to add a point that seems important for me: this natural filtration brings a good brilliance and a good visual aspect in the glass. So we still need to fine the wine with egg white. Nevertheless, with the tannin structure being riper than the past, we have adapted the number of egg white per barrel. We are currently using on average 4-5 egg whites per barrel at Léoville Lascases. In the past, after the second world war, it was customary to use on average 7 egg whites per barrel in the Médoc. Moreover, it was frequent to fine the wines twice at the beginning of twentieth century (after vinification and at the end of ageing)," says technical director Michael Georges.

Fining is rare in the New World, where it's usually viewed as a technique strictly for tannin management. "We used to use egg whites, but recently the tannins have been riper and we find we don't need it," says Mark de Vere at Mondavi. Following the view that today's viticulture and vinification produce riper tannins, Doug Shafer at Shafer Vineyards says directly, "If you need to fine, that means you messed up in fermentation." At Abreu Vineyards, Brad Grimes says, "There is no fining, no reason to fine at all." A few New World producers have a more traditional view, such as Dominus (under French ownership), where Tod Mostero says, "I believe wines were fined because fining makes wine finer. It takes out the more aggressive tannins and there's also an anti-microbial effect by the action of lysozyme" (another protein in egg whites).

At the end of the day, the character of the wine reflects decisions on when to harvest the grapes (meaning just how ripe they are), whether "adjustments" are made to increase alcohol (by adding sugar before fermentation) or to increase acidity (by adding tartaric acid), the levels of tannins extracted from the grapes or added from the oak, and whether the wine is fined before bottling. The character of Cabernet Sauvignon will be influenced by whether the wine is made as a single variety or whether it is blended with other varieties, typically Merlot, Cabernet Franc, or Petit Verdot. But if winemakers all over the world say that they harvest grapes when they are ripe, and if they are more or less agreed on the parameters of viticulture and vinification, and the blends are generally similar, why are their wines different?

Any view of Cabernet Sauvignon's typicity has to take into account the improvements in viticulture in the past two decades, which have narrowed vintage variation by improving quality in poorer vintages. And style is influenced by the much wider geographical range of producers. Until the 1980s, Cabernet Sauvignon was defined almost exclusively by the left bank of Bor-

*Most wines
dominated by
Cabernet Sauvignon
come from the New
World.[33]*

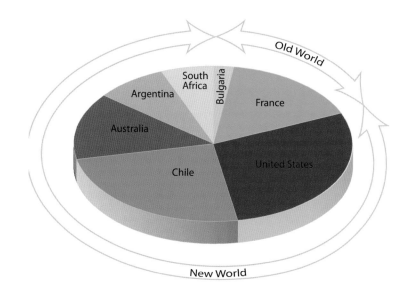

deaux: a wine with moderate alcohol, refreshing acidity, and mid weight fruits
often showing a herbaceous edge. Today a wine labeled as Cabernet Sauvignon is more likely to come from the New World, with higher alcohol, lower
acidity, and fruits whose impression on the palate can approach the exuberant.
But this description might also apply to some modern Bordeaux. Is this change
a natural continuation of a steady evolution of style or does it reflect the new
capacities of modern viticulture and vinification? What should we now expect
of Cabernet Sauvignon?

2

European Classicism

CABERNET SAUVIGNON is not, strictly speaking, a product of Bordeaux. Bordeaux produces blended wines, dominated by Cabernet Sauvignon on the left bank, and by Merlot on the right bank. There is virtually no wine made exclusively from Cabernet Sauvignon. Yet until the 1970s, Cabernet Sauvignon was virtually synonymous with Bordeaux: there was little or no wine of equivalent quality containing the variety produced anywhere else. Through this period, the character of the left bank wines is essentially the story of the struggle to reach ripeness for Cabernet Sauvignon, and the means used to compensate when this did not happen.

It would be a mistake to view Bordeaux as a monolithic region of wine production. Bordeaux is divided into two broad subregions, each with its own character and distinctive mix of grape varieties. The river is the major dividing line. Upstream from the Atlantic, the Gironde estuary (the largest estuary in Europe) divides into the Garonne river (which runs through Bordeaux) and the Dordogne. Extending along the west side of the Gironde, the peninsula of the

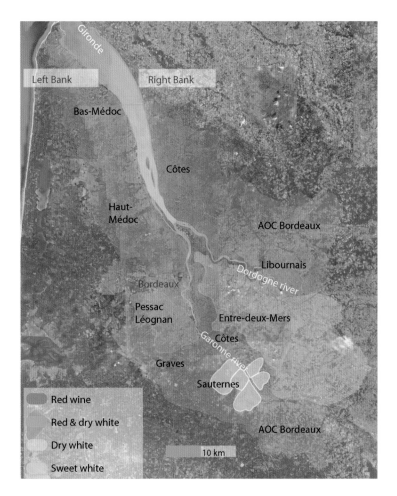

The Gironde estuary and Garonne river divide Bordeaux into the left bank and right bank.

Médoc lies to the north of the city of Bordeaux. The Médoc is divided into the northern half of the Bas-Médoc and the southern half, nearer the city, of the Haut-Médoc.[1] Immediately to the south of the city, running along the west bank of the Garonne, is the region of the Graves. Together the Médoc and the Graves make up the left bank. The right bank includes everything to the east of the Gironde and Garonne.

A small temperature differential is the key to the difference between left and right banks. This is not so much a matter of temperature due to the weather, but results from the terrain. The soils of the left bank are gravelly, but the right bank has more clay. Air temperatures are closely similar, but the clay-based soils do not retain heat as well as gravel. The difference is just enough to allow Cabernet Sauvignon to ripen on the left bank but not on the right bank. Curiously, considering how close they are, the left bank also gets a little more sunshine than the right bank, which again helps Cabernet Sauvignon to ripen.[2]

Bordeaux was too cool a climate to grow grapes successfully when wine production first came to France, and the first vineyards were established

Cabernet Sauvignon is grown on gravel soils in the Médoc (left: at Château Montrose), while Merlot is grown on clay soils, especially in St. Emilion and Pomerol (right: at Château Pétrus).

around Marseilles. When the Romans arrived in 56 B.C.E., Bordeaux was an important commercial center, but there were no vines in the vicinity.[3] During the first century C.E., new grape varieties became available that would ripen in more northern climates, and viticulture developed in a region extending from the southeast towards Bordeaux itself.[4,5] By the fourth century, viticulture around Bordeaux became sufficiently prevalent for the poet Ausonius, who was born and lived nearby, to write a poem extolling the vines and rivers of the region.[6] Bordeaux remained a commercial center after the collapse of the Roman Empire (476 C.E.), and there are occasional references to vineyards from the fifth through eighth centuries;[7] but wine production did not really resume until the reign of Charlemagne at the start of the ninth century,[8] and it's pretty much a black hole until the English takeover of Aquitaine in 1152.

After the Middle Ages, Bordeaux owed its increasing importance as a wine producer as much to commercial ruthlessness (what's new?) as to superior quality. During the fourteenth century, various privileges accrued to the merchants of Bordeaux under the name of the "police des vins" (policies concerning wines).[9] Basically the control of shipping was used to give an advantage to the local producers. Local production was defined in *very* narrow terms. Production in the Médoc was held back by a regulation of 1401 that prevented its wines from being exported from ports in the Gironde; they could be exported only via the port of Bordeaux.[10] (The Bordelais saw the ports of the Médoc as a distinct threat to their monopoly;[11] the law stayed in effect until the seventeenth century.[12]) And although wines from the southeast had acquired a good reputation during the Middle Ages, their ability to compete with those of

Bordeaux remained a major port for wine distribution. Most wine continued to be exported in barrels until the twentieth century. (This view dates from 1908.)

Bordeaux itself was impeded by such regulations until into the eighteenth century.[13] Tight control of distribution remains a feature of Bordeaux to the present day.

By the twelfth century, viticulture was established in Entre-deux-Mers (between the Garonne and Dordogne rivers on the right bank) and around the city of Bordeaux itself.[14] During the thirteenth and fourteenth centuries, viticulture spread beyond the city. Immediately to the south, the Graves was easier to penetrate. One of the oldest vineyards in the Graves was the property of the Archbishop of Bordeaux. At the start of the fourteenth century, when he became Pope Clément V, he gave his private vineyard to the archdiocese: named after him, it still produces wine as Château Pape-Clément. Château Haut Brion has made wine since the sixteenth century, and the monks at neighboring Mission Haut Brion were making wine in the seventeenth century. One of the very first to establish a great reputation abroad, Château Haut Brion was the most fashionable wine in London in the late seventeenth century.

Superficially a less attractive terrain, because of its swampy nature, the Médoc offered restricted opportunities for agriculture, but vineyards were established in the infertile soils of the Haut-Médoc where few other crops could be grown.[15] Production started around Blanquefort, just outside the city, and then extended north. Vineyards were largely confined to a band running along the Gironde. With less favorable terroir, and lying farther from the city of Bordeaux, the Bas-Médoc was not cultivated for viticulture until later. Even by the fifteenth century, production of wine was never more than a secondary culture

The map of Hippolyte Matis of 1716 shows vineyards all around the city.

of relatively small economic importance in the Médoc.[16] Viticulture really took off and became a major economic contributor by the end of the seventeenth century. During the eighteenth century, viticulture became close to a monoculture in some parts of the Haut-Médoc.[17]

Flat and marshy, the Médoc does not at first sight seem a natural place for viticulture. Most good wine-producing areas are relatively hilly, with slopes and angles that give good drainage. The highest point in the Médoc is only just above sea level (43 meters at Listrac-Médoc). The importance of even minor points of elevation is indicated by the number of châteaux whose names refer to hills: Grand Puy Lacoste (a *puy* is a small hill); Montrose, where *mont-rose* may have described a small hill covered in pink heather; Lafite, where *fite* (derived from the Gascon *hite*) means a hillock; Mouton Rothschild has nothing to do with sheep, but may derive from *motte*, meaning a mound; the original name for Léoville Lascases was Mont-Moytié, *mont* meaning mountain! Just as the Eskimos have a million words for snow, so does the original Gascon language of Bordeaux have many words for hill. Anything that stood above the marshes was notable, even if the elevation is barely perceptible.

Today's terrain owes as much to human intervention as to natural features. Until the seventeenth century, the palus (wetlands adjacent to the river) and marais (inland marshes) were so extensive in the Bas-Médoc that conditions for human habitation were regarded as marginal. The modern terrain results from a progressive draining of the marshes over the past four centuries. While the results are most dramatic in the Bas-Médoc, marais have been drained

Vineyards extend to about 200 m from the Gironde, where swamps and woods are close to the river.

throughout the Médoc, extending right to the city of Bordeaux. Today the remaining marais are preserved wetlands.

The reconstruction of the Médoc started when Henri IV engaged Dutch engineers to drain the marshes in 1599. The work continued over the next two hundred years.[18] As a result of successive drainage projects, now only the palus extending out immediately from the river remain of the original swampy terrain in the Haut-Médoc. The effect of the drainage on viticulture is mostly indirect: few vineyards are on drained land, but some are close to areas where drainage has lowered the water table. While the terroir of the vineyards was not created by the drainage, the environment has certainly been much influenced by it.

Water in all its forms is a major viticultural issue in Bordeaux. The humidity of the maritime climate encourages fungal diseases. Epidemics of oïdium (powdery mildew) have been a problem ever since vines have been grown here. Water supply to the grapevines is a mixed bag. On the one hand, much of the terroir in the Médoc has the desirable feature that the level of the water table falls around the time of véraison (when the grapes change color). Limiting the

the supply of water to the roots in the later part of the growing season is ideal for encouraging the grapevine to put its energy into making fruit instead of vegetative growth. But water supply above ground can be an issue. Irrigation is not allowed, but this is not usually a problem, because Bordeaux has a rainy climate. Indeed, rainfall can be a problem: there is often too much, or more to the point, rainfall at the wrong time—typically it rains around the equinox of September 21, just coming up to harvest. It is rare to have a harvest in Bordeaux completely without rain. And drainage after rainfall is a perpetual issue in the Médoc. The major producers started to install drainage systems under their vineyards in the nineteenth century. Where does all the human intervention in the water supply leave the claim of the Bordelais that the terroir of Médoc is naturally perfect for growing Cabernet Sauvignon? And, indeed, when and how did Cabernet Sauvignon come to be the grape variety of choice?

   The first grape variety associated with the region was Biturica, named for the Bituriges tribe who lived on the left bank of the Gironde and founded the

The Gironde is an omnipresent influence in the Médoc. The former palus (swamps) immediately along the river are either built up or undeveloped, but a monoculture of vineyards runs inland from this strip.

city of Burdigala (later to be known as Bordeaux).[19] (The Bituriges were known for their production and consumption of barley beer before the Roman invasion, after which they took up wine.[20]) It has been proposed that Biturica was the same as, or later developed into, the variety subsequently known as Bidure or Vidure.[21] Exact relationships to modern varieties are hard to determine because of the use of overlapping names and different usages in the Médoc, Graves, and right bank. However, Bidure was very likely one of the Cabernets, most likely Cabernet Franc (or possibly its relative, Gros Cabernet).[22]

The oldest overt reference I can find to Sauvignon comes from the end of the seventeenth century. "The Sauvignon is a black grape, quite large and long, which [ripens] early and has a very good spicy taste. Sauvignon Blanc has the same qualities. Both are rare and little known."[23] The description suggests that a relationship was recognized between black and white varieties, but it's not completely clear whether Sauvignon Noir was equivalent to Cabernet Sauvignon.[24] During the next century, Cabernet came to prominence on the left bank. "Cabernet is most cultivated in the Médoc, which makes its wines superior," said a writer in 1787.[25] But an old vineyard map of Haut Brion shows that there was no Cabernet Sauvignon there in 1763, so clearly it was not yet thought to be the best variety for the Graves.[26]

Cabernet Sauvignon expanded early in the nineteenth century on the left bank; Cabernet Franc and Malbec were the dominant varieties on the right bank. Lesser varieties fell out of favor in the Médoc, and the best varieties were recognized as Cabernet, Carmenère, Malbec, Petit and Gros Verdot, and Merlot. "The first four cépages are used in the grand crus of the Médoc; blended with intelligence, their product is most distinguished," said William Franck in

This marais just north of St. Estèphe is traversed by a drainage canal and shows typical wetlands vegetation, which is often turned into pasture.

1845.[27] Considered to be less delicate than Malbec, Merlot was an also-ran at this point.[28]

Cabernet Sauvignon was not always recognized as the most superior variety for the area. During the first half of the nineteenth century, opinion varied as to whether Cabernet Sauvignon or Carmenère was the best grape for the left bank.[29] The first specific focus on Cabernet Sauvignon is thought to have come from Baron Hector de Brane (proprietor prior to 1830 of Brane Mouton, which was later to become Mouton Rothschild). Armand d'Armailhacq also grew the grape at his property and advocated its use in his book (published in various editions from 1855). It was during the second half of the nineteenth century that Cabernet Sauvignon really took over. "Cabernet Sauvignon is certainly the most highly regarded cépage in the Médoc. For several years it has spread, especially in Pauillac and St. Julien, where it is cultivated almost exclusively," d'Armailhacq noted.[30] The first counts of individual grape varieties date from this period (historically the different varieties had been intermingled, so it would have been difficult to assess relative proportions). Various communes of the Médoc varied from 40-75% Cabernet, with the rest planted to Merlot and Malbec. Pessac (the northern tip of the Graves) had half Cabernet, with a quarter each of Merlot and Malbec.[31]

Following the devastation caused by phylloxera at the end of the nineteenth century, the pattern of varieties simplified. Cabernet Sauvignon increased in the Médoc at the expense of Cabernet Franc. Carmenère largely disappeared. It was a relief for vignerons not to have to handle Carmenère, which ripened so late that it was marginal, and was also vulnerable to the fungal disease oïdium. (Carmenère became almost extinct in France, but was rediscovered in Chile in the 1990s.[32]) Petit Verdot disappeared from the Graves. Malbec did not take very well to the necessary grafting on to American root-stocks, and was largely replaced by Merlot. (Malbec is still grown in Cahors, just southeast of Bordeaux; the local name for the variety is Cot.[33]) By the turn of the century Merlot had become the major black grape on the right bank.[34] The pattern of plantings did not change much over the next half century.

Prior to the introduction of rules controlling geographic origins, Bordeaux had suffered from a century or more of adulteration with stronger wines from warmer regions. All this had to stop when new rules were introduced in 1911. The rules did more than exclude distant sources. Previously there had been vigorous debate as to whether Bordeaux should continue to include wines from neighboring areas. When the rules were defined, the boundaries for Bordeaux were restricted to the department of the Gironde. This brought a halt to the close historical connection with the wines just to the east in the Dordogne. Bergerac had started exporting wine to England in 1254, and the wines were transported along the Dordogne river through Bordeaux. Indeed, they were often included in the assemblage in Bordeaux. Their exclusion led to a rush of vineyard plantings in Entre-deux-Mers to replace them.[35] (Today the blend of grape varieties in the Dordogne resembles Bordeaux's right bank.[36])

The introduction of the system of appellation d'origine contrôlée (AOC) in 1936 caused the next significant change, by restricting the varieties that could be grown. The motives for introducing the system were to protect quality wine from imitations, but from the very beginning it was decided that merely protect-ing authenticity was not sufficient, so there were rules to ensure quality and enforce a concept of what was typical for each region. This has effectively fro-zen Bordeaux into the varieties of the early twentieth century. The system went beyond defining the character of Bordeaux into creating a hierarchy of more detailed *appellations* within the generic Bordeaux AOC. Every bottle of wine within the system now carried on its label the name of its appellation.

The AOC divides Bordeaux into many subregions; there were as many as 57 different appellations at one time, although some have now been amalga-mated. AOC Bordeaux is the generic descriptor for the whole region, and is the lowest level of the hierarchy. Slightly more restrictive, Côtes de Bordeaux de-scribes wine coming from broad regions adjacent to the river on the right bank, and Entre-deux-Mers describes the region between the Garonne and Dordogne rivers. Graves is a large area on the left bank to the south of the city. All of these descriptions can be used for either red or white wine. On the left bank, Haut-Médoc describes wines from the southern part of the Médoc, and Médoc is used to describe wines from the Bas-Médoc (Bas is dropped because it is considered to be pejorative). Both can be used only for red wine.

The top wines come from much smaller areas. On the left bank, these lie to the immediate south and north of the city. Pessac-Léognan split off from the

In spite of its reputation as the perfect terroir, Bordeaux has drainage problems everywhere, from the high water table on the left bank to the clay soils of the right bank.

Graves in 1987 and produces the best wines, both red and white, from south of the city. Within the Haut-Médoc to the north, there are six communes: going up the Gironde from Bordeaux come Margaux, St. Julien, Pauillac, and St. Estèphe; a little inland are Moulis and Listrac. Like the Haut-Médoc itself, the communal AOCs apply only to red wine. The equivalent appellations across the river lie in the Libournais (not itself an appellation but a general description for the area centered on the town of Libourne on the Dordogne). The top appellations here are St. Emilion and Pomerol, both exclusive to red wine based on Merlot and Cabernet Franc.

The nature of Bordeaux wine historically, and indeed the very name of "claret," is not much of a guide to its style today or to the character of Cabernet Sauvignon. Claret is an anglicization of "clairet," meaning light-colored,[37] and dates from the Middle Ages, when wine was required to be "clar, bon, pur" [clear, good, and pure].[38] Categorized by color, wine could be white, claret, or red. The white was held in high esteem, claret was sold to consumers, and the red (which gained its color from prolonged contact with the skins after fermentation and therefore became somewhat bitter) was given to the workers.[39] This was effectively the inverse of current attitudes that more color means more extraction which means more quality! Claret was probably the color of a rosé.[40]

At the beginning of the eighteenth century, a major source of supply for England came from wines seized at sea during the war with France. These were

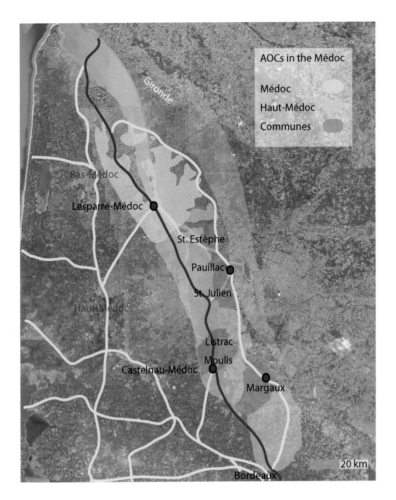

The Médoc peninsula is divided into two appellations, the Médoc to the north, and the (higher quality) Haut-Médoc to the south. Within the Haut-Médoc are the individual communes where the best red wines are produced.

advertised as "New French Clarets."[41] After the war was over, punitive taxation, in the form of discriminatory duties on French wine, made it unprofitable to export ordinary wine to England. The barrier was overcome by exporting premium wines, and it was during the first half of the eighteenth century that a demand for fine wines arose.[42] Yet during this period, all wines, including the finest, were commonly "improved" at source or in London by blending with stronger wines from the south of France or from Spain.

They don't make Bordeaux like they used to—well, perhaps they never did. In the nineteenth century, Claret, as experienced in England, was more alcoholic, deeply colored, and richer than the wine that had been produced from the vineyards in Bordeaux.[43] How much Cabernet Sauvignon went into the wine, and what influence it exerted on style in this period, especially after "improvement" seems doubtful. It was only after 1911 that "Bordeaux" wine had legally to come from Bordeaux, so it was not until the twentieth century that a buyer could be sure a bottle exclusively represented grape varieties grown in Bordeaux.

A major source of wine for blending with Bordeaux was Hermitage, in the northern Rhône.[44] An idea of what effect this had on the flavor comes from Château Palmer's recent experiment in recreating the nineteenth century wine by blending Syrah (from a secret source "somewhere between Cornas and Côte Rôtie" in the northern Rhône) with wine from the château's estate in Margaux. Only a couple of hundred cases have been produced (with the wine selling at the same price as Château Palmer itself). Legal restrictions mean that the wine can be labeled only as Vin de Table, so it cannot carry an identification of origin or vintage; it is described as Château Palmer Historical XIXth Century Blend, and the label carries a discrete notation of the lot number to identify the vintage (L20.07 indicates the 2007 vintage).

The wine was made in 2004, 2006, 2007, and 2010. The proportion of Syrah in the blend has closely followed nineteenth century practice, with 15% in 2004 and 2006, and 12% in 2007. These vintages were relatively weak in Bordeaux, so the blend is duplicating the nineteenth century objective of strengthening the wine. The result is an interesting wine, but one that more resembles its minor component from the northern Rhône than the traditional character of Margaux (page 340). At least in the first few years after the vintage, it's the aromas and flavors of Syrah that are most obvious. Will the wine revert to reflect more the character of Margaux in the future? The blend was not tried in 2005, because it was felt the Syrah would not do much for the ripe Cabernet of the year, and it remains to be seen what the effect will be in the great vintage of 2010.

Of course, when they used to "hermitager" the wine in the nineteenth century, everything—both Bordeaux and Hermitage—was more muted, but if the relative effect was at all similar to Palmer's new blend, the "typicity" of claret at the time must have been very different from what you might expect looking back from today's varieties in Bordeaux. Varietal character no doubt strengthened in the wine once blending with foreign sources was banned. The trend to authenticity was further enhanced as the producers took over responsibility for determining style.

The development of Bordeaux after the medieval period relied on the growth of a powerful merchant class, the negociants, who actually matured and in due course sold the wine. The negociants would buy wine from the producers soon after the vintage, transport it to their cellars in Bordeaux, and mature it to suit their clientele. The original producer was unknown to the ultimate buyer, and did not become important until much later.

In the fifteenth century, the wine was sold under broad regional headings, such as "red Gascon." By the sixteenth century, wines from some places began to attract higher prices.[45] During the eighteenth century, wines from individual producers were recognized, and the best were classified. During the nineteenth century, "château" became a successful marketing term implying a significant

Negociants had vast subterranean caves in Bordeaux where most wine was matured until the last part of the twentieth century. Barton and Guestier were established in 1802 on the Quai de Chartrons, where they matured their wines.

producer with a good reputation; in 1855 only a handful of properties were described as "châteaux," but by the turn of the century most producers were known as châteaux.[46] The importance of the châteaux increased further after Baron Philip de Rothschild persuaded others to follow his example of bottling his own wine at Château Mouton Rothschild from 1924. This removed the responsibility for maturation from the negociants, and château-bottling slowly became an imprimatur of quality, although it did not become common practice until the 1960s, and it became compulsory only in the 1990s.[47]

The use of "château" might be taken to imply a certain grand scale of production. This is and isn't true. When viticulture developed in the Médoc in the sixteenth century, vineyards were largely local affairs. They were mostly based on rather small holdings, although there was a tendency to amalgamation of parcels held by the larger seigneuries (the grand estates).[48] The Church was relatively less important here than it was in Burgundy, where it was a major landholder and at the forefront of technical developments.[49] The proprietors in Bordeaux came from the parlementaires—the equivalent of the upper middle classes—rather than from the nobility, and most of the vineyards were rented out or managed at a distance.[50] During the seventeenth and eighteenth centuries, some of the seigneuries gave rise to today's more important estates; most of the important châteaux were established by the nineteenth century.

The concept of "grand vins" developed in the first quarter of the eighteenth century. These were the forerunners of the great Cabernet-dominated clarets of today. In an address to the king in July 1725, the authorities in Bordeaux remarked that, "All the wines of this province are different in quality and price. Some that the English call grand vins are bought under this name at an excessive price; they are a class apart and should not be confused with the other wines."[51] What a prescient view of today's market!

Today's hierarchy began to be established when the wines of Pontac (Haut Brion), Latour, Lafite, and Margaux were individually recognized, selling at 4-5 times the price of other wines from the Médoc.[52] By the 1723 vintage, one English importer could write: "the four topping [superior] growths of La Tour, Lafite, Château Margaux and Pontac are exceeding good."[53] Haut Brion was in the forefront. Its proprietor, Arnaud de Pontac, established a restaurant in the City of London where Haut Brion was appreciated by notables such as Samuel Pepys: "M. Pontack, the son of the President of Bordeaux, imported to England some of the most esteemed claret to establish a tavern with all the novelties of French cookery."[54]

Why were the Médoc and the Graves the regions where the grand vins developed? Their initial advantage may have been due to the Willie Sutton effect. (Willie Sutton was a bank robber, who when asked why he robbed banks, said, "Because that's where the money is.") The Médoc and the Graves were where the parlementaires invested in estates.[55] By the mid-eighteenth century, vines had become the major crop in the large estates of the seigneuries,[56] and revenue from wine had become the landholders' major source of income.[57] By contrast, the estates on the right bank were much smaller, as indeed they remain today, and wines of equivalent quality did not develop there, most notably in St. Emilion and Pomerol, until the second half of the twentieth century.[58] It is because the terroir of the left bank, where most investments were made, is well suited to Cabernet Sauvignon that Bordeaux made its historic reputation with this variety.

Given the differences between the focus on Cabernet Sauvignon on the left bank and Merlot on the right bank, you might well ask why all this wine is labeled under the common rubric of "Bordeaux." The answer is surely that the concentration, indeed the monopoly, of distribution through the city of Bordeaux caused the wines to be marketed through the same channels. There are no separate generic appellations such as Rive Gauche and Rive Droit to represent the broad division into left and right banks, although most generic AOC Bordeaux comes from the right bank.[59] Claret, however, strictly speaking, describes only the wines of the left bank that historically were exported to England, and has therefore become indissolubly associated with a Bordeaux blend based on Cabernet Sauvignon, although the term itself originated well before Cabernet Sauvignon was grown in Bordeaux.[60]

Within much of the AOC system, the name of the appellation is a principal guide to quality. Burgundy is famously divided into a steeply ascending hierarchy, based on geographical location, from generic Bourgogne, to regional AOCs, village AOCs, premier crus, and grand crus. Ascending the hierarchy, quality increases as the size of the appellation decreases. Premier and grand

The châteaux of the Médoc were usually constructed after the wine had become established. Château Margaux is an exception that was constructed earlier, and is famous for the grandeur of its tree-lined approach allée.

crus are located within village AOCs, village AOCS are located within regional AOCs, and the regional AOCs lie within the generic Bourgogne AOC. Bordeaux is different. There is a flat hierarchy, with individual AOCs of varying quality all lying directly within the generic Bordeaux AOC.[61] The only real exception consists of the six communes of the left bank (Listrac, Moulis, Margaux, St. Julien, Pauillac, St. Estèphe), which lie within the Haut-Médoc AOC, and Pessac-Léognan, which occupies the best part of the Graves AOC.

Quality on the left bank (and in the top appellation of St. Emilion on the right bank) is assessed by a system that is independent of geography and whose origins predate the AOC system by almost a century. It was an incidental outcome when the wines of the Gironde were displayed at the Universal Exposition in Paris in 1855. The Chamber of Commerce commissioned a wine map of the Gironde and asked the local brokers to draw up a list of the leading wines. This list placed the top châteaux (producers) into five categories of Grand Cru Classé (classified growths), simply on the basis of their relative market prices. At the peak of the hierarchy are the five Premier Grand Cru Classés (Lafite Rothschild, Latour, Margaux, Haut Brion, and Mouton Rothschild, the first four as classified in 1855, and Mouton promoted in 1973). Never revised apart from Mouton's promotion, and now surely set in stone, this list continues to dominate Bordeaux even today, although as a detailed classification it is seriously out of date.[62] (There were 57 châteaux in the original classification, but due to divisions, there are 61 today.[63]) The 1855 classification was so outstandingly successful in increasing the visibility of the Grand Cru Classés that price rather than terroir has been the basis for classification in Bordeaux ever since.[64]

All but one of the Grand Cru Classés are from the Médoc (the exception being Château Haut Brion in the Graves). This reflected the fact that the wines of the left bank were better known, and more highly priced, than those of the right bank. By 1855, Cabernet Sauvignon was widespread in the Médoc and had become the dominant grape at the very top châteaux, so the classification might be taken as the very first list of the top wines based on Cabernet Sauvignon. If the classification were repeated today, which is to say if wines were ranked solely on recent prices, the first growths would retain their positions at the top, next would come a group known as the "super-seconds," which include some of the second growths and others from lower levels, and then would come about half of the rest from the original classification. A subsequent classification, the Cru Bourgeois, applies to châteaux that were not included in the 1855 classification;[65] the best would be included in the list of Grand Cru Classés in any reclassification today.

The one constant factor in the great wines of the left bank has been their high proportion of Cabernet Sauvignon, but other varieties have changed. Environmental disaster has been the spur to changing the plantings in Bordeaux more than once. The massive change caused by phylloxera at the end of the nineteenth century was almost matched by the replanting caused by the great freeze of the winter of 1956, which killed off many vines (especially on the right bank). Collateral damage resulted when the authorities forced producers to plant a high-yielding cultivar of Cabernet Sauvignon (reliable but not of very high quality), and it took some years for the effect to be reversed. At all events, following the great freeze, Merlot climbed steadily, Cabernet Sauvignon overtook Cabernet Franc, Malbec started its final decline, and a large number of miscellaneous varieties began to disappear.

The rules for what is permitted in the AOC have been steadily strengthened, but it was really only between 1964 and 1988 that the last of the inferior varieties were squeezed out.[66] Until the 1950s, the AOC covered only half of the vineyards of Bordeaux, but today it includes virtually all vineyards in the region.[67] Since 1998, only six black varieties have been permitted in Bordeaux: Cabernet Sauvignon, Cabernet Franc, and Merlot account for more than 80% of plantings, but Petit Verdot, Malbec, and Carmenère are also legal. Only three white varieties are grown: Sauvignon Blanc (and its subvariety Sauvignon Gris), Sémillon, and Muscadelle.[68]

Bordeaux's great reputation is based on its red wines (with a nod of exception to the sweet whites of Sauternes), but the exclusive focus on reds is a phenomenon of the last half century. In Bordeaux as a whole, white wines were in the majority until the end of the 1960s. The major transition to red wine occurred during the next two decades, reaching its present level of 90% by the end of the 1980s.[69] The driving force here was commercial; white wine from Bordeaux simply was not selling. Of course, the change affects only the right bank and the Graves; the Médoc has been almost exclusively devoted to red wine all along (although in the past few years some other top flight châteaux have imitated Château Margaux—which has long produced a white wine[70]—and begun to produce small quantities of dry white wine. Because of appellation regulations, this can be labeled only as AOC Bordeaux.)

Along with the increased restrictions on permitted varieties has come a further simplification, in the form of increasing focus on Merlot at the expense of other varieties. Cabernet Sauvignon is far from an endangered species, but it is only a quarter of all plantings in Bordeaux as a whole. When the inferior varieties were squeezed out in the 1970s and 1980s, plantings of both Merlot and Cabernet Sauvignon increased; but since then there has been a steady increase in Merlot and decline in both Cabernet Sauvignon and Cabernet Franc. Bordeaux as a whole has the most Cabernet Sauvignon of any wine region in the world. But Cabernet Sauvignon is the majority grape in less than 15% of the wines, almost all from the Médoc or Pessac.[71]

Vintage variation is probably more extreme in Bordeaux than anywhere else Cabernet Sauvignon is grown. Partly this is because it is one of the cooler climates to start with, traditionally on the edge for ripeness, so temperatures below average push the Cabernet Sauvignon into herbaceousness. Of course, recent vintages have gone the other way, most notably in 2009 and 2010, which, at least as judged by alcohol levels, were the richest ever. Yet Bordeaux has a surprising capacity to retain freshness: the only year in which it seemed to me to lose it completely was 2003, the year of the *canicule* (heat wave). The 2009 and 2010 vintages in Bordeaux achieved a reputation en primeur (when the wines were tasted from barrel) for atypically lush wines, high in alcohol and low in acid: great vintages but pushing even further the trend towards New World styles, but my first tasting of 2009 from bottle revealed very satisfactory freshness (Υ page 311). As described for Lafite Rothschild by its Director, Charles Chevalier, "The wine has had good evolution, the exuberance we had at the beginning is no longer there; at the en primeur I was not sure we were in Bordeaux, now we are coming back into Bordeaux."

The reputation of the 2009 vintage had made it seem that traditional communal differences might be obscured by the rising tide that is lifting all fruits to higher and higher levels of ripeness, dampening differences between communes that come out more sharply when grapes strive for ripeness. But not a bit of it. The wines of Pessac-Léognan tend to show a soft, smoky quality of cigar box, very classic for Graves, the Haut-Médoc has firm fruits with acid support, Margaux comes off just a bit more elegant, with refined fruits some-

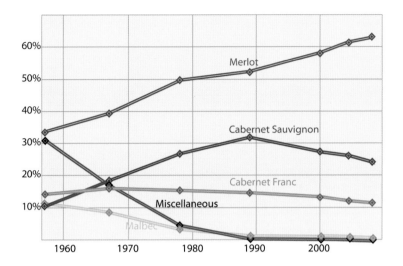

Concentration on the major grape varieties occurred in the 1970s and 1980s, followed by focus on Merlot through the 1990s and 2000s.[72]

times showing a faintly herbal or mineral impression, and St. Julien shows that precise delineation of tight black fruits. Pauillac is less typical for me, sometimes showing a slightly hard edge that I usually associate with St. Estèphe. (Over on the right bank, the best St. Emilions seem to be displaying more the fine-edged richness of ripe Cabernet Franc than the Merlot, while Pomerol tends to full blown ripe Merlot, the one area that lives up directly to the reputation of the vintage.)

So what is the true nature of Bordeaux? Although the vast majority of wines today are based on Merlot, it is for defining the character of Cabernet Sauvignon that Bordeaux became famous. Is Bordeaux abandoning its role as the guardian of Cabernet Sauvignon's typicity? Why is it then that attempts elsewhere to emulate Bordeaux focus on Cabernet Sauvignon? Or do they—is Cabernet Sauvignon from the New World in fact more like the fruitier, Merlot-based wines of the right bank than the traditional austere wines of the left bank? And indeed, how is the left bank changing to meet competition from the New World, not to mention the challenge from the right bank across the river?

3

The Bordeaux Blend

CABERNET SAUVIGNON is not the most important variety in Bordeaux on the numbers: with under a quarter of plantings, it is a distinct second to Merlot. But for more than a century after the 1855 classification, it remained unchallenged as the dominant influence in the greatest wines of Bordeaux, the Grand Cru Classés of the Médoc, spreading a halo over the other wines of the left bank. In the past half century there has been competition from across the river, with a steady rise to prominence of the top wines of the right bank. Dominated by a blend of Merlot and Cabernet Franc, or even Merlot alone as for Château Pétrus, these wines now challenge the great first growths for leadership in the market. Yet attempts in other regions to emulate or compete with Bordeaux focus on challenging the wines of the left bank. "Bordeaux blend" is synonymous with wine dominated by Cabernet Sauvignon, for all that these wines are a small minority in Bordeaux itself.

If Bordeaux were classified according to the proportion of Cabernet Sauvignon, it would be divided into three subregions: Médoc/Pessac-Léognan,

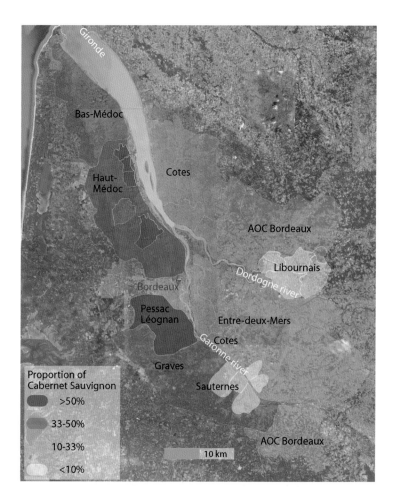

Cabernet Sauvignon is more important on the left bank than the right bank. Its highest concentration is in the Haut-Médoc, especially in the communes. There is almost an equal area of Cabernet Sauvignon on the right bank, but it represents a much lower proportion of the overall plantings.[2]

Graves, and the right bank. Cabernet Sauvignon is the most important grape in the Médoc peninsula, where it is a clear majority of plantings in the major communes (St. Estèphe, Pauillac, St. Julien, and Margaux), and also in Pessac-Léognan, the northern part of Graves. It's just under half of plantings in the rest of the Haut-Médoc and Médoc (and somewhat less in the communes of Moulis and Listrac).[1] It is just over a third of the Graves (excluding Pessac-Léognan), where Merlot is the most important variety. On the right bank, it is generally around 20%, although rarely above 10% in the Libournais. Of course, there are some individual châteaux with higher proportions.

The key to understanding the style(s) of Bordeaux is blending. This has been a key feature of the region ever since different grape varieties were intermixed in the vineyards—now, of course, each variety is grown in its own separate plots. Already by 1787, blending varieties was regarded as the route to successful winemaking: "In all four areas (Entre-deux-Mers, Graves, Médoc, and the Palus [close to the river]), vignerons are convinced that it is best to cultivate

*Cabernet Sauvignon
dominates the Médoc,
and is important in the
Graves, but is of much
less importance on the
right bank.[4]*

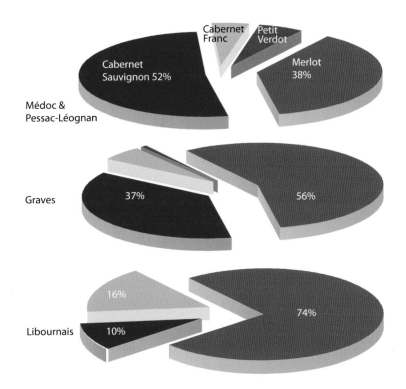

Médoc &
Pessac-Léognan

Cabernet
Sauvignon 52%

Cabernet
Franc

Petit
Verdot

Merlot
38%

Graves

37%

56%

Libournais

16%

10%

74%

many varieties in order to make good wine; they plant varieties that are preco-
cious in the colder terrains and those that mature later in the drier places."[3]

Blending in Bordeaux is a typically pragmatic solution to the problem of
growing grapes in a marginal climate (marginal at least for the varieties being
grown), by offering some protection against the vagaries of vintage variation.
Cabernet Sauvignon does not ripen reliably every year on the left bank, so
blending with varieties that ripen more easily offers two advantages: adding
riper flavors to the wine than can be obtained with Cabernet Sauvignon alone;
and being able to vary the composition of the blend to respond to failures and
successes each year. It also allows more vineyard area to be cultivated, since
Merlot will ripen in spots where Cabernet is not successful. (On the right bank,
of course, Cabernet Sauvignon is even harder to ripen and so is generally replaced by Cabernet Franc, but the same principle applies).

Even today, with warmer vintages and better viticulture, there is still significant variation in the blend each year: Cabernet Sauvignon may do better in a
warmer year, but fail to ripen in a cooler year; but Merlot may become too ripe
in a really warm year although ripening well in a cooler year. Cabernet Sauvignon may go from being the dominant variety to less than half the blend from
one year to the next on the left bank. Vintage character therefore depends not
only on overall ripeness, but on the proportions of each variety that end up in
the blend. This is a contrast with the other great French wine region, Burgundy,

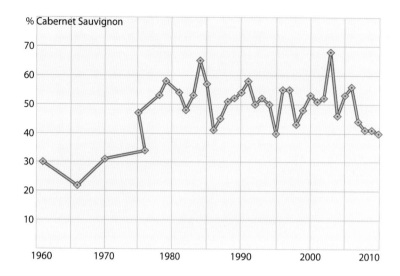

Château Palmer has fluctuated between 40% and 68% Cabernet Sauvignon, with the vintage, since the 1980s. The vineyard has 47% Cabernet Sauvignon today.[5] Some of the famous older vintages, including 1961 and 1966, had even lower levels. Was Palmer 1961 the greatest Merlot ever made[6] (with due apologies to Château Pétrus)?

where red wine comes exclusively from Pinot Noir; in a sense, Burgundy gives a more direct impression of vintage conditions, since each wine represents production from the very same vines every year, compared with Bordeaux's bias towards whichever varieties did best each year.

The blend has changed significantly with time. In the eighteenth century, there were far more varieties than today, and Cabernet Sauvignon emerged as the quality leader by the end of the century. For the first half of the nineteenth century there was still some question as to whether Cabernet Sauvignon or Carmenère was the best variety, so these two were probably the dominant varieties of the blend. During the second half of the century, Malbec became a more common partner for Cabernet Sauvignon on the left bank. Phylloxera changed everything, of course, and Merlot—previously somewhat disdained—came into a prominence that has steadily increased for the past century. The simplification of varieties resulting from phylloxera, followed by the replanting forced by the great freeze of 1956, means that today the only other significant black varieties are Cabernet Franc and Petit Verdot.

There is virtually no Carmenère, although a tiny amount was recently reintroduced at Château Brane Cantenac, and used in their blend for the first time in 2011. There was still some Malbec at Château Gruaud Larose until recently, but the last year it was used in the blend was in 2007 (for the second wine). "What to do with the Malbec was a real debate. The vineyard manager said it was a nightmare to look after, but the technical director wanted to keep it. The Malbec was planted on one of the best plots for Cabernet Sauvignon, so they decided it was a nightmare and replaced it with Cabernet Sauvignon," says general manager David Launay. Owner Jean Merlaut says that, "Malbec may be okay on the Côtes, but in the Médoc you get good Malbec one year out of ten or maybe twenty." Indeed, the last holdout for Malbec in Bordeaux is the right bank area of the Côtes de Bourg, where it is about 5% of plantings.[7] (The nineteenth century has been recapitulated in South America, albeit under somewhat different conditions from Bordeaux. Today blends of Cabernet Sauvignon and Carmenère are produced in Chile, and blends of Cabernet Sauvignon with Malbec are found in Argentina; see Chapter 7.)

The intensity of the left bank and the richness of the right bank are modern features. When the châteaux were classified in 1855, the style of the wine was very different from today. It was a light red color with less than 10% alcohol, and less than a quarter of modern tannin levels.[8] Tannins give the wine the structure needed for aging, so this would have been partly responsible for the much shorter life of the wines, typically less than 10 years in the mid eighteenth century. The wine was matured in Baltic oak,[9] which must have given a somewhat different flavor bias than the French oak used today.[10] (French oak probably became widely used only after the first world war, when the sources of Baltic oak dried up.) The typicity of Cabernet Sauvignon during the period of classification would have been influenced by its blend with Cabernet Franc and Malbec.[11]

In spite of the vicissitudes of phylloxera and the change in cépage composition from Malbec to Merlot, there was little change in style by the start of the twentieth century.[12] Wines remained light and were consumed relatively young, although a market for older wines, particularly those of the top châteaux, which were drunk for one to two decades after the vintage, had developed in England.[13] During the first half of the new century the concept seemed to develop that great vintages would be tannic and undrinkable when young and would require time to age.[14] This was very likely a measure of desperation developed in response to poor vintages, especially the terrible run of the 1930s. But the concept took hold, and until the most recent two or three decades it was generally accepted that a Bordeaux that was pleasant to drink when young would not age well. "Red Bordeaux is... delicate but firm... but its characteristic softness and subtlety come only with age," said Alexis Lichine, the proprietor of Château Prieuré-Lichine, in 1967.[15]

Since then things have changed. I am inclined to divide the time since the second world war into three periods. The Traditional Period lasted until 1982, what I think of as the Middle Period started with the vintage of 1982 and lasted until around 2004, and then the Modern Period includes recent vintages. Changes of style during each period influenced the view of the typicity of Cabernet Sauvignon. Lichine's comment would no longer apply even to Château Prieuré-Lichine (perhaps especially so since the style changed in the late nineties following a corporate takeover; indeed, I wonder whether Lichine, who is buried in the vineyard, would even recognize the wine).

From 1945 until 1982, wines were made along much the same lines as during the first half of the century, but with increasing technical expertise. Much of the reason for improved winemaking lay with changes introduced by the great oenologist Émile Peynaud. There was more use of new wood (a subject for some criticism at the time[16]), and more consistent alcohol levels. Grapes were usually harvested once they reached around 11.5% potential alcohol, because higher sugar levels caused over-vigorous fermentation, which pushed up temperatures and risked the development of volatile acidity. Producers were freed from this constraint when temperature control of fermentation became available in the 1970s. Alcohol was generally increased to 12.5% by chaptalization. Picking Cabernet Sauvignon at (relatively) low sugar levels went hand in hand with high acidity and a tendency to herbaceousness. Vintage fluctuation remained considerable, from extremes such as the great vintage of 1961 to the terrible vintages of 1972 or 1977. Most châteaux produced only a single wine; variations in the blend were used to even out quality. But basically the wine you saw each vintage was a reflection of the combination of the climate and terroir in that year.

Vintage conditions produced a dramatic change in 1982. Ripe grapes gave wines that were rich and relatively fruit-driven, with softer tannins than usual, and low in acid to the point at which some critics were doubtful about their longevity. There was a great controversy as to whether wines that were not overtly tannic and acidic had the potential for aging.[17] Eventually it became apparent that the wines in fact were aging very well, and 1982 now has turned into a classically developing vintage—although it took twenty years. Sometime after year 2000, I noticed a reversion to more classic character, with faintly herbaceous tones appearing in many of the wines, in delicious balance with the maturing fruits. The 1982 vintage was a harbinger of things to come, and over the next two decades more vintages followed in the new style, richer, more opulent, and softer, with notable peaks in 1990 and 2000. Looking back, 1982 seems to have been a case of 'you ain't seen nothing yet.'

Change has not been due solely to natural conditions. Certainly vintages have been warmer on average. But producers took advantage of the more favorable conditions to harvest their grapes later (aided by developments in viticulture giving better control of grapevine development). A reduction in yields has led to a general increase in concentration since 1982. The new criterion of "phenolic ripeness" has replaced the previous basis for judging readiness in terms of sugar levels or sugar/acid balance. Phenolic ripeness lacks any precise definition: most producers judge it by taste and by criteria such as the color and looseness of the seeds; some actually measure tannin levels, but at all events the basic intention is to judge maturity by overall ripeness. This results in harvesting at higher sugar levels and lower acid levels than previously. One corollary is increased alcohol level in the wine. Another is an increase in the total amount of tannin. Measured by the IPT (index of total polyphenols), this increased from an average of 5 g/l in 1982 to 6 g/l in 2005.[18]

Superficially not much has changed at Château Lafite Rothschild. The harvest in 1881 was performed by hand, and it was still manual in 2011. Of course, criteria for selecting berries have changed, as have means of transport. View of 1881 from Illustrated London News; photograph of the 2011 harvest, courtesy Gavin Quinney.

But most producers will tell you that a change in the *character* of the tannins, from vegetative to riper, is equally important (although there is no objective way to measure this).[19]

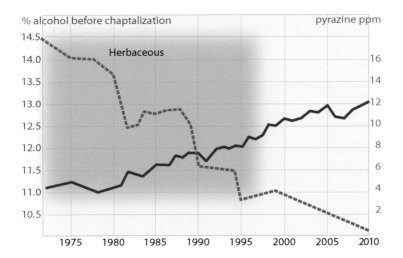

Pyrazines decline with increasing ripeness (roughly measured by sugar level) and probably dropped below the level of detection (indicated by the green square) during the 1990s[20].

During the transition period from 1982 to 2004, the left bank underwent its most striking change of style: the replacement of herbaceousness with fruitiness. Herbaceous aromas depend on the levels of pyrazines at harvest; and the decline in pyrazines in Cabernet Sauvignon is the most important consequence of the transition to harvesting later in order to get greater phenolic ripeness. Because pyrazines are destroyed by exposure to light, the extra few days before harvest can push levels below detection. Of course this varies with the vintage, but in the nineties harvests became regularly prolonged to ensure that pyrazines were routinely below detectable levels. No one measures pyrazine levels as a criterion for harvest (perhaps they should?) but producers everywhere are anxious to avoid herbaceousness in Cabernet Sauvignon. Young wines from Bordeaux rarely show herbaceousness any more.

The decline in herbaceousness is not due solely to the reduction in pyrazines. The word that cannot speak its name is Brett, shorthand for Brettanomyces, a spoilage yeast that infects wine (most often via contaminated wood barrels). Low levels add leathery aromas that meld into the herbaceous aromas of pyrazines. At higher levels, the aromas turn to barnyard, mousy, and ultimately Band-Aid. Brett is controversial because some producers believe it can add complexity at low levels; while to others, especially in the New World, it is anathema, and any level is considered a fatal flaw. "All wines in Bordeaux were contaminated with Brett in the seventies," says negociant Bill Blatch, "we did not even know what the cause was then." Some of what was taken for characteristic herbaceousness, especially when it tipped over towards medicinal overtones, was almost certainly due to Brett rather than pyrazines. Improvements in winery hygiene mean that Brett is rare in Bordeaux today.

Each variety contributes its own character to a blend. The most powerful, Cabernet Sauvignon, has the most structure in the form of tannins, and gives the left bank wines their longevity. On the right bank, Cabernet Franc plays something of an equivalent role, but with more of a leafy, tobacco quality. In the context of Bordeaux, the Cabernets can be overwhelming without the softening effect of Merlot, which offers a generous fleshiness to round out the palate. (Or conversely, Cabernet Franc adds structure and freshness to the dominant Merlot on the right bank.) The last variety, Petit Verdot, is usually used on the left bank only in small quantities, adding a faint spiciness and density that lends interest to the fruit quality of the wine. Wines on the left bank often contain all four varieties, in proportions that vary each year depending on conditions. The dominance of Cabernet Sauvignon can give the wines of the left bank a touch of austerity, compared to the fuller, fleshier, and more overtly fruity wines dominated by Merlot on the right bank.

To what extent do vintages have general styles determined by variations in proportions of the different cépages in the blend? "Vintage conditions aren't always easy to understand—in 1994 there was no Merlot in Lafite, but at Latour there was the maximum," says Director Charles Chevalier at Lafite Rothschild. And it's not always easy to relate differences in style between vintages to simple changes in cépage composition, although certainly some years stand out by being more or less driven by Cabernet Sauvignon—1996 was a "Cabernet year," for example, and the wines are more clearly characterized by acidity and herbaceous overtones. It's by no means always true that "Cabernet years" are the best years. The difficulty in generalizing about varietal character was explained by Jean Delmas when he was the winemaker at Château Haut Brion. "An experiment with separate vinification, conducted at Château de Pez in 1970, showed some common errors concerning the cépages. I tasted blind Cabernet Sauvignon, Merlot, Cabernet Franc, and Petit Verdot. The blind tasting allowed us easily to identify the characteristics of each cépage, the roundness and richness of Merlot, the powerful tannins of Cabernet Sauvignon, the slightly aggressive, vegetal character of Petit Verdot, and the freshness of Cabernet Franc. We were all wrong. The wine that was fat and long on the finish was Petit Verdot. The wine that was complete and tannic was the Cabernet Franc. The slightly acid wine was the Cabernet Sauvignon. And the lightest wine was the Merlot. There is no single truth for each cépage, but a different situation in each year."[21]

A perfect illustration of how the varieties complement one another in the blend came from a tasting when I visited Château Lascombes a year after the 2010 vintage. The individual varieties had been maturing in barriques since the vintage, and there was also a blend (𝒯 page 331). The Cabernet Sauvignon had power and structure but was hard and lacked aromatics, the Merlot was sweet, ripe, and rich, and pushed the mid palate at you, and the Petit Verdot was intense, spicy, and perfumed (a little goes a long way). The blend was clearly a more complete wine than any of its components. There was no Cabernet Franc, on which opinion is divided in the Médoc.

At Château Pontet Canet in Pauillac, Jean-Michel Comme told me, "The 2-4% Cabernet Franc is totally necessary; without it the wine is not so good. People at the great growths are suppressing the Cabernet Franc and I cannot understand it. With it, the tannins in the blend are finer. Those who have suppressed it may have just tasted it alone; it's difficult if you taste it together with Cabernet Sauvignon in the same line of glasses. The taste of Cabernet Franc as a single variety is not the relevant criterion; it's the same with Petit Verdot, it needs to be blended." At Château Montrose, where Nicolas Glumineau would have liked to increase the Cabernet Franc, he said the problem was that "people have always planted Cabernet Franc on terroirs that weren't good enough for Cabernet Sauvignon or Merlot." At Château Rauzan-Gassies in Margaux, Anne-Françoise Quié feels that things have changed. "We used to say Cabernet Franc is for the attack and Merlot is for the mid palate, but that's not true any more. Cabernet Franc is going out because if you can ripen Cabernet Franc you can ripen Cabernet Sauvignon." Of course, these different views may partly reflect differences between Pauillac, where the Cabernet Sauvignon is always masculine, and Margaux, where the style is more feminine.

At Rauzan-Ségla, John Kolasa explains the divergence of views. "Both views of Cabernet Franc are true. You use Cabernet Franc only three years out of ten; you would get greater reliability with Cabernet Sauvignon. Here I don't think the Cabernet Franc is worth it, we've pulled it up (in the main estate) and we're replacing it with Cabernet Sauvignon." Insofar as there's any consensus on Cabernet Franc, it's that the problem on the left bank is the lack of calcareous soils. Where Cabernet Franc shines is on the plateau of the Côtes around St. Emilion, where the soils are based on a substratum of limestone. "On the left bank, Cabernet Franc mostly does not give concentrated wines—it's not interesting on gravelly or sandy soil," explains Gabriel Vialard at Château Haut-Bailly in Pessac-Léognan. Paul Pontallier at Château Margaux expresses a common view of Cabernet Franc on the left bank. "Cabernet Franc produces great wine but it's not as regular as Cabernet Sauvignon, sometimes it's good but it's very small, only 1-2% here. In our conditions it never reaches the extraordinary quality or harmony of the Cabernet Sauvignon."

The issue with the fourth variety, Petit Verdot, is due more to climate than terroir. Never planted in more than small amounts, Petit Verdot used to be considered to be necessary for increasing the strength of the wine, but it was always difficult to ripen. That has changed with global warming, and plantings seemed to be increasing at the start of the new millennium. But already the trend may be reversing. "It was really needed to bring color, alcohol, tannin—nearly a vin de presse or a vin de gout. I like it because it brings some flavors that don't exist in Cabernet Sauvignon. But with global warming it loses part of its interest; now it is getting a bit rich and rustic," says Philippe Blanc at Château Beychevelle. That reservation is echoed by Michael Georges, who

Changes in grape varieties planted at the classified growths show a trend for increasing Merlot and decreasing Cabernet.

The total plantings include grapes used for the second wine as well as for the grand vin.[22]

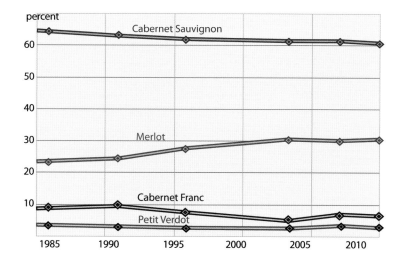

says, "We don't use Petit Verdot in Lascases. The problem comes in the aging, it gives an impression of dryness. For us the tannins are too rustic. And it gives very high degrees—15% in 2009 and 2010." At Château Rauzan-Ségla, John Kolasa has found an interesting compromise. "With the weather conditions we've been having with the extremes, Petit Verdot has become a little too strong, a little too difficult to blend. We had the idea of cofermenting the Petit Verdot with Cabernet Franc and it seems this gives you interesting material to add to the blend."

For all that the numbers show a small decline in the overall proportions of Cabernet Sauvignon, the perception everywhere on the left bank is that global warming is increasing its importance. Whether this is because of the positive view that Cabernet Sauvignon can now succeed in locations that used to require Cabernet Franc or the negative view that Merlot and Petit Verdot are becoming too alcoholic and rustic, the common impression is that producers would like to have more Cabernet Sauvignon. There's a certain amount of swapping terroirs, because criteria for selecting sites have changed. "Fifty or sixty years ago Cabernet Sauvignon was planted in cool places because it starts later than Merlot and there's less risk for frost. Now we have our Cabernet Sauvignon in the warmest places to have good maturity," explains Jean Merlaut at Château Gruaud Larose. This also may be contributing to the change to a riper style. But it's a slow process, given that a vineyard usually has a life of 25 years or so; those at their peak today represent decisions taken in the conditions of two or more decades ago.

As its preferred temperature range indicates, Cabernet Sauvignon is a grape for moderate climates. Within the context of Bordeaux, it does best in the warmer spots. And Cabernet hates to get its feet wet, meaning that it needs good drainage. The combination means that gravel soils, which are (relatively) warm and drain well, are the best locations. In Bordeaux, these are provided by the gravel mounds, which form a line of (slightly) elevated outcrops more or less parallel with the Gironde. "Gravel mound" is a geological description, which refers to the structure of the subsoil, although you do of course also often see a gravelly soil surface. Gravel mounds are quite large, typically 5-6 km long, and 1-2 km wide.[23] They consist of topsoil on compact sand, on top of a gravel bed that can range from a few centimeters to 2 or 3 meters in depth. The deeper the better. Below that are alternating layers of compact sand and clay lens. The gravel mound forces the grapevines to send their roots down deep, in the best cases several meters to the water table, which ensures an even supply of water during the growing season. The warmest spots on the left bank are centered on the gravel mounds; [24] perhaps this is what gives the great communes that crucial advantage in maturing Cabernet Sauvignon.

So how well does terroir match up with plantings of Cabernet Sauvignon? Virtually all the classified growths are located on gravel mounds.[25] The vineyards of the first growths are on the best terroir, with deep gravel mounds of up to 9 meters and a relatively low water table.[26] The only one not to conform completely is Château Margaux, where some of the vineyards are on bedrock rather than gravel (and some people consider that in fact this makes it the best terroir in the Médoc).[27] But there is not much geological evidence to support any hierarchy of terroirs among the other classified châteaux, at least to an extent that would explain the differences in their positions in the classification.[28]

Heterogeneity of soils is common in the Médoc. Although the generalization is that there are sandy swamps close to the river, gravel mounds just inland, and clay-based soils farther inland, there can be great differences even within a single vineyard. Each château has a mix of terroirs, usually including more gravel-based terrains where Cabernet Sauvignon is planted, and more clay-based terrains where Merlot is planted, and it would be hard for analysis of terroir to justify the difference, say, between second and fifth growths.

Does terroir explain the characters of the communes? The traditional view is that St. Estèphe produces the tightest, sturdiest wines, and Pauillac the most powerful; St. Julien is a touch lighter and more precise in its focus; Margaux is the most feminine and elegant. To the south in Pessac-Léognan, the classic description refers to cedar and a touch of cigar box. Does this reflect the character of the blend, the properties of Cabernet Sauvignon grown in each commune, some adherence to a common style by the châteaux—or is it a figment of the imagination?

Certainly there are differences in terroir between the extremes. The soils in Margaux tend to be a little lighter, with fine pebbles; this contributes to the elegance of the wines. The soils in St. Estèphe tend to be a little heavier, and there is a touch more clay; correspondingly the wines have a tendency to a little more hardness, especially when young. The best vineyards tend to be close, but not quite adjacent, to the river—there is an old Médocian saying that the

Gravel mounds provide the best terroir in the Médoc, forcing vines to develop deep roots.[29]

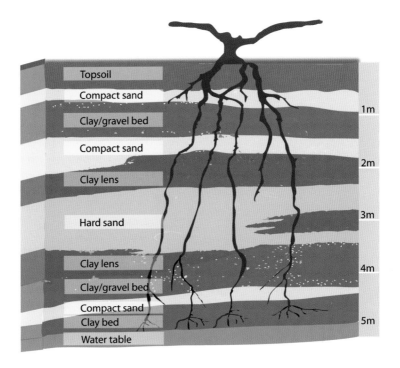

Topsoil

Compact sand

Clay/gravel bed
                                                                        1m
Compact sand

Clay lens   2m

Hard sand   3m

Clay lens   4m

Clay/gravel bed

Compact sand

Clay bed   5m

Water table

best vines can see the river—and the gravels become less distinct, and the wines not so fine, moving inland. "It's very easy to spot the best terroir in Pauillac, you don't need to be a geologist, you just need to be on top of the hill (although hill is a relative term), able to see gravel, and you look ahead and see the river," says Jean-Charles Cazes of Château Lynch Bages.

But it would be a fine taster who could always tell the difference between St. Julien and Pauillac. I sometimes think the reputation of Pauillac for that unique combination of power with elegance—what in another context Michael Broadbent has called the iron fist in the velvet glove—actually relates to the fact that Pauillac has three of the first growths (Lafite, Latour, and Mouton), giving a lift to the average intensity of its wines. If you compare wines that are at the same level in the hierarchy, say Léoville Lascases and Ducru Beaucaillou in St. Julien versus Pichon Lalande and Pichon Baron in Pauillac, can you really make the case that the differences between them represent the communes rather than the characteristics of viticulture and vinification at each château?

I suspect furthermore that differences were brought out in the past by marginal conditions. There's a much larger difference, especially for Cabernet Sauvignon, between grapes that are almost ripe and grapes that are just ripe than between grapes that have passed the point of ripeness by differing levels. So in past vintage conditions when Cabernet Sauvignon was struggling to reach ripeness, the difference between Pauillac and St. Estèphe might be exaggerated compared to a warm vintage of today when the issue is just how ripe to let your grapes get before you pick them. But the essential character of each commune is still a point of faith in Bordeaux. "The lesser wines have become better," agrees Paul Pontallier, "but the stylistic differences between appellations have not diminished. For other reasons, the differences between wines [at different levels of the hierarchy] have narrowed."

The best vineyards are located on a series of gravel mounds parallel with the Gironde.

Yet the typicity of Cabernet Sauvignon comes through the various blends from each of the communes. Whether a Médoc wine comes from the southernmost commune of Margaux or the northernmost commune of St. Estèphe, its structure comes from the character of Cabernet Sauvignon. In a classic (these days a euphemism for cooler) year, the structure takes the form of a touch of herbaceousness with some evident tannins; in a warmer year, now more typical than not, the tannins may be subsumed by the ripeness of the fruits, but underneath those fruits will be that firm texture. I'm inclined to the view that warmer vintages and modern methods of viticulture and vinification have narrowed the range, but there are still differences between communes.

Because it is larger and more heterogeneous, Margaux is distinct from the group of communes to its north. Anne-Françoise Quié, whose family owns Château Croizet Bages in Pauillac and Rauzan-Gassies in Margaux, says that,

Four soil profiles illustrate the rapidity with which terroir can change in the Médoc. From left to right are podzosol (acid, infertile, sandy clay-gravel), peyrosol (classic gravelly soil), planosol (heavy clay: more suitable for Merlot), and brunisol on sand (closer to the river). The first is from the Clos du Marquis, all others from l'Enclos of Château Léoville Lascases. Profiles show the top meter of soil.

Photographs courtesy Michael Georges, Château Léoville Lascases.

Are the mounds of gravel besides this vineyard along route D2 in Margaux being removed as the ground is prepared for replanting or being added to improve the terroir?

"What is interesting in Margaux is that there is of course a blend of grape varieties, but there is also a certain blend of soils. You see the difference partly in that harvest lasts four weeks in Margaux but is much shorter in Pauillac."

Contrasting opinions on the true typicity of Margaux are reflected in different views of the relationship of its two top châteaux, Margaux and Palmer. Like the other first growths, Château Margaux is dominated by Cabernet Sauvignon (ranging in recent vintages from 72% to 90%). By contrast, Château Palmer, nominally a third growth but in practice one of the super-seconds, is famous for an unusually high content of Merlot (so that its Cabernet Sauvignon ranged from 40% to 68% over the same period).

When I asked Nicolas Glumineau, formerly of Château Montrose, now at Pichon Lalande, whether communal specificity still exists, he said, "Yes, but you can't think globally. Palmer no longer produces a Margaux, but Château Margaux does." Taking the view that the Médoc is Cabernet, the contrast between Châteaux Margaux's refinement and the greater power of Lafite, Mouton, or Latour might be taken to typify the differences between the communes of Margaux and Pauillac.

But Bill Blatch, a much-respected negociant whose annual vintage report sets the scene in Bordeaux each year, sees it differently. "Château Palmer is the only real Margaux remaining today because all the other châteaux have replanted their best terroirs with Cabernet Sauvignon. Their attitude is that, 'we make great wines with Cabernet Sauvignon so we should plant it on our best terroirs.' But Margaux used to be characterized by the quality of its Merlot—growing it on gravel was what gave the feminine quality to the commune."

Cabernet Sauvignon is planted on a gravel outcrop at Château Montrose. The Gironde can just be seen in the background.

The importance of Merlot is certainly felt strongly at Château Palmer (⍑ page 340). As Directeur General Thomas Duroux explains, "Palmer is a unique case in Margaux and in the Médoc generally, with a large proportion of Merlot, basically 50% in the vineyards, due to the enthusiasm of a past proprietor, who planted Merlot not only on the clay terroirs but also in the best gravel terroirs that usually would be planted with Cabernet. Palmer has Merlot on the tops of the slopes, which are warmer and where there is deep gravel. The point is that it's not just a matter of the temperature or ripening potential of these locations, it's a matter of complexity; the tops of the hills have more complex soils and give more complex wine. Château Palmer is a Margaux wine because its Cabernet Sauvignon has the purity and finesse, but Palmer has its unique character because its Merlot also has precision."

The implicit view in the Médoc is really that Cabernet Sauvignon should be grown on the best terroirs. When I put this point directly to the châteaux, the answers tended to be a bit evasive. "Each cépage is grown on the terroir that is best for that cépage," was the general response. But at Château Léoville Barton, Anthony Barton was straight about it, as he always is. When I asked whether Cabernet Sauvignon was always planted in the best terroir, he surprised me by saying, "That's an embarrassing question." He went on to explain, "There's one plot where they made a mistake, and planted Merlot, but it is gravel terroir and would give great Cabernet. Of course," he adds ruefully, "it gives lovely Merlot too." But as and when it needs to be replanted—he's not sure when it was planted but probably in the late sixties or seventies and so may be coming up for renewal sometime soon—it will be replanted to Cabernet Sauvignon.

Château Margaux has a traditional organization of its vineyards, with Cabernet Sauvignon tending to be planted on the best-drained gravel soils, and Merlot on clay-based soils with higher water retention. Soil types can change rapidly over short distances.

The upper map divides the vineyards of Château Margaux according to gravel or clay content; the lower map shows block plantings of each variety.

In a historical context where the climate was marginal, and Cabernet Sauvignon as the last ripening variety was the most marginal, yet clearly the most distinguished, inevitably the best terroirs were regarded as those that ripen the Cabernet most reliably, which means the gravel mounds close to the river. Merlot tended to be planted *faute de mieux*, on soils richer in clay where Cabernet would not ripen reliably enough. (Château Palmer's Merlot on clay soils usually harvests ten days after the Merlot planted on gravel soils.) The clay-rich soils are generally found along the river and then farther inland, confining Cabernet Sauvignon to a relatively narrow band parallel with the river. The correlation between soil and plantings is rarely exact, because historically there was less information about soil types, but is becoming closer when vineyards are replanted in the light of current knowledge.

Certainly the big distinction is between gravel and clay soils, as is clear from the experience at Château Margaux. "Cabernet Sauvignon means little without knowing where it grows. We grow Cabernet Sauvignon in different terroirs here. We are lucky to have the diversity of soils. We grow Cabernet Sauvignon where it does best, on the gravelly soils, but we also grow it in front of the cellar where there is clay. And the two wines are absolutely different, you would never believe they are made from the same grape. So the influence of the grape is much less than the terroir. We have Merlot on both gravels and clay, when we taste the wines blind we always make a family of the two wines coming from the same terroir, not from the grapes. So each group represents its terroir," maintains Paul Pontallier.

As the climate has become warmer, two trends have combined to extend the areas where Cabernet Sauvignon is likely to be cultivated. Not only do warmer vintages make it possible for Cabernet to ripen outside of the original terroirs, but the higher temperatures are pushing Merlot to higher sugar levels and to more intense extraction than really suits the blend. Indeed, quite a bit of Merlot is relegated to second wines because it is too powerful for the grand vin (which is why second wines sometimes have higher alcohol levels than the grand vin, an interesting reversal of the old tradition that higher alcohol equals better quality). Switching to Cabernet brings things back into better balance. A similar issue applies to Petit Verdot, which like Cabernet Sauvignon ripens late, and historically was used in small amounts because there were so few places where it would ripen well.

A revealing comment about views of terroir came from Sylvie Cazes, then Directrice at Château Pichon Lalande, who says, "If it's great terroir for Petit Verdot, it's even greater terroir for Cabernet Sauvignon." Along the same lines, Jean-Michel Comme at Pontet Canet says, "The greatness of terroir is shown by the percentage of Cabernet Sauvignon in the vineyards." Cabernet Sauvignon über alles!

So is it the Cabernet Sauvignon that gives each commune its typicity? I'm certainly inclined to the view that it's more important than the Merlot, if only because the Cabernet has taken the best terroirs, and the Merlot is planted on those clay-rich soils farther inland that don't differ so much from place to place. This is a historical consequence of the pattern of plantings; as the case of Château Palmer shows, you can certainly produce distinctive Merlot by planting it on the terroirs that bring out the best in Cabernet Sauvignon. The problem with Merlot is that it tends to be bimodal: it changes quickly from under-ripe and herbaceous to over-ripe and jammy. In warm climates, the window for harvesting can be too narrow to be practical. In Bordeaux, this has not been a problem until recent years, but because there is a certain sameness to the locations where Merlot is usually planted, I believe it provides less distinction between the communes. It's difficult to make direct comparisons, because there are few cases where wines are made in exactly the same way in different locations, but Châteaux Grand Puy Lacoste and Haut Batailley in Pauillac are both owned by François-Xavier Borie, who says that, "The Merlots of Haut Batailley and Grand Puy Lacoste show less difference; there are more differences between terroirs with Cabernet Sauvignon."

Perhaps the real issue is that gravel soils show more differences, and this would be reflected in whatever variety is grown; it just happens that in the Médoc it's usually the Cabernet. Clay soils differ less, and in the Médoc are usually planted with Merlot. So it may be more that some terroirs are more expressive than that some varieties respond more than others. In this context, I asked general manager Frédéric Engerer at Château Latour whether he felt the character of Latour would show in the same way with a different variety? "I don't know. With the same variety, I measure huge differences in quality between the different parts of the appellation. I would think this would be true with another grape variety. Maybe we should plant some Syrah but it is a bit complicated. You would see the same effect. The question (you are asking) is whether Cabernet Sauvignon is neutral enough as a variety to express the terroir better (than another variety)."

Is Cabernet Sauvignon truly the measure of greatness? It's certainly true that the first growths of the Médoc have the most Cabernet, followed by the super-seconds.[30] Would the more reliable ripening resulting from warmer climate conditions make it logical to move towards wines of 100% Cabernet Sauvignon? Because assemblage usually is done before the en primeur tastings in April, individual varieties are usually kept separate for only a few months. It's difficult to form any opinion based on tasting such young barrel samples. But some châteaux keep back some samples of the individual varieties, to see how they mature individually. So here is an opportunity to re-examine past blending decisions.

Château La Lagune organized a tasting to compare the grand vin with the Cabernet Sauvignon vinified alone for a series of vintages from the first decade of the twenty first century (Y page 314). It was fascinating to see the effect of deconstructing the blend for the warm vintage of 2000 and the cool vintage of 2002, and then for the recent super vintages of 2009 and 2010 (still in barrel). Here in order to show the full potential of the Cabernet, it is vinified as a monocépage in 100% new oak. The final assemblage, by contrast, relies on 50% new oak.

From the 2000 vintage, La Lagune's Cabernet Sauvignon alone shows maturation along typical lines for Bordeaux, with the fruits becoming more savory, but there's an absence of presence on the mid palate that is filled in by Merlot in the final wine in classic style. The grand vin itself is at a perfect transitional moment. In 2002, the Cabernet is surprisingly full, but it shows a savage austerity that is tamed and compensated by the Merlot in the final blend, which is rather a gentle wine, and now ready to drink. In 2009 and 2010 the comparisons come off completely differently. The 2009 Cabernet Sauvignon is the height of elegance and finesse, very refined; it feels quite complete across the palate and you think that maybe it could make an elegant wine by itself. Its purity of fruits is impressive. But then by contrast the grand vin shows an extra dimension of complexity, and you gain the impression that it will evolve beautifully, whereas the Cabernet alone might become too austere. In 2010, the Cabernet is positively savage, with massive tannins giving an impression of an elemental force that needs to be tamed. Even the Merlot in 2010 in the Médoc often is quite tannic. However, the blend shows a balance that should evolve well, although this powerful wine will take some years to resolve.

I gained the same impression at Château Rauzan-Gassies in a comparison of Cabernet Sauvignon with the final wine from several vintages (⍭ page 346). Here an assemblage of Cabernet Sauvignon from all the plots was matured in exactly the same way as the lots that went into the blend, but only in two year old oak in order to preserve maximum varietal character. In cooler vintages, the Cabernet is clearly missing something on the mid palate: that's the traditional argument for filling in with Merlot. In a warm vintage, the Cabernet gives an elegant impression, with precision of fruits, and you are almost convinced it could make a complete wine. But then when you taste the blend, the extra dimension is clear.

An unusual case in which I actually did prefer Cabernet Sauvignon alone came from a comparison at Château Lynch Bages of all four individual varieties with the final wine for the 2006 vintage. This sample of Cabernet Sauvignon had it all: more fruit presence and more structure than any of the other varieties. The left bank wines of 2006 tend to be somewhat flat, not so much tannic or hard as simply lacking fruit character, and I've certainly had final wines from other châteaux that were less generous than the Cabernet Sauvignon from Lynch Bages. The overall blend at Lynch Bages appeared less rounded and fruity than I would have expected from the Cabernet Sauvignon alone, and if all the Cabernet Sauvignon had been at this level, it might have been tempting to bottle it alone.

You don't often get a chance to rethink the blend retroactively. In 1999, the blend at Léoville Lascases was 62% Cabernet Sauvignon, 18% Cabernet Franc, and 18% Merlot. Tasting the individual varieties in 2012, the Cabernet Sauvignon gave the most complete impression, although with a stern herbal edge (⍭ page 334). The Cabernet Franc was more refined and elegant than the other varieties to the point of making the Merlot seem a little rustic, although it was surprisingly fresh for Merlot. Not surprisingly, the Cabernet Sauvignon was the most closely related in character to the bottled wine, in which more develop ment is evident than with any of the individual varieties, bringing greater complexity, with red fruits mingling with traces of sous bois. The blend has certainly taken its superficial softness and roundness from the Merlot, but you can see the spartan structure of the Cabernet Sauvignon coming through the fruits; in fact, in some ways it seems more evident than it did in the sample of Cabernet Sauvignon alone (perhaps because the combination of fruits has less weight than the Cabernet Sauvignon alone), but the overall balance is rescued by the freshness of the finish. There seems no doubt that the blend is more complex than its components.

After we tasted the single varieties and the grand vin, technical director Michael Georges made some new blends to see what the effect would be of increasing each variety by another 10%. I liked the blends with more Cabernet Sauvignon or Cabernet Franc; they seemed to me to have at least as good a balance of fruit to structure as the grand vin. I could believe that either of them might be Léoville Lascases. But the blend with additional Merlot seemed to be unbalanced, almost to have a rusticity that had lost the character of St. Julien: I would not believe in this as a Léoville Lascases. Further experimentation suggested that the ideal blend might have just 5% more of each Cabernet; this seemed to show just a touch more finesse than the grand vin. "Perhaps we should wait ten years to do the assemblage," said Michael Georges, but then we agreed that this might have some adverse financial consequences.

For me this tasting also cast an interesting light on the question of whether assemblage should be done early or late. Some people believe that the sooner the cépages are blended, the better they marry together, and the better the final wine. The earliest practical moment is after malolactic fermentation is finished. Others hold the contrary position, that you are better able to judge the quality of each lot if you keep the individual cépages separate until the last moment, just before bottling. I felt that the retroactive blend with 5% more of each Cabernet had more youthful liveliness than the grand vin, but then it might of course have developed differently had this been the blend from the beginning. As a practical matter, the châteaux are under pressure from the en primeur system to commit to a blend before the April tastings in order to show the wine to potential buyers; it would be interesting to see what they would do if they had a free hand.

These tastings seemed to answer the question: given that vintages have become warmer, does the traditional rationale for a blend still hold? It's probably true that in the past it would really not have been possible to make an acceptable wine from Cabernet Sauvignon alone; now it could be done in warmer vintages, but the results would not be so good as the blend. When I asked Jean-Michel Comme at Pontet Canet whether they still need so much Merlot, he was frank. "Sometimes we wonder. But Médoc wines are wines that need to be blended." Looking at the aging of individual varieties, I'm inclined to think that the key in the Médoc may be to add just enough Merlot to soften the more spartan structure of Cabernet Sauvignon, but only just enough, and to stop before it shows too much influence.

The very best lots of Cabernet Sauvignon might stand alone, but this would be tantamount to extracting special cuvées, which is not in the tradition of the Médoc. Indeed, experiments along these lines usually confirm producers in their belief in the conventional wisdom. "We made a selection of the very best plots, but when we compared it with the blend, we preferred the blend," says Director Charles Chevalier at Château Lafite Rothschild. Château Haut-Bailly in Pessac-Léognan came to the same conclusion about its block of hundred-year-old vines. "We thought about doing a garage cuvée from the old vines in 1995, but decided it would change the character of Haut-Bailly. We did bottle one barrique of old vines. The old vines cuvée showed as stronger in tannins but not as complex as the Haut-Bailly itself," says Gabriel Vialard.

Nowhere in Bordeaux does Cabernet Sauvignon reign more supreme than at the first growths of the Médoc, where it is usually more than 80% of the blend. Not surprisingly, at Château Latour, general manager Frédéric Engerer is passionate about Cabernet Sauvignon. My visit did not get off to a very promising start when Frédéric said that he disagreed completely with my view of blending. "You look at single varieties, you look at the blend, you say the blend is better, so Cabernet needs Merlot. This is absolute nonsense. It's all a matter of Cabernet Sauvignon—it's the quality of Cabernet Sauvignon alone that determines the quality." So I thought I would pursue the key question. "You've never made a wine that is 100% Cabernet Sauvignon?" "No, but we've tried. Every year we taste the final blend without the two vats of Merlot, and honestly, I always prefer the ones with the Merlot because there's a little essential touch from the old Merlot vines that adds interest in the blend. But among individual vats, Cabernet Sauvignon is always top... There's a noblesse to Cabernet, you know, it has everything, freshness, purity of line, fruit: when we have ripe Cabernet Sauvignon it's at 13%, and inevitably the Merlot is at 14%... The only reason that we put in some Merlot is that it's old, it's located on gravelly soil, it behaves like Cabernet Sauvignon; the Merlot is as masculine as the Cabernet Sauvignon." This is a common view at the first growths: the Cabernet Sauvignon is superb, but there are some plots of Merlot that give such good results it would be a crime to leave them out. "We've never made a hundred percent Cabernet Sauvignon because we have one fantastic plot of Merlot that always goes into the grand vin. It comes from a gravel terroir," says Paul Pontallier at Château Margaux.

The gravel terroirs are the most distinguished in the Médoc, and they express themselves through the predominant Cabernet Sauvignon, but it's not easy to see the effects directly because the wines are blended. One complication in relating terroir and wine is the relatively large and dispersed nature of

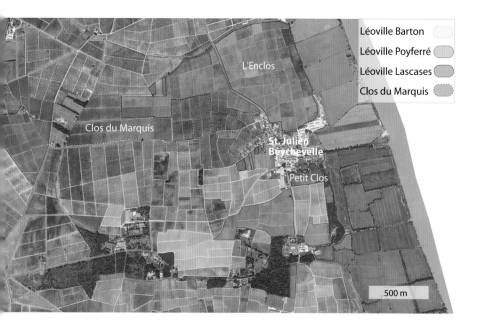

The Léoville estate was divided into three châteaux whose vineyards remain intermingled. Léoville Poyferré is the most broken up. Léoville Barton has common ownership with Langoa Barton (vineyards are to the south of the Léovilles). Léoville Lascases divides its wine into the château bottling, from L'Enclos to the east, and the Clos du Marquis from the vineyards to the west.

most châteaux' vineyards. Take the typical example of the three Léovilles. Léoville was a single estate, one of the largest in the Médoc, in the late eighteenth century. Partly resulting from division during inheritance, partly from complications arising from seizures during the French Revolution, the estate became split into three parts.

Léoville Lascases was established in 1815, Léoville Barton in 1826, and Léoville Poyferré in 1836. A somewhat piecemeal process meant that none of the three châteaux emerged with a single contiguous block of vineyards. And of course since the châteaux were established, they have sold and purchased individual plots of land so that their vineyards today are generally somewhat larger than when they were created. In the case of Léoville Lascases, there has always been a distinction between L'Enclos, which is the major source for the wine under the château name, and the Clos du Marquis, produced as a separate bottling since 1904.[31]

Clos du Marquis was later used to describe the second wine of Léoville Lascases, which mostly came from the vineyards to the west of the main road through the town. Since 2007 this has once again become a separate wine, representing its own vineyards, and now there is another name for the second wine (Petit Lion du Marquis de Lascases). So if we now consider the old Léoville estate to be divided into four parts, there are the 55 ha of Léoville Lascases, 43 ha of Clos du Marquis, 80 ha of Léoville Poyferré, and 48 ha of Léoville Barton. Within each of these substantial areas there is significant variation of terroir: and furthermore each of the three Château Léovilles produces a second wine as well as a grand vin. So it is not straightforward to relate the character of the wine to terroir.

The cadastral map (land register) for the part of Saint-Julien-Beychevelle including the Léoville estates shows the original tiny plots, many of which have now been amalgamated.

Indeed there are relatively few cases where it's possible to see the direct effects of terroir. Each château has a diversity of terroirs that is different from the next, and of course there are differences in winemaking. Châteaux Léoville and Langoa Barton are an unusual example where two adjacent châteaux have been under the same ownership for a long time. "The two vineyards are run as one property and equal care is bestowed on both. And yet it can be said that always, whether the wine be good, bad or indifferent, the Léoville turns out to be the superior of the two," Ronald Barton maintained.[32] No one has been able to define whatever difference in terroir might be responsible (ⵖ page 333).

Another case is the pair of Châteaux Haut Brion and Mission Haut Brion, just to the south of Bordeaux (well, actually, now all but surrounded by the expanding suburbs of Bordeaux). One of the oldest wine-producing properties in Bordeaux, Haut Brion has been in the hands of the Dillon family since 1935; and in 1983 they purchased La Mission Haut Brion. Perhaps there's a slight difference in exposure, but there's not much difference in terroir to the eye: the vineyards run contiguously across two small slopes, and are planted with a similar mix of cépages; there's a fraction more Cabernet Franc and less Merlot at Haut Brion. They share a microclimate, which usually starts the harvest one or two weeks before the rest of Bordeaux; this may be partly due to warmth from the surrounding city, but it was also true in the nineteenth century. Harvest usually starts one or two days earlier at La Mission.

Yet in spite of these close similarities, there's a consistent difference in the wines. La Mission is always immediately charming in its youth; Haut Brion is more restrained. Directeur Jean-Philippe Delmas says, "For Mission the wine comes to you, for Haut Brion you have to work to catch everything." The only

Haut Brion and Mission Haut Brion are surrounded by the suburbs of Bordeaux and separated by the main road.

difference in the vineyards is that Haut Brion is planted at 10,000 vines per hectare, while La Mission is planted at 8,000 vines per hectare. Jean-Philippe thinks this is the significant factor, and also explains why alcohol tends to be higher in La Mission. More plants per hectare require fewer grapes per vine for the same yield, he says. As and when the vineyards need to be replanted, he plans to bring La Mission up to the same 10,000 as Haut Brion: it will be fascinating to see whether the styles converge (Υ page 325).

To the south of Bordeaux, the region of Graves is somewhat of a halfway house between the Médoc and the right bank, with an average of just over one third Cabernet Sauvignon, but in Pessac-Léognan, the most prestigious part of the Graves near the city, the blend is very similar to the Médoc. Although dominated by Cabernet Sauvignon, the wines give a less powerful impression than those of the Médoc. "Pessac gives a wine that is more tense, with good acidity, good length; in the Médoc they are more full bodied, more muscular. We get hints of cedar and liquorice where they get fruit in the Médoc. Haut Brion is always suave, Lascases is more powerful. But when we look at the technical analyses, between Pessac and St Julien there is no difference, but the personalities are different. The wine is more intellectual in Pessac, they always have class here, it's the quality of the acidity," says Rémi Edange at Domaine de Chevalier.

Aside from Châteaux Haut Brion and Mission Haut Brion, the top châteaux in Pessac are Pape-Clément, Haut-Bailly, Domaine de Chevalier, and Smith Haut Lafitte, more or less equivalent in the market to second growths of the Médoc. An interesting contrast here is between Pape-Clément, which has become the epitome of the "modern" style, and Domaine de Chevalier, which is determined to keep to tradition. Pape-Clément was inherited in 1959 by Bernard Magrez, who now has an extensive portfolio of properties in Bordeaux and elsewhere. "In 1960-65 there was about 60% Cabernet Sauvignon; this resulted from decisions taken in the 1930s-40s. This gave a typicity to the wine that was solid. This was entirely a reflection of the terroir... We planted over some years with Merlot and Petit Verdot; the proportion of Merlot has increased, and Cabernet Sauvignon must now be about 55%. After 30 years we had a wine that has become rounder and perhaps the Merlot became a bit too high. There were years when Merlot brought a certain typicity and years when it wasn't so successful. Today the amount of Merlot does not embarrass the elegance. The wine is easier to drink young but that won't stop it aging," Bernard told me. But he does not believe that Pape-Clément has changed any more than other châteaux. "No, I don't think so. The typicity is the terroir, that we can't change, this is what gives character to the wine. One can't make a wine international." Even allowing for the effects of warmer vintages, however, it seems to me that Pape-Clément has been getting steadily richer, with warm, deep, black furry fruits showing a character moving towards the right bank. According to negociant Bill Blatch, "It's the quality of Merlot that makes Pape-Clément what it is."

"The role of the Grand Cru Classé is to carry the values of the history of French wines," says Rémi Edange, staking out Domaine de Chevalier's position. "The idea here is to keep the savage taste, the typicity of Domaine de Chevalier is not the technique of making Cabernet Sauvignon, it is to express the terroir." However, savage is the last word I would use to describe Domaine de Chevalier: its style is the epitome of elegance, with a real precision to the fruits (Y page 317). The wine is essentially a blend of two thirds Cabernet Sauvignon and one third Merlot (with a little Petit Verdot, relatively unusual for the Graves). "There's almost no Cabernet Franc because there is no chalk in the soil," says Rémi Edange.

The international style pays off. Château Pape-Clément has been steadily improving its relative price; Domaine de Chevalier is somewhat underrated. Smith Haut Lafitte has been moving in a more international direction, although not so forcefully as Pape Clément, and under the ownership of the Cathiards has changed from a solid, even rustic wine, into a more generous representation of Pessac-Léognan. "We have to listen to our consumers (sometimes). The

Americans showed what they like, now the Chinese. There is an influence because we want our wine to be referred, we want to make wine that pleases our customers," says Daniel Cathiard. This has improved its relative market position.

While there is not much question but that the best Cabernet Sauvignon-dominated wines of Bordeaux come from the four top communes of the Médoc and from Pessac-Léognan, they represent only part of the total production from the wider areas of the Haut-Médoc, Médoc, and the Graves. A few of the Grand Cru Classés lie in the Médoc outside the great communes, as do a fair number of Cru Bourgeois. Although there are no classified growths in the communes of Moulis and Listrac, lying just to the west inland, there are some fine Cru Bourgeois making wine in the tradition of claret. The smallest appellations in the Médoc, Moulis-Listrac's combined size and total production are comparable to Pauillac or St. Estèphe. The soils are a combination of gravel with clay and limestone, and Listrac has the highest point in the Médoc (43 m), which should count for something. The best two châteaux are generally considered to be Chasse-Spleen and Poujeaux, located on the plateau at the village of Grand Poujeaux, on top of a small rise with pebbly soils in the Moulis appellation. At Poujeaux, they like to say that Pijassou in his famous study of the soils of the Médoc said that Poujeaux is more Lafite than Mouton. The wines tend to be lighter than those of the great communes, but in the same general style, tending to elegance rather than power.

Across on the right bank, Cabernet Sauvignon is much less important; in fact, its proportion is lowest in the most important areas, St. Emilion and Pomerol. However, there is an exception at the northwest corner where St. Emilion abuts Pomerol. Here there is an extensive plateau of gravel-based soils, the Graves of St. Emilion. It's usually described as surrounding the two great châteaux of Cheval Blanc and Figeac, but actually extends farther into Pomerol. (The gravel here actually comes from the Massif Central, whereas the gravels of the Médoc originated in the Pyrenees.) Cabernet Sauvignon is concentrated at Château Figeac, where its 35% of plantings is by far the greatest on the right bank. The grand vin is usually equal parts of Cabernet Sauvignon, Cabernet Franc, and Merlot.[33]

The history of the plantings of Cabernet Sauvignon at Figeac is part tradition and part design. According to current owner Eric d'Aramon, when his father-in-law, Thierry Manoncourt, inherited the estate in 1947, there was already a significant amount of Cabernet Sauvignon. "Thierry investigated and bottled the cépages separately for several years to see how each evolved and what it would bring to the blend. The Malbec was bringing the most beautiful red color, but after a while (the taste) became diluted. By contrast the Cabernet Sauvignon, which was harsh when young and difficult to taste, with aging developed refined flavors and became the backbone of the wine. In the

The gravel plateau extends from St. Emilion into Pomerol.

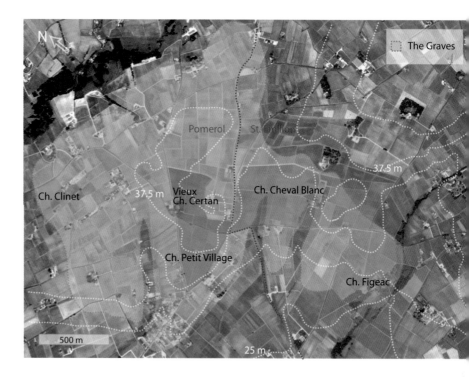

'inconvenience' of 1956 [when many vines were killed by a winter freeze], they took out all the Malbec and put in more Cabernet Sauvignon. When I asked Thierry why Cheval Blanc was growing Cabernet Franc and we were growing Cabernet Sauvignon, he said 'we have different soils.' 'But, I said, you told me that Cheval Blanc and Figeac are on the same 60 ha band of gravel.' 'But Cheval Blanc is on the slope going down to Pomerol and they have more clay in the soil.' Indeed, Figeac's best Cabernet Franc comes from the plot closest to Cheval Blanc."

Figeac is one of those wines whose development can be deceptive. It can still sometimes seem harsh when young, but with age develops a characteristic nutty softness. It does not have the sharp precision of St. Julien or the soft power of Pauillac; it reflects St. Emilion more than the left bank, but certainly it has more structure than the average St. Emilion; the core of Cabernet Sauvignon is surrounded by the generosity of St. Emilion. It requires aging. Eric d'Aramon recollects that, "When I did my first tasting for the assemblage with my father-in-law, I was very concerned about the results. Every cuve that he selected for the grand vin, I selected for the second wine and vice versa. I was really worried about his reaction but he explained to me, 'you have been selecting the vats for drinking now, I am selecting them for future potential'. After that it was alright and we agreed on everything."

The Cabernet Sauvignon is key to its unique style. "We love Cabernet Sauvignon. Each time we try to put more Merlot in the blend we don't like the

Château Figeac is the largest Grand Cru Classé in St. Emilion.

blend. The soil here is made to make elegant wines, that means Cabernet Franc and Cabernet Sauvignon, and each time I put in more Merlot to make something more up to date, the wine is dull, it lacks complexity," says Eric. An insight into Figeac's unique blend came from a tasting that included a separate bottling of the Cabernet Sauvignon from 1989 (⊤ page 320). This vintage of Figeac has never shown its typical richness and nuttiness; critical opinion has always regarded it as inferior to the 1990, possibly indicating the difficulties of ripening Cabernet Sauvignon on the right bank. But the Cabernet Sauvignon alone tastes like quite a complete wine in the model of a linear Cabernet Sauvignon, certainly sparser than Figeac itself, but with deep fruits to balance the herbaceousness. I could easily drink this for dinner, thinking it was a Médoc from, say, 1985. This example made it clear what the Cabernet Sauvignon brings to the blend and showed that it's the characteristic generosity of the right bank Cabernet Franc and Merlot that makes Figeac distinct from the left bank. The problem with the 1989 seems more likely to have been with the Merlot!

Following a line from Figeac towards Pomerol, the proportion of Cabernet Sauvignon goes down, and Merlot goes up. I asked Eric whether this represents terroir or tradition? "I am sorry to say both. The road (between the communes) is historic and probably reflects old culture of crops," he told me. Just across the border, there's typically less than 10% Cabernet Sauvignon. The most curious story comes from Château Petit Village. For a long time, it appeared to have by far the most Cabernet Sauvignon (17%) in Pomerol, but then abruptly in 2010 the proportion dropped to 7%. I wondered whether they had decided that Cabernet Sauvignon for some reason was not so successful after all, but it turned out that a plot of old vines that had survived the frost of 1956, which had been thought for fifty years to be Cabernet Sauvignon, was really Cabernet Franc.[34] They are a bit sniffy about this at the château. "We do have some Cabernet Sauvignon on the estate, however not much (less than 7%), and our main concern there is Merlot, the main grape variety on the estate. We do not feel that speaking about Cabernet Sauvignon here is relevant to the style and personality of the wines from Petit Village," said Marie-Louise Schÿler of AXA (who own Château Petit Village). This is a pity, because a plot of Cabernet Franc that could masquerade as Cabernet Sauvignon for over half a century might have something rather interesting to contribute to the future of the right bank, especially given the difficulties created by the warming climate trend.

Indeed, you might think that warmer vintages (when Merlot has sometimes been pushed to the limits) could argue for introducing Cabernet Sauvignon on to the right bank. At Château Ausone, the Premier Grand Cru Classé just outside the town of St. Emilion, they are experimenting with Cabernet Sauvignon and Petit Verdot. The experimental parcels are mostly close to the retaining walls just under the château. Ausone is a blend of (more than half) of Cabernet Franc with Merlot, but maître de chai Philippe Baillarguet says it's almost certain some Cabernet Sauvignon will find its way into the blend in the next few years. "Cabernet Sauvignon is treated here somewhat like Petit Verdot is treated in the Médoc," he says.

Château Ausone lies just to the south of the town of St. Emilion.

Tasting barrel samples from the 2011 vintage at Ausone, the Cabernet Sauvignon makes an interesting comparison with Cabernet Franc, not so elegant, not so refined, with a definite edge of hardness giving the impression that there isn't quite enough generosity of fruit to balance the structure. Indeed, like Petit Verdot, you feel it might be too strong by itself, but would definitely add structure to the blend. At all events, owner Alain Vauthier plans to increase the proportion of Cabernets in Ausone. "Merlot is very plastic, Cabernet Sauvignon is more complicated, but in top terroirs I have more Cabernet Franc than Merlot. But it may good to have a soupçon, perhaps 2% of Cabernet Sauvignon, in Ausone. The aim is to arrive at 65-70% Cabernet Franc. The problem is that you have to have Cabernet Sauvignon very ripe, so people tend to plant Merlot," he says.

At the northern tip of wine production on the right bank, the Côtes de Bourg has a dilemma in becoming stuck between Merlot that is too ripe and Cabernet Sauvignon that does not ripen enough. "In spite of all our best efforts it is really difficult to get Cabernet Sauvignon to ripen. We are wondering whether the Cabernet is necessary; but I think it's still necessary today, it brings freshness. We have a problem with Merlot becoming too ripe and the alcohol too high. It will lack freshness if this continues. Wines need roundness and ripeness—look at the New World—it's possible in the Médoc," says Stephan Donze at Château Martinat. "The difficulty with Cabernet Sauvignon is to get ripe berries without botrytis. The period for harvest is very short because Cabernet Sauvignon botrytizes easily," explains Jean-Yves Bechet at Château Fougas. "The Merlot goes to 14% alcohol, the Cabernet Sauvignon only to 12%. But even though there is a difficulty in getting Cabernet Sauvignon mature, it is better than a monocépage Merlot, because it gives structure," he adds. In spite of these difficulties, it's striking that the two most successful wines of the Côtes de Bourg are those with the highest proportions of Cabernet Sauvignon.

Château Roc des Cambes is owned by François Mitjavile of St. Emilion's Château Tertre Rôteboeuf, and follows the same forceful, generous, style. The driving force at Roc des Cambes seems to be its history; the mix of varieties has scarcely changed since François purchased the property in 1987. Its 12 ha of 45 year old vines are 80% Merlot and 20% Cabernet Sauvignon. "The terroir of Roc des Cambes is homogeneous, argile-calcareous soils with a southern exposure, and there are no differences between the plots where Cabernet and Merlot are planted. The only change made to the original vines has been to pull out some Cabernet Sauvignon on soil that was too sandy; this is being replaced with Merlot. The terroir is perfect for Merlot. In dry years we get a superb maturity of Cabernet Sauvignon, we like the effect of having the Cabernet Sauvignon, it's more a matter of the aromatic complexity it brings than the structure. We have never looked for structure, we look for maturity. There is short maceration with fermentation at high temperature to avoid over extraction," says Nina Mitjavile. The wine has something of the same exotic quality that characterizes Tertre Rôteboeuf (Ⲑ page 349). The vintage that gave me pause for thought about the general criticisms of Cabernet Sauvignon in the Côtes de Bourg was the 2000, which unusually was half Cabernet Sauvignon and half Merlot. It seemed at its peak in 2008, but had become more complex by 2012, when it was hard to disentangle fruit and savory influences. It made me regretful they can't increase the Cabernet Sauvignon.

At Château Fougas, which is usually a quarter Cabernet Sauvignon, I don't think I would describe the wine as *claret* because it doesn't quite have that tang of dominant Cabernet Sauvignon, but it seems more like a half way house between right bank and left bank than a typical right bank wine. There's good structure with the fruits, although there isn't quite the *power* of Cabernet Sauvignon of the Médoc. But the wines age well (Ⲑ page 322). Today Fougas Maldoror vintage 2000 may be close to its peak, with just a little tertiary development, but good enough fruit concentration and underlying structure to go on for another decade. (Maldoror is a cuvée that today represents the majority of production.)

All across the left bank, an important development with significant effects on style was the introduction of second wines at many châteaux. Some châteaux have always produced a second wine, by declassifying lots that were deemed not good enough to put in the grand vin bearing the château name. Château Latour produced a second wine as early as 1810.[35] During the nineteenth century, the first growths would periodically produce second wines from declassified lots that were matured to a lesser standard.[36] Their second wines typically represented about a quarter of total production, and sold for about a third of the price of the grand vin.[37] By the start of the twentieth century, some châteaux in the tier below the first growths were also producing second wines. During the twentieth century (when it was hard to sell even the grand vins), second wines diminished in importance, and did not revive until the 1980s.[38]

Selection all along the line has been a sea change in the past quarter century. One of Bordeaux's most famous oenologues, Michel Rolland, recollects that, "At the start of my career (in 1985), assemblage in Bordeaux was simple enough; the oenologue followed the proprietor's instructions to set aside the worst cuvée. Inevitably, the proprietor would ask later, 'Don't you think we could use half of this cuvée?' More volume was more money."[39] Today there is selection at all levels from sorting the berries that go into the fermentation vat to deciding what use to make of the individual cuvées after fermentation.

In 1975 there were fewer than a hundred second wines in Bordeaux; by year 2000 there were almost six hundred. At first, second wines were mostly produced by declassifying lots that did not make the grand vin. The second wine would not be as good as the grand vin, and it would correspondingly be matured in a less demanding way, intended for earlier consumption, but it would bear a distinct relationship to the grand vin: in another year, production from the same plots that had gone into the second wine might instead go into the grand vin. It used to be said that the second wine gave the consumer a chance to look at the style of the grand vin, but in an earlier-maturing, less demanding way, and of course at a lower price.

Driven by the relentless increase in the prices of wines from the top châteaux, the nature of second wines has changed steadily. The only formal definition of a second wine is that the producer has a more expensive wine that actually carries the name of the château. The second wine usually carries some play on the name, such as Moulin, Petit, Cadet, Fleur, Chapelle de Château Quelquechose. The implication remains that it is closely related in origin and style to the grand vin. But this can be quite misleading. Second wines first took off in the Médoc, and almost all significant châteaux in the Médoc now produce a second wine. For a long time, second wines were less common on the right bank (partly because of the much smaller size of the properties), but today many of the leading châteaux of the right bank also have second wines.

Only about half of the wine that goes into second wines today actually represents declassified lots that might have gone into the grand vin (most often because they come from recently replanted vineyards where the vines are considered too young to produce great wine). The other half tends to come from inferior vineyard plots that are never used for the grand vin. There's also a strong tendency for the second wines of the left bank to be Merlot-based, whereas the grand vins are dominated by Cabernet Sauvignon.[40] Coupled with less use of new oak and a reduced period of maturation in oak, this results in a wine with a style distinctly more approachable than the grand vin.[41]

The division between the grand vins and the second wines has been steadily widening. The grand vins remain as driven by Cabernet Sauvignon as ever; in fact, allowing for variations in response to individual vintage conditions, the

Second wines usually have a name closely related to the grand vin. Château Latour used the description, grand vin, long before it was commonly used to mean the principal wine of a château. Forts de Latour, which actually comes mostly from a separate vineyard, is one of the best second wines.

Grand vins contain a higher proportion of Cabernet Sauvignon than the vineyard plantings.[42]

Second wines contain less Cabernet and more Merlot.

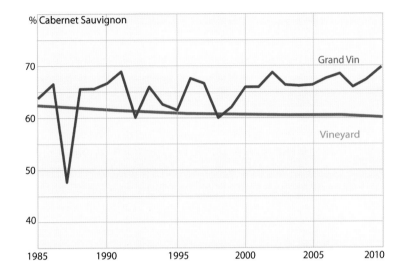

proportion of Cabernet Sauvignon may have increased slightly in the past decade. (This may reflect the run of warmer vintages, in which Cabernet Sauvignon has been better able to ripen. Aside from that, the only trend in the blend of the grand vins is a slight decrease in Cabernet Franc and slight increase in Petit Verdot.)

Conflicting trends between more Cabernet Sauvignon in the grand vin and more Merlot in the vineyard mean that you can no longer draw inferences about the nature of the wine from the plantings of varieties. Over the past two decades, Cabernet Sauvignon has declined a few percent in the vineyards, but the grand vins of the Grand Cru Classés have continued on average to be about two thirds Cabernet Sauvignon. The châteaux have been planting more Merlot in order to make their second wines! This makes it evident that second wines have become profit centers in their own right, and are no longer simply a way to mop up lots that are not successful enough to include in the grand vin. Often enough they have become a separate brand in all but name.

Indeed, second wines have become increasingly important. When second wines were used principally to improve the quality of the grand vin, they would increase in proportion in poor vintages, but in the past few vintages they have been approaching 50% of production irrespective of the character of the vintage. Because total production has increased about 50%, this means that the grand vin has stayed more or less steady in amount. All the same, almost a quarter of the châteaux now produce more "second" wine than grand vin; has the second wine has been turned into the regular production, with the grand vin becoming a more exclusive cuvée?[43] Will second wines become more typical of left bank production than the grand vins? Is the left bank losing its heart? At the least, in asking how the left bank defines the typicity of Cabernet

Sauvignon, we have to exclude a large part of its production and focus specifi-cally on the grand vins.

Is there a risk that the increasing emphasis on second wines will lessen the typicity of the communes? There's certainly a case for saying that their bias to-wards an earlier-drinking style based on more Merlot contributes to greater similarities. If close to half of production is devoted to second wines, the lines between communes may well become blurred. Does this mean that communal specificity is, after all, more a matter of winemaking choices than a reflection of the intrinsic character of each commune?

For all this criticism, second wines seem to have improved significantly in the past few years. As recently as five or ten years ago, many seemed to be more a brand extension into a cheaper line than a genuine reflection of the grand vin. But with the 2009 and 2010 vintages, many seemed to reflect their origins more clearly. Admittedly these were vintages in which it should have been difficult to make ordinary wine, but the increasing focus on second wines has created a situation in which the second wines represent the public face of the château more clearly than the grand vin. This creates pressure for quality. "Second wine used to be a dumping ground—everything was put in it—but now it's much more an independent brand, and there is selection for it. The second wine of a great year today is better than the grand vin of a minor year previously. I think the second wines of 2009 and 2010 are superior to the La-grange of 1985, for example," says director Bruno Eynard at Château Lagrange. Of course, the corollary of introducing selection for the second wine is that there must be a third wine, and indeed many châteaux are expanding to have a hierarchy of wines, often taking the form of a grand vin, second wine, and communal AOC.

Second wines (and third wines!) make it clear that blending is no longer simply a matter of protection against the vagaries of climate: it is a tool for di-recting the style of the wine. The high proportion of Merlot in the second wines of the Médoc, and the possibility of using this in the traditional way to com-pensate for any deficiencies in Cabernet Sauvignon, brings back the question of how far grand vins might move towards focusing on the very best lots of Cab-ernet Sauvignon. But the view in Bordeaux is that even when Cabernet Sauvignon is ripe enough to avoid herbaceous flavors, still it can be a little ungiving on the mid palate. There probably simply isn't enough Cabernet Sau-vignon that would be really complete in itself: even if only a small amount of Merlot is used, still its fleshiness is essential to complement the Cabernet Sau-vignon.

In the New World, however, as typified by Napa Valley, Cabernet Sauvi-gnon reaches full ripeness in most years; indeed, some might consider that it reaches over-ripeness. The idea that it then fills in the palate completely is the oenological rationale for making a monovarietal. Is this just a matter of ripeness? Bill Harlan, of Napa's Harlan Estate, thinks it's also a pragmatic issue. "Part of the issue with hundred percent Cabernet Sauvignon is that Bordeaux has too much variability in the weather, they can't take the risk of one variety. I guess once a decade it's a problem here; that's a risk you can take," he says. Certainly if you look at the past ten years in Bordeaux, it's more the other way round, with one or two years when Cabernet might be a candidate for a mono-varietal.

But tastings, whether of monovarietal bottlings or of barrel samples before assemblage, generally convinced me that even in Languedoc and Provence, which are significantly warmer than Bordeaux, Cabernet Sauvignon by itself makes a less complete wine than as a blend, whether that blend is with conventional Bordeaux varieties (principally Merlot) or with Syrah or Grenache (ⴳ pages 350-356). Somehow an extra complexity comes from the assemblage. Is this a feature of the grape variety or is it representative of conditions in France? Now it is time to ask whether there is a difference in the New World and whether Cabernet Sauvignon in Napa Valley or elsewhere achieves full complexity or benefits from a blend.

And the other question to take on board is whether Merlot is always the perfect partner for Cabernet Sauvignon. Arguing that Merlot provides the perfect fleshiness to fill in the mid palate is somewhat *post hoc ergo propter hoc:* Merlot initially came to prominence not so much because of its own merits, but because of the deficiencies of Malbec. Looking at South America, you can get an impression of what Bordeaux might have been like before the transition by comparing traditional Cabernet-Merlot blends with Cabernet-Malbec blends from Argentina. Malbec also complements Cabernet Sauvignon, but differently from Merlot: it is smooth and supple rather than fleshy and rich. And going back to an even earlier era, blends of Cabernet Sauvignon and Carmenère from Chile show that when the Carmenère is fully ripe, its refined tannins complement the firmer tannins of Cabernet Sauvignon. Even within the history of Bordeaux there are therefore precedents for a variety of blends, and we should return to the question of whether a warming climate argues for their resurrection or even—quelle horreur!—for new blends.

4

American Renaissance

CABERNET SAUVIGNON production was almost insignificant in Napa Valley until the 1970s. Although Cabernet was grown in Napa as early as the 1880s,[1] it was not acknowledged in its own right (with the first varietal-labeled wines) until the 1930s.[2] But most wines were labeled with generic names, and little was made from high quality varieties. It was only with the revival of winemaking in the 1970s that Napa Cabernet developed as the paradigm for the New World expression of the variety. Since then Cabernet Sauvignon has become the international variety *par excellence*, produced everywhere. Napa Valley remains at the very forefront of the challenge to Bordeaux; indeed, it was in Napa Valley that Cabernet Sauvignon first showed the ripe style of the modern era. Over recent decades, the story of Cabernet Sauvignon in Napa has been the struggle to control its ripeness.

Attempts to imitate Bordeaux in California go back to the nineteenth century, but imitation was more in marketing than winemaking. From the 1860s, Zinfandel was regarded as the finest grape for making Bordeaux-style wines; by

Napa Valley is north of San Pablo Bay, an hour from San Francisco.

the 1880s it was the most widely planted grape in California, and was the basis for most "claret."[3] Although Cabernet Sauvignon was used in wines that were often labeled as "Médoc" during the first two decades of the twentieth century, Zinfandel continued to be a common component.[4] (Zinfandel also played another interesting role in the development of Californian wine. Although almost all wine was sold under generic names, Zinfandel was probably the first grape to be bottled under a varietal name, in the 1880s.[5])

Wine production in California started when Franciscan monks introduced what became known as the Mission grape.[6] From the south it spread up to Santa Clara and Sonoma Valleys, and then to Napa Valley, which became established as the leader in premium wines at the start of the twentieth century. But all attempts to produce fine wine in California were thwarted by Prohibition. When production resumed in 1933, the demand was for sweet, fortified wines. Prohibition had eliminated most fine grape varieties in the United States, and most wine was made from cheap, over-productive, varieties.[7]

After Repeal, Napa Valley was at the forefront of wine production in California, and since then has only reinforced its position as America's best known wine-producing region. Napa Valley itself is really quite a confined area. About 30 miles long and generally less than a mile wide, it nestles between the Mayacamas mountains to the west (separating Napa from Sonoma) and the Vaca mountains to the east. Looking across the valley, a difference is immediately apparent between the Mayacamas Mountains, which are covered in vegetation, and the Vaca Mountains, which have a distinctly scrubby appearance. Weather comes from the Pacific, and the east is drier than the west, because rainfall gets blocked by the Mayacamas Mountains.

Napa Valley has an abundance of that surprising key feature for wine production in California: fog. This is not usually welcome in wine-producing regions, but the climate in California would normally be too warm for fine wine production, and is rescued only by the regularity of the cooling fog. Almost all the top regions for wine production are in valleys that are cooled by fog rolling in from the Pacific Ocean. (The exceptions are vineyards at high enough elevations that cooling comes from the altitude.) Morning fog is fairly reliable in Napa, usually clearing around midday.

Because a high pressure system settles over the California coast each summer, the growing season tends to be warm and dry. Except for the absence of rain in the summer, the climate is perfect for agriculture. Irrigation fills the gap. Conventional wisdom is that climate in Napa Valley escapes the European rule that temperatures become warmer going south; the northern end is decidedly warmer than the southern end. The reason is that the more open southern end gets cooling breezes from San Pablo bay, whereas the narrow northern end is effectively closed. At the very southern end, Napa itself is close in temperature to Bordeaux; but Calistoga at the far north is more like the south of France, and it becomes too hot to grow Cabernet Sauvignon on the valley floor.

Fog rolls into Napa Valley from the Pacific most mornings, and disperses around midday.

The Mayacamas Mountains to the west are covered in evergreens.

Before it was devoted to viticulture, Napa Valley grew a variety of products ranging from wheat to fruit orchards. Still recovering from Prohibition, wine production was already increasing when the shortage of imports from Europe caused by the second world war led to a move towards producing fine wines in California, with Inglenook, Beaulieu, Beringer, and Louis Martini at the forefront.[8] The rise, and sometimes fall, of these wineries epitomizes the vast changes in Napa Valley over the past half century.

The history of the old Inglenook winery in the Rutherford region encapsulates the history of Cabernet Sauvignon production in Napa Valley. Finnish sea captain Gustave Niebaum, who made his fortune trading furs in Alaska, decided after a visit to France that the gravelly loam soils of Rutherford resembled Bordeaux and might reward attempts to produce the same blend of wine. He planted Cabernet Sauvignon, together with Cabernet Franc and Merlot.[9] Under the leadership of Niebaum's great nephew, John Daniels, Inglenook produced a series of famous Cabernet Sauvignons between 1933 and 1964. It's a sign of the lack of interest during this period that Inglenook made a profit for only one year in its existence.[10] Falling on hard times, it was sold to United Vintners in 1964, and became part of Heublein in 1969; then quality collapsed. The winery and vineyards were subsequently resurrected by film director Francis Ford Coppola under the name of Rubicon Estate.[11] (The Inglenook name was owned by The Wine Group, who sadly used it for jug wine, but it was sold to Coppola in 2011, and will now again be used for the wines from the estate.)

*The hills to the east
are dry and scrubby.*

About twenty years after Gustave Niebaum planted Inglenook, Georges de Latour came to the same conclusion and planted Beaulieu's first vineyard, later to be used for the famous Private Reserve wine, on an adjacent plot. The wine was created by André Tchelistcheff, America's most famous winemaker in the period after Prohibition. It was a measure of things to come that the emphasis was on Cabernet Sauvignon. Mike Grgich, who was at Beaulieu through the 1960s recollects that, "They pointed out on the label '100% Cabernet Sauvignon'. However, I discovered that in the vineyard #1, from where the grapes for the Private Reserve Cabernet [came] there was about 5% Merlot. I kept it a secret as the company did." Tchelistcheff made the Private Reserve from 1938 until his retirement in 1973, although Beaulieu Vineyards was sold to conglomerate Heublein in 1969. There's a strangely parallel history for Inglenook and Beaulieu, both started by men of vision, but encountering economic difficulties in maintaining quality standards, with the wineries ultimately ending up lost in the corporate maw of Heublein (which therefore has the distinction, if that is the right term, of wrecking both of what might have become Napa's First Growths).

The acknowledged leaders, Inglenook and Beaulieu, marched to the beat of somewhat different drums. "If the standard of quality of wine, for some particular reason (vintage deficiency, etc.) was not corresponding ideally to the vintage denomination of Inglenook wines, George Deuer (the winemaker), with John Daniel tasted the wine together, and they said, 'We are going to sell every

The Inglenook winery was the birthplace of Cabernet Sauvignon in Napa Valley in 1879. It is no longer used as a winery but was purchased by Francis Ford Coppola and became the headquarters of Niebaum-Coppola in 1975. It was renamed as Rubicon Estate in 2005 after the vineyards of the original estate were restored, but now is known as Inglenook again.

thing bulk, to the competitor. There will be no Inglenook label.' That was the only wine château of California, due to the wealthy background of the owner, that permitted themselves to do such a thing. Beaulieu, which was fed by the business, never was able to eliminate a vintage... Beaulieu produced excellent wines, but Beaulieu was a commercial organization, where there was compromising," André Tchelistcheff recollected.[12]

The history of Louis Martini and Beringer is a little different, but both end up in conglomerates. Both wineries go back to pioneers of the nineteenth century, both survived Prohibition by producing sacramental wines, and turned after Repeal to producing quality varietal wines from their own vineyards, but ultimately ended up sold to large producers (Beringer to Fosters of Australia in 2000, Louis Martini to Gallo in 2008). Both still produce quality wines, but as part of much larger facilities for general wine production.

Napa Valley ranges from artisanal production to corporate scale. Many elegant tasting rooms are set in gracious surroundings, but aerial views show that much wine is actually made in semi-industrial facilities. Some wineries emphasize their historic origins. Beringer advertises that it is the oldest continuously operating winery in Napa Valley (since 1892), and has its tasting room in the historic mansion originally constructed for the Beringers' residence. Yet across the street is a huge plant where wine is made by Treasury Wine Estates, Beringer's corporate parent. Before it was chic to be artisanal, when Louis Martini constructed a new winery at the end of Prohibition, however, they proudly extolled its size and technical capacity.

The striking architecture of the Mondavi winery set the standard for developments in Napa Valley in 1966. Until then wineries were mostly utilitarian.

Photograph courtesy Mondavi.

The early difficulties in establishing a market for high quality Californian wines are clear from an assessment of the top wines by Life Magazine in 1954. A distinguished jury spent a day selecting the best imported and domestic wines.[13] The names of most of the top imported wines would be well up in a comparable list today. None of the Californian wines would make the grade. The top domestic "claret" was the Inglenook Cabernet, but there was no premium for quality: it was one of the cheaper wines in the domestic list, and its price was below every wine on the imported list.

The pioneers of Cabernet Sauvignon were pretty much lost in a sea of bulk wine. By 1961, almost the only quality grapes in Napa were some small parcels of Cabernet Sauvignon, a meager 150 ha in all. Some date the modern era in Napa from 1966, when Robert Mondavi opened his winery, almost the first new winery to be built in Napa since Prohibition.[14] The differences between the sleek new lines of Mondavi's winery and the traditional construction of the Inglenook mansion symbolize the transition to Napa's new role. New wineries have been the driving force in Napa's revival: three quarters of Napa's current 400 wineries have been established since 1966.[15]

Even by the start of the 1970s, Cabernet Sauvignon production was a mere 5% of total plantings; varietal-labeled wines altogether were about 30% of premium production.[16] Cabernet Sauvignon became the most common black variety during the planting boom of 1968-1974 (and Chardonnay became important in the whites). There was a pause for the rest of the decade, and then in the 1980s, Cabernet Sauvignon took off exponentially. Today Cabernet Sauvi-

Conditions were primitive in Napa in 1896 when Beaulieu (right) was established on Route 29.

gnon amounts to more than half of the red wine, and 40% of all production in Napa Valley. It accounts for about a quarter of the Cabernet Sauvignon plantings in California, but only about 12% of all production, a measure of the fact that yields are lower in Napa. While Napa is the leader, quality Cabernet Sauvignon is also produced in adjacent (but cooler) Sonoma Valley (where yields are comparable to Napa), and farther south in Monterey and San Luis Obispo.[17]

Napa Valley shows the same general trend as Bordeaux in shifting towards red wine, although less dramatically. Bordeaux went from 50% red in 1964 to 90% red today; Napa has gone from 60% red in 1964 to 76% red today.[19]

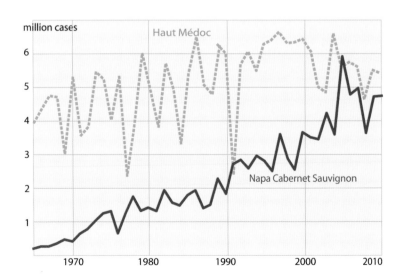

Growth of Cabernet Sauvignon in Napa Valley has been exponential since the 1970s until leveling off recently. By comparison, red wine production in the Haut Médoc has increased relatively less and shows more yearly fluctuation.[18]

The new Louis Martini winery at St. Helena in 1933 had a production capacity of about 6 million cases, and claimed to maintain perfect conditions of 50 °F for maturation. The wines were all named by reference to French types.

ONE REASON FOR THE EXCELLENCE OF OUR DRY WINES

BURGUNDY — CLARET — RIESLING — SAUTERNES — CHABLIS AND MANY OTHER VARIETIES

OUR 1,250,000 GALLON PLANT AT ST. HELENA, NAPA COUNTY

Insulated and ventilated so that a constant temperature of 50° F is maintained regardless of outside weather conditions. Underground storage facilities are used for aging wines under ideal conditions.

L. M. MARTINI GRAPE PRODUCTS

BRANDIES, SWEET AND DRY WINES

WINERIES: KINGSBURG AND ST. HELENA, CALIF.   MAIN OFFICE: KINGSBURG, CALIF.

With about 7,900 ha now devoted to Cabernet Sauvignon, Napa's production is roughly comparable to the Haut Médoc in Bordeaux, which has 10,700 ha of black grapes. Production levels have been converging.

The rapid pace of growth, coupled with the disappearance of the old pioneers, means that the new producers of the 1970s and later have defined the meaning of Cabernet Sauvignon in Napa Valley. The pioneers defined the heart of the valley, with Inglenook and Beaulieu in Rutherford, and Louis Martini and Beringer in St. Helena. Rutherford remains absolutely prime territory for Cabernet production, but in the past fifty years vineyards have expanded considerably, especially on to hillsides or mountain tops that would have been hard to cultivate previously. So what in fact does it mean today when the label on a bottle of wine says "Napa Valley"?

The collision between the three tectonic plates that created the valley some 150 million years ago left detritus of a great variety of soil types, with more than 40 different soil series classified in Napa.[20] A major factor is the consistent difference between the warmer, and more fertile, valley floor, and the cooler terrain of the slopes to the west and the east. And moving from south to north, the soil changes from sediments deposited by past oceans to a more volcanic terrain, which also is prevalent on the mountains.

Definition of individual regions, or more specifically identification of those locations where particular varieties grow best, developed slowly after the growth of the 1960s. The spur for the realization that not all sites in Napa Valley were created equal had been the definition by University of California

The Beringer winery is just across the street from the historic mansion that is used as the tasting room. Like other large wineries, its appearance somewhat resembles an oil refinery.

professors Albert Winkler and Maynard Amerine in the 1940s of heat zones in Napa Valley. Classifying California into five zones according to average temperatures during the growing season,[21] they recommended suitable grape varieties for each region.[22] Among the varieties recommended for the cooler, southern part of Napa Valley were Cabernet Sauvignon and Chardonnay, but it was not until the 1960s that growers paid much attention.

With the extension of grape growing from the valley floor where it resumed after Prohibition to the mountain slopes planted after the revival of the seventies, there is considerable variation not only of terroir but also of climate. In fact, the most important determinant of climate may be elevation, rather than position along the valley. The original definition of heat zones mapped Napa into three zones, with the Carneros region at the southern end the coolest in zone 1, Napa itself in zone 2, but Oakville and St. Helena in warmer zone 3.[23] More recent data confirm a gradual increase in average growing season temperatures going up the valley, but put the whole valley floor into zone 4, with conditions becoming significantly cooler moving up in elevation into the mountains on either side.[24]

To the casual tourist—of whom there are more than five million annually—driving up Route 29 on the western side, or back down the Silverado trail on the eastern side, Napa Valley might appear quite homogeneous, a veritable sea of vines stretching across the valley between the mountains on either side. The land appears flat until close to the mountains. Taking any cross street between the two highways, you travel exclusively through vineyards. The Napa river in the center of the valley seems unimportant. The impression of dense plantation is true for the center of the valley, where three quarters of the land is planted with vines, but this apparent consistency is somewhat deceptive.

The heart of the valley is characterized by alluvial fans, formed by streams that flowed out of the mountains. When a stream opens out on to a valley floor, it deposits sediment as it flows. Over time, the sediment causes the watercourse to shift sideways, creating a fan-like area of sediment. Alluvial fans run continuously along the west side of the valley; the series is more broken up along the east side. Known locally as "benches," the most famous are the Oakville Bench and the Rutherford Bench, where production of fine wine started in the nineteenth century. (Valley floor tends to be used in two senses in Napa. Generally used as generic description to distinguish terrain between the mountain ranges as opposed to the actual slopes, it is not pejorative. Sometimes it is used more disparagingly to distinguish fertile soils from the alluvial fans.)

Sediments become finer, and the soils that form on them become richer, as an alluvial fan widens out. Beyond the fan, soils on a valley floor can be too rich for producing fine wine. And the Napa river is not as toothless as it appears; fifteen miles of the river are currently being restored, adding 55 ha of floodplain.[25] The intention is to stop the river from flooding the low-lying areas in the vicinity of the town of Napa. To accomplish the renovation, 43 producers have agreed to take vineyards out of production. Of course, so close to the floodplain, these are unlikely to be the best vineyards in the valley. Indeed, on either side of the Napa river in the center of the valley, the soil is less appropriate for fine wine production.

"Terroir isn't everywhere. In fact, terroir is in very few places. I have five wines and one is a terroir wine," says Doug Shafer of Shafer Vineyards. "Hillside Select is a special place; it's planted with one hundred percent Cabernet Sauvignon, but it could be Merlot or Cabernet Franc and the special quality of the fruit would still come through." Doug feels that hillsides make better wine than flat lands, but that the gap has narrowed. "Originally we didn't have the tools to make wines from the valley floor. Changes in viticulture mean now you can make wine from the valley floor that is nearly as good as the hillside. You have to work harder; we used denser planting and canopy management to reduce yields. This was not possible ten years ago."

Well before any regulations were introduced, Napa Valley became an imprimatur of quality on the label. Following the precedent of the French system of appellation contrôlée, the AVA (American Viticultural Area) system was introduced in 1976. This defines a pyramid of wine-producing regions. A broad Napa Valley AVA covers the whole region: as the result of a highly political process, the boundaries go well beyond the valley itself and were drawn to include all vineyards regarding themselves as producing Napa Valley grapes.[26] Covering a total area of 90,000 ha, which represents about half of Napa County, the AVA has about 18,500 ha of vineyards. Given the variation between the south and north, and between the valley floor and the mountains, this implies a certain lack of coherence.

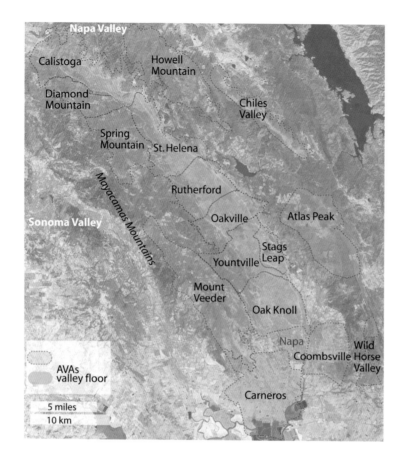

Napa Valley has several smaller AVAs within it.[27]

(Carneros connects Napa and Sonoma valleys.)

AVAs are defined at the instigation of producers in a region, and there are presently fifteen smaller AVAs within the all-encompassing Napa Valley designation.[28] They extend from appellations defining the central valley to mountainous slopes on either side. (Producers often use the term appellation rather than AVA, and will talk about their appellation or sub-appellation wines.) The sub-AVAs tend to have more integrity, and often indicate higher quality wines. About 40% of the vineyards are in the old areas, stretching from Yountville through St. Helena, at the heart of the valley.

Are there really discernable differences between AVAs in the valley? The answer is yes and no. There may be a core to each sub-AVA, but unfortunately the same sorts of political considerations came into play when defining the sub-AVAs that had much reduced the coherence of Napa Valley. The original proposal for the Stags Leap District, for example, expanded to the west, south, and north as producers on the edges clamored to be let in.[29]

The boundaries of the AVAs don't always make it easy to tell whether a particular wine has come from a valley or mountain. The AVAs in the valley often extend up the slopes of the mountains on either side. Pritchard Hill is well known for mountain Cabernets from the vineyards of Bryant, Chappellet, and

Climate mapping by Winkler originally divided the valley into three zones going from south to north. More recent data suggest the main difference is between the valley floor and the slopes and mountains on either side.[30]

Zones are defined in terms of degree days (a calculation of time above the minimum growing temperature for the grapevine). Zone 1 is less than 2,500 degree days, zone 2 is 2,500-3,000, zone 3 is 3,000-3,500, zone 4 is 3,500-4,000. However, the exact number, and therefore the zone, depends on the method of calculation, and is less important than the relative gradations.[31]

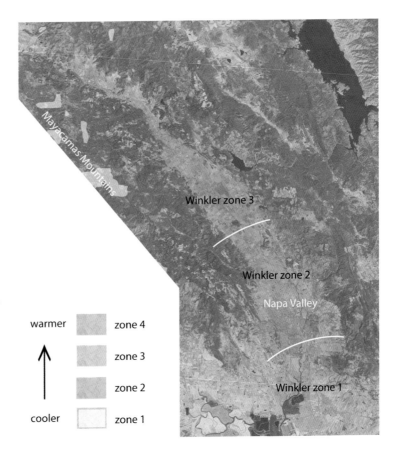

Colgin, at elevations ranging from 120-330 m—but is included as part of the St. Helena AVA!

The best case for integrity is made by the most famous appellations of the valley proper. The supposed characteristic of Rutherford is a dusty note in the wines. Whether Rutherford Dust is real or is a marketing ploy has been long debated. "The tannins of wines from Rutherford give the sensation you get by running your hand backwards along velvet," was an imaginative description by one producer. I do find a similar quality to the tannins in the wines of several producers. I would not describe it as dusty, more as a sort of slightly sharp tang to the tannins on the finish, but it does give a distinctive tannic grip. But there are other producers whose wines typically have more massive or tighter tannins. I would be prepared to concede a commonality in which firm tannins give the wines a quality I might be inclined to call Rutherford Grip.

In Oakville, the more common pattern in my tastings has been a quality of taut black fruits supported by fine-grained tannins that reinforce an impression of elegance. Does Oakville play St. Julien to Rutherford's version of Pauillac? "Oakville is about expressing big berry fruits, a rich character with black olives, and more open tannins," says Mark de Vere of Mondavi. Some wines display a

Looking from the Silverado Trail, vineyards extend across the valley to the Mayacamas mountains.

much softer style, with more overt, opulent black fruit aromatics extending from blackcurrants to cassis, and you might argue that they have deserted the communal specificity by going for more approachability in their vinification.

"Cabernets in Stags Leap tend to have richer fruit, with a softer texture," says Doug Shafer, whose winery was instrumental in establishing the AVA. Shafer's Hillside Select, one of the top wines of the AVA, which comes from the vineyard rising up behind the winery, epitomizes this quality, with a style of opulent fruits showing evident aromatics (Y page 412). Doug supports his case by recollecting that when Shafer showed its first 100% Cabernet Sauvignon, it was so approachable that people refused to believe it had no Merlot.[32] But in Stags Leap District generally, I get less impression of consistency today, with many wines that are forward and approachable, with soft black fruits on the palate, supported by nuts and vanillin on the finish, and tannins noticeable only as a soft, furry presence in the background. These are nice enough for something to drink immediately, but I wonder how it represents Cabernet typicity to make wines that are so fruit-forward and lacking in tannic structure. Again it's a producer's choice, but seems more common in Stags Leap.

There may be a typicity that distinguishes each AVA if you let it express itself. In any of these appellations, however, you can make soft, forward, fruity, wines with lots of nutty vanillin, using appropriate winemaking techniques to bump up the appeal. Let's at least say that unless you know the producers' styles, the name of the AVA has little predictive value.

The area of the Napa Valley AVA extends far beyond the obvious tourist trails. Well off to the east are Howell Mountain, Chiles Valley, and Atlas Peak. To the west are Diamond Mountain, Spring Mountain, and Mount Veeder. Driving up the twists and turns of the densely forested roads into the mountains is a completely different experience from meandering along the center of the valley. Vineyards here are sparsely planted, occupying perhaps 5% of the total land, contrasted with the monoculture in the valley itself.

The big difference in Napa is really between mountains and valley: these terrains have different climates and soils. With vineyards often above the fog line, the climate in the mountains is quite distinct from the valley itself, where fog is the dominant (and saving) influence. The playoff is that temperatures are reduced by the elevation, but increased by the lack of fog. There is often more diurnal variation. Mountain vineyards have primary soils with more mineral or volcanic character, compared with the more alluvial soils deposited by water flow in the valley. Couple the climatic changes with the differences in the soils, and you may ask what connection exists between the mountain vineyards and those in the valley to justify both being labeled under the same Napa AVA.

It's striking that the first wineries constructed in Napa Valley after Prohibition were in completely different locations. Mondavi was founded at Oakville in 1966 in the heart of the valley proper, while Chappellet was constructed in 1967 on the isolated heights of Pritchard Hill. Yet Mondavi was the driving force, the one to emulate, as tasting rooms sprung up all along route 29 and the

The heart of Napa Valley, between Napa and St. Helena, has a monoculture of vineyards, extending across the narrow valley, and confined by the mountains on either side.

Silverado trail, over the next decade. With some notable exceptions, such as Diamond Creek in 1968, and Dunn in 1972, plantings in the mountains did not really gather sway until the late seventies. Today about 14% of the vineyards and 20% of the wineries are on the mountains (mountain vineyards tend to be smaller).[33] However, there's a growing tendency to plant Cabernet Sauvignon on hillsides and mountains rather than on the valley floor.

There is quite a bit of talk in Napa about "mountain tannins." Grapes grown on the mountains tend to have higher, and sometimes more aggressive, tannins; getting the tannins ripe at higher altitudes may require a long hang time, with the incidental consequence of later harvests. The grapes protect themselves from the combination of more sunshine (especially higher ultraviolet radiation) and greater wind exposure by increasing their production of anthocyanins and tannins. All this contributes to a tighter structure, especially when the vineyards are above the fog line.

The distinctive quality of the mountains is emphasized by Pride Mountain Vineyards, located right on top of Spring Mountain, actually straddling the line between Napa and Sonoma. Fitting into neither AVA, most of the wines carry a complicated label giving the percentage coming from each side of the border. The factor determining style, of course, is the location (above the fog line), not whether the vineyards are in Napa or Sonoma. Cabernet takes several forms here, from the Estate bottling to the more elegant Vintner Select and the larger-scale Reserve, but all have a definite structural backbone (⟦page 405).

The clearest demonstration of mountain tannins may come from Howell Mountain, on the other side of the valley, where AVA regulations require vineyards to be above the fog line. A tasting of barrel samples from Howell Mountain at David Abreu showed that the interplay of fruit and tannins can practice an unusual deception. At first taste, the wine was surprisingly soft, round, and chocolaty: where were the famous mountain tannins, I wondered?

A series of alluvial fans occupies the west side of the valley and also part of the east side.

Then 30 seconds later, the finish closed up completely with a massive dose of tannins. That's Howell Mountain for you. "Of all the appellations I would say tannins define Howell Mountain more than any other AVA," says Phillip Corallo-Titus of Chappellet.

Unlike the European system, the statement of an AVA on the label applies only to geographical origin; there is no additional implication of quality, grape variety, or style. When the rules were being discussed in 1979, André Tchelist-cheff was sarcastic about the construction of AVAs. "We are not solving the basic elements of appellation, we are not controlling the varietals, we are not controlling the maximum production; I mean we are just trying to fool the consumer that we have appellation of origin."[34]

An AVA label only requires that 85% of the grapes come from the AVA: my view is that this is nowhere near good enough. Considering the premium you pay for Napa Valley, a wine labeled from Napa should have only grapes from Napa. As for vintage, the rules have finally been tightened to specify that wine from an AVA must have 95% of its grapes from the stated vintage. For grape variety, the rule is 75%; this is probably as good as we are going to get, since it started out as 51% when the first federal regulations were introduced in 1936, and was increased (against some opposition) to 75% in 1983.[35] The 75% rule leaves a lot of wiggle room, far too much in my opinion. I would like to see all the rules replaced with a 95% lower limit!

The argument for allowing that 25% of other varieties is that you make a better wine; for Cabernet Sauvignon, this most often means softening with some Merlot. But it leaves open the possibility of including lower quality varieties. More to the point, perhaps, it's an interesting question whether there's a difference in taste profile between a 100% Cabernet Sauvignon and a 75% Cabernet Sauvignon. Should there be different descriptions for wines that are 100% of the variety and wines that have other varieties included?

Diamond Mountain
130-530 m

Howell Mountain
184-675 m

Spring Mountain
184-675 m

Pritchard Hill
120-330 m

Atlas Peak
230-790 m

Valley
0-75 m

Mount Veeder
183-650 m

Vineyards in the mountains have significant elevation above those in the valley itself, and conditions are quite different.

Varietal-labeled Cabernet Sauvignon is Napa's main challenge to Bordeaux, but there is another option for producers who want to include more than 25% of other varieties. The Meritage category was introduced in 1988 by a group of producers to describe wines based on a Bordeaux blend. This really means left bank blend, since although the wines are blended from the traditional Bordeaux varieties, including Cabernet Sauvignon, Merlot, Cabernet Franc, Petit Verdot, and Malbec, they are usually dominated by Cabernet Sauvignon. Meritage has few restrictions on the exact blend, and perhaps for this reason has not really impacted the mainstream.[36] In fact, it seems to be disappearing. There are also wines that are described simply as "proprietary reds," and which can contain any mix of varieties, but which usually have Cabernet Sauvignon as the most important variety.

There is also still some "claret" produced in Napa Valley. The term itself now has been reserved by the European Union for wine produced in Bordeaux—in my view an example of protectionism almost as blatant as banning use of "Méthode Champenoise" for sparkling wine made using the same methods as in Champagne. Claret is not a geographical description, after all, but a casual name introduced by English wine merchants to describe left bank wines. A handful of producers currently making a Napa "claret"—mostly based on Bordeaux varieties—are grandfathered.[37]

"Napa Valley is more a concept than a sense of place—it has become a brand and a style in itself," one producer said to me. "Napa Cabernet is the only New World wine ruler that's being used internationally—it wins price, volume, and scores. The reason it's the market winner is because the word

Bryant Vineyards is the Pritchard Hill area at an elevation of 130 m overlooking Lake Hennessey. It is within the St. Helena AVA.

Napa is a brand," says Leo McCloskey, of Enologix, a company that advises producers on how to increase the impact of their wines in the marketplace.[38] The question about Napa is to what extent there is uniformity of style, and how important are climate and land as opposed to winemaking? It's probably fair to say that winemaking with Cabernet Sauvignon is less variable than with some other varieties. The most significant factor affecting style is the choice of when to harvest, and certainly the trend towards achieving greater ripeness by later harvesting has played to Napa's general strengths: lots of sunshine and not much water. Insofar as there is a common style, it's an emphasis on ripe fruits that is encouraged by the climate.

Napa's character as a young wine region was prolonged by the need to re-plant many of the vineyards in the nineties. One of the glories of old vineyards is the extra concentration produced in the wine as the vines age. There's no exact measure for what the French would call Vieilles Vignes, but after about twenty years, the yields drop. Perhaps because the lower yields are achieved naturally, the extra concentration seems to have a focus and intensity that is not produced by simply reducing yields by extreme pruning. You might expect the vineyards that were planted during the boom of the 1970s now to have venerable old vines. Unfortunately, a problem with phylloxera put paid to that.

Because of its European origins, Vitis vinifera has no resistance to phyllox-era; it must be grafted on to resistant rootstocks from American species of Vitis. Early plantings in Napa used the St. George rootstock, a cultivar of Vitis riparia, which is highly resistant to phylloxera. Its disadvantage is that it can lead the vine to be too productive. New plantings during the 1960s and 1970s tended

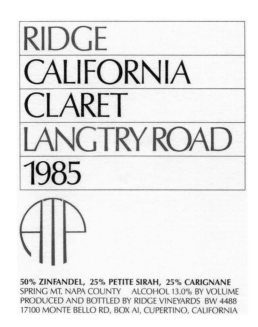

RIDGE
CALIFORNIA
CLARET
LANGTRY ROAD
1985

50% ZINFANDEL, 25% PETITE SIRAH, 25% CARIGNANE
SPRING MT. NAPA COUNTY   ALCOHOL 13.0% BY VOLUME
PRODUCED AND BOTTLED BY RIDGE VINEYARDS BW 4488
17100 MONTE BELLO RD, BOX AI, CUPERTINO, CALIFORNIA

Old habits die hard. Even into the 1980s, Ridge was producing a "claret" largely made from Zinfandel, and containing none of the Bordeaux varieties.

to use AxR1, a rootstock recommended by the Enology Department at the University of California, Davis for its reliability. AxR1 is a hybrid between Vitis vinifera and Vitis rupestris (AxR1 stands for Aramon[39] x Rupestris); like many hybrids with some vinifera parentage, it is not really very resistant to phylloxera.[40] The university should have known better, because by the late 1980s, quite predictably, phylloxera was enthusiastically feeding on these rootstocks; unfortunately, by then about 75% of plantings in Napa and Sonoma were on AxR1.[41]

The need to replant vineyards in the 1990s was not entirely a bad thing. "As growers were forced to replant by phylloxera, a lot of the unspoken issues—rootstocks, clones, spacing—became issues for discussion," says Anthony Bell, who had been horrified to find when he came to Beaulieu in 1979 from South Africa that Napa had made itself so vulnerable by planting on a single rootstock. "This was something all Europeans had been told you didn't do," he says.

It's hard to find a consensus on how vines should be planted and pruned in Napa. Driven by the nature of the available equipment, early plantings were widely spaced. In the early 1970s, spacing at 8 x 10 or 8 x 12 foot was typical. This gives 1,000-1,125 vines/ha, compared to 6,000-8,000 in Bordeaux. Because soils are more fertile in Napa than in Bordeaux, a wider spacing may be appropriate to accommodate the greater vigor of the individual vine, but as tractors have become available that can span narrower rows, the spacing has usually been somewhat reduced.

The only old vines in Napa today are those planted on St. George before the phylloxera epidemic. Sometimes this was the result of calculation, sometimes it was luck, and sometimes *force majeure*. When Al Brounstein created Diamond Creek Vineyards in 1968, he was under pressure to plant AxR1, but he stuck to St George because it had a good record in the mountains.[42] When Cathy Corison purchased her vineyard in Rutherford in the 1990s, the price was reduced because it was thought to be on AxR1—but in fact turned out to be on St. George, and at over forty years old, the vines today are some of the oldest in the valley. When Chateau Montelena planted vineyards in 1974, they tried to do the conventional thing and use AxR1, but it was in so much demand they couldn't get any, so they used St. George. "We were lucky rather than smart," Bo Barrett recalls happily. A side effect of the replacement of AxR1 since the nineties has been an increase in ripeness; the new rootstocks encourage lower yields and more rapid ripening.

Replanting as the result of the AxR1 debacle forced attention on the selection of the cultivar as well. Clones attract more attention in Napa Valley than perhaps anywhere else that focuses on Cabernet Sauvignon. Until the early nineties, there was little choice, but then the French ENTAV clones from Bordeaux became available as well as the old clones that had been propagated from vines previously grown in California. The question about the move towards the ENTAV clones is whether material that was selected in a relatively cool period in Bordeaux will necessarily give the best results in Napa's warmer and drier climate. The most concern is about clone 337, which might compensate for lack of ripeness in Bordeaux, but which really emphasizes lush fruits and supple tannins in the context of Napa (see Chapter 1).

The nature of the high end has changed somewhat since Napa started concentrating on Cabernet. In 1974, many of the top wines were "Reserves," coming from Beaulieu, Mondavi, or Louis Martini. That has changed. "Reserve really didn't mean much, although the term was popular at the time. Benziger destroyed the use of the term by making a bulk wine. I always resented that. It was quite different from Estate but even that has been diluted now. Today I am amazed that some of the big producers have Estate wines with the California appellation, which to me is ridiculous," says Richard Arrowood, one of the first winemakers to focus on single vineyard wines (in Sonoma).

Today the top wines tend to come from single vineyards, often enough carrying the name of the sub-AVA in which they are located. (However, worried about possible dilution of identity, Napa Valley vintners sponsored a law in 1990 that all wines attributed to any AVA within Napa should in addition mention Napa Valley.[43]) Is the switch in emphasis from reserve bottlings to single vineyards a mark of a maturing wine region? Does this bring Napa more into line with Bordeaux? Well, it remains true that in both cases, the main selling point is the brand, whether or not that brand is associated with geography. But you could make a case that some of the top wines in Napa are more clearly associated with specific terroirs than they are in Bordeaux.

Two eras in Napa are
revealed by replanting
at Beaulieu, around
1946 as widely spaced,
individual vines, and in
2003 as more closely
spaced rows of vines
on a modern trellis.

Photographs courtesy
Beaulieu Vineyard and
Joel Butler MW.

Although there is a definite move towards single vineyards, there are still some leading wines based on barrel selections. It may be true that single vineyards become more interesting at very small production levels, but blending produces more complexity at higher levels. "Separate vineyard wines from the mountains and valley would be like putting handcuffs on us. Not all lots turn out great every year and quality bounces around the valley like a ball. There's wide variation in sources from year to year. In a cool year, St Helena and Calistoga make the best lots, in a warm year it's Napa and the hillsides," says Chuck Wagner, explaining that Caymus Special Selection is usually a blend of one quarter from mountain sources and three quarters from the valley (Ⓨ page 383).

Selection has become increasingly important even for single vineyard wines, since many leading wines also have second wines.[44] It seems a fair question to ask whether selection reduces the impression of the wine as representing terroir and vintage. Vineyard manager Caleb Mosley at Araujo estate says that selection is more a way to take out those parts of the vineyard that have underperfomed. "There are always some plots that you work really hard but which cannot be made to give top results no matter what you do," he says. His colleague Burges Smith turned the tables by asking me whether removing one fermentation lot that had problems—for example too much volatile acidity—would qualify as reducing expression of time and place. I guess it's a fine line when you deviate from the principle that terroir means expression of the vineyard, the whole vineyard, and nothing but the vineyard.

Although terroir is emphasized at many top vineyards, they are not necessarily representative of the AVAs in which they are located. Michael Silacci says that, "Our emphasis is on a vineyard designated wine. Opus is just Opus. There isn't any single external reference point, although by default the wine is Napa and Oakville. To think about expression of each vineyard site is more of a European perspective." When I said I thought perhaps this had reversed, and terroir may be more important in Napa than in Bordeaux, Michael said he thought this could be true if Napa weren't so concerned with ripeness: "Going from ripe to over-ripe fruit tends to mask terroir," he believes.

Superficially, Napa Valley offers a similar range of wines as Bordeaux, from introductory offerings under $10 per bottle to cults or icons above $100 per bottle. At lower price levels it has something of the same problem as Bordeaux: high costs in Napa make it difficult to compete with varietal Cabernets from the southern hemisphere with lower costs. Moving up market, the recent recession took a toll, with some significant price cuts forced on wines at the top end. Prompted partly by the wish to maintain quality (and exclusivity), and partly by difficulties with the economy, a trend to follow Bordeaux into second wines has accentuated in Napa. As in Bordeaux, the second labels have a variety of origins: for cult wines produced in small quantities, they usually come from declassified lots; at larger producers they may represent different sources of material.

Vintage variation is the inevitable companion to expression of terroir. Napa has come a long way from the era when the Wine Institute (an advocacy group representing producers) used the slogan, "Every year is a vintage year in Cali-

All types of training systems for Cabernet coexist in Napa. Vertical shoot positioning, with a dense canopy of shoots trained vertically from a cordon was a standard, but cordon training (top left) has become less popular because the large number of pruning cuts increases susceptibility to the disease Eutypa. It now tends to be replaced by cane pruning when the shoots come off the head of the vine and are aligned on a trellis (top right). Some of the more unusual pruning systems are the Geneva Double Curtain, which splits the canopy into two parts (bottom left) or freestanding bush vines (bottom right).

fornia."[45] That was behind the belief that persisted through the seventies that wine is made by winemaking.[46] Site location and vineyard management were all but dismissed as relevant factors, and it was assumed that California's climate ensured perfect ripeness every year. "The predominant thinking at the time was that every variety would give good results if planted in a good place," Bill Phelps recalls. Matching terroir to varieties and taking account of climatic variation came later. Today at top producers there is more concern to represent the terroir, and recognition that each vintage is different. Indeed, there's a certain disdain at the top Napa producers for technological advice from graduates of the Enology Department of the University of California, Davis. "Graduates from Davis know how to take care of chemicals and things," Fred Schrader says somewhat dismissively. Recollecting Napa's revival, Paul Roberts of Harlan Estate says, "There was the era of students from Davis who came here and said: 'That's how we make wine—going after the correct numbers.' This lasted into the eighties. Today there is more purity and less intervention; we measure numbers but we don't let it drive winemaking." That's the artisanal view.

Ownership in Napa is divided between wineries and grape growers. The wineries claim to own roughly two thirds of the vineyards,[47] but the true number is probably nearer one half.[48] Many of the famous single vineyards belong to individual estates, so the wine is made by a single producer, but some are owned by growers who sell grapes to multiple producers, creating an opportunity to see what different winemakers make of the same terroir. (The largest single private landowner in Napa Valley is Beckstoffer Vineyards, which has several top vineyards in Oakville, Rutherford, and St. Helena, among its roughly 400 ha.)

Some of the top sites in Napa Valley have long histories, with potential that was recognized more than a century ago. At the heart of the Oakville area is the To Kalon vineyard, a parcel of almost 100 ha originally purchased by Hamilton Crabb in 1868 (the name is Greek for "most beautiful"). Further purchases brought Crabb's total to more than 150 ha. Half of the land was planted with hundreds of grape varieties within a few years. Wine was produced under the name of To Kalon vineyards; the best known was "Crabb's Black Burgundy," which actually was made from the Italian Refosco grape.[49] But Cabernet Sauvignon was also grown there in the 1880s. The 1882 vintage was described as: "Wine of moderately dark garnet color, with a vinous flavor, accompanied by a perceptible, light bouquet; fair acid and medium astringency. Body, good; condition, clear. The wine promises very well."[50]

After various vicissitudes, including changes of ownership, Prohibition, and destruction of the original winery, the vineyard fell into various hands. The major part of more than 100 ha became part of the Stelling Estate in 1943, and almost all of this eventually ended up with Robert Mondavi, whose new winery

Looking down the To Kalon vineyard from the apex of the alluvial fan, there's a slight gradient down to route 29. The scrubby hills beyond the Silverado trail are in the background.

was positioned at the edge of the original To Kalon vineyard.[51] (Mondavi also purchased another 120 ha of land immediately to the north, which is now part of the Mondavi home estate.[52])

A minor part of the original To Kalon estate, a plot of 36 ha, was purchased by Beaulieu Vineyards from the Crabb estate in 1940. As Beaulieu Vineyard No. 4, it became the heart of Beaulieu's Private Reserve, but was sold to Andy Beckstoffer in 1993. Beckstoffer sells grapes to a variety of producers, and some of Napa Valley's most expensive Cabernets come from this parcel.[53] It's a measure of the reputation of the vineyard that its grapes sell for more than five times the average price for Napa Valley Cabernet Sauvignon.[54] The last, smallest part of the original To Kalon vineyard is a parcel of 8 ha that Crabb himself donated to the University of California; this now forms their Oakville Experimental Station. (Probably the most expensive terroir for an experimental station anywhere in the world!)

The To Kalon vineyard occupies the top half of the Oakville Bench—the apex of the fan is more or less at the top of the vineyard. The terroir is a gravelly loam, forming a gradual slope (only just noticeable to the eye) from an elevation of about 75 m at the base of the mountains to 50 m at the highway. Of course, To Kalon is large for a high quality vineyard, roughly three times the size of the average Grand Cru Classé of the Médoc, so it has significant variation. "Up by the hills it's grand cru terroir, and the wine goes into the Reserve, towards the middle it's premier cru level, and the wine goes into the Oakville Cabernet, down by route 29 it's village territory and the wine goes into a Napa bottling," says Mark de Vere, expressing Mondavi's view (Y page 399). Tasting

The To Kalon vineyard extends from the highway to the edge of the mountains. The major part is owned by Robert Mondavi (winery at bottom right). Beckstoffer has a single large parcel, Opus One has two parcels, and the U.C. Davis experimental station has a small plot.

barrel samples of Cabernet Sauvignon made this quite clear. A sample from vines close to the road gives an austere, fresh, light impression. "This is about having classic Napa Valley Cabernet," says Mark. From the middle of the vineyard, the wine is fuller on the palate, but still has a fresh impression. "This is powerful, rich, and obvious, but not at the level of sophistication we want for the Reserve," explains Mark. Wine from close to the hills is fuller, but more restrained and less obvious. "This has the elegance and finesse we look for in the Reserve." For a barrel sample it seems remarkably complete.

Just across the road from Mondavi, Opus One was one of the first collaborations between Bordeaux and Napa winemakers, created as a joint venture between Robert Mondavi and Baron Philippe de Rothschild in 1979. When it was announced, the news was seen as a validation of Napa as a winemaking region. Before Opus One had its own vineyards, grapes came from Mondavi's holding of To Kalon, so the first vintage in 1979 was really more of a super-cuvée than Opus One as it later developed. The first estate vineyard was established when Mondavi sold the 14 ha Q block of the To Kalon vineyard to the new venture. Further vineyards directly across route 29 were purchased in 1983 and 1984, and another 19 ha of To Kalon were transferred after Constellation took over Mondavi in 2004. The wine was made at Mondavi until Opus One's winery was constructed in 1991. The wine is easy to underrate in the early years, when it tends to be somewhat dumb, and to retain a touch of austerity. Relatively close spacing makes the vineyards look more European than most. "The assumption from the beginning was that there should be a Bordeaux blend," says Michael Silacci, but there's always a high content of

Cabernet Sauvignon (usually over 85%). In terms of aging, the 2005 is showing beautifully now, and the 1995 shows the extra elegance of another decade's age (Ⳙ page 402). The very first vintage remains vibrant today.

There is probably no clearer example of the French influence on Napa than Dominus winery. It's located on the old Napanook vineyard, which was one of the first vineyards in Napa Valley, planted on the Oakville alluvial fan by George Yount in 1838. The vineyard was bought by John Daniel, owner of Inglenook, in 1943, and he kept it when he sold Inglenook in 1970. Dominus was first produced as a partnership between Christian Moueix of Château Pétrus in Pomerol and John Daniel's daughter, and then in 1995 Christian became sole owner. The change in varietal constitution over the years is one sign of the difference between Napa and Bordeaux. Explaining the history, "When Dominus started we had 21% Merlot; now it's only 0.2%. Cabernet Sauvignon has gone from 65% to 85%. The initial plantings were prejudged from Bordeaux, that you could transpose percentages from Bordeaux to Napa and it would work," says winemaker Tod Mostero.

One of the first changes Christian made in 1996 was to introduce a second wine, called Napanook after the vineyard, for lots that didn't fit the profile for Dominus. Wondering what effect the introduction of Napanook had on Dominus, I compared the last vintage of the old regime with the first Dominus of the new regime (Ⳙ page 392). The difference seemed more apparent in style than quality as such; Dominus 1995 shows perfumes of soft, ripe, gentle red fruits, but Dominus 1996 gives a more mineral impression of black fruits with more structural support. In short, Dominus 1995 seems more typically New World and Dominus 1996 seems more Bordelais. Although that's partly characteristic of the vintages, it epitomizes the style since then. Dominus is one of the more restrained Cabernets in Napa: ownership may reside on Bordeaux's right bank, but the style is definitely left bank. Some attitudes come straight from France. "We still make wine that is intended to be aged, you can probably start to drink five years after the harvest, but I consider that it doesn't really begin to become expressive until it's ten years, sometimes twenty," says Tod. I could see that taut, restrained style of vintages of the past decade foreshadowed in the 1996 vintage, whereas 1995 seemed to be more like Napanook of today, which shows a more forward, approachable style.

At the northern end of the valley, just to the east of Calistoga, the Eisele vineyard is another of Napa's famous sites. It was first planted as a vineyard in 1886; this was around twenty to thirty years after much of the valley was planted to wheat, but the soils here were too poor, and probably vines were the first crop to be planted. There was a variety of cépages, originally Zinfandel and Riesling, but nothing very distinguished until Cabernet Sauvignon was planted in 1964, when it was field grafted on to the old roots. Quality really began with the Eiseles, who were Bordeaux collectors—perhaps that's why

Eisele vineyard is in Simmons Creek Canyon, a protected area to the east of the Silverado trail (running parallel to the bottom of the image). Elevation rises from 111 m at the lowest point to 134 m at the edge of the mountain. Simmons Creek (dry most of the year) runs through the vineyard.

they planted Cabernet. At first the grapes were used only to make a wine for home consumption, but Paul Draper of Ridge Vineyards made the first commercial release in 1971; this was the one and only vintage of Ridge Eisele. In 1972 and 1973 the grapes were sold to Mondavi (reportedly for the Reserve Cabernet Sauvignon). In 1974, Conn Creek Winery produced the second vineyard-labeled release, and then from 1975 the grapes were sold to Joseph Phelps, who made a famous wine. "Phelps Eisele 1975 was the benchmark wine for years and years," Fred Schrader said, when I asked him what was the first Napa cult wine. Phelps continued to produce its Eisele Cabernet until Bart and Daphne Araujo purchased the vineyard in 1990. The following year was the last vintage of Phelps Eisele and the first vintage of Araujo Eisele; since 1992 there has been only the Araujo bottling.

Eisele has an unusual terroir. The vineyards are on an alluvial fan coming straight off the Palisades mountains, but they are not very fertile, and fertility *decreases* going away from the mountain. Going up the slope you get more clay soils and higher vigor, the opposite of the usual order. Pebbles washed down from the Palisades to make a thick layer of subsoil about one foot deep all over the western block of the vineyard, which is effectively bisected by Simmons Creek. The creek—dry most of the time, but prone to fill up and even flash flood—is full of large round pebbles. The pebbles get smaller as you move away from the hillside. This is the most gravelly part of the vineyard, and in true Bordeaux style, it is planted entirely with Cabernet Sauvignon. The blocks on the eastern side are planted with a variety of cépages, mostly Merlot and Syrah for the blacks, and at the farthest east, some white varieties.

The vineyard occupies half of a V-shaped canyon that extends into the Palisades. The unique feature of the microclimate is the breeze that cools the vineyard in late afternoon, created by updrafts from the Palisades that suck in cooler Pacific-influenced air from Sonoma. This balances the warmer temperatures at the north end of the valley, which might otherwise make the site too hot for Cabernet Sauvignon. The blocks where Cabernet Sauvignon are planted have good drainage (all those pebbles), so water stress develops earlier in the season (before véraison); this affects the cycle of the vine through the growing season and gives better balance, according to vineyard manager Caleb Mosley.

As at other special vineyards in Napa, the site is more representative of itself than the local AVA. Eisele is in the Calistoga AVA but the site has its own strong identity, says Director Jimmy Hayes. "We make a kind of wine that speaks not just of place but also of the time," he says, referring to vintage variation. In addition to the Cabernet Sauvignon, there are also bottlings of Syrah and Sauvignon Blanc from the vineyard. In the early days, the Phelps Eisele was 100% Cabernet Sauvignon, as were the first two Araujo vintages, but since then the wine has been a blend, usually 85-95% Cabernet Sauvignon with some Cabernet Franc and Petit Verdot, sometimes also a little Merlot (⟲ page 372). The Araujos believe in blending: the Eisele Syrah usually has about 4% Viognier, in classic Rhône style, and the Sauvignon Blanc is a blend of Sauvignon Blanc, Sauvignon Musqué, and a little Viognier.

It's difficult to compare the Cabernet from Eisele before and after 1991 given vintage variation and differences in age, but it's interesting that in the one year that both Phelps and Araujo released an Eisele bottling, the wines today show more similarities than differences. The Araujo shows more complex, attractive fruits and is more open; the style of the Phelps is more reserved (in line with earlier Eisele vintages and with their Insignia blend of the period). Of course, differences seen today may be partly due to bottle variation. But a savory aromatic thread, somewhat reminiscent of the French garrigue, runs through both wines. Perhaps this is what others have called minerality in the wine, but whatever you call it, there's an impression in comparing the wines side by side that the vineyard is expressing its terroir.

When Hamilton Crabb planted the To Kalon vineyard, it was just a matter of clearing the land and digging in the grapevines. Switching the use of the land to viticulture, especially as it becomes a monoculture, creates a certain change in the environment, but the terroir remains recognizably the same. This has not necessarily remained true as vineyard plantings have extended to mountains. When the first vineyards were carved out of mountain sites around Napa in the 1960s and 1970s, no one thought much of it (aside from questioning whether the sites were appropriate for the intended varieties). By the 1980s, people began to object to terraforming. One trigger was the construction of Atlas Peak Vineyards. As described by the project manager, Dick Peterson, "There are D10 Cats up there. This is a moonscape, but we're ripping it. We'll put terraces in there…We'll fill that canyon with rocks the size of Volkswagens, then cover

Viader Vineyards is on Howell Mountain (although outside the AVA) on a 32-degree slope overlooking Bell Canyon (a source of the drinking water supply for St. Helena).

it up with some muck from the caves we're digging."[55] Mountain reconstructions became controversial. When Delia Viader constructed her vineyard on Howell Mountain, environmental damage to Bell Canyon Reservoir below led to civil law suits and criminal charges.[56] Today the growth of mountain vineyards has slowed dramatically. Given the much higher costs associated with creating and maintaining mountain vineyards, it's not surprising that they should include a concentration of high-end wineries; indeed, many of Napa's cult wines come from mountain sites.

Perhaps at the end of the day (environmental issues aside) the question is not whether a terroir is natural or artificial, but whether it is good for growing grapes. Or in the context of Cabernet Sauvignon, what's the difference in making wine from grapes grown on a mountain as opposed to in the valley? Indeed, it's curious that attempts in Napa to produce wines like Bordeaux should focus on mountain vineyards. Bordeaux, after all, is pretty flat, and the principal distinction between sites is whether they are gravel-based or clay-based. But Bill Harlan at Harlan Estate (on the mountain above Oakville) and Al Brounstein at Diamond Creek Vineyards (on Diamond Mountain) felt that vineyards in the valley would not give the small berries that they needed for the highest quality Cabernet Sauvignon. "I wanted to create a first growth in California. All at once I started looking for a totally different type of land that would produce the best fruit, not necessarily look nice. Historically the best

Harlan Estate, which made one of the first "cult" wines in Napa, is on the mountain slopes at Oakville, looking out over Martha's Vineyard, To Kalon, and Napanook, lower in the valley.

wine produced in America over a long period of time was the Rutherford Bench, but after studying soils I became convinced we wanted to be on the hillside with good drainage," says Bill Harlan. "Al felt that grapes from hillsides suffer more, and would give more intensity," Phil Ross at Diamond Creek recalls.

Is Cabernet Sauvignon a terroir grape? This is not entirely a silly question. It's accepted that Pinot Noir and Riesling are terroir grapes, in the sense that different locations close to one another can give consistently different wines, even when all other factors except the sites themselves appear to be identical. Similar emphasis on terroir for Cabernet Sauvignon is lacking. Certainly it is accepted in Bordeaux that it gives its best results on the gravel mounds, and indeed, vice versa: the gravel mounds are considered to be the best terroir because Cabernet Sauvignon does so well there. (But there is really only one choice in Bordeaux: gravel or clay—and the clay is too cold and drains too poorly for Cabernet.) In any case, almost every Bordeaux wine is a blend from several varieties grown on a diversity of terroirs. There are no bottlings to display the qualities of single vineyards, so we are left only with the broad generality that Cabernet Sauvignon does best on gravel.

Ironically in view of the New World's slow acceptance of the significance of terroir, it is to Napa we have to turn to ask what effect individual sites may have on the character of Cabernet Sauvignon. Although most of Napa's top wines today come from individual, named vineyards, relating the character of the wine to the vineyard is not necessarily simple, since there's variation in clones or age of the vines, and each producer has his own practices in viticulture and vinification. What's needed to make a real comparison is for a single producer to bottle Cabernet Sauvignon from different vineyards planted with similar cultivars of around the same age.

After he founded Diamond Creek Vineyards on Diamond Mountain, Al Brounstein was fond of saying, "I produce a Bordeaux wine in a Burgundian way."[57] His 9 hectare vineyard was planted in 1986 with Bordeaux varieties, largely Cabernet Sauvignon obtained directly from the first growths in Bordeaux. (Al famously smuggled the cuttings in via Mexico: he was not one to be diverted from his objectives of quality.) The first wines showed evident differences between different parts of the property, so Al divided the estate into separate vineyards, and bottled each separately. This is exactly what we need to see whether and how the site influences Cabernet Sauvignon.

Volcanic Hill is the warmest site, facing south, with soils based on volcanic ash. At Red Rock Terrace, facing north, the ferrous soils are not quite as warm. Relatively flat, Gravelly Meadow is a cooler site, with soils reflecting its name. Harvest lasts a month, usually in the order Volcanic Hill, Red Rock, Gravelly Meadow. A little farther off, Lake Vineyard is the coolest microclimate on the property, in fact to the point that it has made a wine in only thirteen years to date. (Anywhere else, they would perhaps conclude they had the wrong variety, and plant something less demanding, but Phil Ross says that they stay with it because when it does work, the wine is wonderful.) The blend is similar for each vineyard, with about 86% Cabernet Sauvignon, and the rest from Merlot, Cabernet Franc, and Petit Verdot (this last coming from a small, separate vineyard plot near Lake Vineyard).

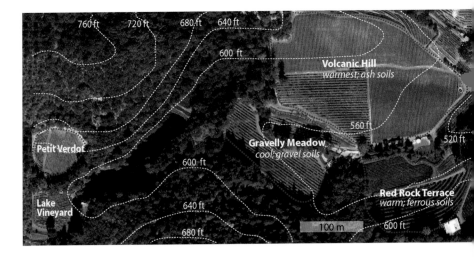

Diamond Creek has several adjacent vineyards, each with distinct soil and microclimate.

The Volcanic Hill vineyard at Diamond Creek on the upper slopes is bordered by woods and faces south. Red Rock Terrace is in the foreground.

Volcanic Hill provides a fascinating comparison with the other vineyards (ϒ page 390). When you compare wines produced on volcanic terroirs versus sedimentary terroirs for other varieties, there is a consistent pattern: volcanic soils produce wines with a tauter quality, a sense of tension, compared to the rounder, broader flavors produced on sedimentary soils. The effect is less pronounced with Cabernet Sauvignon than it is with Pinot Noir or Riesling, but it follows the same general lines. Volcanic Hill gives an impression of taut, precisely delineated, black fruits, whereas Red Rock is more forward, brighter, open, although in the same elegant style. Perhaps it is a flight of imagination encouraged by the name, but Gravelly Meadow does seem to have more of an underlying mineral, earthy, texture. With a greater sense of austerity, Volcanic Hill ages more slowly than the others.

A significant part of the difference between the vineyards is in the tannic structure—taut for Volcanic Hill, elegant for Red Rock, earthy for Gravelly Meadow—so will the characteristic differences between the wines narrow as the tannins resolve with age? I tasted all three vineyards from 1994 to see whether the differences among current vintages were still evident after nearly twenty years. With the moderate alcohol of the early nineties (12.5%), and delicately balanced palates, these were clearly all food wines, with some convergence in style compared to younger vintages. The fruit spectrum was similar in all three, just a touch more aromatic than you would find in Bordeaux of the period, but there were indeed differences in the tannic structure, although not exactly what I expected based on the younger vintages. Volcanic Hill seemed the most mature, savory elements mingling with lightening fruits; Gravelly Meadow seemed the most precise and elegant, a tribute to the conventional wisdom that gravel goes with Cabernet; and Red Rock showed the most evident tannic structure. What else can this be but reflection of terroir? Going back a little further, when I tasted the 1992 Volcanic Hill early in 2012, if I had been told it was from Bordeaux, I would have thought about the 1986 vintage. There's less savory development than in Bordeaux, perhaps due to the high proportion of Cabernet Sauvignon.

Another mountain vineyard shows the effects of differing altitudes. Across the Mayacamas Mountains in Sonoma, the top of Alexander Mountain was converted to vineyards for the Stonestreet Estate, purchased by Jesse Jackson in 1995. This is a vast vineyard site: at the top, the vegetation is scrub; lower down there are bay trees, and oils can drift on to the vines and berries, making a slight aromatic contribution to the wine. Soils change significantly: there are red ferrous areas, gray stone areas, and impenetrable serpentine. A series of single vineyard Cabernet Sauvignons comes from sites within the estate, distinguished as much by elevation as soil type. The vineyards range from below the fog line, to within the fog bank, to nicely above the fog line. "Blending in (other varieties) would cause loss of site specificity, the focus here is expressing single vineyards in a Burgundian model," says winemaker Graham Weerts. Certainly the four single vineyard wines were all distinct (⟑ page 415), with the sense of structure becoming more evident with elevation, perhaps due to the effects of increasing luminosity on tannin production.

Sonoma County is about twice the area of Napa County, but has a comparable area of vineyards: reflecting their relative positions in the hierarchy of California wine regions, the crop is somewhat larger, but its value is somewhat less.[58] Napa's intense concentration on Cabernet Sauvignon for reds and Chardonnay for whites has led to its being viewed as the leader for both, but in fact

Vineyards on Alexander Mountain are in steep terrain. Oils from bay trees (in the foreground) at lower elevations may contribute to the character of the wine.

Photograph courtesy Jackson Family Vineyards.

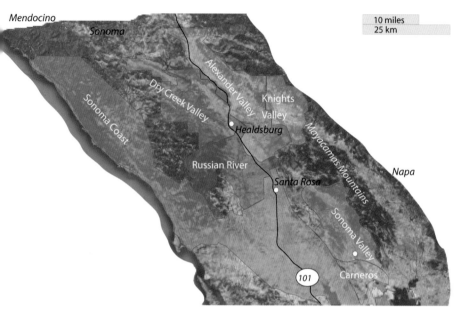

Mendocino

Sonoma

Alexander Valley

Dry Creek Valley

Knights Valley

Sonoma Coast

Healdsburg

Russian River

Mayacamas Mountains

Napa

Santa Rosa

Sonoma Valley

101 Carneros

10 miles
25 km

Sonoma County has 15 AVAs (some contained within others). Only the major areas are shown here.

Sonoma produces three times as much Chardonnay as Napa and almost as much Cabernet Sauvignon.[59] Cabernet is the most important black variety grown in Sonoma, but Sonoma is more diverse, since it produces almost as much Pinot Noir. "In Napa, Cabernet is king, but in Sonoma it's more one of a variety of grapes," says winemaker Margo Van Staaveren at Chateau St. Jean.

The feeling in Sonoma is quite different from Napa. As you drive up to Sonoma from San Francisco, the valley is much less confined than Napa Valley. The Coastal Range is well off to the west between Sonoma and the Pacific, and the Mayacamas Mountains are away to the east. Driving right through Sonoma, route 101 is a highway with the usual depressing industrial developments on either side once you enter the valley above Petaluma. This is quite a contrast with the chic wineries and tasting rooms along route 29 in Napa. However, when you get off the beaten track, there are numerous winding roads running through hillside slopes patterned with vineyards; wineries are indicated rather discretely. Several of the valleys come together at Healdsburg, a gentrified town just off the freeway. The average scale of production in Sonoma is smaller; vineyards are divided among 1,800 growers, compared with 600 vineyard owners in Napa.

Sonoma is on average cooler than Napa, with growing season temperatures in Santa Rosa, on the edge of the Russian River Valley, up to a degree less than Napa.[60] This is why Pinot Noir can succeed in Sonoma while it is rarely successful in Napa. By the same measure, Cabernet Sauvignon might be expected to show more of a cool climate character. Microclimates are if anything more important in Sonoma than Napa, with wide variation in soils and temperatures. There's more Cabernet Sauvignon in the warmer valleys, Alexander, Dry

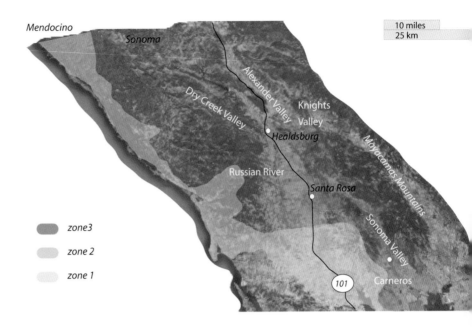

The climate becomes steadily warmer moving inland. Alexander Valley and Dry Creek Valley are variable, but are the warmest sites, together with parts of Sonoma Valley.

Creek, and Sonoma, and very little in Russian River, which has a sharp focus on Pinot Noir.

Although there's a great diversity of soil types in Sonoma, possibly it's more to the point that terrains vary from valley floor, to rolling hills, to mountainous. Russian River Valley is the most consistent, with some vineyards on the flat land along the river, and the rest on low, gentle slopes. The most dramatic contrasts are to be found in Alexander and Sonoma Valleys, which vary from vineyards on relatively fertile flat soil in the center to vertiginous slopes up to several hundred meters of elevation on the mountains.

My recollection of styles from the first Cabernet Sauvignons I tasted from Sonoma in the seventies is that they were distinctly leaner than Napa, not so surprising given Sonoma's slightly cooler climate. (Those wines would have come from valley floor sites that today would probably not be regarded as optimal for Cabernet.) That leaner quality does not seem to be true today; certainly as judged by alcohol levels, the Cabernets of Sonoma are right up there with Napa.[61] "Sonoma even to a greater degree than Napa has more vagaries in climate and terroir. It probably was true that Sonoma Cabernet was leaner than Napa in the seventies but not so much now. There is more knowledge now about where to plant Cabernet, we know it needs to be in the warmer sites on hillsides, it used to be on the valley floor," says winemaker Richard Arrowood, who was there right at the beginning, producing Cabernet Sauvignon first at Chateau St. Jean and then later at Arrowood. Part of the reason the difference has apparently lessened may be the increased concentration on growing Cabernet in mountain vineyards, which may be more similar between Sonoma and Napa than are the valley floors.

The Monte Rosso vineyard occupies a peak at 375 m in the Mayacamas Mountains with direct exposure to San Pablo Bay, fifteen miles away.

Photograph courtesy Louis Martini.

Perhaps because of that initial leanness, there seems to have been more concern to soften the Cabernet with other varieties in Sonoma. "Green bean character in Cabernet Sauvignon was typical in the 1990s. Then Parker came along and it became unacceptable," says Rob Davis, who has been making wine at Jordan Vineyards since the seventies (page 394). "The wines made in the seventies were fairly extracted; there wasn't this 'I want to take it home and drink it tonight'—you really had to lay them down. We thought that blending would make a softer wine," says Margo Van Staaveren, who has been at Chateau St. Jean throughout. This was the impetus for Chateau St. Jean's introduction of Cinq Cepages in 1990, a wine made from all five classic Bordeaux varieties (page 386). "The idea was to have approachability, accessibility, and ageability; they weren't accessible wines we made in the seventies," she recollects. "I have Napa envy, they get the lush rich textures that are not so easy to come by in Sonoma," she adds.

Opinions have oscillated on blends versus varietals. "The early vineyard designates were all 100% Cabernet Sauvignon. There weren't a lot of the other varieties—when there was a blend the cheapest variety was the Cabernet Sauvignon!—you couldn't find the other varieties," Richard Arrowood recollects about the early days at Chateau St. Jean. Things went in the other direction at Arrowood, where Richard made the wines through the nineties. The two top wines were the monovarietal Cabernet Sauvignon from the Monte Rosso vineyard and the Réserve Spéciale, a blend from several vineyards. The reserve has undergone an interesting transition. "With the reserve at the beginning we

The rusty red appearance of the iron-rich soils lives up to Monte Rosso's name.

started with a blend, but we wanted to get more structure," says current winemaker Heidi von der Mehden. The Reserve was a classic blend of four Bordeaux varieties until 1993, but then changed to a 100% Cabernet Sauvignon. I think this may have been a mistake; comparing the 1997 monovarietal with the 1993 blend, there seems to be a certain something missing (⟁ page 378). I'm inclined to the view that it is only an exceptional site in Sonoma that will make a really successful monovarietal Cabernet. The exception that proves the rule is the Monte Rosso Vineyard.

Probably the most famous vineyard in Sonoma, the Monte Rosso ranch has 100 ha of vines spread out over 250 ha at the peak of the mountain with views across to San Pablo Bay. As the name suggests, it has rocky, red volcanic soils; most of the topsoils are 18-24 inches deep, based on pure rock. Exposure to the bay ensures cool breezes all day and keeps up the acidity in the berries. It was originally planted by Emanuel Goldstein in the early 1880s with a wide mix of varieties. The vineyard was wiped out by phylloxera and replanted in 1890, when Zinfandel became a significant part of the plantings. Some of these old vines still remain as blocks of Zinfandel or field blends with Alicante and Beaunoir. When Louis Martini took over the vineyard in 1938, they concentrated on Zinfandel and Cabernet Sauvignon. (In the interim, they called the wine Monte Rosso Chianti.) Among the plantings from 1938, the surviving Cabernet Sauvignon vines are probably the oldest Cabernet in the USA. The old plantings are mostly on the St. George rootstock; in 1955 they started to switch plantings to AxR1, and all that has had to be replanted.

Vines planted as individual bushes in 1938 at the Monte Rosso vineyard are probably the oldest Cabernet Sauvignon in the United States.

Following the sale of Louis Martini, since 2002 the Monte Rosso vineyard has been part of the Gallo Empire. Louis Martini takes the bulk of production, but still sells grapes to other producers.[62] There have been experiments with various blends, but the monovarietal Cabernets from Monte Rosso certainly stand out. What I especially liked about Louis Martini's Monte Rosso Cabernet was the precise expression of black fruit without the jammy overtones that often accompany big wines in Napa (Y page 398). Arrowood's Monte Rosso is perhaps a touch more precise, and Sbragia's a little softer (Y page 402). The common thread is a sense of elegance, a fine structure supporting the fruits.

In due course, there will be a fascinating comparison between Monte Rosso and the adjacent vineyard, Amapola Creek, planted by Richard Arrowood as his latest venture (Y page 377). Just below Monte Rosso, the land, which has similar ferrous soils, was cleared and planted mostly with Cabernet Sauvignon. The first vintage in 2005 was a monovarietal; subsequent vintages have included a little Petit Verdot. "I like Petit Verdot because of the additional structure you get and the aromatics that it carries. I've considered Malbec, I think it would add something, but the difficulty with Malbec is getting the right clone that won't shatter. Most of the Malbec in California is ordinary," says Richard.

The conventional wisdom is that Russian River is suitable for cool climate varieties. So it was not surprising that when I mentioned I was visiting Dehlinger, everyone said, "Well if you find out how they produce Cabernet

Sauvignon in Russian River, let me know." Indeed, Dehlinger produces one of the very few—perhaps the only—Cabernet Sauvignon in the heart of Russian River. So I asked whether it was a problem producing Cabernet Sauvignon in an area better known for Pinot Noir and Chardonnay. "When I started out, all the wineries were making everything, but now the region has become type-cast—Merlot comes from Sonoma Valley, Pinot Noir from Russian River, etc. So Cabernet from here is an oddity," says Tom Dehlinger. In fact, when he started planting the vineyard in the early seventies, he was advised by famous viticulturalist Albert Winkler of U.C. Davis, who had devised the degree day system for assessing which varieties should be planted where. "The degree days are similar to Bordeaux, so someone should do that (plant Cabernet)," Winkler told him. "This is cool climate Cabernet production. It might be similar to Bordeaux, but certainly it is substantially warmer than Burgundy," Tom says today. You might think this would argue for a Bordeaux-like blend rather than a monovarietal, but production has oscillated, starting with a monovarietal, switching to a blend with Merlot from 1992, and then back to monovarietal from 1998 (Ⴓ page 389). The problem with the blend has actually been more with the Merlot (which wasn't planted in the best place) than with the Cabernet. I actually rather liked the blends I tasted from the nineties and feel sorry they're not still being made.

A variety of unusual blends are being made at the only other place in Russian River where I found Cabernet Sauvignon, but this is the slightly warmer area of the Chalk Hill sub-AVA. At Chalk Hill Estate, the sites where they grow black grapes are too warm for Pinot Noir, which is how they came to Cabernet Sauvignon, planted on hill tops where the soil is based on red volcanic rocks and the exposure is warm south-facing. They also have quite a bit of the old varieties Malbec and Carmenère, and a little Petit Verdot. The Estate Red is a blend of all varieties, but the higher-end wines, made in small quantities for the wine club, are blends of 80-90% Cabernet with just one of the other varieties. I tasted these expecting to get a clear bead on what Carmenère or Malbec adds to Cabernet Sauvignon in a blend, but I was thwarted in being unable to see any special effect (Ⴓ page 381). This reinforces my view that other varieties don't really show directly in blends in California until they are close to the limit for varietal labeling (25%); up to that point the Cabernet is quite dominant.

The doyen of Cabernet Sauvignon in California in the modern era might not be in Napa or Sonoma at all, but in the Santa Cruz Mountains just south of San Francisco. Wine production started at Ridge in the nineteenth century, although it lacks the continuous history of Beaulieu or Inglenook, having closed during Prohibition; it was revived in the 1960s. Another couple of peaks along the mountain range, Martin Ray established his winery in the 1940s. After he left in 1970, it became the Mount Eden vineyard. Both Ridge and Mount Eden have a long history with Cabernet Sauvignon. The vines for both properties

Vineyards on Santa Cruz mountains look out over Silicon Valley.

Photograph courtesy Ridge Vineyards

originated with a selection brought from Margaux in the nineteenth century by Emmet Rixford (no one is sure whether the wines actually came from Château Margaux or merely from the Margaux appellation). The vines passed through Rixford's La Questa vineyard to Mount Eden, and on to Ridge (which also had some selections from the old Fountain Grove vineyard in Sonoma). The original plantings are still propagated by selection massale at both wineries.

The Santa Cruz mountain appellation has roughly equal amounts of Pinot Noir, Chardonnay, and Cabernet Sauvignon (and then a mix of other varieties), indicating that this is cool climate for Cabernet Sauvignon. The style is distinctly more moderate than the North Coast of Napa or Sonoma. With vineyards at altitudes from 400 to 800 m, exposed to cooling influences from the Pacific only a few miles away, the climate is distinctly cooler. "Santa Cruz is more soil-driven than fruit-driven and appeals to a more Eurocentric style. Alcohol levels here are usually lower," says winemaker Jeffrey Patterson at Mount Eden. Today the Cabernet Sauvignon is a blend at the varietal limit, usually with 75% Cabernet Sauvignon, and the rest mostly Merlot. Until 2000 there was also a monovarietal Cabernet Sauvignon made from old vines planted by Martin Ray in the 1950s (on their own roots!) They had to be replanted because they had essentially stopped producing. We tasted a very interesting comparison between the blend and the Old Vine Reserve from 1994 (Y page 399). The two wines come from the same mountain top, same scion. You see the same relative difference as elsewhere: the monovarietal is more precise, tighter, less developed; the blend has lost that precise delineation of fruits, but has gained some roundness, development, and flavor variety. In terms of the development of old wine, I preferred the blend, although the Old Vine Reserve certainly had something extra from the concentration of the old vines.

The topsoils in the mountains are thin, based on shale. At Ridge, there is an unusual terroir, with a fractured layer of limestone overlaid with green stone (a highly friable sedimentary rock). The vine roots penetrate easily through the green stone and can go into the limestone. Is it the terroir that's responsible for the minerality in the wines or just better retention of acidity due to the cooler climate? The wines are long lived. "The natural instinct of the vineyards here is to make a 25 year wine," says Jeffrey Patterson. And that is certainly true of Ridge, where the Cabernets begin to develop well after a decade and may last for three or more decades (🍸 page 407).

In Europe there's a direct linear relationship between grape varieties and latitude. Going from north to south in France, there is Pinot Noir in Burgundy, Cabernet Sauvignon in Bordeaux, Syrah in the northern Rhône, and Grenache in the southern Rhône. Each variety on this line progressively likes warmer temperatures. It's very Cartesian, very logical, very French. Such logic does not apply in North America, which is a jumble, from Pinot Noir in southern California, to Cabernet Sauvignon in northern California, to Pinot Noir in Oregon, and back to Cabernet Sauvignon in Washington State. Local climatic conditions are more important than latitude. In California the dominant influence is most often the exposure to fog. In Washington it is the Cascade Mountains, about fifty miles to the east of Seattle, which divide the very wet Pacific regions from the very dry desert on the other side.

The history of wine production in Washington was dispiriting until recently. After Prohibition, wine produced in the state had a protected market. Until this was abolished in 1969, wineries produced rubbish from Concord grapes or worse.[63] After 1970, all but three of the existing wineries closed, and plantings of Vitis vinifera began. Almost half of all production in the State today comes from wineries owned by Stimson Lane, a subsidiary of U.S. Tobacco (the largest single properties being Château St. Michelle and its sister company Columbia Crest),[64] but there's a host of small producers. This makes the industry unusually bifurcated, as almost two thirds of vineyards are smaller than 6 ha. There are more growers than producers; statistics reveal that more than half the crop is purchased rather than estate grown,[65] but because Château St. Michelle owns or controls a large number of vineyards, for other producers probably less than a quarter of the crop consists of estate grapes.

Red wine production is just in the minority in Washington, about 48% of the total annual production of 8 million cases. In black grapes, Cabernet Sauvignon (36%) just leads Merlot (34%), with Syrah coming a distant third (16%).[66] (Whites are split between Riesling and Chardonnay.) The criticism that Washington hasn't found its defining variety isn't quite fair: in reds it is clearly

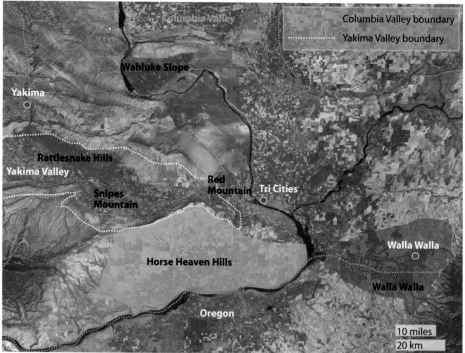

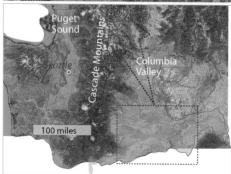

Columbia Valley AVA (inset left) contains most vineyards in Washington and extends to the border with Oregon. The most important sub-AVAs lie in the south of Columbia Valley (above). Rattlesnake Hills, Red Mountain, and Snipes Mountain lie within Yakima Valley; Walla Walla extends over the border into Oregon.

focused on Cabernet Sauvignon and Merlot, either as a varietals or blends. "Napa sits at the top of the pyramid, but Washington in time will define Cabernet character," says winemaker Bob Betz MW. Insofar as there's any subregional concentration of varieties, the focus shifts from whites to reds as it becomes warmer moving from west to east.

It's a popular myth that Washington is too cool and too wet to produce fine wine. That might be a reasonable description of Seattle (where annual rainfall is around 36 inches), but the climate on the eastern side of the Cascade Mountains is a rain shadow, with virtually no rainfall during the growing season (total rainfall is less than 10 inches); viticulture is made possible only by irrigation. The average growing season temperature is similar to Bordeaux, but this is a bit misleading because Washington has a modified Continental climate, meaning that there is extreme diurnal variation: while daytime temperatures can be hot

Harsh winter conditions are reflected in an old training system using two trunks to ensure the vine's survival in case one is killed by winter cold.

(more than 27 °C or 80 °F, with spikes up to 38 °C or 100 °F not uncommon during July), at night it can drop to a few degrees above freezing, well below the 10 °C (50 °F) limit at which the vine shuts down photosynthesis.

The problem for Vitis vinifera comes from the very cold winters; as recently as 2004, a winter freeze destroyed the harvest in Walla Walla. A corollary is that the season starts late—bud break is several weeks later than Napa—but the more important factor is the distribution of heat during the growing season. In Washington the heat tends to be early, in July, with ripening occurring during a cooler period in September, whereas in Napa the relationship is the reverse and it can be very hot when the grapes are ripening in September. The cooler end to the growing season makes for a more moderate impression in Washington's wines. Joel Butler MW says that, "Whereas August makes the wine in Bordeaux, September makes the wine in Washington." In cool years, the problem for Cabernet Sauvignon, as a late-ripening variety, can be that the season ends abruptly with the first freeze, before full ripeness has been achieved. "It doesn't matter when the season starts, it has to end October 1—after that you're living on borrowed time," says winemaker Bob Bertheau at Chateau Ste. Michelle. But one compensation is that the northerly location ensures extra hours of sunshine (about two hours more per day than in California).[67]

The geography east of the cascades was created by the formation of a vast lake to the northeast of Washington at the end of the last Ice Age. Forming ice dams that constantly ruptured, Lake Missoula periodically flooded the area that

Comparing the scrub of the unplanted slope on the left with the adjacent vineyard shows that only irrigation makes viticulture possible in Columbia Valley.

is now Columbia Valley.[68] Flood is an inadequate term for a wall of water that scoured areas at several hundred meters elevation down to the base of basalt.[69] The floods deposited a variety of glacial and post glacial materials; the debris created soils that are mostly sandy on the basalt base.[70] This may be why phylloxera has never taken hold; almost all the vines are planted on their own roots. Some areas have a richer topsoil of loess blown by the wind. The east of the Cascade Mountains is an arid plateau at 300-600 m, interrupted by hills, with the appearance of a high desert (the northern latitude enhances the effect of the dry climate); compaction of sand onto the basalt base sometimes gives an impression of dunes. Although there are exceptions, the general homogeneity of soils means that climatic variations, reflecting temperature, sun and wind exposure, and altitude, are generally the most important variables of vineyard sites.

In an area stretching over 150 miles—roughly the same as the distance from cool Burgundy to the hot Southern Rhône—it's hard to describe a single defining character. Although there are significant climatic variations in daytime temperatures across the region, the extreme diurnal variation is a single common factor. This has a significant effect on ripening. It's fair to say that where Cabernet Sauvignon is grown, it achieves ripeness at high alcohol levels, while retaining acidity, and without developing the over-ripe notes that can be characteristic of warmer regions. "The biggest difference is that when we get the fruits ripe at 15% alcohol in Washington they are still fresh, whereas in Napa (or Barossa) they get flavors of prunes," says Joel Butler. Winemaker Bob Bertheau of Chateau Ste. Michelle made wines in Sonoma before coming to

Walla Walla vineyards are islands in an arid landscape overlooking the Blue Mountains.

Washington. "The biggest difference moving up from California was having to adjust to the tannins and color. Maceration and extraction times that worked in California did not work in Washington, and I learned my lesson the hard way by making some pretty tannic wines." Structure is a big issue. "We have more structure than you would find in California and I don't know why—if you look at the numbers, there isn't an obvious reason. There's a vibrancy of fruit and structure to the Washington wines, it's not just the acidity" says Bob Betz of Betz Family Winery (page 418). That said, the range of styles in Washington extends from forceful fruits in a New World style to wines that seem more European except for the high alcohol.

The AVA system in Washington is frankly a mess. The first AVAs were Columbia Valley, Yakima Valley, and Walla Walla. Columbia Valley is such a vast area that it includes 99% of all grapes planted in the state! This is so meaningless that some producers are switching to Washington State as a description, because they feel it has better recognition. "So far as most people are concerned, Columbia Valley might as well be in Chile," says Jamie Brown of Waters winery in Walla Walla. At the other extreme from Columbia Valley is tiny Naches Heights, the latest AVA (created in 2012). "We have a new AVA that has only 40 acres planted, 21 different grape varieties, and no vines over five years old: how is that an AVA?" asks Greg Harrington of Gramercy Cellars. Except for Columbia Gorge (an extension of Columbia Valley) and Puget Sound (an irrelevance), all the AVAs lie within Columbia Valley.[71] The big question is the integrity of these smaller AVAs: to what extent do they really depend on terroir or climate to produce a characteristic style of wine?

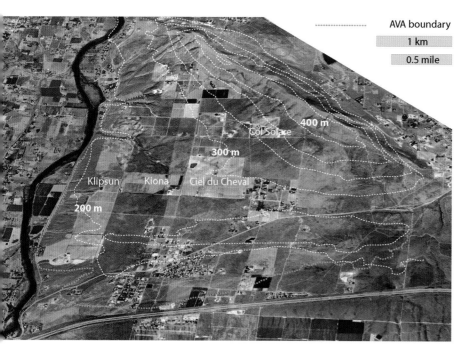

AVA boundary
1 km
0.5 mile

Red Mountain AVA is a slope running up from the river to the ridge. (More vineyards have been planted since this view was taken.)

Many wine producers are located in the area around Woodinville, just to the north of Seattle, but there are virtually no vineyards in the vicinity.[72] The larger producers (including Chateau Ste. Michelle, the largest of all) have their own facilities, of course, but many boutique operations are indicated by stretches of wineries in warehouses of a semi-industrial area known colloquially in the wine trade as the North Ghetto. During harvest, grapes are trucked daily across the Cascade Mountains from the vineyards.

The Walla Walla AVA goes pretty much as far south as Washington gets: in fact it spills over the border into Oregon. When the AVA was created in 1984, there were only four wineries and 25 ha of vineyards; today there are more than a hundred wineries and 730 planted hectares. Terroirs vary from hills to the plain; the most common plantings are Merlot, Cabernet Sauvignon, and Syrah, although there really isn't any single focus yet. But as one of the oldest AVAs, Walla Walla at least has good name recognition. "Any time you put Walla Walla on the label it sells faster," says Greg Harrington. "Walla Walla is the most diverse AVA, because of soil types, and the diurnal shift from north to south. Roughly every mile means another hundred foot of elevation and inch of rain," says Jamie Brown of Waters. A tasting of barrel samples from 2011 at Leonetti showed the range from three vineyards extending across Walla Walla, where harvests differ by about three weeks. Reflecting increasing content of clay in the soil, there was a pretty impression from Seven Hills, greater intensity at Loess (Leonetti's home vineyard), and a masculine spicy density at Uplands (Ⴤ page 428).

The Kiona Vineyard on Red Mountain looks southwest across to Horse Heaven Hills (left) and Rattlesnake Hills (right), with Yakima Valley in the gap between them.

The best known vineyards are Pepper Bridge and Seven Hills, both owned by Pepper Bridge Winery. "Pepper Bridge has more clay, giving a darker, more structured wine," says winemaker Jean-François Pellet. The Walla Walla Cabernet is a blend from both vineyards, and there is also a separate bottling from Seven Hills (Ɣ page 431). A reserve wine called Trine is a blend, and it's an insight into Washington that this has less Cabernet Sauvignon (it is 44% Cabernet Sauvignon with 38% Merlot and the other Bordeaux varieties). Grapes from Pepper Bridge are the basis of Walla Walla bottlings from several other producers, including Chateau Rollat (Ɣ page 419), Gramercy (Ɣ page 427) and Waters (Ɣ page 434). Walla Walla is felt to have a distinct character: "The mark of Walla Walla is a black olive or tapenade note," says Joel Butler.

Horse Heaven Hills comes to the immediate west of Walla Walla. (As you might imagine, there are many interesting ideas about the origin of the name.) The second largest AVA after Yakima (excluding the all-encompassing Columbia Valley), it's important in terms of numbers, accounting for about a quarter of all Washington's production. The climate is ameliorated by the Columbia River, aided by winds coming through the Columbia Gorge to the west. The focus is on Merlot and Cabernet Sauvignon. Horse Heaven Hills has smoother, darker, fruits, as typified by its most famous vineyard: "Champoux has more floral notes compared with the earthier notes of Walla Walla," says winemaker Rick Small of Woodward Canyon. As you might expect from the size of AVA, it is difficult to establish a distinctive typicity, but Champoux is considered to characterize the best of the AVA so far as Cabernet is concerned.

Red Mountain does not have red soils, nor is it really a mountain (more a steep slope), but it's the most prestigious of the Washington AVAs. (The so-called red is something of a dry, dusty, orange-brown, and the name is claimed to come from a local grass that turns red in the Spring.) Perhaps the prestige is due to its small size and corresponding homogeneity. "It's essentially a south-western-facing slope of homogeneous soil types, with very high heat units, and low-vigor, low-nutrient soils," says Tom Hedges of Hedges Family Estates. Its exposure means that sunlight hours are higher than elsewhere. Cool nights on the mountain slopes help to keep up acidity and make for structure in the wine.

One of the warmer AVAs, Red Mountain focuses on Cabernet Sauvignon, Syrah, and Merlot, more or less in that order. Some of the state's most prized vineyards are located here. Running up the slope, Klipsun, Kiona, and Ciel du Cheval are the best known. There are about thirty growers, but less than a dozen wineries. Kiona both sells grapes and makes wine, but Ciel du Cheval and Klipsun sell all their grapes. The producers who purchase Red Mountain grapes come from all over the state. Red Mountain's concentration of top vine-yards for Cabernet Sauvignon dates back almost to the beginning. "In 1975 when we started we had no idea what varieties would do well," says Scott Wil-liams who established the Kiona Vineyard (⊤ page 428). "The focus on Cabernet goes back to when we started selling grapes after a couple of years and the producers said, these are good, they are ripe and don't have herba-ceous flavors." But Red Mountain can verge on too hot. "This is a warm spot, and our bugaboos are over-ripeness and high alcohol." What does this do for Cabernet Sauvignon? "Most of the producers to whom we sell Cabernet use it as the backbone of a blend, there are not many people bottling straight Caber-net Sauvignon from Red Mountain, that probably tells you something," says Scott.

Comparing the other regions, Wahluke Slope is warm, but not quite as warm as Red Mountain, as temperatures are moderated by the proximity of the river. "This is the closest to California that you're going to see in Washington," says Joel Butler, "with plummy fruits, soft tannins, and high alcohol." Rattle-snake Hills claims to be homogeneous with regards to climate. A little cooler than Red Mountain,[73] it is located within Yakima Valley. Climate is roughly equivalent to warm vintages in Bordeaux. Vineyards always have some eleva-tion, as the AVA starts at 250 m and rises up to 900 m, but need to be located in spots with good air drainage to avoid frosts and winter kill. The best known vineyard is DuBrul, known for its finesse, and represented in the wines of sev-eral producers including its owner, Côte Bonneville (⊤ page 424).

While it's a strength of Washington that vines can be planted on their own roots—there are very few grafted grapevines—it's surprising that little attention has been paid to clonal variety. Almost all the Cabernet Sauvignon is clone 8 (essentially the same as clone 7), one of the oldest Californian heritage clones.

This is a potential weakness in offering less diversity in the source material. Perhaps it drives a trend towards obtaining diversity by blending from different sites. "I believe that blending vineyards makes for more interesting wines. There can be a oneness to single vineyard sites, although there are differences due to vine age, pruning, blocks etc.," says winemaker Bob Bertheau.

The large proportion of vineyards owned by growers means that the focus for winemakers is often on identifying the best sources for grapes. "I think the state has a blending culture, winemakers are used to getting in the car and driving over the state to look for sources," says Greg Harrington of Gramercy Cellars (Υ page 427). Although there are single vineyard bottlings from some of the top sites, in terms of Washington overall, this is the exception rather than the rule: the top wines more often are blends from different sites. Fewer than a quarter of the Cabernet Sauvignons I tasted on a recent visit to Washington came from single vineyards. Of course, this does not help the recognition of individual appellations.

There's an interesting difference between Cabernet Sauvignon and Syrah. "I make almost exclusively single vineyard wines for Syrah to capture terroir, and I believe the Syrah captures that when it's in the cooler sites and can't get super ripe; the aromatics drive Syrah but that's a thing you can't get with Cabernet. This wouldn't work with Cabernet because you'd get pyrazines, whereas a Syrah picked at under ripe levels wouldn't really be under ripe but a Cabernet would. They need to be treated differently, Washington's big mistake is not realizing that. For Cabernet, the key is blending from different sites. I don't believe you have all the bullets in the holster if you do single vineyard wines; you end up with over-ripe or green wines depending on your site," says Jamie Brown of Waters (Υ page 434).

With plantings of Cabernet Sauvignon dominated by a single clone, you might argue that clones play a much smaller part in Washington than elsewhere. Or perhaps considering the lack of diversity this implies, clonal selection plays a much *larger* role than elsewhere, since the uniformity significantly restricts the potential expression of different sites. A tasting at Col Solare of four different clones suggested that the reputation of Red Mountain for big, bold Cabernet might partly depend on the interaction of clone 8 with this site. Clone 8 showed typical Red Mountain character: strong tannins on the edge of harshness pointing in the direction of rusticity. Clone 6, usually the most herbaceous of Cabernet clones, gave a more herbal impression. Clone 2 showed pure, linear, aromatic fruits, while clone 10 had fragrant aromatics bordering on delicacy. There's clearly potential for bringing out more diverse character from Red Mountain by experimenting with other clones.

Not all of the top vineyards are in sub-AVAs, some are only in Yakima Valley or even the general Columbia Valley AVA. The best known vineyards tend to be those that were established earliest: given the rapid expansion of the past

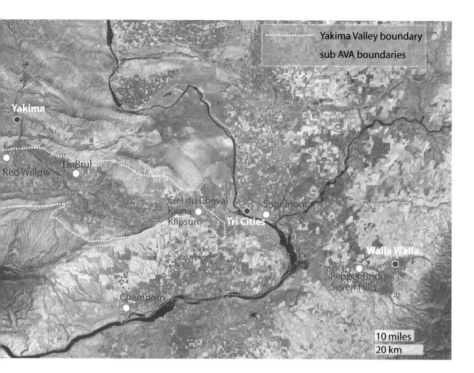

Yakima Valley boundary

sub AVA boundaries

Yakima

Red Willow

DuBrul

Ciel du Cheval
Kiona   Sagemoor
Klipsun   Tri Cities

Walla Walla

Pepper Bridge
Seven Hills

Champoux

10 miles
20 km

Top vineyards for Cabernet Sauvignon are widely dispersed.[74]

decade, views on which sites are best for Cabernet Sauvignon may change as vines age in the younger vineyards. There is general agreement that the Champoux vineyard in Horse Heaven Hills, first planted in 1979 as the Mercer Ranch, is one of the best, if not the best, site for Cabernet Sauvignon. Some 60% of the 70 ha vineyard is planted with Cabernet Sauvignon (the other major grape is Riesling, an illustration of the unusual character of Washington that lets these varieties be cultivated together). Champoux has a definite character: dark but smooth, as seen in the wines of Quilceda Creek, almost the only producer whose wines might be regarded as having a cult following (ɪ page 432). Champoux is the most important source for Quilceda Creek, and a major concern is to protect its character. "Blending from different sources doesn't really work out that well; each vineyard has its own character and you lose it," says owner Alex Golitzin. "Champoux is power coupled with finesse, layers of perfume, you can't get it elsewhere. The expression of Quilceda Creek is the Champoux, it is always dominant: we blend with other sources, but not enough to lose the character of Champoux." So only a little wine from Red Mountain is blended with the Champoux to add ripeness, but not too much. The mark of Quilceda Creek for me is its crystalline precision, the sharp delineation of the black fruits (very much a pure Cabernet—usually more than 97%).

Producers give the impression that the decision on whether to make mono-varietal Cabernet or a blend is somewhat pragmatic, depending on available

sources of grapes. There doesn't seem to be the same philosophical commitment on either side of the divide as there is in Napa. Perhaps this is a
consequence of the reliance on purchasing grapes from growers as opposed to
estate bottlings. Although most of the leading wines carry varietal labels, about
half have more than 90% Cabernet Sauvignon, and the other half fall between
90% and the 75% limit (not very different from the distribution in California).[75]

Washington offers a unique reversal of the usual relationship between Cabernet Sauvignon and Merlot. Elsewhere, Merlot is used to flesh out the mid
palate or to soften the Cabernet. In Washington, Cabernet Sauvignon develops
ripe tannins, but the tannins in Merlot can be quite aggressive, giving a monovarietal Merlot more structure than a Cabernet! "We use Merlot to give more
structure to the Cabernet Sauvignon, and Cabernet Sauvignon to soften the
Merlot," says Joel Butler. "There have been way too many blind tastings when I
have mistaken Merlot for Cabernet," says Bob Betz. "The Merlot can be—I
don't like that word bigger—but more generous, often with even more structure
than the Cabernet," says Jean-François Pellet at Pepper Bridge. "The Merlot can
be complex enough that often enough in blind tastings I would challenge people to pull them out of a Cabernet lineup," says Chris Figgins at Leonetti. If
there's a trend, it's the reverse of the traditional relationship in Bordeaux, to
strengthen the Cabernet by adding Merlot.

Could the unusual Merlot character result from lack of clonal diversity?
Washington is dominated by plantings of Merlot clone 3. "The clone we are
using in Washington is the one everyone in Bordeaux has got rid of because it's
too phenolic and aggressive," says winemaker Rick Small at Woodward Canyon. It's described briefly as having "more tannin, less fruit" in one
comparative study.[76] It will be interesting to see whether a switch in recent
plantings to a newer French clone will result in a more conventional relationship between Merlot and Cabernet.[77]

An illustration of the relationships between the varieties came from a tasting
at Long Shadows in Walla Walla, which is a consortium of seven consulting
winemakers. Each winemaker sources grapes according to the type of blend he
wants to make, and resident winemaker Gilles Nicault oversees production
(☞ page 429). Randy Dunn's Feather Cabernet Sauvignon is finely textured, but
less rich and structured on the palate than Michel Rolland's Pedestal Merlot.
Philippe Melka's Pirouette Bordeaux blend seems more right bank than left
bank in character. And the Chester-Kidder "New World blend" of a majority
Cabernet Sauvignon with minority Syrah tastes more like a Syrah than a Cabernet Sauvignon.

The stern character of Merlot in Washington may be becoming less of a
problem as the region matures. "In Washington we used to use Merlot for the
opposite reason from what you might think, because it's more powerful, and
the Cabernet Sauvignon needed more power, but what's been happening in

Plantings go up the arid slope at Col Solare's vineyards on Red Mountain.

past years as Cabernet has been planted in better areas is that you don't need Merlot so much... I think a little Syrah is useful in the leaner years to add a little richness and weight," says Marcus Notaro at Col Solare. One interesting insight into the use of Syrah came from a comparison at Chateau Ste. Michelle of the 2008 and 2009 Canoe Ridge Cabernet Sauvignon. The 2008 was more reserved, and the 2009 had more showy aromatics, so you might think the first has Merlot and the second has Syrah, but it's actually the other way round: the ripe vintage of 2009 had Merlot to calm it down, and the cooler vintage of 2008 had Syrah to bring more fleshiness (♟ page 420). "We wanted to broaden the 2008 and tighten the 2009," says Bob Bertheau.

It's curious that although Syrah is the third most important black variety, it's usually regarded as separate from the dominant Cabernet Sauvignon and Merlot when it comes to blending. There has been little experimentation with Cabernet-Syrah blends. (One exception is at Efeste, where the top wines are Cabernet Sauvignon and Syrah varietals, but the second wine is a blend of declassified lots from the two varieties; ♟ page 425.) Most varietal-labeled Cabernet Sauvignon, and most blends, follow the traditional Bordeaux model. When Syrah is included, it's usually less than 5%. "There's always been some Syrah in our Walla Walla Cabernet Sauvignon. It adds just an additional breadth, but I'm hoping now the Cabernet Sauvignon vines are older, it may not be necessary," says Rick Small of Woodward Canyon (♟ page 434). At Long Shadows, Syrah has gone from 11% to zero in the Pirouette blend. "2004 was a cool vintage, and at first the wine was austere. We wanted to make a Bordeaux blend, but Philippe Melka felt he didn't know Washington State well enough and needed Syrah. In 2006 it declined, and was zero in 2007. Now he doesn't feel the need of it," says winemaking manager Gilles Nicault.

Alcohol levels are on the minds of Washington producers, but the issue does not seem to be as sensitive as in Napa. Sometimes appearances can be deceptive. When asked why he had said that the alcohol level was 14.7% on one wine where the label stated 14.1%, one winemaker said simply, "I lied on the label." There's the same general defense of high levels as elsewhere. I asked at Quilceda Creek if they were worried about being pushed into high alcohol levels? "Yes." What are you going to do about it? "Nothing. It's not a problem if the wine is balanced," says owner Alex Golitzin. Alcohol levels ranged widely in the wines I tasted, but I can't say that I noticed any consistent difference in ripeness between wines below 14% and wines over 16%. It's reasonably convincing that ripeness in most sites doesn't develop until over 14%, but I'm not convinced you have to go to the extremes over 15%: I wonder how perceptible the difference in ripeness would be if those producers who are getting over 15% harvested a percentage point sooner. And if you do have to go over 15%, perhaps one should ask whether this is the right site for the variety? "The key to Washington is that you really have to stay with cooler sites, but with a strategy of picking earlier we do get punished in the cooler vintages," says Greg Harrington.

Although stated alcohol levels have been similar over the past few years in Washington and Napa (averaging about 14.5% between 2007 and 2009), sometimes I found the alcohol more noticeable in Washington. I suspect this is because in Napa it is hidden better by the jammier fruits. Against a more acid background, alcohol can push the tannins to give a tart bitterness on the finish of young wines that for me is often a marker for Washington. Although many producers claim they are struggling to keep ripeness down, they say ruefully, "You wouldn't like the wines if we picked earlier." But higher levels are partly market driven, or at least driven by a perception that, whatever consumers may say, the preference is for wines with higher alcohol. "If I thought our customers would follow us, we would go for lower alcohol," says Rick Small of Woodward Canyon. I realize that 14.5% has become the new 12.5%, but at the end of the day, I felt that the wines I tasted over 14% all would have been more elegant with a percent less alcohol; and I would enjoy a bottle for a dinner, whereas, balanced or not, they can be fatiguing to drink rather than merely to taste at these high alcohol levels.

It's hard to get a bead on the potential for aging because even ten years ago, most vines were still rather young. It will be another decade or so before the last rash of plantings mature enough to judge their potential. But wines from the first vineyards give some idea. In my tastings, several wines were caught at that tipping point where fruits are hinting at becoming savory. Betz's Père de Famille 2000 seems at its peak, Woodward Canyon 1999 still seems fresh and youthful, Col Solare 1998 is at a perfect point of development, showing subtle mineral and savory elements, Chateau Ste. Michelle's Canoe Ridge 1998 shows classic herbal and savory development, and the Cold Creek 1998 is more overtly savory. The only wines that seemed too old were those that had been over oaked, a failing that probably would not occur today. From these experiences, it seems that 12 years is around the point to catch the first stages of development, with longevity extending to around 20 years. As the vines age, these periods should be pushed back further. An experience with a 1976 Cabernet Sauvignon from Chateau Ste. Michelle was especially promising: still lively and vibrant, not very developed, its ability to retain character suggests there may be real longevity in Washington wines.

So what does North America tell us about the typicity of Cabernet? Today Napa and Sonoma are more similar than different, with a tendency to emphasize power of extraction over elegance. The best wines, however, have precisely delineated fruits, with good aging potential, although I would drink most before they turn twenty. Washington has sharper acidity and the more tightly defined edges that go with it. Today's top wines probably peak a few years earlier than California. The biggest stylistic distinction in California may be between wines from mountain sites and those from the valley; in Washington, all sites are relatively elevated, so the style is closer to the mountain wines of California than to those in the valleys. Almost all of the American wines have a distinct New World aesthetic, most clearly seen in more intense fruit aromatics compared with Bordeaux. And as they tend to have higher levels of Cabernet Sauvignon than are typical in Bordeaux, they offer a more direct perspective into the typicity of fully ripe Cabernet.

5

The Pursuit of Ripeness

CABERNET SAUVIGNON was virtually synonymous with Bordeaux until 1976, when everything changed at a famous blind tasting. The results were so shocking that some of the judges tried to grab their score sheets in order to destroy them. A California Cabernet Sauvignon had come out ahead of Bordeaux. (The judges were French.)

The impetus for the event was a plan to hold a tasting of Californian wines in Paris in conjunction with the American bicentennial. Steven Spurrier, an English wine expert, had bought a wine shop in Paris in 1970 and started the Académie du Vin to teach expats about French wine. By the mid seventies it was the leading place in Paris for wine education. A tasting of California wines would be an interesting and different way to publicize the shop and school.

The tasting was to consist of six Californian Cabernet Sauvignons and six Chardonnays, matched for comparative purposes by four red Bordeaux and four white Burgundies. A distinguished panel of experts was assembled to judge the Californian wines (the inclusion of French wines was not mentioned).

Top vineyards in Bordeaux overlook the Gironde. Vineyards are densely planted.

The tasting was blind, not so much as to make a direct comparison between the wines, but to prevent the French judges from putting down the Californian wines by reflex. No one in Paris was much interested in Californian wines, and the only person from the press who could be persuaded to come was George Taber of *Time* magazine.

The white wines were tasted first, and a Chateau Montelena Chardonnay from Napa Valley came top, ahead of a Meursault Charmes premier cru from Guy Roulot, both of the 1973 vintage. This sensitized the judges, who paid a fair amount of attention to trying to decide whether wines were French or Californian when they tasted the reds. But Stag's Leap 1973 Cabernet from Napa placed first, ahead of three Bordeaux from the 1970 vintage: Mouton Rothschild, Montrose, and Haut Brion.[1] Ridge Monte Bello from the Santa Cruz Mountains was in fifth place. The tasting became known as the Judgment of Paris, and was highly controversial in France: some of the judges were criticized publicly for their participation.

Was this a fair comparison? The only real point for criticism might be that wines from Bordeaux and California age at different rates, and six year old Bordeaux might be somewhat less approachable than three year old Napa Cabernet. But in any case, the order of wines is not the issue: the point is that the judges were completely confused about which wines were Californian and which were French. That was a major accomplishment in itself for Napa Valley.

The news came as a shock in Napa. The immediate effect was to sell out the wines that had won—the Chateau Montelena Chardonnay and Stag's Leap Cabernet. But the more important, longer term effect was to validate the con-

Top vineyards in Napa are close to the mountains. Vineyards are less densely planted.

cept of high-end wines from Napa. Bo Barrett of Chateau Montelena recollects that up to then, it had been an uphill battle to get the wines into distribution on the East Coast. "The practical consequence was that distributors would take the wines," he says. The effect on style was to reinforce the view that Napa should compete with Bordeaux. "The Paris tasting had the effect that if we won there, we must be as good, and we should make wine more like Bordeaux," says Fred Schrader. And the tasting emphasized the importance of new wineries: almost none of the Napa wineries in the tasting existed before the 1960s.[2]

As soon as the revival of Napa began in 1970—vineyard areas had declined until 1969 and then began to increase again—Cabernet Sauvignon had become a focus. When the Judgment of Paris occurred, Napa had started on the path to making Cabernet Sauvignon its dominant grape. Yet this was not a foregone conclusion. It was clear that the future lay in premium varieties, but which varieties? Throughout the seventies and eighties, Cabernet Sauvignon production was only about twice the level of Pinot Noir. Napa did not really achieve its mature focus until the 1990s, when Cabernet far outstripped Pinot.[3] As it became clear that Cabernet Sauvignon should be the black grape of choice, what were the producers' stylistic aims?

Asked whether Cabernet Sauvignon was the obvious variety of choice when Joseph Phelps was established in 1973, Bill Phelps responded, "Hardly. The first three years Riesling was the main variety. It wasn't clear Cabernet would be the future until the late seventies. At the start we planted Riesling, Pinot Noir, and Cabernet Sauvignon. During the 1980s we realized we couldn't do every variety and we focused on Cabernet Sauvignon." (The first winemaker,

Walter Schug, was German, which might have had something to do with the emphasis on Riesling.) But "Joe Phelps was a pragmatic businessman. One factor was that Riesling gave cash flow straight away whereas you have to wait three years to sell Cabernet."

Discussing Phelps's top wine, Insignia, Bill Phelps explained, "Insignia came about by accident. 1974, the first year of Insignia, was a really good year, the best vintage of the seventies in Napa. A special lot was set aside and then we decided we would do this every year. We did not want to call it a reserve because the term was so widely used already. We conceived it as changing each year to release the best cuvée—at the time we thought it could be Cabernet, Merlot, Syrah, whatever happened to be best. It was a proprietary blend [in fact the first Proprietary Red in Napa] because there was no commitment to any variety."

But when you decided on Cabernet, were you trying to compete with Bordeaux, I asked? "Absolutely. The model was the first vintage of Insignia in 1974. Joe made it like a Bordeaux and really wanted it to be a blend. In fact, the second vintage was 80% Merlot." It has since settled down to be a Cabernet-dominated blend, typically with around 80% Cabernet Sauvignon (⟨ page 404). Have objectives changed since the first vintage? "Our style has changed. This was a decision. As Napa came into its own, we realized what was in the material and we could rely on the vineyards. In the 1970s, things were driven by winemaking, now they are more driven by what happens in the vineyards. There's still a strong affinity with Bordeaux, but now we have established our own identity."

The Médoc was already covered with vineyards at the start of the twentieth century.

The transition took quite a while. Rosemary Cakebread recalls, "I came to the valley in 1975. For California Cabernet, and specifically for Napa Valley Cabernet, I think it's fair to say the model was Bordeaux; there was no question about that. It was primarily pure Cabernet Sauvignon but there was a lot of experiment in blending with Cabernet Franc or Merlot." Some change was part of an inevitable learning process, says Phil Ross at Diamond Creek. "In the old days the wines were rustic and very tannic, you needed to wait twenty years to drink. Our wines today are much more approachable and can be drunk younger. This has happened naturally as we have got better at viticulture and vinification." Bill Harlan, who established Harlan Estate in 1984 with the explicit intention of producing a "first growth" in Napa, says, "I think the shift was really that everywhere in the world people learned how to make better wine. The game changer for California was taking the pressure off from trying to make Bordeaux in California."

Chuck Wagner, who joined his parents to start Caymus in 1971, has a similar recollection. "In that era, winemakers didn't have a direction. In 1973 we made all three varieties and the Cabernet came out dark and balanced, just by using my father's home winemaking skills. That was the first indication that Cabernet was the grape. Every year after 1973 the story became more conclusive that Cabernet was complete by itself. The reason we grew anything else besides Cabernet was the fear that the market wouldn't stay interested in Cabernet, but by 1990 we felt it was here to stay, and we eliminated all varieties except Cabernet Sauvignon." Describing the subsequent change in style, Chuck says, "The old style would be tart and bitter, with pronounced tannins and

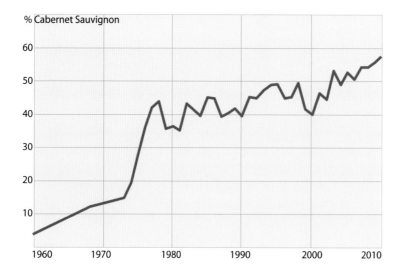

% Cabernet Sauvignon

Napa made its commitment to Cabernet Sauvignon in the 1980s.

The percent of Cabernet Sauvignon in plantings of black grape varieties has been rising steadily.[5]

and higher acidity, trying to emulate Bordeaux. The new style would be ripe, with acidity in balance but never becoming a focus point, devoid of bitterness, containing more but riper tannins. The newer wines are a blend of two components: sweet fruits and tannin texture. I used to think Bordeaux had wines of texture and Napa had wines of flavor. But now Napa has flavor and chalky texture" (Ⓨ page 383).

Fred Schrader, who has been associated with cult wines since the early nineties, thinks the change in style is an appropriate reflection of conditions in Napa. "In the mid eighties, people wanted to make wine just like Bordeaux. I was never part of that school, my attitude was why do we care? The climate and actually the seasons here are different. We have a hotter climate, with riper berries; we are more fruit forward. We should not try to emulate, we should try to make something that reflects who we are." Anthony Bell dates a deliberate change to riper styles from the early nineties, and attributes it to Robert Parker's influence. "When I was running Beaulieu, by the late eighties, we were trying to change the style of our wines. By the mid nineties we were in our stride. Probably the period from 1990-1995 was when things changed." Anthony quotes a telling example of the change in style. "Today the reserve wines are made from grapes picked at the end of the season, but when I joined BV the Reserve was made from grapes picked first—because they came from the healthy vineyards that gave the best quality grapes." Another skeptic about the ripe style, Paul Draper of Ridge Vineyards in Santa Cruz, put the transition a little later, but also puts the blame on the critics. "Napa Valley now has a view of what ripeness is that is completely out of synch with what they thought up to 1997, when the wines were over-ripe and the critics praised them. The sweetness covered the tannins. But now the wines are falling apart. Now they say that if it doesn't show intense over-ripe black fruits it isn't ripe," he says.

There was some confusion between means and ends in the early attempts to emulate Bordeaux. "With regards to copying the Bordeaux model I'm not so sure we were copying the wine so much as copying the viticulture, but it doesn't work here, we are too warm," says Rosemary Cakebread. It was taken for granted that the principal grape should be Cabernet Sauvignon, and if it was blended with other varieties, they were the usual suspects: Merlot, Cabernet Franc, and Petit Verdot. A split between those who believe that pure Cabernet Sauvignon gives the best results and those who believe in the sanctity of blending continues to this day, but almost no one has questioned the nature of the blend. Yet if it's true at one extreme to argue that Cabernet in Napa does not need to be rounded out by other varieties, why isn't it equally valid to ask whether the principle agent of softening (when necessary) might be something other than Merlot? John Caldwell, who has long experience in growing different varieties in his nursery, thinks that Syrah does better than Merlot in fattening up the Cabernet Sauvignon. With regards to the other varieties, Cabernet Franc in Napa seems to play a similar role as it does in Bordeaux, bringing perfume and freshness, and a sense of precision to the fruits. I sometimes wonder, given the extra intensity of Cabernet Sauvignon in Napa, whether Petit Verdot, with its intense spicy character, really complements the Cabernet Sauvignon, as opposed to driving the wine to further extremes.

The best contemporary bird's eye view of the relative states of Bordeaux and Napa comes from Robert Parker's annual reviews of the vintage in the *Wine Advocate*. Before the Napa revival, an early issue commented, "The better Bordeaux are elegant, delicate wines that possess incredible subtlety and complexity, whereas the best California Cabernets are massive, powerful, assertive wines often bordering on coarseness." Parker went on to comment that the California Cabernets did not age well beyond a few years, compared with Bordeaux's greater longevity.

As Napa began its revival, the general view was that Bordeaux was about elegance, and California was about power. "It has always been my feeling that if the consumer wanted a lighter style Cabernet based wine, a French Bordeaux was just perfect, and if a more powerful wine were desired, then an offering from California was the solution," Robert Parker commented in 1984.[6] Here is a perfect description of the attractions of California Cabernet: "California's Cabernets in the seventies became world famous by making exactly what their warm climate and rich soils dictated, fruity, ripe, fat, intense, full bodied wines... Most consumers loved the big, rich wines for their explosive fruit and mouth filling gustatory pleasures."

Perhaps responding to criticism that the wines were too alcoholic and rich, or perhaps because vintages went in opposite directions in Bordeaux and Napa, there was a reversal by the mid eighties. Throughout the seventies, Bordeaux had a series of poor vintages; 1975 and 1978 were hailed as top vintages at the time, *faute de mieux,* but in retrospect there was much less there than met the eye. Napa had a good vintage in 1973 and a top vintage in 1974, followed by a series of decent vintages. The situation reversed in the eighties. Bordeaux had an unprecedented vintage in 1982, destined to set the tone for the next three decades, followed by good vintages in all years except 1984 and 1987. But Napa had a series of disappointing vintages from 1980 to 1983. Added to this swing was a currency fluctuation that made California more expensive relative to Bordeaux.

By 1986 Parker was excoriating the vintners in California. "Many California vintners were in search of more finesse and elegance in their wines and became convinced (or should I say confused) that bland, innocuous, technically perfect and squeaky clean wines that had perfect pHs, perfect acidity, and just the right amount of alcohol, but little flavor, would somehow be considered more elegant and satisfying than wines with dynamic and distinctive regional characters and personalities. In short, many California wines began... to look alike and taste alike."[7] Parker placed much of the blame with advice from the University of California. "They taste and smell... as if all the oenologists from the University of California are using the same magic formula... Technical perfection is preferred over a wine with character and dimension."[8]

In due course the pendulum swung back to a view that Napa Cabernet should offer the authentic richness of California. But in the meantime, driven by warmer vintages and following the international trend, Bordeaux also had moved to a richer style. Descriptions of recent top vintages in both places show more similarities than differences. "The 2007s are not as tannic, backward, or powerful as the 2001s were early in life, nor as exuberantly opulent and voluptuous with as intense fruit, charm, and seductiveness as the 2002s were at a similar stage. There is a freshness, delineation, and laser-like focus in the finest 2007s that speaks well to the continuing development of terroirs."[9] "[The 2010s are] concentrated and rich, yet also have higher acid numbers and lower pHs than 2009, thus giving the 2010s a freshness and precision that is the paradoxical characteristic of this vintage... Add the extraordinary concentration of flavor and the high polyphenol levels with tannins that are often off the charts in terms of analytical readings, and readers can see that this is a massively concentrated vintage."[10] Which comment applies to Napa and which to Bordeaux? Substitute different vintages, and the first comment could well apply to Bordeaux and the second to Napa rather than the other way round. Is this convergence an inevitable result of climate change or is it a deliberate move to satisfy consumer demand? Has Napa defined a new style and is Bordeaux now emulating it?

The move to the riper, more "international" style was partly driven by critics who scored the wines highly—or perhaps more to the point, scored restrained wines poorly. Certainly attempts at a European aesthetic in Napa were criticized. There was a long-running difference of opinion between Mondavi and the *Wine Spectator* over style. The *Spectator's* lead critic on California, James Laube, commented in July 2001, "At a time when California's best winemakers are aiming for ripe, richer, more expressive wines, Mondavi appears headed in the opposite direction... [Winemaker] Tim Mondavi and I have different taste preferences... He has never concealed his distaste for big, ultrarich plush or tannic red wines. I know he can make rich, compelling wines, yet he prefers structured wines with elegance and finesse... the attempt to give his wines more nerve and backbone has come at the expense of body and texture...he's decided to turn his back on a climate ideally suited for producing ripe, dramatic wines, and rein in those qualities so that the wines show restraint rather than opulence."[11] Tim Mondavi replied, "I am concerned... that while global wine quality has improved tremendously, there appears to be a current trend toward aggressively over-ripe, high in alcohol, overoaked wines that are designed to stand out at a huge tasting rather than fulfill the more appropriate purpose of enhancing a meal."[12]

There you have the whole debate in a nutshell. Yet after this was all said and done, the style at Mondavi seemed to change in the direction of greater richness. I first noted a change in style with the 2003 vintage. "This is distinctly in the more modern style with more weight and alcohol, and less elegance," my tasting note reads. By the 2005 vintage, I noted, "In contrast with the Mondavi wines of a decade ago, this is somewhat brutal in the modern style." But at a recent tasting, I felt these wines actually had come around, and more recent vintages had reverted to a more elegant style (Υ page 399). It's hard to defy the rush to ripeness: the price is likely to be lack of critical acclaim.

The single factor with the most effect on wine style is probably the date of harvest. Early harvests focus the wine on freshness (at the risk of herbaceousness); later harvests focus on dense extraction (at the risk of the jamminess associated with dehydration). And the conditions of harvest can have an important effect on fermentation, because the temperature at which the grapes are picked influences the start of fermentation. It can be warm during the day at harvest time in Napa, so night picking has become more common. This means that the berries come in cool enough to delay the start of fermentation, creating a natural cold maceration. The general consensus on vinification seems to be for cold maceration for a few days, closed-top stainless steel fermenters, pumping the juice over the cap to keep it moist, running the wine off directly into barrels after fermentation, performing malolactic fermentation in the barrel, and maturing the wine for up to two years in oak. The major difference in winemaking between Bordeaux and Napa is that chaptalization may be necessary in Bordeaux (albeit not in some recent hot vintages), whereas acidification is usually necessary in Napa (albeit not in the unusually cool 2011 vintage). Recent climatic oscillations make these generalizations dangerous!

Shafer Vineyards harvest Cabernet Sauvignon in Stags Leap District at night for the Hillside Select bottling.

Photograph courtesy Andy Demsky.

Of course, there's a wide range of styles in Napa: some producers have stayed faithful to the original attempt at European restraint, while others have enthusiastically searched for greater ripeness. The issue was well put by Anthony Bell. "We are blessed with sunshine in California, but the sunshine that is our friend at the beginning of the season becomes our enemy at the end. You can't take California sunshine out of the wine, it will always be there, but you can have a European sensibility in the wines." Anthony is among a number of producers—others who are commonly cited are Corison, Spottswoode, Togni, and Dunn—who follow European stylistic imperatives. To make restrained wines in Napa Valley means pulling back against the tide—in the majority view, not fully using what the fruit can give you. But the question is really whether the maximum is the optimum?

Cathy Corison is known for producing one of the most restrained Cabernets in Napa. "I'm looking for wines that are powerful and elegant. Cabernet Sauvignon is almost always powerful but not necessarily elegant. I've always had the same stylistic goal, nothing has changed. My wines are California wines so they are fruit-driven, but there is more to it than that," she told me. My general impression of the Corison Cabernet, which is a blend from three vineyards between Rutherford and St. Helena, is that it somewhat resembles what would happen in Bordeaux if they made monovarietal Cabernet. The wines showcase precise black fruits, outlined in cooler vintages by a tight acidity supported by fine-grained tannins, not exactly austere but certainly restrained, giving way in warmer vintages to a softer palate with more velvety textured tannins (⊤ page

386). They age slowly: the 2001 was on the verge of beginning its development at the end of 2011.

Another winery known for its generally restrained style is Spottswoode, located in St. Helena, with a vineyard close to the Mayacamas Mountains where wine was being made in the nineteenth century. A measure of their commitment to a classic style is that most of the vineyard is planted with their own selection of Cabernet Sauvignon, and when they tried planting clone 337, they ended up pulling most of it out because they felt the wine became too flavored with cassis. The wines have changed from pure Cabernet Sauvignon twenty years ago to a blend with other Bordeaux varieties today, and current winemaker Aron Weinkauf says, "We are still fairly early pickers but that's partly because we are one of the warmer sites, but in more recent years we haven't shied away from going after ripeness." The traditional style here is certainly restrained, and the wines definitely need to age (Ⴓ page 389): the 1992 vintage was at perfection in December 2011.

On the top of Spring Mountain, Philip Togni also believes that ageability is more important than instant gratification. All the same, the wines are probably more approachable in their youth than they used to be. "I used to claim that if the wine wasn't pretty terrible coming out of the fermenter it would never amount to anything, but I no longer believe that," he says. His Cabernet is a blend with Merlot, because, "It seemed to me that Cabernet needs some roundness at the center." He is unusual in being one of the holdouts who still picks on Brix. "If we hit 25 Brix by mistake we have exceeded 14% alcohol by mistake. We have made a concession over recent years, we look at grape seeds, but we don't wait until they taste ripeness. We would like to steer close to the way things were in the Médoc fifty years ago." What sort of result does this produce in the context of Napa? Whereas the ripe character of the 2007 vintage may have been overdone at some producers, at Togni it gave a restrained wine that's almost ready to drink now (Ⴓ page 416). But other recent vintages were more reserved, and I was uncertain when they would come around. I quite liked older vintages from the nineties for their Bordeaux-like savory development.

On the other side of the valley, Dunn Vineyards, which Randy Dunn first planted in 1972, is the doyen of Howell Mountain. Dunn has been famous for its traditional style, meaning that the wines require a very long time to come around. They are probably the slowest to develop, and possibly the longest lived, in Napa Valley. "Randy always liked French wine, the older the better," says his son Mike, the current winemaker. The style is partly a consequence of natural conditions on the mountain and partly due to winemaking choices. With lots of extraction, the wines always have a strong tannic structure. The same style runs through the Howell Mountain and Napa Valley bottlings; the former comes mostly from the estate, and the latter has a strong core from

Howell Mountain (⅄ page 393). The style lightened a little after some changes in 2002, but still has a sternness reminiscent of traditional Bordeaux. Mike Dunn feels that his winery is something of a holdout. "Is there a character to Howell Mountain? In the past, Howell Mountain had a character similar to ours, but now many producers are making wines that don't reflect this, and apply a more modern style. There's no longer a style character for Howell Mountain as a group given the move to higher alcohol levels."

I found another outlier for style at Viader, where the Proprietary Red is a blend of Cabernet Sauvignon and Cabernet Franc, generally around 60:40, but varying with the vintage. Delia Viader explained her stylistic objectives: "I always had a very clear stylistic aim, I wanted to make a wine more in the St Emilion style, but elegant. I don't go after fruit, fruit, fruit, fruit, I want elegance. Like St. Emilion because it's not in your face, there are not the dominant Médoc tannins. It's the quality of tannins that are the big criterion." The wine needs at least seven years aging, she says. Coming from Howell Mountain, but outside of the AVA, the wine has typical mountain austerity, with the aromatics of Cabernet Franc often quite dominant even though it's the lesser component (⅄ page 415). The 2002 seemed at its peak when I visited.

So it's perfectly possible to get restraint in Napa Valley in the form of wines that may be austere when young, but which age well. "There's a big generality about Napa Cabs, that they've become ripe, even over-ripe, but there are some people who have stuck to their guns, aiming to make wines that are balanced and drinkable," says Rosemary Cakebread. Wines like this are definitely in a minority, often regarded as being out of the mainstream. "I would be happy to have the wines described as traditional, but I do not like to be called old fashioned, since it's only 10-15 years since this was a common style. I think there is a sea change and people are backing off the over-ripe style and moving back to lighter wines," says Cathy Corison. The counter argument was put by Phillip Corallo-Titus at Chappellet. "The first year I was here [as assistant winemaker] the grapes had to conform to the winemaking style of the winemaker. [When I took over] I took a broader view in interpreting our grapes, so they could fit the market (make a more approachable wine) and yet still reflect Pritchard Hill." High up on Pritchard Hill, Chappellet today is making wines in a big, bold style (⅄ page 385).

Although Napa may have started out trying to compete with left bank Bordeaux, the focus today is generally on a riper style that in some ways has more affinity with the Merlot-driven wines of the right bank of Bordeaux. But there's a direct focus on Cabernet Sauvignon. It's a striking difference that Bordeaux has a universal belief that Cabernet Sauvignon needs to be blended to make a complete wine, whereas in Napa there's a strong view that it makes a complete wine by itself. Most wines in Napa Valley (as in the New World generally) are now varietal-labeled, whereas this is illegal in Bordeaux. Of course, varietal

The most common style in the Médoc is to have between one half and two thirds Cabernet Sauvignon, but 100% Cabernets are the most common style in Napa, although they are not quite in a majority.[13]

The inflection point at 75-80% for Napa represents an accumulation of blended wines just above the minimum level for varietal labeling.

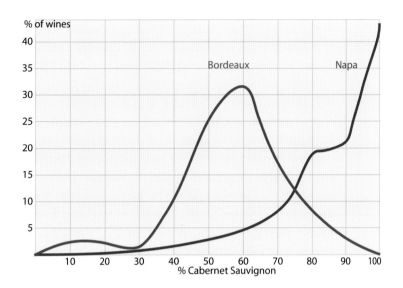

labeling in Napa does not mean that a wine is 100% Cabernet Sauvignon. Indeed, at first the situation in California was not in fact too different from that in Europe: before 1983, when the limit was raised to 75%, a wine could be labeled with a varietal name so long as it had more than 50% of the variety. At the limits, Napa Cabernet Sauvignon would not necessarily have been much different in varietal composition from a Médoc.

So the question in comparing Bordeaux with Napa is not so much whether we are comparing blended wine with monovarietal wine as to whether the comparison is really between wines blended from the same mix of varieties, but with a higher proportion of Cabernet Sauvignon in Napa? The answer is only partly: the vast majority of Cabernet-based Napa wines have more than 75% Cabernet Sauvignon (almost half are monovarietals), and the vast majority of Médoc have less than 75% (and there are no monovarietals). The most common styles are 100% Cabernet Sauvignon in Napa and about 60% Cabernet Sauvignon in Bordeaux.

Blending may have started as a pragmatic response to climatic variation in Bordeaux, but centuries of experience have brought it close to an act of faith. Putting the case at its most extreme, "In the New World, they make a single varietal—why? Because they sell the taste of fruit, we sell the taste of the earth," says Rémi Edange at Domaine de Chevalier. Blending is integral to the character of Bordeaux. "People in Australia and the New World have terrible problems because they have simplified everything by selling grape varieties. Today they are trying to go to appellations. Bordeaux has been intelligent enough to realize this previously and to maintain the identity of each château," says John Kolasa at Rauzan-Ségla. Although there are experiments in vinifying the single varieties alone, the general reaction in Bordeaux is that the best block of Cabernet Sauvignon might make a fantastic wine by itself, but there is always a gain of complexity (if also perhaps a reduction in power) by blending in the best lot of Merlot. Monovarietals find their way to the bottled wine only *faute de mieux*, as at Lafite Rothschild in 1961 (100% Cabernet Sauvignon) or 1994 (99% Cabernet Sauvignon).

Whether or not to blend is a matter of preference in Napa. Whereas in Bordeaux there is a correlation (albeit fairly rough) between increasing prestige (and price) and increasing proportion of Cabernet Sauvignon, in Napa the cult wines at the top are divided between varietal-labeled Cabernet Sauvignon and Proprietary Reds (mostly Bordeaux blends). For the most part there's a split between those who believe in blending, and therefore add other (usually Bordeaux) varieties to all their Cabernets, and those who believe in the inviolability of Cabernet and never blend it. There's a tendency, when a producer makes both regular and reserve bottlings, for the reserve to have more Cabernet Sauvignon than the estate bottling, or occasionally even to be 100% Cabernet while the estate is blended, which perhaps indicates where Napa's heart lies. On the other hand, Don Bryant, whose 100% Cabernet was one of the first cult wines, told me, "I noticed a year ago that of the top twenty wines in Parker, all but mine were blends. I was not happy about that." He has now introduced a Bordeaux-style blend, called Bettina after his wife, which comes from grapes at three top vineyards outside of the Bryant Estate (￼ page 381).

The rationale for making monovarietal Cabernet Sauvignon is that the grapes ripen more reliably in Napa than they did in Bordeaux: full of fruit, the mid palate does not need to be filled in by Merlot or other varieties. This view was reinforced by early difficulties with the other Bordeaux varieties. "One reason why there wasn't a movement to Cabernet Franc or Merlot in the eighties was because the clonal material available was so poor it wouldn't ripen properly—the Cabernet Franc was more like the Loire than Bordeaux, the Malbec used to shatter, and we couldn't obtain Petit Verdot. So it was an economic decision: you don't want to plant something that will fail. But Cabernet was proven: clone 4 and clone 7 were known to make good wine. There wasn't so much fear about planting Cabernet Sauvignon," says Rosemary Cakebread, formerly of Spottswoode, and now making her own wine at Gallica.

The general perception is that Napa has been moving away from monovarietal wines since then. "One thinks of all-Cabernet Sauvignon wines as a seventies thing," said one commentator, but in fact almost half of Napa Cabernet Sauvignon is pure or almost pure variety. Proponents of monovarietals who argue that Cabernet Sauvignon achieves a full flavor spectrum in Napa without needing assistance from other varieties, sometimes take this argument to the logical conclusion of saying that you can *only* really appreciate the full varietal force of Cabernet Sauvignon if you don't weaken it with other varieties. "I do not blend my Cabernet Sauvignon. Why dilute or even alter the King of red wines?" says Jeff Smith of Dusinberre Cellars. Cathy Corison, who is definitely not into the blockbuster style, says that, "At least on the Rutherford bench, I believe that nine years out of ten, Cabernet can do better anything the blending varieties can do. Rutherford gives you the entire range of fruit flavors that Cabernet can give all in one glass." Fred Schrader, who produces wine in a more powerful style, seconds the motion. "I love the idea of blending clones, it gives complexity, but I don't see any point to blending anything other than Cabernet. The most honest expression of Napa is to make 100% Cabernet."

In an interesting contrast with the growing emphasis in Napa on single vineyards, some producers believe that blending gives the most complexity, but the way to do it is to take advantage of Napa's soil diversity, and blend Cabernets from different sites. On the other hand, there is a good proportion of blended wines, and John Caldwell, a grower who brought in many of the clones, and who also now produces wine, says, "I have sold grapes to many wineries over the last 25 years and know their blending styles and I think you will find that most do blend. You know why? It tastes better." One view is that blending becomes more important for mountain vineyards. "The focus here from the start has been on blending. I think if you are a hillside Cabernet producer you should think about blending. The hillsides have more tannins and in order to rein in those tannins you need other varieties to calm down the astringency," says Ry Richards at Chappellet.

The issue of whether to blend with Merlot is two-sided: Cabernet achieves higher ripeness in Napa than in Bordeaux, but the Merlot is rarely successful. "Oh, the Merlot question again," said former winemaker Helen Keplinger at Bryant Vineyards, raising her eyes to heaven, when I asked why Merlot isn't successful in Napa. The relative accumulation of sugar is not the issue in Napa, where Merlot had higher sugar levels than Cabernet in the seventies, was more or less the same level through the eighties and nineties, and in recent years has actually been just a tad lower.[14] This may reflect differences in growing conditions or in harvest decisions, but means that potential alcohol levels are not a factor in deciding whether or not to blend Merlot with Cabernet. The issue in Napa is more that the Merlot tends to add a rustic quality to the wine.

At Opus One, where they are conscious of French ownership, and the wines are a traditional blend with from 77% to 97% Cabernet Sauvignon, depending on the vintage, Michael Silacci believes that Cabernet Sauvignon is the most successful of the Bordeaux varieties. "Merlot starts unripe, gets sweet, but stays green: it very rarely gets to phenolic ripeness in Napa. It does okay in cooler seasons. Cabernet Franc handles water stress *too* well; the vines seem fine, but then you find dry tannins in the wine. Petit Verdot doesn't handle water stress at all," he told me. John Caldwell, whose nursery has grown a wide range of varieties over the years, says, "The Merlot deal is going away, it just doesn't (reliably) make great wine, it makes it only one year in three. Malbec could be an excellent replacement." The answer is that it's just too warm for

Merlot in Napa Valley. Merlot can be successful if there is a cooler spot in the vineyards; at Harlan Estate, the Merlot is planted at a site that used to have Cabernet Sauvignon, but couldn't ripen it. Fred Schrader was forthright about varieties in Napa. "If you are growing anything other than Cabernet north of Yountville, you ought to have your head examined. So in order to do a blend, you would need to source the Merlot from Carneros [a cooler area]."

Recent issues affecting the blend are somewhat different in Bordeaux, where Merlot always achieves higher ripeness than Cabernet Sauvignon, typically equivalent to a percent or more extra alcohol. In the cooler vintages before the recent warming trend, Cabernet often needed to be chaptalized to bring it up to the same sugar level as the Merlot, which might not require chaptalization. While producers are happy to have riper Cabernet, there is increasing concern about the parallel effect with Merlot. "I'm a firm believer in the issue of global warming, I think there is no doubt about it, we've never had such good Cabernet as now. I'm sure that in very good years, which are more and more common today, Cabernet Sauvignon is a more interesting variety, it has more noblesse. We have benefited from global warming but we benefit far more with Cabernet Sauvignon than with Merlot. With Merlot we are far closer to the drawback than the benefits, especially on the right bank. Although we are not high alcohol producers, the Merlot reached 15% in St Julien. I'm absolutely sure the right bank will be 16% and this is not consistent with making great wine," says winemaker Philippe Blanc at Château Beychevelle.

"There are two main factors for higher alcohol," says Paul Pontallier at Château Margaux. "The soil and the variety. Clay soil always produces more alcohol. Alcohol for Cabernet Sauvignon grapes harvested from the best gravel soils in 2009 and 2010 was between 12.7 and 13.1%. Our two or three plots on clay soils reached 14%. We see the same difference for Merlot, 13.5-13.7% on gravel, up to 15.5% on clay. In the same conditions Merlot always produces about 1% more alcohol than Cabernet Sauvignon." Given that most of the Merlot in Bordeaux is planted on clay, this is the nub of the problem.

More than the alcohol per se, the question is what happens to the blend. "I don't think the level of alcohol is a problem, it's the balance. With global warming it will become more difficult to produce quality Merlot: just look at Napa Valley where the Merlot is not successful. It's a question mark whether Palmer will be able to keep the same proportion of Merlot in its vineyards. I hope so because it is the style of Palmer," says Thomas Duroux at Château Palmer. The general dilemma was captured by Jean-René Matignon at Château Pichon Baron. "In our best terroir we have some Merlot—we don't know who planted it there—and we are thinking of replacing it with Cabernet. But we are concerned that if we do this, the [remaining] Merlot won't be good enough to put in the blend." So what to do about the Merlot? "In hot vintages Merlot can be unblendable, so it goes into the second wine. It's already driven people to use higher proportions of Cabernet Sauvignon in the hot years. In 2009 and 2010 the Merlots were over 15%: if we can't put them in the wine, it messes up the whole thing," says negociant Bill Blatch.

"Climate change is more a problem for châteaux with more Merlot," says François-Xavier Borie of Grand Puy Lacoste. Indeed, there are the first signs now of a movement back towards Cabernet Sauvignon. "Global warming obliges us to reduce the proportion of Merlot, it's not a matter of over-ripeness in the Merlot, but the alcohol level is too high. The replacement is intended to maintain the character of the wine. Merlot was always planted historically be-cause Cabernet Sauvignon wasn't so successful," says Didier Cuvelier at Château Léoville Poyferré. But terroir may be a limitation. "Plantings depend on the soils. We would be happy to grow more Cabernet Sauvignon, but unfor-tunately we know that Cabernet Sauvignon will not do well on some clay soils. It's much more a matter of soil than climate," says Paul Pontallier of Château Margaux. But he feels that the general change in climate has been beneficial. "The last fifteen years have been more favorable not just because temperatures have been higher but because it's been drier. We've made great wine in cool conditions but never in wet conditions. Temperature is not such a big issue as rain, which is always the key to success or failure."

The first growths, which have the highest proportions of Cabernet Sauvi-gnon, are the most sanguine about climate change. Paul Pontallier again: "As long as we have a minority of Merlot, the increase in alcohol is not a problem. It has relieved us of the period when it was necessary to add sugar. Now in most vintages we do not add sugar. We find ourselves with alcohol around 13.0%, 13.2% has been the highest. We have indeed increased the proportion of Cabernet Sauvignon in the first wine but as usual the reasons are not clear, the Cabernet Sauvignon is probably better, the Merlot is not quite as good—but there is no one simple reason. It's a trend but many things have contributed."

Perhaps there are really two interlinked issues about blending: under what conditions is Cabernet Sauvignon complete in itself; and if blending is advan-tageous, what are the other appropriate varieties. Is it axiomatic that a blend should use the traditional Bordeaux varieties in places where the climate and terroir are quite different from Bordeaux? After all, Bordeaux is relatively cool and humid, whereas most other places that grow Cabernet are warmer and drier. (Not to mention that those other varieties have changed significantly over time in Bordeaux, from Carmenère, to Malbec, to Merlot.) Reversing the ques-tion, should difficulties with today's principal blending variety mean that it's better to make a monovarietal, or should alternative varieties be considered for the blend?

If the global warming trend continues, could Merlot have run its course as the best partner for Cabernet Sauvignon in Bordeaux? Would one solution be to go back to the old varieties of Malbec or Carmenère? Carmenère actually ripens after Cabernet Sauvignon; in fact the problem with Carmenère is that its flavor spectrum can be quite herbaceous, similar rather than complementary to Cabernet Sauvignon, if it does not reach full ripeness. It's somewhat of a game of double or quits. Blends with Malbec and with Carmenère are the norm in Argentina and in Chile, where the most successful wines tend to convey a smooth elegance, with more supple tannins to complement the more evident structure of Cabernet Sauvignon (see Chapter 7). It's an obvious contrast with the fleshier qualities of Merlot, especially on the mid palate. The switch to Merlot in Bordeaux coincided with a relatively cool period, when an earlier-ripening variety offered obvious advantages, but in today's warmer climate perhaps Bordeaux's classic style might be better retained by reversing that transition. Of course, there is still extensive vintage variation. "In 2004 and 2007, we really needed the Merlot, but maybe in the next fifty years the Merlot will disappear," says Michael Georges, technical director at Château Léoville Lascases, before adding hastily, "I exaggerate, of course."

Bordeaux today has average growing season temperatures around the same as the Northern Rhône twenty years ago, so perhaps they should consider planting some Syrah. Just as Malbec was replaced by Merlot as a result of phylloxera in the nineteenth century, so might Merlot be replaced by Syrah as a result of global warming in the twenty first century. Except, of course, that things were flexible then, and now the varieties are fixed by Appellation Contrôlée rules that make change illegal. But it's not illegal in the New World, and in Napa, Mendoza, and Chile, it often seems that a small proportion of Syrah gives an interesting aromatic lift to the blend. I suspect that in these places it would be more widely used in place of Merlot if it wasn't for a residual adherence to the tradition of the Bordeaux blend.

I'm prepared to buy the argument that in warmer climates—maybe even sometimes in Bordeaux in really warm vintages such as 2009 or 2010—Cabernet Sauvignon by itself can make a wine that seems complete across the palate when it is young. Youthful enthusiasm can fill the mid palate with fruits. The trade-off compared to a blend is that monovarietal Cabernet Sauvignon shows greater purity of fruits, but more linearity: the blend diffuses the purity, but broadens the flavor spectrum. There can certainly be room for both styles. But when the wines age, there is a tendency for the differences to widen. Purity of fruits in young monovarietal Cabernet Sauvignon can begin to seem a bit narrow in an older wine, and that intrinsic spartan character can come through. Certainly the wine matures as it ages, but does it develop as much complexity as a blend? At the least, it is slower to develop those delicious savory notes of tertiary development that meld with the lightening fruits, which for me mark the moment when the wine is at its peak.

Aging is clearly not just a matter of varietal composition, since as a general rule, Napa Valley wines seem to reach a comparable point to Bordeaux in about half the time, say ten years compared to twenty, when other conditions are comparable. The Cabernet-dominated blends of Chile and Argentina seem to age a bit faster yet, reaching the savory tipping point in five to ten years (whether this is due to the difference in the blends, using Carmenère in Chile and Malbec in Argentina, or to younger vines, or other conditions, is impossible to say). But judgment on this issue depends very much on what style of wine you like. If you are committed to a primary fruit spectrum, if savory development is a step too far, then monovarietal Cabernet may well be the wine of choice. If tertiary development is when the wine really becomes most interesting, blends may offer more satisfaction.

Another question about aging is how it will be affected by the increase in alcohol (and decrease in acidity). A seemingly relentless increase in ripeness has made alcohol levels a controversial issue everywhere wine is produced. Many producers give a wide range of information about their wines, the detailed varietal composition, the vineyards from which the grapes were sourced, harvest conditions and date, the Brix at harvest—but often enough, the actual alcohol level is missing from the technical sheets. And unfortunately, the level that's stated on the bottle by law need be no more than a distant approximation.[15] But with modern technology there is absolutely no reason why alcohol should not be stated on the label within 0.1 or 0.2%.

There's a trend for alcohol levels to be understated on the label, because producers are responding to a belief that consumers react against stated high alcohol, but actually prefer the taste of it.[16] When I surveyed alcohol levels in Napa and Bordeaux, I received some surprising hostility from producers. "I would expect you'd have a more profound interest in what we do here in Napa Valley than tracking our wines' alcohol levels. I can't participate in the study… Whatever the results, it sends the wrong message to wine lovers the world over," said one producer. I wonder what that message would be?

A more measured, and common, response was to say that alcohol is not the main issue: the question is whether the wine is in balance. While that is true up to a point, doesn't it evade a major issue, which is the effect that alcohol has on style? Certainly wines can remain balanced with alcohol at 14%, perhaps even higher, but they have a different flavor spectrum and impact on the palate than wines with 12.5% alcohol. In my view, it's not the alcohol alone that impacts the style, but the associated levels of higher extraction and richness that go along with getting grapes to very high sugar levels. The wine may be balanced, but the balance has to be different if the alcohol is not to stand out. High alcohol gives Cabernet Sauvignon an impression of very deep rich fruits, with a touch of aromatics: the wines are big, bold, forceful, and fruit-driven. The extra richness may show well at a tasting, but will wines with high alcohol accompany food as well, will they be so elegant, and will they age so well? Or will we be left with the grin of the alcohol?

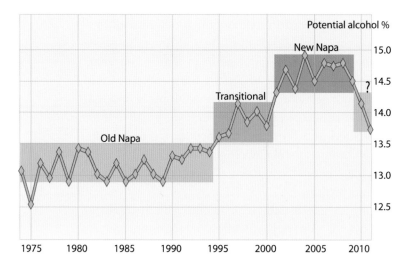

*Alcohol levels in Napa
were in a steady range
of 13.0-13.5% until the
mid nineties; the first
vintage over 14% was
1997; and this became
the norm in the
2000s.[17]*

Alcohol levels of Napa Cabernet have increased more or less steadily since the seventies. What you see in the grapes may not be exactly what you get in the wine, because rising levels have pushed some producers to reduce alcohol by watering back[18] (addition of up to 7% water is legal in California;[19] the amount of water added is sometimes described ironically in "Jesus units") or by more sophisticated interventions using techniques of reverse osmosis or spinning cone (which extract volatile components from wine[20]). The change in Napa from moderate alcohol levels (around 13%) to high levels (over 14%) was triggered by the warm 1997 vintage, but did not become set until the new century. It remains to be seen whether this is a permanent effect, as levels certainly fell back in 2011 and 2012, and enthusiasm has been expressed about the potential of 2012 for producing ripe but more balanced (for which read less alcoholic) wines. (The alcohol levels are usually a little lower in wines from the mountain AVAs, about 0.25-0.5% less than those from the valley floor.[21])

Certainly attitudes have changed. One Napa Valley producer said to me recently, "We are lucky to be able to craft such balanced wines that high alcohol to date has not been an issue." The wines she was discussing were 14.8% and 15.1% alcohol! In fact, there's a range of attitudes from reluctant acceptance of high levels to a belief that this is what consumers want. "Our wines are right around 15% alcohol, that's where we want them to be. Lower alcohol for us comes with greener flavors," says Phillip Corallo-Titus at Chappellet. Thinking back to the old era, Doug Shafer recalls, "We started pushing ripeness in 1990-1991. We decided to pick at 24-25 Brix and guess what?—black fruit, no veggie or herbal character. People liked it better... I've watched the alcohol debate from the sidelines and picking at 28-29 Brix is ridiculous. We went rich earlier, but rich enough is rich enough." The balanced view expressed by Mark de Vere at Mondavi is that, "Alcohol levels are not ideal but we are not worried about it. Usually people don't notice the alcohol level until they read the label.

Alcohol levels in Bordeaux were centered on 12.5% until the mid nineties, and increased over 13% only in the mid 2000s.[22]

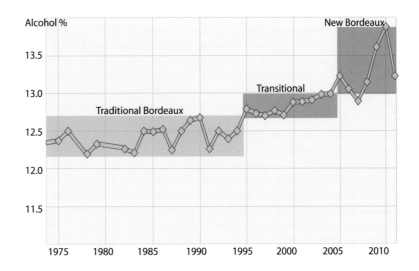

We think you can get a wine that is balanced even if it is fairly high in alcohol; it's not something we want but it's not something we would want to manipulate out of."

Historically, it might seem oxymoronic to put "approachability" and "Cabernet Sauvignon" in the same sentence, yet many Napa Cabernets can be drunk virtually upon release. This does not seem to be much affected by whether they are pure Cabernet Sauvignon or blends. At the Napa Premiere tasting early in 2012, when the 2007, 2008, and 2009 vintages were tasted blind from a variety of producers, I found that most 2007s were either ready now or would be within the year. Many were made in a soft, approachable style, evidently intended for short term consumption. Now 2007 was a notably ripe vintage that lends itself to this style, but it seemed to me that winemaking was actually more important than vintage, because the 2008s and 2009s (generally less ripe and concentrated) from producers with a consciously approachable style were pretty much as ready as the 2007s. Generally low acidity in all three vintages left me doubtful about aging potential. The low acid makes the best wines quite approachable, with a soft, velvety or furry palate, but in other cases the impression remains a little flat. It was a contrast with my tasting of the 2009 vintage from Bordeaux, which I expected to be flabby from the warm conditions, but where the wines had that characteristic Bordelais lift of freshness, and were in fact much livelier than any of the Napa vintages (Y page 311).

Many producers say that aging is important, but advances in viticulture and vinification give more fruit and riper tannins, enabling the wine to be both approachable and ageworthy. Of course, it all depends what you mean by "approachable." I mean that the tannins are no longer bringing bitterness to the finish and they're not preventing me from appreciating the fruits, even though the underlying structure may be evident in the background. By this criterion, I

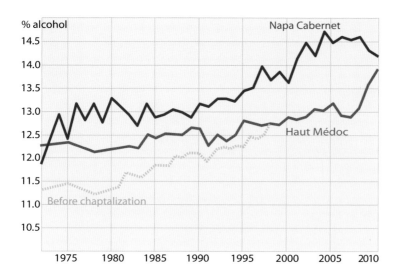

Grapes have always been riper in Napa than in Bordeaux, but the difference was narrowed by chaptalization.[23]

often find I would prefer to wait a year or two after the producer regards the wine as ready to drink. When I asked Tom Dehlinger, who makes relatively reserved Cabernet in the cooler climate of Sonoma's Russian River Valley, whether his view had changed on the relative importance of approachability and aging, he had an interesting perspective. "I think probably the view of what is immediately drinkable has changed more. We care about aging but if a wine was not ready to drink at five years old, I would not be happy. I definitely want a full-bodied rich wine. I want the tannins to be mature. I want to make the most flavorful wines, I'm not in the school of thought for making lower alcohol wines. If someone doesn't like the alcohol levels at which grapes get ripe here, they should go to another region for their wines. Going back to lower Brix at harvest would be a mistake."

Until 1982, the big issue in Bordeaux was getting the Cabernet to reach ripeness. A major difference from Napa is that until the end of the 1990s, around one percent of the alcohol level of Bordeaux was due to chaptalization. There's a stylistic difference here: a wine with 12.5% natural alcohol will probably be richer and riper in its overall impression than a wine where one percent of the alcohol is due to adding sugar before fermentation. Most producers in the Médoc say that they have rarely chaptalized since 1997, as warmer vintages (and better viticulture) have achieved greater ripeness at harvest.[24] No doubt the vintages since 1982 have been warmer and riper, with 1985, perhaps 1989, and then 1990, and 1995 standing out as examples of the "new" style in the next decade, but it's really in the new century that you see the effect in full force, with exceptional years in 2000, perhaps 2003 (although that year remains atypical), 2005, 2009, and 2010. Chaptalization may have returned in 2011, and I have some skepticism as to how much it diminished after 1997, as records of the French tax authorities show significant taxes con-

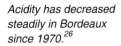

Acidity has decreased steadily in Bordeaux since 1970.[26]

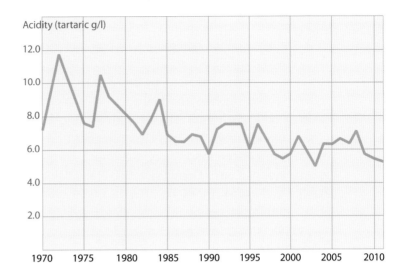

tinued to be paid by producers in Bordeaux on their reported use of sugar through 2000.[25] But I may have been asking the wrong question. "People who say they stopped chaptalizing in 1997 are liars—but you should have asked if they stopped enrichment [i.e., concentration, which uses alternative techniques such as reverse osmosis]," François-Xavier Borie told me at Château Grand Puy Lacoste.

The struggle to reach ripeness may not have ended completely in 1982—there were still some poor vintages to come, such as 1984, 1991, and 1997—but after the nineties, the problem switched from too little sugar to too much at harvest. In terms of ripeness of style, Bordeaux has come farther since the seventies than you would expect from the increase in alcohol levels in finished wines. The change at harvest is really from around 11.5% potential alcohol to around 13.5%.

Alcohol was such an insignificant issue in terms of consumer concern that it was not even stated on the label until the mid eighties.[27] But throughout the seventies, the Cabernet-based wines of the left bank were generally in a range of 12-12.5% alcohol. Even the unprecedently warm vintage of 1982 produced only a handful of wines at 13% alcohol. Slowly alcohol levels began to rise, moving over 13% after the nineties, but with that 1% differential between Bordeaux and Napa more or less maintained. Although the 1982 vintage started the change in style, it was more than a decade later before the change in alcohol level became really noticeable (perhaps because natural alcohol replaced chaptalization before the overall level went up). The really dramatic increases of 2009 and 2010 brought Bordeaux clearly into the same orbit as Napa, with alcohol levels reaching record heights, and some wines close to 15%. It's a mark of the new Bordeaux that even in the 2011 vintage, when the exuberance fell right off, average alcohol levels stayed over 13%. The parallel between

Bordeaux and Napa is striking: both left traditional territory behind at the end of the 1990s, and then entered a new phase around 2005. A secondary effect is that acidity has declined steadily in Bordeaux as ripeness has increased (acidity is usually maintained in Napa by adding tartaric acid at fermentation).

Is increased ripeness the main cause of higher concentration and alcohol levels? "You know I think the problem is more complex. Some of the increase comes from lower yields," says Jean-Michel Comme at Château Pontet Canet. "Increase in concentration is due as much to pruning and lower yields as to global warming," says Dominique Befve at Château Lascombes. Jerome Juhe at Château La Lagune draws the obvious conclusion. "One possibility to counter global warming would be increase yields again, as the lower yields have led to more concentration and higher sugar levels."

For the first part of the twentieth century, yields were reduced by the state of the vineyards (which often included many dead vines) and climatic conditions. Some vines were overproducing while others were not producing at all. For most of the twentieth century, the priority was to increase yields to economic levels. "We were almost bankrupt in the seventies, when yields were around 15-20 hl/ha," recollects Jean-Charles Cazes of Château Lynch Bages. The good vintages of the 1980s brought much higher yields, well over today's limit of 45 hl/ha in the communes of the Médoc. Since then it's become commonly accepted that reducing yields leads to higher quality. "People used to gain their living with the yields; this is the first generation to work more for taste than quantity," says Rémi Edange of Domaine de Chevalier.

Since the 1980s, there has been more focus on increasing concentration by reducing yields. One picture tells the story. After Suntory purchased Château Lagrange in 1983, a huge new building with three chais was constructed to hold enough barriques to handle the current production. "In the old days I remember all three chais full to the ceiling, now one of the three is empty," says director Bruno Eynard. "When I started yields were 65 hl/ha in a good year, 55 hl/ha in a poor year, but today they are 40-45 hl/ha." There's some skepticism as to just how far this needs to be taken to ensure quality. Jean-Michel Cazes takes the view that extremely low yields in Bordeaux can be a sign of poor quality rather than the reverse: "It's not that you don't produce fine wines with 20-25 hl/ha, but it's not necessary, at least in Bordeaux... A low yield in a well maintained vineyard with homogenous production of 40 or 45 hl/ha with old vines is perfect."[28] At Château Gruaud Larose, owner Jean Merlaut takes a similar view. "We are not in a race to get to the smallest yields. It's a good way to increase the price, but Bordeaux is probably one of the rare regions where you can get good yields without losing the structure. The proof is 1982, 1961, 1945 where there was no selection—but the wines are still magic today." It's clear that quality increases when yields are reduced to around 45 hl/ha for Cabernet Sauvignon (the yield needs to be somewhat lower for high quality with Pinot

Noir), but when yields are pushed down to 25 hl/ha, it's at least arguable that the main effect is on scarcity of production rather than on quality.

Green harvest (vendange vert) is one way to reduce yields. It's done by pruning the number of berries, some time after flowering, but most often at the point when the berries are small and green and the yield can be predicted. When introduced in the eighties, it was a controversial technique much favored by a group of producers on the right bank, the so-called *garagistes*, who used it to help decrease yields dramatically. Now it is common everywhere. One of the first major châteaux to use it was Pétrus, and the story goes that the producer was denounced in the local church in Pomerol for wasting God's bounty.[29] It remains controversial because the vine tends to compensate by increasing the size of the remaining berries. At Château Sociando-Mallet, perhaps the most distinguished of today's châteaux in the Médoc omitted from the 1855 classification, proprietor Jean Gautreau says forcefully, "I'm contre-courant," arguing that, "Vendange vert is more to increase the price than the quality; the garage wines were a catastrophe for Bordeaux. What is a grand wine of Bordeaux—finesse and elegance in the aroma and taste. We make normal yields, we have good terroir, there is no green harvest, we can make 80% grand vin. 15 hl/ha for a grand vin—it's nuts." He's not in favor of the

Véraison, when the berries change color, is a critical stage en route to ripeness. Uneven development in this bunch is shown by berries at all stages from green to full change of color. More uniformity in ripeness levels will be achieved by sorting at harvest time.

Photograph courtesy Suzanne Wooton, Avatar Vintners.

trend to higher alcohol but admits its inevitability. "I would prefer 11.5% alcohol to 13%, but you have to live in your time. But you can't assure optimal maturity at 12%, the tannins aren't mature. But I prefer a wine at 13% with fully ripe flavors to one at 12% with green flavors."

A major factor in the march to ripeness has been the change from harvesting at a specific sugar level to waiting for "phenolic ripeness." This has no exact measure. As grapes mature, the tannin content increases, but more importantly, the nature of the tannins also changes from harsher to better rounded. The taste of the grapes changes: a ripe berry should come away cleanly when picked, the skin becomes almost nutty to chew, and the color of the seeds turns from green to brown. Waiting for phenolic ripeness usually means that grapes are picked at one or two percentage points higher in potential alcohol, and with significantly lower acidity, than if harvest were decided simply on sugar and acid levels. Prolonged ripening also has an effect on the aroma and flavor spectrum of the wine, since volatile molecules as well as the phenols change significantly during the extra period on the vine.

With the pre-eminent role of ripeness in setting style, winemakers have become increasingly involved with viticulture and setting harvest dates. When Michel Rolland, originally from Pomerol and now one of the world's most famous flying winemakers, visited Napa for the first time in 1985, he was astounded by the gap between viticulture and vinification. "In the winery, no one knew the origin of the grapes. I deduced that the oenologue had never been in the vineyards and had not analyzed the maturity of the grapes. When I said I was going to taste the berries, people were dumbfounded."[30] Recollecting the transition, "We saw the winemaker getting out into the vineyard, previously you would see your grapes for the first time on the crush pad," says Don Weaver of Harlan Estate. Genevieve Janssens at Mondavi sees the winemaker's role as crucial in the transition to greater ripeness. "In the 1970s in Napa, the people we were observing were Bordeaux, and they were picking early, so we thought we should do that, and all the contracts with vineyards called for picking below 23 Brix; you were penalized if you went higher, and the vineyard manager, not the winemaker, decided the date of harvest. In the nineties there was a revolution—in the vineyard they are inclined to say winemakers are magicians, they can make wine from anything, and we were getting tired of that—and then the winemakers started to determine the date of harvest."

Getting to higher ripeness levels has been assisted by warmer growing temperatures and by canopy management to control the exposure of the berries to sunlight. More uniform ripeness also has been helped by improvements in handling the berries, especially the introduction of sorting tables. Introduced in the 1990s, the first sorting tables were fairly rudimentary devices in which the grapes were emptied on to a moving belt, and any unsuitable material was

This mechanical sorter separates individual berries by size.

identified by eye and removed. A major effect was much better removal of MOG (material other than grapes) as well as any undesirable berries. Various mechanical devices followed, including vibrating tables and meshes that sorted berries by size. The latest development is optical sorting, in which parameters for size, color, wrinkling, and so on can be adjusted by a computer program, and then the machine scans the berries with a laser and removes those that do not fit the criteria.

The continual refinement of sorting might appear to have somewhat different effects in Bordeaux and Napa. In Bordeaux it led to the removal of extraneous material and unripe berries. Bill Blatch of Vintex comments that, "Getting out the green berries makes a big difference, and can bring you up a percent in alcohol." In Napa, especially for those producers who pick very late, it's more a matter of eliminating those raisined, dehydrated berries that have gone too far. "It does a better job with less wastage—it pulls out 2% of berries with better results than human eyes, which pull out 4%," says Michael Silacci of Opus One. But whether sorting is more concerned with eliminating MOG, unripe berries, or over-ripe berries, it has a very definite universal effect on flavor spectrum: the berries have greater uniformity.

There's not much difference in terms of technological intervention between Bordeaux and Napa. While some options are available at the low end only in the New World—such as using cheaper staves or chips to replace expensive oak barrels—there's not much difference for premium wines. Many Bordeaux châteaux have reverse osmosis machines (useful for extracting water when it rains at harvest time) locked away in back rooms; any producer in Napa can take advantage of a commercial service for reducing alcohol levels by reverse osmosis or spinning cone. But it remains equally obscure in both Bordeaux and Napa what goes on behind the scenes: I could find no producers in Bordeaux who admitted to chaptalization, and no producers in Napa who admitted to alcohol reduction.

The optical sorter extracts berries that do not fit a set of parameters. The green berry at upper left is about to be excluded from the stream.

Bordeaux has lurched towards greater ripeness rather than progressing smoothly. The first impetus was poor weather. "The 1970s were the worst decade, a complete disaster with the weather and still with young vines resulting from replanting after the freeze of 1956. This led to a drive to get more sugar [into the grapes at harvest]. In the mid eighties Pétrus was the first to do a green harvest, Haut Brion did its first green harvest in 1988, followed in large volume in 1989. Since then cover crops have been introduced," recollects Jean-Philippe Delmas at Château Haut Brion. There followed two decades with opposing characters: the wet nineties and the hot 2000s.

Warmer temperatures are definitely a driving force, but (with the exception of 2003 where torrid temperatures drove the style), this is an overall trend rather than a single determinative factor for any particular year. Abrupt jumps in ripeness occurred in 2000, 2005, 2009, and 2010. But the climate is more an enabling force than directly driving the style. At the heart of the transition to a riper style is a conscious determination to avoid any overt herbaceousness in the wine. I think this is a mixed bag. I certainly carry no candle for the strongly herbaceous wines of the poorer vintages of the past. But do you have to go to the extremes of massive fruits to avoid herbaceousness? Is it really necessary to let the berries become so ripe that alcohol levels rise over 14%? When I asked producers in Bordeaux whether and how far they feel this stylistic change should go, the general response is that the wines are better now, that they have gained approachability when young without losing the ability to develop when older. The châteaux proprietors do not go so far as the Burgundians—who are prone to claim that they make wine exactly as their fathers and grandfathers made it—but they tend to deny any change in style beyond reflecting what the vintage brings. But a change in alcohol from under 12.5% to almost 14%, accompanied by more tannins and greater extraction all round, makes it undeniable that a change is under way.

"It's multifactorial" might be the new cry of Bordeaux, or at least of the left bank. Whenever you ask about the effects of rising temperature, whether long term climatic changes are creating increased pressure on rising alcohol levels or lower acidity, there's a response that the climate isn't really a problem because the causes are multifactorial. When asked about problems with rising alcohol levels in the Médoc, they say that's a problem for the right bank, with its high concentration of Merlot. "Merlot brings the alcohol, it is more a problem on the right bank. The future of Bordeaux is Cabernet Sauvignon, forget the right bank," says general manager David Launay of Château Gruaud Larose.

Phenolic ripeness is almost synonymous with tannin management, since tannins are by far the major phenolic component of wine. Yet while there is significant convergence worldwide in viticultural techniques designed to produce riper wines, there is less consensus about managing tannins during vinification. In addition to tannins that come from the grape itself (mostly from the skin), wines pick up tannins when matured in new oak (and to a lesser degree from barrels that are one or two years old). The general principle is that the stronger the wine, the more it can withstand, or indeed is complemented by, exposure to new oak. It's probably fair to say that there is generally more extensive use of new oak in the New World. Indeed, high use of new oak in Napa is a major difference from Bordeaux, where two thirds of châteaux use 60% or less new oak; only 15% use 100% new oak.[31]

The move towards what is sometimes pejoratively called the new international style is an issue in all the classic wine regions of Europe. Fathers and sons stopped speaking to one another over the clash between modernists and traditionalists in Barolo, and Brunello di Montalcino suffered from the same divide, although without such personal animosity. In Rioja some producers solved the problem by making two wines: one in the traditional style, and another under a new label in the modern style. In Bordeaux it is rarely so clear cut. It is not always easy to pick out the extreme examples of modernists and traditionalists in each commune, itself an indication of the generality of the trend. So to what extent has Bordeaux narrowed the gap with Napa, which is almost universally in the modern camp?

When I asked producers in either Bordeaux or Napa about their stylistic objectives, the answers were more similar than different: "to express the character of the vineyard by making the best wine we can at optimal ripeness" would be a fair, if cynical, summary. Napa producers say that the combination of climate

Opus One is matured exclusively in new oak, in a splendid semi-circular barrel room.

and terroir gives wines that are richer at optimum ripeness than in Bordeaux. Some force is lent to this argument by the fact that even in the early days when they were trying to emulate Bordeaux, the wines still had greater alcohol. It's also true that climate forced Bordeaux producers in 2009 and 2010 into higher alcohol levels than they wanted. Certainly the disconnect between sugar accumulation and phenolic development means that warmer seasons will produce higher sugar levels at equivalent levels of phenolic ripeness.

But as a certain American President might have said, it all depends on what you mean by ripeness. When harvesting was fixed by Brix, it was easy, because Brix is a precise measure of the level of sugar in the grapes, but phenolic ripeness is loosely defined. Does the definition of ripeness in Bordeaux equate to a point that Napa producers consider still to be green; does the Napa definition of ripeness go to a level that the Bordelais consider over-ripe? To what extent is the difference due to climate and how far to differences in perception?

In Napa, producers who dissent from the common style usually attribute its dominance to an attempt to satisfy what are darkly described as "powerful critics." It is certainly true that there is a correlation between critics' scores and alcohol levels (and for that matter, between alcohol levels and price).[32] "Being good Americans, if a little is good, more must be better," is how Bo Barrett of Chateau Montelena sums up the prevailing attitude. The extent to which style is a matter of choice is indicated by producers who say that they've pulled back from super-ripeness in order to make wines with lower alcohol.

The direction of movement is still towards greater ripeness in Bordeaux, and the extent to which market forces may be the most important driving factor is indicated by abrupt transitions at some châteaux, especially after a change of ownership. When a château changes hands, there's a common trend: to move to a new, more intense, more extracted, more "modern" style. This has been seen most dramatically outside the Médoc, with Château Pavie in St. Emilion—famously converted after Gérard Perse bought it in 1998 to a wine loved by Robert Parker and loathed by Jancis Robinson in the 2003 vintage—and with Château Pape Clément in Pessac, which Bernard Magrez added to his portfolio (by inheritance) in 1985, and which subsequently became richer and more extracted. The verdict of the market has been quite clear: both have increased significantly in price after the change in style relative to others that were formerly at the same level. And the promotion of Château Pavie in 2012 to the very top class of classification in St. Emilion confers an official recognition, as it were, that the international style is more important than tradition.

Other examples are more ambiguous. In most cases, the impetus for the sale was that the old proprietor had lost interest (or lacked resources) and the château was palpably under-performing. Even if you regret the passing of the traditional style, it's hard to criticize the change when the wine was poor before the transition and was so clearly technically improved afterward. Take Châteaux Prieuré Lichine and Lascombes in the Médoc, purchased by American investors in 1999 and 2001, where the style went from rather faded, perhaps one might say tired, to modern and bright. Others that might be put in the same category are Château La Tour Carnet (another Magrez property, acquired in 2000), La Lagune (acquired by the Frey family in 1999), and perhaps Pichon Baron (purchased by AXA in 1987). One example of a forceful change by an existing owner is Léoville Poyferré, where Michel Rolland was brought in as consultant in 1995, and the style has since been modernized (page 335). Everywhere in Bordeaux, it's a one-way street to modernity.

Change may be inevitable even where there is a conscious attempt to maintain traditional values. I've always viewed Château Montrose as one of the most traditional châteaux: its wines can take a decade or so to come around, but my goodness, do they justify the wait! They go from a tough hardness in the early years to a savory elegance after twenty or thirty years that absolutely typifies St. Estèphe for me. The 1970 came around in the past few years and now puts most other wines of the vintage to shame. I thought perhaps this era had come to an end when the Bouygues brothers purchased the château from the Charmolües in 2006, but was reassured when they hired Jean Delmas, recently retired from Château Haut Brion, as consultant winemaker.

Château Montrose has one of the simplest châteaux of the Grand Cru Classés.

The question, "Has the style of Montrose changed in the past twenty years?" produced an emphatic NO! from (former) general manager Nicolas Glumineau when I visited Montrose recently. However, they are making better balanced wines, less austere than earlier vintages, which perhaps were too masculine, he allows. Nicolas sees the tannins as the key feature in the character of Montrose (and indeed Cabernet Sauvignon in general). "We can get more precision and earlier integration of tannins," he says. Being more approachable now does not mean the vintage will not last as well. "In the seventies and up to the eighties, it needed fifteen years before the tannins integrated into the wine; the difference today is that the tannins are riper and integrate better and sooner. Tannin integration is a permanent question with Cabernet Sauvignon, but much less so with Merlot. The characteristics of Cabernet Sauvignon are its tannins, and quality is about getting them riper and well integrated into the wine."

Has Bordeaux in general changed? "Probably more so on the right bank than the left bank, because Merlot is more flexible and responds to changes in the cuverie, but Cabernet Sauvignon is a more powerful variety. Also in the Médoc we are more attached to the personality of the growths. We [at Montrose] are very attached to Bordeaux wine, we do not want to make the sort of wine that you cannot place on a map," Nicolas says. But he comments ruefully that if you want to adapt your wine to the global demand, to make interna-

Cos d'Estournel is by far the most exotic winery in Bordeaux.

tional wine in a more jammy style, it's better to plant some Merlot, since it adapts to a variety of soils.

Some producers feel they have been able to take advantage of changing conditions to make the wines they want. Before he left Château Cos d'Estournel, Jean-Guillaume Prats was a believer in the new style. "Global warming is a key component to the evolution of Cos, we are now producing wines which have extraordinary levels of phenolic ripeness. Because of the phenolics they drink well at an earlier age. I doubt whether we will produce any more vintages like 1975, 1986, and 1996, which required fifteen years to come around. My taste favors intensity and richness in the wines; I like Napa Cabernets. Vintage variation is just as great as thirty years ago except that the scale has been moved to a higher level of ripeness. But it's not variation in quality, it's variation in style," he maintains. On the general trend, "Yes, Bordeaux has changed," he says. "We are not producing wines that are too tannic (1975, 1986) or unripe (1997) and they have much better organoleptic properties. Change is driven by global warming and prosperity. The major change in criteria for harvesting is willingness to take a risk by leaving grapes long on the vine or dumping them on the sorting table."

The comparison between Cos d'Estournel and Montrose—the two second growths of St. Estèphe—encapsulates both the trend and the resistance movement in Bordeaux. The difference is epitomized by the styles of the buildings:

Montrose straightforward and workmanlike, but the exoticism of Cos d'Estournel reflecting its first owner's time in the Orient. Contrasted with the traditional style of Montrose's wine, Cos d'Estournel is one of the most modern. The quintessence of a wine driven by Cabernet Sauvignon (𝚼 page 339), Château Montrose has softened in the past decade through improvements in viticulture, not any change in plantings. Cos d'Estournel has changed more overtly. It has become progressively more modern in the past twenty years: its fruits are more forward and lush, it is more delicious when young, and there is more evident sense of ripeness to it. In terms of Bordeaux's past, it seems less overtly Cabernet-driven (𝚼 page 317). But here is a surprise; while Montrose has stayed steady between 62% and 72% Cabernet Sauvignon in the past twenty years, Cos d'Estournel has increased from an average of 57% in the nineties to 76% in recent years. Merlot has decreased significantly. Yet it is riper and richer than ever before. Is there a more telling demonstration of the change in the character of Cabernet Sauvignon? Merlot is no longer always needed to get to ripeness. The correlation between increased ripeness and increased Cabernet seems positively New World-ish.

The change in Bordeaux over the past two decades was highlighted by a tasting at Château Léoville Lascases to compare the 1996 and 2009 vintages of three Delon properties, Château Potensac (a Cru Bourgeois), Clos du Marquis (formerly the second wine, now a separate wine), and Château Léoville Lascases itself (𝚼 page 334). Both vintages were "Cabernet years," but even allowing for age difference, it seemed to me that 1996 showed the traditional character of Bordeaux, whereas 2009 showed the new, modern Bordeaux. A certain sparseness of structure comes through on all three wines from 1996, which for me relates to the wines of the seventies: while there's still a superficial roundness to the fruits, as they continue to develop and lighten, the relatively lean structure of Cabernet Sauvignon shows through. Quality in 1996 shows itself in better defined structure going up the hierarchy. With the 2009s, the effect is more an increase in the concentration of youthful fruits as you ascend the scale. Potensac should be drunk now, Clos du Marquis could be started now, and even Léoville Lascases itself is quite approachable. In Potensac and Clos du Marquis, the structure isn't really much in evidence: what you sense most is the ripeness of the fruits. Léoville Lascases is a great wine in the tradition of St. Julien, with elegance and finesse, and a most refined structure. What is most responsible for the change from 1996, I think, is the increased ripeness of Cabernet Sauvignon, not so much in the extra fruit density, but more in the increased maturity and ripeness of the tannins, replacing those formerly tight or even harsh tannic edges with roundness and elegance. Indeed these wines are a tribute to the fact that Cabernet Sauvignon has become ripe rather than herbaceous.

Bordeaux has long been famous for its capacity to age. Indeed, for much of the twentieth century the mantra was that the wines would reveal their quality only with significant age: they could not be appreciated young. I suspect this idea may have originated as a marketing ploy to sell the wines in the first half of the century; they were certainly quite horrid when young as the result of a run of poor vintages. Things are quite different now. "1982 was the year of transition. Before then only very ripe vintages would be able to mature. One problem was that we used to harvest too early. Now we are achieving better maturity, more vintages will age well, and they will last just as long," says Didier Cuvelier at Château Léoville Poyferré. Today's concern about tannic structure has made Bordeaux far more approachable when young; it's a fair comment that many vintages now will age better than would have been possible previously, but the great unanswered question is whether the wines of great vintages will age as long, and as gracefully, as those of the past.

Aging has not been a similar issue with Napa, as the wines have generally been ready to drink sooner, but the best wines do show significant aging potential. My first experience with California Cabernets was when I purchased cases of the Napa and Sonoma 1974 and 1978 vintages in the late seventies. I was generally disappointed: few of the wines aged well beyond five years, and none lasted a full decade. (These were the wines of new producers who were making a stir at the time, such as Sterling, Jordan, Chateau St. Jean, and I might have done better to have tried more established wines such as Heitz Martha's Vineyard or Ridge Monte Bello.) The wines I laid down did not show a graceful conversion to a savory spectrum, but lost their fruits to reveal a slight residual sweetness or sparse tannic structure. But perhaps this was not a fair experiment given the young age of vines and producers at this point. Since then I have had mixed experiences: some wines have aged brilliantly, such as 1985 Chateau Montelena and Caymus Special Selection, showing well early in 2012; others from the mid nineties have shown the same sort of collapse I experienced in wines from the seventies.

By way of pushing this comparison to the limits, I recently compared wines from the classic 1970 vintage in Bordeaux with Cabernet Sauvignons from the 1974 vintage in California, really the first vintage that put California on the map as a potential competitor to Bordeaux (☐ page 372). The two top wines in the tasting absolutely typify the character and quality of Bordeaux versus California. The Pichon Lalande had that delicious balance of fruits and herbaceousness; as it gets older it turns more savory. The Mount Eden Cabernet Sauvignon (coming from an old plot of ungrafted wines on Santa Cruz Mountain) has that warm impression of sweet, ripe red fruits; age has brought a faint impression of piquancy that adds complexity. Ultimately it will become sweeter and simpler.

The Californian wines are aging well, but they are staying ripe and sweet and warm, and showing impressions of red fruits rather than becoming savory. The best are absolutely delicious, but it's not obvious what further evolution will occur if they are kept longer. To what extent is this because most are 100% Cabernet Sauvignon or simply a consequence of the warmer climate? The Californian wines that made great reputations in their day remain the leaders. Heitz Martha's Vineyard has lost some of its density, and its style is less evidently European. Ridge Montebello shows more evident savory notes. Diamond Creek Volcanic Hill is every drop a mountain Cabernet, just a touch behind the Mayacamas (from Mount Veeder).

Bordeaux was more surprising with some reversals of reputation. From Margaux, Châteaux Giscours and Brane Cantenac, generally considered to be slightly rustic and overcropped in the era, showed better than more classic wines from Pauillac or St. Julien. The issue with the Bordeaux as they age is just how savory you like your wine, as ultimately they can turn herbaceous and medicinal. On this showing, typical or not, the best showed more complexity than California, but usually were less delicious. The difference is not so much that Californian Cabernet doesn't age so well as Bordeaux, as that it ages differently.

I've often been tempted to join the lament that Bordeaux is losing its way, that it has succumbed to an international style emphasizing fruit rather than savory character. Part of my concern was alleviated when I discovered that the 1982s—so rich and lush and un-Bordeaux like when first released—are now reverting to a more classic flavor spectrum. If 2000 and 2005 do the same, I shall be very happy. And it is hard to characterize vintages such as 2001, 2004, or 2006 as overly international. So it comes down to how 2009 and 2010, with their intense extraction and high alcohol, will perform as they age in bottle. I admit I find it hard to see how a wine at over 14% alcohol can mature like classic Bordeaux, but there have been surprises before.

No one in Bordeaux seems to regret the passing of the old style although no one admits to choosing to change their style. Some attitudes never change. Notwithstanding the modernization of recent years, Bordeaux's reputation for resistance to change (or at least for admitting its existence) is well deserved. In an interview with the Director at one chateau, I tried to establish how the changes as seen from the outside are viewed within Bordeaux. I asked whether they were worried about the rising levels of alcohol? "No, not at all. Cabernet Sauvignon is a low alcohol variety, when it ripens it's never very high. We don't have that problem." Do you have a problem with Merlot becoming overripe in the warm years? "Not at all, quite the contrary. Our terroir keeps the Merlot fresh." Have the differences between communes narrowed with riper vintages? "No they have stayed the same." Has Bordeaux deserted its old markets with the recent price increases? "No, not at all, we are still in every major market."

As Cabernet Sauvignon became increasingly popular worldwide, prices have increased steadily, more or less doubling every decade in both Bordeaux and Napa. Bordeaux prices are certainly more subject to vintage fluctuation. Partly this may be because there are more climatic swings in Bordeaux, but it is also a consequence of the en primeur system. Whereas most Napa wines become available on the market only after they are in bottle, most Bordeaux wines are sold in an en primeur campaign during April to June after the vintage. Consumers have no direct exposure to the wines: they have to rely on reports from critics who have tasted barrel samples. This exacerbates price variation: in a good vintage it creates demand that pushes up prices, but in a poor vintage, fewer people can see the point in buying the wines two years before they are bottled.[34] In good vintages, en primeur prices can seem a (relative) bargain, but when Bordeaux has a run of poor vintages, such as 1991-1994, prices dip en primeur, and sometimes fall further on the secondary market. Napa shows less direct variation with vintage and more dependence on the general economy. Dramatic price changes in Bordeaux in 2005 and then again in 2009 and 2010 may have decoupled the old relationship, in which the average price of Bordeaux ran about a third above Napa,[35] since Bordeaux's recent sharp increase (partly driven by demand from Asia) was accompanied by a decline in prices in Napa (caused by troubles with the domestic economy).

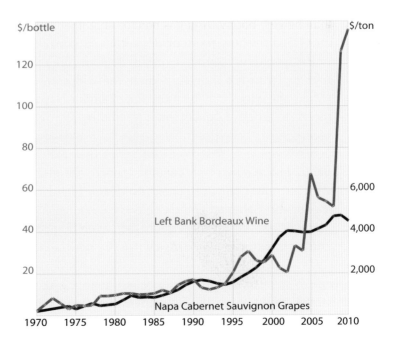

Prices for Bordeaux and Napa have increased more or less in parallel, although Bordeaux shows more fluctuation with vintage.[33]

Looking back, Napa's attempt to rival the style of Bordeaux may have peaked in 1985: the best 1985 Cabernets of Napa would stand up well against the best Bordeaux of that vintage, or perhaps if you wanted to place things on a really equal footing, against Bordeaux 1982. As they have evolved from the lushness of the first twenty years, the 1982 Bordeaux now have a faintly herbaceous tinge to provide a delicious counterpoise to the opulent fruits. The best 1985 Napa Cabernets still show ripe, rich fruits, fuller on the palate than Bordeaux, but often balanced against a very faint herbaceousness. That speaks to the imperatives of vinification at the time. Perhaps no wine better epitomizes the closeness of the challenge than Phelps Eisele (⍦ page 378). The opening bouquet is a delicious dead ringer for old Bordeaux, but then the palate offers a richness that Bordeaux did not achieve for another decade. The ripe fruits are cut by a faintly medicinal impression of leather and tar: this is a faint touch of Brett (the aroma of Bordeaux of the sixties and seventies, a cynic might say).[36] This would never be permitted today in Napa (and perhaps not in Bordeaux either). I will concede that a touch of Brett might make the wines seem more similar, but the whole balance of ripe fruits, moderate alcohol, and the structured quality of Cabernet brings the Eisele remarkably close to the aims of Bordeaux in the following decade. Of course, since then, Napa has followed another path, towards even greater ripeness, more fruit and alcohol, and generally more extraction. Perhaps that is why 1985 remains my favorite Napa vintage, just as 1982 Bordeaux would be my choice for drinking today.

Even though recent years have brought some convergence as Bordeaux has followed Napa into a richer, more extracted style, I'm not sure they are really alternatives: Bordeaux still tends to be lighter with refreshing uplift at the end, and Napa to show more obvious fruits. Bordeaux still defines the elegant end of the spectrum: moving into other regions, the Bordeaux blend remains dominant in Tuscany's Bolgheri (where the wines are more aromatic), in Australia (where the wines may be more forceful than Napa), and in South Africa (which reverts to a herbal quality more resembling Bordeaux). The historical Bordeaux blends have been resurrected in Chile and Argentina, where the ability to achieve ripeness has produced wines that would have been envied in Bordeaux in the nineteenth century. Indeed, the global pursuit of ripeness means we can now compare classic Bordeaux blends of Cabernet Sauvignon with Merlot and Cabernet Franc to blends at equivalent ripeness with Carmenère or Malbec. The big question is whether, even if each region is well adjusted to its current blend, climate change will force new blends.

6

Mediterranean Blends

CABERNET SAUVIGNON was a latecomer to the Mediterranean. The Romans brought the first vines to the area around Marseilles. Suited to the warm climate, these varieties would not ripen in Bordeaux, where the development of cooler climate cultivars started later, perhaps with an ancestor of Cabernet Franc. In due course this led to Cabernet Sauvignon. Recognized as a variety of exceptional quality by the nineteenth century, Cabernet Sauvignon slowly migrated to the Mediterranean basin. Its presence is recorded across Languedoc and Provence in a survey during the 1860s by the great ampelographer Jules Guyot, although it was never more than one of many varieties grown in the area. As the region came to focus on mass production of cheap wines, Cabernet became inappropriate, and disappeared almost completely.

Today Cabernet Sauvignon has once again become an important grape in the Languedoc, France's southernmost wine region. With a third of the country's Cabernet Sauvignon, Languedoc is now second only to Bordeaux. With perhaps typical disdain, the Bordelais are dismissive of Cabernet production

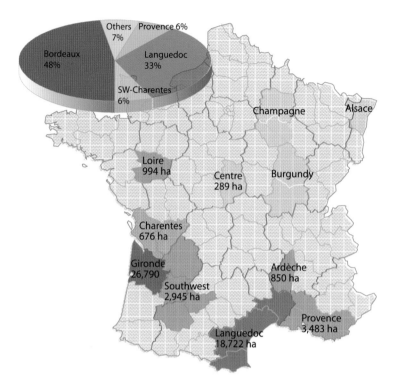

Cabernet Sauvignon in France is concentrated in Bordeaux and the Languedoc.[2]

elsewhere in France. "It's a big mistake," the Directeur at one second growth blurted out when I asked what he thought about growing Cabernet in the Languedoc. "There isn't any Cabernet in Languedoc," one senior figure on the Bordeaux wine scene said, when I mentioned that I was visiting Cabernet producers there.

Whereas Bordeaux is subject to the cooling influence of the Atlantic, the Languedoc offers a warm Mediterranean climate. Atlantic influence is supposed to extend to the western edge of the Languedoc, where in the vicinity of Carcassonne, the small AOCs of Cabardès, Malepère, and Limoux allow some Cabernet Sauvignon and other Atlantic varieties to be included in the blend.[1] Otherwise, Cabernet Sauvignon is not permitted in the various AOCs of the region, which INAO has insisted on keeping focused on traditional southern varieties, Syrah, Mourvèdre, and Grenache being the best of them.

The rise of Cabernet Sauvignon in the Languedoc is a relatively recent development: there was no Cabernet Sauvignon to speak of in the region in the 1970s. There's more than an element of bucking the system here, because Cabernet's exclusion from the AOCs means that it is confined to the nominally lower level of Vin de Pays. (This is also true of Provence.) One can only speculate on how much more Cabernet Sauvignon there might be in Languedoc and Provence if it were allowed in the AOCs. (This of course is one of the reasons why INAO is excluding it!) Indeed, some Cabernets are labeled simply as table

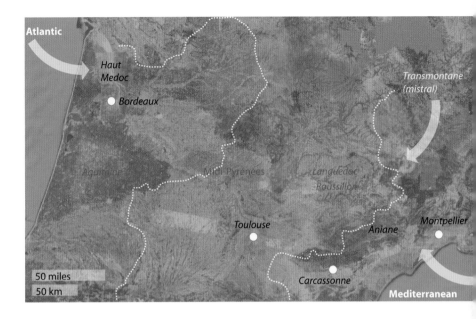

It is only 250 miles from Bordeaux to the Languedoc, but the climate changes from Atlantic to Mediterranean influence.

wine under the generic description of Vin de France, because producers have found even the regulations of the Vin de Pays (or IGP as it has now become) to be too restrictive on the proportions of cépages they want to blend.

Investigating how the typicity of Cabernet is represented in the Languedoc, I could find only a handful of producers making distinguished wines. Traveling from Bordeaux through the Languedoc to Provence, I first encountered the best known example of Cabernet Sauvignon in France outside Bordeaux: Mas de Daumas Gassac (near Montpellier). Then farther east near Saint-Rémy-de-Provence, I came to Domaine de Trévallon, where Cabernet Sauvignon is blended in equal proportions with Syrah. Along the way, I encountered a series of variations on Cabernet Sauvignon, ranging from monovarietal wines, blends with Bordeaux varieties where the Cabernet varied from a minority to a majority, and blends in various proportions with non-Bordeaux varieties ranging from Syrah to Grenache. There were also some interesting blends where Petit Verdot (never more than a very minor element in Bordeaux) became a major component.

I started my tour at Finca Narraza in Roussillon, just north of the Pyrenees not far from Perpignan, where Corinne and Gérard le Jan have a twenty year old vineyard of Cabernet Sauvignon. Interestingly, there's just as much vintage variation here as in Bordeaux. Cabernet does well when the climate is Atlantic, but can be difficult to handle when it rains and the wind comes from the mountains, or when the weather is too hot and it ripens too quickly. The main cuvée is an equal blend of Cabernet and Syrah, and it's fair to say the wine shows more the aromatic influence of the south than of Bordeaux.

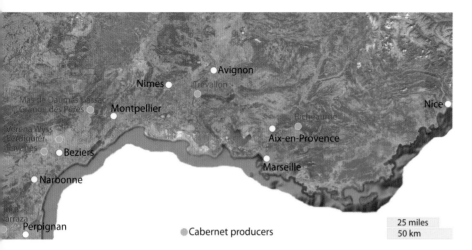

Interesting Cabernet producers are few and far between, but extend from the western edge of Languedoc (west of Perpignan) into Provence (to the east of Aix-en-Provence).

●Cabernet producers

25 miles
50 km

An interesting opportunity to see what a Bordeaux blend achieves in this region came from Verena Wyss, near Pezenas (￼ page 358). In the Belcanto cuvée, the structure of the Cabernet comes through quite clearly, but the aromatics are more those of the south, fruity and perfumed, than in the more savory tradition of Bordeaux. "There is no problem ripening here; it is warmer and drier than Bordeaux. The training system needs to protect the fruit against excess heat, the opposite of tradition in Bordeaux where it needs to ensure good sun exposure. The problem here is not getting good maturity, it is avoiding over-maturity; the only answer is to harvest when the grapes are ready and not wait too long," says Verena.

Another insight came from the ability of Petit Verdot to ripen reliably in this climate, which enables Verena to produce the La Tonga blend of 60% Cabernet to 40% Petit Verdot. Here I felt that the spiciness of Petit Verdot dominated the palate, making an attractive young wine, but I wondered whether it would age well. I received a partial answer when I visited Marc Benin at the Domaine de Ravanès, just a little farther west, where there is both a 100% Petit Verdot and a 50:50 blend of Petit Verdot with Merlot. "I don't want to make a Bordeaux, I want to make a wine of the Languedoc, but with the Bordelais varieties. Here the Petit Verdot achieves the same maturity as the Cabernet Sauvignon and gives an interesting, structured wine," Marc told me (￼ page 355). Tasting these wines from 2002 and 2000 showed that Petit Verdot really matures very slowly indeed: I was left uncertain whether it would ultimately develop the same interest with age as Cabernet Sauvignon.

But a vertical tasting of monovarietal Cabernet Sauvignon from 2007 back to 1995 showed some difficulty in getting a complete structural balance. The youngest vintage showed nicely concentrated fruits, but still had a good way to go to maturity. "The Cabernet can be too strong. It's not ready to drink straight away, you need to wait 3-4 years to sell it, this is a marketing problem," Marc said, explaining why he now blends the Cabernet with Merlot. Older vintages showed nice development, much along the lines of traditional Bordeaux, with savory and even herbaceous elements coming out. I was left with the impression that, just as in Bordeaux itself, blending produces a more complete and complex wine. A similar classic impression came from the Cabernet-Merlot blends at Domaine de Perdiguier, close by, where I revisited the question of the typicity of Cabernet Sauvignon in the south (⟲ page 354). These wines sufficiently resembled Bordeaux AOC to provoke me into realizing that by now I had made the transition into looking for something different in the south.

The pioneer for Cabernet Sauvignon in the Languedoc is Mas de Daumas Gassac, where winemaking began as the result of an accidental encounter. Aimé Guibert had bought a house and land at Aniane, near Montpellier, as a country residence. The family was considering what sort of agricultural use they might find for the land when a family friend, the famous geographer Henri Enjalbert, remarked during a visit that the terroir reminded him of Burgundy's Côte d'Or and would make a remarkable vineyard. The Guiberts were not much impressed with the local grape varieties. They did not feel that the climate was right for Pinot Noir, and as Bordeaux drinkers they naturally gravitated towards Cabernet Sauvignon. Emile Peynaud, the doyen of Bordeaux oenologists, became an advisor, and a Cabernet-based blend was created.

The blend has changed over the years, but has generally consisted of around 80% Cabernet Sauvignon with the remainder coming from a wide range of varieties, some Bordelais, others more exotic: initially they were mostly Malbec, Tannat, Merlot, and Syrah; by 1990 they were described as Cabernet Franc, Syrah and Merlot; and today the label just says "several other varieties." One reason for adjusting the blend may have been to calm down the tannins, as some criticism had been expressed of rustic tannins, and current winemaker Samuel Guibert says freely that the wines could be tough and tight for the first few years. In the mid nineties, there started to be more elegance and finesse in the young wines, he says, probably as a result of increasing vine age.

Daumas Gassac is not looking for the modern jammy fruity style. "We belong more to the Bordeaux 1961 attitude—wine with 12.5% alcohol and good acidity. Only 15% new oak is used to get finesse. We don't make a Cabernet wine; we make Daumas Gassac. The wine is no more typical of Bordeaux than it is of Languedoc," says Samuel Guibert. "The influence of Bordeaux comes from the fact the knowledge comes from Bordeaux, which unfortunately now is in the hands of banks and insurance companies. We live and breath what we make here, they are owners, we are artisans," Samuel told me. When I asked whether he felt that Bordeaux had deserted its heritage, Samuel laughed and said, "I'm not going to fall into that trap." But clearly they feel at Daumas Gassac that they are perpetuating old traditions of winemaking and style.

*The soil at Mas de
Daumas Gassac is red
and rocky.*

*Photograph courtesy
Mas de Daumas Gassac.*

The avowed intention is to produce a "grand cru" of the Languedoc, but these are not always obvious wines to characterize in the context of Cabernet Sauvignon. Perhaps the character of the wine depends on whether Atlantic or Mediterranean influences predominate during the vintage. I find something of a split, with some vintages tending more towards the savory, which I see as Atlantic influence, while others are softer and less obviously structured, which is more what you might expect of the Mediterranean. The differences for me really came out with age, and were typified by the 1982 and 1983 vintages, the former tending more towards classic savory characteristics of Bordeaux, the latter more towards the soft, perfumed quality of the south (Υ page 352). Cabernet is more obvious in the Atlantic vintages; it can be more difficult to perceive in some Mediterranean vintages And aging potential can be deceptive. I felt that some recent vintages, such as 2005 or 2001 would have only a

Vineyards at Mas de Daumas Gassac are individual parcels surrounded by woods and trees to keep the environment as natural as possible.

Photograph courtesy Mas de Daumas Gassac.

few years' potential longevity, but then I came to the 1988 which is still going strong. Today's wines may more elegant, with notes of the garrigue cutting the black fruits of the palate, but perhaps they are not so long lived as those from the eighties.

At Daumas Gassac they tried the traditional local varieties of Carignan, Grenache, and Syrah for a while, but eventually pulled them out because it was felt they over produce and lack finesse in this terroir. Almost adjacent, however, is the Domaine de la Grange des Pères, where the attitude is almost the antithesis of Daumas Gassac, but the wines are equally interesting. Daumas Gassac today, albeit way off the beaten track, is a modern facility with a snazzy tasting room, and a constant trek of visitors. Laurent Vaillé established Grange des Pères soon after Daumas Gassac; his first vintage was 1982. Grange des Pères has a utilitarian appearance; it's not especially easy to make an appointment with Laurent who is nothing if not reticent, but the rendezvous, if successful, takes place in the working cave, where samples can be tasted from barriques. The wine is a blend of roughly equal proportions of Syrah and Mourvèdre with a minor component of 20% Cabernet Sauvignon. Minor, but essential. "The Cabernet Sauvignon is like salt in food. I do not want Cabernet Sauvignon to dominate my assemblage. Grange des Pères should have a southern character, but with freshness, and that's what the Cabernet Sauvignon brings," says Laurent.

The Cabernet is planted in the coolest spots, and is always the last variety to harvest. Syrah is planted quite close by, and ripens reliably to make a rich, deep component of the wine. The Mourvèdre is planted a few kilometers away on a hot, south-facing terroir. Tasting barrel samples, you can see what each variety brings to the blend. All are rich and powerful with a good level of tannins, the Syrah full of rich, deep black fruits, the Mourvèdre distinctly spicy, and the Cabernet herbal and fresh. It's not so much the acidity of the Cabernet as such, but the tightness of its structure that freshens the blend (⊤ page 350). Without it, the wine would have more of that jammy fruit character of warm climates. So here the Cabernet in effect is playing a moderating role on the forceful fruit character of the other varieties: almost exactly the opposite of the role it plays elsewhere as a "cépage ameliorateur" in strengthening weak varieties. The wines can be quite aromatic when young, but have long aging potential; the 1994 seemed at the midpoint of its development in 2012 and should be good at least for another decade.

The pioneer for blending Cabernet Sauvignon with Syrah was Eloi Dürrbach, who planted the vineyards at Domaine de Trévallon, near Saint-Rémy-de-Provence, just south of Avignon, in 1973. Vineyards were blasted out of the calcareous rocks, and the first vintage was harvested in 1976. Cabernet Sauvignon and Syrah were planted in the belief that historically a blend of the two had made excellent wine in Provence before phylloxera struck at the end of the nineteenth century. I am unable to substantiate this idea, but if it was a misunderstanding, it was a happy one.[3] At all events, Eloi Dürrbach should take full credit for introducing the idea in modern times.

In the (relatively) cool microclimate at Trévallon, the two cépages play the traditional complementary roles: Cabernet Sauvignon can be austere, but Syrah softens it (without acquiring the jammy notes of the southern Rhône). The wine started out as an appellation contrôlée, in the Coteaux des Baux en Provence, but in 1993 the rules for red wine in the appellation were defined to exclude more than 20% of Cabernet Sauvignon on the grounds that it would not be "typical." (Typical of what, one might ask: poor quality?) INAO demanded that Cabernet Sauvignon should be reduced and Grenache should be included. As this was not acceptable, Trévallon became a Vin de Pays des Bouches du Rhône (yet another example of the authorities undermining the AOC by excluding its best wine).

Barrel samples of the two varieties before assemblage (which takes place just before bottling) show more similarities than differences: both cépages display dense black fruits with good tannic support; the Syrah is just a touch more aromatic and the Cabernet just a touch sterner. The interesting comparison is with a pre-assemblage blend, made because there wasn't enough of either separate cépage to fill another foudre. The increase of complexity is obvious, combining roundness with precision, sternness with aromatics. Usually the Syrah is a little more evident as an influence than the Cabernet, says Antoine Dürrbach, but it varies from year to year. There is no attempt here at instant

The vineyards at Trévallon are covered with stones that remained after the rocks were dynamited and bulldozed to create the vineyards.

gratification: usually the wine does not open up for ten years, he told me, but then it will last another decade (Y page 357). Indeed, the 2001 vintage was just beginning to open up in October 2011. As the wine ages, it tends to show its Syrah element more strongly, and Cabernet recedes. It's hard to characterize the wine in terms of other regions—it's been variously taken for Bordeaux or Hermitage according to circumstance, says Antoine—but I would be inclined to say that it has something of the aromatics of the south combined with the texture of Bordeaux. The whole is certainly greater than you might expect from the sum of the parts tasting the individual varieties. Whether or not a Cabernet-Syrah blend was a top wine in the nineteenth century, it's certainly one now.

My next stop to investigate blends of Cabernet with southern varieties was at Domaine Richeaume, farther east in Provence, located just underneath Mont Sainte Victoire. The backdrop to the vineyards could be a painting by Cézanne. There's a small production of monovarietal Cabernet Sauvignon, and blends of Cabernet Sauvignon with either Syrah or Grenache (Y page 356). The Cabernet gives the impression that seems to prevail all the way from Bordeaux to Provence: more precision and elegance than the other varieties or even than the blends, but less complete, not quite filling in entirely on the mid palate. Syrah by itself goes the other way: lovely aromatics to the fore, but not very fine-grained. The Cabernet-Syrah blend, Columelle, is a good compromise: Syrah aromatics with that structure of Cabernet underneath. I wasn't quite sure with the Cabernet-Grenache blend, oddly called Tradition, whether Grenache was filling in the fleshiness the Cabernet lacks by itself, or whether the Caber-

Ferrous oxide makes the soil red at Domaine Richeaume, close to Mont Sainte Victoire.

net was giving structure to an amorphous Grenache, but it did not seem to me that the marriage was as complementary as Cabernet and Merlot.

There are certainly interesting wines, based on Cabernet Sauvignon or containing a significant proportion of it, in Languedoc and Provence. They are not a challenge to Bordeaux, not because they are necessarily inferior, but because their overall flavor spectrum is different: whether the Cabernet is a monovarietal, blended with Bordeaux varieties, or blended with other varieties, it takes on at least a partial tinge of the aromatics of the south. None of the top wines are appellation contrôlée, as they are considered more typical of themselves than the prevailing standard. And they have not been imitated to any significant extent by others. So they create no halo effect to lift up the region. And in terms of the total production of Cabernet Sauvignon in Languedoc and Provence, my attempts to identify wines of character might account perhaps for a couple of hundred of the twenty thousand hectares. What are they doing with the rest?

With more than half the vineyard area of Cabernet Sauvignon compared to Bordeaux, but with higher yields, the Languedoc has the potential to produce almost as much Cabernet Sauvignon as Bordeaux.[4] So where on earth does all this Cabernet go? The pattern of production is very different from Bordeaux. The vast majority of Cabernet Sauvignon in the Languedoc goes into big brands, sold under the Vin de Pays d'Oc (or now IGP d'Oc) at price levels that are roughly comparable to AOC Bordeaux. Some of it is blended, but not necessarily with the same varieties as in Bordeaux. The majority may actually go into varietal-labeled wine; in fact, the Languedoc is France's largest source for varietal-labeled Cabernet Sauvignon, and if you want a European wine labeled as Cabernet Sauvignon, this is where you will find it. (The authorities would not release any official figures for production of Cabernet Sauvignon in the Vin de Pays of the Languedoc, but I calculate there must be around 10 million cases of Cabernet Sauvignon or wines based on Cabernet. This compares with a total production for generic AOC Bordeaux of around 25 million cases, most of which has Cabernet Sauvignon only as a minor component.) What does this do for the reputation of the variety in France?

Should the Bordelais be quite so disdainful of the varietal-labeled brands under the Vin de Pays labels? Given the inroads that have been made into the market at the level of Bordeaux AOC by varietal-labeled New World wines, isn't the Languedoc a more insidious threat since it combines the mystique of being French with the varietal labeling that appeals at this level of the market, and a more forward, fruit-driven style? Well that depends to some extent what you expect of Cabernet Sauvignon and what you expect of the Languedoc.

"I expect sunshine in a glass, from Languedoc wines, Cabernet Sauvignon or Merlot can be too plump," says Rosemary George, who wrote the definitive book on the wines of the region. If you are looking for a typical wine of the south, Cabernet may not be the best variety to bring out that southern warmth. By contrast, if you are looking for those faintly austere notes of traditional Bordeaux, the Languedoc may not be the right place to bring out typicity. But if you are simply looking for a reliable drink at modest price, and have no particular expectation of typicity of place or variety, will Cabernet fit the bill better than the traditional varieties?

To compare the attractions of Bordeaux AOC and varietal-labeled Cabernet Sauvignon, I held a tasting with two criteria: the wine should come in a bottle; but it should cost less than $15 (£10). There was no difficulty finding wines from the Languedoc, but it is relatively difficult to find Bordeaux based on Cabernet Sauvignon at this price level: most are based on Merlot. Although the Cabernets from the Languedoc are monovarietals or close to it, they tasted surprisingly like the blends of Bordeaux, which had from 65% to 20% Cabernet Sauvignon. My general impression was of the similarity of the wines from both regions: there's a convergence of style on soft, supple fruits with an impression almost of sweetness on the palate, reinforced by a touch of high toned aromatics suggesting black cherries or plums. Fruit concentration is usually a bit lacking, and yields appear to be on the high side. If there is indeed a common objective, the warmer climate of the Languedoc gives it an advantage. If there's any consistent difference between the regions, it's that there's a tendency to greater aromatics in Languedoc and to more tannic dryness in Bordeaux. The lower yield limits of the AOC did not seem to give Bordeaux any advantage in concentration over the more relaxed attitude of the Vin de Pays of the Langue-doc. In fact, the main difference between the two sets of wines was price, with Languedoc offering a significant advantage. It was a rare wine in this tasting that showed typicity of Cabernet, in the sense of any character extending be-yond the simple, direct, slightly aromatic fruits, but where I could find typicity, the wines were just as likely to come from Languedoc as Bordeaux. The moral is that it's hard at this level if you expect Cabernet Sauvignon to be more than a marketing term on the label.

Going east from the Mediterranean across to the Black Sea, it seemed at one time as though Bulgaria might become the source for inexpensive Cabernet Sauvignon in Europe. Wine has been produced in Bulgaria for centuries, virtu-ally across the entire country. At the start of the twenty first century, there were around 120,000 ha of vineyards (about the same as the total in Bordeaux), with Cabernet Sauvignon as the most important variety (about 15% of plantings).[5] During the 1980s, an emphasis on international varieties led to some success in exports, with Bulgarian Cabernet Sauvignon at around £3 ($5) becoming common on the British market. Following the collapse of communism, the in-dustry was thrown into disarray, and sales fell sharply from their peak in 1995. Winemaking has not managed to break out of the straitjacket of the lowest lev-els, and it's difficult today to find Bulgarian Cabernet that would cast light on the typicity of the variety.

Across the Mediterranean from France, the wheel has come full circle. The Romans carried vines from the coast of Italy to the coast of France. Now the compliment has been repaid, with Bordeaux varieties firmly rooted on the coast of Tuscany. Perhaps it is ironic that within France itself, there is decreas-ing use of Bordeaux varieties going east along the Mediterranean; but the Tuscan coast takes its model mostly from Bordeaux. The left bank is the inspira-tion: about two thirds of the wines are Cabernet Sauvignon blended with Merlot and Cabernet Franc, although there are some wines based on Merlot. There's also experimentation in blending Cabernet with Syrah and other varie-ties. Called the super-Tuscans, the description of these wines reflects their origins outside of the traditional system. They have spread from the coast across Tuscany, although when you go inland to the Chianti region, blends of Cabernet Sauvignon with Sangiovese become equally common. Indeed, Cab-ernet-Sangiovese blends run the full gamut from wines where a little Sangiovese has been added to freshen the Cabernet, to Chiantis where a little Cabernet has been added to beef up the Sangiovese.

Cabernet Sauvignon is not entirely a newcomer to Tuscany. Some produc-ers are quick to tell you that Cabernet Sauvignon has been grown in Tuscany for several hundred years, so its presence is not quite such a culture clash as you might imagine. While there's an element of truth in this, and Cabernet Sauvignon was certainly grown in Tuscany in the nineteenth century, it was

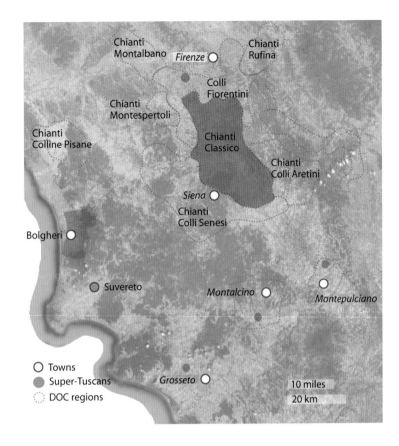

Super-Tuscans are concentrated in the areas of Bolgheri and Chianti Classico.

Bolgheri and the Chianti Classico area each have around 70 super-Tuscan wines, and there are about 50 in outlying areas.

always regarded as a foreign variety, and the focus was on using it to improve indigenous varieties rather than making a separate wine. A survey of foreign grape varieties growing in Italy in 1903 said, "Even the best Tuscan wines improve notably if Cabernet is added in small quantities. Especially worthy of note are the results obtained by blending Cabernet with Sangiovese."[6] Moving to make it the dominant variety raises the question of how this reflects Tuscan terroir. In charge of winemaking at Antinori, Renzo Cotarella says, "I have my idea of the super-Tuscans. I think a wine should be considered a super-Tuscan (only) if it is a Sangiovese blend because Sangiovese is the representative of Tuscany."

Super-Tuscans can come from anywhere in Tuscany, but most come either from the coastal region of Bolgheri or from the Chianti region. In the seventeenth century, the area around Bolgheri was under the control of the Gherardesca Counts, who encouraged agriculture, including planting vineyards.[7] In fact, several of today's leading wines in Bolgheri come from parts of what was originally the Gherardesca's huge estate, occupying the entire north of the area. The estate was divided in the mid twentieth century. Clarice della Gherardesca inherited half the estate and married Marquis Mario Incisa. This was the area that became Tenuta San Guido, including a tract of land called

Sassicaia (meaning place of the rocks). Her sister, Carlotta, married Marquis Nicolò Antinori, from the Florentine family that had become a major wine producer. Their property became the Guado al Tasso estate, in due course part of Antinori's Florentine Empire. The Ornellaia estate occupies part of the original holdings that Carlotta gave to her son, Lodovico Antinori. Bolgheri Castle and the surrounding farm and vineyards remained in the direct hands of the Countess of Gherardesca.

The traditional wines of Tuscany are based on the Sangiovese grape, usually blended with other local varieties.[8] Most production is in the various Chianti appellations between Florence and Sienna. (Chianti itself must be more than 80% Sangiovese; inclusion of a minor part of Cabernet Sauvignon has been legal since 1996.) Wine has actually been produced in the coastal area around Bolgheri since the seventeenth century, but was of little consequence, quantity rather than quality being the primary driving force. Produced from Sangiovese or Trebbiano, the wines were reds, whites, and rosés of no particular distinction. No one ever thought the area had the potential to produce fine wine until the first super-Tuscan, Sassicaia, from the San Guido estate, became available in the early seventies. It's impossible to over estimate the importance of Sassicaia in creating the super-Tuscans: its success was like a shock wave that still resonates. All over Tuscany—not just around Bolgheri—producers took Sassicaia's success as a signal that they were not restricted to indigenous varieties, and that Cabernet Sauvignon might be the basis for a successful wine representing their terroir.

The origin of Sassicaia actually goes back to soon after the Marquis Incisa's acquisition of the Tenuta San Guido estate. Occupying 650 ha, it extended from Castiglioncello in the hills, where a vineyard had been planted in the nineteenth century, up to the coast. Trying to imitate Bordeaux, in 1944 the Marquis planted a hectare each of Cabernet Sauvignon and Cabernet Franc in the area of the historic Castiglioncello vineyard.[9] Elevated and facing east, the initial site was chosen because it was a myth at the time that exposure to winds from the sea would bring bad weather and poor wine, says current winemaker Sebastiano Rosso. The vineyard remained more or less experimental, with the wine consumed only in the family, but in 1965 the plantings were extended to new vineyards closer to the sea, slightly less elevated (at 100 m above sea level compared to Castiglioncello's 350 m) and more exposed. The crucial step towards commercial introduction was the intervention of Marquis Incisa's cousin, the Marquis Antinori, who agreed in 1972 to start marketing the wine from the 1968 vintage.[10] There was no precedent in the modern Italian system for producing Cabernet Sauvignon in Tuscany, so the wine was sold only as Vino da Tavola. Sassicaia rapidly achieved legendary status as a rival to the top wines of Bordeaux. The 1985 is generally reckoned to have been one of the best wines produced in Italy. Sassicaia's style is elegant, with Cabernet Sauvignon

The Castiglioncello vineyard where Sassicaia started is a 2 ha clearing about 2 miles into the forest beyond Bolgheri, just below the castle of Castiglioncello, well inland from the area where most vineyards have since been developed.

Photograph courtesy Tenuta San Guido.

providing structure and Cabernet Franc bringing freshness, more left bank than right bank as it lacks the superficial fleshiness of Merlot (Ⲧ page 364).

With Sassicaia setting the paradigm for a Cabernet blend, others followed, often trying to establish their own variations on the mix of Bordeaux varieties. Immediately adjacent to Sassicaia, another part of the historic estate was used by Lodovico Antinori to create Tenuta Dell'Ornellaia in 1981 (now owned by Frescobaldi). Here the vineyards were planted with Cabernet Sauvignon and Merlot. The first vintage was harvested in 1985, and the winery was constructed in 1987. Among the vineyards are the seven hectares of the Masseto hill, where the clay is several meters deep, and the Merlot performed so well that it was diverted to a separate wine. As a result, Ornellaia itself actually did not contain much Merlot until the subsequent purchase and planting of another vineyard, at Bellaria a little to the south, which is more exposed to sea breezes (actually those breezes can be pretty windy sometimes). Merlot peaked at around a third of the blend, but more recently has been decreasing to make room for a little Cabernet Franc. A comparison of Cabernet Sauvignon barrel samples from Bellaria with the Ornellaia home vineyard alone gives lie to the old myth that it would not be possible to produce great wine in sites exposed to the sea breezes; the wine from the Ornellaia vineyard is better rounded, massive rather than precise at this stage, but the wine from Bellaria offers an extraordinary expression of pure, precise fruits (Ⲧ page 363). Ornellaia itself is certainly a "bigger" wine than Sassicaia, more prone to emphasis on fruit ex-

Bolgheri vineyards are on a plain running down to the sea. The climate is maritime.

pression, with a characteristic opulence emphasized by a drop in Cabernet Sauvignon over the years from more than three quarters to only about half.

Just after Sassicaia's appearance on the market, another branch of the super-Tuscans originated on one of Antinori's estates in Chianti. Tignanello was first produced in 1970, labeled as Chianti Classico Riserva Vigneto Tignanello; it was a traditional blend of 75% Sangiovese, 20% Canaiolo, and 5% of the white grapes Trebbiano and Malvasia. But in 1971 it contained more Sangiovese than was allowed in Chianti at the time, and was labeled as a Vino di Tavola. White grapes were no longer included from 1975. It has included Cabernet Sauvignon since 1978. Since 1982 it has been a blend of 85% Sangiovese, 10% Cabernet Sauvignon, and 5% Cabernet Franc. Antinori describes it as "the original super-Tuscan," and claims it was the first Sangiovese to be aged in barriques and blended with a nontraditional grape variety.

A Cabernet-based super-Tuscan, Solaia, is also produced at the Tignanello Estate, creating an interesting opportunity for direct comparison with Guado al Tasso, which is produced at the largest estate in Bolgheri, also under Antinori's ownership. The influence of sea and wind gives Bolgheri a maritime climate compared to the Continental climate in the Chianti area: it's consistently about 1 °C cooler at Bolgheri during the growing season.[11] Winemaker Marco Ferrarese at Guado al Tasso says, "The Cabernet in Solaia is more linear, stronger, like stainless steel. Cabernets from Bolgheri are more rounded, more generous." Attributing the thought to Guado al Tasso's Director, he adds, "Solaia is like Catherine Deneuve, and Guado al Tasso is like Sophia Loren." Is the difference due to terroir and climate or to grape varieties? Guado al Tasso started

Chianti vineyards are on hills and valleys with varying exposures. The climate is Continental.

in 1990 as a Cabernet Sauvignon and Merlot blend, with tiny amounts of Syrah; the Syrah was increased to around 10% in 1996; and then was replaced by Cabernet Franc in 2007. Solaia is a blend of three quarters Cabernet Sauvignon to almost one quarter Sangiovese, with a small touch of Cabernet Franc. But Marco sees terroir as more responsible. "Bolgheri has identity, with similar aromas and sweet tannins. It can be difficult to tell whether you have Cabernet or Merlot sometimes. So whatever gives the identity, it's not the variety." Guado al Tasso is a classic representation of Bolgheri today; the structure of Cabernet Sauvignon is evident, but there is a plush overlay. Tasting vintages from the very first to the most recent provides a fascinating insight into the evolution of Bolgheri (Υ page 361). At the start of the nineties, a blend of Cabernet Sauvignon with Merlot could achieve elegance; today the Merlot has been cut back and Cabernet Franc introduced to maintain the effect.

Super-Tuscans divide into those from new wine regions and those produced from nontraditional varieties in established regions. No one knew what to make of Sassicaia or Ornellaia or the other wines from Bolgheri, because they were completely outside the traditional classification system for both varieties and location. By contrast, Chianti Classico is historically the oldest region for producing wine in Tuscany. Tignanello was the first wine to buck the system, first by ignoring rules that reduced quality and then by introducing a foreign variety. Its success led other producers to follow, some concentrating on Sangiovese, but others following Bolgheri's lead into Bordeaux varieties. These super-Tuscans have been as successful as the wines from Bolgheri, but as they were excluded from the local system also had to be labeled as table wines.

When it became embarrassing that some of the most expensive wines in Italy were labeled only as table wines, a new category of IGT (Indicazione Geografica Tipica), roughly equivalent to Vin de Pays in France, was invented in 1992. This still remains the label for wines produced in the Chianti region that do not conform to the regulations for Chianti. (It continues to be used for some, including Tignanello, that could conform now that the rules for Chianti have been overhauled.) A new category of DOC, equivalent to AOC in France, was created in Bolgheri for its wines. In fact, Bolgheri has two levels of DOC; most producers use Bolgheri Superiore for their top wine, while Bolgheri DOC is used for lower level wines.[12] Most of Bolgheri's wines now bear one of these labels, although there are still a few labeled as IGT Toscana. But whether the official name is Bolgheri DOC or IGT Toscana, the wines continue to be known colloquially as super-Tuscans. Overall, more than a third of the super-Tuscans come from Bolgheri, more than a third from the Chianti region, and the rest from Maremma (south of Bolgheri) or Montalcino (south of Chianti).

The very idea of the IGT classification is to allow producers freedom to do as they wish, so the other side of the coin is a lack of stylistic coherence. "Tuscany is a large area with much variety. Given the wide variety of grapes that might be used, there is really no such thing as a super-Tuscan," says winemaker Axel Heinz at Ornellaia. "People ask me why there is no vintage chart for super-Tuscans," he says with some amusement. As an approximation, you might say that the wines of Bolgheri tend to a certain softness, perhaps plush rather than opulent, whereas those from the Chianti area tend to a certain freshness. This is partly due to climatic differences and partly due to the more common inclusion of Sangiovese in the Chianti area. Farther south in Maremma, the wines are richer and bigger, more overtly New World in style.

Today the majority of wines produced in Bolgheri are based on a Bordeaux blend;[13] about half of the super-Tuscans from the Chianti region are dominated by Cabernet Sauvignon, the other half by Sangiovese. In Bolgheri there is no history to guide expectations, but in the Chianti area, it's generally the same producers who make the best Chiantis who produce the most interesting super-Tuscans. Is this due to better skill or to better terroir? It seems that at least the super-Tuscan phenomenon has given them the chance to break out of the constraints of Chianti, especially the limitations on price imposed by its reputation. Most producers now regard their wines under the IGT Toscana label as their flagships, with Chianti Classico DOCG playing a distinct second fiddle in terms of reputation. Certainly, the super-Tuscans produced in the Chianti area generally sell for significantly higher prices than traditional Chianti.

The Bolgheri DOC runs from the hills at the east to the main road adjacent to the coast. It extends from just south of Bibbona, past the town of Bolgheri itself, to the south of Castegneto Carducci. This is sometimes called the amphitheater of Bolgheri, because the area is a semi circle, bordered by the sea to the

The vineyards of Bolgheri extend from the hills, which lie about 4 miles inland, towards the coast.

west, and protected by the ring of hills to the east. The main area, in the northern third of the commune, with the town of Bolgheri at its eastern edge, is close to a monoculture of vines. Moving along to Castegneto Carducci, the vineyards are more widely dispersed. When you drive along the Strada del Vino, which runs parallel and close to the hills at the east, much of it passes through woods, and there are only occasional stretches with a series of wineries in succession. Overall about 20% of the total area of the DOC is given to vineyards (about 1,150 ha). The mix of black grape varieties is greatly reminiscent of the communes of the Haut Médoc: 49% Cabernet Sauvignon, 26% Merlot, 8% Cabernet Franc, and 7% Petit Verdot (the other varieties being Syrah and Sangiovese; there are also some plantings of white varieties). Although the rules admit a wide range of possibilities, and the wines can be based on Cabernet Sauvignon, Merlot, or Sangiovese, the emphasis in Bolgheri DOC is on left bank blends. But the Consorzio admits that, "This frame work does not offer the possibility of defining one single style for the wines of Bolgheri."[14]

The remarkable feature about Bolgheri's history is that the terroir of the original Castiglioncello vineyard where it all started is completely different from the terroir that is now generally associated with the DOC. Castiglioncello is well into the hills, but virtually all the vineyards of the DOC are on a plain that slopes gently down to the sea. It was more the Marquis Incisa's determination to produce fine wine, and continued experimentation with plantings, that created the environment for Bolgheri's success than any direct extension from the first vineyard.

What about the climate and terroir make Bolgheri suitable for Cabernet Sauvignon? The parallels with Bordeaux are only superficial. Both have mari-

Most of the coastal region from Bolgheri to Maremma originally consisted of swamps, the last of which were drained only in the 1930s ("the only good thing that came out of Fascism," one local producer commented).

time climates with relatively flat land much of which was drained from swamps. (The area of Maremma south of Bolgheri was considered a dangerous malarial swamp in Roman times.) The soils are quite stony to the east, but it's the Tuscan galestro (a mixture of schist and clay); there is more sand moving down towards the coast. Bolgheri is warmer than Bordeaux (by 1-2 °C on average). Contrary to the conventional wisdom at the time when Castiglioncello was planted, it is now thought that the best terroirs are on the plain at the foot of the hills between Bolgheri and Castegneto. Weather variations are less extreme in Bolgheri than Bordeaux; it is not usually a problem to ripen Cabernet Sauvignon, but (similar to Bordeaux), some vintages are getting too warm for Merlot. Sangiovese, the traditional grape of Tuscany, is not usually very successful here; it tends to be over productive. With more consistency across vintages, for the most part varietal composition does not change so widely each year as in Bordeaux.

How important is the terroir in Bolgheri? Crucial, according to Angelo Gaja, famous for his Barbarescos (and Barolos) in Piedmont, who established the Ca'Marcanda winery in 1996. "It was difficult when I came here because there was no historical record, all the new vineyards were planted in land that was not vineyards before. Although I am not a Burgundian, land is important for me, so I investigated. There was research done in 1987 to discover whether there was land similar to Sassicaia. They transferred the research to a big map. There was one copy, given to the town hall, and I asked to see it in 1993. No one had asked to see it before, and they had stored it, but no one knew where it was. I went there four times and finally they found it—it was a very large piece of paper, as big as this table (about six by two meters). It was like a harlequin with 11 colors, there was land with sand, land with rocks, etc. For me it was impossible to read, I asked a friend, a producer, to look at it with me. I asked him, what is the color of Sassicaia's land, he showed me the yellow, and there was yellow also at Ornellaia and Guado al Tasso. And this yellow here (I asked)—this is a very rich family, they could buy you many times (he said). But I called them and asked to talk with them. I visited 17 times, making many different proposals to rent the land, and my wife said, 'You are losing time, these are Ca'Marcanda people' (this means endless negotiations without ever signing a deal). But the eighteenth time their sister was with the two brothers, I had not met her before, she said that renting did not make sense, so why don't we sell it to Mr. Gaja?" Located more or less adjacent to Guado al Tasso, Ca'Marcanda has a variety of soils, including "white land," a calcareous terroir that is used for the Camarcanda cuvée, which has the highest content of Cabernet Sauvignon at 40%. Based on Merlot, the Ca'Marcanda wines are delicately balanced, with fruits typically turning savory after about five years (Ⴟ page 360).

The second most important grape variety in Bolgheri, Merlot is present in more than half the wines. Is the warming climate threatening this varietal composition? Angelo says that, "I have to admit and recognize that climate change is introducing some problems for Merlot. It has a tendency to increase the sugar level rapidly. It is Merlot that pushes the alcohol level up. Good diurnal variation in the Bolgheri terraces makes it possible to maintain good acidity but it requires patience. Merlot becomes very ripe. We must be very careful. We work with the Merlot, we harvest when it reaches 15% alcohol, but the wine overall is 14 or 14.5%." Everyone recognizes that the Masseto hill is an exception with its high clay content, and Axel Heinz of Ornellaia says, "Merlot can soak up water from the soil, that is probably the secret of Merlot at Masseto, and why it isn't jammy and over-ripe... It's always a problem to find the right site for Merlot. It has been popular in Tuscany because it is easy to manage, making wines of good quality, and is a good blending partner. That said, we are coming to realize that in some sites it is reaching its limits. It's in the warmer sites, especially to the south, where we have seen some difficulties. It's not any more a grape variety to put everywhere, you have to be more selective about sites. The tendency is for warm years to use less Merlot and more Cabernet Franc."

Bolgheri has been finding its identity over the past two decades, but the reference point remains Bordeaux, although more in the sense of using a Cabernet blend and making a wine of comparable quality than in directly emulating the style. "I think today we are in a situation where we want to express what is specific to this area. Even though we have more direct connections with Bordeaux, we try not to refer to Bordeaux in order to work on what is making our wines particular," says Axel Heinz, who also consults in St. Emilion. But he sees some convergence in recent vintages. "Some of the recent Bordeaux vintages have been much closer to what a Bolgheri Cabernet Sauvignon would be than people used to think," he says. "Bolgheri is a Mediterranean version of the Bordeaux climate. The 2010 is probably as close as you can get to Bordeaux."

The focus in Bolgheri is on varietal combinations resembling Bordeaux's left bank—typically about two thirds Cabernet Sauvignon, with Merlot as the second variety, and a small amount of Cabernet Franc—but the characteristic softness of the palate in some ways more resembles Bordeaux's right bank. I wonder whether this is what the right bank would produce in Bordeaux if it warmed up enough to ripen Cabernet Sauvignon reliably? "Bolgheri has a special combination of opulence, ripeness, and freshness. There's an almost exotic ripeness in the nose, but not explosive like young California Cabernet Sauvignon, there is a spiciness, a mintiness, and in the mouth there's sweetness, but compared to the other southern wines they always finish dry and fresh, that's the special feature of this place," says Axel.

The blend has a magical importance. "It's a Bordeaux blend but in the mind of the artisan I would like to make a wine that follows *our* ideas, that speaks the Tuscan language," says Angelo Gaja. At his neighbor Guado al Tasso, Marco Ferrarese says, "Our ambition is to make wine you can compare with Bordeaux. In the last twenty years Bolgheri has developed its identity and style. The blend is similar. The style is quite different. The wine is warmer with the character more oriented towards red fruit, the acidity is lower, the tannins are sweet and rich. So the wine is ready to drink at two years, but with good longevity. So we look at Bordeaux but we have our identity."

Everyone agrees that the character of Bolgheri shows a certain softness to the tannins. "We feel it in the grapes, we have softness in the tannins, there is always roundness in the mouth, this is the style of Bolgheri," says Fabio Motta of the Michele Satta winery, where their I Castagni single vineyard wine is a blend of Cabernet Sauvignon and Syrah with a little of the indigenous grape Teroldego (Ⓣ page 362). One driving force here is Michele's love of Syrah and wish to avoid too great a focus on international varieties. There is some skepticism about Merlot. "We planted Merlot at the beginning of our history, but I'm sure if Michele had the chance he wouldn't do it now. It can be too hot for Merlot. The cycle is very short for Merlot between véraison and harvest, with lots of sugar but few polyphenols developing. Masseto is the only exception, they have a different soil, like Pomerol," says Fabio.

Bolgheri's reputation for lushness can make it difficult for producers who strive for elegance, as in the experience at Batzella, one of the smallest producers in Bolgheri with only 8 ha. "We started looking at the blends in 2005, when the market was still focused on big, powerful wines. We made our blend, but our consultant warned us that the market wanted bigger wines," says winemaker Khanh Nguyen (Y page 359). But the market is changing. "Ten years ago we paid less attention to elegance and aromas, now we have changed completely, we start with aromas, we are concentrating on fine tannins and aromas, the body and the power have become less important. In Bolgheri the wines normally are powerful, our work during vinification is to obtain freshness and elegance," says Marco Ferrarese at Guado al Tasso.

Would more use of Syrah be the way forward if the climate continues to warm? "Well the Syrah also would be pushing it in terms of sugar content," says Angelo Gaja. Does the greatest complexity come from the Bordeaux varieties? "If the global warming becomes a problem for Merlot, we would be able to reduce the quantity of Merlot to perhaps 30% and increase Cabernet Franc. I am reluctant to change the formula but if global warming obliges us to change it, the grape variety that will benefit will be the Cabernet Franc. We have good results with Cabernet Franc here," says Angelo. So the wheel comes full circle to Sassicaia, which has stayed true to its blend of Cabernet Sauvignon and Cabernet Franc since its inception.

The last word should go to the Marquis Nicolò Incisa, whose father started it all at Sassicaia. "Cabernet Sauvignon in Bolgheri represents a warmer climate; the wine always has elegant tannins, even compared with Bordeaux. With Sassicaia we have established a style that is quite different from other Italian Cabernet Sauvignon and from Bordeaux. I think we have proved that Cabernet Sauvignon for each region has a different style and Sassicaia has a definite personality." Have others followed the style created by Sassicaia? "I think they are doing something different, because when they came out the style of wine was being influenced by the New World and everyone started to look for a lot of extraction and alcohol. Now the market is looking for less extraction, but it is difficult for them to go back. It is difficult because of Merlot, most of the wines with a high percentage of Merlot are over-ripe, but we are looking for freshness. This gives longevity."

Bolgheri has focused on high end wines since its beginning. "Even the least sophisticated producers have internalized the idea that this should be an area for high quality production. No one is making cheap wine, we don't risk becoming like Chianti which has been ruined by the extremes between good and bad," says Franco Batzella. But in recent years there has been the same increasing trend as in Bordeaux towards the production of second wines. At Ornellaia, the second wine, La Serre Nuove, is the result of declassification; at San Guido, about 20% of the production of Sassicaia is usually declassified to Guidalberto; but at most producers the second wine is essentially a separate brand at lower price. At Guado al Tasso, the eponymous lead wine comes from different vineyard plots from the second wine, Il Brucciato, although up to around 5% of Guado al Tasso may be declassified in any year. The second labels are usually more approachable, although this is a relative concept since few Bolgheri wines are really tight at the outset. Are they still super-Tuscans? Well, there's a tendency to call any wine under the IGT Toscana label a super-Tuscan, although of course the label can be used for its original intended purpose—to allow the production of wines that do not conform to DOC requirements—at any price level. Let's say that the concept is fairly elastic.

Soon after Bolgheri itself became established, the idea of producing Cabernet Sauvignon in coastal areas spread to the area around Grosseto, about 75 miles to the south. With land prices rising in Bolgheri (they are now similar to those in the much longer established area of Montalcino), Maremma (the province around Grosseto) became the latest hot area for wine production. Part way from Bolgheri to Grosseto, and a bit farther inland, about ten miles from the coast, is Suvereto. It's a small, hilly area, with about fifteen producers. Although it is a subcategory in the DOC Val di Cornia, the important wines are labeled as IGT Toscana. Tua Rita's Redigaffi, a 100% Merlot, and Montepeloso's Gabbro, a 100% Cabernet Sauvignon, have placed Suvereto on the map. Although the distance from Bolgheri may be short as the crow flies (about 20 miles), the climate changes significantly: it is 2-3 degrees warmer in Suvereto than in Bolgheri (although not as warm as the more southern part of Maremma). Tua Rita's famous Merlot is planted on clay-rich soils on the lower slopes, and Montepeloso's Cabernet Sauvignon slightly higher up on friable soil with a base of petrified clay. The Montepeloso vineyard, on the hill of Montepeloso, was planted with Sangiovese, Cabernet Sauvignon, and some white varieties when Fabio Chiarelotto purchased it in 1998. He started replanting and also purchased another, slightly smaller, vineyard on the Fontanella hill, about 3 km away. Even in this limited area there are distinct differences between the vineyards: Montepeloso is exposed to southern winds, but Fontanella gets northwest-west winds and more rainfall, so the work in the vineyard is quite different.

"My idea was to make an Italian wine, I wanted to shape an Italian Tuscan blend, to get away from those wines pumped up with international varieties," he says. He is a purist: "The wines of Bolgheri are too commercial, too manipulated." Perhaps it's ironic that he has had his greatest success with Gabbro, a one hundred percent Cabernet Sauvignon. "We started research, planting varieties and grafting, with varieties that had been here before the international approach started. I did not want to follow that path, but at the same time, I had the feeling that Cabernet would do well here, and since there was no real history here, I decided to start with Cabernet, get a reputation, and then work on the Italian project. When we purchased the winery and tasted the separate Cabernet lots, we were impressed by how complete the Cabernet was."

Gabbro came initially from Cabernet Sauvignon on the Montepeloso hill, and was an immediate success. As the replanting program has proceeded, its

The Montepeloso hill (right) is viewed from the Fontanella vineyard. Both have petrified clay subsoil (left).

source has switched more towards the Fontanella vineyard; in 2008 the wine came equally from both vineyards. Barrel samples show Montepeloso as richer, and Fontanella as more obviously structured. What are the stylistic objectives for the blend? "A reference point for sure is the old style California Cabernets from the period when they were elegant, before they became brutal, when they followed a direction I can see here, not as an imitation but as an expression of Cabernet, like Ridge Monte Bello or Heitz Martha's Vineyard." With this precedent in mind, and recognizing the warm climate of Suvereto, it's not surprising that Gabbro is a monovarietal Cabernet Sauvignon. "I tried a little Cabernet Franc in early vintages but I preferred 100% Cabernet Sauvignon; it is such a great variety when it is ripe that it doesn't need anything else, it's a complete variety. The Cabernet Franc gave more freshness but the wine was more diluted. I liked the Cabernet Franc by itself but it doesn't work in the blend." The wine is rich and complete, extremely dense, and even a little tough, when released, but progressive softening as you taste through the vintages suggests this is merely a feature of youth (⅄ page 365). To my mind it is more New World than Old World. The acid test is what happens to all that dense fruit as the wine ages; the wines only begin to open out after ten years, so it is still too early to say.

Several Chianti producers have expanded on to the coast, usually in Maremma, but generally with a different name and style of production for the new winery. Brancaia is an interesting exception where the same name is used for both Chianti and Maremma. In fact, the entry-level wine, Tre, is a blend coming two thirds from Maremma and one third from the Chianti region, a rare use of the IGT Toscana label to allow blends from all across the region. The

Chianti vineyards are usually inclined at varying angles, often interspersed with olive trees or other vegetation, and overlooked by hilltop towns.

super-Tuscan Illatria comes exclusively from Maremma, and from its first vintage in 2002 was a blend of 60% Cabernet Sauvignon with 30% Sangiovese and 10% Petit Verdot. With the 2009 vintage, the blend changed to 40% Cabernet Sauvignon, 40% Petit Verdot, and 20% Cabernet Franc. The wine has become much "bigger," and now demonstrates the massive quality of Maremma; in fact, I found a barrel sample of Cabernet Sauvignon to show more elegance than the final blend, which is presently dominated by the Petit Verdot (Y page 366).

Whereas the "average" super-Tuscan in the coastal areas has a distinctly left bank blend, a Cabernet-dominated super-Tuscan from Chianti is likely to have more Cabernet Sauvignon, sometimes 100%, and if there is a blend, Sangiovese is typically the second variety.[15] To what extent is this responsible for the difference in character, and to what extent is the difference intrinsic to the Cabernet Sauvignon? "The Cabernet tends to be leaner and tighter in Chianti, it does not have the generosity that Bolgheri has. Ours seem broad and opulent, theirs seem linear and tight by comparison. It's less opulent, it has more of a Chianti character—the Sangiovese and Cabernet Sauvignon in Chianti both have a very Chianti-like touch to them," says Axel Heinz.

The origins of Cabernet Sauvignon in Chianti are rooted in scandal. After its expulsion from the DOC to become a Vino da Tavolo, Tignanello went for broke in including Cabernet Sauvignon in its 1978 vintage. Others took heed of the message, planting Cabernet Sauvignon in order to strengthen Sangiovese. Making good wine in the region had not been easy. "People bought sugar and brought in wine from elsewhere—it was a black economy. The role of the oenologue was to be the link to buy the wine from the south!" recollects Luca di Napoli of Castello dei Rampolla, with some disgust. "We started planting Cabernet Sauvignon in the late seventies, the intention was to blend it to reinforce the Sangiovese. We took out the Malvasia, Trebbiano, and Canaiolo. We wanted to make a wine that would stand by itself. It was going to be a Chianti, but it wasn't quite legal. We were the first people to plant Cabernet Sauvignon and it was a scandal—we had to leave the association. It was the same later with Petit Verdot; Petit Verdot wasn't allowed in Italy so it was illegal." In fact, Rampolla produced what has become their super-Tuscan, Sammarco, from an equal blend of Cabernet Sauvignon and Sangiovese in 1980, but since then it has moved towards today's blend of 90% Cabernet Sauvignon with 5% each of Sangiovese and Merlot. In 1996, Rampolla introduced Vigna d'Alceo, a blend of 85% Cabernet Sauvignon with 15% Petit Verdot. Sammarco shows the heritage of Chianti in an elegant, almost savory, quality, whereas Vigna d'Alceo is more the modern super-Tuscan with intense black fruits (page 371). So perhaps variety does have something to do with style.

They seem to be somewhat torn in Chianti between a wish to express the terroir, whether through the traditional Sangiovese or through Cabernet Sauvignon, and the demands of the market to concentrate on single varietal wines. Alessandro François at Castello di Querceto expresses the dilemma. "I produce Chianti Classico without an international variety because in my opinion it must retain the character of the past. When we started to produce international varieties our idea was to find the maximum link between the varieties and the terroir. We wanted to produce the expression of our terroir."

At Querceto, there's a long history of single vineyard wines, since Alessandro's grandfather planted a vineyard of Sangiovese that has produced a pure varietal since 1904. Alessandro views La Corte, the descendant of this wine, as the first super-Tuscan. He describes the process of defining the blend for his super-Tuscan, Il Querciolaia. "We tried 50% Cabernet, the Sangiovese disappeared, we tried 10-15% it was not enough, so we decided about 30%." That's a pretty fair description of the character of Cabernet-Sangiovese blends. There are two other single vineyard wines at Querceto, Cignale (90% Cabernet Sauvignon; the rest is Merlot) and Il Sole di Alessandro (100% Cabernet Sauvignon). All of the wines show a tendency to elegance, with the fruit density and roundness decreasing, and savory elements increasing, moving from the 100% Cabernet, through Cignale, to Il Querciolaia (page 369). I wasn't sure how this expressed the character of each vineyard, as opposed to the varieties, but, "It is not easy in my opinion to define typicity for Cabernet Sauvignon of Tuscany. The situation we have in Tuscany is completely different, not just province by province, but from one valley to the next, there is considerable difference in the soil and microclimate depending on altitude, distance from the sea. The particularities of these wines are very varied," says Alessandro.

Querciabella is a more recently established producer, making wines in an elegant style since 1974. The owners have always been interested in Bordeaux, but first planted Cabernet Sauvignon with the intention of using it to strengthen their Chianti. One thing led to another, and in 1981 they produced their first vintage of Camartina, a blend of 70% Cabernet Sauvignon with 30% Sangiovese; there were only 3,600 bottles, matured in barriques, with a wonderfully moderate 12.5% alcohol. What is the stylistic reference? "We want it to be like Tuscany, we have Cabernet growing here, but we want it to taste like here," they say, telling the story that, "A group of Bordeaux winemakers visited, they were quite reverent about the Sangiovese, and then we pulled out Palafreno [a 100% Merlot] and a winemaker from St. Emilion said, 'This is astounding, it is not the quality, it's that it's not *our* Merlot, it's *Chianti*." With regards to the Cabernet blend, winemaker Manfred Ing says, "With Camartina we want the fullness and richness but still to maintain the elegance; by giving a little Sangiovese to the Cabernet we bring out the elegance of Cabernet Sauvignon." Barrel samples from different vineyard areas—Cabernet Sauvignon is planted in a wide variety of small plots, usually on galestro and clay, making up 5-7% of the total area—show that the Cabernet Sauvignon itself is elegant rather than powerful. It ages well, developing a delicious savory quality after about ten or twelve years (ᵀ page 369).

The Cabernet based super-Tuscans in Chianti tend to go to two extremes: blends with Sangiovese (you feel there is just so much Sangiovese they *have* to try blending some with Cabernet); and monovarietal Cabernets. There is a wide range of expression in monovarietal Cabernets, from the fresh, savory impression of Nozzole's Il Pareto, to the sterner impression of Castagnoli's Il Buriano, to the very modern expression of Villa Cafaggio's Il Cortaccio. At Nozzole, Giovanni Mazzoni says, "We didn't want to compete with the great Cabernets of France, we wanted to demonstrate the character of Cabernet grown in our terroir. It was always the intention to make a Cabernet that would compete with Chianti, so it needs to be elegant. Il Pareto became too powerful, so we have eased back (around 2008) to look more for elegance." One change, which is becoming common in the region, was to start using some tonneaux (500 liter) instead of barriques (225 liter), to reduce oak influence (ᵀ page 368). At Rocca di Castagnoli, they are conscious of market forces driving towards single varietal wines, and Il Buriano is a selection of the best grapes (ᵀ page 370). At Villa Cafaggio, the big distinction is between production of Chianti Classico as opposed to IGT Toscana. They picked the best terroirs for the IGT wines, with two south-facing plots, one for varietal Cabernet Sauvignon, one for varietal Sangiovese, adjacent on the same hill (ᵀ page 372).

With super-Tuscans all over Tuscany, and soils and climates so very varied, what do the Cabernet-dominated super-Tuscans tell us about the specificity of the variety? They vary from wines heavily dominated by Cabernet Sauvignon to those in which it less than half of the blend. From the extremes of the rich New World-like wines of Maremma, to the soft tannins of Bolgheri, to the freshness of Cabernet from Chianti, one common feature is evident: there is no trace of herbaceousness. In the blends, each region seems to reinforce its intrinsic properties rather than go for complementarity. So in Bolgheri, those soft, full, furry tannins tend to be softened yet further by Merlot, whereas in Chianti, a fresher, more herbal edge tends to be emphasized by adding Sangiovese. Different typicities for Cabernet that reflect the characters of the regions are supported by the choice of blending partner. It's difficult to disentangle the effects of soil from climate, but climatic differences, and changes in exposure, may be more important in determining character, since soils that aren't appropriate are avoided anyway. Ageworthiness may not yet match Bordeaux, but there is significant longevity as the top wines tend to begin their maturation only after a decade. It's hard to see super-Tuscans as great values these days, but I'm inclined to view the best wines as good alternatives to their equivalents in Bordeaux, especially if you are looking for a style between the traditional reserve of the left bank and the opulence of the right bank.

7

Southern Challenge

CABERNET SAUVIGNON is just as dominant in the southern hemisphere as in the northern. Chile has the most plantings, and Cabernet Sauvignon is its most important variety. Australia comes next, although Cabernet Sauvignon plays second fiddle to Shiraz. Argentina has significant plantings, although the concentration on Malbec, and a large remaining amount of Bonarda, push Cabernet Sauvignon into third place. Cabernet Sauvignon is the most important black variety in South Africa. It is fair to say there is a convergence of stylistic objectives, with a focus on ripe, forward, fruits in the New World style.

There's a certain commonality to the history of wine production in the southern hemisphere. Vines were brought from Europe by early settlers and used to make a somewhat rough wine, sometimes fortified and sweet to hide its deficiencies. Only towards the end of the twentieth century did production begin to focus on dry wines from quality varieties.[1] In South America and South Africa, the early moves towards quality were stymied by political or financial crises. The growth of Cabernet Sauvignon is more or less a direct indication of

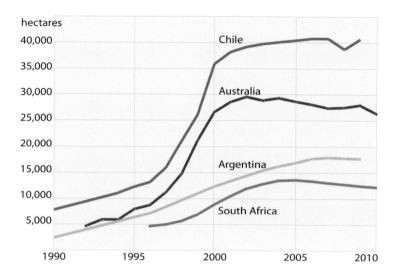

Plantings of Cabernet Sauvignon have followed similar growth patterns in wine-producing countries of the southern hemisphere.[2]

the eventual move to quality, and is strikingly parallel in southern hemisphere countries. Plantings first became significant in the first half of the 1990s, accelerated sharply during the second half of the decade, slowed after the turn of the century, and reached a plateau or declined in the past five years.

All southern hemisphere producers favor those fuller fruits of the New World, but Chile's premium Cabernets offer a sense of restraint holding back the fruits from too overt an expression. Tannins are usually supple rather than aggressive. Fruits are fuller in Argentina, tannins are softer, and producers say they have less pyrazines as the result of the more Continental climate and the luminosity of higher altitudes. Although South Africa is warmer, styles vary from soft opulence to frank herbaceousness. Australia offers a range from (relatively) cooler climates to the full-blown expression of ripe aromatic fruits. Then the wheel comes full circle, going across the Tasman Sea to New Zealand, which is the only New World Cabernet-producing region to be cooler than Bordeaux. There's a fascinating difference in attitudes between Chile and Australia, because in Chile the lower level wines tend to be pure varietals, while the premium wines are blends; in Australia the Cabernet-Merlot blends are distinctly second tier compared to varietal Cabernet Sauvignon.

The strong French influence on winemaking in Chile might seem surprising since the country was settled by the Spanish. Grapes were originally brought to Chile by Spanish settlers in the sixteenth century,[3] but the modern industry dates from a new wave of wineries established between 1860 and 1880[4] by industrialists who had made their fortunes in mining (usually copper), and looked to gain prestige from owning wineries. These included wineries that remain a major force in the industry today.[5] As a result of the war with Spain for independence in 1810, France became the primary cultural influence on the nouveau riche. "They were so snobbish they went to France instead of

Spain for influence," says Claudio Naranjo at Los Vascos. Connections between viticulturalists made it natural for the new vineyards to be planted with varieties from Bordeaux.[6] Indeed, for many years Chile produced wine under the general description "Bordeaux."[7]

The revival of the industry in the 1990s shows a contrasting mixture of influences. French influence is strong, and Bordeaux especially is often cited as a reference point, but the wines followed the New World mode, emphasizing varietal labeling rather than the French priority for place of origin. As the industry developed in the eighties and early nineties, the focus on varieties was assumed to be the only way to go. The New World created the market for varietal-labeled wines, and it's far more practical to break in at entry-level with a wine placed in the context of a known variety than to try to gain recognition for unfamiliar place names. This strategy demands some adherence to the style favored by the new consumer: forward and fruity.

Chile vies with the United States to be the world's largest producer of varietal-labeled Cabernet Sauvignon, but Cabernet Sauvignon is relatively far more important in Chile, accounting for about a third of all wine production.[8] Chile became well known for its good value entry-level wines, with Cabernet Sauvignon at the forefront. There's a certain rueful admission among producers that this initial success has backfired on attempts to produce higher quality wines, because it created an attitude among consumers that Chile does not produce premium wines. "When we started, we were producing wines of low price. It's a bit of a challenge to get Chile perceived as a premium wine producer," says Isabel Guilisasti, of Concha y Toro, who started producing one of Chile's first "icon" wines, Don Melchor, in 1987. She draws an interesting contrast with Argentina. "Argentina is totally different, they started to export at high prices, so the perception of Argentine Malbec is completely different from the perception of Chilean Cabernet Sauvignon." The challenge to Argentina is on the minds of Chilean producers. "It has become difficult for Chile to become known as a serious place for wine production, Chilean wine in the nineties was just good value, then there was an evolution, with more varieties in the blend. With higher prices people did not think Chile was just for cheap wines. The proposal is to strengthen more and more, and by 2020 to be ahead of Argentina," says Claudio Naranjo.

Moving up from entry-level, many of the wines are blends. "When new investors from all around the world were coming to Chile in the nineties, it was a huge question in the industry whether we should keep wines labeled as varieties or whether we should go in the European direction of blends. All the industry was asking what we should do to make wines of higher class. Most of the high end went for the blend decision, very close to the French concept," says Isabel Guilisasti.

Merlot and Carmenère are superficially similar during the growing season, but Carmenère leaves turn a characteristic red at the end of the season (top of vineyard), whereas Merlot stays green.

Carmenère and Merlot are the other significant black varieties, although therein lies a story. Merlot was thought to be the only other significant variety, until visiting French ampelographer Jean-Michel Boursiquot observed in 1994 that much of it was really Carmenère. It took the rest of the decade to sort it out, but finally it appeared that probably about two thirds of the "Merlot" was really Carmenère. Aside from varietal-labeled Cabernet Sauvignon or Carmenère, the most common wines are blends of the two (sometimes with smaller amounts of the other Bordeaux varieties). But Carmenère is not a simple substitute for Merlot: it brings sleek tannins to complement the firmer tannins of Cabernet Sauvignon, rather than the mid palate fleshiness of Merlot. "Carmenère gives us the attack Merlot doesn't have. Here we view Carmenère more like they view Cabernet Franc in France," says viticulturalist René Vasquez at Altaïr.

The term "icon" is bandied around a good deal in Chile. It's a buzzword indicating a signature wine, the very best produced by a winery. In practical terms, icon wines vary from a reasonable $30 to around $100. One winemaker let the cat out of the bag when asked to define an icon wine. "The marketing people say," she said, "it has to have a story, to be connected with a family, you have to have good terroir, it must be hand crafted, and you have to have recognition with good reviews." Marketing aside, many of Chile's icon wines are seriously good, and should not be dismissed because they do not yet com-

Furrow irrigation is used for vineyards in Chile and Argentina. Water runs from an irrigation channel at the edge of the plot down a furrow along the row.

mand the prices of cult wines from other countries. Today only a quarter of the icon wines based on Cabernet Sauvignon carry a varietal label.[9] This is a tribute to the French influence, as expressed by Patrick Valette, who makes wine at both Neyen de Apalta and Vik. "For me the beautiful wines always are blended, the blend gives more complexity."

The imperatives of viticulture in Chile are distinctive. Although it generally becomes cooler going south (away from the equator), position on the east-west axis is a major factor. "I want to emphasize how dramatic the influence of the coast is," says winemaker Marcelo Papa at Concha y Toro. "The Pacific is our main source of cool climate." Vineyards lie between the Andes and the Coastal Range of low mountains about 50 km in from the coast. Elevation within this relatively narrow band is important. The soil changes from stony close to the Coastal Range, to alluvial in the center, and then volcanic near the Andes.

The terrain is an arid desert on both sides of the Andes. While total rainfall may meet the minimum level required by the grapevine, rain falls only in the winter, so irrigation in the summer is crucial. Water comes from run-off from the Andes, and global warming may pose a future problem in limiting the supply. Increasingly regulated, this may become the limiting factor in the growth of viticulture. The original method of irrigation was to construct channels—indeed, there are many gracious lines of old trees running along channels constructed in the late nineteenth or early twentieth century. Extended to vineyards, channels run along the ends of the rows and water is sent down deep furrows along each row. The roots of the vines are submerged when the channels are opened every two weeks or so.

As drowning kills phylloxera, this may be partially responsible for its absence from Chile: it could become a problem as furrows are replaced by drip irrigation in modern vineyards. So far, most vines are ungrafted. In Argentina, where there is phylloxera, but many vineyards are still surviving on their own roots, the type of irrigation has a significant effect on the choice of plant material. "When you use drip irrigation, self-rooted plants die after five years because of phylloxera. So if you use drip irrigation you have to have grafted vines. When you use the old method of furrow irrigation, periodically there's enough water to kill phylloxera," says Hervé Birnie-Scott of Terrazas de los Andes.

There's unusual diversity in the Cabernet plant material in Chile. Selection massale is the most common method for planting new vineyards; and gaps created when single vines die are often filled simply by sticking a shoot from the adjacent vine into the missing space. Within a year or so, after it has rooted, the connection is cut, and voila! there is a new vine. But no one is certain phylloxera will remain absent, so some producers are planting on resistant rootstocks as a precaution. This may require using clones for the scion. As Alvaro Espinoza at Antiyal explains, "When you plant on rootstocks you have to use clones, because the scion needs to be virus free: if there is any virus it is released by interaction with the rootstock. That is a reason for using selection massale. It's also a cost factor as grafting costs five times more." Most Cabernet Sauvignon was planted during the 1990s, so there are as yet few really old vines.

Coming up to harvest in Chile in 2012, it was not obvious how Cabernet Sauvignon came to be the grape variety of choice—it seemed too hot (admittedly 2012 was a hot year, forcing an early harvest). What makes the difference is the extreme diurnal variation. One day, temperatures were as low as 10 °C overnight, and there was a fog so thick in the morning that you could hardly see; by mid afternoon the temperature was over 30 °C with a full sun. Coming up to harvest in Bordeaux, the temperature range is more likely to be 14-24 °C. "Bordeaux is completely different, with lower daytime temperatures but much warmer nights. There is more diurnal variation in Chile. Bordeaux gets earlier ripening because vines start work earlier in the morning, here they need an extra hour or two," says Marcelo Papa, winemaker at Concha y Toro. So although this is a warmer climate than Bordeaux, it is not as much warmer as you might expect from the average temperatures.

Wine producing regions in Chile are usually divided into three broad areas: the Aconcagua region to the north; the central valleys south of Santiago; and the southern region of the Itata and Bio Bio valleys. The rush to plant Cabernet

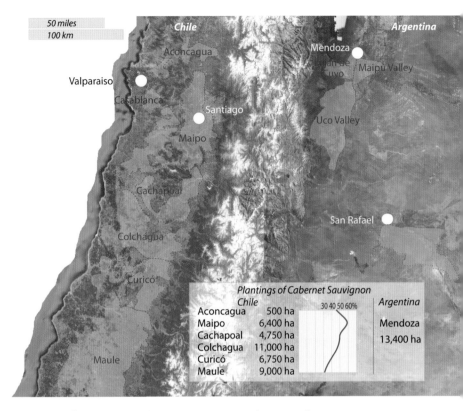

Cabernet Sauvignon in Chile is concentrated to the south of Santiago, declining from 60% to 30% of plantings going south from Maipo. In Argentina it is represented more or less pro rata in all regions, but Mendoza is the most important.[10]

Plantings of Cabernet Sauvignon		
Chile		Argentina
Aconcagua	500 ha	
Maipo	6,400 ha	Mendoza
Cachapoal	4,750 ha	13,400 ha
Colchagua	11,000 ha	
Curicó	6,750 ha	
Maule	9,000 ha	

Sauvignon—the area doubled in only five years between 1997 and 2001—has led to its expansion into a variety of terroirs. In a reversal of the usual relationship between quality and latitude (for the southern hemisphere), the higher quality regions are in the north of the country. There is some Cabernet Sauvignon in Aconcagua, where vineyards run right up to the base of the mountains, but most quality production is in the valleys to the immediate south of Santiago: Maipo, Colchagua, and Cachapoal. By the time you reach as far south as Maule Valley, production is more focused on bulk wine.

The official appellations (D.O.s) are based on the major valleys. This is a bit of a mixed bag in terms of conveying the character of the wine, as many valleys stretch from the Andes to approaching the coast. The appellation scheme was extended in May 2011 to add three new terms: Coasta (coastal regions), Entre Cordilleras (the central region to the east of the Coastal Range), and Andes (bordering the mountains). So a description of D.O. Aconcagua Coasta would imply a relatively cooler region than D.O. Aconcagua Andes. There is also a hierarchy of subregions and zones within the valleys, again a mixed bag since the units are political rather than geographical. Apalta Valley, a sub valley within Colchagua that is becoming known for quality Cabernet Sauvignon and Carmenère, has no official recognition, but there is a D.O. based on the local town of Santa Cruz, away from the main concentration of vineyards!

Sprawling around and to the south of the capital, Santiago, Maipo Valley historically has been Chile's most important region for wine production. It extends from the Coastal Range to the Andes. French varieties were first planted in Maipo when the major wineries were established in the nineteenth century. Although this is where Chile first developed its reputation for Cabernet Sauvignon, and remains important, it's no longer at the cutting edge. Fine wine is also produced in the valleys immediately to the south, Cachapoal and Colchagua (sometimes grouped together under the general description of Rappel Valley). The focus in the three valleys is on black varieties in general, and on Cabernet Sauvignon specifically. Variations in microclimates, running against the general temperature gradient, mean that it's often a bit warmer in Colchagua and Cachapoal, with harvest a couple of weeks earlier than Maipo. Within the major valleys are many subvalleys, with most running north-south, others transversal on an east-west axis. The transverse valleys have a more direct maritime influence from ocean breezes.

Driving south into Maipo Valley from Santiago, at first there is not much impression of the importance of viticulture or even of agriculture. There are pockets of vineyards here and there, well separated from one another and from the occasional orchards of fruit trees. Going farther south through Maipo and into Cachapoal, agriculture becomes more evident, with stretches of fruit orchards, and vineyards of table grapes grown under pergolas. Viticulture is more evident in individual sub valleys. It's very different from the monoculture you see in more developed wine-producing regions. When you reach Colchagua Valley, the sense of viticulture is more evident, especially in sub valleys such as Apalta, where several well known vineyards line the main road through the valley—Casa Lapostolle, Alpha Montes, and Neyen de Apalta among them.

Although you are always conscious of the mountains on either side, the major valleys vary from quite constricted to relatively broad. The sub valleys are narrower. Most of the vineyards are not in direct view of the majestic Andes, but are surrounded by the foothills to the Andes or the Coastal Range, showing as an arid ochre-colored scrub of small bushes and sometimes cactus. And where the Andes can be seen, they are not so white any more: in Maipo Valley, near Santiago, in fact, they often simply disappear into a haze of heat and pollution during the growing season.

Maipo Cabernet Sauvignon has a reputation for a minty character. There's some controversy whether this is intrinsic or due to volatile oils blowing from eucalyptus trees on to grapevines. I asked Francisco Baettig, chief winemaker at Errázuriz, whether people have been chopping down the trees a bit. "More than a bit, they have totally got rid of them. The amount of eucalyptus character today has gone almost to zero," he says. (Actually, eucalyptus is not the only aromatic influence in the area; the indigenous Boldo tree in central Chile has leaves somewhat like bay leaves, with a light camphor-like aroma.)

The leaves of eucalyptus trees have volatile oils that can blow on to grapevines. Sticking to the berries, this can give wine a minty or even medicinal aroma.

At the northeastern edge of the Maipo valley, one of Chile's first, and most famous, vineyards was planted by Manuel Antonio Tocorno in 1841. At Puente Alto, just south of Santiago, it is now threatened with being encircled by the city. The original planting included a wide variety of grapevines from France, including "cavernet Sauvignon colorado y blanco" from Bordeaux, and "pinot colorado y blanco" from Burgundy.[11] The estate was purchased by Alfonso Chadwick of Errázuriz in 1942, when it was replanted with Bordeaux varieties, reaching a total of 400 ha.[12] Under the name of Viña Tocornal, it became famous for its production of the red wine Tocornal Fond de Cave. Under the agricultural "reforms" of the 1960s (which all but destroyed Chilean viticulture), Chadwick was forced to sell the vineyard, and most of it was acquired in 1968 by Concha y Toro, one of Chile's largest producers.

Today the vineyard has been split into three parts. From 1972, Concha y Toro produced the Marqués de Casa Concha, and then in 1987 they set out to make an icon wine, Don Melchor. Almost a decade later, in 1996, Concha y Toro partnered with Baron Philippe de Rothschild to produce Almaviva from a 40 ha section of the vineyard. Back in 1968, the Chadwick family had kept 25 ha, from which 15 ha were replanted in 1992 with field selections of Cabernet

Sauvignon (12 ha) and the other left bank varieties. The first vintage of Viñedo Chadwick was the 1999, intended to be the Chadwick flagship wine. So here is a rare opportunity in Chile to see three different producers' interpretations of wine at the highest quality level from a single vineyard area.

Puente Alto is an alluvial fan of the Maipo River. Right at the foot of the Andes, it's considered cool climate for Maipo. Cool breezes from the mountains keep temperatures moderate during the growing season, which runs later and longer than in the more southern valleys. At Viñedo Chadwick, I asked Francisco Baettig how he sees the terroir manifesting itself in the wines presently being produced at Tocornal. "The common thread between the three major wines, Viñedo Chadwick, Almaviva, and Don Melchor, is in my opinion, the quality of the tannins. I think nowhere else one finds such fine grain tannins in a Chilean Cabernet Sauvignon. I would also mention as a common thread the purity of fruit and the freshness of it. In one word I think the common thread is elegant and refined Cabernet Sauvignon," he says.

Don Melchor is the most traditional of these wines, usually close to 100% Cabernet Sauvignon; recent vintages have contained 2-9% Cabernet Franc. The vineyard has soils based on gravel terraces, but varying from sandy clay, to loam, to volcanic rocks. A tasting of barrel samples from different parts of the vineyard showed a variation from light and elegant on sandy soils to more rounded, blacker fruits on clay soils. One block gave an impression of Maipo's traditional minty character. The Cabernet Franc was unusually well rounded; it is usually sharper in Maipo. The assemblage gave a more complete impression than any of the individual parcels, and even at this early stage showed its hall-

The small Puente Alto D.O. lies at the northeastern corner of Maipo Valley, close to the Andes. The old Tocornal vineyard at the heart of the D.O. is now split between Concha y Toro, Almaviva, and Viñedo Chadwick.

Photograph courtesy Concha y Toro.

mark elegance. In fact, in a vertical tasting of the past decade, "elegance" was the word most often found in my notes, reflecting the very fine structure, sometimes almost delicate (Υ page 440). The richness of the fruits and the higher alcohol are the indications of New World origin.

Also close to 100% Cabernet Sauvignon, Viñedo Chadwick gives a restrained impression. Reflecting that strong varietal constitution, it can show faint hints of herbaceousness to cut the elegant fruits, but overall it gives a slightly softer, sweeter impression than Don Melchor (Υ page 440). Perhaps its New World origins are just a touch more evident. There's that crystalline purity of line you get from fully ripe Cabernet Sauvignon, and perhaps a sharper focus on terroir, reflecting the smaller area for this wine compared with the greater diversity of terroirs in the blocks for Don Melchor.

Almaviva started as a frank attempt to make a Bordeaux blend. "Baron Rothschild wanted to start with the same sort of blend as Mouton, but then it turned out the Merlot was not Merlot, it was Carmenère, there is no chance we would go back to Merlot because we like the quality of the Carmenère. Within Chile this is probably *the* place that can give a similarity to Bordeaux. But the typical Bordeaux blend would not give the best result because the Merlot does not do so well," says winemaker Michel Friou. The typical blend is about three quarters Cabernet Sauvignon to one quarter Carmenère, with a little Cabernet Franc. Almaviva is smooth and silky, soft and very approachable even when young, but the first vintage (1996) is still lively (Υ page 436). Age does not seem to develop the same complexity as in Bordeaux, as even the oldest wine did not have much tertiary development.

Vineyards in Maipo Valley are often on plateaus close to the foothills.

About half an hour south of Santiago, more or less in the center of the historical area for winemaking in Maipo Valley, Santa Rita is one of the oldest and largest wineries. They consider themselves, together with Concha y Toro, to be the most traditional producers in Chile. Their top Cabernet Sauvignon is Casa Real, a selection from the best plots. There's an interesting contrast with another of their top wines, Triple C, an unusual blend of two thirds Cabernet Franc to one third Cabernet Sauvignon, with just a touch (5%) of Carmenère. Surprisingly, I felt that the monovarietal Casa Real might be aging more rapidly than the Triple C, which displayed those characteristic leafy notes of tobacco, perhaps akin to an absolutely top Chinon in a great year (⟲ page 446).

One of the big questions about blending is whether Carmenère will ripen fully. Carmenère is the last variety to ripen, typically a month after Cabernet Sauvignon (a great contrast with Merlot, which is earlier), and in much of Maipo the climate is right on the edge. It's definitely easier to ripen Carmenère in the slightly warmer areas of Colchagua and Cachapoal. In a revealing comment on climate and varieties, winemaker Germán Lyon at Pérez Cruz, in the southern part of Maipo, told me, "When we started with Petit Verdot, we thought that if we can ripen Carmenère, we can ripen anything. We are at the

Photograph courtesy Santa Rita.

limit for Carmenère, it performs well on the flat or valley but here [at a slight elevation on the slopes] it takes longer."

Merlot is rarely successful. "Merlot is a terrible variety for us. It used to be a good variety for us when it was Carmenère. Perhaps it's a matter of material, the plants we have are not the best. Merlot needs clay and good water retention. We have been making a mistake in Chile in where we have planted Merlot, we planted Merlot where it was suitable for Carmenère," says Alvaro Espinoza at Antiyal. The main difficulty is water management. "The Merlot collapse problem is dehydration. Merlot naturally has a small root system. If the soils don't have enough humidity, the plant does not do well. Even if it is very warm, Merlot does not completely close the stomata, we call it an optimistic variety. The result is that it loses too much water by dehydration," says Francisco Baettig.

Huddled under the Andes and relatively narrow, Cachapoal Valley runs north-south, with most vineyards right at the foot of the mountains. It is less well known than the valleys to its immediate north and south; much of the wine has been labeled with the more general description of Rappel Valley.[13] Right into the foothills at the end of a sub valley, Viña Altaïr produces two

Vineyards in Apalta Valley are surrounded by foothills where the arid, ochre-colored earth can be seen through the scrub.

blends, both about three quarters Cabernet Sauvignon. The top wine has Syrah as the major partner; the second wine (called Sideral) has Carmenère (Υ page 436). With a consulting French winemaker, Altaïr was committed from the start to the notion of blending. The only issue was whether the blend should be based on Cabernet or Syrah. They liked the quality of grapes in this area: "It is not as strong as the Maipo Cabernet Sauvignon, it is more in the French style, and we don't want to be French but the balance is more like Bordeaux with high natural acidity," says Claudia Gomez. In an interesting revelation of attitudes in Chile, she adds that, "Altaïr is more serious, it is not so exuberant. Altaïr is Old World, Sideral is New World."

Going on south, Colchagua Valley falls into two parts. The eastern half runs north-south, between the Coastal Range and the Andes. Relatively protected from the ocean, it can be warm during the day, but quite cold at night. Moving towards the west, the oceanic influence strengthens, and the climate is generally cooler. Approaching the Coastal Range, the valley turns north and is parallel to Cachapoal Valley. Colchagua is one of the most rapidly growing areas in Chile, especially with its newly recognized subregions, including Apalta, a small sub valley which is approaching a monoculture of vines, and offers a microcosm of the forces driving wine production in Chile. Apalta is now recognized as prime terroir for Cabernet Sauvignon, but it was only in the early nineties that Viña Montes pioneered plantings here.

It's impossible to say whether Montes's success owes anything to the classical music that plays to the maturing wines in the barrel room—Gregorian chant was coming through the speakers when I visited—but the original tiny operation has grown enormously. A modern winery constructed on Feng-Shui principles is used for producing the icon wines, and there's a much larger winery elsewhere for the other brands. The top wine is Montes Alpha M, a classic Bordeaux blend with 80% Cabernet Sauvignon. The intent was to express the elegance of the Apalta Valley (less powerful than Colchagua as a whole), and the inaugural vintage in 1996 created a great deal of interest in Apalta. A soft, sweet, ripeness gives a gentler impression than you see in Maipo (page 443).

A mile or so farther along the road, at the very end of the valley, is Neyen de Apalta. Apalta Valley may have recently become fashionable, but Neyen de Apalta has the oldest Cabernet Sauvignon vines in Chile—several hectares planted in 1892. Until 2003, the grapes were sold off, but then winemaker Patrick Valette—his family used to own Château Pavie in St. Emilion—was brought in to make the wine. Following the French imperative, what could the result be but a blend? In this case, Carmenère is usually the majority component. The wine shows the typical soft, silky elegance of Apalta Valley, and makes a good case for the quality of Carmenère when it's fully ripe (page 444). That case is taken even further at Casa Lapostolle, a sleek operation under French ownership. The top wine, Clos Apalta, is typically 60-70% Carmenère and 15-20% Cabernet Sauvignon, with some Merlot or Petit Verdot depending on the year.[14] Once again there's that silky, almost perfumed qual-

Neyen de Apalta has several hectares of fruit-bearing Cabernet Sauvignon vines that were planted in 1892.

ity, of fully ripe Carmenère, with tannins that seem finer and smoother than those of Cabernet (⟙ page 438).

Two contrasting images round out the impression of Colchagua. Several kilometers from Apalta towards the coast, Los Vascos was established in 1986 as a joint venture between Château Lafite and a large Chilean landowner (since replaced by the Santa Rita group who are a sleeping partner). Los Vascos occupies a sub valley of 4,000 ha, with 600 ha planted, mostly to Cabernet Sauvignon. There have been vineyards here probably since the eighteenth century, and the property includes some sixty year old vines. Only 40 km from the Pacific, the transversal valley gets maritime breezes. It's just a little cooler than Apalta. The scale of the operation is indicated by manager Claudio Naranjo's casual comment, "We have a little Chardonnay." That turns out to be 20 ha! There are three red wines: a varietal Cabernet Sauvignon, the Gran Reserva, and the top wine, Le Dix. The Gran Reserva is a blend that is about three quarters Cabernet Sauvignon, with Syrah, Carmenère, and Malbec. "Until 2004 it contained only Cabernet Sauvignon, but the market was going fast—faster than the producer—and the idea was to make a more cosmopolitan wine," says Claudio Naranjo. Le Dix, which was introduced to celebrate the tenth anniversary of the Rothschilds' arrival, is 85% Cabernet Sauvignon, 10% Carmenère, and 5% Malbec. "Cabernet Sauvignon is a nice variety but sometimes it is too linear, it needs more dimensions, this was the impetus for introducing the extra varieties into the blend," says Claudio.

Los Vascos illustrates two aspects of Chilean viticulture. The varietal Cabernet Sauvignon is determinedly an entry-level wine; vineyards are farmed to purpose, so yields are higher, and there is some machine harvesting. But even if it inevitably lacks much varietal typicity, it is an extraordinary value: it would be difficult for Bordeaux or Napa Valley to match this quality at this price (⟙ page 442). Le Dix is a more ambitious wine, refined and elegant, with more of a cool climate impression than you usually get in Colchagua; it's interesting, but its target is more at the Cru Bourgeois level than the Grand Cru Classé. Perhaps Lafite does not want to compete too directly with its properties in Bordeaux.

One of the first foreign collaborations in Chile, Los Vascos presents an interesting contrast with the most recent, the foray of Norwegian billionaire Alex Vik into Colchagua. Viña Vik also occupies a large valley, well actually a series of contiguous small valleys, totaling around 4,200 ha. It's a stone's throw from Apalta Valley, but because there's a mountain in between, it's a very bumpy hour away by road. What sold it to Vik, who had originally been looking for vineyard locations in Argentina, was the constant breeze all summer. The first 300 ha were planted in 2006, and plans are to increase the planted area to around 480 ha. But the intention here is to have only a single wine, an icon aiming at the $100 price point. The expanse of the area means there are wide

Avocados (on the hill) are a more profitable crop than grapevines (foreground) in Aconcagua Valley.

variations in soils, which coupled with various exposures, make for significant variety in the plots. Barrel samples from the coolest areas show herbal character, while those from clay-rich sites are round and chocolaty. With Patrick Valette as winemaker, the choice of a blended wine based on Cabernet Sauvignon was set; although the initial vintages have shown rather wide variations in varietal composition as the vineyards have been coming on line, the plan is to settle down around 60% Cabernet Sauvignon. The first two vintages show tight structure, precise fruits, and a tendency to elegance (Υ page 448).

Driving north from Santiago the general impression is quite different from the south. For a hundred or so kilometers, aside from the industrial developments that peter out along the road, all you see are foothills covered in scrub. But as you enter Aconcagua Valley, everything turns green, a canopy of trees covers the road, there are agricultural crops next to the road, and beyond them are vineyards planted on the slopes. A transverse valley, Aconcagua runs almost from the coast to the Andes, and offers significant climatic variation. Wine production is only a small part of its agricultural activities: the fertile environment supports many other crops. Indeed, near Errázuriz, the surrounding hills are planted with avocados—economically a more desirable crop than grapes. "I consider the avocado trade to be the main threat to Aconcagua simply because it's so profitable," says Ireneo Nicora of the von Siebenthal winery.[15]

When Don Maximiano Errázuriz established his vineyard in Aconcagua in 1870 he was bucking the trend: almost all the major wineries were established in Maipo close to Santiago. It's just a little warmer here than in Maipo: average growing season temperatures at Errázuriz are about 1 °C higher than at the Tocornal vineyard. That may not sound a lot, but it can be the difference between Carmenère ripening fully or not. Errázuriz has been a driving force for quality, with their icon wine Don Maximiano (given the subtitle, Founder's Reserve) being one of the Chile's first attempts at top quality, in 1983. Don Maximiano started as a 100% Cabernet Sauvignon, but in 2003, after winemaker Francisco Baettig took over, it moved to a blend with Cabernet Franc, Petit Verdot, and Syrah. "We wanted to enhance the palate of the Cabernet, now it's usually around 85% with the other varieties, which bring acidity and structure, it will age differently but Cabernet will always be a variety that will age well," says Carolina Herrera, a winemaker at Errázuriz. Tasting a vertical that spanned the change, I felt this was a good decision: the extra varieties bring more breadth and range of flavors (⌕ page 441). But Don Maximiano remains very much a classic Cabernet Sauvignon, with some vintages showing more of a European heritage, others seeming more New World, according to vintage conditions.

Seña is another sign of the times. One of the first international joint ventures in Chile, with its first vintage in 1995 after Eduardo Chadwick persuaded Robert Mondavi to become involved, ownership reverted entirely to Errázuriz in 2004 when Mondavi was sold to Constellation. The first vintages came from grapes selected from Errázuriz's vineyards, but in 2000 Seña acquired its own vineyards; as they have come on line, the proportion of grapes from the estate has been steadily increasing. Seña also became more of a blend after Francisco took over as chief winemaker. Until 2002, Cabernet Sauvignon was usually more than three quarters of the blend, but from 2003 it has been just above half. Carmenère and Merlot are the other major varieties.

About half an hour to the west of Errázuriz, the Seña estate is a cooler site, about 2-3 °C less, as the result of breezes blowing from the ocean. "This is the freshest place in the valley where you can plant Cabernet Sauvignon, which is what we are looking for," says viticulturalist Eduardo Gonzalez. Perhaps because of the cooler climate, perhaps because the blend is closer to that of Bordeaux, the wine has a slightly more European feel than Don Maximiano; not so much when it is young, when the fuller fruits of the New World dominate, but when it ages, developing a delicious savory counterbalance to the fruits (⌕ page 447).

Producers in Chile today are as conscious of terroir as producers anywhere. Relating regional character to the formal D.O. descriptions is limited by the large sizes of the D.O.s, but it might be fair to say that Cabernet from Aconcagua tends to be well rounded, Maipo tends to show elegance (and is no longer minty), from Colchagua there is more overt structure, and Apalta gives a soft silkiness. Running through all regions is that sense of restraint coming from the maritime influence on the mountainous terrain.

Is anyone conscious of the subregions besides the producers? "Chile is Chile. Sometimes Chile is South America," says Claudia Gomez of Altaïr.

There's agreement that more recognition of regions would be good for Chilean wine, but some doubt as to how best to achieve this. "There's recognition of the valleys now but not of the sub areas within the valleys. You know what the biggest problem is, it's based on political divisions, on communes; it's not based on geography. We cannot use actual place descriptions, but have to use communes. We need to create appellations that are related to terroir but we should not become as specific as the French or Spanish," says Francisco Baettig at Errazuriz. Marcelo Papa at Concha y Toro says ruefully that it will take time. "I don't think individual appellations have significance for the consumer, not at this time, consumers follow more the brand. We need to do it that way, I don't know if it will take ten or a hundred years. In the eighties, people used to look for Napa; now they look for To Kalon," he comments. At the high end, the running issue is that terroir needs to fit into the context of a regional identity. Once you lose the varietal tag, the brand or the region becomes the point of identification. Although there are certainly some well known brands at the icon level, they won't have any halo effect to lift up other, less well known wines, unless regional identification comes into focus.

The need for better regional identity plays out against two contrasting forces: a move towards blends at the top levels; and a wish to represent the effects of individual terroirs on single varieties. There's a general feeling that blends may make better wines, but varietal Cabernet Sauvignon may better express terroir. "When I work with a single variety or block, the wine gets like a line in the mouth, but when I blend the wine gets more dimensions. If you are purist and you want to express a single place, it should be a single variety, but maybe it's not the best wine. You should be conscious of this. You want to express the place or you want to make the best wine—that is the question," says winemaker Germán Lyon at Pérez Cruz.

Is an increased proportion of blends a function of a maturing wine industry? "Making blends is an evolution in Chilean winemaking. Chile was very varietal at the beginning, but now there are more varieties and more blends. Another story is, let's go to the different valleys. Chile has to invent. Now the division of regions is more sophisticated. Because France, Italy, Spain, the traditional producer countries, have always talked about regions, we have this contradiction, we are talking about varieties. We have to say this is a Cabernet from Colchagua by the coast, we have to find the way to identify varieties with regions to be successful. Colchagua, Maipo, and Casablanca are well known, but not the others," says Claudio Naranjo at Los Vascos.

Producers are clear about the trade-offs in making top wines either as blends or varietals: it depends on objectives. "It's a matter of style. If you want the typical elegance, you just need the Cabernet Sauvignon, but if you are looking for more complexity, maybe the best idea is to blend. The intent with Casa Real is to express the terroir of the vineyard," says winemaker Tomás Vial at Santa Rita. Style, not quality, is the issue. "Maybe sometimes you could make a better wine if you blend, sometimes not, it depends on the year. I think the Cabernet Sauvignons in this area are quite pure—in other areas it may be more necessary to blend. I don't believe it's a matter of quality, it's a matter of approach, what you want to do as a house. At Almaviva we set out to make a blend, at Concha y Toro we set out to express the typicity of this area," says winemaker Marcelo Papa.

Like everywhere else, Chile is wrestling with the issues of ripeness and high alcohol. They are not so defensive about alcohol levels in Chile as they are in Napa (typically levels run about 14%), but it remains a concern. "It's the wine-maker's nightmare, the alcohol level. We should worry. The market is looking for lower alcohol and more drinkability. I would be happy to make the same wine with one percent less. The usual answer is the balance. I think we should worry but not compromise the quality of the wine," says winemaker Andrea Leon at Casa Lapostolle.

There's been the usual evolution from moderate alcohol at the start, to a steady increase in the twenty first century, and some producers would now like to back off a bit. "In the early nineties, alcohol was 12.5%, 13% max, but the wines were green. From 2003 we moved to 14.6-14.9%. I want to move back to where we were at 2002, with 14.1-14.2% with nice fruit, very vibrant, with good balance," says Marcelo Papa at Concha y Toro. Producers started out anxious to ensure full ripeness, but as they gained experience, realized they did not need to go so far. "The problem was that when the vines were too high, grapes did not ripen, so the focus was on planting to get the sun. So the rows were planted east-west, looking for more exposure. I realized five years ago we have lots of sun in Chile. So now there is netting in the fruiting zone to reduce exposure on the north side of the row, which is exposed all day. New plantings are now done in north-south rows," says Francisco Baettig at Errazuriz, with self-deprecating irony.

Summarizing the trend, Francisco says that, "Chile historically went looking for ripeness, personally I think we moved a bit far in that quest. Today I think we are going back, not to become green, but looking for elegance and finesse." Winemaker Germán Lyon at Pérez Cruz is following the same path. "Five years ago I was following Robert Parker and the *Wine Spectator*, I was harvesting over-ripe grapes, but I asked myself, why am I doing this, I would prefer to make wines with lower alcohol and more freshness." Patrick Valette at Viña Vik also sees this as a recent movement. "Everything has been changing in Chile in the past five years. In the 1990s people were concerned to have very powerful concentrated wine in the Parker style, they were not so concerned with acidity. Today we are going back to produce wine with more acidity; there has been a big difference in viticulture, we are picking earlier, that gives you a different maturation."

Netting is used to protect the ripening berries from excess sun exposure at Viñedo Chadwick.

Chile is in an interesting position between the Old and New Worlds. The Cabernet-dominated wines have a restraint that speaks to Europe: they are not exuberant or boisterous. But they do have a somewhat fuller impression on the palate, with higher alcohol, and they do not always achieve that natural lightness you find in Bordeaux. Although they are usually more approachable when young, the best have aging capacity. "Should your wines be ready to drink on release?" I asked Andrea Leon at Casa Lapostolle. "Well in that case we'd have to hold them five years longer, the finance people would not be happy." Five years is about the point at which most of the icon wines approach their maturity, but usually the tannins are sufficiently supple that they can be drunk well before that. The difference with Bordeaux narrows at the point when the wines begin tertiary development, which for the most part is a lot sooner in Chile: some tertiary signs may show by five years, and by ten years may be fully fledged. Given that the very best wines I tasted were still lively after two decades (albeit past their peaks), that vines are getting older and viticulture is getting better, it's reasonable to expect greater longevity in the future.

Like other New World countries that initially seemed to have the advantage that vintages were consistent and reliable, Chile now shows more vintage variation. Partly this is due to expansion of vineyards into a wider range of areas, with more climatic variation, so one vintage chart does not fit all, and partly (perhaps due to global warming?) there is more intrinsic variation. "We used to say, how can vintages be so different in Bordeaux, but after 1997 every thing changed here. Every year was the same in the nineties, then around 1997, 1998 the vintages started being different, hot versus cool, dry versus wet. Since 2000, everyone says the odd years have been good. Weather can be quite local, it can be different at Los Vascos from Apalta Valley," says Claudio Naranjo.

It's only about a hundred miles (less than 200 km) across the Andes from Santiago to Mendoza, but the weather conditions and terrains are completely different for grape growing. Chile has a maritime influence; Argentina is pure Continental. Vineyards in Chile start around 250 m of altitude and go up to about 650 m. Argentina starts where Chile leaves off: the plateau around Mendoza is higher than the vineyards in Chile. Compared with Cabernet's restrained character in Chile, in Argentina the fruits are more forward and the wines are softer. Peering over the Andes, each side views the other with a (relatively friendly) skepticism. "Here if you go 50 km you are at the coast, in Argentina you are 1,000 km from the coast and you have to go higher to get freshness. The main difference in the wines is that the tannins are far softer in Argentina," says Dennis Murray of Viña Montes. Across the border: "Here there is a Continental climate with no marine influence. Mountains stop precipitation. This allows another expression of Cabernet Sauvignon, especially compared to Chile; here there is much less pyrazine due to the higher altitude and diurnal variation. What I like about Cabernet Sauvignon here is that it's always on the fruity edge, sometimes the ripe fruity edge. Like Napa, that's always the case here, we can have ripe Cabernet Sauvignon," says Hervé Birnie-Scott of Terrazas de los Andes in Mendoza.

Chile and Argentina share a focus on varietal wines and on blends resembling nineteenth century Bordeaux. In Chile this is an accident resulting from the confusion between Merlot and Carmenère, which was never a major variety in Bordeaux, and has been all but lost there since the replanting caused by phylloxera. In Argentina, the lost variety is Malbec, which was the second most important variety in Bordeaux on the left bank, and the major variety on the right bank, until it was displaced by Merlot at the end of the nineteenth century. Malbec did not disappear entirely from view in France, since under the name of Cot, it is the basis for many wines in Cahors, just over a hundred miles from Bordeaux. Malbec is not a new craze in Argentina: it has been important since the start of the twentieth century when there was a fury of planting.

The popular image of Malbec from Argentina today does a disservice to the potential of the grape. Certainly it can make a forward, fruity wine, with soft and supple black fruits on the palate, and just enough underlying support not to collapse. But you can make entry-level wine in this style from many varieties—Merlot, Cabernet Sauvignon, Syrah—if you find appropriate conditions. With old vines and lower yields, when treated as a noble variety, Malbec can make an interesting wine, showing a black fruit palate with a characteristic velvety smoothness and fine, elegant tannins giving support for aging. Under peak conditions, this may be a more interesting blending partner for Cabernet Sauvignon than Merlot, because the tannic structure is complementary: the more supple character of Malbec adds smoothness to the tighter structure of Cabernet Sauvignon. It doesn't fill in on the mid palate in quite the same way as Merlot, so the wine tends more to elegance than fruit-driven power. Perhaps the closest comparison with Merlot is when the Merlot is grown on gravel like the Cabernet, producing a finer result than Merlot on clay.

Mendoza is by far the most important wine region in Argentina, with 70% of the vineyards and 80% of all production. From its latitude you would think it was a warm climate, but the high elevations of the vineyards reduce temperatures and make for greater diurnal variation. Originally the area was a desert with a sandy soil, but irrigation has transformed it for viticulture. There is little phylloxera, so most vines are not grafted. The town of Mendoza nestles right under the Andes. Just to its south is Luján de Cuyo, surrounded by a monoculture of vineyards, running up the slopes to the base of the Andes. Immediately to the east of Luján de Cuyo is Maipú Valley, and to its south is Uco Valley. Farther south and west comes San Rafael. Malbec and Cabernet Sauvignon are found everywhere, but the quality leader for Cabernet Sauvignon is the relatively small area of Luján de Cuyo.

Altitude is an important determinant of style in Mendoza, where vineyard elevations vary from 800 m (on the plateau at the foot of the Andes) to 1,450 m (well into the mountains). With an average drop of 0.6 °C per 100 m, the difference between the lowest and highest vineyards (within 50 km of one another as the crow flies) is comparable to going from the northern limits of France to well into Spain.[16] So the climate ranges from hot to cool all within a short distance. Higher altitudes provide lower temperatures, greater diurnal variation, increased luminosity, and more wind and lower humidity. The vine responds by toughening its skin. Up to about 1,000 m in altitude, the color becomes more intense and violet, and the quantity of tannins increases.[17] (Production of anthocyanins is partly a defense mechanism to protect the grape from ultraviolet radiation, so increased solar exposure causes increased anthocyanin production in black varieties.) The harvest occurs about a month later at the highest altitudes compared with the lowest.

Soils in Mendoza are highly heterogeneous, generated by the glacier and rivers that flowed down from the Andes. Deposits vary with the (sub) region. Generally there is more sand and rocks near the Andes. As a high altitude desert, the layering of deposits that would occur with a greater water supply doesn't happen here, so the variation is quite extreme. The general approach of producers who try to match terroir to varieties is first to identify the right microclimate by altitude, then to look for the appropriate soil type at that altitude.

Vineyards in Luján de Cuyo extend from 1,000 m elevation directly to the south of the town, rising up a continual slope towards the Andes at about 1,400 m.

Malbec grows so successfully in Mendoza that it all but stifles competition, creating an unusual situation in which Cabernet Sauvignon has to fight for space on the best terroirs. "Does Cabernet Sauvignon play second fiddle to Malbec in Mendoza? I think so. There isn't any competition because Malbec is so dominant, but there could be competition if Cabernet Sauvignon was more popular. Malbec is so well adapted to Argentine culture because it is less demanding. Mendoza is still fairly wide open, but the answer is yes, Malbec is occupying some land that would be better suited for Cabernet," says Paul Hobbs, who makes wine in both Mendoza and Sonoma. Paul sees some problems at present: "In Mendoza there are blends with all Bordeaux varieties. What determines whether to blend? When the Cabernet is absolutely top qual-

Vertical shoot positioning is used to make a high, dense, canopy in Mendoza, to protect the grapes at the bottom from excessive sun exposure.

ity it is rarely improved by blending, but it is easier to find that situation in Napa than in Mendoza. Mendoza Cabernet is a little more rustic, somewhat more monolithic; it's big but doesn't have the refinement of the layers you can get in Napa." But there is great future potential: "Mendoza can stand shoulder to shoulder with the competition, why stop at Napa, it could compete with Bordeaux, although not the very top. Mendoza is Argentina's equivalent to Napa. As sub-AVAs develop in Mendoza they will be equivalent to top regions in Bordeaux."

Given the dominance of Malbec in Mendoza, it takes a certain nerve to plant Cabernet Sauvignon in your best vineyards. The undoubted pioneer was Nicolás Catena. Recollecting his early ventures into Cabernet, he told me, "When I started I knew nothing about Cabernet Sauvignon although my father was a fan of Malbec wines. I went to Napa and I fell in love with Cabernet Sauvignon. For me it was the best wine I have tasted in my life. I came to the conclusion that Cabernet Sauvignon was the king of the varieties. I decided to produce in Argentina a Cabernet Sauvignon that would compete with the best in the world. I have to admit that all my decisions on what to plant and where were based on hypotheses, I must say, pretty poor hypotheses. I had produced a pure Cabernet Sauvignon in the late 1980s when Cabernet Sauvignon was not at all important here—Malbec was important. I produced a Cabernet Sauvignon for export in 1990, and I was very pleased with that Cabernet

Sauvignon. I was having dinner with Jacques Lurton from Bordeaux and he said, this tastes like a Cabernet Sauvignon from the Languedoc. His comment was extremely relevant for me because his reputation was made in Bordeaux. I said, he's right, I have to change immediately, no more Cabernet Sauvignon from hot climates, I should go to the cooler sites. So I took risks. One was that there would not be enough ripeness, it would be too cool. My technicians said I was crazy. We planted Cabernet farther south and then went up in altitude. We decided—it took about six years—that Cabernet Sauvignon from cooler climates was better."

Catena have vineyards in many terroirs, and barrel samples of Cabernet Sauvignon from the 2011 vintage provided a fascinating exercise in relating tannic structure to soil and altitude. The wine from the lowest vineyard (Angélica at 800 m with sandy-clay soils) was the softest and least acidic. The wine from the highest vineyard (Adriana at 1,480 m with gravelly-calcareous soils) was the tightest, with mountain tannins hidden underneath the fruits. There wasn't an exact correlation with altitude in between. Most of the wines seemed likely to benefit from blending, although those in the middle, La Pirámide (940 m with deep clay soils), and Nicasia (at 1,180 m the liveliest of the flight), seemed the most complete. Cabernet Sauvignon and Malbec show more or less parallel reactions to these terroirs. Malbec is more supple, with a range varying from raciness to fruity. Cabernet Sauvignon shows more variation depending on vintage conditions. It would be interesting to follow the development of these terroir-driven wines if they were bottled separately.

Catena regards even the single variety wines as being blends. "The reality is that our 'single variety' Malbecs are actually blends of special lots from different altitudes. These components are very different, one from the other, so there is more than enough complexity in these single variety wines," says Laura Catena. "For our Nicolás Catena Zapata blend, the main components are Cabernet Sauvignon from La Pirámide at 900 meters elevation and Malbec from Adrianna at almost 1,500 meters elevation, so actually here we are choosing a Malbec from a cooler climate than the Cabernet Sauvignon," she explains. "For the Nicolás Catena Zapata blend we like to have the Cabernet Sauvignon character dominate in the nose and the Malbec dominate in the finish, so we adjust the blend to preserve the classic style of this wine."

Catena's top wines today are the single vineyard Malbecs and the eponymous Nicolás Catena Zapata blend, which is usually about three quarters Cabernet Sauvignon to one quarter Malbec (although it has varied from 95% to 52% Cabernet). Under the Catena Alta label, there is a varietal Cabernet Sauvignon that is blended from the various high altitude vineyards (some vintages have also contained some Malbec). The Nicolás Catena Zapata blend and the varietal Catena Alta shows the same relationship as elsewhere: the blend has more breadth and flavor variety, the varietal wine is purer but more linear

(⟲ page 449). Nicolás Catena agrees that blends are more complex. "We have introduced two blending processes with Cabernet Sauvignon: one is blending different microclimates; the other is blending Cabernet Sauvignon with Malbec. Our conclusion is that the blend is better than Cabernet Sauvignon from a particular vineyard, although we are not completely sure yet... The Malbec drops a bit with aging, and Cabernet Sauvignon holds the aging better. When you get into the flavors coming with age, my conclusion is that the blend of Cabernet Sauvignon with Malbec is more complex than Cabernet Sauvignon alone." The blend shows its Malbec component in the form of a smoother, tighter, impression on the palate than a blend with Merlot: in terms of Bordeaux, a move towards the style of Margaux rather than Pauillac. Indeed, the style at Catena is more towards elegance than power, and this comes through on the Malbecs as well as the Cabernets.

Catena produces several single vineyard Malbecs, but not Cabernets. This is due mostly to market considerations. "With Malbec we think this is something really new, consumers are experimenting. We discovered that different microclimates produced really different flavors of Malbec but we don't know what the preference of the consumer would be. So with Malbec we offer the consumer different flavors, each corresponding to a different microclimate. With Cabernet Sauvignon it is different because the best is very well defined. For me today there are two regions that define Cabernet Sauvignon, Bordeaux and Napa. If a consumer will compare you, it will be with these two. To introduce a new Cabernet flavor would be really risky," says Nicolás Catena, explaining the background to Cabernet production. "When I met Robert Mondavi, I said, what we are trying to make is a Médoc. He corrected me, and said, a Premier Grand Cru Classé. When we enter the world of Cabernet Sauvignon, we need to produce something similar, if we are not able to produce something like Médoc, forget it."

Catena also has a collaboration with Château Lafite in the form of Bodega Caro. The principal wine is a blend with Cabernet Sauvignon as the main variety. Since the first vintage in 2000, the composition of the blend has varied quite a bit. Winemaker Estela Perinetti says, "In cooler years we use more Cabernet. At the beginning the Malbec had more rustic tannins so we needed to use more Cabernet Sauvignon. Then we got better tannic structure with the Malbec and we reversed. Now we are going back to more Cabernet Sauvignon because it gives better aging." Caro shows the same silky tannic structure as Nicolás Catena Zapata, but seems to age a little faster by turning more savory sooner (⟲ page 449).

The French influence shows at another significant Cabernet producer, Terrazas de los Andes, an offshoot of Champagne producer Moët et Chandon. In 1958 Chandon expanded for the first time beyond the borders of Champagne by starting a winery in Argentina (Bodegas Chandon), for producing sparkling

Vineyards in Mendoza go up to elevations of 1,500 m in the Andes.

Photograph courtesy Terrazas de los Andes.

wine. Terrazas was their first move into dry wines, a brainchild of Hervé Birnie-Scott, who came to Mendoza twenty years ago to work on the "new wines." At Terrazas, they believe that altitude is the most important factor in terroir. Their vineyards range from 900 m to 1,500 m, with different varieties planted at different elevations. Syrah and Cabernet Sauvignon are planted in the lowest vineyards: Malbec and Merlot are planted at cooler elevations of 1,050-1,150 m. But even the lowest elevations would qualify as mountain vineyards within the context of, say, Napa Valley. "We play with the altitude like in France they play with the latitude," says Hervé.

I asked Hervé whether the decision to focus on varietal wines was a marketing decision or because they express the terroir better. "The dominant influence was the United States and Australia, driving in the direction of varieties. If you go through the phone book, under M you will find Malbec, but where would you find 'blend?' We produced what people wanted to buy. Commercially there was a feeling that Malbec was just a table wine, and there was pressure to produce Cabernet Sauvignon. But from outside Cabernet Sauvignon was boring and the Malbec was discovered. The driving force was the journalistic view—the next big thing for you is the Malbec," he says.

The top Cabernet here is the single vineyard Los Aromos, at 980 m the highest elevation at which they grow Cabernet. Yet the wine is refined and pure, with that directness of 100% Cabernet, but no signs of harsh mountain tannins (page 450). The Reserva range is made in a more obviously approachable New World style. Terrazas also has a collaboration with Château Cheval Blanc to produce a Cabernet-Malbec blend, Cheval des Andes, and interestingly this actually has a firmer character than the single varietal Los Aromos.

Recognition of subregions by consumers hasn't yet gone beyond Mendoza, but there's already a clear distinction in the market for purchasing grapes. "We pay different prices for Malbec from different places, and to a lesser degree for Cabernet Sauvignon," says Hervé. This discrimination is purely internal so far, but in due course I would expect to see more precise location of origin making its way on to the label. "Sub-appellations? You are absolutely in the middle of the debate among winemakers. We know that we have to sell less Malbec and more Mendoza. You will see more and more single vineyards, starting with the Malbec. Each berry of Malbec has to be merchandized and the best way is to say which vineyard it came from. The future will be to speak about wines of individual areas, Malbec from Altamira or Cabernet Sauvignon from Perdriel," is Hervé's view. Not surprisingly, there are differences of opinions on this issue. When I asked the Catenas whether consumers were ready to recognize sub-appellations, they replied simultaneously: Nicolás said yes, but his daughter Laura said no.

The difference between varietal Cabernet Sauvignon and the dominant blend is surprisingly similar in Chile and Argentina, although in Chile the other variety is Carmenère and in Argentina it is Malbec. Both provide tannins that are softer and silkier to complement the sterner structure of the Cabernet Sauvignon. Malbec perhaps offers a slightly more lush impression, although Carmenère can be very smooth when it is fully ripe. Usually I found the blends to be more interesting than the varietal Cabernet, especially as the wine ages, when varietal Cabernet can show quite a spartan backbone. Whether blends or varietals, the wines in Chile show more restraint compared to the more open, forward quality of Argentina.

Although there are differences, there is also a certain commonality to the Cabernets of Chile and Argentina, but I was struck as the result of a visit to Bodega Weinert by how much this depends on a consensus to winemaking. At Weinert, winemaker Hubert Weber marches to the beat of a different drum. "The new style of winemaking is not very friendly for aging; if you concentrate on blackcurrant aromas and intensity, aging potential is reduced. Bodega Weinert is classic winemaking—I am not looking for intensity of young aromas, I am looking for complexity of flavor. The wine spends up to five years in 2,000 liter casks of old wood. Gran Reserva is the model," he says. Hubert has the contrarian view that Malbec has greater aging potential than Cabernet. "I like to have Malbec only from Luján de Cuyo, where the soils are heavier, Cabernet from the south where it is stonier," he says. His top wine in most years is the Cavas de Weinert, a blend of Cabernet Sauvignon, Malbec, and Merlot. The blend stays constant in varietal composition, and is produced only when all three varieties are of sufficient quality. "The blend gives more complexity but not more aging," is his view. The wine makes a distinctive impression: the absence of new oak allows the primal quality of the fruits to come through, showing a savory, almost savage, impression with age (⟐ page 451). And the wines certainly age: vintages were lively back to 1977. Younger vintages seemed more dominated by Cabernet, older vintages more by Malbec.

In years when there is an exceptional variety, a single varietal is made under the Estrella name. The Estrella Cabernet Sauvignon from 1994 is still intense, barely showing the austerity of the variety; a Merlot from 1999 shows refinement, and seems to be aging scarcely any more rapidly than Cabernet Sauvignon. As you go up the scale at Weinert, the wines start out fruitier with faintly savory overtones, and then at the top of the scale the fruits are still there of course (in fact they are more intense) but the savory and even animal notes become predominant. You might say that the wines show an increasingly European flavor spectrum.

A European aesthetic also shows itself in the wines of South Africa—in fact they are sometimes considered to be a halfway house between Old and New Worlds—although the climate is decidedly warmer in Stellenbosch, where the best Cabernet Sauvignons are produced. In fact, Stellenbosch is one of the warmest places where Cabernet Sauvignon is grown. Although nominally part of the New World, wine growing is long established in South Africa, where the first vines were planted in 1659. The center of South Africa's wine industry, Stellenbosch is about 40 km east of Cape Town, and about 10 km from the coast: cooling breezes from False Bay are an important feature, especially for south-facing vineyards. The most common terroir is sandstone over a granite base. Vineyards extend from the flat plain on to mountain slopes. Production in Stellenbosch is split about one third white to two thirds red, with Cabernet Sauvignon occupying about a third of the plantings of black varieties.[18]

The majority of Cabernet Sauvignons from Stellenbosch are aimed just above the entry-level market, the hallmark being soft, supple fruits, with just enough structure in the background to justify the varietal label. In that regard, they are not terribly different from comparable wines from other places: they certainly fit a market, but it's hard to get a good sense of place or variety. Some are 100% Cabernet Sauvignon, but some producers believe that only the best Cabernet stands alone; the next level down needs to be blended. "The best Cabernet Sauvignon gets kept for the single vineyard Cabernet Sauvignon and the Estate Cabernet Sauvignon. The batches that are slightly greener or harder are blended into our Red which is a blend containing all five Bordeaux varieties as well as Shiraz," says David Finlayson of Edgebaston. Yet if you look at the very top wines, they tend to be Bordeaux blends. Alcohol is usually high, between 14.0 and 14.5%, but is rarely obtrusive.

The general style of the entry or mid-level Cabernet Sauvignons is for the wines to be nutty rather than savory, with overtones of vanillin, giving the im-

Vineyards in the Simonsberg Ward of Stellenbosch are on a rolling plain running up the slopes of the mountains.

Photograph courtesy Warwick Wine.

pression that a lot of new oak was used (⅋ page 453). It seems that South African producers haven't backed off from new oak as much as their counterparts elsewhere. Certainly Stellenbosch is capable of a variety of styles, from the extremes of the ripe, rich, extracted international style of Edgebaston to the restrained black fruits with classically herbaceous overtones of Vergelegen (one of the grandest of the old Cape estates, originally established in the seventeenth century). Of the pure Cabernet Sauvignons, perhaps the closest to a European style is the flagship Lady May bottling from Glenelly, established by May de Lencquesaing after she sold Château Pichon Lalande, although even here there are some of those overly aromatic overtones of the New World. The wines that stand out most distinctly are the mountain Cabernets, coming from vineyards at significant elevation in the mountains: Stark-Condé (600 m above Stellenbosch) and Cederberg (1,000 m elevation 250 km north of Cape Town) both give impressions reminiscent of the mountain Cabernets from Napa, although the fruits are not so intense.

Within Stellenbosch, the Simonsberg Ward focuses the most sharply on Cabernet Sauvignon. This is a small appellation—although the wines are usually labeled just as Stellenbosch—referred to casually as "Cabernet country" by the local producers. The appellation is restricted to areas with rust-colored (ferrous) clay soils based on decomposed granite. The soils are relatively fertile, which calls for some serious canopy management to keep yields down. Vineyards on the slope of the Simonsberg mountain go up to 500 m, cooler on the southwest-facing Stellenbosch side than the north-facing Paarl side. Clay content increases going down the slope. White grapes tend to be planted on the higher slopes, black grapes lower down.

"Our Simonsberg appellation has a silver thread of defining characteristic that runs through it. It is a slightly herbal, sometimes minty, but never green flavor with big structure, big body and it can be picked easily by those in the know. We have found over the past thirty years that we cannot in fact impact the thread that runs through the wines that much through oenological manipulation. Vintage variation tends to exaggerate or deaden these characteristics, but they are always there," says Mike Ratcliffe of Warwick Wines. As elsewhere, however, criteria for harvesting have a big effect. "The sloped, ferrous rich, red soils, which range from loamy to clay/shales that we have, are renowned for giving different styles of Cabernet Sauvignon, ranging from quite herbal /minty through to cassis and dark chocolate flavors. Ours tend to be the latter but if we pick too early, we get the more herbaceous style," says David Finlayson of Edgebaston. Thelema Mountain Vineyards, at 370-640 m occupying one of the highest locations on Simonsberg Mountain, even capitalizes on this by producing a Cabernet Sauvignon called "The Mint," from a single vineyard close to an avenue of eucalyptus trees lining the approach to the winery. Personally I find its overall impression to be more herbal than minty.

The impression of the Bordeaux blends is more overtly European than the monovarietal Cabernets, and with more than three or four years of age they tend to show some savory development. They have higher alcohol and do not exhibit Bordeaux's refreshing uplift, but tending towards the herbaceous end of the flavor spectrum rather than overt, bright, fruits, they are closer to Bordeaux in style than they are to Napa. All have some ageworthiness. Meerlust's Rubicon, one of the longer established Bordeaux blends, which has been made since 1980, was my favorite, and seemed a dead ringer for Bordeaux. The best of the South African Bordeaux blends might be regarded as equivalent to good Cru Bourgeois in the northern parts of the Médoc.

Cabernets from South Africa and South America are the most restrained in the New World. While it's true that the breakthrough into the market came from entry-level wines, there are now serious efforts at quality which, if they do not yet rival top wines of Bordeaux or Napa, certainly compete with mid to higher tier wines. The big question is where the focus will be in the future.

8

Antipodean Range

CABERNET SAUVIGNON has a wider range of styles in Australia than any-where else. At one extreme, if there is anywhere that applies the full New World treatment, meaning maximum extraction of flavor, it is Australia. The spotlight in Australia is certainly on Shiraz, which is about half of black grape plantings.[1] Cabernet Sauvignon has about half the acreage of Shiraz, so in terms of production is about a quarter of all red wine. At first, not much distinc-tion was made in style: Cabernet Sauvignon tended to be treated in much the same way as Syrah, giving intense, aromatic, wines. But more recently there has been a transition to a more reserved style coming from cooler locations. There's a rough division between Barossa, McLaren Vale, and Langhorne Creek as warmer sites, contrasted with Coonawarra and Margaret River as relatively cooler sites, where Cabernet Sauvignon is the main focus. These are the quality leaders (the first four in South Australia), and together account for about a quar-ter of all the Cabernet Sauvignon plantings.[2]

The best known area of South Australia, Barossa Valley is a little on the warm side for Cabernet Sauvignon. A popular tourist destination only an hour from Adelaide, it is known for its powerful, aromatic Shiraz. It is fair to say that the Cabernet Sauvignon follows the same stylistic imperative: it is bold and exuberant, with strong blackcurrant aromatics. Cabernet Sauvignon is about 10% of Barossa's total production. South of Adelaide in slightly cooler climates, the proportion of Cabernet Sauvignon increases in McLaren Vale and Langhorne Creek, where the style is more toned down, and it becomes the most important variety in Coonawarra, where the fruits seem more elegant and precise, and it amounts to about half of all production. Over in Western Australia, it is similarly important in Margaret River, where it is about half of all red wine.

There are conflicting views in Australia about what Cabernet should represent. One young Barossa winemaker's experience when he visited Bordeaux in 2000 epitomizes the gap between the new breed of winemakers in Australia and expectations based on European experience: "I had not grown up with European wines, but I traveled with a group of winemakers who had been brought up on Bordeaux wines. We visited châteaux including the first growths and they were oohing and aahing about the wines, but I couldn't see it. There wasn't any fruit, and they talked about fruit developing with age, but that doesn't happen; the wines were thin and tannic and they tasted of Brett. I thought they were rubbish." They tend to be more sympathetic to the European aesthetic in Coonawarra and Margaret River, especially the latter, where the whole impetus behind winemaking was the identification of the similarities of the climate to Bordeaux. "For all our varieties here our benchmarks are Burgundy and Bordeaux. That means the style of wine you make is an attempt to capture key aspects of Burgundy and Bordeaux, except we are in Margaret River," says Keith Mugford of Moss Wood, one of the pioneer wineries in Margaret River.

The roller coaster of fashion has dominated winemaking in Australia perhaps more than anywhere else. Until the 1950s there was really no alternative: wine was sweet and fortified. It was only in the 1970s that production of dry wine overtook the fortified styles. "During the boom of the seventies, suddenly you weren't a weirdo to drink red wine," says Drew Noon MW of McLaren Vale. In the eighties there was a Chardonnay boom, until fashion turned back to reds in the nineties. In fact, the Australians attribute their reputation for big, bold wines in a massively fruit-driven style to the discovery of Barossa Shiraz by Robert Parker in the nineties. "Shiraz was regarded as a workhorse—with one or two exceptions like Grange and Hill of Grace—until Robert Parker discovered it," says winemaker Pete Bissell of Balnaves in Coonawarra. Until then, Cabernet was regarded as the most promising variety.[3] Now it is an also-ran, except in Coonawarra and Margaret River.[4]

Cabernet Sauvignon is grown predominantly in South Australia.

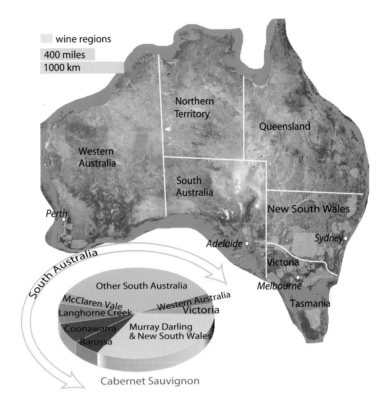

wine regions
400 miles
1000 km

Northern Territory

Queensland

Western Australia

South Australia

New South Wales

Perth

Adelaide

Sydney

South Australia

Victoria

Other South Australia

Melbourne

McClaren Vale
Langhorne Creek

Western Australia
Victoria

Tasmania

Coonawarra

Murray Darling
& New South Wales

Barossa

Cabernet Sauvignon

Barossa may not be a leader in defining trends in Cabernet Sauvignon, but Australia's best known, and probably most prestigious, Cabernet Sauvignon has its heart in Barossa. The label on Penfolds Bin 707 Cabernet Sauvignon says South Australia, but the core of the wine usually comes from the Kalimna Estate, just north of the town of Nuriootpa, where the vines may be the oldest surviving Cabernet Sauvignon in the world. Block 42 is 4 ha of old Cabernet, planted before 1888. Occasional vines that have died have been replaced individually. Adjacent to it, block 41 has vines that are 40-60 years of age.

Penfolds produce a bewildering array of wines with different bin numbers (taken from the old storage bins at the historic Magill cellar). Bin 707 is the flagship Cabernet, a multi-region blend coming from a variety of sources that have changed with time. First made in 1964, Bin 707 was discontinued after 1969, because Cabernet Sauvignon of the required quality was not consistently available, but production resumed in 1976. In recent years a major component has come from Block 42. Fruit from Coonawarra has been included since 1976. Other sources include Padthaway and Wrattonbully.

It's one hundred percent Cabernet Sauvignon, but Bin 707 has more in common with Grange, Penfolds' iconic Shiraz, than with other Cabernets. "Bin 707 is always matured in 100% American oak, in a bigger style, with less varietal dependence. 707 is like Grange, it's almost a style within itself," says

Block 42 is a 4 ha plot, surrounded by trees, at Penfolds' Kalimna Estate in Barossa Valley. Vines were originally grown as individual bushes, but now have been converted to a trellis.

winemaker Steve Lienert. Distinguished as it is, Bin 707 is not as expressive of Cabernet typicity as other wines from Penfolds. Another multi-region wine, Bin 407, sourced from Coonawarra, Wrattonbully, and McLaren Vale, has been produced since 1990 as a 100% Cabernet designed to be more typical of the variety than Bin 707. "The 707 style is a lot bigger, more concentrated, with darker fruits, and completes fermentation in American oak just like Grange. Bin 407 goes to oak only after blending," says Steve. Moving to a different style altogether, the latest development is Bin 169, a pure Cabernet varietal produced at the same quality and price level as Bin 707 (Bin 407 is less expensive) since 2008, but coming completely from Coonawarra. "What is Bin 707: it's 707—it happens to be a Cabernet; Bin 407 is more frankly a Cabernet; Bin 169 is definitely a Cabernet," says Penfolds' chief winemaker Peter Gago (☙ page 458).

None of the Cabernets from Barossa are for the fainthearted: all are bold, often aromatic and spicy. It would be fair to say that Barossa is at the limits of ripeness for Cabernet Sauvignon, but that the concentration on Shiraz has perhaps been at the expense of producing some interesting Cabernets, albeit in a bigger style. There is a certain rueful admission among producers of Cabernet in Barossa that they are swimming against the tide. "We've got old vines, we've got the climate, what's the problem?" asks Cameron Ashmead of Elderton Wines (☙ page 456). He feels that Cabernet has not been given a fair chance in Barossa. "Cabernet has never been planted in the best spots in Barossa—Shiraz

Block 42 contains what may be the oldest Cabernet Sauvignon in the world, planted by 1888.

has been. If we planted Cabernet in the best spots you might get the same consistency as Shiraz," he says.

How far Bin 707 is a winemaking stylistic choice is emphasized by tasting Block 42 separately. The special quality of Block 42 was recognized when it was first used to make an individual wine, called Grange Cabernet, in 1953. In 1963 it was produced as Block 42, and then in 1964 it was the (100%) source of Bin 707. In some vintages there is a Cellar Reserve, an estate wine coming largely from Blocks 42 and 41,[5] or less often, a Block 42 bottling.[6] But Block 42 by itself has nothing like the stylistic imperatives of Bin 707; it has a precision of fruits that contrasts with the massive intensity of Bin 707, and you might even describe it as delicate (Y page 458). In fact, it's an amazing contrast with other Cabernets from Barossa, and you can only speculate whether this is due to the age of the vines, clonal variation, or the terroir of the block.

McLaren Vale is as far south of Adelaide as Barossa is to the north. In fact, the first vines in South Australia were planted at the northern edge of McLaren Vale in the 1830s. That area is now part of the suburbs of Adelaide. It's generally a little cooler than Barossa (although there is significant variation across McLaren Vale).[7] "McLaren Vale Cabernet is like a cross between Coonawarra and I hesitate to say Barossa because it's more chocolate and fat and not about structure. In McLaren Vale, Cabernet ages longest and wines from the sixties are still drinking well," says Chester Osborn of d'Arenberg. But Shiraz is top

It's not often you see Cabernet Sauvignon grown in a region where palm trees thrive, but Seppeltsfield Road in Barossa Valley is definitely a warm spot.

dog. "With the boom after 1990 everyone went for Shiraz, and Cabernet was pushed back. It's easier for us to sell a single vineyard Shiraz than Cabernet," he says, explaining why there is a series of Shiraz wines from single vineyards, but only one top Cabernet (the Coppermine Road bottling) (⊤ page 461).

There's a sense in McLaren Vale that they could establish a better reputation for Cabernet if they weren't let down by producers who make extravagant wines, and if only the market would let them. "A lot of people have made the over-ripe style, in the past 20 years they have made almost dry red styles," says winemaker Kim Jackson at Shirvington Wines (using dry red in the pejorative Australian sense). "McLaren Vale is a richer style than Coonawarra or Margaret River. We've never had any issues with ripening Cabernet in this region," she adds. The style at Shirvington more resembles the classicism of Coonawarra than the stereotype of Barossa (⊤ page 462).

Farther south across the Adelaide Hills lies Langhorne Creek, not entirely an obvious place for vineyards given all the warnings on the road about flooding (prone to occur in the winter). Although it's a little cooler than McLaren Vale, once again the trend-setting wines here are southern varieties. But talking of old vines, here at the Brothers in Arms Metala Vineyard are some of the oldest vines in South Australia. Adjacent vineyards with 1.5 ha of Cabernet Sauvignon and 3.5 ha of Shiraz were planted in 1891. Interestingly that's still more or less the proportion of Cabernet to Shiraz grown in the region. Here blends of Cabernet Sauvignon and Shiraz are traditional. "A unique feature of the Langhorne Creek microclimate is that it allows you to grow Cabernet and Shiraz, and get both perfectly ripe. There are few regions that can perfectly ripen both varieties and we make both varietals and blends—you name it, we make it," says Guy Adams of Brothers in Arms (page 463).

"Langhorne Creek is a good region for Cabernet Sauvignon, but it is not treated with much respect. Langhorne Creek is capable of more, it is not ambitious enough, it's a great pity, they grow too many tons/acre," says Drew Noon MW, whose winery is in McLaren Vale, but who makes Cabernet Sauvignon from a small vineyard in Langhorne Creek (page 464). "My aspiration is to make the wine to be able to keep for a long time. What we mean is that they taste like young wines when they are old, we don't want them to taste like old wines, we want them to age gracefully and slowly," he says. The wines of McLaren Vale and Langhorne Creek are more in line with Barossa than Coonawarra, but with less opulence.

"There's a sense that Cabernet comes from Coonawarra or Margaret River, Shiraz comes from McLaren Vale or Barossa," says Paul Shirvington of

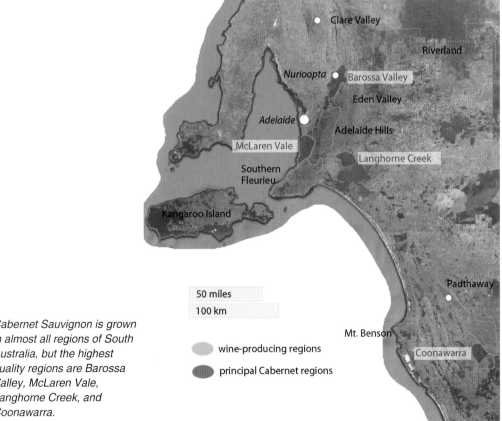

Cabernet Sauvignon is grown in almost all regions of South Australia, but the highest quality regions are Barossa Valley, McLaren Vale, Langhorne Creek, and Coonawarra.

Cabernet Sauvignon and Syrah were planted at the Metala vineyard in Langhorne Creek in 1891, so the original plots now contain vines of more than a hundred years old, on their own roots. This Cabernet is shown just after bud break.

McLaren Vale. But although Coonawarra and Margaret River are certainly the defining regions for Cabernet, their production is small in the context of Australian production. Coonawarra is devoted almost exclusively to black varieties, while Margaret River has 40% black varieties, but the most important single grape variety in each area is Cabernet Sauvignon, which translates into roughly two million cases of Cabernet from Coonawarra and well under a million from Margaret River.[8] (By comparison, the Haut Médoc or Napa Valley produce roughly 5 million cases of Cabernet-based wines each year.) Coonawarra and Margaret River each regard the other as their main challenger for defining Cabernet Sauvignon in Australia. In the Australian context, the wines are described as mid bodied, but you wouldn't say that compared to Bordeaux; there is generally speaking higher alcohol and greater viscosity here than in Bordeaux. Reflecting their relative climates, this is more evident with Margaret River.

Part of Australia's past disdain for the concept of terroir may have come from the fact that climate has generally been recognized as the most important indicator of which varieties do best in each region. Coonawarra was probably the first place in Australia that attracted any interest in terroir, but today there is also more interest elsewhere. Growers at McLaren Vale have just completed a detailed geological survey dividing the area into several subregions. The Barossa Dirt project has the target of defining subregions for Barossa and Eden Valleys. But the surveys are used more to identify the best sites, for planting the most fashionable varieties, rather than to distinguish terroirs for planting different varieties. In Coonawarra, where Cabernet is king, it tends to be planted on the Terra Rossa soils that are the best terroir; in McLaren Vale and Barossa, when Cabernet was fashionable it was planted on the best terroirs, where today Shiraz is routinely planted: there is no distinction between which terroirs might be more suited to Shiraz or more suited to Cabernet, it's simply a matter of which variety the market dictates is most in demand.

Coonawarra may be the exception that proves the rule. Isolated midway between Adelaide and Melbourne, it occupies what appears to be a flat wasteland. Most of the vineyards are concentrated in a contiguous block close to the town of Penola. There is some dispute as to whether it's really the flattest place in Australia; there is in fact an imperceptible slope from 67 m elevation at the south dropping to 63 m at the northern end of the vineyard concentration. The climate is a couple of degrees cooler than Barossa, tipping the balance for optimum growth from Shiraz to Cabernet Sauvignon.[9] The surrounding area is known as the Limestone Coast, and accounts for about 20% of wine production in South Australia (or 8% of all Australia); the quality heart of the region, Coonawarra is about 20% of the Limestone Coast.

The road to Coonawarra could almost have been built by the Romans, it's so straight and flat. Given the reputation of Coonawarra for having one of the few absolutely distinctive terroirs in Australia, it's ironic that driving along the main road you can see why terroir might be dismissed. Vineyards to the left, vineyards to the right, all are absolutely indistinguishable, with the same spacing, a similar pruning system with arms spread out in a cordon, and the only apparent variable being the orientation of the rows (some north-south parallel with the road, others east-west perpendicular to it). Winery succeeds winery, each in its own large square block, in what appears to be a contiguous monoculture of vineyards.

But in fact Coonawarra has a special terroir, the Terra Rossa, a reddish-brown soil on top of a limestone ridge. The combination of the coolest climate in South Australia with its unique geology is widely taken to be responsible for the quality of the wine. It's generally been thought that the Terra Rossa soil, given its red color by a high concentration of ferric (iron) oxide, is the crucial feature, but in fact the key is the subsoil.[10] This is an unusually permeable limestone, which gives good drainage of excess water, but retains enough moisture to nourish the vines even in dry periods. The Terra Rossa is just high enough to be clear of the water table.

Unfortunately, Coonawarra is not synonymous with Terra Rossa. The area of Terra Rossa is a cigar-shaped strip that extends for a kilometer or so on either side of the road through Coonawarra. To the west, it is replaced by heavy, black soils; going east, it peters out into sand. There was a great deal of political infighting when the GI (geographical indication) of Coonawarra was

The famous Terra Rossa of Coonawarra consists of rusty red gravelly loam above a base of limestone.

established. The rules mandated that the GI must be defined by an unbroken line, so to include some of the outcrops of Terra Rossa, intervening areas had to be included. But of course the GI extends far beyond the area of Terra Rossa, which is about a quarter of the whole area. Unfortunately, only about half of all vines in Coonawarra are on the Terra Rossa soils, although there is a tendency for Cabernet Sauvignon to be concentrated on it.[11]

The small size and lack of apparent variation in the area hide disparities on the north-south or east-west axes. There's significant temperature difference from north to south: it's cooler in the south by about one degree, resulting in as much as two weeks retardation in ripeness. There's more Continentality in the north, and more cloud cover in the south. The dividing line is more or less defined by the V & A Lane, which runs across the region just north of the town of Penola. "Years ago they used to say you couldn't make good wine south of the V & A Lane. This is not true, of course. We have some vines from the V & A area and we regard these unofficially as subregion wines that give ripeness with moderate sugar," says Sue Hodder at Wynns.

*The boundary for the
Coonawarra G.I.
extends far beyond the
Terra Rossa.*

On the east-west axis the main difference is the character of the soils. On
the Terra Rossa strip itself, the main distinguishing feature is the depth of the
Terra Rossa before you hit the limestone base. To the east, the sandy soils give
more aromatic wines; there's a tendency for Shiraz to be planted here. To the
west, the black Rendzina soils are distinctly more fertile and poorly drained.
This results in more vegetative growth, and tends to give a more leafy or herbaceous character. (Should the black soils have been included within the
boundaries of the region? Not really.) Putting together the north-south and east-
west variation, Pete Bissell of Balnaves says, "I think there are six regions in

The best vineyards of Coonawarra are located in a flat plain immediately northwest of Penola.

Coonawarra that produce different characteristics:" quite some complexity for a small area without much visible variation.

There's no doubt about the quality of the Terra Rossa terroir, but the focus on Cabernet Sauvignon is relatively recent. The origins of winegrowing in Coonawarra go back to John Riddoch, who started sheep farming in 1861. From 1890 he divided 800 ha of his land into four hectare allotments called the Coonawarra Fruit Colony, and by 1897, 120 ha were planted with vines.[12] A winery was built in 1891 (the original buildings are now part of Wynns Coonawarra Estate). His great grandson, Peter Rymill, who started the Rymill winery, recalls that, "We have the old records and they made a blend of Shiraz and Cabernet in 1895. Coonawarra was Shiraz for most of its history."

Established as a producer of fine "claret" by the end of the nineteenth century, Coonawarra fell into disarray for the first half of the twentieth century. Its renaissance started with the purchase of the old Riddoch vineyard by the Wynns family in 1951. The Wynns started planting in what is today the Johnson vineyard. "Johnson is a Cabernet-Shiraz vineyard which is an example of the thinking of the time. The oldest vines here are Shiraz and it's still a defining feature of Coonawarra to have Cabernet-Shiraz blends. They were called Claret at the time. The Shiraz here was still called Hermitage until 1994," says

Coonawarra Wine Cellars was producing wine from the Coonawarra Fruit Colony in the 1890s.

Wynns' winemaker Sue Hodder. The first varietal-labeled Cabernet Sauvignon was released in 1954. Others followed Wynns' lead into Coonawarra, and by the end of the 1960s many of the major producers had purchased land. "Shiraz did well and became dominant. In 1951 there were only 10 acres of Cabernet Sauvignon. When 100 acres of Cabernet were planted at the Balnaves farm in 1971, they doubled the area of Cabernet in Coonawarra," says winemaker Pete Bissell at Balnaves. Slowly the balance shifted towards Cabernet, and the tipping point from Shiraz to Cabernet happened in the late nineties. Today's vineyards mostly date from then, so the vines are less than twenty years old.[13]

The general impression of Wynns' wines is that savory elements are integral right from the start, although of course they become clearer as the fruits begin to recede with age (Υ page 421). "This is typical of Wynns and a bit less for Coonawarra as a whole," says Sue Hodder. "For Wynns, it's important to have varietal typicity, and for the wine to age well." It's fair to say that Wynns' wines fit the preconception of Coonawarra as a cooler climate, tending to elegance rather than power. A lot of people talk about the mintiness of Coonawarra, although personally what I see is a savory or herbal note akin to sage, but more to the point is the edgy linearity of the fruits. "There's a beautiful linearity to the Coonawarra fruits; people don't want to see too much ripeness," says Wayne Stehbens at Katnook (Υ page 466).

As one of the early producers to move into Coonawarra, Lindemans have one of the older vineyards. St. George was planted in 1890, and pulled out in the 1930s; then 12 ha were planted in 1967, and expanded to 16 ha in 2010. The original vines are an old heritage selection, supposed to have come from the vines planted by John Riddoch. "When it was planted in 1967 it was a significant proportion of Australian Cabernet," says winemaker Brett Sharpe. "St George is never a big wine, never ever," he says. "It has an unusual tannic structure, angular at first, and then showing finesse." A vertical tasting is a study

South Australia has a combination of established vineyards and modern technology.

of the evolution of Cabernet Sauvignon in Australia (Υ page 468). The style is elegant, with fruits supported by a lacy acidity, some vintages becoming savory with age, others tending more to fragrance and perfume. The 1976 (the second vintage made) remains lively, although it's now time to drink up.

Two of the top wines in Coonawarra, Balnaves' The Tally and Parker Coonawarra, are made by the same winemaker. Pete Bissell describes the character of Coonawarra: "What we are doing here in Coonawarra, which is different from what other people are doing, is to make wines that not only have flavor but that have texture. The typical Roseworthy attitude [Roseworthy is Australia's leading school of enology] is to emphasize varietal intensity—the more intensity the better, whereas Europe, especially Bordeaux, is about structure and balance and secondary complexity. We try to do something between the two. Coonawarra has that typical Australian sweet mid palate, but also a finer, grainier finish to the wine. We are making wine for people who are tired with fruit bomb styles and are looking for something more interesting, that's where we think our niche is for Coonawarra."

The Tally is usually a blend of three vineyards; the best two ferments from six parcels are selected to maintain consistency from year to year (Υ page 465). Parker Coonawarra, which styles its flagship wine as Terra Rossa First Growth, comes from a single vineyard and makes a more open declaration of vintage variation (Υ page 471). If you want to see purity of Cabernet fruits, Parker

Mechanization is common in Australia at all price levels. These old vines still show the results of "hedge pruning" in earlier years.

Coonawarra is where to come. It's classic Cabernet, with that precise definition of black fruits, elegant and sometimes even a little austere, turning a touch savory after about a decade, but with every indication of more development to come. The Tally has a firmer style, very tight at first, and beginning to open out after a decade. Asked to define the difference, Pete Bissell says that, "Parker Coonawarra has some Merlot which has a softening effect, but its vineyards are in a different region, which gives a prettier, more perfumed, profile. The Tally is a more masculine, stronger style." My own view is that I see Parker Coonawarra as very fine, very elegant—a Margaux-like finesse if you will—and The Tally is clearly an edgier wine with more tension, somewhere between Pauillac and St. Estèphe in terms of Bordeaux comparisons. Parker Coonawarra is one of the most refined wines made in Coonawarra—personally I think it is one of the closest challenges to Bordeaux coming from Australia—and perhaps for that reason ranks one notch below the more muscular The Tally in Langton's classification of Australia's top wines.

Western Australia's sense of isolation from the rest of the country hasn't changed much in the past century. In 1933 a referendum provided an overwhelming majority to secede from Australia. (The results were over ruled on procedural grounds by the British Parliament.) Most people say there would be the same result again if the referendum were repeated today. So when Margaret River started to produce wine, its reference points within Australia were somewhat limited. Efforts to prevent phylloxera from coming into the region meant, and still mean to this very day, that grapevines cannot be imported even from elsewhere in Australia, greatly restricting the available choices. To some degree this has worked unexpectedly well, focusing plantings on a selection of Cabernet Sauvignon that seems well suited to the area, and by chance often resulting in the choice of Malbec as a partner rather than Merlot. On the other hand, you have to wonder how far the views of Margaret River's potential are biased by the limited range of cultivars.

"In the late sixties Margaret River was dead, there was no future here and people were leaving," says Nick Power of the producers' association, describing the scene in 1966 when John Gladstones[14] suggested that it might be a suitable place to grow high quality winegrapes. The possibilities were brought to public attention by a letter in the *Busselton Margaret Times* in July 1966 when Gladstones pointed out that, "Growing season (summer) temperatures between Busselton and Margaret River are almost exactly the same as those districts in France and elsewhere making the world's greatest table wines."[15] This led several entrepreneurs to try their hands at planting vineyards (among them several physicians from Perth).[16] Vasse Felix was the first commercial vineyard to be established, with 4 acres of Riesling, 2 acres of Cabernet Sauvignon, and a few rows each of Malbec and Shiraz.[17] The choice of grape varieties was based more on availability than any match with terroir. "We planted Cabernet, Riesling and Traminer, because these were the only cuttings we could get. You couldn't get Merlot, Sauvignon Blanc, Sémillon, Chardonnay or Pinot," Di Cullen recollected about the foundation of Cullen a year or so later.[18]

Margaret River offers a completely different impression from Coonawarra. It's a large region, representing the eastern half of the promontory. Although there are some concentrations of vineyards, especially in the Wilyabrup area, and in Wallcliffe around the town of Margaret River, the main impression of the region is heavily forested, with vineyards and grazing pastures occurring as individual islands in the forest. There is no impression of monoculture, except for the groups of vineyards at the center. Soils are quite heterogeneous, from the best gravelly loams close to the Leeuwin Ridge, a protective line of low hills running parallel with the coast, to areas that are fit only for pasture. The general trend in planting is to put Cabernet or Chardonnay on the best soils—which is to say those with the most gravel—and other varieties elsewhere.

Subregions were distinguished on the basis of geography by Gladstones in 1999, and the big issue in Margaret River is whether they should be officially recognized. There has not been any further work to define them, although producers refer to them all the time. There's a big annual tasting when producers compare wines from all over Margaret River divided by subregion. "When you drink a Bordeaux you are always thinking about its origin—does it come from St Julien or Pauillac? In Margaret River lots of people are trying to make a wine to a style. The people who are against the subregions are just making wine; they don't care about the origins," says Stuart Watson of Woodlands. Andrew Watson adds, "There tends to be a lot of discussion about subregions, but what's disappointing is that a lot of it's about Wilyabrup versus others, but I think it should be about all the regions."

The Margaret River wine region is a large promontory, extending 50 miles north to south, and 15 miles across, bounded by the Indian Ocean to the west and the Southern Ocean to the south. The eastern boundary is line of longitude 115 18'. The region is divided unofficially into six subregions, as defined originally by John Gladstones on the basis of catchment areas for the rivers. In the northern regions, the coastal influence comes from the Indian Ocean; in Karridale it comes from the cooler Southern Ocean.

Cabernet Sauvignon dominates in the north, but white varieties are more prominent south of the town of Margaret River. The dividing line for Cabernet Sauvignon is more or less around the town of Witchcliffe; most people feel it is too cool for Cabernet Sauvignon in the Karridale area to the south. And the moderating effect of the coast is progressively lost once you move more than 5 miles or so inland. The result is that the focus for Cabernet Sauvignon is in Wilyabrup and the western half of Wallcliffe. To the north, Yallingup can be a little warm, and Carbunup has fallen victim to larger scale, more commercial plantings making entry-level wine, driven by tax incentive schemes of the eighties and nineties.

Defining styles for subregions on the basis of tastings is fraught with difficulties because many producers have vineyards, or buy grapes, from multiple subregions. Indeed, although a variety of styles was evident at a horizontal tasting of the 2007 vintage, it was not possible to correlate them directly with producers' locations (Ⓨ page 477). It's only the occasional bottle that actually carries a subregional identification—and that's almost always for Wilyabrup.

"The characteristics of subregions extend almost to stereotype," says Teresa Gibellini, vineyard manager at the Glamorgan vineyard in Yallingup (a significant source of grapes for Vasse Felix). "I've had winemakers stand up and say they won't take any Chardonnay fruit from north of (the town of) Margaret River. But the Glamorgan vineyard is 300 m over the Wilyabrup line, it's on a slope, and produces excellent fruit. It's a preconceived idea of winemaking when the first question is, where is the vineyard?"

You have to turn to barrel tastings to form an overall view of differences between subregions. An unusually wide range came from a tasting at Stella Bella; the winery is in Karridale, but grapes are sourced from vineyards all the way from Wilyabrup to the very southern end of the region (Ⓨ page 487). The Cabernet from Wilyabrup is firmer, more aromatic, more evidently fruity than from regions farther south, and often is the only sample that gives the impression of being a complete wine. As you come down into Wallcliffe, there's a more restrained impression, perhaps less broad in flavor, more precisely delineated, with more evident structure. From the Forest Grove area in the northern part of Karridale, there's a distinctly leaner impression. The Suckfizzle vineyard is the farthest south in Margaret River—"Logic will tell you this is too far south to grow Cabernet," says winemaker Stuart Pym—but it's only a touch leaner on the finish than Forest Grove, with more obvious hints of herbaceous influence.

One reason for Wilyabrup's dominance in Cabernet Sauvignon may be that the first plantings were here, so the vines are the oldest. At the core are three of the first wineries to be established, Vasse Felix, Moss Wood, and Cullen. Before he established Vasse Felix, Tom Cullity spent weekends digging holes in possible properties; his success in identifying the best terroir was indicated by a tasting of barrel samples in which the Cabernet Sauvignon from Tom's Vineyard was far and away the most complete. On the other hand, the vines were also by far and away the oldest (original plantings from 1974). The style at Vasse Felix is quite firm; the wines need time to come around, but they are elegant rather than blockbusters, and age well to the point where wines from the late seventies are still fine if only the corks have held up (Υ page 490). The belief here in Malbec as a blending partner shows in the smooth refinement of the tannins. The partner variety at Cullen is Merlot; but the style is similarly elegant, if perhaps a little more linear, and with not such long aging potential (Υ page 482).

The third of the trio, Moss Wood, is perhaps the most Bordelais in style, but of course that's a relative statement (Υ page 486). "In terms of structure we probably have more in common with Margaux, or perhaps Graves," says winemaker Keith Mugford. Beyond that, I see a richer tone to the palate, and less acidic uplift on the finish. Keith recalls how objectives shifted in the early years. "In 1982 we started to sell wine into the British market. 1983 was a classic Margaret River year with ripe Cabernet. 1984 was a cooler year and we took it to England and all they would do was damn with faint praise. And then 1985 was warm and they loved it. We realized they didn't want to buy Bordeaux from us, they wanted to buy Margaret River Cabernet."

A common feature in all three wineries is the lack of irrigation. "The old vineyards were all dry farmed—there was no infrastructure for irrigation. In the late seventies and early eighties people started irrigating. The big difference (in dry farming) is that the roots go down, you don't have all the moist roots close to the surface, there is more emphasis on fruit production and less on vegetative growth," says viticulturalist Bruce Pearse. More recent vineyards are usually irrigated, but Fraser Gallop, planted in Wilyabrup in 1999, was unirrigated. Showing how views have changed since the original plantings, "It was considered a folly and very adventurous to plant without irrigation. I took a different view—this is a proven area for unirrigated Cabernet and unproven for irrigated," says owner Nigel Gallop. The wines show a growing tendency to elegance in recent vintages, perhaps reflecting the increasing age of the vines (Υ page 482).

The firm tannic structure of Wilyabrup stands out in the wines at Woodlands and Juniper Estate. At Woodlands the lead Cabernet Sauvignon shows that linear purity of black fruits, with a touch of austerity, and hints of herbaceousness coming out on the finish; it ages well for at least thirty years (Υ page 492). At Juniper Estate, the fruits show the stern character of Cabernet Sauvignon, and the style is masculine, with firm tannins that need time to come around in the bottle (Υ page 484). Different producers' styles show a range in Wilyabrup from firm to elegant, and even in some vintages to soft, but a common feature is the breadth of the flavor variety and impression of completeness in the fruits.

Some wineries in Margaret River have sleek tasting rooms, but many are utilitarian, often with tanks outside or in open barns.

Wine production in Wallcliffe started just after Wilyabrup. Today it is dominated by the southern Mafia of Cape Mentelle, Leeuwin Estate, Voyager (Ⱡ page 491), and Xanadu (Ⱡ page 493). Is there any commonality of style? There's certainly a good sense of structure in Leeuwin's famous Art Series, which shows a definite sense of restraint in cooler years, turning to elegance in warmer years (Ⱡ page 485). The first vintage, 1982, remains vibrant today. The doyen of the Wallcliffe area is Cape Mentelle, one of the first wineries to be established there, in 1971. "As things evolved they tried quite a few varieties, including Gewürztraminer and Riesling. After a few years of experimentation they came to the conclusion that the region is best suited to Bordeaux varieties, although Chardonnay has a big place in the north," says winemaker Rob Mann. Vineyards are becoming better defined. "Over time we've learned which varieties work best, now we're looking at where they work best," he says.

My tasting notes going way back draw parallels between Cape Mentelle's Cabernet Sauvignon and the left bank wines of Bordeaux—often comparing Cape Mentelle with the Cru Bourgeois of the Médoc, but noting the higher alcohol as a give-away of origins. A vertical tasting spanning five decades confirmed those views, at least so far as older vintages are concerned (Ⱡ page 479). The wines continue to be lively after almost fifty years of age (although you have to work hard to find a bottle that's not let down by the poor quality of corks available at the period).[19] The peak vintage in my view was the 1993, caught right at that delicious transition from fruity to savory. "We're making wine more like Bordeaux used to be than it is now," says Rob Mann.

Climate is a major difference between Margaret River and Coonawarra: Coonawarra is on average about two degrees cooler during the growing season. But another difference is that there is little overlap in their clones of Cabernet Sauvignon. Its isolation through quarantine rules has meant that Margaret River has mostly grown a single selection, which can be traced back to the Houghton Vineyard in Swan Valley (a much warmer area than Margaret River) in the 1930s. This may have started out as a selection of 38 plants, narrowed to 24 or 20 according to different accounts, and possibly further. The details aren't entirely clear, except that it originated in cuttings brought from South Africa in the nineteenth century. Historically this was probably the major part of Cabernet Sauvignon plantings in Western Australia—although there's a tendency for people to say, 'Oh, it's Houghton,' when they don't know the origin. Clone 126 from South Australia was introduced into Western Australia in 1969, but was not planted until 1989; it's been the majority of plantings since then, and so is probably the majority of vines today. Clone SA125 arrived together with SA126, but is not so commonly planted.[20] "I don't think the Houghton clone has been limiting, I think it's been an advantage," says Keith Mugford of Moss Wood, expressing a common view in Margaret River. Whenever I was able to compare samples of Houghton with SA125 or SA126, I found the Houghton to be more complete, but of course there is a bias in that the vines were always older.

The clones grown in Coonawarra have very little overlap with Margaret River, so you have to wonder how far characteristics such as herbaceousness might reflect clonal properties rather than climate or terroir. The three major clones in Coonawarra are SA125, CW44, and Reynella. SA125 (and SA126) originated in 1941 at the Dorrien vineyard in Barossa Valley, and is one of the most widely planted clones in South Australia. CW44 was selected from Richardson's block in Coonawarra, and gives higher yields than SA125. The oldest in origin, Reynella is actually a selection, not a single clone, and can be traced back to a vineyard planted in McLaren Vale in the mid-1840s. (The vineyard was sold by Constellation to provide suburban housing amidst a certain amount of protest about loss of heritage.) Reynella is known for its inconsistency in yield. Both Reynella and the two Dorrien vines may have originated with cuttings from St. Julien's Château Léoville Barton in 1837.

"It's only in the past five years there's really been interest in clones. People used to ring up and say, we need 20,000 Chardonnay plants, any clone, any rootstock, we need it now. But now people are more judicious," says Nick Dry at Yalumba Nursery in Barossa Valley, where they have developed clones of Shiraz and Grenache from older vines, and are looking at the properties of some existing Cabernet Sauvignon clones. Attempting to define how these clones perform in Coonawarra, and extending the range to some new clones, Yalumba have planted an experimental plot of 5.6 ha on their estate with a variety of clones, some on their own roots, some on rootstocks. Wines are made in small fermenters at Yalumba's winery in Barossa.

I tasted samples from the 2012 vintage, all vinified in the same way (stainless steel with the same yeast), and adjusted to the same pH. SA125 stood out as the darkest, with the most intense fruits and firmest tannins (these were the lowest yielding vines), but there was an interesting difference between SA125 on its own roots, where the acidity was aggressive, and SA125 on the Paulsen rootstock, which was softer and better rounded. (It was striking that the perceptible acidities were quite distinct, although both wines had the same pH.) CA44 was lighter and more aromatic, and gave a generally leaner impression. Other clones showed quite a range from softer and fruitier to sterner and more tannic. Once again it seemed that you are abandoning an important source of diversity by focusing on any one clone, no matter how well it seems to perform in a given vineyard. The differences between these wines, made from different clones in adjacent rows of the same vineyard, reinforced the question as to what would happen if a wider variety of plant material was available in Coonawarra and Margaret River.

The availability of clones can have more widespread effects than forcing uniformity. "One clone has basically ruined the reputation of Merlot in Australia," says Nick Dry at Yalumba Nursery. "I think most people would agree that Merlot in Margaret River has been pretty atrocious," says Pete Dillon of Brookland Valley. "If there was a better clone of Merlot you would be hit by the rush to plant Merlot," says Nick Power of the Margaret River producers' association. In effect, winemakers are looking for something to round out Cabernet, but have found that the available Merlot will not do the job. When I tasted Merlot barrel samples in Margaret River, they tended to be fresh, and even tannic, rather than offering the mid palate fleshiness that would complement Cabernet Sauvignon. Curiously, the only Merlot clone that has been available in Australia, D3V14, came from California (where it is known as fps1). In Australia, the problem is that it's distinctly stalky unless you push it to very high potential alcohol levels to get ripeness. Which all goes to show that conditions in California may not predict success in Australia (although Merlot is not exactly known for its success in Napa Valley).

The Australian market has a definite bias towards varietal wines. "Australia consumers are about straight varietals, blends are looked at more skeptically," says John Rymill. A varietal wine must have more than 85% of the named variety, but as you go up the scale, from estate bottlings to single vineyards, or simply from lower to higher price points, varietal-labeled wines tend increasingly to be 100% of the variety. However, that said, there is a difference in the choice of varieties that are blended with Cabernet Sauvignon.

Small fermenters are used to make wine from the experimental plantings of different clones.

Margaret River takes a positively Bordelais view of blending. Blending part-ners in varietal Cabernet in Margaret River are most likely to be Malbec and/or Petit Verdot. By chance, Malbec was available when the early plantings were made, and as Mark Messenger of Juniper Estate says, "Forget Merlot when the Malbec is good." "Malbec is amazing in Margaret River, it gives richness in the cooler years that aren't so generous," says Paul Attwood at Leeuwin. "It doesn't matter how many times we look at Cabernet Sauvignon in the barrel, adding a little Malbec brings a touch of fruit," says Virginia Willcock at Vasse Felix. Could this contribute to a smoother character in the varietal-labeled wines compared to Coonawarra? When a wine is actually described as a blend in Margaret River, however, it's most often a Cabernet-Merlot blend.[21] But these blends are distinctly also-rans compared with the varietal Cabernet, often be-cause the best lots of Cabernet are selected for the varietal wine, and what isn't good enough to stand alone is blended with Merlot.

Coonawarra shows the influence of South Australia in its tendency to view Shiraz as an alternative to Merlot. "Our Shiraz is a lot stronger than our Merlot and we have that historical record with Syrah—the Cabernet–Shiraz blend is a deference to history—and Merlot is planted in second and third tier vineyards so it hasn't had a good run", comments Sue Hodder of Wynns. Around Ade-laide, Cabernet-Shiraz blends are the most common form of expression. Some of them are considered to be their top wines by the producers. Yet there are conflicting views about Cabernet-Shiraz blends in Australia. At Majella, where one is the top wine, Bruce Gregory says, "The Cabernet-Shiraz blend for us is typically Australian; our objective was to make a blend with the best parcels of Cabernet Sauvignon and Shiraz" (Ⳁ page 470). What does typically Australian mean? "Cabernet has a strong structure, Shiraz has spice and mulberry fruits. When they are put together you get a wine with wonderful structure but rich across the palate, whereas Bordeaux blends are more akin to straight Cabernet," says Brett Sharpe at Lindemans. A contrary view comes from Chester Osborn, at d'Arenberg, where the top wines from Shiraz and Cabernet Sauvignon are varietals, and blends of Cabernet are with Bordeaux varieties (Ⳁ page 461). "I don't blend Shiraz and Cabernet. As Shiraz ages it develops a nice spicy character. Cabernet develops more a sage impression, and as they age they fight one another." My general impression of Cabernet-Shiraz blends is that the aromatics of Shiraz easily come to dominate the Cabernet fruits and as soon as there's more than quite a small amount of Shiraz, the wine feels distinctly more Shiraz-like. Perhaps this doesn't really matter in Barossa, where the Cabernet Sauvignon often achieves a pungency that resembles the Shiraz anyway.

The styles of Coonawarra and Margaret River have changed somewhat in parallel with Bordeaux. In Bordeaux the tipping point was the 1982 vintage: up to the seventies, wines tended to herbaceousness; from the nineties the style was more fruit-driven. The change may have come a little later in Margaret River. "A little herbaceousness was acceptable in the eighties. Margaret River had a reputation for producing pretty green character until the late nineties. I remember seminars on how to reduce green fruit character," says viticulturalist Bruce Pearse. "Those herbaceous characters of capsicum (green peppers) were more accepted and even considered as the target style twenty years ago. The wines that put Margaret River on the map (winning the Jimmy Watson trophy in 1983-1984) were more herbaceous," says Glen Goodall at Xanadu. "The trend is bigger and better at the expense of varietal typicity. At high ripeness and alcohol, the lines of varietal integrity blur," he adds.

Another important factor is like the dog that (didn't) bark in the night. Brett is almost totally absent from wines of Australia, but (indirectly) has a significant influence on the fruit-forward style. Brett stands for Brettanomyces, a spoilage yeast that can infect wine to give it strong medicinal overtones. At high levels, it makes a wine undrinkable. At low levels it can give a wine leathery overtones that add complexity against the fruits, merging into the natural herbaceousness of Cabernet Sauvignon: it sticks out more with other varieties. Until the 1970s, it was common in Bordeaux and Burgundy. Many New World winemakers feel that since Brett is due to a spoilage yeast, it's a fatal flaw in wine; no level is acceptable. This view is especially strong in Australia, where the more fanatic winemakers on the subject are known as "Brett Nazis." Their position is reinforced by the fact that judges at wine shows (an important feature of the Australian wine scene) automatically throw out any wine with any trace of Brett.

The practical problem with Brett is that it's very difficult to control. "A little bit of Brett is like being a little bit pregnant," says Pete Dillon at Brookland Valley winery. "From the winemaking angle I have to eliminate it because you can't be the master of it," says Glen Goodall at Xanadu Wines. Is there an inconsistency given that when Margaret River winemakers took Bordeaux as their model, Brett was still common there? "Yes, but I don't like those wines any more. Brett interferes with wine's primary aromas, I don't like it. It's basically a winemaking fault," says Keith Mugford at Moss Wood. "A wine is never better with Brett than without it," says winemaker Pete Bissell at Balnaves. The final word goes to Wayne Stehbens at Katnook. "I hate Brett. You can get good enough character from the grape and nature without worrying about what is essentially a spoilage character. I sterile filter every wine that goes to bottle."

Brettanomyces' ability to infect wine is strongly influenced by acidity, and it's common for Australian winemakers to increase acidity to ensure there will be no infection. "As ripeness increases, acidity decreases. That was probably the reason for the Brett epidemic of the late nineties," explains Glen Goodall. I suspect the reaction, acidifying to eliminate Brett, explains the palpable sensation of acidity, slightly disjointed from the rest of the palate, that is common, especially in the Cabernets of Coonawarra. Of course, one reason for adjusting acidity is that wine tastes flabby if acidity is too low. But adjusting acidity to exclude Brett infection may raise the level to a point at which it becomes noticeable, and can seem disjointed in the context of the ripe flavors of the palate.[22]

The same thread of concern that wines should be ready to drink when released runs through Australia as elsewhere, but many of the top Cabernets from Coonawarra and Margaret River do have good aging potential. Some producers focus on drinkability for all wines except the very top tier, where consumers are more accepting of the need to delay. At Yalumba, where the top Cabernet is The Menzies and there is a second wine called Cigar, Dan Newson says, "Prior to 2002, we had really nice wine but it had to be put away for 10 years; consumers didn't like it. Changes in the vineyard have made the wine more approachable. In terms of ageability, wine needs to be drinkable on release. Instead of compromising Menzies, we introduced Cigar in a more approachable style" (Υ page 475). I was impressed generally with a number of wines that seemed to reach their peak after a decade, including Balnaves' The Tally, Parker Coonawarra First Growth, Lindeman's St George, Wynns' single vineyard wines and John Riddoch from Coonawarra, and Leeuwin Art Series, Cape Mentelle, Moss Wood, Vasse Felix, and Woodlands in Margaret River.

What is the aging potential of Cabernet Sauvignon from Australia, or perhaps more to the point, what are the wines like when they reach their peak?

The question is complicated by the fact that the corks sent out to Australia right up to the point when they switched to screwcaps—in the early 2000s for most producers—were truly terrible. This is all the more frustrating because some older bottles where the corks were good have been really splendid. Four wines from the 1970s make the case. Yalumba's 1970 Galway Reserve Vintage Claret (a blend of 90% Cabernet Sauvignon with 10% Shiraz) from Barossa (⟁ page 460), and Lindeman's 1976 St. George Cabernet Sauvignon from Coonawarra (⟁ page 468) are still lively and interesting, although it's time to drink up. In Margaret River, the Cabernets from Cape Mentelle in 1979 (⟁ page 479) and from Vasse Felix in 1978 (⟁ page 490) have that characteristically delicious blend of mature fruits with herbaceous overtones; both are good for a few years yet. Coming forward into the eighties, the first vintage of Leeuwin Art Series Cabernet in 1982 (⟁ page 485) similarly gives quite a left bank impression, and the Moss Wood Cabernet from 1986 (⟁ page 486) has the tar and leather of old Bordeaux; both are distinguished from Bordeaux by that slightly more viscous impression on the palate. Any of these wines would show well against wines from the Médoc of the same period. The difference with Napa Valley is epitomized by a comparison of two wines from the 2001 vintage: seeming at a similar stage of development, both have smooth, elegant, precise Cabernet fruits, but the Leeuwin Art Series from Margaret River has a faint leanness showing as a barely detectable (and delicious) touch of herbaceousness, while the Mondavi Reserve from Napa has a silky, plusher, quality showcasing those rich fruits of California (⟁ page 399).

Current vintages in Australia are almost all bottled under screwcap, so producers expect the wines to stay fresh for longer. Certainly the wines will age more slowly; to what extent this will also change the balance during aging, as fruits decline and savory influences come up, remains to be seen. Will the higher degree of ripeness (and the constant pressure to make wines that can be consumed upon purchase) change the aging pattern of the current vintages? Well, you could ask the same question of Bordeaux.

One reason for the softer impression of much Australian Cabernet compared to Bordeaux is barrel fermentation. This is somewhat misleading as a description, as fermentation in the barrel is a technique used for white wines; it is not practical for red wines because of the presence of large amounts of skins and seeds. In conventional winemaking, fermentation continues until all the sugar has been converted to alcohol, and then (or after a few days delay to allow further extraction), the juice is drained off and the skins are pressed. An alternative technique that's sometimes used in Australia is to press the juice off the skins before fermentation has been completed, typically when there's another 4% or so of alcohol to go. Fermentation is then allowed to complete in barriques. That's what it means when you see "barrel fermentation" on the label of a bottle of red wine. The resulting wine has softer, more rounded, tannins; in fact, a

Cabernet Sauvignon becomes more like Merlot; does this reduce the need for blending with Merlot? Some producers use a mixture of lots, with some pressed off early, but others pressed off immediately after fermenting to dryness, or macerated on the skins for several days after fermentation, to achieve something of the same textural variety you might get with a blend of grape varieties.

There is no such thing as a cool climate in mainland Australia, but Coonawarra and Margaret River are relatively cool ends of the warm climate spectrum. The real thing is found in New Zealand, which for the most part is too cool a climate for Cabernet Sauvignon, but Gimblett Gravels in the north is the world's most recent area for growing Cabernet Sauvignon. It's recent in the sense that there were virtually no vineyards until the 1990s, but more so in that the area did not even exist until the Ngaruroro river flooded in 1867. The river had previously flooded many times, depositing gravel in the flooded areas, but in 1867 it permanently changed its course, exposing 800 hectares of gravel-rich terrain of the old flood plain. It's part of the Hawkes Bay region, which was (and still is) a significant area for wine production, but the terroir of Gimblett Gravels is unique.

A couple of degrees warmer than Hawkes Bay itself, Gimblett Gravels was regarded with disdain as unsuitable for any agricultural use until the first vineyards of black varieties were planted in 1981;[23] ten years later there were still only 20 hectares planted. Large companies started to purchase land in the early 1990s. This led to a great clash. In 1988, a concrete company purchased 150 hectares with the objective of mining for gravel. Alan Limmer, a soil chemist who was one of the early pioneers and had planted the Stonecroft vineyard in 1982, led the fight to keep the land for viticulture. In 1997, the company conceded defeat and sold its land, which became the Craggy Range vineyard. Today most of the 800 hectares are planted with grapevines, and the area is among the most expensive viticultural land in New Zealand.[24]

The majority of plantings are black varieties, led by Merlot and Cabernet Sauvignon, followed by Syrah.[25] The Cabernet Sauvignon is usually blended with Merlot. (In terms of single varietal wines, Merlot and Syrah are the most common among the reds.[26]) Cooler than Bordeaux, Gimblett Gravels has more Merlot because it ripens earlier and gives better yields than Cabernet Sauvignon, but Steve Smith MW of Craggy Range says that, "The blends tend to be more right bankish [in varietal composition] and the character of the wine more left bank... Merlot in Gimblett Gravels can actually be quite tannic and therefore I believe the wines are probably closer to left bank in style because of the gravelly soils creating a more taut linear palate profile. In a way they are more Graves-like than anything." But he says that at Craggy Range, "Our actual preference is for higher and higher proportions of Cabernet Sauvignon and it wouldn't surprise me that within a decade, once we have more plantings of the most desirable clone/rootstock combination (this is a big deal) that we end up

The deep gravelly soils of Gimblett Gravels are excellent for Cabernet Sauvignon.

Photograph courtesy Villa Maria Group

with Cabernet Sauvignon closer to 30% or 40% or maybe equal to Merlot, particularly in the warmer vintages" (Y page 496).

Tightly defined by the gravel soils, Gimblett Gravels is unusually homogeneous, so there is little impetus to focus on single vineyard bottlings.[27] Vineyards farther from the river are slightly more prone to frost, and there are variations in the relative depths of gravel and silt: as might be expected, the tendency is to plant Cabernet Sauvignon on the more gravelly plots, and Merlot on the plots with more silt, but these are fine differences.[28] "I believe the future is that the greatest wines will be made from assembling parcels from the very best parts of each vineyard, possibly even the appellation considering its relative homogeneity," says Steve Smith. "The best wines will be based every year on... a blend that is consistent with the house style. This is how Bordeaux works and this I believe is the model that works for us."

Is Gimblett Gravels too cool to produce a monovarietal Cabernet Sauvignon in the New World style? "Not really," says winemaker Alastair Maling MW of Villa Maria. "You could make a pure Cabernet Sauvignon probably five years out of ten, but you would not have continuity in the years when it's not possible. If you make a Cabernet-Merlot blend, you have some wiggle room." Villa Maria's Hawkes Bay bottling is a blend with more than half Merlot, while their Gimblett Gravels blend has a majority of Cabernet Sauvignon; in each case, the basic decision was which variety should dominate, and then the exact blend depends on the year (varying from 55-88% Merlot with the Hawkes Bay, and from 55-75% Cabernet Sauvignon with the Gimblett Gravels). This is a typical model for the region.

A tasting of the 2009 vintage identified a range of styles (ⵏ page 494). All of these wines give more of an Old World than New World impression, with the fruits held back by the structure, and often in the background rather than right at the forefront; there's a definite impression of cool climate. With one exception, the wines were blends; Cabernet Sauvignon ranged from 38% to 70%, but the proportion of Cabernet Sauvignon seemed to be a less important determinant of style than the choice of other varieties. Malbec has a tendency to bring smooth, silky, tannins and to give the wine an overall sense of refinement, but the wines can seem to simplify with time. Cabernet Franc tends to bring a precise, lively, elegance. Merlot is more of a question mark, filling in the mid

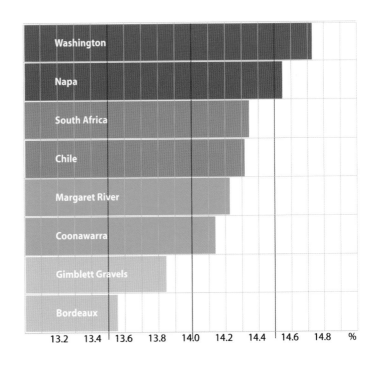

Average alcohol levels in Cabernet Sauvignon from the 2009 vintage show that Bordeaux remains the most moderate and Washington the highest, although they are the two regions with the highest latitudes.[29]

palate in traditional manner, but tending perhaps to a touch of rusticity in the tannins when the wines are young, giving an overall impression resembling the Cru Bourgeois of the Médoc, but with more grip as the wines age. In general, it's not the acidity that gives away the cool climate origin, but a certain angularity to the fruits, and a sense of lack of generosity in the structure of the Merlot.

For all the fuss about alcohol—"if the wine is balanced why do you care about the level?"—alcohol levels are as good a guide as any to the general relationships between styles of different regions. Alcohol levels in the southern hemisphere usually average between 14.0 and 14.5% alcohol, a relatively narrow range, varying with vintage conditions. Gimblett Gravels is the exception, at just under 14%. The northern hemisphere has a wider range, with Bordeaux definitely at the low end, typically under 13.5%, and Napa Valley and Washington State certainly at the high end, usually over 14.5%. Coonawarra and Margaret River are the most moderate regions in the New World (aside from even-cooler Gimblett Gravels). If you go back thirty years, everywhere except Napa was about 12.5% (sometimes with assistance from added sugar in Bordeaux), but those days are gone. If you want wine with moderate alcohol and a restrained character to replace Bordeaux, Coonawarra, Margaret River, or Gimblett Gravels come closest in terms of style. South Africa, Chile, and Argentina are halfway houses; and Napa Valley, Washington, and South Australia (except Coonawarra) are at full throttle.

9

Cults and Icons

CABERNET SAUVIGNON dominates by far the cults and icons of the wine world. The Premier Grand Cru Classés of Bordeaux's left bank are virtually unique in having been icons for two or more centuries. In the past two decades, they have been joined by cult wines from Napa Valley, marked increasingly by the concentration and power produced by extreme ripeness. Aside from Cabernet Sauvignon, top wines from the right bank of Bordeaux have become icons in the past fifty years, and some collectible wines from other regions and varieties have achieved iconic status, but for no other place or variety is there the density of cults and icons found with Cabernet Sauvignon.

Perhaps the first icon wine was Shedeh, a red wine sufficiently prized in ancient Egypt for amphorae to be buried with King Tut.[1] By the time of the Greeks, the best wines were considered to be sweet styles from the Aegean islands. In ancient Rome, the sweet white Falernian wine (made from partially dried grapes grown on the slopes of Mount Falernus near Naples) was considered the connoisseur's choice; the especially fine vintage of 121 B.C. became

Château	Second Wine	Vineyards	Cabernet Sauvignon	Production (Grand/Second)
The first growths are dominated by Cabernet Sauvignon (in the Médoc) and are among the larger producers.				
Latour	Forts de Latour	80 ha	80%	15-16,000 / 18,000
Mouton Rothschild	Petit Mouton	84 ha	83%	16-18000 / 5,000
Lafite Rothschild	Carruades de Lafite	103 ha	70%	15-20,000 / 15-20,000
Margaux	Pavillon Rouge	92 ha	75%	12-13,000 / 16,000
Haut Brion	Le Clarence de Haut Brion	51 ha	50%	10,000 / 7,000

known as Opimian after the name of the Emperor. In a foretaste of the mark of cult wines, Pliny remarked that the highest prices were paid only "in a fit of extravagance and debauchery."[2] Flaunting their ability to provide such wines became the mark of the nouveau riche.

Long before they were sanctified by the 1855 classification, the leading châteaux of the left bank became identified as a breed apart. The four châteaux of Lafite Rothschild, Latour, Margaux, and Haut Brion became the first icons of the modern wine world. The first to be recognized was Haut Brion, known originally as Pontac, and then as Ho Bryan, before the modern spelling was adopted. By the start of the eighteenth century, the top wines were maintaining their superior position by setting prices in unison, led by Châteaux Margaux and Haut Brion.[3]

Over the next century, there was increasing focus on individual châteaux, and the brokers in Bordeaux developed a series of classifications to guide pricing in each vintage. Although there were changes in the hierarchy through the various classifications, the same group of four always headed the list.[4] When the châteaux were classified in 1855, the four first growths maintained a significant price separation from the other châteaux, which showed a more or less continuous price distribution, headed by Mouton Rothschild.[5] Virtually the only change in the primacy of the first growths since the seventeenth century has been the de facto addition of Mouton Rothschild in the early twentieth century, confirmed by its formal promotion to first growth status in 1973 after a fifty year campaign by Baron Philippe de Rothschild.[6]

Mouton's change of status naturally raises the question of whether promotion might be appropriate for other châteaux. But whether or not this is so, Mouton is a unique case. Baron Philippe ascribed Mouton's omission from the first growths to extraneous factors: "There was not the faintest trace of anything that might in the judges' eyes justify the word 'château'. In that era, an impos-

Mouton Rothschild commissioned labels from different artists, starting in 1924 with a design from Jean Carlu.

The design was considered revolutionary and even described as "Bolshevik."

The prominent statement on the label that the wine was bottled at the château was another novelty at the period.

ing building, a true 'château' counted for as much as the wine... And Baron Nathaniel had been proprietor for only two years. And he was English!"[7]) Actually, there were only five 'chateaux' at the time of the classification. And the fact is that for the rest of the nineteenth century, Mouton averaged 80% of the price of the first growths. It closed the gap to maintain parity in the 1920s after its first label by a famous artist appeared in 1924.[8]

How have the first growths been able to maintain their iconic position over centuries? Is it because their terroirs are so superior to all others that the wines are always better? Or is it due to a self-reinforcing circle in which early success provided the resources needed for continuing improvements in viticulture and vinification that were always a step ahead of the competition? Could it even be that the imprimatur of "Premier Grand Cru Classé" provided a marketing advantage that continues to resound down the decades? There's more than an element of truth in all of this, and Mouton is the exception that proves the rule: its promotion owes as much to Baron Philippe's forcefulness as to the wine itself.[9] Part of the reason the first growths remain supreme is the barrier they maintain to any other château breaching their price level (partly as a result of Bordeaux's monopolistic distribution system). Although critics may rate châteaux in the group of "super-seconds" higher than the first growths in some vintages, the market remains immune to any change in the price hierarchy.

The historic nature of Bordeaux shows in the lists of top wines over time. Bordeaux is not static, but change occurs by reordering existing châteaux in the hierarchy rather than by introducing new producers. Virtually all châteaux on the list of leading left bank wines have existed for at least a century—although their second wines are new. (Change has been more obvious on the right bank, partly due to the emergence of small production "garage wines," which for a period rose to the top of the critics' ratings and to the highest prices. But Cabernet Sauvignon plays little part in the garage wines; all are based on Merlot.)

As one of the oldest Châteaux in Bordeaux, it is fitting that Haut Brion has a classical facade.

The same five wines—the first growths—were at the top of the price list for left Bank Bordeaux in 1982 and 2010 (and for that matter in 1855). The next ten contain a good proportion of wines that have been prominent for a century, although the order has changed over the past three decades, and some wines have risen up the hierarchy.[10] Critical opinion changes more rapidly than price, but the top wines listed by whatever criteria remain recognizable.

There is little controversy about the icons of Bordeaux. The First Growths are the First Growths, always have been, and always will be, is pretty much the attitude. Perhaps this lack of argument is because, ever since the 1855 classification, market price has been stamped as the definitive measure of success in Bordeaux, and (whether due to intrinsic quality or to self-fulfilling reputation) they have stayed firmly at the top. Of course, once you pass a certain financial point, in which price is completely decoupled from the costs of production, resources become more or less irrelevant to quality. That point has certainly now been passed for the super seconds as well as the first growths, and perhaps if it were not for the calcifying effect of the 1855 classification, some of the super-seconds would challenge the status of the first growths.

I am inclined to divide Bordeaux's first growths into two groups. Châteaux Latour and Mouton Rothschild are usually the most powerful. Although Lafite Rothschild is adjacent to Mouton Rothschild, its style is different, more elegant

The ecclesiastical origins of La Mission Haut Brion show in its cloister.

and precise, as also are Château Margaux and Château Haut Brion. The first growths of the Médoc are heavily dominated by Cabernet Sauvignon (averaging 82-84% in recent vintages), but Haut Brion in the Graves to the south stands alone, with less than 50% Cabernet Sauvignon in most recent vintages.

Haut Brion is by far the longest established of the first growths. In the late seventeenth century, the top wines available in London were distinguished as Médoc and Pontac. "Médoc" referred to several wines, including what were to become Lafite Rothschild, Latour, and Margaux, but "Pontac" referred specifically to what was to become Haut Brion.[11] A famous entry in Samuel Pepys's diary from April 10, 1663 notes that he "drank a sort of French wine, called Ho Bryan, that hath a good and most particular taste that I never met with."[12] Within a few years, Haut Brion had in effect become Bordeaux's first cult wine, selling to the cognoscenti at Pontack's Head, the restaurant in London run by the son of Arnaud de Pontac, Haut Brion's proprietor.[13] Jonathan Swift complained that the wine was expensive at 7 shillings a flagon.[14] Visiting Haut Brion in 1677, the philosopher John Locke commented that its price was rising "thanks to the rich English who sent orders that it was to be got for them at any price."

The owners of Château Haut Brion seem to have felt a distinct superiority at the time to La Mission Haut Brion. As the result of his visit, Locke perceptively summarized Haut Brion's advantages in terms of terroir: "The vine de Pontac, so much esteemed in England, grows on a rising open to the west, in a white sand mixed with a little gravel, which one would think would bear nothing; but there is a such a particularity in the soil, that at Mr. Pontac's, near Bourdeaux the merchants assured me that the wine growing in the very next vineyards, where there was only a ditch between, and the soil, to appearance, perfectly the same, was by no means so good."[15] Presumably this was a reference to La Mission Haut Brion!

Haut Brion was the only wine of the Graves to be included in the 1855 classification.[16] The puzzle is the complete absence of any mention of La Mission Haut Brion. Notwithstanding the disdainful comparison with Haut Brion in 1677, the terroirs are not so different. Certainly Haut Brion maintained its pre-eminent position in the hierarchy over the next two centuries, but it is hard to believe that the difference was so great that La Mission Haut Brion did not merit inclusion at any level. But while the brokers' records divided the Médoc into eight price groups (five levels of classified growths and three of bourgeois), Graves was divided into Haut Brion versus the rest (which priced out collectively below the classified growths).[17] Records at Mission Haut Brion suggest that its price at the time of classification was just below the fifth growths.[18]

As its name suggests, La Mission Haut Brion had monastic connections; in fact the land (probably already functioning as a vineyard), was donated to the Congregation of the Mission in 1664. Under the monks, the wine apparently became quite well known during the eighteenth century, and was said to have been drunk by the ecclesiastical notables of the period. The property was confiscated at the Revolution, and the modern era starts when it was acquired in 1821 by the Chiapellas, a family of ship owners from New Orleans. Certainly it was well known soon after the classification: in 1862 it was awarded a gold medal at the Exhibition in London.[19] Cocks and Féret, the standard reference, listed it in third place in Pessac in 1868, after Haut Brion and Pape Clément.

During the first part of the twentieth century, both Haut Brion and Mission Haut Brion fell into decline. Haut Brion's revival started when the property was acquired by Clarence Dillon, a New York banker, in 1935. La Mission Haut Brion had previously been sold to the Woltners in 1919, who managed it through the twentieth century until they sold it to Domaine Clarence Dillon in 1983. Since then, both properties have been under the same management, with the same winemaker. Today it can sometimes be hard to draw a line in terms of quality between the two châteaux. In terms of price, La Mission Haut Brion occupies a position just below the first growths. It's hard to say whether it should be reclassified as a first growth or a super-second, but in a side by side tasting of the two wines, certainly there are some vintages (albeit a minority) in which I have preferred La Mission to Haut Brion (☒ page 325). But no one could quarrel with Haut Brion's inclusion in the first growths, even though it may no longer be *primus inter pares.* Although it often has as much Merlot as Cabernet, the overall impression on the palate shows that restrained, faintly austere quality of a wine dominated by Cabernet. If I were to pick one of the first growths as the antithesis to the Napa cult wines, Haut Brion would be a leading contender.

Moving north, the next first growth is Château Margaux. Wine production probably dates from the sixteenth century, when one third of a 265 ha estate was devoted to viticulture. Red wine production dates only from the eighteenth century—previously the red and white grapes had been vinified together! But as soon as the brokers started to classify the wines of Bordeaux in the early eighteenth century, Château Margaux was included in the group of four first growths. By the end of the century, ownership had passed to the proprietor of Château Haut Brion, and after he lost his head in the French Revolution, Château Margaux was purchased by the Marquis de la Colonilla, an absentee owner whose foremost interest was in the prestige that came from its ownership. His main contribution was to construct the grand château, one of the first to be built in the Médoc. Like other châteaux, Margaux had its ups and downs through the twentieth century. In 1949 it was purchased by the Ginestets, an important negociant family in Bordeaux, but they were forced to sell after the negociant business collapsed in the crisis of 1974. An attempt to purchase by an American company, National Distillers, was blocked by the French government, who insisted on a French purchaser; but a Greek magnate, André Mentzelopoulos, was then allowed to buy the property, on the rather tenuous grounds that he owned the Félix Potin supermarket chain in France. Since then, Château Margaux has remained in the hands of the Mentzelopoulos family.

"The walled vineyard behind the park is the heart of the quality of the château," said Emil Peynaud.[20] Clear on maps from the eighteenth century, the vineyard is adjacent to the main approach to the château. Since then the estate has expanded farther into the appellation of Margaux, with the area of vines both expanding and contracting under different owners. The estate runs down to the Gironde (and includes one of the islands in the river), but the vineyards are inland from the château. At the time of the 1855 classification, the château had 81 ha of vineyards. During the early twentieth century, when quantity became more important than quality, vineyards expanded to 92 ha, but by 1949 they had declined to about 60 ha. The Ginestets then undertook a significant reconstruction of the estate, by purchasing or swapping vineyards. Even more change came with the major investments of the Mentzelopoulos era, when large areas were replanted. Today there are 87 ha in the Margaux appellation. Parcels around the château are mostly Merlot except for one of Cabernet Sauvignon. Cabernet Sauvignon is on the gravels to the north of the chateau. When Mentzelopoulos took over, some of the Cabernet Franc and Merlot was replaced with Cabernet Sauvignon, so the proportion is now higher than in the

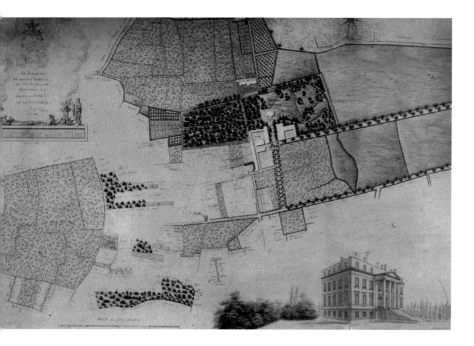

An early nineteenth century map from the Colonilla period shows Château Margaux as standing in its own park, with its major vineyards close by.

early eighties. But there has been little change since then; the average age of the vines now is 35 years.

Château Margaux went through a distinctly difficult patch before Mentzelopoulos took over—the last good vintage before the Mentzelopoulos era was perhaps the 1959—but continued improvements have brought the wine well back to first growth standard. "Improvements have largely been in viticulture, what we have added in winemaking is more precision, all the technology has helped, but there hasn't been any breakthrough. But in viticulture the great advance has been that in almost every vintage we can harvest ripe grapes. What has happened in the vineyards has more influenced the quality. For example we see in 2011 a selection that didn't exist before. Those wines that used to go into the grand vin now go into the second wine; this selection is a considerable change," says Paul Pontallier, Margaux's Directeur.

Pavillon Rouge du Château Margaux is one of the oldest second wines in Bordeaux. (The first vintage was 1908. There is also a much smaller production of the Pavillon Blanc du Château Margaux, usually considered to be one of the best white wines of the Médoc.) The relationship between grand vin and second wine may be the most striking change in the past couple of decades. Today the production of second wine usually exceeds that of the grand vin, but it is subject to a selection that's probably more severe than used to apply to the grand vin. I asked Paul Pontallier whether he thinks that Pavillon today achieves a higher standard than Château Margaux itself twenty or thirty years ago? "It's an unpleasant thing to admit, but I think so. Twenty years ago, Château Margaux would have been made in different conditions. What would have been Pavillon then would go into the third or fourth wine today."

If there is a single descriptor I would use for Château Margaux, it is "elegant" (⟁ page 338). There's a supple core of black fruits, melding imperceptibly into a velvety surround. The lineage shows clearly from the 1959 through the 1982 to current vintages, with increasing richness, but still displaying that characteristic supple, elegant, style at the core. People often associate violets with Margaux, but if there were such a thing, I think black strawberries would be the perfect description.

Château Lafite vies with Château Margaux for the description of the most refined wine in Bordeaux. In the seventeenth century, it was part of the vast Seigneurie of Ségur; already the wine was well known in England. After the Revolution, ownership was somewhat obscure, but the wine came out at the top of the 1855 classification. Baron James de Rothschild bought the property in 1866, just twelve years after his cousin Baron Nathaniel had purchased what was then Château Brane-Mouton. Since then, Lafite has hardly ever dipped below its pre-eminent position, although it did have a bad patch in the 1960s.

Located right at the northern border of Pauillac with St. Estèphe (the Jalle du Breuil drainage channel between the two appellations lies at the edge of the vineyards), Lafite's estate covers 178 ha. The 112 ha of vineyards are divided into two major areas: the hillsides around the château, and the adjacent Carruades plateau to the west (there are also 4.5 ha just across the border in Saint Estèphe). Two wines are produced from the estate: Château Lafite Rothschild itself, and the second wine, Carruades de Lafite.

Château Lafite purchased the Carruades vineyards in 1845. The terroir was considered to be virtually the equal of Lafite itself; and Brane-Mouton (as it was at the time) also tried to purchase the property. "Half an hour after the sale was completed (for 96,000 Ff), the Gérant of Mouton came to offer 100,000 Ff."[21] At first the wine was bottled separately. (In 1868, Lafite produced three wines: a grand vin, the Vin de Carruades at about three quarters the price of the grand vin, and a second wine at about half the price of the grand vin.[22]) During the twentieth century, Carruades de Lafite became a second wine, representing declassified lots from all the vineyards. At one time, Moulin de Carruades was used to describe the wine, but since 1985 the second wine has again been called Carruades de Lafite.

Until recently the grand vin and second wine had a consistent relationship, with Carruades typically selling at around a third of the price of Lafite itself. But the market for both wines has been significantly distorted recently by the great interest from China. Always brand conscious, the new Chinese consumer regards Lafite Rothschild as the premier of the Premier Grand Cru Classés, and its price accordingly has shot up in the Chinese market. Indeed, for the past two years, the price of Lafite Rothschild (and also other leading châteaux) on the

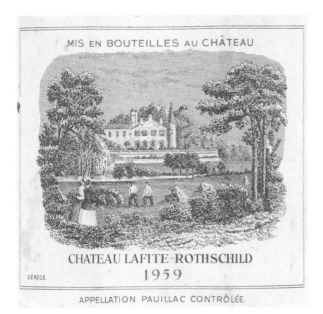

Redolent with tradition, Château Lafite's classic label has not changed in more than a century.

auction market has followed the price of the Shanghai stock index (down as well as up).[23] But the most striking demonstration of the pulling power of Lafite's name is the effect on the price of Carruades; for the 2004 vintage, Carruades has been trading recently at almost the same price as Mouton Rothschild![24] (This brought it to about half the price of Lafite itself.)

The quality of Carruades is not in question—it has always been one of the best second wines of Bordeaux; and since the nineties, its grapes also have been subject to selection. "I think there is an evolution everywhere but especially on the second wine. I started in 1983, the second wine was made as everything that did not go into the grand vin. But now the second wine is also selected; we sell off (unsuccessful) wines to the negociants. It was necessary to increase the quality of the second wine to make it a little more regular," says directeur Charles Chevalier. But it borders on the ridiculous for its price to be the same as the grand vin of another first growth. Does this mean Lafite has made the reverse transition from an icon to a cult in the original meaning of the term (an irrational religious belief)?

Lafite Rothschild marks a great contrast with its immediate neighbor, Mouton Rothschild. Even though the vineyards are almost interdigitated, Lafite is the epitome of refinement and Mouton of restrained power. Nowhere do you see the contrast more strikingly than in the wines of the 1945 vintage. Although the Lafite has perhaps begun to fade a bit in the past few years, it still shows those ethereal layers. Mouton remains incredibly youthful in its overall impression; somehow you feel you can never penetrate its core. (These wines are all the more amazing given the appalling conditions in Bordeaux in 1945, just

The view of Château Lafite has not changed since the label was drawn.

towards the end of the second world war. It's hard to believe that today's vintages, as impressive as they are today, will be this good in 2075!)

The vineyards of Mouton lie on a small hill (rising to the dizzy heights of around 30 m), and it's thought that motte, local dialect for a mound, might be the origin of "Mouton." The area falls into three parts. To the north and south are deep gravels with a low water table (more than 2.5 m down). Forcing the vines to develop deep roots, this is prime terroir for Cabernet Sauvignon. Soils are more varied in the central area, and the water table is higher. Cabernet Franc is grown here, and most of the Merlot stretches around the periphery to the north, in blocks that have more sand and clay. There are also some small blocks of Sauvignon Blanc and Sémillon, used to make the white wine, Aile d'Argent. The soil determines what varieties can be planted. "The water table is the key factor. There have been small changes towards Cabernet Sauvignon with one or two plots of Merlot replanted with Cabernet Sauvignon," says technical director Eric Tourbier. But the vineyards are mostly unchanging, and because of the high proportion of Cabernet Sauvignon (second only to Château Latour among the first growths), they are not too worried about rising alcohol. "13-ish percent is the highest we've had," says Eric. The age of vines, averaging around fifty years, may also help.

Four wines are produced by the winemaking team at Mouton Rothschild (ignoring Mouton Cadet, which as a large volume brand comes from quite dif-

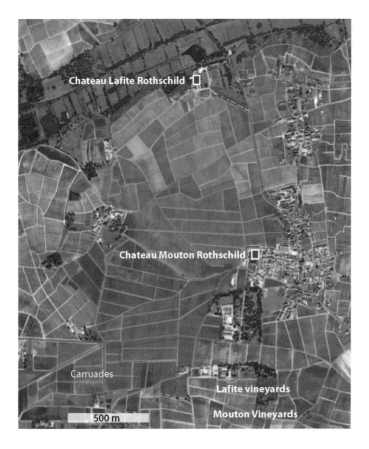

The vineyards of Lafite Rothschild and Mouton Rothschild are closely juxtaposed. The major vineyards of Lafite are immediately to the north of Mouton; the Carruades plateau is immediately to the south.

ferent sources on the right bank, and is produced at a separate plant). The second wine, Petit Mouton, is made in the smallest proportions of any second wine for a first growth, varying from 10-25% of the production of Mouton Rothschild itself. And then two adjoining châteaux are also under the ownership of Baron Philippe de Rothschild: Château Armailhac (at one time known as Mouton-Baronne-Philippe) just to the southeast; and Château Clerc Milon (just to the northeast). There is a clear sense of hierarchy at Mouton: "The cuvées are selected after malolactic fermentation for Mouton, and the Petit Mouton is made: Petit Mouton should be better than d'Armailhac," says Eric Tourbier.

Mouton is sometimes felt to show more vintage variation than the other first growths, but the words most often used to describe the grand vin are flamboyant, extravagant, exotic (Y page 340). Perhaps it has more distinct aromatics than the others; my most dramatic instance of this was when a spicy perfume filled the room as the 1998 (not a great vintage generally on the left bank) was poured. After the great 1945, the next vintages that stand out above the crowd are the 1959 (better than the 1961 in my opinion), and then the 1982. There's that impenetrable black core of fruits softening out into a velvety spiciness. The most amazing quality is perhaps the way the initial impression of dense, ripe, sweet fruits can remain into old age.

So how does Mouton differ from Château Latour, also known for its high content of Cabernet Sauvignon and corresponding power? At the southern boundary of Pauillac, the heart of Château Latour is the Grand Enclos, consisting of 47 ha extending between the D2 road and the river. Most of the vineyards were replanted in the 1920s, and some of the best plots date from then, but there was also extensive replanting in 1963, after new British owners bought the château. "The Grand Enclos originally was Cabernet Sauvignon with some complantation with Cabernet Franc. This was replanted with Cabernet Sauvignon alone," explains general manager Frédéric Engerer. This was more *faute de mieux* than a calculated decision. "When we took over in July 1963, the vineyards were in a terrible state, and we had to replant many of the vines. There was extensive complantation [intermingling of varieties]. Everywhere there were dead vines, but because they were dead you couldn't tell which variety they were; by habit we planted Cabernet Sauvignon, because it is the great vine of the Médoc," recalls Jean-Paul Gardère, who was in charge of viticulture from 1963 to 1989.

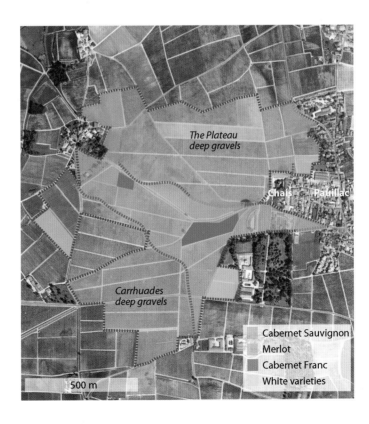

The vineyards of Mouton Rothschild have deep gravels to the north and south, with a central area where the water table is higher (shaded in green). Cabernet Sauvignon fills the vineyards except for Merlot, mostly at the periphery, and Cabernet Franc, in the central area. The chais surround the château just on the edge of the town of Pauillac.

The Plateau
deep gravels

Chais   Pauillac

Carruades
deep gravels

Cabernet Sauvignon
Merlot
Cabernet Franc
White varieties

500 m

The old chai at Mouton Rothschild dwarfs the small château

When I discussed Latour's character with Frédéric Engerer, he felt that the terroir of the Grand Enclos trumps everything else. "The character of Latour depends on the terroir. The nobility of the whole thing is just the terroir. I know your feelings for Cabernet Sauvignon, I don't want to diminish its importance, but it needs the terroir. The Cabernet Sauvignon is just the instrument, it is just the tool to express differences between terroirs. You see huge differences in the Cabernet Sauvignon from different plots." So I asked whether he regards Latour more as blend of Cabernet Sauvignon from different plots than a blend of varieties? "Well, Latour is a single vineyard, only a limited number of plots make the grand vin. I want to plant Cabernet Sauvignon instead of Merlot in some areas. First growth terroir maybe allows Cabernet Sauvignon (alone) to make great wine." So should they go to Cabernet Sauvignon alone in the best areas? "That's a very good question. The [increasing] maturity of Cabernet Sauvignon, especially the flesh around the tannins, makes Merlot more and more unnecessary. The main cause is better viticulture and canopy management. When

Merlot is planted in the best areas, they would probably make an even greater Cabernet Sauvignon. But the decision may be to put in Merlot in some places. All the bottom slopes are harvested separately—we call this the Cabernet d'Argile (Cabernet from clay). It may be better to plant Merlot in these areas, so there may be a few rows of Merlot in the lower, wetter, areas. Otherwise the question is what to do when you could make either good Merlot or Cabernet?"

A fascinating comparison of Latour's three wines from 2009—the communal Pauillac, the Forts de Latour second wine, and the Latour grand vin—showed the same massive style (Y page 332). Although Cabernet Sauvignon content increases from half in the Pauillac, to two thirds in Forts de Latour, and to 90% in Château Latour, there's little palpable sense of the expected increase in structure. Paradoxically, the increasing fruit density going up the hierarchy balances the structure more effectively so that it becomes less obtrusive, and vice-versa. Although the appearance becomes inkier, the fruits become more reserved and restrained, less evidently fruity, going from Pauillac

Adjacent to the famous tower, the buildings of Château Latour are low and unassuming.

to Forts to Latour itself, as they come into better balance with the structure. Even the Pauillac needs time to soften and come around, and in spite of the density produced by the vintage, the Forts and Château Latour will require years to show their complete range of flavors.

Would it be fair to say that the black fruits of Latour are more direct, more mainstream, less extravagant, although just as concentrated and ripe as those of Mouton Rothschild? It's a fine judgment as to which is longer lived. They used to say that the 1928 Latour took fifty years to come around to be drinkable; certainly when I had it in 2000, it was still going strong. In more recent vintages, even Latour 1945 cannot compete with the youthfulness of the 1945 Mouton. In 1959 the Mouton triumphs, whereas in 1961 Latour is the wine of the vintage (a remarkable tribute to its terroir given the terrible state of the vineyards at time). Trying to pin down relative qualities is perhaps a distinction without a difference.

It would be an even more difficult question to define which is first among the super-seconds, a group of wines defined solely by that criterion so dear to the Bordeaux marketplace: price. Most of the super-seconds are second growths, but they have been joined by some others that would undoubtedly be promoted in any reclassification. With the sole definition that their prices are

between the first growths and the rest of the pack there can be some uncertainty where you draw the line.

Léoville Lascases defines itself as a member by its history of trying (unsuccessfully) to challenge the first growths in price. Cos d'Estournel, Pichon Lalande, Ducru Beaucaillou, Palmer, and perhaps Lynch Bages, are established members of the group. More recently Pichon Baron, Pontet Canet, and possibly Montrose have been competing for admission. If the group were extended to Pessac-Léognan (it's usually described only in terms of the Médoc), Mission Haut Brion would be at the head of the group, and Pape Clément and Haut-Bailly would be contenders.

It was Léoville Lascases's avowed aim to be included with the first growths, and proprietor Jean-Hubert Delon came close to pushing his price to first growth levels in some years, most notably 1997 when there were reports that his prices had risen above the first growths.[25] But this was only temporary, and since then the price has been marked more by a sense of competition with the other super-seconds. M. Delon's attitude towards Léoville Lascases's position was quite forceful: he withdrew from the Conseil des Grands Crus Classés in 1998 "because it had become a means for commercial promotion of a disputable classification, and thereby for misinforming the consumer."[26]

Château Léoville Lascases originated with a vineyard planted on a gravel mound in the Mont-Moytié estate at the end of the seventeenth century; at that time, the mound was surrounded by marshes which regularly flooded at high tide. This makes Léoville Lascases today one of the most visible beneficiaries of the old draining of the marshes. Twenty years before the Revolution, the estate came into the hands of the Marquis de Las-Cases; after the revolution the estate was divided, but the major part was later restored to the family. By 1840, there were three Léovilles, and all were classified as second growths in 1855. The Delon family inherited a share in the Lascases part in the twentieth century and in due course became sole owners.

The major vineyard of Léoville Lascases is a single walled block, L'Enclos, which runs from the D2 down to the Gironde. This is the northern boundary of St. Julien and the vineyard is adjacent to the Grand Enclos of Château Latour, which marks Pauillac's southern boundary. The 55 ha of L'Enclos are the basis for the grand vin of Léoville Lascases. Resembling Château Latour again, Léoville Lascases has another vineyard of about 45 ha just to the west. At the start of the twentieth century, it was used to produce a separate wine. Later this became the basis of the second wine, Clos du Marquis, but in 2007 it returned to becoming a separate wine; there is now a new second wine, Le Petit Lion de Lascases.

The entry to L'Enclos is through the famous gate on the D2 road. Vineyards run from the road to within perhaps 300 m of the river. The gentle slope down to the river is slight but evident to the eye. Proximity to the river has an important climatic effect: there is 10% more humidity at the boundary close to the river than at the D2, and the temperature is 1.5 degrees lower. There is a lot of diversity to the soils, which can change within a few meters. On a path parallel with the Gironde, towards the river the soil is clay and sand; on the other side, stretching up towards the D2, it is distinctly gravelly. Léoville Lascases is strongly biased towards Cabernet: altogether the property is two thirds Cabernet Sauvignon, with another ten percent of Cabernet Franc, which is entirely in L'Enclos. "In the enclosure the encépagement is tending to move more towards Cabernet Sauvignon," says technical director Michael Georges.

How does Léoville Lascases fare on the scale of cults and icons? The wine is not as powerful and dense as its immediate northern neighbor, Château Latour, nor quite as plush as Pichon Lalande; perhaps, if this is not too imaginative, that's the difference between St. Julien and Pauillac. But it has distinctly more weight than the other Léovilles, and this perhaps is due to the terroir of L'Enclos (Υ page 334). It's very refined, and there's a definite concern to maintain tension. It is often the best wine of St. Julien, the only other pretender to the crown being Château Ducru Beaucaillou.

If Léoville Lascases is St. Julien's equivalent to Château Latour, Ducru Beaucaillou is the equivalent to Château Lafite. And it's a marker of modern Bord-

The famous gate of Léoville Lascases marks the entrance to L'Enclos, a contiguous block of 55 ha stretching from the D2 to the Gironde, that is the basis for the grand vin.

eaux that the Delons at Lascases and the Bories who own Ducru Beaucaillou both have an ascending hierarchy of châteaux in their portfolios. Lalande Borie was part of the vineyards of Château Lagrange until the Bories purchased it in 1968; now it is treated as one level of a brand that includes Croix de Beaucaillou (nominally the second wine of Ducru Beaucaillou) and the grand vin, Ducru Beaucaillou itself. There are 35 ha at each property (Croix de Beaucaillou is regarded as a property in its own right). It's a descending hierarchy: Ducru may be declassified to Croix de Beaucaillou, which may be declassified to Lalande Borie: but never the reverse. They give a clear impression of the Médoc's view of the importance of Cabernet Sauvignon: ascending the hierarchy in the 2009 vintage, Lalande Borie is 50% Cabernet Sauvignon, Croix de Beaucaillou is 75%, and Ducru Beaucaillou is 85%. There have been only Cabernet Sauvignon and Merlot in Ducru Beaucaillou since 2004 (Cabernet Franc was last included in 2003). The measure of Ducru Beaucaillou is its sheer refinement (Ⴕ page 319). Some people apparently find Ducru Beaucaillou *too* refined, but I view it as a classic example of St Julien.

Just across route D2 from Château Latour is the old Pichon estate, with Pichon Baron retaining the vineyards closest to the road and Pichon Lalande having plots inland. This leaves the château of Pichon Lalande isolated between the vineyards of Latour and Pichon Baron. (Standing on the edge of Latour's vineyards, the terrace of the château at Pichon Lalande offers one of the best views of the famous *Tour.*) Pichon Lalande is Léoville Lascases's clos-

Pauillac
Latour
Forts de Latour
Pichon Lalande
Pichon Baron

St. Julien
Léoville Lascases
Clos du Marquis
Léoville Poyferré
Léoville Barton

The southern part of Pauillac is closer to St Julien than it is to the northern part of Pauillac. The Grand Enclos of Château Latour runs to within sight of the river, and is separated by the vineyards of Pichon Baron and Pichon Lalande from the separate vineyards of the Forts de Latour. L'Enclos of Château Léoville Lascases is adjacent to Latour's Grand Enclos, and is separated from the vineyards of the Clos du Marquis by part of Léoville Poyferré.

est competitor in the super-seconds (⅂ page 346). The main difference in styles may be due to the high proportion of Merlot at Pichon Lalande compared with the concentration on Cabernet Sauvignon at Léoville Lascases, but this may be about to change. "Pichon (Lalande) historically has been a property that for various reasons has had a lot of Merlot. A previous owner bought the property in 1927, and at that time it was very difficult to ripen Cabernet Sauvignon so he planted a lot of Merlot. In 1995, which was a Merlot year, it was an advantage for Pichon Lalande, which was one of the best wines that year. Sometimes it is an advantage, sometimes not. Now we know how to ripen Cabernet Sauvignon and in the last years of May-Éliane Lencquesaing there was a tendency to plant Cabernet Sauvignon wherever it was possible. When Roederer arrived in 2007 they did a study of soil and topsoil and started a ten year program of planting. We aim to use as much Cabernet Sauvignon as possible in the grand vin when it is a Cabernet year. In 2011 we have only 8% Merlot," says former director Sylvie Cazes.

The château where Merlot is most important, however, is undoubtedly Palmer. Indeed, there is no question about Château Palmer's status, but you might ask what it is doing in a list of Cabernet icons since only half of the vintages of the past two decades have more than 50% Cabernet Sauvignon. Certainly Palmer is *sui generis,* the only one of the Grand Cru Classés of the Médoc to consider Merlot of equal importance to Cabernet. Although classified only as a third growth in 1855, Palmer has been a leading member of the group just below the first growths for at least the past fifty years.

The origins of Château Palmer are relatively recent as the Médoc goes.[27] After arriving in Bordeaux with the Duke of Wellington during the Napoleonic wars, Major General Palmer purchased a series of vineyards over the next couple of decades. During the 1820s he assembled a domain with 82 hectares of vineyards in Cantenac, which in due course was named after him. Just before the 1855 classification, the property was acquired by the Pereires, a Jewish Portuguese family of bankers. Somewhat competitive with the Rothschilds, they purchased Palmer just a week after the Rothschilds purchased Mouton. They constructed today's château and steadily improved the property.

By the twentieth century, Palmer's reputation was up with the second growths. It appears at this time to have been heavily dominated by Cabernet Sauvignon; in the 1920s, Merlot was less than 3% of the plantings.[28] The modern era of Palmer started when the Pereires sold the property in 1938 to a syndicate of several negociants, which with various changes has lasted until the present. The manager until the 1950s was Édouard Miailhe, who substantially increased the proportion of Merlot to as much as 60%. He was succeeded by Jean Bouteiller, who reduced the proportion to 47%,[29] but the unusual feature of having Merlot on some of the best terroirs remained unchanged.

The quality of the Merlot gives Château Palmer a softness at its core, a sort of plush, velvety quality, which is different from the opulence of ripe Cabernet Sauvignon. Yet all the same, the wine has that unmistakable structure of Cabernet, albeit tempered at the edges. It was the 1961 vintage that lifted Palmer above the other second growths. Given its long established reputation, it would be unfair to say that the 1961 vintage made Palmer's name, but it is fair to say that by dominating this top vintage from the Médoc, Château Palmer placed itself on the list of icon wines of the twentieth century.

The quality of the 1961 Palmer was not recognized immediately.[30] When prices were first released, Palmer was in its usual position with the second growths. By the late seventies, it became apparent that the Palmer of this vintage was exceptional, and at the start of the eighties, its price rose above that of neighboring Château Margaux; by 1986 its price was above the rest of the first growths. It hasn't quite had the staying power to maintain that position; since the 1990s, Château Latour has been recognized as the best wine of the 1961 vintage, with Palmer, Mouton Rothschild, and Haut Brion in a group with varying price order close behind.

The relative pricing accords well with my own experience of tasting the wines (⅄ page 340). When I tasted Palmer 1961 in the late eighties, it was every bit as impressive as the best first growths, with dense, seamless, layers of black fruits all encased in its typical velvet sheen. One might have guessed at a fifty-fifty split of Cabernet Sauvignon and Merlot, but actually it was just under a third Cabernet Sauvignon and just over a half Merlot. By around year 2000, the density was lightening a little (in contrast with Château Latour which seems timelessly unchanging). Allowing for the usual range of bottle variation in a fifty year old wine, at its best it is still splendid today, its poised feminine elegance making a contrast to the sheer grandeur of the Château Latour. It's a fantastic demonstration of the potential of Merlot on gravel soils.

No one knows what lifted this vintage of Château Palmer to such heights. Michael Broadbent, who certainly tasted as many vintages of Palmer as anyone when he was in charge of Christie's wine department, said, "I am not a huge Palmer fan and have always considered that its 1961, one of the greatest wines of that vintage, was a fortunate aberration,"[31] but I do not believe it was entirely an accident. The 1959, 1962, and 1966 vintages all show much of the same character. (The 1966 had even less Cabernet Sauvignon than the 1961, but the exact blend in 1959 and 1962 is unknown.) I am not sure Palmer has ever recaptured that combination of precision with softness. Is it a coincidence that these great vintages coincided with the period when Palmer had its greatest concentration of Merlot in the vineyards?

Should Palmer be on the list of icons? There is no doubt that the 1961 is one of the iconic wines of the twentieth century. I would like to feel that current vintages show the same unique character of the sixties, with that dense sheen of Merlot surrounding the core of Cabernet, but I am not completely convinced of the consistency. More recent vintages have seemed to me to oscillate between Palmer's distinctive profile of the sixties and a more Cabernet-dominated impression, depending on the year. The vintage showing the clearest lineage back to 1961 in my view is the 1983 (which has remained better than the 1982). The view at the château is that Palmer should surmount individual vintage variations in composition. "Palmer is not a Cabernet-driven or a Merlot-driven wine, it is a blend-driven wine," says director Thomas Duroux. But to my mind, high "Cabernet years," such as 2006 and 1996, do not entirely seem to suit Palmer's style. On the other hand, it's an open question whether the effects of global warming in causing Merlot to ripen more rapidly will prove to be more of a threat to Palmer than to the other châteaux. (In 2003 they dealt with the heat by using an unprecedented proportion of Cabernet Sauvignon—more than two thirds). Recent vintages such as 2005 and 2009 have given an impression of more opulence.

What makes the first growths unique as group? Perhaps it is their sophistication, not so much when the wines are young—they can be lovely, of course,

The flags signify Château Palmer's history of ownership by a French, Dutch, and English syndicate.

but they do not display their full complexity—but when they age. After twenty years or more, as the tannins resolve and the fruits begin to meld into more savory aromas and flavors, there's that impression of seamless layers of flavor, impossible to disentangle and difficult to describe. I am inclined to think that one reason for this infinite variety is the blend; there may be only a small proportion of varieties other than Cabernet Sauvignon (except for Haut Brion), but Cabernet Sauvignon needs their contribution as the wine ages. Indeed, for all that the first growths are marked by the highest proportions of Cabernet Sauvignon in the Médoc, it is not necessarily the years with the most Cabernet Sauvignon in the blend that have been the most successful.

Are the first growths truly distinct from the super-seconds? In some years some super-seconds have equaled or exceeded the first growths in critical acclaim immediately after the vintage (although never in price!). It remains to be seen whether this will be sustained into the long term. It may be too early to tell. The super-seconds separated as a group during the eighties, and consolidated their position during the nineties,[32] but it was not really until then that success brought the rewards required to support the level of investment for absolute quality. The first growths probably have a decade or more's start on the super-seconds in that regard. We need another decade to see whether the super-seconds of the nineties will rival the first growths as developed wines. But whether we confine the cults and icons of Bordeaux to the first growths or ad-

Inglenook was famous for its varietal-labeled Cabernet Sauvignon from 1933 to 1964. The 1941 vintage became legendary and can be found under two labels. One proclaims that it is made from the "true Cabernet grape" (left); the other (right) has the same label that was used through the 1960s. Some labels had the description "Classic Claret" added.[34]

mit the super-seconds to the club, it's striking that these are all wines that were well established in the hierarchy of two centuries ago.

The history of the cult wines of Napa Valley is quite different from that of the icons of Bordeaux. It's not just that the timescale is measured in decades instead of centuries, but that the cults have changed even over the past twenty or thirty years. The acclaimed wines of the period from Repeal in 1933 to the renaissance of 1966 no longer exist, or at the least no longer have their former prominence. Most of the new wave wines that replaced them in the sixties and seventies have fallen from favor. The majority of today's cult wines originated in the eighties or later; roughly a third had their first vintage in the 1990s, and another third in the 2000s. Indeed, the majority of the wines in the top positions today did not even *exist* in the eighties. Only a handful of the top-ranked wines of recent vintages in the *Wine Advocate* were also on the list for the mid eighties.[33] Is this because the former cult wines missed a beat, and either lost their quality or at least failed to capture the modern spirit? Or is it that cult wines are a creation depending on managed scarcity, and the novelty of new producers helps to create famine?

Another difference is that today's top wines of Napa Valley are almost all produced in vanishingly small amounts; the median is about 500 cases per year, usually available only to a mailing list (often there is a wait of several years to get on the list). By contrast, most of the top wines of the eighties were produced in several thousands of cases and were available in general distribution. The total production of all of the current cult wines is less than the annual production of a typical classed growth château in Bordeaux. Managed scarcity is splendid for marketing, but can we really view such small production wines as a fair comparison with the grand vins of the Médoc? As a proprietor of a medium sized château in St. Emilion said to me, perhaps a little sourly, "It is easy enough to produce high quality wine on a miniscule scale by using all the tricks of viticulture and vinification, but the real issue is to get quality wine when you have tens of hectares to cultivate." The counter-case is put by Doug Shafer, whose Hillside Select is made in small, but reasonable quantities (2,000-2,500 cases; ϒ page 412). "The criticism of the cult wines is silly. There are lovely wines out there and if they were lost by blending into 10,000 case lots, it would be sad."

Most cult wines of Napa are akin in style as well as scale to the garage wines of St. Emilion, which used low yields and intense extraction to achieve powerful results, often in a lush style, in the small quantities disparaged by more conventional producers. Of course, Bordeaux and Napa have both moved towards a richer, more extracted style that has partly been achieved by adopting some of the methods of the garagistes for lowering yields and increasing concentration. This is accentuated in Bordeaux by diverting an increasing proportion of production into second wines, but even so, the grand châteaux of the Médoc still produce tens of thousands of bottles of their grand vins. In Napa the action is more with a new group of producers focusing on intense production from single vineyards.

Napa cults and Bordeaux garage wines differ in at least one important aspect. The reputation of the garage wines was built on their novel methods of viticulture and vinification, which often produced extraordinary results in spite of coming from relatively uninteresting terroirs. The cult wines of Napa come from sites chosen for their potential in producing wine in the desired style. There is quite a concentration of mountain sites among them—Harlan on Oakville Mountain, Bryant and Colgin on Pritchard Hill, Diamond Creek on Diamond Mountain—and other special sites, such as Abreu's Madrona Ranch at the foot of Spring Mountain, or the Eisele vineyard in Simmons Creek canyon. To what extent do the cult wines owe their success to choosing sites that naturally allow production of low yields of small, intense berries, and to what extent do they share with garage wines extremes of viticulture and vinification that maximize extraction and intensity?

By contrast with the stability of the icons of Bordeaux, not only have the cults of Napa risen to fame more recently, but also they are highly controversial. One winemaker drew a distinction between the first cult wines and the situation today. "The top six cult wines were built in the nineties, Screaming Eagle, Colgin, Harlan, Araujo, Bryant, and Abreu. Some of the new wave Cabernets are based on bigger is better, they are built on density and extract," she said. Then she took it back. "My 'bigger is better' thought was not applicable to Napa Cabernet—please do strike that from the record," she emailed me.

But this indeed is the general criticism of the cult wines. "The grapes come from a rocky hillside, but really they could come from anywhere. This over-

Harlan Estate is perched on a hilltop at 150 m elevation, surrounded by vineyards on the slopes.

extracted, super-tannic wine simply wipes out all traces of origin. It sells for about $400 on release and commands incredible prices in charity wine auctions," said Larry Walker about one leading cult wine in his book on the wines of Napa Valley.[35] Certainly it is undeniable that the cult wines of today do not tend to be the most restrained. Putting aside personal preferences about style, the first question is whether a cult wine stands as a distinct representation of its origin, or whether ripeness and extraction have eliminated that sense of place. But I think one has to go further, and ask what happens as the wine ages. As the tannins resolve, as the fruits lighten and turn to a more savory spectrum, does the wine become more interesting, does it show more sense of time and place? In a somewhat different context, in the past there have been wines of such massive structure that they took decades to come around: I'm not really suggesting that today's wines with super-ripe massive fruits will necessarily fit into that same model, but before rushing to judgment, I'd like to know what they taste like at, say, twenty years of age: do they acquire more subtlety? Is sheer fruit concentration a comparable obstacle to appreciating young wines from Napa like tannins used to be in Bordeaux?

I had somewhat of a preconception when I set out to investigate California cult wines. Based on experiences at past tastings of current vintages, I thought they would be likely to be highly extracted, alcoholic, impossible to distinguish, and generally brutish. What I experienced, especially in tasting older vintages, was quite different. Certainly there are wines following the old precept, bigger is better, where extraction obscures any possible nuances, but the top wines can be refined, with finesse and elegance, and increasing layers of complexity as they age. Like all California wines, they tend to be richer in extract and higher in alcohol than their European counterparts, but the best are well balanced enough that this is scarcely noticeable on the palate.

Who defines the cult wines of today? The precedent of the 1855 classification would argue for price as the basis—sometimes extraordinary, but at all events reaching well above the tier of wines below. Certainly the cult wines of Napa and the garage wines of St. Emilion share an attraction for some powerful critics, who seem blown away by their sheer intensity. Many feel that the underlying force in the phenomenon is the opinion of Robert Parker in the *Wine Advocate*. This is perhaps especially true for wines where there is no prior history to lend support. Recognition in the *Wine Advocate*, can lead to immediate reputation. High ratings are important. "I want to get to the next level," Don Bryant told me, when we were discussing the Bryant Family Estate Cabernet. It turned out that he meant moving from 97 Parker points to obtaining 100 points.

The creators of the first cult wines were no doubt ambitious, but probably did not foresee just how far they would rise above the others. There's general agreement that a small group of people started the movement. Paul Roberts of Harlan Estate draws a parallel with the creation of the garage wines in Bordeaux. "A handful of wines were emerging at the same time, Harlan, Colgin, Screaming Eagle, Bryant. It was a perfect storm. It was the first time in several decades that new people had come into the valley, bringing new ideas. And there was a shift to people who came into Napa bringing independent sources of finance. But this was happening elsewhere in the world at the same time, for example, St. Emilion."

Bill Harlan set out avowedly to establish an "American first growth wine-growing estate" in Napa. But what does this mean in the context of Napa? The Bordeaux precedent says that first growths have more of what you find in the second growths, but exactly what is this? Should the wine be more elegant? more concentrated? more ageworthy?—more exactly of what? Some people think that more extraction is the key. "There was a move almost overnight to move into that more extracted style. Harlan was at the front of it; you might say that Harlan defined the trend," says Anthony Bell, who at that time was at Beaulieu.

Harlan's vineyards are part of a stunning estate in the hills above Oakville. Just opposite the famous Oakville Grocery on route 29, you take the road up into the hills to the west. As you enter the estate, you go up a long, winding drive between rows of olive trees. The vineyards are on slopes, some terraced, planted with the typical Bordeaux varieties, although "We never publish the exact breakdown as it forces the discussion into varietal composition instead of sense of place," says Paul Roberts. Aside from the 1998, which was pure Cabernet Sauvignon, the wines have generally followed the mix of plantings in the vineyard and have been about 70-75% Cabernet Sauvignon. "Bill and the team looked at the historical makeup of the first growths and loosely based the planting percentages on that makeup," says Paul. The wine is labeled as a Proprietary Red to give complete flexibility in winemaking. There is also a second wine, The Maiden, which tends to come from the youngest vines, but the decision on which lots go into the estate wine versus The Maiden is not made until about 14 months into maturation. "The important thing about The Maiden is that it has the hallmark of the property," says Paul.

A vertical from 1991 to 2007 demonstrated a more austere style than I expected (ᵠ page 394). The wines could not be more different from the caricature of the over-extracted cult wine. "If we extracted anything close to what the grapes could give us, we would make undrinkably austere wine," says winemaker Cory Empting. Perhaps responding to the increasing age of the vines, Paul Roberts says that, "In the early days we were a late picker, now we are an early picker." The younger wines show structure as much as overt fruit; clearly they are built for aging. While they may become approachable sooner than Bordeaux, the vintages from the 2000s showed a sense of reserve, with the fruits opening out slowly and promising interesting development in the future. Paul says that the wines usually close up for 18-24 months when they are 6-7 years old, after which the secondary character emerges: at around 12 years they begin to show a signature sous-bois. The 1995 seemed the most elegant of the vertical, and at its peak. The Maiden bears something of the same relationship to the Estate wine as a second wine to the grand vin in Bordeaux, with a more open, approachable character.

Bryant and Colgin are the other two wines often mentioned in the same breath as Harlan. Both are located on Pritchard Hill, Bryant just above Lake Hennessey at about 130 m, and Colgin higher up in the woods, above 300 m, near the site of Chappellet, the first winery to be established on Pritchard Hill. Since the first vintage in 1992, Bryant's principal wine has been a 100% Cabernet Sauvignon from the estate vineyards. Recalling the decision to make a varietal wine, Don Bryant told me, "I like Cabernet, that's one thing. Cabernet Sauvignon was the best grape and fetched the best prices. I was not thinking about Bordeaux at all; there were many 100% Cabs at the time." More recently (in 2009) the Bettina Bordeaux blend, coming from a mix of David Abreu's vineyards, has been added. "Most of the industry has gone away from the 100% Cabernet. Cabernet often has holes that need to be filled in, unless you have a really special spot; the Cabernet here makes really complete wine," says Brady Mitchell at Bryant. Judging from the first vintage, Bettina remains pretty true to the imperatives of Cabernet Sauvignon; in fact, I would say that it is sterner than Bryant itself. My marker for Bryant is its suppleness, turning to delicacy in the most refined older vintages, such as 1996, which is hard to relate to the caricature of California cult wines (ᵠ page 381).

Colgin made its first splash with the 100% Cabernet Sauvignon from the Herb Lamb vineyard. Located outside of St. Helena at an elevation around 200 m on the lower slopes of Howell Mountain, the vineyard was planted in 1987, and Colgin bought grapes from the first vintage in 1990 until the vineyard had to be replanted in 2008 (unfortunately it had been planted on AxR1 rootstock).[36] Ann Colgin also bought her own estate on Pritchard Hill and planted it in 1998, and since 2002 the IX Estate wine has been a blend close to the vineyard plantings, usually 75% Cabernet Sauvignon and 15-20% Merlot, with the rest split equally between Cabernet Franc and Petit Verdot. In addition, Colgin also produces the Tychson Hill 100% Cabernet and the Cariad Bordeaux blend, both coming from other vineyards. Colgin has retained its reputation through the switch from Herb Lamb as its principal source of grapes to the IX Estate wine, although I see a difference of style. "We don't like the idea of bigger. We're looking to balance the power on the palate that Napa naturally brings with some delicacy. We have fantastic weather and if there's a challenge here it's to capture balance in the wines so they can age," says winemaker Allison Tauziet. Certainly the style seems to have evolved in the direction of increased refinement: the current IX Estate wines seem tighter and more precise compared to the bigger, broader character of Herb Lamb of the nineties (page 387).

Judged by price, Screaming Eagle is without question California's leading cult wine. It may have reached that position as much by accident as design, but it has never been toppled from its pedestal. One of the few cult wines of the nineties that is not based on mountain vineyards, Screaming Eagle has around 20 ha of vineyards that occupy most of a small amphitheater on the west side of the Silverado trail. The whole area is surrounded by woods; along the north and west sides, it is bordered by narrow strips of other producers' vineyards. Local real estate broker Jean Phillips purchased it as an investment in 1986, when it was mostly planted with Riesling, except for a few rows of Cabernet Sauvignon, 80 vines in all. The grapes were sold off, except for the Cabernet, which made such an exceptional wine that the rest of the vineyard was replanted with it in 1987. Some Merlot was also planted in 1987, and some Cabernet Franc in 1988.

A wine was made from the 80 old vines in the 1991 vintage but it was not released. The 1992 was the vintage that hit the press, with about 175 cases produced. No one knows what proportion the old vines were of this first release, because there are no records from the early years, but I calculate that they must have accounted for less than 10% of the wine,[37] which makes the success of this vintage, based largely on five year old vines, even more remarkable. "[The] debut vintage is the extraordinary 1992 Cabernet Sauvignon, one of the greatest young Cabernets I have ever tasted," said Robert Parker in the *Wine Advocate*. With a score of 99 points, there was no looking back.

The terroir is an alluvial fan over a base of volcanic gneiss, with the soils changing from gravel at the east to more loam at the west. Describing the vineyards, "Conventional thinking is that Cabernet does well on gravel and Merlot on clay, but some of our best Cabernet is on the west side where there is more clay. We have Merlot in most places but we prefer it on the gravel. It's very site specific. Cabernet Franc is mostly on gravelly soil, with a little on loam," says winemaker Nick Gislason. Tasting barrel samples of the separate varieties indeed identified an unusually refined Merlot from vines planted in 1987 on gravel. It gave a supple impression on the palate but with a taut underlay showing very fine, ripe tannins, and overall a finely textured structure for Merlot. This was from 2010, which was an unusually tannic year at Screaming Eagle, so perhaps it is not completely typical, but it was strongly reminiscent of the elegant Merlot of Château Palmer, also planted on gravel soils where most people would plant Cabernet Sauvignon. I suspect this makes a significant contribution to the sense of refinement in the wine (⟰ page 411). Blending is used much as in Bordeaux to even out vintages; cooler years have more Merlot in the blend, warmer years have more Cabernet Franc.

My impression of the 2009 and 2010 vintages was distant from descriptions of a lush cult wine. The style seemed refined and elegant, albeit with the fullness of Napa: somewhat along the lines I imagine a first growth in St. Julien might have achieved in 2009 or 2010. Since Screaming Eagle was sold to new owners in 2006, and a new winemaking team was installed, it's possible that these wines will evolve differently from those of the early years. The only change that's foreseen in the future is that "Cabernet Franc will have a bigger role in our future warmer years, just because we will have more blocks to

The stark simplicity of Screaming Eagle's label belies its position as California's most expensive wine.

Wine was made at Screaming Eagle in this tiny stone building under Jean Phillips's proprietorship. Today there is a new underground winery.

Photograph courtesy Screaming Eagle, © Fred Lyon.

blend with," according to estate manager Armand de Maigret. "We are going for a style with delicacy and finesse, with a floral character, not so much a heavy hitter wine," says Nick Gislason. Certainly these wines were a far cry from most of the other 2009 and 2010s that I tasted at the same time. "A lot of people in the valley think that 2009 was not as good as 2008, and 2008 was not as good as 2007, but I would like to reverse that (speaking specifically of Screaming Eagle)," says Nick.

There are wines made today in Bordeaux that you might place in Napa at a blind tasting, but twenty years ago the greater ripeness of Napa was usually distinct. The Heitz Martha's Vineyard 1974 was the first wine from Napa that fooled me at a blind tasting into thinking it came from Bordeaux. I had to be shown the bottle to be convinced I had made a mistake. This hundred percent Cabernet Sauvignon comes from a 14 ha vineyard on the Oakville Bench, just above the To Kalon vineyard. The vineyard itself is not easy to find; there are no signs or directions—perhaps Heitz don't want it covered in day trippers. The winery is somewhat to the north, on route 29 in St. Helena.

The vineyard was owned by Tom and Martha May, and after a handshake deal, Joe Heitz started to produce wine from its crop in 1966. It was one of the first single vineyard wines of the modern era. The wine is often said to have a

The eucalyptus trees at the edge of Martha's Vineyard may have something to do with its famous minty aroma. The Opus One block of To Kalon is on the far side of the trees.

minty taste, and even the Heitz web site mentions the string of eucalyptus trees at the edge of the vineyards close to the base of the mountains, but Joe Heitz is reputed to have believed that the mintiness actually was a property of the vines (which are claimed to come from a proprietary clone producing unusually small berries). (But when Opus One acquired a block of the To Kalon vineyard on the other side of the trees, they did not like the minty taste in their wine, and cut down some of the trees.) With some shade from the mountains close by, Martha's Vineyard is a little less sunny than some others; possibly this contributes to a slightly cooler climate impression and lower alcohol. "For more than two decades, Heitz Martha's Vineyard was the benchmark by which California cabernets were judged," said Frank Prial of the New York Times in 2000.[38] More recently it has of course followed the inevitable trend towards greater extraction and higher alcohol, but the wine remains relatively restrained for Napa (Y page 396). 1974 probably remains its greatest vintage.

Ridge Monte Bello goes back even farther than Heitz, with its first commercial vintage dating from 1962. The modern history of Ridge began when a group of engineers from Stanford University bought the property on the Santa Cruz Mountains south of San Francisco in 1959 and started producing Cabernet Sauvignon from vines that had been planted in the 1940s. Over the next few years they expanded the vineyard area from 6 to 18 ha (introducing Zinfandel from 1964), and production grew to about 3,000 cases. Paul Draper, a

Stanford philosophy graduate who had been making wine in Chile, joined in 1969 because he was so impressed with the 1962 and 1964 Cabernets (both monovarietal). "It was the first time I tasted California wine, outside of the old Inglenook and Beaulieu wines, with the complexity of Bordeaux. Those two wines were the reason why I joined Ridge. The wines were completely natural," he told me.

Ridge Vineyards is actually an amalgam of several different vineyards all planted along the Monte Bello Ridge, which runs roughly northwest to southeast. Both terroir and climate are different from Napa and Sonoma on the North Coast. This explains the moderate character of the wines. "We are too cool here to do what Napa is doing and anyway I don't like the style. My reference point was Château Latour, until Bordeaux began to change. We stayed with the style of moderate alcohol. For the first forty years it was 12.9%, now it is around 13.1%," Paul says. Because the vineyards are located literally on a ridge, every parcel has a slightly different exposure and has been planted accordingly with the intention of achieving even ripening. "When I say fully ripe I get into a definition that has become—I shouldn't say controversial—but California has a totally different interpretation of what ripeness is. In the Santa Cruz mountains the average temperature is the same as Bordeaux but the nights are cooler and for that reason we retain acidity much better than elsewhere in California, such as Napa. We have never added acidity but sometimes we have had to precipitate it out."

His prescription for winemaking was set by a nineteenth century text from Bordeaux, as modified by a book on winemaking in California at the time.[39] I asked whether he feels that he is preserving the old traditions of Bordeaux better than they are at source? "Yes, many in Bordeaux have new equipment, such as sous vide concentration, they use lots of enzymes, etc," he says, not exactly with disdain, but certainly with a feeling that it's not the way he would care to make wine. "In Bordeaux to my mind they over extract and then they have to go back and fine—this was the origin of the traditional treatment with 6-8 eggs per barrel." Here it's only exceptional lots that are fined with egg whites; Paul feels that the fining leaves a mark on the wine, with the egg whites giving a chalky quality to the tannins. In nineteenth century Bordeaux, he says, they did trial fining before deciding. In the 1930s or 1940s (perhaps because of the run of terrible vintages in the 1930s) the tradition arose of using 6-8 egg whites.

The one break with tradition is Ridge's use of American rather than French oak, although Paul points out that Bordeaux used to mature its wines in oak from the Baltic, and an experiment in Bordeaux around 1900 with various sources of oak actually produced better results with American white oak than with local oak. French oak is used at Ridge only for an experimental 5%; the rest is American. The key is that the oak is air dried for two years: American oak got a bad name for winemaking because it was kiln dried, Paul believes.

The Monte Bello vineyards are located along a mountain ridge.

Photograph courtesy Ridge Vineyards.

Monte Bello is a blend, and perhaps not surprisingly considering Paul's traditional imperatives, closer to Bordeaux in its varietal composition than to a Napa Cabernet. The transition took a while, from the monovarietal of the early sixties, to a wine with over 90% Cabernet Sauvignon in the eighties, and then to a range over the past two decades from a minimum of 56% to a maximum of 85%. Merlot is always the second most important variety, with smaller amounts of Petit Verdot and Cabernet Franc. Monte Bello is a long-lived wine; Paul thinks it begin to show its characteristics around 9-12 years of age, and develops until it is 20 or 30 years old.

Judged by the point at which I first detect savory development in Monte Bello, I'd actually place the development just a little slower than that, up to fifteen years, depending on the vintage, before it's first noticeable, and with development clearly evident by twenty years (⛾ page 407). Tasted early in 2012, the 1992 was well developed, in fact it was time to drink up. But the 1990 was just perfection, on that cusp of fruits turning savory, with years ahead. Paul Draper and I saw the 1984 and 1985 differently, the winemaker's opinion being that 1984 is ready to go but 1985 still has a distance, whereas I saw them the other way around. Be that as it may, the 1978 was still showing well, and had declined so gently from the last time I tasted it, three years previously, as to emphasize the parallel with Bordeaux, where a wine may continue to be completely enjoyable for a decade after it shows the first signs of decline. As for really old vintages, the 1974 was only just past its peak at 35 years of age, and the 1964 was rather tertiary but still enjoyable at 45 years. I can't help but wonder how much the moderate style of the wines is a key factor in ensuring such longevity.

The main challenge to Bordeaux from within Europe comes from an unexpected place: Italy. Italy certainly has its famous wines: top Barolos and Barbarescos hold a place in the icons and cults of the wine world, and some Brunello di Montalcinos might also qualify, but Sassicaia, as the wine that broke the mold, is a special case. Sassicaia's difference is that it represents Italy's first success with an international variety, with the famous 1985 vintage regarded as the equal of any Bordeaux. It was the first time any other place in Europe produced a wine based on Cabernet Sauvignon to rival Bordeaux. Sassicaia retains an almost mythical reputation, especially among producers in Tuscany, who often refer to it as having created a new arena for wine production.

The original production of Sassicaia, starting in the 1940s, was typical of today's wine neither in its origins nor in the cultivar. Replanting a historical vineyard on the estate, the first vines were at Castiglioncello, in the hills above Bolgheri. Marquis Mario Incisa planted the vines densely at 10,000 to the hectare, and had them pruned low, anathema to local custom. Yields were low. Local reactions to the wine were completely hostile, but ten years later, the early wines were showing well, so the Marquis extended the vineyards, this time into a site at San Guido where an old olive grove had been destroyed by frost. The choice of the original vineyard was based on the belief of the time that exposure to the sea must be avoided. "We thought the reason why the wines of Bolgheri were not good was the winds from the sea, but we realized it was because no one was making an effort to make good wine. The first vineyard was planted in 1944; in 1959 we planted some vineyards down here [the present location at San Guido], it was ten to fifteen years before we decided these vineyards were good enough," recalls Marquis Nicolò Incisa today.

Sassicaia's vineyards now are at the estate just outside the town of Bolgheri, in the plain between the hills and the sea. The vines are different also. "The Cabernet Sauvignon we used in the first vineyard [at Castiglioncello] was quite different from those used today, but the style of wine is very similar, maybe it is a little richer but it has the same elegance. The vines for Castiglioncello came from a vineyard planted early in the twentieth century. We sent the leaves to Bordeaux to identify the origins, but it's not found any more in Bordeaux," the Marquis told me.

Sassicaia became a commercial venture when Antinori became responsible for distribution in 1972. Their oenologist, Giacomo Tachis, took over manage-

Sassicaia is in the heart of Bolgheri.

ment of the vineyard and winemaking. "I brought forward all the times in the winemaking process, from the vintage to transferring to barriques to bottling, so the wine should be fresh and fragrant. The length of ageing fell by more than two years to a maximum of twenty two months. I succeeded in getting rid of all extraneous vines, and of reducing the percentage of Cabernet Franc from 30% to 15%," he recollected.[40]

The Marquis started out trying to make a wine like Bordeaux, but Sassicaia took on its own life and character. How long did this take? "After twenty years of comparing the wines, we found our wine was different, and even people from Bordeaux said our wine was more approachable when young, the tannins are always softer than Bordeaux, but the wine has great potential for aging. Usually when you have a wine that is easy to drink when young, you feel it will not last, but our wine has potential to improve with age. This is what makes Sassicaia different from wines of this region, you can enjoy it young, but it will improve with age," says the Marquis.

The hallmark of Sassicaia for me is its elegance. Not beefy or brawny, the constant blend of 85% Cabernet Sauvignon to 15% Cabernet Franc does not give the austerity that might result in Bordeaux, but shows refinement rounded out by that characteristic softness of Bolgheri. "Having a good result with Cabernet Franc we decided to stay with it. Merlot is very popular but Cabernet tannins are more elegant, especially if you want a wine that will improve with age," says the Marquis. The latest vintage impresses with its suppleness, older vintages by their delicate combination of fruits with savory development (☥ page 364). The estate seems to have gone through a bad patch in the late nineties, but current vintages are back on form.

I suppose the existence of cult wines that challenge the first growths poses the immediate question of how their styles compare. Is this a competition for increasing intensity and power, as the reputation of California cults for being "big" wines might suggest? But the more important question goes beyond the issue of what gives the most immediate gratification: how do these wines age and when does that primary burst of enthusiasm give way to something more complex?

Since most of today's cult wines originated in the early 1990s, it's not yet possible to get a really long perspective, but I compared the first growths from Bordeaux with Cabernets from California for the 1995 vintage (☥ page 374). A slightly cooler vintage in both Bordeaux and California, 1995 provides a good basis for comparison. Not quite as well regarded as the much hotter 1997 vintage in California or the more tightly structured 1996 vintage in Bordeaux, it's still a very good, roughly equivalent, vintage in both. Rounding out the tasting, there was also Sassicaia, and Penfolds Bin 707 from South Australia.

Wines were tasted blind, but in most cases it was obvious which were from Bordeaux and which from the New World. The difference between Bordeaux and Napa was not in the perception of alcohol (although the New World wines were on average one percent higher), but more in the sweetness of the fruits and the texture. Bordeaux had more evident freshness (rarely herbaceous any more, at least at this age), whereas California Cabernet had a characteristic finish of sweet, ripe, red fruits, with lower acidity. (The same difference showed in comparing 1970 Bordeaux with 1974 Napa Cabernet, here with a move towards a savory herbaceousness in Bordeaux compared with retention of those warm, soft, fruits in California Cabernet; ☥ page 372.)

There was a wide spread of opinions about individual wines, the most common divide being whether the Bordeaux were too tight and linear, and whether the California were too soft and ripe. Given the extra ripeness of California, it seemed likely that the Napa Cabernets might show more resemblance with the St. Emilions than with the left bank wines, but in fact Cheval Blanc and Ausone stood out in this tasting for the refinement of their tannins, driven by Cabernet Franc. The closest resemblance with California came with Pauillac (Latour or Lafite Rothschild) and Haut Brion. There were extremes in both directions. Château Margaux seemed a throwback for Bordeaux, thin and herbaceous, almost medicinal. Colgin's Herb Lamb's vineyard went over the top into a thick, jammy, wine.

The top four wines split between Old and New World. Screaming Eagle and Harlan (both incidentally or perhaps not so incidentally Bordeaux blends as opposed to 100% Cabernet) were the top two New World wines. Although Screaming Eagle placed well, it was controversial, being loved or loathed, but there was agreement that (if you liked it) it was delicious rather than complex. The Harlan was more generally liked, on this showing rather youthful, although previously I have found it more developed and savory.

The top two wines from Bordeaux were Lafite and Latour. Lafite was the wine that most clearly evolved to show its breed over a longer period of time. It did not place top in the tasting, but as we continued to taste afterwards, there was agreement that it had advanced to first place; strengthening in the glass, it slowly developed those seamless layers of flavor characterizing Lafite. Although Latour made the top five, this was one of the wines on which opinion was divided as to whether the acidity or ripeness will win out over time.

The aging pattern of these wines did not seem generally different from that of the wines from the seventies: Bordeaux moves towards the herbaceous, Napa moves towards the overtly delicious. In Bordeaux, perhaps you tend to see the structural outlines more clearly with age; in Napa you see the fruits more clearly. Bordeaux changes its flavor spectrum more, while by reducing an intensity that obscures the lines of fruit, Napa shows that less is more. But (unfortunately) none of the 1995 wines gave the impression they would benefit from cellaring for another decade.

In spite of all the challenges, Bordeaux still retains its position as a reference point for Cabernet Sauvignon (whether blended or otherwise) at the top level. Although it cannot compete at the lowest levels against the frank appeal of the fruit-driven varietals from the New World—or even for that matter against the corresponding wines from Languedoc—at the top level it remains hard to equal. This is not just a matter of the reputation of the first growths dating from 1855, but extends throughout what you might regard as the scale of the Grand Cru Classés. At the lower end of this scale, or perhaps at the top end of the Cru Bourgeois scale, there is competition from interesting wines in the New World. South Africa perhaps provides the closest match in style, with its blended wines following Bordeaux quite closely in the assemblage, although the wines tend to be a little thicker. Chile and Argentina offer an interesting variation on the theme, with Cabernet-Carmenère and Cabernet-Malbec blends tending towards a refined impression: the tannins in Carmenère and Malbec are finer than those of Merlot when the grapes reach full maturity, giving the wines a refined tautness rather than the filling in on the mid palate that comes from Merlot in Bordeaux. But it is rare in South America to find a wine that has the sheer presence on the palate of the top Grand Cru Classés. That is more common in Napa or Sonoma, but here the problem can be that a blend with Merlot introduces rusticity, while a monovarietal Cabernet can become somewhat linear as it ages. It is difficult to find that combination of power with elegance, and the refreshing uplift on the finish of the top Bordeaux, although the top wines from California have a rich smoothness that can only be admired.

Not surprisingly, cults and icons are concentrated in the longer established wine regions. The dramatic increase in prices with the 2009 and 2010 vintages confirmed Bordeaux as the leading source of icons. The first growths are *hors de prix*, and the super-seconds run at prices comparable to the cult wines of Napa. Given the lack of any classification, definition of cult wines in Napa is more subjective, but they are roughly equivalent in number to the icons of Bordeaux. (When does a cult wine become an icon? After two hundred years might be an only partly facetious answer. Cults may come and go, witness the changes in Napa over two decades, but icons are there for the long haul.) The most noticeable difference in terms of the market is the much smaller production level of most Napa cults: managed scarcity is certainly a significant factor in their success. Diversion of an increasing proportion of production to second wines is also a factor in maintaining demand for the first growths of Bordeaux, but even as the grand vins turn more towards special cuvées, their production remains an order of magnitude greater than most Napa cults.

The top wines of regions other than Bordeaux and Napa include some very fine wines, but only a handful have attracted the same level of intense interest. Is this because of a difference in intrinsic quality or lack of effective marketing? It may be more because of the absence of a long-term track record, and also the lack of major reputation for the surrounding region. It's noticeable that those rare cases of cult Cabernets outside of Bordeaux and Napa usually have a context where there's some halo from other top-regarded wines in the region. It's hard to build a cult wine in isolation. But I expect some of these wines to rise into the stratosphere of those that are sought after as they age, even if current market fashion does not push them to cult status.

Vintage Chart for Cabernet Sauvignon

This chart places on a rough numerical basis the comments about vintages that follow in the tasting notes. These are specific for Cabernet Sauvignon (or blends based on it). The numbers are only a *very* approximate guide to vintage quality: in any region there will be subregions that rise above or fall below the average, and there will be producers who have unexpected successes or failures. It's useful to see the average extent of variation, and to be able to see what regions performed best in a particular year, but for the character of a vintage, see the tasting notes.

	2011	2010	2009	2008	2007	2006	2005	2004	2003	2002	2001	2000
Bordeaux	87?	95	95	88	87	86	94	89	88	87	90	93
Napa Valley	86?	88	89	90	93	90	91	92	88	92	93	86
Washington	88?	89	92	89	92	90	92	91	90	89	92	89
Bolgheri	90?	90	92	87	95	88	87	94	87	86	94	89
Chianti area	90?	90	91	89	93	90	89	95	89	80	94	88
Mendoza	88?	91	90	89	88	92	93	89	88	93	88	88
Maipo	88?	87	89	90	92	89	91	89	88	87	91	88
Stellenbosch	85?	87	92	87	88	90	89	87	93	88	90	88
Coonawarra	86?	90	89	88	87	92	90	91	90	89	91	90
Margaret River	90?	91	92	91	90	86	91	92	87	89	88	88
		1999	1998	1997	1996	1995	1994	1993	1992	1991	1990	
Bordeaux			88	87	85	92	91	86	85	80	80	94
Napa Valley			89	85	93	90	92	94	90	92	92	91
		1989	1988	1987	1986	1985	1984	1983	1982	1981	1980	
Bordeaux			92	89	84	91	90	80	88	94	85	80
Napa Valley			85	80	90	89	92	90	80	85	84	86

Producer Profiles & Tasting Notes

Bordeaux

Vintage variation has always been a paramount factor in Bordeaux, partly because the climate historically has been marginal, partly because there are large changes from year to year in the varietal character of the blend depending on the climatic conditions. Freakish conditions in 2011 with erratic rainfalls during the summer made for rather uneven results. Conditions in 2010 and 2009 are famous for the unprecedented ripeness and alcohol levels (many wines up to 14%), with 2010 having the reputation for better freshness. John Kolasa of Château Rauzan-Ségla describes them as "American" and "British" vintages to make the point that 2009 is more exuberant, and 2010 is (relatively) more restrained. The 2009s may be ready relatively soon, although as the baby fat wears off, it's apparent that they have good structure, and estimates for when they will be ready may need to be put back; but the 2010s will take longer. Among previous vintages the great reputations go to 2005 (uniformly ripe and round, but still with firm tannins that make it too young) and 2000 (a similar reputation to 2005 but now beginning to show some variation as the wines age). Under-rated vintages are 2001 and 2004, both quite classic in style, meaning in the modern context that there is some restraint to the fruits; but the wines are aging very nicely. Most 2001s have reached their peak; the 2004s should drink well for another three or four years. Given the readiness of 2004 and 2001, there's not much advantage today in looking at 2008 or 2006. The Bordelais feel that the 2006s will come around like a classic vintage, but I have some doubts, because there is a lack of generosity in the fruits, giving a slightly hard, flat, impression. 2007 and 2002 were weak vintages, both quite drinkable, and at their best quite attractive in a light, forward, style, but without much character; the hot vintage of 2003 is at another extreme, where far too many wines now taste cooked. Going back earlier, there are several interesting pairs of successive vintages. 1996 shows pressing acidity and it's unclear whether and when the wines will come around, whereas 1995 is nicely rounded but just below the concentration of an absolutely top year. 1990 shows well now with classically rounded fruits, and 1989 is generally similar but more variable and less concentrated. 1986 is a tougher, more classic vintage, while 1985 is more like 1995, simpler and more generous. The great vintage that started the modern era, 1982, is now developing in a more classic style with traces of herbaceousness deliciously cutting the fruits.

The 2009 Vintage on the Left Bank

My overall impression of the vintage is far more traditional than would be expected from the *en primeur* reports, which emphasized the richness and unprecedented alcohol levels in the wines. This is definitely a ripe vintage relative to Bordeaux's history, but it is not over-ripe. With a handful of exceptions of wines made in an overtly "international" style, the wines all fall within the parameters of traditional Bordeaux: fruits are supported by good acidity, there is a tendency towards the savory rather than the forcefully fruity, and some tannic support shows its bones on the finish. The more approachable wines may be ready to start drinking in as soon as three or four years, but already in the first year after release it has become apparent that there is a stronger underlying structure than was initially apparent. Often the ripeness of the fruits does hide tannic support, but the vintage is not as obviously destined for very long aging as some others—I would be inclined to think more in terms of 15 years than 20 or 30 years. As many of the wines have already developed a restrained austerity as overt opulence. Most are well balanced "food wines" in Bordeaux's traditional pattern, unmistakably Bordeaux in their freshness and aromatic profile. The Bordelais often describe the vintage as "exuberant," and I suppose it is by comparison with older vintages of Bordeaux, but by comparison with, for example, Napa Valley Cabernets of recent years, it seems restrained and fresh. The following notes are for châteaux that are not profiled individually; wines were tasted in January 2012.

Pessac-Léognan

Château Carbonnieux
Classic nose of smoky cigar box and cedar. Touch of acidity on the palate cuts the smoky black fruits, ending in a touch tart on the finish. Good structure supports the mid weight fruits, more austere than opulent. 13.0% *88* Drink 2016-2023.

Château de Fieuzal
Floral and perfumed hints on the nose lead into sweet ripe mid-weight fruits on the palate. A touch of chocolate cuts the bitterness of the tannins on the finish. It's a bit lacking in presence on the mid palate, in fact, the nose is more interesting than the palate. 14.0% *87* Drink 2015-2021.

Château Haut-Bergey
Just a touch of the traditional cigar box and cedar on the nose with a faint suggestion of minerality. Sweet ripe fruits are nicely balanced on the palate with a touch of chocolate on the finish. 14.5% *88* Drink 2016-2021.

Château Latour-Martillac
Black fruit nose has hints of blackcurrants cut by touch of smokiness. Rich, round, black and chocolaty on the palate, straightforward and direct, intended for more immediate drinking. 14.0% *87* Drink 2015-2020.

Château Malartic Lagravière
Restrained nose with traces of black fruits. Direct fruits on the palate, supported by good acidity and light tannic backbone. Touch of cigar box on finish. 13.5% *87* Drink 2015-2020.

Château Smith Haut Lafitte
Fresh black fruit nose with a touch of vanillin and coffee. Full black fruits on palate with firm tannic support, lots of extract. In a modern style but not going so far as Pape Clément. Tannins need time to soften. 13.5% *91* Drink 2017-2026.

Château Larrivet Haut Brion
Fresh impression on the nose. Mid weight smoky black fruits on the palate. Acidity emphasizes the tannic support, giving a slightly hard impression at this stage. 13.5% *88* Drink 2016-2021.

Château Pape Clément
Black fruit nose makes rich impression. Full deep, smoky, black fruits on palate are supported by firm, chocolaty tannins with touch of vanillin on finish. Well rounded fruits but still with the typical freshness of Bordeaux. Top notch result, but is it losing the character of Graves? 13.5% *91* Drink 2015-2024.

Haut-Médoc

Château Cantemerle
Slightly smoky black fruit nose. Quite crisp acidity pushes the fruits back on the palate. If the acidity settles down, this may become light and elegant. 13.0% *87* Drink 2016-2023.

Château Citran
Light nose with acid impression. Good acidity supports medium weight fruits on palate, emphasized by light tannins on finish. Still tight, needs time. 13.0% *87* Drink 2016-2022.

Château La Tour-Carnet
Immediate sense of extraction to the black fruit nose. Palate shows the modern style with those black fruits edged by vanillin. Dense firm tannins on the finish. Still fresh, however. *89* Drink 2016-2022.

Margaux
Château d'Angludet
Soft black fruits on nose follow through to palate. Nice balance in a tight style, just a touch lacking in obvious structure, so more likely to be good for the medium than long haul. 13.5% *88* Drink 2015-2022.

Château Brane-Cantenac
The light fruits on the nose seem more red than black. There's a traditional impression on the palate, with freshness showcasing the black fruits. Generally an elegant wine that will mature to softness in the medium rather than long term, as the tannic structure is not very evident. 13.5% *88* Drink 2015-2022.

Château Cantenac Brown
Modern impression on nose of forward black fruits. Palate shows dense firm black fruits with overtones of vanillin—very pleasant, but does it represent Margaux? 13.0% *89* Drink 2016-2022.

Château Desmirail
A slight savory herbal impression brings character to the nose. There's a nice balance on the palate of black fruits, acidity, and fine-grained tannins. This has the typical delicacy of Margaux and marks progress towards restoring the reputation of this Grand Cru Classé. 13.0% *90* Drink 2016-2025.

Château Du Tertre
Fresh black fruit nose. Traditional impression on the palate of those black fruits supported by fresh acidity, but it hasn't quite come together (yet). A fraction tart, tannins a touch rustic. 13.4% *88* Drink 2016-2024.

Château Giscours
Touch of herbaceousness in the form of bell peppers on the nose. The black fruits of the palate are a little on the full side for Margaux (often the case with Giscours) and tannins are just a fraction rustic. A little on the heavy side for Margaux. 13.7% *88* Drink 2015-2024.

Château Kirwan
Red and black fruit mélange on nose. A little sharp on the palate and a bit disjointed at this point. Perhaps it needs more time to come together. 13.0% *88* Drink 2015-2024.

Château Prieuré Lichine
Very faint herbal notes to the black fruit nose. Not quite fully internationalized but definitely modernized. Nicely balanced in an elegant Margaux style—in fact more typical of the elegance of the commune than some other vintages have been here. 14.0% *90* Drink 2015-2024.

Saint Julien
Château Saint Pierre
Touch of austerity to the nose. Nice depth to the elegant black fruits on the palate, which make quite a traditional impression. Good supporting acidity and light tannins. Perhaps a touch short on the finish. 13.5% *89* Drink 2016-2026.

Château Talbot
Savory elements join the black fruits on the nose. Smooth and elegant on the palate with a touch of herbaceous bell peppers coming out on the finish to give a most traditional impression. Good overall balance, 13.3% *89* Drink 2014-2026.

Château Branaire Ducru
Faint sense of minerality on nose. Slightly savory impression on palate, almost mineral, fruits more red than black, light and elegant, quite typical for St. Julien. 13.5% *89* Drink 2016-2025.

Château Gloria
Fresh nose offers savory, herbal, impression. Fine-grained on the palate, with mid level fruits, but somehow lacking that extra dimension in the middle. 13.5% *89* Drink 2016-2026.

Château Langoa Barton
Fresh red and black fruits mingle on the nose. Nicely balanced fruits on the palate are supported by good acidity. Light tannins are unobtrusive in the background. This should offer medium term longevity, but somehow fails to excite. 13.0% *88* Drink 2014-2025.

Pauillac

Château Clerc Milon

A suggestion of asperity on the nose, but superficially soft fruits on the palate at first; then the firm tannins underneath become apparent. This is typical Pauillac but a little lacking in generosity at the moment, just a touch hard on the finish. 13.5% *88* Drink 2016-2026.

Château d'Armailhac

Brooding black fruit nose is rather reserved. It's a touch hard on the palate; the fruits are there but don't really release their flavors. Blind you might think more of St. Estèphe than Pauillac. 13.5% *88* Drink 2016-2027.

Château Grand Puy Ducasse

Black fruit nose has some savory and herbal overtones. Nicely rounded fruits on the palate, just a touch hard on the finish with a slight sense of bitterness from the tannins. Needs time. 13.5% *88* Drink 2016-2027.

St. Estèphe

Château Cos Labory

Tight black fruit nose. Appealing black fruits on palate, with just a touch of the expected hardness of St. Estèphe. Good acidity and firm tannins. Workmanlike but not exciting. *88* Drink 2016-2027.

Château de Pez

Nutty nose is quite distinct. Soft fruits on the palate, slightly rustic tannins on the finish. Still needs time. *88* Drink 2016-2027.

Château Lafon Rochet

Austere black fruit nose. The hardness of St Estèphe is evident on the palate. Black fruits not really releasing their flavors yet. Firm, tight tannins. 13.5% *88* Drink 2017-2026.

Château Les Ormes de Pez

Tight black fruit nose accurately predicts the palate with a touch of that typical hardness of St. Estèphe. Not very generous. A distinctly old line impression. 14.0% *87* Drink 2016-2026.

Château Phélan Ségur

Tight restrained nose. More giving on palate that you would expect from the nose, in fact the fruits have a roundness approaching Pauillac. Nice balance of fruits to acidity and tannins. A good result for the mid term. 14.0% *89* Drink 2016-2027.

Château Batailley

Château Batailley started out as a single estate, but after it was split in 1942 into Batailley (occupying the larger part) and Haut Batailley, both parts retained their classification as Grand Cru Classés. Château Batailley has stayed in the same family lineage since then, although it was transferred by marriage into the Castéja holdings, which include several other châteaux as well as the Borie-Manoux negociant. Today's 67 ha of vineyards are dominated by the Cabernet Sauvignon that rules in Pauillac, with an average vine age of forty years; the château has not succumbed to the modern trend to plant more Merlot. This is a very traditional property, even to the extent of having no second wine. However, any declassified lots go into the Pauillac produced by the negociant business. "Introducing a second wine would inflate the price of Batailley, do people want to pay fifty percent more?" asks Frederic Castéja. "And we are making a wine that is ready to drink," he argues, "so do we need a second wine?" With few concessions to the modern style, the wines show a certain four square quality, but they have their aficionados. Wines were tasted at Château Batailley in October 2011.

2010

(Barrel sample) Restrained nose with impression of black fruits showing a touch of aromatics (as might be expected at this stage). Lush on the palate with the tannins showing as a distinct dryness on the finish. This will be a very nice wine when the tannins resolve in a couple of years, clearly made in a style for early drinking. 13.5% *88* Drink 2015-2020.

2009

There's a traditional impression on the nose of restrained, slightly acidic, black fruits with those slightly austere notes of Cabernet Sauvignon. The fruits are surprisingly soft and forward on the palate, with furry tannins receding into the background, but not much sense of structure. Made for relatively short term consumption, this is a nice wine, which if I had blind I would place as a good Cru Bourgeois. 13.4% *87* Drink 2014-2020.

2008

A traditional nose here, with a touch of herbaceousness, well perhaps really more herbal than herbaceous, with black fruit aromas. Traditional balance on the palate, with a touch of austerity to the black fruits, but there's a nice balance with acidity and tannins vis à vis the fruits. This is about ready to start drinking. This is a creditable result for the vintage and will do well in the short term. 13.0% *87* Drink to 2017.

2006

Rather restrained nose with some black fruits. Palate shows freshness with mid-level concentration of fruits. At first the wine seems almost fleshy and lacking backbone, and then some acidity comes in with tannins drying the finish; as this takes over, you feel the problem is the lack of concentration on the mid palate (very typical for the year). 13.0% *87* Drink 2011-2019.

1996

A very faint touch of sous bois on the nose overlays the black fruits on a relatively complex nose. The palate remains lively although I'd still like to see a touch more concentration. There is fresh acidity with a touch of the classic austerity of Cabernet Sauvignon; some tannins dry the finish. Superficially this fits the classic description of Pauillac, but I'm not quite convinced: I think the basic issue is that a bit more fruit concentration is needed. 12.5% *88* Drink to 2017.

1986

Faintly herbal and savory nose, rather austere in character. Dry and classic on the palate: a really traditional Bordeaux. But for all the difficulties of the vintage, I rather like it, better than some of the "easier" vintages. Nice balance, still fresh, lively black fruits, more herbal than savory: a very proper and traditional claret. *89* Drink to 2019.

1985

More savory on the nose than the 1982, the sous bois just a touch more evident. The balance on the palate seems more mature with savory elements more in evidence relative to the black fruits, but there is less overall fruit concentration. Seems to be a touch hollow in the mid palate, although some tannins are still evident from the dry finish. *87* Drink to 2016.

1982

Maturing color but still quite dark. Savory elements to the nose verge on sous bois, but are less evident on the palate, which shows mid weight, black fruits with a touch of sous bois coming back on the finish. Nice enough balance, but a little lacking in concentration at the end of the day. Should decay gently over the next decade. *88* Drink to 2018.

1975

A savory nose with some herbal overtones and a touch of pungency. The palate offers a contrast: sweet ripe fruits, interestingly showing less tertiary development than 1986, and much less austerity. The only criticism might be that the fruits remain too simple and primary. Some criticism after 35 years! It comes and goes in the glass, first developing a more herbal note, than simplifying finally to seem a little monotonic. *88* Drink to 2016.

Château Beychevelle

Château Beychevelle is supposed to take its name from the end of the sixteenth century when it came under the ownership of the Duc d'Epernon, an admiral in the French navy. Ships were required to lower their sails when passing the estate on the Gironde, so Beychevelle is supposedly a corruption of baisse voile (lower sail). The story is reflected in the drawing on the label of a boat lowering its sail, and the second wine is called Amiral de Beychevelle. The huge estate covers 250 ha, of which about 90 ha are planted. Although the terroir is mostly gravel based, Beychevelle has one of the highest proportions of Merlot in the area. "We are trying to go towards more Cabernet Sauvignon in the blend. But it takes time. We started mapping vineyard soils to find what soils were adapted to the varieties that are grown here; previously they planted Merlot where I think we could grow Cabernet Sauvignon. We have little clay here, we have maybe 6 ha, the majority is gravelly-sandy, it doesn't get the best out of Merlot. The question is, if the vineyard should change, is the vineyard ready to replant?" says director general Philippe Blanc. Looking to the future, he says, "The wines will be a little stricter, leaner in one sense, elegant with finesse—with more muscle, fat, freshness. We'd like to see the Cabernet reach 65% here." Classified as a fourth growth in 1855, Beychevelle has more or less maintained that position ever since, generally reflecting the finesse and elegance of St. Julien. Unlike the usual tendency to make the second wine more approachable by emphasizing Merlot, at Beychevelle the Amiral tends to have more Cabernet Sauvignon. The same relationship between Beychevelle and Amiral shows in both 2009 and 2005, with a touch more austerity on the second wine due to its greater content of Cabernet Sauvignon, and more roundness but also depth and structure on the grand vin, although everything is lifted to a greater level of ripeness in 2009. Wines were tasted at Château Beychevelle in June 2012.

Amiral de Beychevelle, 2009
Typical Cabernet impression of fresh black fruits, following through to a light, elegant, palate, but with chocolate undertones. The Amiral is lighter than the Beychevelle but also a little more austere (perhaps because it has 58% Cabernet Sauvignon compared to Beychevelle's 48%). The light underlying structure is a good balance to the fruits, with unusually classic representation for a second wine. This should age nicely for the mid term; drink over the next decade. 13.6% *87* Drink 2013-2022.

Amiral de Beychevelle, 2005
Touch of garnet at rim shows start of development. Black fruits have hints of spices. Nicely balanced, developing in the elegant style of St. Julien. Given the softness on the palate, you would not think this was three quarters Cabernet Sauvignon, although there is a well defined structure. There's a slightly fresher impression than the grand vin, almost a tighter impression on the palate, because the fruits are less well rounded. 13.0% *88* Drink to 2019.

Château Beychevelle, 2009
More fruit evident than the Amiral, but still with classic mineral freshness of St. Julien. More generous on the palate, but also more evident depth and supporting structure. Very much in the character of St. Julien, elegant rather than powerful, with supple tannins giving a furry finish with chocolate overtones. Oak is evident in the soft impression of vanillin and nuts on the finish. Fine, but will be finer yet when the planned increase in Cabernet Sauvignon occurs. 13.8% *89* Drink 2015-2025.

Château Beychevelle, 2007
Quite fresh nose shows a touch of herbaceousness, but very soft on the palate, almost chocolaty. The usual dry character of Beychevelle is somewhat subservient to the relatively unstructured character of the vintage, so this should be enjoyed in the immediate future. 13.0% *87* Drink to 2018.

Château Beychevelle, 2006
Although the content of Cabernet Sauvignon was high this year, there's a definite sense of roundness to the fruits on the first impression, with hints of spices. Following through, the palate is taut and elegant, with mid weight black fruits showing as blackcurrants and blackberries. Many wines from this year give a rather flat impression, but here instead, if it's not too contradictory, is a sort of soft tautness—a superficial softness, but with quite tightly defined fruits underneath 13.0% *88* Drink 2013-2022.

Château Beychevelle, 2005
Rather restrained on the nose. First palate impression is of furry, chocolaty, tannins coating soft fruits—softer than the Amiral—and then the structure kicks in on the finish and you see the underlying strength of the wine for aging. Beautifully balanced, elegant, black fruits have lost the initial fat, but not yet started into mid development. The quality of the grand vin shows in a roundness that's absent from the Amiral. 13.0% *90* Drink to 2027.

Château Beychevelle, 2002
Some developed impressions here with herbal savory notes and a touch of sous bois. Not a Merlot year, but the wine is quite soft, with black fruits supported by supple tannins. The char-

acter of the vintage shows itself in a slight flatness on the finish, a basic lack of generosity. 13.0% *88* Drink to 2018.

Domaine de Chevalier

A relatively recent estate, dating from the eighteenth century, Domaine de Chevalier forms its own terroir with a contiguous block of 50 ha of vineyards surrounded by a pine forest. The estate fell into disarray during the nineteenth century and was revived at the start of the twentieth century under the Ricard family. Present owner Olivier Bernard purchased the estate in 1983. Following a traditional style, the wines have elicited mixed reviews, tending to fall out of favor with those who advocate powerful wines in the modern style, but liked by those who prefer precision and elegance. They are not fans of modern techniques at Domaine de Chevalier. "The idea here is to keep the taste, the typicity of Domaine de Chevalier is not the technique of making Cabernet Sauvignon, it is to express the terroir. This is the terroir of the purist. It's possible to transform Cabernet Sauvignon or other wines with technology, but it's a crime, a blasphemy against the terroir," says manager Rémi Edange. The division between grand vin and the second wine makes no concessions: all barrels are tasted by a group of five, and all five must agree for a barrel to be included in the grand vin. Wines were tasted at Domaine de Chevalier in June 2012.

2010
(Barrel sample.) Elegant, pure, black fruit nose—even at first impression you can see the purity of the fruits, with that classic crystalline quality. Showing presently as black cherries and plums (still with some aromatics of the barrel), this makes a very refined impression, with tannins quite tight on the finish. There is lovely fruit concentration, and already some flavor variety; even though this has yet to start its aromatic development, it promises to become a classic. 14.1% *92* Drink 2017-2030.

2009
The beginnings of some aromatic complexity show in the initial impression of blackcurrants and black cherries. This is softer on the palate than 2010, rounder and broader in its flavor spectrum, but conveys a strong sense of a fine underlying structure. This will develop in parallel with its sister vintage, but will be ready sooner, and will remain broader: the 2010 will be the more classical vintage for Domaine de Chevalier. 13.5% *91* Drink 2016-2028.

2005
The initial impression has the fruit-driven character of the vintage but is relatively reserved. The fruits are holding back on the palate in the way of young Bordeaux, or perhaps more specifically, the château. The plushness of the vintage takes the edge off, but still the style has that taut precision of finely delineated fruits. Oak shows as a smoky influence on the finish. The tension in the wine needs time but should develop into great finesse. The style here is unwavering, although its refinement may make it less successful in the marketplace. 13.0% (November 2012) *91* Drink 2015-2030.

2004
Very restrained nose with faint hints of Cabernet austerity. There's a rich initial impression, but cut by a rather dry finish (characteristic of the year, perhaps, but exacerbated here). This feels like a Cabernet-driven wine. How much will that dryness soften with time and will this happen before the fruits dry out? Although I like wines in the classic style, this is a little too dry even for my taste. 12.5% (October 2011) *88* Drink to 2018.

Châteaux Chasse Spleen & Poujeaux (Moulis)

Chasse Spleen is the largest château in the area, with 103 ha plus another 3 ha used for white wine. It was Château Gressier Grand Poujeaux until 1820, when it was divided: one part became Gressier, and one part became Chasse Spleen. The Merlauts bought it in 1976; they bought Gressier Grand Poujeaux in 2003, but the chateaux continue to be independent. There are five wines: Chasse Spleen (which uses all four varieties), Oratoire (which comes from young wines), Heritage (an Haut Médoc), Gressier Grand Poujeaux, and Blanc de Chasse Spleen. Rival Château Poujeaux was purchased by the Cuvelier's of St. Emilion's Clos Fourtet in 2008. Cabernet Sauvignon occupies about half of the 52 ha estate. Without any overt intention to change the style, the consulting oenologist changed from the left bank to the right bank, and they try to be more precise about the harvest. In addition to the grand vin, there is a second wine, La Salle de Poujeaux, and an Haut Médoc (Haut de Poujeaux). Wines were tasted at the châteaux in June 2012.

Château Chasse Spleen, 2010
Black fruit nose with hints of spices and white pepper. Nice fruit density, quite an elegant balance, tannins seem refined. This is generally a good reflection of the lighter character of the appellation. Allow a couple of years for the tannins to resolve—there's still some dryness on the finish— and this should show an elegant representation of Moulis. 12.5% *88* Drink 2014-2022.

Château Chasse Spleen, 2009
The nose is quite fresh with spices and herbs. Full and round on the palate, showing as extra ripeness and roundness compared to 2010. The elegant style of Château and appellation show through. In spite of the high alcohol, the wine remains true to type, this vintage showing more as black cherries than blackcurrants. Finely textured tannins bring refinement to the structure. Global warming has brought Moulis closer to the character of the major communes. 14.0% *90* Drink to 2022.

Château Chasse Spleen, 2006
A little development shows in the appearance. There's an impression of black fruits, minerality, and gunflint on the nose. This is a bit flat compared to 2009 or 2010, but still very creditable. The usual elegant fruits are supported by light tannins, but there's an absence of fleshiness on the mid palate. It's a little muted. 12.5% *86* Drink to 2018.

Château Poujeaux, 2006
A slightly nutty black fruit impression on the nose. This is a gentle wine, nicely rounded, with better liveliness and freshness than many of this often flat vintage. There's a slight touch of heat on the finish. "I chose 2006 to taste because I think it's more dominated by Cabernet Sauvignon," says winemaker Christophe Labenne. Fruits here are light and elegant, with those structured lines of Cabernet Sauvignon. Moulis certainly produces a lighter wine than the great communes, but it's nicely balanced. 13.0% 87 Drink to 2018.

Château Cos d'Estournel

The wine is as showy as the château, and is considered by many to be more Pauillac in style than St. Estèphe (Château Lafite Rothschild is adjacent). The wine became one of the original super-seconds under the ownership of Bruno Prats, which lasted from 1971 to 2000, when the château was sold to Michel Reybier. Bruno's son, Jean-Guillaume, then became the general manager, until leaving in 2012. A major investment led to the building being under construction for several years, but now a new splendid underground *chai* has been finished. I find the wines attractive when young, full of ripe Cabernet flavor, but I seem to be alone in worrying that they will not have the longevity I look for in St. Estèphe. Yet Jean-Guillaume Prats says that, "The current wines will be capable of long aging because they have high acidity and phenolics. Even though acidity is less than it used to be, pH still has remained low [enough]." I have always found the second wine, Pagodes de Cos, named after the exotic building, to be a little superficial (although many would not regard that as a fair criticism of a second wine).

Château Cos d'Estournel, 2008
A little muted on the nose, with just some hints of black fruits. Very smooth, ripe tannins with good finish and a slight rasp. Some chocolate notes develop on the finish. A nice enough result for the vintage, but not a stayer. 13.5% (October 2011) *88* Drink to 2018.

Château Cos d'Estournel, 2006
Sweaty mineral nose with faint hints of gunflint, opening into acidity in the glass, although the fruits are relatively soft and well rounded. Quite deep chalky tannins, with a rasp on the finish suggesting structural support for some development. Acidity is lower than most in this vintage. 13.5% (May 2010) *88* Drink to 2020.

Château Cos d'Estournel, 1996
This wine has been up and down in tastings, perhaps due to condition problems. The best recent bottle had an attractive nose with a touch of exotic perfume, turning to nutty black fruits. The palate has rich, ripe fruits cut by a touch of bell peppers. The nature of the vintage shows itself in the tannins, which bring a bitter touch to the finish. But the rich opulent style of the château served the wine well in this vintage, countering what became a medicinal quality in some wines. Overall impression is rich and spicy, relatively soft for St. Estèphe, as Cos now so often is, but cut by those bell peppers to give complexity. 13.0% (October 2011) *90* Drink to 2019.

Château Cos d'Estournel, 1990
Ripe fruit notes, hints of blackcurrant jam. Spicy and rich on the palate with slightly roasted notes, strong tannic support showing, with some bitterness intensifying in the glass and taking over. Are the fruits drying out in spite of their superficial richness? 13.0% (October 2010) *88* Drink to 2017.

Château Cos d'Estournel, 1985
This bottle seemed disappointing. Quite dark garnet appearance for age, showing a red fruit nose with raspberries and strawberries and some intimations of jam: surprisingly New World in style. Black fruit palate with some bell peppers showing retronasally, still seems rather tight, but rather pressing acidity on the finish. 12.5% (March 2010) *89* Drink to 2017.

Château Ducru Beaucaillou

The name of Ducru Beaucaillou is a reference to the beautiful pebbles (beaux caillou) in the vineyard. It was actually part of the Beychevelle estate until the Duc d'Epernon sold it off in 1642. Subsequently it was supposedly known as Maucaillou (bad pebbles), until it was decided that pebbles were good, and it acquired its present name: an early example of marketing speak, perhaps. By the time of the 1855 classification, when there was no question about its status as a second growth, Ducru had been appended for the name of the current owner. The Borie family purchased the estate in 1941, when it was in quite poor condition. In 1970, Jean-Eugène Borie purchased a further 32 ha from Château Lagrange; although this could have been included in Ducru Beaucaillou, instead it was bottled separately under the name of Château Lalande Borie; in effect it is now the Borie's third wine, as a second wine, Croix de Beaucaillou, was introduced in 1995. There was an awkward patch in the late eighties, when contamination with TCA led to many wines being corked; but aside from that, Ducru Beaucaillou has had no threat to its position as a super-second. Vineyards are all around the château in a single block, with a perceptible slope from the château down to the Gironde about 700 m away with natural drainage. Drainage has been installed in places where there is less slope. The vines of Ducru Beaucaillou are exclusively Cabernet Sauvignon (75%) and Merlot. Wine were tasted at Château Ducru Beaucaillou in June.

Château Lalande Borie, 2009
Restrained on the nose with an impression of fresh red fruits. Fresh, almost crisp, on the palate, with a tart impression, fruits more red than black, and a touch of heat on the finish. Even though this is a lighter style of Bordeaux, it still needs a little time. 13.5% *87* Drink 2013-2020.

Croix de Beaucaillou, 2009
A darker color than Lalande Borie, this shows more classic sternness to the nose, and a lot more weight and roundness on the palate. Now we turn to black fruits, showing as blackberries tinged with blackcurrants, and you can see something of the style of the grand vin—second wines are certainly coming on. There's a good sense of refined structure on the mid palate with the fruits showing the restrained elegance of St. Julien. 13.5% *89* Drink 2013-2022.

Château Ducru Beaucaillou, 2009
Not so much darker than Croix de Beaucaillou as more purple in hue. Restrained nose gives impression of tight black fruits. Lots of concentration here, with the deep, black fruits matched by tight tannins, but closed at the moment. Typical of the top level of St. Julien vis à vis Pauillac, the restrained elegance shows a fine texture of taut tannins, promising long life in the classic style. Fruits are certainly full, but not overbearing; reports of excess exuberance were over rated. 13.6% *93* Drink 2016-2031.

Château Ducru Beaucaillou, 1996
Quintessential St. Julien, claret in the old style. Herbaceousness of Cabernet Sauvignon is tamed by the fruits (or vice versa). This is slowly maturing, full-throated Ducru, with a core of dense fruits turning savory, a distinct touch of herbaceousness on nose and palate, but making a delicious counterpoise to the sweet fruits. There's the elegance and precision of St. Julien, more than a touch of austerity reflecting the character of the vintage, but this is as good as the vintage gets. 13.0% (October 2011) *92* Drink to 2019.

Château Ducru Beaucaillou, 1995
Some garnet hues show development, with minerality, gunflint, some savory, herbal notes of tarragon, a touch of sous bois showing on the nose. The palate shows more fruit vis à vis savory character, a touch nutty, but tannins remain quite dry on the finish. Cabernet Sauvignon comes through clearly as the dominant influence (although at two thirds it wasn't an especially high proportion this year), bringing a slightly spartan impression. The fruits are beginning to dry out, so best to drink in the near future. 13.0% *90* Drink to 2017.

Château Ducru Beaucaillou, 1985
By the late eighties, Ducru was having problems with TCA that spoiled many bottles, but this one was an outstanding effort. The restrained nose is very faintly smoky, developing notes of bell peppers in the glass. Much fuller on the palate than the nose would suggest. Smooth and opulent, with deep black fruits, a lovely balance, and years to go. The overall impression is of that harmonious quality that marks the super-seconds and first growths. 12.7% (March 2010) *92* Drink up.

Château Ducru Beaucaillou, 1970
Oh for the days when giants walked the earth and claret was claret. With its limpid color, elegant lacy structure, and light but complex layers of fruits, this could only be a classic claret. The fruits are just now beginning to dry out, but in the way of old Bordeaux the wine is likely to remain delicious for several years yet. There's a classic Bordeaux nose of underlying black fruits with herbaceous and faint barnyard overtones. A seamless and timeless palate of savory black fruits. It's the height of elegance and finesse. This slightly mushroomy bell pepper notes are cut by the sweetness of the fruits. This does not of course show the sheer density of recent releases, aficionados of cult cabernet would probably not like it, but for my money this is close to perfection. (February 2011) *94* Drink to 2017.

Château Figeac (St. Emilion)

From the seventeenth to the nineteenth centuries, Figeac was an enormous estate, extending from St. Emilion into Pomerol. As an agricultural estate, it had a variety of crops, with vines being cultivated in parts of the estate that were not good enough to grow cereals or to use as pastures. Several of today's famous châteaux have vineyards on what was originally part of the Figeac estate, including neighboring Cheval Blanc, and La Conseillante across the Pomerol border. The estate has been in the hands of the present family since 1892, coming by marriage to the Manoncourts, and into the hands of Thierry Manoncourt in 1947. Today it is managed by Thierry's son-in-law, Eric d'Aramon. From the Manoncourt era, Figeac has been regarded as one of the top châteaux of St. Emilion; at the top of Premier Grand Cru Classé B, its official standing was just below the two châteaux (Cheval Blanc and Ausone) classified as Premier Grand Cru Classé A. With its equal proportions of Cabernet Sauvignon, Cabernet Franc, and Merlot, Figeac is sui generis, without doubt the right bank's leader in Cabernet Sauvignon. Perhaps fashion has partly overtaken Figeac with the rise of the extremely lush style of modern St. Emilion (in the reclassification of 2012, Pavie and l'Angélus were jumped over Figeac into class A), but Eric d'Aramon says, "We are not looking for high alcohol. I was the latest to pick 20-30 years ago, now I'm in the average." Although current vintages are certainly more approachable than those of the past, this is still a wine that benefits from age, perhaps more so than other St. Emilion's given its unusual assemblage. Wines were tasted at Château Figeac in June 2012.

2010
(Bottled one month ago.) Quite a stern black fruit nose with a definite sense of structure at the first impression. With taut fruits and tense tannins, this is quite hard at the moment, with structure somewhat evident ahead of the fruits. This is one of the cases, where at least for the foreseeable future, the 2010 will not show as well as the 2009. This should be a long lived wine, very much in the classic character of Figeac, but it will take a few years for the tannins to resolve; a promising sign is that the wine does soften a little in the glass to give just a faint sensation of that nutty elegance typifying Figeac. 13.75% *90* Drink 2017-2032.

2009
The first impression gives a sense of spicy black fruits, more rounded, more typically St. Emilion, less typically Figeac, than 2010, although the firm structural backbone is evident through the fruits of blackberries and blackcurrants. Tannins are just as dry as 2010 on the finish, but less evident against the more exuberant fruits of the 2009 vintage. Restrained and holding back right now, but even so, certainly more approachable than 2010. Figeac's character becomes more evident in the glass. 13.5% *91* Drink 2015-2027.

2003
Development shows a garnet hue on the rim and the first impressions of sous bois just evident on the bouquet with some mineral hints of gunflint. Lightening up a touch, this is almost at the tipping point for turning from fruity to savory. The wine remains fresh, but the giveaway of the vintage is a touch of hardness on the finish, a faint suspicion of cooked tannins on top of the usual nuttiness. The tannins will probably outlast the fruits, so drink fairly soon. 12.5% *88* Drink to 2016.

2000
This is a classic Figeac, poised between left bank and right bank. The first impression shows generous black fruits with those slightly nutty overtones that are characteristic of Figeac; and then the structural support of Cabernet Sauvignon becomes obvious in the ripe, round, tannins on the finish. The overall impression is well balanced, which is to say the primary enthusiasm of youth has blown off, but it is still very lively: no signs of tertiary development yet. It's more youthful—and promises greater longevity—than some left bank wines of equivalent status where the fruits are not fulfilling their early promise. Over a longer period it begins to seem a little monotonic and tiring, even too rich and nutty, but I would expect a wider range of flavors to develop over the next decade. 13% (October 2012) *90* Drink to 2027.

1990
A decade ago this was showing as typical young Figeac, with somewhat direct fruits, not very complicated. Since then in the confounding style of the château it has put on weight and come round enormously. Two years ago, there was a classic nose with some herbaceous aromas, in fact more typical of the left than right bank, until the finish turned nutty in the glass in the typical style of Figeac. Since then, a slightly sharp touch to the nose has developed to raise the question of volatile acidity. Fruits remain sweet and ripe on the palate, but appear a bit simpler in variety and with less of a herbaceous overtone than two years ago. There's a slight sense of dilution creeping in, creating a risk this may fade rather than develop. 13.0% (October 2010) *90* Drink to 2018.

1989
There's a slightly musty quality on the nose with a flatter flavor profile than 1990, and less well rounded fruits. There's a lack of fleshiness on the mid palate. It fills in a bit in the glass but leaves the impression that it's missing the usual roundness brought by the Merlot. A little dry on the finish, it's a touch lacking in acid uplift. 13.0% *87* Drink to 2016.

1970
Classic nose, and as so often with Figeac you might easily take this for a left bank Cabernet. Sweet ripe fruits still dominate the palate, noticeably sweeter than the 1966, cut by a classic bell pepper herbaceousness, but with a softer touch than the Médoc. Aficionados of modern Bordeaux might find it less concentrated, but its delicacy is a perfect accompaniment to food. Still vibrant and not slacking off much. (November 2010) *93* Drink to 2017.

Cabernet Sauvignon, 1989
A touch of sous bois on the nose leads into an impression of minerality, and then a fugitive whiff of herbaceousness. This tastes like quite a complete wine in the model of a linear Cabernet Sauvignon. The fruits have turned savory, very much Cabernet Sauvignon with that pure structure, with tannins just beginning to resolve. The structure is certainly sparser than you usually see with Figeac itself, but the fruits deepen and round up in the glass, and are quite long and ripe enough to balance the herbaceousness—but this was a hot vintage that probably displays the Cabernet Sauvignon at its best, possibly it would not show so well from a cooler year. I could easily drink this for dinner, thinking it was a Médoc from, say, 1985. (*89* Drink to 2017).

Château Fougas (Côtes de Bourg)

Jean-Yves Bechet bought Château Fougas in 1976, and in 1993 started to make the Maldoror cuvée from a single hectare; it was only 10% of production then. The estate was converted to biodynamic viticulture, quality improved, and slowly Maldoror was increased to its present proportion, about 90% of production. In effect it has gone from a special cuvée to becoming the grand vin. Its proportion of 25% Cabernet Sauvignon is more or less constant each year; the Cabernet vines are now about forty years old, which no doubt contributes to the quality. "Cabernet Sauvignon is difficult here, but when we get ripe Cabernet Sauvignon, its taste is extraordinary, with lots of structure," says Jean-Yves. Wines were tasted at Château Fougas in June 2012.

Château Fougas, Maldoror, 2009
A mélange of spicy fruits with suggestions of blackcurrants gives an initial impression of ripeness. The extra ripeness of the fruits in this vintage is evident on the palate, with firm tannins in support. This is still a little too young, but the tannins that still dry the finish should soften within a year or so to let the elegant fruits of blackcurrants, plums, and cherries come through. The elegant style of this wine would be a credit to a grander appellation. 13.0% *91* Drink 2013-2024.

Château Fougas, Maldoror, 2008
More overt impression of black fruits here, more rounded than 2006, with that slightly nutty, soft quality of Merlot trying to break out of the structure of the Cabernet Sauvignon. This still needs a little time to come around. 13.0% *88* Drink to 2021.

Château Fougas, Maldoror, 2006
Black fruits show on the nose with a slightly spicy impression, leading into a relatively stern palate. There's no shortage of fruit, and this isn't as flat as the 2006 often was in the Médoc. Fruits are holding the firm, slightly rustic, tannins in balance, but aren't quite generous enough to overcome them. 13.0% *87* Drink to 2019.

Château Fougas, Maldoror, 2000
The first beginnings of tertiary development show on top of lively fruits with notes of spices. Smooth and elegant, with a slightly nutty aftertaste, in some ways more like the refinement of the left bank than the overt plushness of the right bank. This vintage should easily age for another decade, becoming steadily more savory and interesting. 13.0% *90* Drink to 2022.

Château Fougas, Maldoror, 1993
This was the first vintage of the Maldoror cuvée at Château Fougas. In this vintage (and also in 1994) it was 100% Merlot, compared to the proportions of 75% Merlot to 25% Cabernet Sauvignon since then. The nose is more perfumed than savory. It's quite smooth and elegant, but is beginning to lose the fruits, although there's only a faint savory touch showing on the finish, where a faint herbaceous whiff comes out. This vintage is fading very gently now, marking the limits of longevity. *88* Drink to 2016.

Châteaux Grand Puy Lacoste & Haut Batailley

The character of the Médoc is encapsulated in the name of Grand Puy Lacoste, as Grand Puy means a small hill, and the château is sited at the top of a gravel mound, with vineyards running down from it. A clear lineage can be seen through the vintages of Grand Puy Lacoste, with a refined style whose elegance is emphasized by the fine texture of the tannins. The 1990 is beginning to lose fruits, the 1995 remains at a perfect balance, and the 2000 is now at a perfect balance, if anything a touch more developed than the 1995. The style comes through even the lushness of the 2009 vintage. You might almost regard it as a half way house between the traditional power of Pauillac and elegance of St. Julien. By contrast, Haut Batailley, under the same ownership, shows a more four square style, verging on rustic, perhaps a throwback to old views of Pauillac, with a touch of St. Estèphe. Given that the châteaux are close together, that the plantings are similar, and that vinification is in the same hands, what can the difference be due to but the vagaries of terroir? This is further emphasized by a relationship between the styles of Châteaux Batailley and Haut Batailley, both in that four square style beloved of traditional British claret drinkers, which no doubt was the style of the château before it was divided in 1942. "Haut Batailley matures more quickly than Grand Puy Lacoste, which has more aging potential," says owner François-Xavier Borie. Wines were tasted at Château Grand Puy Lacoste in June 2012.

Château Grand Puy Lacoste, 2009
A taut refined impression on the nose, its characteristic elegance in evidence. There's that tightly defined, almost crystalline, edge to the fruits, with support from fine-grained tannins. In contrast with the reputation of the vintage for exuberance, this shows the classic elegance of the chateau. 13.5% *91* Drink 2016-2028.

Château Grand Puy Lacoste, 2000
Barnyard notes extend to impressions of sous bois on the nose. This has reached its tipping point, with the fruits turning savory. It's now at a delicious point of balance where it's difficult to tell whether fruit or savory impressions are dominant, whether the driving force is the black fruit or the developing sous bois. Classically in flagrante delicto. 13.0% *92* Drink to 2018.

Château Grand Puy Lacoste, 1995
Developed notes on the nose with a touch of barnyard, more clearly developed on the palate. But it's less obvious than the 2000 vintage, overall it seems to be developing more slowly, with more of a fruit impression evident on the palate and a kick of ripe, sweet, fruits on the finish with only a rather faint touch of sous bois. Tannins are resolving, however. Lovely balance now, but on the verge of beginning to fade. 13.0% *91* Drink to 2017.

Château Grand Puy Lacoste, 1990
A nice mingling of remnant red fruits with developed tertiary aromas. Beautiful balance on the palate seems to be staying at the tipping point. Good fruit density is just holding back the more developed overtones, which are on the verge of breaking through to bitterness on the finish. The brightness that you still see in the fruits of the 1995 has dissipated here. 12.5% *90* Drink to 2016.

Château Haut Batailley, 2009
Black fruit nose with a slightly hard edged impression following through to the palate. Fresh acidity supports the slightly stern fruits. There's a firm tannic structure but the fruits seem less obvious, less forward, than in other wines of this vintage. This is a bit four square and needs a while for the tannins to soften in traditional style. 13.5% *88* Drink 2017-2027.

Château Haut Batailley, 2003
Some developed barnyard notes show before the wine reverts to more youthful impressions, with blackcurrants evident. While it's retained good freshness for the year, this seems much older than the vintage, and I think it's reached its apogee. 12.5% *89* Drink to 2017.

Château Gruaud Larose

"Gruaud used to be the best wine in St. Julien," said owner Jean Merlaut as we looked over the surrounding vineyards from the tower in the middle. "In the forties, Lascases was not so good, Poyferré was not so good. In moments like this we can see the 1855 classification was very well done, because when people renovate the vineyards they return to form." Since 1997, when Merlaut took over Gruaud Larose from Alcatel (the telecommunications group, who had purchased the château from the Cordier family in 1993, making significant investments before selling it on in 1997), there's been a steady program of improvement. After the estate was classified as a second growth in 1855, it was split into two halves; Cordier purchased the first part (Gruaud Larose Sarget) in 1917, and then reunited it with the second part in 1935. Cordier's style, evident in Château Talbot, which they also owned as well as Gruaud Larose, was for a very dry, firm, character, sometimes described as masculine. After Cordier sold their holdings in 1983, Gruaud Larose had several changes of ownership. Quality has been improving steadily under the Merlauts. "Since I have been here we have planted more Cabernet Sauvignon. In 1999 it was 57%, now it is 61%," says Jean Merlaut. "But it takes 30 years to change the vineyards. I started in 1997; in ten years time there will be 70% or so Cabernet Sauvignon." He sees this as representing a return to form. "In the nineties the style of Gruaud was far more classical—what we make now is more like the first part of the twentieth century." Wines were tasted at the château or in London in June 2012 unless otherwise noted.

2010
Overtly fruity nose shows vanillin and nuts from new oak on top of the black fruits. The fruits burst out of the 2010 more clearly than for the 2009. The fruits are so ripe that the firm tannins are pushed into the background, although the structure remains more obvious than 2009. The comparison with 2009 makes the 2010 seem fresher rather than more classical, as the conventional wisdom goes. The taut quality of the fruits is evident here and this is one of the cases where the 2010 may prove to be more interesting than the 2009. 13.5% *93* Drink 2016-2035.

2009
An elegant ruby appearance with a Cabernet-ish nose, showing fine underlying black fruits but a fresh, almost stern impression. The black fruits are elegant and precisely delineated, and there is a taut impression with tannins very much in the background, cutting the exotic exuberance attributed to the vintage, although there's a sort of roundness taking the edge off Gruaud's usual precision. Gruaud has always typified that restrained style of St. Julien; indeed, in older vintages it might be too restrained, so the ripeness of 2009 has really brought it to life. Cedary notes develop in the glass to cut the initial impression of nuts and vanillin. Tannins are firm but fine. This will be most elegant as it matures. 13.6% *92* Drink 2015-2026.

2007
Quite nutty on the nose. Soft on the palate with a glyceriny impression, attractive for current drinking. There isn't much structure in evidence but the wine has retained the characteristic elegance of the appellation, although the nuttiness of the nose carries over to the finish. It's a demonstration of the capacity of Bordeaux today to make attractive wine in vintages that would have been written off in the past. This should drink well for the next three or four years, although without developing much more complexity. 12.5% *87* Drink to 2016.

2006
Quite dumb on the nose. The ripeness of the fruits makes this livelier on the palate than many of this vintage. The wine shows the characteristic black fruits with the elegant, restrained, lines of St. Julien in general and this château in particular. The fruits are tight rather than flat, but there isn't the generosity, that layer in the background that will give future development. It's a good result for the vintage, but doesn't completely overcome the problems of the year; personally I think the lack of follow through on the mid palate indicates that this is best enjoyed soon, although at the château they believe it will be a sleeper. 12.5% *88* Drink to 2019.

2005
The initial impression shows ripe but restrained black fruits, without the cedary and almost herbaceous overtones of 2001 and 2000, but the direct elegance of the fruits gives a similarly clear, pure, linear, view of Cabernet Sauvignon, with precise delineation of fruits on the palate. It's that quality of precision that is the quintessence of St. Julien. This hasn't yet started its savory development, but that should come in the next few years. If there was a criticism at present, it would be the single focus of the fruits, but that's just youthfulness. This can be enjoyed now because the tannins are so refined as to be in balance with the fruits, but you need to wait to get the savory development that will come with time. 12.5% *91* Drink to 2024.

2001
Tight, restrained, black fruits impress with an edge of ripeness just poking through. You might see this as similar in style to 2000, but the fruits being just a touch less sweet and round. This is more open than 2000; it is ready to drink, but less opulent, and there isn't quite the depth of structure or fruit concentration to support the same longevity. 13.0% *89* Drink to 2018.

2000
The nose is more perfumed than herbaceous. Ripe, sweet fruits are round and black, with a faint herbal edge. This vintage is very much in the tradition of Gruaud Larose, with that fine, elegant, tight finish. The overall impression is quite youthful. With its slow development, this vintage should develop well for at least another decade. This seems in the direct line of the older vintages, representing the style of St. Julien; the fruits are riper and more concentrated, but the finish retains that dry, restrained elegance. 12.5% *91* Drink 2010-2024.

1996
This vintage has developed quite a way in the past few years, so the first impression is now savory, showing sous bois and gunflint. Fruits are certainly well rounded for the vintage, but now cut by a classic herbaceousness. There's a delicious balance of fruits to savory, right à point, supported by fresh but not excessive acidity. The impressive feature of this vintage is the way the fruits have emerged from the shell of the early years, to show a lovely level of ripeness that was hidden at first; now they are right at the tipping point. In fact, this vintage shows more overt development than 1989 or 2000. 12.5% *92* Drink to 2020.

1989
There's some variation now among individual bottles, even from impeccable sources. Some show more obvious fruit than is usual for Gruaud; others seem to show more development. There tends to be an intriguing mix of faintly herbaceous aromas with a touch of sous bois. The palate is smooth and round with firm tannins still giving support, but elegant as always. Probably now at its peak, with serious tertiary development about to start. Lovely balance, with a slight rasp on the finish showing you are in Cabernet territory. *91* Drink to 2022.

Châteaux Haut Brion and La Mission Haut Brion

These are grand châteaux, surrounded by their vineyards, although bisected by a main road and railway, and overlooked by the southern suburbs of Bordeaux. There is no perceptible difference between the parts of the property. The terroir is a gravel mound, with the gravel varying in depth from 1 to 7 meters, and a subsoil of clay in an undulating pattern. Viticulture and vinification are the same for both châteaux. Fermentation uses special two-part vats where alcoholic fermentation takes place in the upper part, and then the free-run juice falls into the lower part for malolactic fermentation. Second wines are made by selection. All the grand vin goes into new oak for twenty months. Both châteaux also produce white wine (Haut Brion's white has been Bordeaux's best dry white for a long time, challenged only by Laville Haut Brion, which was recently renamed as Mission Haut Brion Blanc.) Tasting notes concentrate on pairwise comparisons, some from a tasting in 2006, but as the vintages go back to 1975, this is still of interest. Other wines were tasted at La Mission Haut Brion in October 2011. I have also included some tastings of older vintages as a demonstration of aging potential.

Château Haut Brion, 2008
A little darker in color than the Mission. More restrained nose than Mission with only a suspicion of black fruits. Medium fruit concentration. The dominance of Cabernet Sauvignon shows in a certain hardness on the mid palate. There's a touch of heat on the finish. Fresh balance, wine will soften in time, but although the tannins are not pressing they do seem a touch hard. There's a lot of structure here: the question is whether and when the wine will come around. 14.0% (October 2011) *87* Drink 2014-2019.

Château La Mission Haut Brion, 2008
Medium intensity black fruit nose, but showing purity of line. This is more approachable than Haut Brion and the fruits are more obvious, showing as black fruits including blackcurrants on the palate, with elegant, pure lines. Just a touch of hardness shows on the finish (but less than

in Haut Brion). In another couple of years, this should be quite elegant for mid term drinking. 14.0% (October 2011) *88* Drink 2013-2019.

Château Haut Brion, 2003
You might expect a New Wave wine, with very full, forward fruits from this exceptionally hot year, but the Haut Brion 2003 is far from that and shows quite a classical aroma and flavor spectrum. The nose is rather stern, with some notes of leafy tobacco dominating the fruits. High acid accentuates the tannins on the palate, which seem strong and give quite a bite to the finish, and some heat shows from alcohol. Several years are needed for this to come together. 13.0% (March 2006) *92* Drink 2013-2020.

Château La Mission Haut Brion, 2003
There are black fruits on the nose with some hints of tobacco and some faint rubbery notes left from the new oak. Good acidity supports the black fruits on the palate, and some mouth-drying tannins show on the finish together with a little warmth from high alcohol. The overall impression is very good, but lacking the greater concentration (and acidity) of the Haut Brion. (March 2006) *90* Drink to 2020.

Château Haut Brion, 1998
Appearance shows a garnet rim. A little development is just beginning to show as tertiary notes on the nose, which however is still fresh. Development has given this a softer impression than La Mission, but the characteristic herbaceousness of Cabernet Sauvignon comes through to the finish; even though it is a relatively small proportion, it seems to be the driving force in both the Haut Brion and Mission of this vintage. The wine still really hasn't come around. 13.0% (October 2011) *88* Drink to 2019.

Château La Mission Haut Brion, 1998
More youthful appearance than Haut Brion, ruby rather than garnet. Has lost the first flush of primary fruits, but no tertiary development yet. Black fruits have faint savory overtones on the nose. Palate of fresh black fruits has a distinctly austere bell pepper edge of Cabernet Sauvignon. Softens a bit in the glass, but still really needs time—but will it come around? 13.0% (October 2011) *87* Drink to 2019.

Château Haut Brion, 1990
It is fascinating to compare the 1990 with the 1989 Haut Brion. For most Bordeaux châteaux, 1990 was a denser and more concentrated vintage, but for Haut Brion the 1989 may be stronger. The 1990 is a mature color, with a leafy, herbaceous Cabernet nose, and lovely tertiary red fruits coming out on the palate. However, a touch of dilution seems to be creeping into the fruits, marking this down slightly by comparison with the 1989. 13.0% (March 2006) *90* Drink to 2012.

Château La Mission Haut Brion, 1990
The debate as to the relative merits of the 1990 and 1989 is not likely to be resolved in short order. The 1990 is a classic aristocratic wine, with great breed and finesse. It has a lovely nose with a mélange of tertiary fruits; some faintly herbaceous character of Cabernet shows retronasally. The palate is quite developed, with ripe fruits showing tertiary flavors accompanied by hints of tobacco and chocolate, which intensify on the long finish. It is fresh for its age and should have a long life. 13.0% (March 2006) *92* Drink to 2020.

Château Haut Brion, 1989
This may be the wine of the vintage. Its mature garnet color is just a tad darker than the 1990. The nose shows leafy notes, with tobacco coming out. It is softer and more generous than the 1990, with well developed tertiary red fruits on the palate, sweet, and ripe, and some tobacco and chocolate on the long finish. Tannins are beginning to resolve, giving a lovely balance of fruit, acid, and tannins. 13.0% (March 2006) *93* Drink to 2015.

Château La Mission Haut Brion, 1989
The 1989 is a little more forward and exotic than the 1990 and is showing very well. The tertiary fruits of the nose are just a little more developed than the 1990. The sweet ripe fruits of the palate are quite forward and full, and the rich chocolate-coated finish lends an exotic touch. This is showing signs of maturing like the 1964, long, soft, and opulent (whereas the 1990 may mature like the more classical 1966). 13.0% (March 2006) *94* Drink to 2020.

Château Haut Brion, 1982
This is a standout, and has come right around from the early lush qualities that characterized the vintage to an elegant, subtle wine that stands in a direct lineage with the 1961 and the 1945. The nose is quite muted, with some notes of tobacco. The palate is restrained but beautifully balanced with elegant tertiary fruits. The hallmark here is the subtle touch of tertiary notes,

compared with the rather forceful quality of the wines of the late seventies and the more obvious character of the late eighties. Altogether showing as rather soft, but with the underlying structure to last another 20 years, there is real breed and class here. 12.5% (March 2006) *93* Drink to 2025.

Château Haut Brion, 1961

This is a spectacular wine, virtually perfect, and one of the rare cases where it rather than the 1945 is the vintage of the century. The mature garnet color remains quite red in hue. There are quite sweet red fruits on the palate, with the tertiary aromas and flavors increasing complexity by their subtle, rather than overt nature (a feature that is shared with the later 1982 and the earlier 1945). There is just a perfect balance of fruit, acid, tannins, lots of concentration, and seamless layers of flavor. This is just a knockout. (March 2006) 99 Drink now.

Château Haut Brion, 1945

This is a lovely wine, but not as concentrated as the Haut Brion 1961 nor as elegant as the 1945 Lafite. These are of course very fine points of criticism. The fruits seem to be disappearing from the nose, which has some faint tobacco and some notes of gunflint. The sweet ripe fruits of the palate are quite mature and show lots of concentration with rather subtle tertiary notes. The subtlety of the tertiary notes and the ripeness of the fruits marks this as a direct linear ancestor of the 1961 and the 1982. (March 2006) *93.*

Château Lafite Rothschild

Lafite's reputation for wine production goes back to the seventeenth century, and it was recognized as one of the four first growths as soon as the concept of individual Crus arose. At this time it was part of the great Ségur seigneurie that occupied a large part of Pauillac and St. Julien. The Rothschilds acquired the property in 1866. The vineyards fall into two major parts: the main estate around the château; and the Carruades plateau just to the southwest. In addition to the two wines made from these vineyards, adjacent Château Duhart Milon is part of the Lafite portfolio, and there are also some wines under the broader appellations of Pauillac or Médoc (sold as the Barons de Rothschild Collection). Domaines Baron de Rothschild (Lafite), as the holding company is known, also owns Château L'Évangile in Pomerol and Château Rieussec in Sauternes, not to mention the Los Vascos estate in Chile (page 442) and the Bodegas Caro joint venture with Catena in Mendoza (page 449). Wine were tasted at Lafite Rothschild in June 2012 unless otherwise noted.

Carruades de Lafite, 2011

(Barrel sample.) Fresh black fruits on nose with just a whiff of blackcurrants. Quite tight and constrained on the palate, showing elegant but tight fruits with firm tannins. At this moment this gives an impression of combining the tautness of St. Julien but with the power of Pauillac. Slowly fruits of red and black cherries release in the glass. There's a touch of heat on the finish. Very fine. *89* Drink 2017-2028.

Carruades de Lafite, 2009

Slightly nutty nose yet with some savory undertones. Round, elegant, soft, yet there is that underlying sense of the power of Pauillac. Although the tannins are supple, the wine is very restrained; the Cabernet seems more dominant than its proportion of 50%. The palate softens a little in the glass but the nose remains muted. The tannins need to resolve to release the elegance of the fruits. Even as a second wine, this is not for instant gratification, but needs time. 13.5% *90* Drink 2016-2031.

Château Lafite Rothschild, 2011

(Barrel sample.) Dark purple color, almost inky. Slight impression of nuts as well as black fruits on the nose. Fruits are more rounded, deeper, concentrated than on the Carruades, in fact more Pauillac-ish. Tight and reserved with fine tannins evident on the finish. A very fine, classic structure for aging. *92* Drink 2017-2032.

Château Lafite Rothschild, 2009

Restrained nose with faintly nutty tones of blackcurrants. Softer and rounder, yet more concentrated, than Carruades. Tight grained tannins create a very fine texture, and dry the finish. That hallmark core of elegance, of precision to the fruits, runs through the wine. Even after only a few months, the initial exuberance has calmed down. It's that smooth roundness on the palate and the long velvety finish that tells us this is Lafite; that quality of seamless layers of flavor is already beginning to show. 13.4% *94* Drink 2018-2038.

Château Lafite Rothschild, 2003
Even the first growths are not immune from the effects of the super-hot vintage, and already this is showing signs of over-development. Still a deep color although some orange is showing at the rim, a bit sooner than you would expect from a first growth in a top year. Very fat on nose and palate, quite nutty with a Merlot-ish impression, ripe fruits of blackcurrants and black cherries, deep concentration, but slightly jammy overtones coming through on the finish are suggestive of over-ripe fruits and a limited longevity. 12.9% (March 2010) *90* Drink 2011-2021.

Château Lafite Rothschild, 1978
Perfumed, herbaceous nose. Palate shows lots of bell peppers, but somewhat lacking in counterbalancing fruits. The character of Pauillac is just detectable, but this was not a top year for Lafite. 12.0% (May 2011) *88* Drink to 2019.

Château Lafite Rothschild, 1975
Light nose is slightly acid and vegetal, leading into a classically herbaceous palate, but nicely balanced, elegant, and subtle. This is not a great vintage of Lafite, but the layered finish goes into a classical delicacy. The ethereal quality of Lafite comes through. (February 2012) *89* Drink to 2016.

Château Lafite Rothschild, 1945
Early in the twenty first century the wine appeared to be in a stable, timeless state, the epitome of elegance, with seamless layers of flavors dominated by red fruits, a quiet nose of mature claret, and a long finish from which the tannins have resolved. Since then there has not surprisingly been significant variation between bottles. Those reconditioned at the château seem to be just a fraction simpler in their representation of fruits than those under original corks. The best continue to show the ethereal layers of flavor that characterize top vintages of Lafite, supported by good acidity, but with a touch of bitterness or oxidation variously coming through to the finish, and suggesting that unless the bottle is guaranteed to be of pristine provenance, it's time to finish up. (October 2009) *95* Drink now.

Château Lagrange

Château Lagrange somewhat recapitulates the history of the times in Bordeaux. Production dates from the eighteenth century, and the château was classified as a third growth in 1855. Shortly after, financial troubles forced a sale; a new proprietor poured money in. The difficult period at the start of the twentieth century led to several changes of ownership, and the château declined. Parts of the vineyard were sold off, including the 32 hectares that became Château Lalande Borie. In 1983 the château was sold to the Suntory group, who have made major investments. Château Lagrange is part of a portfolio of investments in wine producers, including a share in Château Beychevelle. Lagrange is a large estate with 118 ha of vineyards in a single block, and the facilities, including 92 cuves of stainless steel in a huge cuverie built in 2008, give an almost semi-industrial impression. Even 25 years on, construction continues: the central courtyard is currently being replaced to create a new grape reception center, complete with optical sorting. "Lagrange is more a unit in terms of administration than geography. There are four types of terroir, more or less representing points of the compass," says director Bruno Eynard. The best terroir is white gravel in the northwest quadrant used for Cabernet Sauvignon and Merlot; ferrous soils with large pebbles in the southeast are used for Cabernet Sauvignon and Petit Verdot. Other areas have clay or sand and are used more for Merlot. Since 2006 they have been increasing the proportion of Cabernet Sauvignon (and decreasing Petit Verdot), but to my mind the wine has all the same moved to a lighter, more modern, fruit-forward style. Wines were tasted at the château in June 2012.

2009

Black fruit nose with overt blackcurrants, red cherries, and plums, with vanillin and nuts in support, in a fruity upfront style. "The 2009 is more modern," says Lagrange's Directeur, Bruno Eynard; comparing it with the 2000 vintage, you can see the change in the character of the tannins. The approachable style makes the wine ready to drink, with a soft impression of supple tannins, and just enough acid support. This conforms well to the general impression of the vintage given by the en primeurs; other wines have shed the baby fat to show more restrained structures, but the Lagrange continues to showcase its upfront fruits. The fact that it has 73% Cabernet Sauvignon is a real marker for the significance of greater ripeness in Bordeaux. 13.4% *88* Drink 2015-2023.

2008

A slightly warm, nutty, impression; elegant and modern, with just enough structure to relieve it of the accusation of the international style, refreshing but without the bones for longevity. 13.0% *87* Drink to 2017.

2005

The nose is stem relative to the more exuberant palate, but there is a still a good grip in the background. Nutty black fruits tending towards blackcurrants are supported by supple tannins. Good balance with the tannins resolving; the wine is close to its peak (is it a bit discouraging it is peaking so soon?). This is certainly in a forward style, although to be fair, that is at least partly due to the character of the vintage, and I wouldn't go so far as to call it "international," although the château is moving in that direction, and there is something of a right bank impression to the wine. There is a risk that the nutty character will take over as it ages as this doesn't seem to have Bordeaux's usual refreshing uplift on the finish; already the structure is disappearing into the background. 13.0% *89* Drink to 2019.

2000

Garnet appearance shows some development. Still relatively fruity on the nose, now with some herbaceous undertones showing through. Almost at a turning point, with the lightening fruits giving more a red than black impression, and that herbaceousness coming back on the finish. Although this has almost the same varietal composition as 2009, the Cabernet is much more in evidence. The sensation of slight dilution, which first became apparent about five years ago, is now more evident, allowing those herbal tannins to show through on the finish, so you wonder how much longer the fruits will hold out. 13.0% *89* Drink 2005-2020.

1995

Restrained nose gives more sense of herbs and spices than direct fruits. This is an elegant vintage, nicely balanced on the palate, with the fruits just beginning to lighten and turn savory. This doesn't show the overt Cabernet character of 2000 or the roundness of 1990. It has a very nice balance, but even acknowledging it has the classic elegance of St. Julien, I would have liked just a touch more concentration. 12.5% *90* Drink to 2020.

1990

Tertiary development shows as herbaceousness extending to sous bois. Nice balance here, with rounded fruits evident on the palate (more evident than in 2000). The low proportion of Cabernet Sauvignon this year shows as a distinct softness, but there still seems to be plenty of fruit density to carry the wine forward. You have the impression that the determinant of style in this vintage was more the assemblage (that is, the low proportion of Cabernet) than a conscious attempt to go for opulence. 13.0% *90* Drink to 2024.

Château La Lagune

This is of one of the exceptional châteaux in the 1855 classification that are not in one of the famous communes. Located just south of Margaux, it is the first château you come to driving up to the Médoc from Bordeaux. It's a living illustration of the power of the 1855 classification, because it declined throughout the first half of the twentieth century until in 1954 there were only 4 hectares left. Revived following its purchase by Georges Brunet in 1954, it was sold to Champagne Ayala in 1961, and then passed to its present owners, the Frey family, when they acquired Ayala in 2000. Today the estate comprises 80 ha, planted to 60% Cabernet Sauvignon, 30% Merlot, and 10% Petit Verdot. The grand vin was half of production in 2010; the second wine, Moulin La Lagune, comes from young vines, and has now been supplemented by a third wine, Mademoiselle L (coming not from La Lagune itself but from adjacent vineyards). The winemaker is Caroline Frey. The style at La Lagune can be quite masculine compared with the châteaux in Margaux to its immediate north. Certainly the recent vintages of 2009 and 2010 are powerful. A tasting at the château in October 2011 compared samples of Cabernet Sauvignon vinified alone in 100% new oak with the final château grand vin.

Château La Lagune 2010
(Barrel sample.) The nose is less obvious than the monocépage Cabernet Sauvignon, perhaps because there's only 50% new oak in the grand vin, whereas the Cabernet sample vinified alone had 100%. The nose shows black fruits with some herbal overtones, including tarragon and black tea. This is certainly a more powerful wine than the 2009. The rough edges of the Cabernet Sauvignon have been rounded out in the blend, but there is no mistaking the overall power, which will take some time to soften. Full of dense black fruits and strong but ripe tannins, this will not be ready to drink for a while: wait at least five years to start. 14.5% *92* Drink 2017-2027.

Château La Lagune 2009
The nose is more restrained and less overtly fruity than the Cabernet Sauvignon alone, but more varied and complex. The wine is rich on the palate, richer than the Cabernet Sauvignon alone and more complex in composition. The elegant structure and tannic backbone promise some longevity. You see the extra roundness and intensity compared with the Cabernet Sauvignon by itself. Curiously the tannins are more evident in the complete wine than in the Cabernet sample. The wine is a neat demonstration of Bordeaux's ability to retain freshness even when alcohol levels are pushed up in warm years (the overall blend of 14% reflects Cabernet Sauvignon at 13.5% and Merlot at 14.5%). The wine should mature well for more than a decade. 13.9% *91* Drink 2014-2024.

Château La Lagune 2002
A herbal nose gives an impression of green tea. The tea notes follow through to the palate of mid weight fruits, with gentle, balanced black fruits coming through to the finish. This is wine in a lighter style, reflecting the vintage, and is ready to drink now. It's not especially complex, and does not have the structure for development, but it drinks well at the moment, and will hold for perhaps five years or so. It is a good result for the vintage and I would enjoy a bottle with dinner. 13.0% *87* Drink to 2016.

Château La Lagune 2000
Dark garnet color shows some development. Mature notes of savory black fruits on the nose. Here the immediate impression is sweet and ripe, quite a contrast with the much drier Cabernet Sauvignon vinified alone. (The Cabernet was 12% compared to 13.5% for the Merlot, and the overall blend came out at 13%). There's a nice balance here, just beginning to show as classic Bordeaux, perhaps a little firmer and broader than Margaux as a whole. There is certainly a ripe impression, but the palate is definitely turning savory; in fact, this is the perfect moment to catch this wine on the cusp. (Critical opinion of this wine was fairly negative following the vintage, but it seems now to have come around.) 13.0% *90* Drink to 2015.

Cabernet Sauvignon, 2010
(Barrel sample.) This is quite a savage wine, the beast compared to the beauty of the 2009, but some of the difference is attributable to the fact that here the malo was performed in cuve, by comparison with the barrique of 2009. How much difference will that make in the long run? It's an impenetrable black color. The intense aromas are quite aromatic, and there is a distinct impression of new wood, although the vanillin is quite subtle. This is rich and dense but all the same somewhat incomplete on the mid palate. The backbone shows as strong tannins drying the finish. It's less obviously fruity and elegant than the 2009. There's an almost brutal impression of an elemental force that needs to be tamed in the assemblage.

Cabernet Sauvignon, 2009
This is a remarkably complete wine for a monovarietal. The régisseur feels that the reason may partly be the malolactic in barrique (not a common practice at La Lagune, but used for the Cabernet in this vintage); the unanswerable question is whether the effect will persist or whether the wine will return to a more usual austerity. It's a dark ruby color, and youthful complexity shows in the nose. The palate shows black fruits tending to blackcurrants, some complex aromatics, and an impression of black tea. Its elegance really comes out in the precision and finesse of the fruits, which show great purity, and there is lovely freshness and balance. It would be interest-

ing to return in a decade to see whether this wine matures along the lines of New World mono-varietals or follows some other path.

Cabernet Sauvignon, 2002
There is a slight savage note on the nose, just a little animal. Fruits are surprisingly ripe on the palate—this was actually quite a good year for Cabernet Sauvignon. The wine gives a fresh impression with the classic austerity coming out just a touch in the dryness on the finish. There's a definite lack of fruit on the mid palate in this cooler year.

Cabernet Sauvignon, 2000
Not quite as deep in color as La Lagune itself. Less complex on the nose, showing savory but austere fruits. On the palate are developing black fruits, with a savory edge, not so much austere as a little dry, with some heat on the finish. Very nice fruits, but classically incomplete on the mid palate. The overall impression is of a wine that isn't quite complete.

Château Lascombes

Château Lascombes illustrates the trends in Bordeaux for both ownership and wine style. It was on the verge of extinction when it was rescued by Alexis Lichine in 1951, although he was never able to bring it to real second growth status. It passed into the hands of Bass Charrington in 1971, and although nominally there was more investment, it remained a perennial underachiever. In 2001 it was acquired as an investment by Colony Capital, an American pension fund group. The purchase price was €50 million, and another €50 million was invested over the next decade. Château Lascombes was then sold for €200 million in 2011 to MACSF, a French pension fund group. The price of the wine increased from €22 per bottle en primeur in 2000 to €72 a bottle for the 2010 vintage. The change in style has been as dramatic as any in Bordeaux, partly due to changes in the vineyard, partly to winemaking. When Colony Capital took over Château Lascombes in 2001, they conducted soil surveys that led to replacing 12 ha of Cabernet Sauvignon on clay terroirs with Merlot, which no doubt contributed to the change to a warmer style. Michel Rolland was brought in as winemaking consultant, and there has been an increase in intensity and richness, making Lascombes one of the more "international" styles in the Médoc. How does this sit with the traditional elegance and refinement of Margaux? Wines were tasted at the château in October 2011.

Château Lascombes 2010
(Barrel sample.) Impenetrable color. Nose shows fruitiness from the Merlot, a hint of perfume, and an impression of intensity. Clearly more complete than any of its components. Curiously, the tannins drying the finish seem more obvious than they were in the Cabernet Sauvignon. The mid palate has filled in, but there is a very dense structured finish, which clearly will need a lot of time. 13.5% *90* Drink 2016-2025.

Château Lascombes, 2009
Dark color. Restrained nose, a very fine savory impression mingling with black fruits. Quite a powerful wine, with evident black fruit aromatics, lots of concentrated fruits, and pretty evident tannic structure. This is rather a powerful wine for Margaux; but even allowing that it's a year further along the road, it does not seem as powerful as the 2010. I'm just a bit doubtful how it will develop as the fruits lighten up. 14.0% *89* Drink 2015-2023.

Château Lascombes, 2005
Dark ruby color. Some austere black fruits on the nose, following through to opulent fruits on the palate, with notes of blackcurrants. Very smooth and elegant with the austerity of the nose almost disappearing on the palate, just a trace of asperity on the finish. But I would not expect great longevity—a decade. 13.5% *90* Drink to 2020.

Château Lascombes, 1995
Some maturity just beginning to show in the color. Development on the nose shows as a touch of savory elements to cut the black fruits. Nice balance but a touch austere and perhaps lacking concentration on the mid palate. There isn't the sheer fruit concentration of later years, and you feel that the wine will slip into old age without ever really reaching a peak. It's not going anywhere. 12.5% *88* Drink to 2018.

Chevalier de Lascombes, 2008
Black fruits show on a slightly muted nose. Very soft and quite opulent in its overall impression, certainly giving the more approachable impression of second wines. Sweet ripe fruits, a touch of the elegance of Margaux: if this is a typical second wine they are getting better. But does it represent Bordeaux's tradition? 13.0% *88* Drink to 2016.

Château Latour

Consistently the longest-lived wine of Bordeaux, the wines of Château Latour have not, by and large, passed through the bad patches that the other first growths of the Médoc have suffered; although Latour was certainly dilapidated when it passed into British ownership in 1962, the wines of the fifties and sixties were probably the strongest in Bordeaux. The best vintages remain impressive even today. The château returned to French ownership when magnate François Pinault purchased it in 1993, joining it to a series of other holdings in the line of luxury goods. The second wine, Forts de Latour, was introduced in 1966; and the generic Pauillac, produced in occasional vintages in the seventies or eighties, was introduced in 1990. The masculine style of Latour runs through all the wines. Wines were tasted at Château Latour in June 2012 unless otherwise noted.

Pauillac, 2009
Intense blackcurrant fruit nose. The initial impression is very stern, almost brutal: this seems more like a barrel sample than a bottled wine, with those tough tannins of extreme youth. It's hard to get through the dense structure to see the underlying fruits. The density is quite remarkable for generic Pauillac, especially given that the wine is half Cabernet Sauvignon and half Merlot. The structure would do credit to a named château but the concern is whether there's enough fruit density to stand up to it. Time is definitely needed. *89* Drink 2017-2026.

Les Forts de Latour, 2009
The nose offers spicy sensations with cinnamon at the forefront. Fruits on the palate are intensely black, with blackcurrants, blackberries, and plums at the forefront. The underlying structure is tight, with firm tannins leaving a bite on the finish—but it's a sense of grip rather than bitterness. The great fruit is partly hidden by the density of the tight supporting structure. This is going to need some time, but it should age for a very long time. 13.6% *92* Drink 2019-2029.

Château Latour, 2009
I asked Frédéric Engerer at Latour, when he thought this wine would be ready to start drinking. "Well it depends on your taste," he said, "if you are new and young to wine, perhaps five years, but we might prefer to wait longer." Personally I think it would be vinicide before a decade is up. The intensity is indicated by the inky appearance. The nose is quite restrained although notes of new oak come out in the glass. The palate is more subtle than the Forts de Latour in that its components are less obvious, principally because of the balance of fruits and structure. There's great fruit density, but it's held back by the structure; on the other hand, the structure is less obtrusive than in the Forts de Latour because of the fruit density. The main impression here is of the reserve of the wine, of a sense of power holding back, so massively constructed that it will take a decade to come around. This will no doubt become a classic like great Latours of the past. 13.7% *94* Drink 2022-2040.

Château Latour, 1996
My impressions of this wine have been somewhat colored by context. In a horizontal of the vintage in October 2011, it appeared a big wine by contrast with the others. A fairly closed nose of black fruits with some bell peppers showed its Cabernet Sauvignon origins; the fruits on the palate seemed dense, but cut by a touch of bell peppers on the finish. At a vertical tasting at the château, after the 2009 it appeared much more developed, with an intriguing mix of perfume and sous bois aromas giving contrasting impressions of liveliness and aging. An almost delicate impression on the palate contrasts with the evident acidity of the vintage. Cabernet Sauvignon certainly dominates the fruit spectrum, restrained with a touch of herbaceousness on the finish. Very much in the leaner character of old style Bordeaux, this doesn't display the usual depth of Latour. 12.5% *90* Drink to 2022.

Château Latour, 1966
The fairly restrained nose gives just an impression of austere black fruits with some plummy tones of blackcurrants barely coming through. The impression of forceful Cabernet with a herbal or slightly medicinal edge coming out more clearly with age is now very similar to that of the Mouton Rothschild. The fatness of the fruits has certainly resolved to reveal the structure more clearly. In terms of sheer expression of Cabernet character, this may now be a little behind the Mouton, a reversal of previous impressions, as Latour previously clearly showed a greater fruit density. It's most impressive for the age but probably should be drunk before its fiftieth birthday. (May 2012) *92* Drink now.

Château Latour, 1964
Another timeless wine from Château Latour that shows absolutely no signs of tiring or aging. Still very dark and color, even some purple in the hue. Quite restrained on the nose with some reserved black fruits, but the palate is quintessential Latour. Dense ripe black fruits, denser than the 66, perhaps not as refined as the 61, hints of blackcurrants, long finish with some faint hints of vanillin. Deep, endless layers of flavor from the sweet ripe fruits. In my experience, the 1964 has consistently been at least the equal of the 1966, and now I think it has the advantage. (March 2010) *96* Drink now.

Château Léoville Barton

I always think of Léoville Barton as a very proper claret, the quintessence of St. Julien, with elegance and freshness counterbalancing ripe fruits. There are no tricks here to enhance ripeness by artifice in the vineyards or cellar, and Anthony Barton is known for picking early to maintain freshness. He has his own view. "A journalist asked me one day, 'Why do you harvest so early?' I replied, 'Why don't you ask the others why they harvest so late?'" he recounts. He regards 13% alcohol as the upper limit. "Absolutely. The Barton wines have never been over 13% and you can make good wine at 12%." But he does want to have full ripeness. These are wines to drink with food; they pass the test that there is no fatigue in finishing off a bottle with a companion. The policy of producing eminently drinkable wines and selling them at a fair price means that Léoville Barton has not risen into the super-seconds, but the wine has stayed true to its traditions, although taking advantage of technical developments to continue improving. Wines were tasted at the château in October 2011 unless otherwise noted.

Château Léoville Barton, 2010
Character and quality jump out of the glass, lively and fresh, with a faint savory touch cutting the black fruits. You can't mistake the fruit concentration, which subsumes the tannins on the textured finish. Initially some dryness is detectable but then it is overtaken by the fruit density. The elegant style of Léoville remains in evidence although this must surely be one of the most concentrated Bartons ever. 13.2% *93* Drink 2016-2026.

Château Léoville Barton, 2009
Black fruit nose with more evident presence than Langoa (which is altogether more muted by comparison, a direct demonstration of the difference between the châteaux). Very fine impression on the palate, with elegant, precise fruits supported by fine-grained tannins. Underlying structure should support good aging. The very model of St. Julien. (January 2012) 13.0% *92* Drink 2015-2027.

Château Léoville Barton, 2004
Brilliant ruby color. Slightly herbal touch to black fruits on the nose that show the usual tight elegance of the chateau. The palate is very graceful. The wine is coming up to its peak from this relatively short lived vintage but should hold for a few years yet. Here is a clear demonstration of the typicity of St. Julien. *88* 13.0% Drink 2011-2020.

Château Léoville Barton, 1996
Medium garnet color. The nose hints more of red fruits than black, with a faintly herbaceous note, but is somewhat subdued. The ripe quality of the fruits on the palate is evident, but even so, there is a slightly hard touch to the finish, characteristic of the vintage, with bell peppers developing slowly in the glass. This was a lovely wine, but the fruits are now beginning to fade, and it is time to drink up. 12.5% (October 2011) *87* Drink to 2014.

Château Léoville Barton, 1989
Quite undeveloped appearance with ruby hue. Nose shows black fruits dominated by blackcurrants and blackberries with some faintly musty overtones that intensify retronasally. There're lots of black fruit on the palate, supported by soft, plump tannins. The intensity of the fruits combined with that faintly musty note give this something of the impression of a New World Cabernet. No signs of tiring yet, good for years. (September 2011) 12.5% *92* Drink to 2020.

Château Léoville Lascases

Before the era of the Marquis Las Cases, indeed before the era of the Léoville estate, this was known as Mont-Moytié. The Moytié family were probably the first to plant vines on what was then a small outcrop standing above the marshes close to the Gironde. As Château Léoville Lascases, the estate was classified as a second growth, together with the two other Léovilles, but it has clearly been the best of the three ever since. Today it is considered to be one of the leading super-seconds. Much of the quality comes from Léoville Lascases's inheritance of L'Enclos as a single block, which is the major source for the grand vin. The more western vineyard of Clos du Marquis was vinified separately from 1902, subsequently became the second wine of Léoville Lascases, and now is vinified again separately. The new second wine is Le Petit Lion de Lascases. Also owned by the Delon family, Château Potensac is a very good Cru Bourgeois farther north in the Médoc. Wines were tasted at Château Léoville Lascases in June 2012.

Château Potensac, 2009
Soft, nutty, and warm on the nose. Soft and supple on the palate, an approachable wine in the modern fashion, a great contrast with 1996 even allowing for the difference in age. You hardly see the structure here, it's all soft, appealing, forward fruits, although the textural impression is quite refined. 14.0% *87* Drink to 2020.

Château Potensac, 1996
Mature appearance. More perfumed than savory on the nose. Surprisingly well rounded for the combination of appellation and vintage. The mature fruits are nicely balanced by acidity; the resolving tannins show a very faint herbaceous edge on the finish, but relatively little tertiary development. This now shows as a vintage in traditional style, but I would have liked to see a bit more flavor variety and savory development. 12.5% *87* Drink to 2016.

Clos du Marquis, 2009
Warm, nutty black fruit nose with notes of semolina. A rounded, glyceriny, impression on the palate, but with refined underlying texture. The nose is quite right bank-ish, but the palate has the refinement of the Médoc; slowly the fine-grained texture becomes apparent. Demonstrating the lush, exuberant qualities of the year, this wine is already ready to start drinking, although it will surely develop more flavor variety in the next two or three years. 13.8% *88* Drink to 2020.

Clos du Marquis, 1996
Developed nose is quite savory and herbal, with an impression of green tea. The palate is less developed than the nose suggests; the lightening red fruits are beginning to dry out, but still show some roundness. But there's less structure here to balance the fruits than with Léoville Lascases, and with the tannins resolving, it is time to drink up. 12.5% *87* Drink to 2016.

Château Léoville Lascases, 2009
This has the exotic nose of all the Delon wines in 2009, with vanillin, nuts, and semolina trumping the fruits, although here the fruits are more serious (for which read concentrated but restrained) than the Clos du Marquis. The black fruit palate, with blackcurrants, plums, and cherries, shows real breed; already quite complex and concentrated, but with a sense of restraint, with that refined texture and finesse that speaks of St. Julien. This should be a great wine in years to come, with a combination of elegance and delicacy as it throws off the baby fat. Indeed, the tannins are so fine that you could almost drink it now, but you would be missing the seamless layers of flavor that will develop a decade from now. 13.8% *93* Drink 2015-2030.

Château Léoville Lascases, 1996
Intimations of herbal complexity on the nose. Palate shows underlying red fruits, developing only faintly savory overtones, with flavor variety showing on the back palate. Acidity is under

control (not always the case in this vintage), and tannins are resolving. This does not show too excessive a dependence on Cabernet character. It's a little dry on the finish, with not much savory development, and it's unclear how much further it will develop, but it's a good result for the year. 12.5% *89* Drink to 2018.

Château Léoville Poyferré

The Cuvelier family were negociants in Bordeaux when they moved into château ownership with the purchase of Le Crock in 1903 followed by Camensac in 1913 (the latter held only briefly). The more significant purchases, however, were of Châteaux Léoville Poyferré and nearby Moulin Riche (a Cru Bourgeois) in 1920. Léoville Poyferré declined in reputation during the sixties and seventies; indeed, at one time it had become known as Voie-Ferré, after the railway, reflecting a metallic taste in the wines. Didier Cuvelier took over in 1979 and started a program of modernization. During the eighties the reputation began to be restored. Didier brought in Michel Rolland as consultant in 1994. "When I hired Michel Rolland, everyone laughed, and said, ho ho, he's from the right bank," he recalls. The main change in the wine, he considers, has been in the maturity of the tannins. Under Didier, replanting has brought the total vineyard area from 48 ha to 80 ha, with Cabernet Sauvignon increasing from 30% to 65%. The relationship between Léoville Poyferré and Moulin Riche has been slightly muddled. "For a long time, Moulin Riche was regarded as the second wine of Léoville Poyferré, but today it is made from its own terroir and a new second wine, Pavillon de Poyferré, in effect has been used for declassified lots from both Moulin Riche and Léoville Poyferré since 1995," explains Didier. In the past two decades, Léoville Poyferré has turned towards a more modern representation of St. Julien, with more suppleness and softness to the fruits. My favorite vintage of a vertical tasting at the château was the 2000, which has reached that delicious tipping point at which savory, herbaceous, notes begin to mingle with the fruits. Wines were tasted at Léoville Poyferré in June 2012.

2009
I've had slightly different impressions of this wine depending on context. At a horizontal tasting of the vintage in January 2012, it seemed to be one of the more "international" in style; new oak was still evident, adding vanillin overtones to the chocolaty fruits. No one could quarrel with the sheer quality of the wine, but I was left wondering how it displayed the typicity of St. Julien. Then in a vertical tasting at the château six months later, still displaying a black fruit nose with chocolaty overtones, but with some hints of herbal development beginning to show, and with the oak evident by inference rather than directly. Fruits are firm but may be closing up a bit. The underlying structure shows some gravelly overtones. In classic fashion, this needs time for the firm tannins to soften. Increasing chocolate overtones on the finish suggest that this will become soft and more opulent with age; already it seems more rounded and softer than older vintages, reflecting the conditions of 2009. In the vertical tasting, its soft opulence seemed to reflect the vintage more than a change of style. 13.0% *92* Drink 2015-2027.

2006
Fresh nose seems more inclined to red fruits than black. Softening on the palate, this is becoming more supple, but still has an acidic edge showing on the finish. There's the classic lightness of St. Julien, in fact this is very much a representative of how this year played out in St. Julien, maturing towards refreshing, clear fruits, savory rather than soft, somewhat like a younger version of 1996. *90* Drink 2014-2021.

2003
This has retained a surprisingly fresh quality for the year, coming round now into something of a mature balance with soft furry fruits dominating the palate. The softness is a fraction deceptive, because underneath the tannins are quite firm, almost stern, with a distinct drying effect on the finish. But there are no cooked fruits and it's only by comparison with the other vintages that this wine seems more international in style. I suspect that the fruits will not be able to outlive the tannins, which will limit longevity, but this remains a good result for the year. 13.5% *90* Drink 2010-2021.

2000
An initial impression of a surge of barnyard aromas suggests some significant development, but the palate is less advanced than the nose suggests. In fact, the palate is quite classic, giving an elegant impression that really captures the character of St. Julien as the wine makes the transition into mid age. The fruits are just beginning to show a savory edge with a slight tang of acidity to freshen the finish, and tannins are beginning to resolve. A lovely herbaceous touch develops on the finish in the glass. 13.0% *92* Drink to 2022.

1996
I've had mixed results with this vintage, ranging from bottles seeming partly to reflect the old, pre-Rolland style, to more successful bottles. As the most successful was the most recent, at the château itself, it's possible the problematic bottles reflected poor provenance. In the vertical château tasting, the 1996 showed as less overtly developed on the nose than the 2000, with more of an impression of red fruits on the palate, and refreshing acidity, but avoiding the excess of many wines of this vintage. Development is beginning to show on the palate but seems to be progressing slowly. Fruits are lightening up now, so I'm doubtful the wine will improve significantly, but it should hold for a few years. 13.0% *88* Drink to 2018.

Château Lynch Bages

"I was asked to explain why Lynch Bages was always so popular in England," recounts Jean-Charles Cazes, who has been in charge of the château since 2006. "I mentioned our hard work in the vineyards, the quality of our wine, all the other factors I could think of." But I was told, "No. The reason is that the name is easy to pronounce." Indeed, Lynch Bages was known affectionately in the old English wine trade as "lunch bags." Jean-Charles's great grandfather purchased Château Ormes de Pez and then started making the wine at nearby Lynch Bages in 1934, which he purchased in 1939. His son, André added Château Haut Bages Averous to the portfolio, and this became the second wine of Lynch Bages. In due course, Jean-Michel Cazes, who joined the château in 1973, expanded the operation by creating the hotel of Cordeillan-Bages, and reviving the village of Bages close to the château. He also played a significant role in involving insurance giant AXA in Bordeaux; AXA now own several important châteaux. When Jean-Charles took over, the estate comprised 100 ha of vineyards divided into three areas, and typically for Pauillac dominated by almost three quarters Cabernet Sauvignon. Following the modern trend, the second wine has been renamed Echo de Lynch Bages, and a third wine (a Pauillac AOC) has been introduced. There is also a white wine, which originated with a mistake when a nursery sent Sauvignon Blanc vines instead of Cabernet Sauvignon. Wines were tasted at the château or in London in June 2012 unless otherwise noted.

2009
There's an immediate impression of a nose driven by black fruits with blackcurrants to the fore, with a chocolate coating. Initially you see the exuberance of the fruits of this vintage, but then the structure kicks in to restrain the finish, which is noticeably dry (and a touch hot). As the initial impact of the fruits recedes, the structure becomes more apparent (IPT was at a record level in this vintage). As it matures, the wine will become smooth, supple, and velvety; it would be a shame to drink now, but it will be possible to start quite soon. 13.6% *92* Drink 2016-2030.

2006
Compared with samples of the individual varieties, you see most clearly the Cabernets, with the Merlot and Petit Verdot receding into the background. Cabernet Franc shows in the freshness of the wine, Cabernet Sauvignon by the structure; the overall blend appears less rounded and fruity than you would have expected from the Cabernet Sauvignon alone, although it is no doubt more elegant. This is a lighter, "classic" vintage, with restrained fruits showing herbal undertones, and tannins evident in the dryness of the finish. There is a decent balance of mid weight fruits to supporting structure, but that characteristic flatness of the vintage shows on the finish. The question as always with this vintage is where the generosity of fruits will come from

to give the needed roundness—the risk here is that the spartan nature of Cabernet's structure will take over from the fruits. 13.0% *88* Drink 2015-2024.

2003
This showed quite well when first released, with a soft, approachable texture, but now has gone slightly flat (although at least it does not show cooked fruits like some wines of this very hot vintage). A little development shows with some slightly savory overtones to the slightly spicy fruits. The flatness on the palate is not so much due to lack of acidity ("the acidity is less refreshing than usual," says Jean-Charles Cazes), but because the fruits don't really come out; you just see remnants of the usual opulence of Lynch Bages on the finish. Behind the black fruits the tannins show a chocolate edge. It's difficult to see the basis for any future interesting development; I would drink soon. 13.0% *87* Drink to 2017.

2001
This has quite developed in the past three years, with savory, animal notes coming out more distinctly, although still quite gentle, but pushing the fruits into the background. Although the palate is turning savory, it still seems less developed than the nose. As the fruits lighten up, the tannins seem more in evidence and less refined. Now at its tipping point, this needs to be enjoyed in the immediate future. 13.0% *88* Drink to 2016.

2000
This vintage has really opened up and developed in the past couple of years, showing a classic nose dominated by savory and herbal aromas, with some suggestions of gunflint. The palate seems a little more backward than the nose; sweet, ripe, and elegant fruits have a just perceptible herbal edge. Fruits are on the verge of developing wider flavor variety with those delicious notes of sous bois, but are still nicely in balance with acidity and tannins, which are still quite firm. As with the 1982 vintage before it, the initial fruity impression has turned more classic (although somewhat more rapidly in this case). 13.0% *90* Drink to 2020.

1999
"This is a more serious vintage than 2001 and will last longer," says Jean-Charles Cazes. The wine shows a mature garnet appearance, but is more perfumed than tertiary on the nose. Quite rounded for the vintage, with those perfumed notes of the nose sustained on the palate and running through the finish. There's a soft, gentle, impression, with the herbaceous notes of Cabernet Sauvignon developing slowly on the finish. A good result for the vintage. 12.5% *88* Drink to 2018.

1996
The nose shows a classic touch of cedar, giving an overall impression poised between perfumed and herbaceous. That spicy herbaceousness strengthens in the glass. The palate has reached a lovely point of balance, between ripe fruits and savory development to come. A touch of dryness on the finish causes a certain lack of follow through, or the rating would be higher, but this shows more attractively than many from this vintage where acidity is too evident. But bottles need to be in perfect condition (this came from the chateau; others of less certain provenance have shown less fruit and more herbaceousness and so have appeared less successful). 13.0% *91* Drink to 2022.

1995
Just a touch more perfumed than herbaceous on the nose, with an impression of black fruits. Now showing as riper and rounder than the 1996, with the impression of greater refinement on the finish given by more polished tannins. It's really only with the direct comparison that you see the slightly more rustic quality of 1996. There the fruit seems lovely at first but then there's a bit of lack of follow through on the mid palate with a slight sense of dilution developing in the glass. Here the wine is more complete, open, round, opulent, with flavors right across the palate, although the underlying structure has resolved so it's getting to be time to drink up. (A blend of the 1996 and the 1995 might be perfection!) 13.0% *90* Drink to 2018.

1990
Some development shows on the nose, with notes of sous bois and gunflint just detectable. The ripe, sweet, fruits of the palate are just cut by the notes of savory development. Herbaceous overtones just show on the finish, bringing complexity. This has reached a perfect point of development at which it's hard to distinguish fruits, perfume, and savory elements. The hallmark of the vintage is that sweet ripeness of the fruits, now balanced by a touch of cedar on the finish, which brings character as it strengthens in the glass. 13.0% *91* Drink now to 2018.

1982
Still quite a dark garnet color, although showing a broadening orange rim. Not a lot on the nose,

some faint black fruits and a barely perceptible touch of herbaceousness. The palate shows the typical core of sweet ripe fruits of Lynch Bages, but also is surprisingly herbaceous given the fleshy reputation of the vintage; another example of a reversion to type. 12.5% (April 2010) *91* Drink to 2020.

1961
Light to medium garnet color, weak nose with some faint fruits. But it absolutely springs to life on the palate: this has it all—ripe sweet fruits, good density, and a judicious touch of herbaceousness to lend complexity. Layers of flavor, endless depth, all the hallmarks of a great year, still showing perfect balance. (April 2010) *95* Drink to 2017.

Château Margaux

Under the name of La Mothe de Margaux, the estate goes back to the twelfth century, but wine production did not start until the sixteenth century. By the end of the seventeenth century, the estate included 265 ha, more or less equivalent to its size today, with a substantial part covered by vines. It was well known in England by the eighteenth century (the 1771 vintage was the first claret to appear in a Christie's catalogue), together with Haut Brion with which it was under common ownership at the time of the Revolution (when the proprietor went to the scaffold). The grand château was one of the first to be constructed in Bordeaux, early in the nineteenth century. Classified as a first growth in 1855, the estate passed through a series of owners, some interested and some less interested in the quality of production, until it was sold to André Mentzelopoulos in 1977. Since then it has gone from strength to strength. Wines were tasted at Château Margaux in June 2012 except as otherwise noted.

Pavillon Rouge du Château Margaux, 2011
(Barrel sample.) Rather stern, brooding, black impression on nose. Dense fruits on palate with slightly nutty aftertaste. Insofar as you can tell at this early stage, this is more approachable than the grand vin because the structure isn't so apparent, but it is pretty dense for a second wine. The style is somewhat similar to the grand vin, but with less roundness.

Château Margaux, 2011
(Barrel sample.) Even sterner and more brooding than the Pavillon Rouge. Great fruit density hides the structure more than in the second wine, but then the austerity kicks in on the finish. Very dense and backward with the highest IPT (measure of tannins) ever recorded at Château Margaux. The vanillin of new oak is evident, but the nuttiness and perfume comes up the glass, suggesting a fragrant future.

Château Margaux, 2009
Perfumed black fruits with a touch of spice at first impression. Infinitely smooth, with a firm, velvety texture of blackcurrants and blackberry fruits. Tannins detectable only indirectly by their dryness on the finish. There's no mistaking the sheer elegance, very long and slightly nutty on the finish, with a terrific sense of refinement showing through. This gives the impression of being almost drinkable now, not so much because of the way the dense fruits hide the tannins, as because of the smoothness of the texture. Ripe and sweet, this is positively seductive. 13.1% *94* Drink 2016-2036.

Château Margaux, 1999
Only a small touch of garnet in the appearance. Not a lot of development showing on nose or palate. The characteristic smooth elegance comes through this vintage. Supple and soft, the difference here is the lack of obvious structure in the background; this is a fine wine, but less generous than usual, without the follow-through of a great vintage, but it has to be said that it falls flat only by comparison with the great vintages. Here you can see even more clearly than in top vintages how Château Margaux defines the elegant end of the spectrum for Cabernet Sauvignon. 12.5% *88* Drink to 2022.

Château Margaux, 1996
The nose gives up a faint impression of black fruits with a tertiary edge. First growth quality is unmistakable on the palate, with that smooth, seamless elegance of black fruits, Cabernet-driven, beautifully cut by a faint touch of herbaceous bell peppers and some notes of chocolate. Aging seems quite slow, with flavor variety and complexity emerging gradually, but expect sa-

vory and tertiary development over the next decade. Still too young really. 12.5% (October 2011) *92* Drink to 2025.

Château Margaux, 1989
Soft perfume of black strawberries. Still seems youthful and elegant with a characteristically fine structure of those smooth, silky, tannins behind the sweet, round, impression of the black fruits. There's flavor variety right across the palate, still fresh rather than tertiary. (Some bottles from other sources, that is, not from the château itself, have shown more development.) Soft, supple, elegant, with lots of finesse; and what marks this as a great vintage is the follow-through, the sense of infinite layers extending through the finish. 12.5% *92* Drink to 2027.

Château Margaux, 1985
This may be the best of the first growths in 1985 and possibly the wine of the vintage. Garnet appearance but dark color for age. Restrained nose, faintly floral, with that touch of violets typical of Margaux, and faint suggestion of raspberries. Dense, concentrated black fruits on the palate, but most elegant, unmistakably a first growth. Ripe tannins have resolved, there is good supporting acidity, and a long, slightly nutty finish. 12.5% (March 2010) *94* Drink to 2020.

Château Margaux, 1983
Until twenty years after the vintage, the 1983 held its own often enough against the 1982 to make it an open question which was the better vintage for Château Margaux. Now it is settling into a really classic representation of Bordeaux, distinctly herbaceous on the nose, stopping just short of bell peppers. Very elegant on the palate, all the refinement of Margaux, very long finish. Very smooth, wonderfully refined, with an extraordinary precise delineation of flavors, but losing out finally after a quarter century to that extra dimension of roundness in the 1982. 12.0% (May 2010) *93* Drink to 2022.

Château Margaux, 1982
It took twenty years to resolve the argument as to whether Château Margaux was better in the 1982 or 1983 vintage, but soon after the turn of the century, the 1982 seemed to pull distinctly ahead; the ethereal and velvety texture lifted this onto another level altogether: what could this but a first growth, and Margaux at that? It has now reached a stage of perfection not to mention classicism. Developed black fruit nose has herbaceous overtones turning more distinctly to bell peppers in the glass. There's a delicious balance of savory black fruits with a herbaceous catch on the finish. There has been a complete reversion to classical type from the lushness of the first decade, with a perfect offset between the black fruits of the palate and the herbaceous overtones of the finish. 12.5% (April 2011) *96* Drink to 2022.

Château Margaux, 1959
Garnet color but still deeply hued. The nose is not much more developed than the 1989, although less intense, with faintly animal, savory aromas. Development is evident on the palate, with the fruits becoming tertiary, quite earthy, almost mushroomy, with those truffly, animal notes of old Cabernet. The basic supple core of fruit is actually richer in the 1959 than in the much younger 1989, so the wine should continue to develop for another decade. This is *the* older vintage of Margaux to drink if you can get it. (March 2009) *90* Drink to 2019.

Château Margaux, 1945
A difficult one to assess, because of two recent bottles I was convinced one was genuine while the other left me doubtful. The first bottle still had good color, a relatively deep red. The nose did show some very faintly raisined notes, clearing after a while to show some faintly herbaceous notes of Cabernet with the tertiary aromas of old Bordeaux and a touch of sous bois. Quite vinous on the palate, showing soft fruits with a touch of tobacco and a touch of nuttiness on the finish. The softness is deceptive because there is still good supporting acidity. Very good depth to the fruits, which remain quite rich and sweet. This seems more fruit forward, if one can say that after all these years, softer, and with less acidity than the Lafite, which may be why it appears less complex. The second bottle showed a somewhat coarser overall character, almost rustic, which aroused my concern. (April 2009). *91* Drink up.

Château Montrose

Château Montrose is not really a cult wine, but perhaps it should be for those who remain committed to traditional Bordeaux. Even with its recent softening, it is as traditional in style as you can get. Located on a gravel outcrop running close to the Gironde, where the gravel mostly goes down a couple of meters to an iron-rich subsoil, its vineyards occupy one large contiguous block. They were recently increased from 70 ha to 95 ha by a purchase of land from adjacent Phélan Ségur (a Cru Bourgeois). This is not quite such a dramatic change as it might seem, since two hundred years ago this land was in fact part of the Montrose estate. This has of course increased production, although only one third of the grapes from the new vineyard go into Montrose, with two thirds destined for the second wine, La Dame de Montrose (introduced in 1984); this is the reversal of the proportions in the original vineyards. There is not a specific intention to make La Dame ready to drink sooner than Montrose, but there is mostly Cabernet in Montrose and mostly Merlot in La Dame. The grand vin may have softened in recent years, but it still always has that massive, solid, structure underneath the fruits.

La Dame de Montrose, 2009
Blackcurrant nose. Lots of deep black fruits on the palate, with supple, ripe tannins, nice weight, medium length finish. Almost ready to drink, which I suppose is appropriate for a second wine.13.0% (October 2011) *89* Drink to 2018.

Château Montrose, 2009
An interesting comparison with the second wine. The grand vin has more intensity and weight with less immediately obviously fruits on the nose, less forward, but more complex with some almost herbal aromatics on the nose. More tannic structure is evident from the lovely long finish. Several years are needed in the true style of Montrose. You might almost say that the grand vin is traditional and the Dame is modernist. 13.7% (October 2011) *93* Drink 2015-2025.

Château Montrose, 2006
An austere wine but with some promise for future development, very much the old style of slowly developing Montrose. Muted nose with just some hints of black fruits. The palate has well rounded black fruits, good supporting acidity, and some solid tannic support for ageing. Tannins are nicely matched by the fruits, with good underlying structure, perhaps just a touch short on the finish. 12.5% (May 2010) *90* Drink 2013-2020.

Château Montrose, 1990
This vintage was hailed as an outstanding wine from the start. It has the best structure of the last quarter century, showing a direct lineage from the 1982 and the 1970. Continuing the way it started, this was a standout at a tasting of 1990 Bordeaux. Classic nose: leathery, sweaty, herbaceous black fruits. Absolutely classic on the palate, with stern fruits, solid, dense, still rather undeveloped. A delicious finish reveals the ripeness of the fruits, cut by a faintly herbaceous aftertaste. Really this still needs another decade! 13.0% (October 2010) *94* Drink to 2025.

Château Montrose, 1985
Classic barnyard nose, very savory, quite tertiary. Lovely balance with edge of sous bois showing. It has reached its peak, the palate is still savory, the tannins are all integrated, but the wine has remained fresh. Faint chocolate notes develop on the finish. Very classic for a year where most wines were a little lighter in style. (October 2011) *92* Drink to 2017.

Château Montrose, 1970
This wine was not as slow as the Latour 1928 to come around, but it took a long time, and was similarly worth waiting for. Now it's at its peak, although showing no signs of tiring. There are full, sweet, ripe fruits, at this stage more elegant than powerful; the traces of herbaceousness that showed on some earlier bottles are absent now, having resolved to little more than a savory hint. Fruits are ripe and black with a touch of blackcurrants. Lovely balance of fruit to acidity, tannins resolving but still enough structural support, giving the impression more of a middle aged wine than an old one. Absolutely a top result. 12.0% (September 2011) *93* Drink to 2020.

Château Mouton Rothschild

Classified at the very top of the second growths in 1855, just after it had been purchased by Baron Nathaniel de Rothschild, Château Mouton Rothschild reached effective price equality with the first growths in the 1920s. During fifty years of campaigning for promotion to first growth, the château's motto was, "First I cannot be, Second I disdain, I am Mouton." Many of the innovations of the Bordeaux marketplace have come from Mouton, starting with château bottling in 1924, and the introduction of communal wine, Mouton Cadet, in 1934. (Mouton Cadet started with declassification at Mouton Rothschild in 1934, was briefly a second wine from Pauillac, and then became a mass market generic Bordeaux AOC with entirely different origins.) Often one of the most powerful wines of Bordeaux, Mouton Rothschild is sometimes thought to be more variable than the other first growths. They used to say that you should buy the wines of the minor châteaux in the great vintages, and the wines of the great châteaux in the poor vintages, and a tasting at Mouton certainly demonstrated the pulling power of the first growths in the less successful vintages. Comparison of 2002 and 1998 is an interesting example of how the first growths pull it off in the minor years, with wines that manage to reflect the traditional character of the château through the prism of the vintage. Not to say that the wines aren't overwhelming in the great vintages. Wines were tasted at Château Mouton Rothschild in June 2012 except as otherwise noted.

2009
"This was a great year, with slow maturation and great equilibrium," says Technical Director Eric Tourbier. Still an inky purple color, it gives a rich, perfumed impression at first blush, with touches of vanillin and nuts still evident. It's quite soft on the palate, with huge depth of fruits, blackcurrants the most evident influence, and the nuts and vanillin coming back on the finish. Supple, furry, tannins are subsumed by the fruits—some people will no doubt commit vinicide and start drinking the wine straight away—but there is that characteristic iron fist in the velvet glove, and this will be a classic in twenty or thirty years. 13.1% *95* Drink 2017-2037.

2004
Dusty appearance with some garnet hues. Ripe, sweet, fruits are faintly gamey, with a classic touch of austerity on the palate. The freshness of the nose reinforces the sense of leanness, with herbal rather than overtly herbaceous impressions. The tightness and angularity of the palate raise the question of whether the fruits have enough generosity to support longer term aging. 12.5% *88* Drink 2011-2019.

2002
"This was an intermediate vintage, good but not exceptional," says Eric Tourbier. It's still a dark color with a tight garnet rim showing the start of development. There's a touch of almost floral perfume on the nose, sweet fruits are quite dense, with good acidity, but not quite the same uplift on the finish as (for example) the 1998. It's quite forward and round, clearly Cabernet but somehow lacking that special character of the bite of the variety, with a faint medicinal touch on the finish reflecting the character of the vintage. 13.0% *89* Drink to 2022.

1998
"This is the reference for us in terms of classic Mouton," says Eric Tourbier. The dark color goes garnet at the rim. Perfume fills the room as it is poured, but the nose seems quite restrained in the glass. Sweet fruits show as blackcurrants, cherries, blackberries, lively on the palate, with a faint touch on the finish that is more herbal than herbaceous, and then that sense of perfume coming back retronasally. Classic balance, with fresh black fruits and the herbaceous quality of Cabernet Sauvignon well under control. 12.5% *91* Drink to 2024.

1983
What a huge contrast with the 82 vintage! Instead of that lushness, here is a much more traditional Bordeaux (and far more developed). Classic faintly herbaceous notes mark the nose, overlaying the dense black fruits that dominate the palate. Good acidity supports a classic style with slowly softening tannins, that herbaceous edge just showing on the fruits, altogether a lovely harmonious balance. This is great if you love traditional Bordeaux, possibly less persuasive if you go for the new international style. 12.0% (October 2011) *92* Drink to 2025.

1982
You imagine you can smell the earth of Bordeaux on the 1982 Mouton, a true wine of terroir. This has now really reverted to classic character. The nose shows black fruits with a herbaceous touch, at a perfect balance. The palate has a delicious counterpoise between the layers of black fruits, dense and very long but still fresh, with a herbaceous edge. It did not seem that way when first released, but it is absolutely classic now, and terroir has triumphed over all. 12.0% (January 2011) *94* Drink to 2026.

1970
There was a problem with corks this year at Mouton, and this example was in pretty bad shape, disintegrating when extracted. But there's a nice bouquet with a touch of herbaceousness and

then lovely fruits on the palate, not quite able to make up their mind whether to be sweet or slightly herbal. This was never regarded as a great vintage for Mouton, and was awfully restrained for many years; it has come around now, but I wonder what it would have been like if the cork had been impeccable. I would put this at second growth not first growth level. (November 2012) *89* Drink to 2017.

1966

This is one of those Moutons that seemed youthful until only five years ago, far more so than the less successful 1970, but suddenly it has begun to show its age. The first impression is the dominance of Cabernet, with herbal overtones melding into a suspicion of herbaceousness tinged with cigar box. Fruits have lightened on the palate, allowing the structure to show through more obviously than a few years back; now this is not so fruity and silky as the 1959. The herbal impression segues into an impression of tobacco, strengthening on the finish. As it all comes together in the glass, the savory fruits round out, retaining those delicious herbaceous overtones. With the lessening density, you might think equally of second growths (which of course Mouton was, technically speaking, at the time). This is unmistakably a great Bordeaux in the classic tradition, becoming sweeter and riper in the glass, but it is now time to drink up. 12.0% (May 2012) *93* Drink to 2015.

1959

Three years ago this appeared quite a bit more youthful. Perhaps this is just bottle variation, but although still a dark appearance, now some age is showing on nose and palate. The immediate impression on the nose is austere, black, Cabernet, with an edge of savory development and faint hints of herbaceousness. Acidity is becoming more noticeable on the palate and gives a faint suggestion of piquancy. This is clearly marked as Mouton by that characteristic mixture of power and elegance, a sort of silky Rolls Royce. Development is indicated by weak but strengthening animal overtones in the glass. It seems to be close to time to drink up. (November 2011) *93* Drink to 2013.

1945

In the past few years, two bottles seemed brilliantly youthful, dark in color and quite undeveloped on nose and palate; another bottle was far more developed in showing a touch of madeirization. Assuming that the last bottle was due to condition problems, the fruit spectrum remains youthful, faintly nutty, softer on the palate than previously, but still with that deep structure, very Mouton-ish. The nose immediately identifies Cabernet Sauvignon with that blend of intense fruits with a faint aromatic edge and just a touch of herbaceous overtones adding complexity that typifies the great Bordeaux vintages of the past—alas, they do not make them like this any more. All this follows through to the palate with dense layers of fruit, ripe but never over-ripe, although still showing some blackcurrant flavors even at this venerable age. In a blind tasting this might well be taken for a wine of twenty years of age, but 60 seems incredible. This typifies what seems to have been forgotten today: it's the balance, stupid. There is a perfect match of fruit, acidity, residual tannin, herbaceous undertones to give a complex mélange of flavors that is difficult to deconstruct. It is hard to believe Mouton will ever make a better wine. (November 2011) *99* Drink to 2025.

Château Palmer

The vineyards today cover 55 hectares in Cantenac, including equal amounts of Cabernet Sauvignon and Merlot, with a small amount (6%) of Petit Verdot. Most of the vineyards are in a contiguous series of blocks around the château with two further separate plots within a kilometer. Until 1997, the second wine, La Réserve du Générale, was produced by declassifying lots from Palmer. Then it was replaced by Alter Ego de Palmer. "We produced Alter Ego with a different philosophy, to produce a wine with its own style and character. For Palmer we choose all the fruit with concentration, power, and aging potential. For Alter Ego we choose the fruit with a lot of freshness and delicate tannins. We adapt our winemaking, with higher versus lower temperatures at fermentation, longer versus shorter maceration for Palmer versus Alter Ego," says winemaker Thomas Duroux. The issue this raises for me is how Alter Ego represents the typicity of Margaux and the château. With rare exceptions (such as 2009), it has not seemed to me to resemble Château Palmer—perhaps that's not a fair criticism as it's intended to be different, but I have a certain expectation based on the history of the estate. For Château Palmer itself, I have included some older tastings notes to indicate stages of development of the more interesting vintages, especially for 1961.

Vin de Table, Château Palmer Historical XIX Century Wine, 2007
Dusky purple color. The nose is driven by deep black fruits, spicy and peppery, with blackcurrants breaking through. The palate is deep, dark, and chocolaty with a velvety texture. All this seems much more to resemble the northern Rhone than Bordeaux, until the tannins kick in on the finish. In terms of the vintage, which was pretty tight in Bordeaux, this is quite a pick-up; you can see why they used to bring wine in from Hermitage for blending. But it does not taste like Bordeaux: there may be only 10% Syrah, but it's dominating the palate aromatically. The trade-off is that it's a much better wine for the blending, but it no longer represents a place of origin. (October 2012) *89* Drink to 2022.

Alter Ego de Palmer, 2009
Full and fruity, but some backbone showing a tannic rasp and a touch of heat. You actually get more impression of a grand vin in style than a second wine. A touch of rusticity reflects youth. Indeed, a major difference from the grand vin is the rougher texture and lack of sense of refinement. 13.7% (October 2011) *89* Drink 2014-2019.

Alter Ego de Palmer, 2005
This wine has been a little deceptive right from the beginning. It has consistently appeared a little simple at first blush, and then has picked up more complexity as it develops in the glass to show some structural support for the fruits. But the nose has now become surprisingly aromatic, showing blackcurrants extending to cassis. These aromatics of ripe or even over-ripe Cabernet contrast with a fresh impression of light fruits and crisp acidity. Initially those blackcurrants give a somewhat Ribena-like impression on the palate, slowly giving way to show the tannic structure in the background. There's a touch of bitterness on the finish. 14.0% (October 2012) *87* Drink 2010-2017.

Château Palmer, 2009
Youthful black fruit aromatics show a touch of overt blackcurrants. Some notes of vanillin reflect the new oak, still in the process of integrating. Velvety and rather blackcurranty on the palate. The firm tannic structure shows in a little bitterness on the finish. The baby fat that was evident upon release a year ago has blown off to reveal more of the structure, making the wine seem less approachable, not so suave. This will become refined and precise as it matures. 13.9% (October 2012) *92* Drink 2015-2027.

Château Palmer, 2005
The nose is quite aromatic, offering blackcurrants with a touch of cassis, giving way to vanillin and tobacco, but it's not so obvious as the Alter Ego. The palate offers a more classic impression than you might expect from this opulent year. This is much in the same style as 2009; in a more or less direct progression, the fruits have receded to allow the structure to show. Deep, dark, concentrated fruits are supported by a firm structure, with just a little tannic bitterness on the finish, perhaps reflecting relatively higher content of Cabernet Sauvignon (more than half in 2005 and again in 2006, but less than half in all subsequent vintages). Perhaps a wine to try in the immediate period after release and then leave for a decade, this should be a classic when it eventually comes around. 14.0% (October 2012) *92* Drink 2015-2030.

Château Palmer, 2000
This vintage of Palmer has always been quite restrained considering the reputation of the vintage for opulence. Four years ago, I thought it was perhaps going through a dumb phase, but if so, it hasn't come out yet. Fruits on the nose are countered by some hints of vegetal expression. The palate has not evolved a great deal in the past few years; it's restrained rather than opulent with a fugitive impression of bell peppers alternating with sweet fruits. Surprisingly closed now, slowly it opens out in the glass to reveal riper fruits than had at first seemed to be there. In terms of earlier vintages, it is more like a denser version of the elegant 1995 than the sterner 1996, but it does not seem to be living up to the high reputation of the vintage. 13.0% (October 2012) *90* Drink to 2018.

Château Palmer, 1996
The nose shows more overt fruit than you usually see with this vintage, quite dark with just a suspicion of herbal overtones. This has recently come around on the palate to reveal black

fruits matched by faintly herbaceous overtones. The impression of medicinal austerity of a year or so ago has much softened in the past year, although classic bell peppers come back on the finish. It's still a relatively tough wine, and concentration falls off a bit on the finish, raising a question mark as to how much further it will develop. 12.5% (October 2011) *89* Drink to 2018.

Château Palmer, 1995

This is like beauty and the beast compared with the 1996; the 1995 is delicate and feminine, the 1996 is sturdy and masculine, almost a metaphor for the classic elegance of Margaux versus the modern trend to power. There's a lovely balance to the nose of red and black fruits with a touch of spice and overall a delicate, floral, impression. The palate shows elegant fruits of red and black cherries with that characteristic fresh uplift on the finish. This is a really pretty wine. The lightness of being may be deceptive in that this may go on and on. 12.5% (May 2008) *91* Drink to 2013.

Château Palmer, 1983

The 1983 Palmer has always been acknowledged as one of the stars of the vintage, and certainly it seems much more youthful than the 1982—many would guess at a decade's separation rather than a year. A little darker than the 1982, fairly restrained on the nose with some development showing in the form of faintly pungent barnyard aromas. Lovely balance on the palate, chocolate edge to the fruits, well-rounded ripe tannins now resolving, complexity added from a faint herbal touch. Denser than the 1982, more of the softness for which Palmer is famous. 12.0% (May 2008) *93* Drink to 2015.

Château Palmer, 1982

A curious convergence is now showing between the 1982 Palmer and the much earlier 1970 vintage. The 1982s opened with great opulence, whereas the 1970s were classically austere, but side by side comparison shows a remarkable similarity now in flavor and aroma spectrum. Many 1982s have been reverting to more classic type over the past decade and Palmer seems to be an extreme example. This vintage is certainly developing fairly fast now, with a faintly brown tinge to its hue. It is quite animal on the nose with barnyard aromas. It is lighter on the palate now, more delicate than powerful; beautifully balanced, ripe, soft fruits show faint herbal notes—but in agreement with conventional wisdom this does not have the weight and structure of the 1983. Quite classic aroma and flavor spectrum make this seem like a denser version of the 1970 (but not so much as 12 years younger). 12.0% (May 2008) *91* Drink to 2016.

Château Palmer, 1970

Restrained but developed nose with some faintly pungent notes of barnyard. Very sweet ripe fruits on the palate are remarkable for the vintage and age, and you might take it for an only slightly younger version of the 1982. Wonderfully lively still, obviously fully developed, but in perfect balance of ripe fruits, supporting acid, resolved tannins but still a fine-grained impression of structure. One of the best of what has become a very variable vintage. 12.5% (May 2008) *94* Drink to 2015.

Château Palmer, 1966

It's not showing the liveliness it had five years ago as age begins to overtake it. Brilliant ruby/garnet color, age showing less in appearance than on the nose, where there are not so much barnyard notes as those faintly nutty, musty notes that old Bordeaux sometimes shows. Soft on the palate, faintly nutty on the finish. Certainly the fruits are beginning to dry out and there's now a touch of dilution but it's in remarkable condition for forty years of age, with those sweet fruits of Palmer still showing through. (February 2010) 12.0% 93 Drink to 2014.

Château Palmer, 1962

Savory notes with some faint gunflint and barnyard develop on the nose, with a faint touch of VA. The warm dense fruits of a decade ago are now being replaced by a more savory flavor spectrum, but the palate retains that distinctive velvety texture of Palmer. There's a leafy, autumnal impression, more Cabernet Franc than Sauvignon, beginning to come out, with herbal notes of sage. It has to be admitted that a touch of bitterness has started to come through in the past few years. My tasting notes suggest that the wine peaked in the mid nineties, but it's falling off ever so slowly, and remains a wine of great character. (January 2012) *92* Drink up.

Château Palmer, 1961

November 2009: Fruit density is diminishing but that core of sweet fruits you get in Margaux is still there, now tinged by just a touch of acidity. A mature color now, with soft fruits on the palate, an impression of mulberries, quite intense and ripe, with a supple, lovely finish. A touch of tertiary development shows as some sous bois on the nose. Still top notch if now exceeded by Latour. *95* Drink to 2017.

November 2007: A decade ago, the 1961 Palmer was right up there with the first growths, but now it does not have quite the density to stay with them, although it is only a slight measure behind. The color is still quite dark with some purple hues. The nose reflects Cabernet more than anything else (although this vintage has a very low proportion). The black fruits are fairly subdued on the nose, but come into their own on the palate, rich, deep, black cherries and blackcurrants, but a little lighter than a decade ago. The tannins seem mostly resolved, but there is no sign of tiring and at least another decade lies ahead.

November 1997: Doesn't have the density of 10 years ago, but absolutely typical Palmer, with that plummy quality, soft and rich, yet with a backbone. Tannins now resolved, but enough fruit density to hold for many years.

Château Pichon Baron

Pichon Baron is one of the early examples of revival by corporate investment. The château and vineyards fell into a poor condition after the Second World War, and by the time the property was sold to the insurance company AXA in 1987, there were only 33 ha of vineyards. AXA invested in winemaking and expanded the vineyards to 70 ha, not entirely successfully since some of the vineyards proved not to be of top quality and now are used for the second wine, the Tourrelles de Longueville. The grand vin comes from the vineyards closer to the château itself. The style of the wine is distinctly Pauillac: powerful, not to say robust. It seems more muscular than that of Pichon Lalande, which was the other half of the estate before the separation into two châteaux in 1850. "There is an overall objective for style. The grand vin is Cabernet style for sure, looking for elegance and finesse, although there can be austerity when young. If it is concentrated and tannic we can bring out aging potential with appropriate maturation in oak (usually 80% new for Pichon Baron)," says Director Jean-René Matignon. Recent vintages display the wine in full flow, and the status of Pichon Baron has been rising into the super-seconds. Wines were tasted at the château in October 2011.

Château Pichon Longueville Baron, 2009
Restrained nose has some intimations of deep blackcurrants with a whiff of cassis giving a sweet note. Sweet ripe fruits follow the nose, intense and concentrated. Good supporting acidity almost brings a touch of piquancy. The overall impression is opulent and almost exotic with a long aromatic finish. With concentration, structure, and texture, this has a long life ahead, good for at least two decades. The fruits are so full that the wine is approachable enough to drink now, but it would be a pity not to wait at least four or five years. Here is the full force of a super-second, with intensity and depth of fruits, yet under control and balanced by good acidity and firm tannins. Modern but not international. 13.8% *93* Drink 2015-2030.

Château Pichon Longueville Baron, 2000
Dark color is just beginning to turn to more mature hue. Nose shows black fruits with the first faint detectable savory notes. Fruits are still quite spicy, but the savory elements from the nose follow through to the palate. Some retronasal nuttiness develops in the glass and the flavors become more savory. Here is classic lightness of Bordeaux and sense of elegance; a graceful wine. Its development is a halfway point between the 1989 and the 2009. The style clearly is following the development of the 1989, but you can see the improvements made since AXA took over in the greater complexity of the aroma and flavor spectrum. 13.2% *92* Drink to 2026.

Château Pichon Longueville Baron, 1996
Nose shows youthful black fruits, supported by the usual good acidity of the vintage, but nicely under control. The main impression on the palate is that very smooth texture of Pauillac with dense underlying fruits. This may revert to type by developing some herbaceousness in the next decade. It's a top result for the year, every drop a super-second. (January 2012) 13.0% *92* Drink to 2021.

Château Pichon Longueville Baron, 1989
A mature hue, garnet with some traces of orange at the rim, but still rather dark. Savory nose has elements of sous bois mingling with black fruits. The wine has come into a delicious balance with the fruits turning savory, and that touch of sous bois cutting the ripeness. There is

fresh acidity with a slight tang on the finish. This is very harmonious and typical of gracefully aging Bordeaux. It reached this stage of development about 3-4 years ago and should hold for several years yet. The 2000 is now proceeding along the same route of development a decade behind, but the contrast in complexity shows the improvements made at the château between 1989 and the end of the century. 13.0% *89* Drink to 2018.

Château Pichon Lalande

Pichon Lalande is one of the trio at the heart of the super-seconds in Pauillac and St. Julien (its close rivals being Léoville Lascases and Ducru Beaucaillou). Resulting from the inheritance problems created by the Napoleonic code, it originated when the original estate at Pichon was split in 1850. Five years later, both Pichon Lalande and Pichon Baron were classified as second growths (although they were still largely being managed as a single estate). The modern era started when Édouard Miailhe of the negociant family acquired the château in 1925. After a difficult period in the seventies, the estate passed to Édouard's youngest daughter, May-Éliane Lencquesaing in 1978. The vineyards expanded from 40 ha to 89 ha, and the estate rose steadily in reputation. It was sold to Champagne Roederer in 2007 (since when May-Éliane has been producing Cabernet Sauvignon in South Africa). Visiting the château today, you get the impression that the new owners feel there are improvements to be made, and certainly there has been a steady program of further investment, especially while Sylvie Cazes (sister of Jean-Charles Cazes at Château Lynch Bages) was Director over the past two years. Aside from improvements in viticulture and vinification, the main change will be an increasing emphasis on Cabernet Sauvignon, but this is likely to take some years to accomplish. Wines were tasted at Château Pichon Lalande in June 2012 or in New York in October 2011 (with bottles coming directly from the château).

2010
(Bottled in May.) Fresh black fruit nose leading into stern tones of blackberry fruits on palate. There's a fair tannic rasp on the finish with some heat coming through. Slowly the fruits round up in the glass and the palate softens. Very good structure gives quite a classic impression, with the wine holding back and certainly needing time. There's a feeling of the old tradition of hardness at the outset, but when the tannins resolve, a few years from now, this should become well rounded, and perhaps even delicate. 13.6% *89* Drink 2017-2029.

2009
There's an immediate impression of the roundness of the fruits, but I wouldn't really call this exuberant, it's within the character of Pauillac, albeit evidently from a very ripe year. There's still that slightly hard edge on the palate that I noted in many Pauillacs when first tasted from this vintage, but cut by a faintly nutty quality. Firm tannins need some time to let the blackberry fruits show through; there is good supporting acidity, but the wine is rather closed, which is often the case for young Pichon Lalande. Altogether this makes a fine impression, and should become elegant as it matures a few years from now. 13.0% *91* Drink 2015-2028.

2006
Ruby appearance is beginning to turn garnet. Restrained nose has just some hints of spices. Fruits superficially show more roundness than you usually see with this vintage, then the flatness of the year shows a bit on the finish. This should improve with time and become more elegant and delicate as it's not overwhelmed by tannins, but it's not evident that the fruits will come out much more. 13.0% *87* Drink 2013-2020.

2005
Medium ruby color already with a touch of garnet. A mellow nose has a very faint touch of nuts. The palate is smooth and fresh, not at all the blockbuster you might expect from the reputation of the vintage. The overall impression is quite classically Cabernet-driven, fruits with a touch of asperity backed by tannins that don't seem very generous, decent structure to age well, although softening a little in the glass to become nuttier. Blind I would put this down as an average rather than great year, and I see some notes that remind me of 1996 or 1975, with a possible imbalance developing between fruit and acidity. In short, more of a throwback to the

classic style than would be expected from 2005. 13.0% (October 2011) *88* Drink 2014-2021.

2004

A garnet touch to the color suggests some development. The fresh black fruit nose gives a faint impression of perfume. Nice balance on the palate between black fruits, just a touch of asperity from the tannins shows retronasally, but overall the tannins are quite soft. This is a good result for the vintage, producing a wine that will drink well now and hold for a few years. A perfect restaurant wine. 13.0% (October 2011) *88* Drink to 2018.

2003

Age indicated by medium garnet color with some orange at rim. Black fruit nose shows black-currants and a touch of cedar, even a faint touch of herbaceousness on the nose, somewhat surprising for this vintage. Rich and chocolaty on the palate, with tannins that are ripe but giving a faint impression of being over cooked. The wine becomes a touch hard on the mid palate in the glass. It may be that the tannins will outlive the fruits. The wine is not falling apart, as many are, but it gives a slightly clumsy impression, not atypical of this vintage. It should be drunk in the near future. 13.0% (October 2011) *87* Drink to 2015.

2000

This wine is full of surprises and has changed yet again. What appeared as herbaceousness two or three years ago now shows as an intense cedary aroma on the nose, following through to palate and finish. The dusky garnet color still appears relatively youthful. It is hard to pick out the fruits on nose and palate against the background of cedar, but they seem to be in good balance with the acidity and tannins. The wine gives a very dry, classic impression: it is lean rather than opulent. 13.0% (October 2011) *90* Drink to 2021.

1996

Classic nose, with fruits turning savory. Classic on the palate, a throwback to the seventies in style, dominated by the Cabernet Sauvignon. Savory black fruits have a touch of herbaceous-ness, with the sense of bell peppers carrying through the long finish. The acidity is less pressing here than in some wines of the vintage. This should continue to mature in the classic style—which is to say savory with vegetal overtones rather than overtly fruity—until the tannins overtake the fruits. However, some bottles with less good provenance are showing development of more overt herbaceousness. 13.0% (October 2011) *89* Drink to 2020.

1985

The hit of a vertical tasting of Pichon Lalande. Lightening garnet color. Classic nose showing bell peppers and a touch of cedar. Acidity is quite noticeable on the palate, which generally follows the nose. Beautiful balance, now à point with savory fruits not yet turning really tertiary. Elegant and delicate, with bell peppers strengthening on finish. Very fine-grained structure. A bit of a surprise that this year should end up with such a completely classic development. 12.5% (October 2011) *92* Drink to 2016.

Château Rauzan-Gassies

Rauzan-Gassies is the smaller part of the original Rauzan estate, which was divided at the time of the French Revolution. The château itself became part of Rauzan-Ségla, so wine is made in a relatively modern building, actually just adjacent to Rauzan-Ségla. Rauzan-Gassies passed into the hands of the Quié family when Paul Quié, a wine mer-chant in Paris who sold Algerian wine, invested in Bordeaux. In 1942 he bought Croizet Bages and then in 1946 followed with Rauzan-Gassies. He had a Parisian view that the vineyard was more an investment than a principal occupation; it was not until his son took over in 1968 that the property was run on the spot. Today it is managed by the third generation of winemaker Jean-Philippe and his sister Anne-Françoise. The es-tate consists of 35 ha, with 25 ha planted to vineyards. There are around 17 individual parcels, all in Margaux. The grand vin is around three quarters of production and is dominated by Cabernet Sauvignon (ranging from 60-85% in recent vintages) and ma-tured in 55% new oak. The second wine, Le Chevalier de Rauzan-Gassies, uses 25% new oak. There are some unusual features in both viticulture and vinification. Machine harvesting contrasts with the common emphasis on manual work at most top châteaux; and in the cellar, malolactic fermentation is initiated by inoculation at the start of alcoholic fermentation, so the two fermentations occur more or less simultaneously. They feel that this preserves the purity of the fruit better than waiting for the MLF (partly because less sulfuring is necessary), and it allows the wine to go into barrel sooner. However, some feel that the wine has a more rustic quality compared with its neighbor, Rauzan-Ségla, where there has been more investment and modernization. The grand vin was compared with Cabernet Sauvignon bottled separately in a tasting at the château in October 2011.

Château Rauzan-Gassies, 2009
More complexity than the Cabernet alone is immediately evident on the nose. There's an impression of red more than black fruits with some savory touches. Of course, there is a significant influence of oak (55% new). The wine is softer than the Cabernet Sauvignon, but it's also lost some of that impression of precision. Yes, it has more flavor variety and will no doubt evolve to greater complexity as a result of the blend. The black cherry fruits of the palate still give a good impression of Margaux, but the precision has been muddied with the softening brought by the Merlot. The difference between the Cabernet Sauvignon alone and the blended wine is not so much in fruit intensity as the increase of savory impressions and, of course, a bit more fat. It's just a fraction four square in style. *90* Drink 2014-2022.

Château Rauzan-Gassies, 1996
Mature developed garnet but still quite dark. This shows more intensity and complexity on the nose than the Cabernet Sauvignon vinified separately, and the savory notes of sous-bois are more evident. The fruits are definitely rounder on the palate as the Merlot has ameliorated the sternness of the Cabernet. This is elegant although it has the high acidity and impression of austerity characteristic of the vintage. Tannins have resolved to leave a nice balance. The wine is now at its peak and I do not see support for further development. 12.5% *88* Drink to 2016.

Cabernet Sauvignon, 2009
Youthful ruby color. Restrained nose shows red cherries with a faint touch of Margaux perfume of black violets. There seems to be a very faint touch of vanillin even though the wine saw no new oak. Well rounded and elegant—very Margaux on the palate, showing that feminine perfumed touch—with interesting enough aromatics, to be a complete wine. Fine-grained tannins give an impression of precision on the finish.

Cabernet Sauvignon, 2006
Color development is just beginning. Restrained nose shows a touch of development with some faint savory elements. This is rounder than the 96—it's come off its initial austerity—and the rounding out has brought some elegance. The light, elegant character is surprisingly close to a complete wine—and makes me believe that the Cabernet conveys the essential typicity of the commune.

Cabernet Sauvignon, 1996
Mature garnet color but quite dark. Developed Cabernet nose, slightly savory and herbaceous with a faint touch of sous bois, and an impression of Margaux perfume developing in the glass. The purity of the fruits comes through clearly. Palate follows the nose, very classic in its spectrum, a tight tannic structure with faintly herbaceous overtones. You can see that what is missing here is the mid palate fleshiness provided by the Merlot. As a varietal, this is a bit tight and austere, it needs the fat of the Merlot.

Château Rauzan-Ségla

The estate created by Pierre de Rauzan, a prominent negociant in Bordeaux, was highly regarded in the seventeenth century, but after it was split in 1763 the part that became Rauzan-Ségla was well ahead of Rauzan-Gassies, although both were classified as second growths in 1855. Rauzan-Ségla's reputation declined under the ownership of the Cruse family during the first part of the twentieth century; after they sold in 1956, it was managed by the negociant firm Eschenauer, and some improvements were made, but it was still relatively run down, and real renovation came with its acquisition by the Wertheimer brothers of Chanel perfume in 1994. Everything is new, from 15 km of drainage in the vineyards to a fermentation facility. "The only old part of the property today is the nineteenth century barrel room," says John Kolasa, who came from Château Latour to manage the vineyards in 1994. But the wine remains true to the traditions of Margaux. "There is very traditional vinification, we are not modern style," he says. Wines were tasted at Château Rauzan-Ségla in June 2012.

Château Rauzan-Ségla, 2009
The nose oscillates between perfume and a faint herbal impression. Its elegance means there is no missing the refinement of Margaux, and there is a precise edge resembling St. Julien. In the past three months the wine has begun to round out, and its generosity becomes steadily more evident on the palate. The vanillin and nutty influences of new oak are still evident, fading into a velvety underlying structure with a slight suggestion of chocolate on the finish. Very good depth to the fruits is well balanced by the structure. This will be ready to start surprisingly soon. 13.5% *91* Drink 2015-2025.

Château Rauzan-Ségla, 1995
This was the first vintage made after Chanel took over. There's a classic impression on the nose with a mixture of red and black fruits cut by herbal overtones. This is quite a tightly balanced wine; the fruits seem a little linear, with the herbal notes stopping just short of herbaceousness. Underneath it is softer than it first appears, but the tannins still need to resolve further to allow the fruits to show fully. Perhaps it's a harbinger of future development that it softens in the glass and the fruits become more supple, and then it reverts to a more overtly herbaceous finish. 12.5% *89* Drink to 2022.

Château Rauzan-Ségla, 1983
This is a classic representation of the appellation and vintage. Elegant fruits, now showing as more red than black, dominate a palate that has a slightly herbal or herbaceous edge just on the verge of turning bitter. An impression of layers of flavor comes across the palate to a dry finish. Still fresh and refined after thirty years, but now it's time to drink up *89* Drink to 2017.

Ségla, 2000
Not showing a great deal of development, this is refined and elegant, and makes a fresh impression. It's a very pure, linear, representation of Cabernet Sauvignon. This second wine follows the general style of the chateau, but at a lower level of concentration and roundness. A nice touch of spiciness develops in the glass. *87* Drink to 2018.

Château Roc des Cambes (Côtes de Bourg)

When François Mitjavile purchased Château Roc des Cambes in 1987, it was pretty dilapidated, but it had good terroir—the story often told is that François put his finger in the soil and decided to buy the property—and old vines. The estate is about 10 ha, with an annual production around 40,000 bottles. As at the Mitjavile's other property, Château Tertre Rôteboeuf in St. Emilion, all the efforts go into the single wine: François does not believe in second wines. "With a homogeneous terroir, it is more interesting not to make a selection for a second wine, because production of a single wine best expresses the variations of the vintage, as the fruits ripen differently every year. A second wine is more suitable for properties which have heterogeneous terroirs," he told me. The young wines at Roc des Cambes are pretty forceful, more evidently so than those of François's other property, perhaps because the fruits in St. Emilion are so much richer as to hide the structure. But as the wines age there seems to me to be something of a convergence in style, with Roc des Cambes becoming more like Tertre Rôteboeuf in its overall balance. The wines are usually 80% Merlot to 20% Cabernet Sauvignon, but the 2000 vintage unusually had equal proportions of each (and remains my favorite). Wines were tasted at Château Tertre Rôteboeuf in June 2012.

2010
(Barrel sample.) The black fruit nose is ripe, smooth, and spicy, but in spite of the richness of the year the style is towards elegance (compared, for example, with a more rustic impression from the less generous 2004). The strength of the vintage shows on the nose, with fruits more

of blackberries than blackcurrants. The very high alcohol is not obtrusive now, but there's the possibility it will become more evident as the wine matures. There's certainly a pretty fair tannic grip to the finish and this vintage will need time, but it will be one of the more elegant years from Roc des Cambes, which as always is showing well above the general level of its appellation. 15.3% *91* Drink 2015-2027.

2004
First impression is almost flamboyant, with exotic spices and nuts highlighting the full blown black fruits, but the palate is then restrained by the structure of firm, round, tannins with those nutty tones of Merlot coming back on the finish. The nose is more exuberant than the palate, where the fruits show the characteristic refreshing uplift of Bordeaux. There is certainly a superficial richness here, but it's hiding the structure in a way reminiscent of St. Emilion. This is definitely powerful rather than elegant, even a little rustic, with the structure tending towards massive. It takes quite a while in the glass, but when the exuberance dies down there is a very good balance, and in spite of the high alcohol this is not a fruit bomb. (It would be an even more gorgeous wine at 1% less alcohol, in my opinion.) There may be a case for opening a few hours before drinking. What would it be like without the Cabernet Sauvignon—without the backbone it might well descend into jamminess. 14.0% *90* Drink to 2021.

2000
I thought this wine was most impressive four years ago, when it was just beginning its development. At that point it showed smooth, elegant, black fruits, with the first beginnings of tertiary development; although lacking the power of Tertre Rôteboeuf, the style is generally similar. Now there is an intensely developed nose of gunflint and tertiary aromas. The palate is less developed than expected from the nose; fruits are lightening, with just a touch of sous bois, or perhaps really more of a mineral impression, coming through to the finish. It seems that the level of savory development has not changed much in four years, although the fruits are now discernibly lighter, allowing a slightly spartan quality to replace the originally more lush impression; no doubt the sparse character reflects the unusually high proportion of Cabernet Sauvignon in this vintage. It should become progressively more savory, with the fruits continuing to lighten, and should be drunk in the immediate future while it stays at this peak. 13.5% *90* Drink to 2016.

The South of France

"Variable conditions" describes the last three vintages (2012-2010), with a drought broken by rain in 2011. 2012 was especially difficult. 2010 alternated between wet and cool in the Spring, to dry and hot in the summer, to storms at the end, giving concentrated but relatively tough wines. The warm year of 2009 was generally good. The dry summer of 2008 with cool spells made for difficulties with ripeness. Cool conditions and winds in 2007 also created problems with ripeness. Wines from 2006 are light and relatively short lived. 2005 was good here as elsewhere, but was often spoiled by rain at harvest. 2004 is the most classic of recent vintages. 2003 was the year of the heat wave, it's an exceptional wine that has survived. 2002 was the disaster of the floods.

Domaine de la Grange des Pères

The winery is the middle of uncultivated fields with not a vine in sight. The Syrah and Cabernet are actually fairly close by, the main difference between their terroirs being that Cabernet is planted in the cooler exposures. The Mourvèdre is 4-5 km away, on a south-facing plot covered in galets (large pebbles), which is rather hot. The Cabernet accumulates sugar more slowly than Syrah, which allows good choice for time of harvesting. Vines are grown low to the ground. Yields are always very low, often below 25 hl/ha. There are only two wines here, one red and one white. Laurent Vaillé is a perfectionist: "any lot that isn't satisfactory is discarded, I don't want to make a second wine." Wines were tasted in September 2012.

Vin de Pays de l'Hérault, 2008

This is an arresting and paradoxical wine. The evident richness of the first impression suggests the New World, with intense blackcurrant fruits and distinctly aromatic notes having a suspicion of piquancy. But then savory overtones cut the aromatics, turning to shades of tobacco in the glass, and the palate presents such precise, refined, black fruits that you are drawn back to Europe; indeed, in a blind tasting I would probably be hesitating between the sheer elegance of Côte Rôtie and the greater power of Hermitage, anyway I would be in the northern Rhône. But then there's that tight, precise, structured edge coming from the Cabernet, definitely a tautness you wouldn't expect from Syrah alone. Alcohol is evidently high, although well integrated with the fruits; some might find it just a touch too much for comfort as it reinforces the aromatic impression. The wine is clearly young now, it can be enjoyed already, although it is a little aromatic for my taste; but the main point is that you are left with the feeling that you are missing out on much potential development when the aromatics will turn savory, perhaps a decade from now. At the end of the day, the wine is sui generis. 14.0% *92* Drink to 2024.

Vin de Pays de l'Hérault, 2007

Openly delicious but quite New World-ish in the pungent aromatics of fresh Syrah with piquant black plums (one might think about Barossa Shiraz in a blind tasting). Good acidity stops this going over the edge into jamminess, but it's the least subtle and most overtly fruity of recent vintages, almost overwhelming, with the aromatic core of Syrah very evident and the structure of Cabernet pushed undetectably into the background. More loose knit than usual, this can be enjoyed in the next few years, but I would be hesitant about expecting longevity beyond a decade. This is heady wine with a strong impression of high alcohol (as much in the style as on the numbers), and it's not obvious whether it will calm down in the future. 14.0% *87* Drink to 2022.

Vin de Pays de l'Hérault, 2001

A warm first impression is accompanied by some faint hints of raisins. but the apparent simplicity is ameliorated by the development of some notes of tobacco in the glass. Slightly aromatic black fruits of Syrah dominate the palate, with those raisiny notes coming back on the aftertaste. The ripeness of the fruits extends almost to an impression of sweetness on the finish. Perhaps this vintage is a particularly slow developer, but the flavor spectrum still seems somewhat primary and straightforward, raising the question of whether it will develop in a savory direction or will relax into a jammy old age. 14.0%. *88* Drink to 2020.

Vin de Pays de l'Hérault, 2000

This vintage definitely gives a more restrained impression than 2001, the impression here being that the rich fruits of Syrah have been better balanced by the structure of the Cabernet Sauvignon. Fruits show as blackberries and blackcurrants cut by a very faintly savory element; good acidity maintains freshness. The typical sweet ripe fruits of Grange des Pères dominate the palate, but are cut by the restraining structure of the Cabernet; while the palate could not be called subtle or savory yet, it shows more flavor variety than 2001. Faint hints of savory development suggest that the wine may be expected to develop more complexity in the next few years. 13.5% *90* Drink to 2022.

Vin de Pays de l'Hérault, 1994

Age has brought lightness and elegance to showcase the spectrum of red fruits. A touch dumb at first, slowly the nose develops enticing notes of spices with a mélange of mature red fruits, and savory undertones. The flavor spectrum resembles the 2000 vintage, but the sense of refinement is much enhanced by the extra few years of age; the wine has made the transition from evident richness to lightness of being. Unlike some younger vintages where it's possible to tease out the influence of one variety or another—the 2001 shows its Syrah forcefully, the 2000 shows the structural contribution of Cabernet Sauvignon—this vintage has now melded into a seamless blend in which the components are hard to disentangle. In seeking to define a broader context, perhaps the closest parallel for the slightly spicy aromatics would be a top Hermitage of the early nineties. Mature red fruits show a slowly developing savory undertone; tannins are largely resolved, but there is still a sense of a fine underlying structure that will support longevity for some years. The only negative note is a touch of heat on the finish. As this is only the third vintage of Grange des Pères, there is no precedent to forecast future development, but the ripe sweetness of the fruits, the fine supporting structure, and some slowly developing subtle undertones, suggest that the wine may take a savory path of development over the next decade. 13.5% *92* Drink to 2022.

Mas de Daumas Gassac

The Domaine is devoted to natural viticulture and vinification. Vineyards are interspersed with original sections of the garrigue, so the total planted 50 ha are made up of about 63 separate small plots. Emphasis here is on minimal treatments of the vines, basically little more than fertilization with sheep manure every three years. The terroir has red glacial soils beneath the local garrigue; the vineyards are on hillsides, where nocturnal currents of cool air create a microclimate that distinguishes the valley of the Gassac from neighboring areas. While day time temperatures are similar between Gassac and (for example) nearby Montpeyroux, the night time minima can be 10 °C lower, to the point at which they drop very close to freezing even in June. The domain is planted predominantly with Cabernet Sauvignon, which makes up 80% of the red wine (Cabernet has varied from as little as 65% to as much as 90%), but the remaining 20% comes from a diverse set of varieties, including Merlot, Cabernet Franc, Tannat, Pinot Noir, Nebbiolo, Barbera, Dolcetto, Tempranillo, Voskehat (Armenia), and Kontorni (Armenia). (The white is similarly eclectic, with a base of Viognier and Chardonnay, but many other minor varieties.) The wines are classified as Vin de Pays d'Hérault. Whether because of the microclimate or the other varieties, the red wine is by no means a typical Bordeaux-like Cabernet, but can more reflect the Southern spices and herbs of the garrigue. I'm inclined to place the wines into two groups, with 2005, 1996, 1988, 1982 more reflecting Atlantic influences, and 2001, 1990, 1985, 1983 more evidently Mediterranean. My favorite was 1988, which seemed to capture the essence of what the domain is about. In addition to the regular cuvées, there is now a Cuvée Emile Peynaud in some vintages, made from the oldest Cabernet Sauvignon vines in one of the original vineyards. This plot is vinified separately, and the decision is made only just prior to assemblage whether to include it in the regular bottling or make a special cuvée (which happened in 2001, 2002, 2007, 2008). Moulin de Gassac is a negociant line that includes purchased grapes. Wines were tasted in June 2012.

Vin de Pays d'Hérault, 2008
This is an elegant wine with Cabernet Sauvignon represented in a lighter style. It's fresh with a slight spiciness and some aromatic complexity. The Cabernet is identified by notes of cedar, with lively fruits on the palate, showing a faint savory touch of the garrigue. For the south this is a restrained style. Good flavor variety across the palate is supported by an unobtrusive structure with tannins well in the background. (August 2011) 13.0% *88* Drink to 2017.

Vin de Pays d'Hérault, 2006
Nose shows fresh red fruits and a touch of nuts with intimations of complexity. Elegant fruits on the palate follow the red spectrum of the nose. There's a touch of savory influence from the garrigue. Opening up in the glass, the wine shows its delicacy, yet with the fine structure and tannic support of Cabernet. It brings back memories of some of the more delicate older vintages of Bordeaux. (August 2011) 13.0% *90* Drink to 2016.

Vin de Pays de l'Hérault, 2005
Still youthful in appearance. A rush of perfume when the glass was filled, then some savory undertones. The sense of perfume carries over to the palate, with a faint aromaticity identifying its southern origins, but quite fresh on the palate, although different from Bordeaux's savory tang. Then a Cabernet rasp shows itself on the finish, which develops more dryness as time passes in the glass, making the wine seem a little rustic. Tertiary development seems about to begin. Moderate alcohol emphasizes the lightness of the style—no heavy handed modern extraction here. The wine certainly rounds up in the glass, so perhaps that initial rustic impression will ameliorate with time. 12.5% *88* Drink now to 2020.

Vin de Pays de l'Hérault, 2001
Maturing now to a garnet appearance and giving an immediate impression on the nose of some development with a whiff of tertiary aromas replacing an initial, more perfumed impression. The palate makes a more savory impression, although still with the soft edge of the south. This now presents quite an elegant balance, indeed, delicate would be a fair description. It's certainly

much lighter than Bordeaux would be from the same vintage. Character is a bit amorphous, the wine somehow fails to declare itself, although it's very appealing for current drinking. 13.0% *89* Drink now to 2016.

Vin de Pays de l'Hérault, 1996
Restrained nose somewhere between perfumed and savory, Smooth palate, but with a faint rasp of Cabernet on the finish. At first the tannins seem just a touch rustic, but then the wine reverts to elegance as the fruits take over. That rasp disappears with time in the glass, although the fruits show a nicely rounded Cabernet character, which is to say just a suspicion of savory development. This is an Atlantic vintage. 13.0% *91* Drink now to 2020.

Vin de Pays de l'Hérault, 1990
Delicate and refined, with just a touch of structure showing on the finish, but a sense of dilution as the fruits begin to lighten, slightly nutty and delicate, with a faintly glyceriny impression on the finish. The fruits are soft and appealing, but does it have enough character? It's superficially delicious, but without any determined structure may not improve any further, and may lose its interest as there isn't really enough flavor variety to withstand much further lightening of the fruits. This is clearly a Mediterranean vintage. 12.6% *88* Drink now to 2016.

Vin de Pays de l'Hérault, 1989
This wine shows the pace of development of 1990, which is to say that the fruits are lightening up, but has the aroma and flavor spectrum of 1988, which is to say that they are Bordelais in character. Faintly leathery impressions on the nose suggest a very slight touch of Brett, which reinforces the sense of relationship with old Bordeaux. An initial impression of a touch of dilution comes initially from the lightening of the fruits, but then is obscured by the soft sweetness of the palate. Not as characterful as 1988, and time to drink up now, but still a lovely, refined, impression. 13.0% (October 2012) *90.*

Vin de Pays de l'Hérault, 1988
There's an impression of Bordeaux here with a faint but delicious herbaceous touch: this wine immediately produced appreciative noises all round. It's right at the tipping point from fruity to savory with just a faint touch of perfume adding to the herbs to show that you're in the south. There's still enough structural support for a few years as the wine continues to develop in the savory direction. You might think here in terms of a Grand Cru Classé from Bordeaux, except that the structure is a bit softer. This takes you back to the time when you could use herbaceous as a description in the context of delicious, and when cabernet was elegant rather than powerful. This is the most classically Atlantic of the vintages. 12.7% *92* Drink now to 2020.

Vin de Pays de l'Hérault, 1985
Following the path of Mediterranean vintages, this is now turning somewhat nutty on the palate, and this is a bit too noticeable on the finish for comfort. Certainly it's soft and appealing, in an overtly southern way, with nice fruits—but not a lot of structure behind. This might be difficult to place as Cabernet Sauvignon in a blind tasting; I think you'd be more inclined to think in terms of warmer climate varieties. No doubt this reflects the brutal summer with very hot conditions through September and October. *87* Drink now to 2016.

Vin de Pays d'Hérault, 1983
Still a fairly dark color. An intriguing slightly floral note on the nose, almost a whiff of violets à la Margaux, conveying a vague sense of garrigue but more floral than herbal. The ripeness of the fruits is evident on the palate, giving a kick of sweetness to the finish. Black fruits on the palate show more as blackberries than blackcurrants, but with a fleshiness on the midpalate, presumably from the Merlot and Syrah. Still youthfully vibrant, and I'm struck by the warm tones of the palate with chocolaty hints on the finish. Age has brought a definite softness rather than the savory development that's common in Bordeaux; in fact, the wine shows surprisingly little tertiary development. (November 2011) 13.0% *92* Drink to 2017.

Vin de Pays d'Hérault, 1982
The immediate impression on nose and palate is that this wine more shows Atlantic influence with a resemblance to the savory development of old Bordeaux. The nose is relatively savory compared to the gentle, soft, perfumed fruits of the 1983, and there's a very slight touch of herbaceousness. This spectrum follows through to the palate, which makes a more classical food wine than the 1983. There is lovely flavor variety right across the palate. A faint impression of cedar develops on the finish, giving a Graves-like impression. There are the first signs of the fruits beginning to dry out, as the wine becomes dumb in the glass to show an austere finish of residual tannins, then reversing itself to let the fruits hang out again. At peak moments there's a lovely balance and classic impression of Cabernet, but it is getting close to time to drink up. (November 2011) 13.0% *93* Drink to 2015.

Vin de Pays de l'Hérault, Cuvee Emile Peynaud, 2001
I do wonder what Emile Peynaud would have thought of this wine, which comes at you in a full knock-your-eyes-out international style. Much darker in color than the Daumas Gassac of the vintage, with an intense nose of pure Cabernet—sweet, ripe, dense, rich, nutty, a touch of vanillin—loaded with new oak. This is a lovely wine: no one could complain about the quality. But it's not simply a more intense version of the Daumas Gassac bottling, it's altogether in a different style, modern where the Gassac is traditional, oaky where the Gassac relies on fruits. I feel about it somehow the same as I do about Petit Verdot; fantastic to taste, you can see at once what a few of barriques of this quality would do to lift the blend, but do you want to drink it by itself? It doesn't seem even to have started to age, it's impressive and would hold its own against New World Cabernets—but I think if I were to split a bottle over dinner, I'd rather have the Daumas Gassac 2001. 13.0% (June 2012) *91* Drink now to 2022.

Finca Narraza

This is a very small producer, run by Corinne & Gérard Le Jan, with a winery behind a shop front in the center of St. Paul-de-Fenouillet. Most of the producers in the immediate vicinity send their grapes to the local cooperative: the Le Jans are unusual in handling their own production and aiming for quality. They have around a hectare each of Syrah and Cabernet, a little less Grenache, some Carignan (and they used to have some Mourvèdre). There are also white varieties. The vineyards are biodynamic. The Cabernet Sauvignon vineyard is about twenty years old; the Le Jans bought it in 2008. Gérard believes you get the most complexity for Cabernet Sauvignon by blending. There are two named cuvées, both with Syrah. The Aeron Du cuvée has equal proportions of Cabernet Sauvignon and Syrah, typically at yields around 20 hl/ha. The top cuvée is the Raoul Blondin, named after the maitre de chai at Mouton Rothschild who interested Gérard in Cabernet; it is 80% Syrah and 20% Cabernet Sauvignon, with yields typically around 15 hl/ha. Wines were tasted at the domain in October 2011.

Vin de France, 2009
Just about to be bottled, this blend of Syrah and Cabernet Sauvignon shows a fruit-driven nose with lots of character. The dense fruits have a good tannic backbone. Nice balance with some freshness to offset the density of the fruits. Cabernet seems to be a strong influence in this vintage. *90* Drink 2013-2019.

Vin de France, 2008
This equal blend of Syrah and Cabernet Sauvignon shows an impenetrable black color. A touch of reduction on the nose rapidly blows off. The black fruits of cherries and plums show an impressive density on the palate, supported by fresh acidity and firm tannins that are integrating nicely. The impression in this vintage is dominated more by Syrah than Cabernet, as indicated by the rich, plummy aromatics. It's a more powerful wine than the 2009, albeit just a touch rustic in its overall impression. It will no doubt show greater smoothness in a year or so and should drink well for up to a decade. 13.8% *89* Drink 2013-2021.

Vin de France, Cuvée Raoul Blondin, 2008
Some savage notes to the stern nose resemble Syrahs of the northern Rhône. The dense black fruits on the palate are ripe and unctuous, deep and long, with a chocolaty texture. The Cabernet Sauvignon gives extra backbone to this basically Syrah-dominated wine. The structure is somewhat buried under the density of fruits but should support aging for a decade. A very fine effort. 13.0% *90* Drink 2013-2021.

Château de Perdiguier

Thirty hectares of vineyards (including 8 ha of Cabernet Sauvignon and 6 ha of Merlot) partly surround the eighteenth century château, although the property also contains 200 ha of cereals; indeed, some of the vineyards immediately behind the château were replaced by cereal because the land proved too sandy for vines. Production started out with a monovarietal Merlot, but then the Ferracis, who have owned the property for three generations, decided that a blend made better wine. The Cabernet-Merlot blends have a distinct resemblance to Bordeaux. Indeed, in Bordeaux-like fashion, Cabernet Sauvignon is planted on the plain near the Orb river where soil is very pebbly, and Merlot is planted on soils with more clay. The entry-level wine is an equal blend of Cabernet Sauvignon and Merlot, which spends 18 months in old oak; the higher level cuvée, the Cuvée d'en Auger, is 85% Cabernet to 15% Merlot, and spends 12 months in new oak. All the wines are VDP (now IGP) des Coteaux d'Enserune. Wines were tasted at the domain in October 2011.

Vin de Pays des Coteaux d'Enserune, 2008
Fresh nose with just a hint of classic bell peppers and cedar. The fresh note continues to the palate where slightly herbaceous tannins show on the finish, which might easily be mistaken for a Bordeaux AOC. A tannic rasp persists a little on the finish. 13.5% *86* Drink to 2016.

Vin de Pays des Coteaux d'Enserune, Cuvee d'en Auger, 2007
This has more evident concentration and roundness than the regular bottling. This vintage is still a deep ruby color with little sign of development. Black fruits on the nose have an austere edge with a touch of smoke and chocolate. The palate of ripe black fruits shows a touch of classic herbaceousness on the finish, but accompanied by a chocolaty texture. Tannic support shows as dryness on the finish. 13.5% *88* Drink to 2017.

Vin de Pays des Coteaux d'Enserune, Cuvee d'en Auger, 2003
Black hue with purple rim. Black fruit nose with some austere herbaceous and cedary notes. Sweet, ripe, rich fruits on the palate are supported by good freshness (a very good result for this awfully hot vintage), with tannins definitely drying the finish. Overall impression is quite unctuous until the tannic dryness cuts in. This really still needs some more time, but the conditions of the year have given a monolithic quality that may not ameliorate. 13.5% *87* Drink to 2015.

Vin de Pays des Coteaux d'Enserune, Cuvee d'en Auger, 2001
Dark color with only a slight touch of garnet developing. Restrained but classic nose with those herbaceous hints of bell peppers. Nicely rounded on the palate with good freshness and attack; the bell peppers come back on the finish. This gives a rather classic impression of a Cabernet Sauvignon-dominated wine, although it's half Cabernet and half Merlot. 13.5% *87* Drink to 2014.

Domaine de Ravanès

When Guy Benin created this domain in the vicinity of Beziers, he did not believe in following conventional wisdom. With the aim of defying the then current reputation of the Languedoc for poor quality, he planted Merlot in 1970-1972, followed by Cabernet Sauvignon, and subsequently Petit Verdot. All of this was illegal at the time, and a certain amount of subterfuge was necessary. Today the Domaine is run by Marc Benin, who studied at Montpellier and Beaune and has a Ph. D. in oenology. He has 5 ha of Cabernet Sauvignon, 6 ha of Merlot, and 2 ha of Petit Verdot out of total plantings of 32 ha. Most of the vines are 40 years old or more. The entry-level wines—including the 50/50 Merlot/Cabernet blend—use no oak, but the Grand Reserve wines use a mixture of 1-year to 3-year oak. Initially a monovarietal Cabernet Sauvignon was produced, but Marc decided that it was too unapproachable when young, and from 2008 switched to a blend with Merlot. All the wines are IGP Coteaux de Murveil (formerly VDP). Wines were tasted at the domain in October 2011.

Coteaux de Murveil IGP, Cabernet/Merlot, 2009
This is the entry-level wine, an equal blend of Cabernet Sauvignon and Merlot, matured in cuves, without oak exposure. The black fruit nose shows some slightly stern notes from the Cabernet. Fruits are quite forward on the palate, where you see the silky fleshiness of the Merlot and don't see much of the structure of Cabernet Sauvignon. This is light and pleasant and will drink well for three or four years, more appropriate for the market, but with less aging potential than the monovarietal Cabernet it replaced. 13.9% *87* Drink to 2014.

Coteaux de Murveil VDP, Cabernet Sauvignon, 2007
This was the last year a monovarietal Cabernet was produced. It's still a dark ruby purple, showing very much a Cabernet nose with austere black fruits. Ripe, rich fruits dominate the palate, supported by ripe tannins. Very good extract but still not quite ready (which creates a marketing problem at the price level of 7 euros). Nice texture: there's no exposure to wood so the forcefulness of the Cabernet fruits comes right through from this good year. 13.5% *88* Drink 2013-2018.

Coteaux de Murveil VDP, Cabernet Sauvignon, 2002
This was a difficult year (the year of the floods in southern France). There's some evolution on the nose, which has lost primary fruits but not yet become tertiary; there are some vegetal over-tones. Fruity on the palate, but a little thin with a herbaceous touch on the finish. Quite agreeable overall, but just a touch herbal for the average taste. 13.5% *86* Drink to 2015.

Coteaux de Murveil VDP, Le Prime Verd, 2002
This wine is a monovarietal Petit Verdot that is matured in (old) oak. It's a medium ruby color with a touch of garnet. Maturity has brought a faint herbal touch to the spicy nose, with a per-fume of the garrigue. The flavor spectrum of the palate has evolved less than the nose—it has lightened up but not really developed tertiary complexity, although a faint touch of savory tarra-gon and the garrigue has carried over to the palate. Dry and smoky on the finish. It's a nice wine, but I'm not sure I see the basis for further development. 14.5% *90* Drink to 2015.

Coteaux de Murveil IGP, Gravières de Taurou, 2000
This is a 50:50 blend of Merlot and Petit Verdot. Still quite dark and ruby in hue. Some smoke, gunflint, and a tertiary touch of barnyard show development. The pure elegant fruits of Petit Verdot show through clearly, with elements of spice, which carry through to the palate and dry finish. Petit Verdot really seems to age very slowly, but on the finish you can just detect the first notes of sous bois beginning to emerge. Nice balance here with herbal retronasal aromas add-ing complexity. A very fine and complex overall impression. 14.9% *89* Drink to 2016.

Coteaux de Murveil VDP, Cabernet Sauvignon, 1998
Here is a classic Cabernet nose, rather mineral with a touch of gunflint and some reduced notes. Fruits of blackcurrants and plums on the palate have a herbal note on the finish, but a general richness that might compare well with Bordeaux's left bank in this vintage. Absence of maturation in oak lets the tight precision of the fruits come through, but the wine would probably have shown as more complete if complemented by a little Merlot. 13.5% *86* Drink to 2014.

Coteaux de Murveil VDP, Cabernet Sauvignon, 1995
Mature color with garnet showing. Fruits are becoming more red than black on the nose with some spicy overtones. Softening on the palate, there's still some intensity, but the wine does not show the Cabernet typicity that was evident on the younger vintages, indicating that fifteen years is about the age limit for the wine, which is now turning towards a more vegetal and herbal spectrum. 13.0% Drink up.

Domaine Richeaume

Domaine Richeaume nestles under the ridge of the long rocky escarpment of La Croix de Provence, with Mont Sainte Victoire in the background. Vineyards extend towards the mountains on red, stony soil. The wines used to be bottled under the Côtes de Provence AOC or the Vin de Pays des Bouches-du-Rhône, but because of restrictions on varietal descriptions resulting from changes in the system, they are now simply bot-tled under the generic Vin de France. The reds are interesting blends of Cabernet Sauvignon, Grenache, and Syrah. Sylvain Hoesch has now taken over from his father, Henning Hoesch, who constructed the modern concrete winery, built into the hillside, in the early 1970s on the site of a former Roman villa. From an initial 2 ha, the holdings have increased to 31 ha, including 5-6 ha of Cabernet Sauvignon, 7-8 ha of Syrah, and 3 ha of Grenache. Three cuvées are based on Cabernet Sauvignon: Tradition (the larg-est production) is an equal blend of Cabernet and Grenache; Columelle is a blend of 50% Cabernet Sauvignon, 40% Syrah, and 10% Merlot; and there is a 100% Cabernet. Unusually for this part of the world, a mix of French and American oak is used for éle-vage. Wines were tasted at the domain in October 2011.

Vin de France, Cuvée Tradition, 2009
Fruity, aromatic nose shows black plums and cherries. The intense aromatics on the palate give this wine a distinct impression of the warm south, with the black fruits subsuming the ripe tannins. Good acidity keeps this refreshing, but the texture is a little rough. Maturation was in equal proportions of American and French oak. 14.1% *88* Drink to 2018.

Vin de France, Cuvée Columelle, 2009
Black fruits drive the nose. Freshness on the palate cuts the ripeness of the fruits, which show the typical aromatics of Syrah. Although the Syrah dominates the palate, there's a sense of restraint and finesse, which is perhaps due to the Cabernet. The overall impression is fine-grained and elegant. 30% of American oak was used here. 14.0% *90* Drink to 2020.

Vin de France, Cabernet Sauvignon, 2008
Some evolution on the nose has occurred in the last year. It's a touch reduced, with some hints of gunflint and a touch of barnyard. The black fruits are quite stern on the palate. This is less open, less overtly fruity than the Cabernet blends. The good fruit concentration comes back on the finish where ripe tannins are evident. The developed notes of barnyard certainly cut the fruits: it's an interesting question whether they will become complex enough to offset the lightening of concentration as further maturation occurs. This wine was matured exclusively in French oak. 13.5% *88* Drink to 2018.

Côtes de Provence, Cuvée Columelle, 2004
When I first tasted this wine a few days after bottling, I was impressed by its combination of concentration and elegance. Two years later it was showing well, but with Syrah appearing more in evidence than Cabernet Sauvignon, providing aromatic fruits to counterbalance the mouth drying tannins. Today I have two conflicting impressions. First, it scarcely appears to be developing: color is still dark with some purple hues, the nose is quite aromatic, and fruits are rich and concentrated. Second, as it gets older, Syrah becomes increasingly dominant and the Cabernet all but disappears: now there are full throttle aromatics, rich fruits with faint hints of chocolate overtones, and the tannins are quite subsumed. As the aromatics of Syrah take over, the wine seems to become more rustic, and without any savory development to counterbalance the fruit aromatics, it may become tiring. In short, it has lost the elegant structure of Cabernet, which leaves it toying dangerously with jammy overtones of ripe Syrah becoming cloying and giving an impression almost of sweetness. In spite of the moderate alcohol, there's now a distinctly warm climate impression to the wine; certainly it tastes richer and more alcoholic than indicated by a level of 13%. At least if you want to appreciate the contribution of Cabernet, it seems this may be a wine that should be consumed relatively young. 13.0% (August 2012) *88* Drink to 2015.

Domaine de Trévallon

The name of Domaine de Trévallon reflects its construction from three valleys, where three separate vineyards were planted after the land was cleared in 1973 by dynamiting limestone rocks in the hills surrounding the domain. The vineyards total 20 ha on soils that remain stony with a mixture of sand and gravel. There are nine separate parcels of Cabernet and nine of Syrah, each individual parcel being surrounded by remnants of the original forest. Viticulture is organic. The white wine (under 10% of production) is a blend of 45% Roussanne, 45% Marsanne and 10% Chardonnay. The red is an equal blend of Cabernet Sauvignon and Syrah. Whole bunches of grapes are fermented in stainless steel, and the Cabernet and Syrah are aged separately in oak for 2 years before assemblage. Maturation is 90% in large foudres, with the rest in barriques varying in age from one to four years. The Cabernet may get a little more barrique treatment because it is harder. Both reds and whites are bottled as Vin de Pays des Bouches du Rhône.

Vin de Pays des Bouches du Rhône, 2004
The first impression is the richness of the wine, with plums and blackcurrants showing aromatic overtones more representative of Syrah than Cabernet Sauvignon, although a sense of tobacco develops. But then the palate shows almost tart fruits, red as well as black, with herbal overtones: here the Cabernet seems more evident. The overall impression is of a wine in which the

south reveals itself more in the herbal and savory notes of the garrigue of Provence than in the fleshy fruits of the southern Rhone. There's a sense that the wine is more or less at its peak; it seems to be maturing along similar lines to the 2001 and so may be expected to be more savory and tertiary in another two or three years. Stylistically this is elegant rather than a blockbuster, an impression that is aided by the moderate alcohol, and in fact it seems to fit into a similar context to Mas de Daumas Gassac (although the assemblage is somewhat different). There's a sense of the complementarity of Syrah and Cabernet in this terroir, with richness counterpoised against savory. 13.0% (August 2012) *90* Drink to 2018.

Vin de Pays des Bouches du Rhône, 2001
This vintage is just beginning to start its evolution. It's a medium density color with some garnet on the rim. The nose is quite developed, showing gunflint with a touch of some tertiary barnyard aromas. The palate is less developed than the nose, showing ripe blackcurrants and plums, but the tertiary notes come back on the finish. Tannins show as dryness on the finish. Personally I'd wait another couple of years for the peak, after which the wine should hold for some time. (October 2011) 14% *91* Drink to 2020.

Coteaux de Baux en Provence, 1993
This gives an impression of a developed cool climate Syrah. The mineral nose conveys somewhat of a savage animal impression. Crisp acidity leads into brambly fruits on the palate, with those animal notes coming back strongly on the finish. There's a contrast between the fruits, which seem precise and sharply delineated by the acidity, with the tertiary development beyond sous bois. The acidity comes close to cutting off the fruits, which however do seem to be smooth and elegant. This may display the limits of winemaking in an unusually cool year. 12.0% (December 2012) *88* Drink to 2017.

Verena Wyss

Verena Wyss and her husband, both formerly architects in Switzerland, bought the domain in 1999. Today there are 38 ha of grounds with 14 ha of vineyards in production, all reconstructed since the original purchase. There is a new winery with stainless steel vats for fermentation. Planted varieties include Viognier and Roussanne in the whites, Cabernet Sauvignon, Merlot, Petit Verdot, and Lledonner-Pelut in the blacks. The vineyards surround the winery, enabling them to be maintained and harvested without much extra help. Terroirs are limestone but rather heterogeneous. Merlot is planted on the areas richer in clay with higher water retention; the Cabernet Sauvignon and Petit Verdot are essentially planted on the same south-facing slope, more or less according to the proportions needed for the wine. By contrast with Bordeaux, the Petit Verdot matures reliably, giving nice small berries. The microclimate in these vineyards is a bit advanced relative to Gabian (the local town). Half of production is white and half red, with a total around 40,000 bottles annually. Wines were tasted at the domain in October 2011.

IGP d'Oc, La Tonga, 2007
This wine is a blend of 60% Cabernet Sauvignon and 40% Petit Verdot. First impressions are intensely aromatic. The classic notes of Petit Verdot are really evident, with a peppery spiciness on the nose showing as all-spice on the palate, which is full of flavor and character. The deep fruits show as blackcurrants and plums, with ripe tannins in the background. The Petit Verdot gives that Rolls Royce sense of power, but does it make the flavor spectrum just a touch monotonic? 13.5% *90* Drink to 2020.

IGP d'Oc, Chant de la Terre, 2007
This wine is a 100% Merlot (but not stated on the label because Merlot has such a bad reputation!) Very fleshy on the nose, with direct black fruits coming up on the palate, very direct with tannins not much in evidence. (Verena calls this the St. Emilion of Gabian.) 14.0% *87* Drink to 2015.

IGP d'Oc, Belcanto, 2007
Belcanto is a Bordeaux-like blend of 60% Cabernet Sauvignon, 30% Merlot, and 10% Petit Verdot. It shows a medium to deep ruby color with a touch of garnet indicating the first development. The restrained nose gives an impression of black fruit with some floral notes. The

underlying structure shows the influence of Cabernet Sauvignon quite clearly, with smooth black fruits supported by ripe tannins. At first the tannins hide behind the fruits, but then they come through to show as dryness on the finish. There's more elegance here than in La Tonga. This is certainly Old World not New World, but shows more overt aromatics than would be found in Bordeaux. 14.0% *90* Drink to 2021.

Bolgheri and the Coast

Vintages are much influenced by local conditions here. Producers say that although 2011 was a cool year in Europe generally, it was a good vintage in Bolgheri, in fact one of the earliest on record. More rainfall than usual in the summer avoided hydric stress in 2010, giving well balanced wines. The 2009 and 2008 vintages illustrate the extremes of the past decade (except perhaps for the atypical conditions of 2003): 2009 was a warm, generous year, while 2008 was a cool year giving acidity and herbal notes. They were preceded by the classic warm year of 2007, generally giving well rounded wines that rarely disappoint. Before that 2006 was more restrained, and 2005 was generally considered difficult, even a bit clumsy in some cases. The 2004 season started and ended late, giving good quality ("textbook perfect" say some producers). Here as everywhere else 2003 was the year of the heat wave; and 2002 was generally disappointing due to problems with rain. Best recent vintages are 2007 and 2004.

Batzella

Batzella is a boutique operation. I'm not sure if it is the smallest producer in Bolgheri, but it must be one of the smallest. Khanh Nguyen and Franco Batzella worked at the World Bank until they decided to retire early and do something different. Initially they decided to start in Montalcino. "Since no one knew us and we were starting without any reputation, we thought we should start somewhere that had a reputation," says Khanh, who makes the wines. They bought and planted an estate in Montalcino, and started selling the grapes, but then 8 ha became available in Bolgheri, and they decided this was more attractive because of the way the region was expanding. They have 1 ha of Cabernet Franc, 1 ha Syrah, 1 ha white varieties, and 5 ha Cabernet Sauvignon, planted with 6 different clones. The first year of production was 2003. There are three levels of wine: a Bolgheri Superiore, a Bolgheri, and an entry-level wine. Yields are slightly lower for Tâm, a blend of 60% Cabernet Sauvignon with 40% Cabernet Franc, which is the top of the line Bolgheri Superiore and spends two years in barriques, than for the Bolgheri DOC Peàn, which has 70% Cabernet Sauvignon and 30% Cabernet Franc, and spends one year in barriques. This is really an artisan operation, in semi-permanent surroundings because of problems obtaining a construction permit, which has finally come through. "It proves you don't need a cathedral to make good wine," says Franco. Wines were tasted at Batzella in April 2012.

Bolgheri, Peàn, 2008
The nose suggests light but slightly stern fruits. There's a nice but light balance of fruits to chocolaty tannins on a furry finish. Just released, this could benefit from another year, but doesn't convey a great sense of typicity. 14% *87* Drink to 2017.

Bolgheri Superiore, Tâm, 2008
Restrained nose gives a sense of freshness. This is still rather young but gives its usual impression of taut black fruits, with tight tannins in support. The direction is for precision rather than power, and you can certainly see the dominant influence of Cabernet Sauvignon. There should be sufficient structure to hold until this softens, but I wouldn't mind a touch more generosity on the palate. 14.0% *88* Drink 2013-2019.

Bolgheri Superiore, Tâm, 2007
Restrained nose offers the usual taut black fruit impression, but more rounded than 2006; as always, the fruits are more generous in the 2007 vintage. Here they tend towards blackberries. Tannins are still fairly tight, making the underlying structure quite evident, with an overall impression of elegance rather than power. The sense is that the wine is about to emerge from its shell. 14.0% *89* Drink to 2019.

Bolgheri Superiore, Tâm, 2006
Just a tinge of garnet in the medium ruby color. The black fruit nose gives a stern impression of developing slowly, with just the first faint intimations of savory elements. Blackberry fruits are supported by firm tannins with a faint chocolate touch on the finish. 14.5% *89* Drink to 2018.

Ca'Marcanda

Angelo Gaja is a force of nature—and not one to do things by halves. Famous for his Barbaresco (and Barolo), where his single vineyard wines are at the top of the hierarchy, he expanded into Montalcino by acquiring the Pieve Santa Restituta vineyards in 1994. Having decided he wanted also to make wine in Bolgheri, he conducted a long and patient search until he identified the best terroirs, followed by a lengthy wooing process until he was able to purchase the vineyards in 1996. There were some small plots of Vermentino and Sangiovese, but most of the land was given over to other crops or was unplanted. "We started planting the vineyards in 1997, every year we planted 7-8 ha, two years ago we reached 100 ha," says Angelo. "We plan a maximum of 120 ha," he says," explaining that this is more or less the limit he sees for artisan production. A striking new winery has been built, largely underground. There are three wines. Promis is a blend of Merlot and Syrah, with a little Sangiovese; Magari is half Merlot with a quarter each of Cabernet Sauvignon and Cabernet Franc; and Camarcanda is half Merlot with 40% Cabernet Sauvignon and 10% Cabernet Franc. Production is around 25,000 cases of Promis, 8,000 of Magari, and 2,500 of Camarcanda. Wines were tasted at Ca'Marcanda in April 2012.

Bolgheri, Camarcanda, 2009
Some complexity is just beginning to emerge on the nose in the form of nuts, cereal, and savory elements. There's an elegant balance with mid weight fruits, quite tightly circumscribed; you could believe there was more than 40% Cabernet Sauvignon. The flavor profile has not really started to develop yet, but the structure is evident underneath the fruits, and promises a good future, although there is still that touch of heat on the finish. *89* Drink 2013-2021.

Bolgheri, Camarcanda, 2007
There's an immediate impression of development with savory notes conveying a faint sense of barnyard and gunflint. This has already reached a lovely point of balance, almost at the tipping point from fruity to savory, with red and black fruits mingling with those savory sensations, and an elegant texture reflecting fine-grained tannins. "I have the impression that this is the most elegant, it is perhaps the character of the vintage," says Angelo Gaja. 14.5% *92* Drink to 2020.

Bolgheri, Camarcanda, 2005
There's less obvious sense of development than in the 2007 and a slightly coarser texture. It's less well integrated, alternating between fugitive herbaceous impressions of Cabernet Sauvignon and jammy fruits of Merlot: you get a sense this wine is having a hard time deciding which way it wants to go. There's some variation in the extent of savory development between bottles; without savory development the fruits seem somewhat monolithic, but when it has started, there is more sensation of flavor variety to relieve the massive quality of the wine. The richness and alcohol identify with the super-Tuscan style but there is also a countering freshness. The wine seems to retreat into itself in the glass as the interplay between faint herbaceous notes and fruitiness changes continuously. This is a good result for a year that was considered difficult, and there's plenty of fruit concentration. This seems to be a case of retarded development, showing as a little hard on the finish at the moment. 14.5% *88* Drink to 2019.

Bolgheri, Magari, 2008
Faint impression of gunflint on the nose. Refined palate is just about to open out, but at present

the fruits are tight, supported by fresh acidity, and showing a refined texture. The blend shows more the purity and tightness of the Cabernet than the roundness of the Merlot; it is pure and elegant but not as concentrated as the Camarcanda. Interestingly the alcohol is less evident than in Camarcanda. 14.5% *89* Drink to 2018.

Bolgheri, Magari 2001
Quite a developed initial impression, savory verging on barnyard. Then showing some generosity as the fruits open out, more red than black, with savory overtones. Perhaps the fruits are beginning to lighten up a bit. There's a touch of gunflint on the finish. 14.0% *89* Drink to 2015.

Guado al Tasso

Guado al Tasso is part of Antinori's Florentine Empire, which has estates all over Tuscany and Umbria. In addition to several estates in Chianti, there are estates in Montalcino and Orvieto. Antinori's most important super-Tuscans are Tignanello (Sangiovese based but historically the first wine to blend in Cabernet Sauvignon), Solaia (Cabernet based, coming from the Tignanello estate in Chianti), and Guado al Tasso (the super-Tuscan from Bolgheri). The home vineyard at Guado al Tasso extends from the hills at the eastern boundary almost to the sea, and there are further vineyards at the northern and southern edges of Bolgheri. The total vineyard area of 300 ha is planted to 100 ha Cabernet Sauvignon, 40 ha Merlot, 50 ha Syrah, 20 ha Cabernet Franc, 5 ha Petit Verdot, and 40 ha Vermentino (close to the sea). Some of the production is transferred to make the Villa Antinori IGT Toscana. There are also 200 ha of cereal (some of this is used to feed their pigs) and 1,000 olive trees. The eponymous Guado al Tasso and a second wine, Il Brucciato, use different dedicated vineyard plots, with 80 ha presently used for Brucciato and 60 ha for Al Tasso. Guado al Tasso is usually about 60% Cabernet Sauvignon, 20-30% Merlot, 10-15% Cabernet Franc, and 1-2% Petit Verdot. Il Brucciato has about 40% Cabernet Sauvignon, with Merlot and Syrah. Guado al Tasso is harvested at yields of 20-25 hl/ha, lower than Il Brucciato, which is about 40-45 hl/ha. There's a small amount of declassification from Guado al Tasso to Il Brucciato, usually less than 5%. Production is about 8,000 cases of Guado al Tasso and 25,000 cases of Il Brucciato. Wines were tasted at Guado al Tasso in April 2012.

Bolgheri, Il Brucciato, 2010
Attractive savory first impression is almost salty. Smooth expression of black fruits on the palate, quite soft, warm, and almost nutty, contrasts with the savory nose. Overall impression is just a fraction lacking in concentration, but elegant rather than chunky, making a good impression for a second wine. There's a touch of heat on the finish. 13.5% *88* Drink to 2015

Bolgheri Superiore, Guado al Tasso, 2009
(Not yet released at time of tasting.) This warm vintage gives a more overt impression of ripe fruits, and is more forward, than the preceding vintages, although it is still relatively restrained. Almost piquant blackcurrant fruits dominate the palate at first, and slowly the structure shows through as the baby fat of the fruits blows off to let a touch of tannic bitterness come through. The monolithic impression should dissipate by the time the wine is released; indeed, with time in the glass the ripeness begins to express itself. 14.5% *90* Drink 2015-2024.

Bolgheri Superiore, Guado al Tasso, 2008
This cooler vintage has brought out the Cabernet character. A savory impression at first with a touch of gunflint, turning to piquant blackcurrant fruits. Sweet and ripe on the palate, but fresh on the finish. Elegant balance with the fruits counterpoised against a smoky texture with a sense of reserve, almost a herbal touch on the finish. The only giveaway that this is a warm climate is a touch of heat on the finish. Flavor variety is just beginning to show; this still needs time. 14.0% *89* Drink 2014-2019.

Bolgheri Superiore, Guado al Tasso, 2007
This is immediately obvious as a Cabernet-based wine in classic tradition, with smoky black fruits restrained by a touch of austerity on the finish. The wine has that right bank-ish quality of Bolgheri in the blackberry fruits supported by soft tannins. Good balance on the palate hides

the alcohol; in fact, this is one of those rare wines where I would estimate the alcohol to be lower than is actually stated. The structure is deceptively hidden behind the fruits, but should support good aging at least until the end of the decade. 14.0% *91* Drink to 2020.

Bolgheri Superiore, Guado al Tasso, 2006

Expression of Cabernet in this vintage takes a more aggressive form than in 2007 or 2008, with a stern impression of tight tannins hiding the fruits. Fruits tend to tart black cherries, with something of the acid tang you usually associate more with super-Tuscans from the Chianti region. An impression of minerality is reinforced by a whiff of gunflint. The overall impression is that the wine simply is not ready yet; it's quite closed now, but when the structure resolves, it should give a fine impression of precisely delineated black fruits. 14.5% *89* Drink 2013-2019.

Bolgheri Superiore, Guado al Tasso, 2004

Still a dark color with only a trace of garnet. Very much an old world impression with faintly animal hints offsetting deep black fruits on the nose, following through to a subtle leathery overlay for the fruits of blackberries and blackcurrants on the palate. This has reached a beautiful point of balance, where the restraint of the Cabernet Sauvignon is the dominant influence, with firm tannins lending supple support, and the overall impression becoming savory. The wine will now soften and gain elegance and become more savory over the next few years. 14.0% (May 2012) *92* Drink to 2022.

Bolgheri Superiore, Guado al Tasso, 2003

This is a wine that shows very well on initial tasting, but does not hold up quite so well during the reality check of a whole bottle with a meal. Initially it seems a very good result for this hot year, in which freshness has been well retained. The immediate impression is of typical notes of Cabernet Sauvignon, slightly cedary or even smoky, giving way to the typical soft plushness of Bolgheri. Slowly the impression in the glass becomes a little thicker; this is the heat of the vintage making its presence felt. The deep black fruits are weighty but not especially aromatic Although there is a faintly savory edge, it is less noticeable than in other vintages. This remains an excellent result for the year, but overall less elegant than usual. 14.0% (August 2012) *88* Drink to 2018.

Bolgheri Superiore, Guado al Tasso, 1990

This first vintage of Guado al Tasso is still going strong. First impressions show more red fruit than black, with a touch of cedar and smoke, and a slowly developing savory or almost leafy element. A Graves-like impression strengthens in the glass with the palate displaying a distinct dryness on the finish. High acidity keeps the wine fresh, with the style tending more to elegance than power; certainly this is not the style of modern Bolgheri. The fruits become sweeter and riper as the wine develops in the glass, filling in more with an impression of black fruits, with some hints of the classic blackcurrants, and that initial savory impression disappearing. This is not a top vintage for Guado al Tasso, because development seems a bit restricted, but there is still life left in the wine, as indicated by the evolution to a more complete flavor spectrum in the glass. 12.5% (September 2012) *90* Drink to 2022.

Michele Satta

One of the pioneers in Bolgheri, Michele Satta started in 1982 with only 4 ha, "but it wasn't a project, he moved slowly into wine production," says Fabio Motta, his son-in-law, an oenologue who is presently in charge of marketing. Today the home vineyard occupies 25 ha at the southern limit of the Bolgheri region. Its gradual development has been responsible for the higgledy piggledy organization of many varieties across the vineyards. Standing at one spot in the vineyard, I could see Cabernet Sauvignon, Merlot, Syrah, Teroldego, Vermentino, and Viognier. Overall, plantings are 30% Cabernet Sauvignon, 30% Merlot, 20% Sangiovese, 10% Syrah, 10% Teroldego, but I Castagni focuses on 70% Cabernet Sauvignon, 20% Syrah, and 10% Teroldego. "I Castagni started with only Cabernet Sauvignon and Merlot. After Michele decided to make a single vineyard wine, he decided to add Syrah and Teroldego. Originally when Michele planted the vineyard he felt he must plant Cabernet Sauvignon because the area is in Bolgheri, but he also wanted to plant his favorite grapes, Syrah and Teroldego. Teroldego has rich color and lots of tannins, but is very soft. This was planted rather than Merlot because ripening is very slow. Probably the Syrah will increase in future," says Fabio. Michele has been an enthusiast for Syrah ever since visiting the northern Rhône, and he introduced a varietal Syrah with the 2007 vintage. There's a small winery on the edge of the home vineyard. It's quite unassuming, with plans to build a second storey with a tasting room, but in true Alice in Wonderland fashion, this has been stuck in the bureaucracy because of fears that carbon dioxide (notably heavier than air) might rise up and kill the patrons. In the meantime, Michele continues to make wine in a traditional manner; no modern gimmicks here. Wines were tasted at Michele Satta in April 2012.

Bolgheri Superiore, I Castagni, 2005
The first impression shows a mix of savory and cereal notes with suggestions of minerality. This is a leaner wine than the 2004 (not surprising considering the characters of the vintages), with the Cabernet Sauvignon showing more clearly here with a certain spartan structure. Curiously a touch of blackcurrants is more evident than in the riper 2004. This is soft in the glass but retains an impression of minerality. 13.5% *88* Drink to 2019.

Bolgheri Superiore, I Castagni, 2004
A savory edge to the first impression, then showing as sweet and rounded on the palate, but with good freshness from uplifting acidity. There's a definite sense of underlying structure, with tannins showing as dryness on the finish, with a touch of heat, but Bolgheri's typical softness comes through. Good balance is aided by moderate acidity. This is not yet really ready, having barely started its development, but it gives a more complete impression than the 2005. 13.5% *90* Drink to 2022.

Bolgheri Superiore, I Castagni, 2003
With more than 30 days at temperatures over 40 °C in this very hot year, Satta did a very hard green harvest to leave only one cluster per branch in order to preserve the fruit. Even so, there's a more obviously fruit-driven impression in this year than usual, leading into a touch of piquant blackcurrants. The heat has translated into increased softness rather than power, with less acidity and freshness than 2004 or 2005, giving a furry finish. So far it's holding up very well. 13.5% *88* Drink to 2017.

Bolgheri, Il Piastraia, 2008
This blend of one quarter each of Cabernet Sauvignon, Merlot, Syrah, and Sangiovese was Satta's first Bolgheri DOC. The initial impression is quite complex, with an almost piquant sensation edging towards savory and herbal notes of sage. The palate doesn't quite fulfill the promise of the nose, perhaps it hasn't really started to develop yet, but it's soft and supple with a furry finish that more reflects the Merlot and Syrah, whereas Sangiovese is more evident on the nose. Slowly some of the animal notes of Sangiovese come through to the palate. The structure is hidden behind the fruits, but this is ready now. 13.1% *87* Drink to 2017.

Ornellaia

Close to the Sassicaia estate, Ornellaia became one of the great names in Bolgheri almost immediately after it was established in 1981 and produced its first vintage in 1985. It was created by Marchese Lodovico Antinori, younger brother of Marchese Piero Antinori of the wine producer Marchese Antinori. The Mondavi winery of California took a minority interest in the estate in 1999, acquired the entire estate in 2002 in partnership with the Frescobaldi family; and then Frescobaldi purchased the estate outright in 2005 after Constellation Brands took over Mondavi. Ornellaia has two separate vineyards: the home estate around the winery; and the Bellaria vineyard just a little to the south (planted between 1992 and 2005). Today four wines are produced. The top two are Ornellaia itself, and the 100% Merlot produced from the Masseto hill. A second wine, La Serre Nuove, was introduced in 1997, and is made by declassifying lots from Ornellaia. Le Volte is more a separate blend (including some Sangiovese) than a third wine, since it includes purchased grapes. Ornellaia's varietal composition has changed somewhat over the years The original intention of a blend of Cabernet Sauvignon with Merlot was somewhat sidetracked when the Merlot from the Masseto hill was diverted into a separate cuvée. Merlot increased in the blend after the vineyards at Bellaria (a slightly cooler site exposed more to the sea) was acquired. Having peaked at almost a third of the blend, now it is back down to around a quarter. Cabernet Sauvignon was around 80% for the first decade, then dropped abruptly to 65% with the 1997 vintage, but for the past few years has been only just above half; it's dropped a little recently as the result of a replanting program. Perhaps reflecting the warmer climate, Cabernet Franc has been increasing (5% in the first vintages, 15-20% in recent years) and Petit Verdot has been included since 2003. The grapes for Ornellaia come roughly half from the home vineyard and half from Bellaria. Ornellaia's level of production has been fairly steady, something over 8,000 cases, although production of La Serre Nuove has increased from 2,500 to 12,500 cases since its inception. Wines were tasted at Ornellaia in April 2012.

Bolgheri Superiore, Ornellaia 2010
(Barrel sample of the final assemblage.) A soft, almost chocolaty impression follows from nose through palate, with the soft black fruits leading into a furry finish. A sense of spice develops. If you wanted to compare with Bordeaux, the softness would push you to the right bank rather than the left, but the strength of the underlying structure becomes evident on the finish. There's somewhat of an impression of the tobacco notes of Cabernet Franc (although there's only 20% in this vintage). But that superficial impression of soft generosity is misleading insofar as this really needs time. *91* Drink 2016-2026.

Cabernet Sauvignon, Bellaria Vineyard, 2011
(Barrel sample.) There's a ripe black fruit impression with spicy overtones showing a touch of cinnamon and nutmeg, complete on the palate with furry, chocolaty tannins. Fruits are very precise and black; there's no mistaking the sheer quality, but it's restrained and fresh. The ripe, fine-grained tannins are subsumed by the fruits but dry the finish. You can see that in a cooler year, that restrained purity might become leaner or austere. The precise yet rounded fruits make you wonder what this would be like if it was bottled as a monovarietal Cabernet.

Cabernet Sauvignon, Ornellaia Vineyard, 2011
(Barrel sample.) Contrary to expectation, given that this site is warmer than Bellaria, the nose seems more reserved and almost stern. But the fruits are rounder and sweeter on the palate, more brooding, with less purity of expression. The tannins not so refined: somewhat stronger, they are really drying on the finish. This is a more forceful wine, more opulent, but also less approachable at this point, massive rather than precise. Overall, this is more the character of Ornellaia than the lot from Bellaria.

Sassicaia (Tenuta San Guido)

Sassicaia stands alone. It's the only wine in Italy to have its own DOC. "Sassicaia was Vino da Tavola until 1994 when we got the DOC. Until that time the proportion of Cabernet Sauvignon and Cabernet Franc was 85:15, so when we had to decide regulations for the DOC we decided 80% should be Cabernet Sauvignon and the rest could be anything," says the Marquis Incisa. It is no longer the most expensive super-Tuscan, perhaps because it has not moved very far in the direction of power and extraction, but has remained true to its original objective of an elegant wine in the tradition of Bordeaux's left bank, although necessarily more Mediterranean than Atlantic in style. Reflecting on changes over time, the Marquis Incisa says, "There is a little difference (in alcohol levels). Twenty years ago it was difficult to get 12%, today we try keep it as low as possible. People say we are picking the grapes too early. People have been reducing yields because they thought it makes higher quality, but this then makes the wine unbalanced. Sassicaia started at 60 hl/ha, when everything else was generally around 100 hl/ha Some people went down to 30 hl/ha but this makes it very difficult to contain the alcohol." The main change has been the move to introduce a second wine. "Until 2000 we made only one wine. We were using 98-100% of our grapes. Since 2000 we have made another wine, and we select... The reason we started making Guidalberto was that we didn't want to increase the production of Sassicaia. The wines with the highest ratings in American journals were all based on Merlot so we thought we must make a wine with Merlot to follow the trend." Guidalberto is 60% Cabernet Sauvignon to 40% Merlot. Wines were tasted at Tenuta San Guido in April 2012.

IGT Toscana, Guidalberto, 2010
The initial impression shows restrained fruits, then a smooth palate, generally following the elegant style of Sassicaia itself but without much overt structure. Nicely made for immediate drinking but without falling over the edge into overly fruity. 13.5% *87* Drink to 2016.

Bolgheri Sassicaia, 2009
The first impression is the softness and suppleness of the palate. Overall this is elegant and smooth, and the underlying structure is skillfully hidden. Aromatics are restrained but there is an impression of layers of softness with very fine-grained tannins at the end, quite surprising given that the varieties are exclusively Cabernet Sauvignon and Cabernet Franc. This is already ready to start. If you wanted to compare with Bordeaux you would think about a top wine from Pessac. 14.0% *92* Drink to 2022.

Bolgheri Sassicaia, 2004
This has been a splendid vintage for Sassicaia from the off, although development of the wine has been quite deceptive. When first tasted not long after its release, it seemed almost Burgundian, with an unusually aromatic fruit spectrum extending to strawberries. Most recently it seemed to be the most Bordelais vintage of Sassicaia I have ever had—not so much in a left bank flavor spectrum as this vintage presently shows Cabernet Franc more obviously than Cabernet Sauvignon—but in its character and sheer refinement. It carries its high alcohol imperceptibly, with good acidity and very fine-grained tannins showcasing the precisely delineated black fruits. Although the tannins seemed almost resolved immediately after the vintage, I think this was a deception practiced by the density of fruits; today there is a sense of a very fine structure underneath the taut, elegant, fruits, and I therefore expect more longevity than might at first sight have seemed evident. The wine now gives the impression of being at its peak at least for the current phase of development; perhaps its very faint savory impression will become more overt in a few years, even turning to delicious sous bois at the end of the decade. 13.5% *93* Drink to 2020.

Bolgheri Sassicaia, 1977
Medium garnet color has browning appearance. Developed nose is very tertiary, suggesting that the palate may have decayed, but actually the wine starts out quite lively, albeit with obviously mature fruits, but an initial slight touch of raisins does in fact begin to decay in the glass, and soon the wine seems too old. You can still see the ripeness of the original fruits, it's interesting to taste, but it is well past its peak.

Montepeloso (Suvereto)

Fabio Chiarelotto started with 9 ha on the Montepeloso hill and then added another 5 ha on the facing Fontanella hill. He makes four wines: the Gabbro Cabernet Sauvignon, Nardo, which is mostly Sangiovese, the Eneo Sangiovese-based blend, and the entry-level A Quo. The blends in Nardo and Eneo have been moving towards the Italian project, to blend Montepulciano, Sangiovese, Alicante, and Marselan (a cross of Cabernet Sauvignon with Grenache). Gabbro, the top wine, spends 18 months in oak (85-90% new). The wine started out with Cabernet Sauvignon from the Montepeloso hill, but as the new plantings at the Fontanella vineyard have come on line, they have formed an increasing proportion of the blend. (Montepeloso was originally planted with Cabernet Sauvignon and Sangiovese at low density in the early eighties. The replanting since 1998 has used higher densities.) Whether it's because of the difference in exposure (southwest at Montepeloso as opposed to west at Fontanella) or the age of the vines (old at Montepeloso but only a few years old at Fontanella), barrel samples show a much richer wine from Montepeloso, but perhaps the blend is more complex. Fabio is considering an old vines selection from Montepeloso (but the issue of course is the effect of taking this out of the Gabbro.) Production of Gabbro has made its way up from a mere couple of hundred cases to about 400 cases today, almost all exported. Wines were tasted at Montepeloso in April 2012.

IGT Toscana, Gabbro, 2010
(Barrel sample.) Here a primal quality, almost animal, is showing (just before bottling). This vintage is certainly more Bordeaux-like and less Mediterranean-like, with a touch of leather lending character. "The wines were vinified in the same way, but 2008 seems modern and 2010 seems more backward," says Fabio. The palate is smooth but shows that characteristic sense of precision, with some blackberries and suspicions of blackcurrants slowly coming out in the glass. Very tight and reserved now, with tannins puckering the finish, so closed that it's hard to assess, but it seems likely that within a couple of years it will begin to release precise, pure, fruits against a mineral background. *92* Drink 2016-2030.

IGT Toscana, Gabbro, 2009
Hints of graphite give the nose a mineral aspect, with stern black fruits in the background, followed by a faint herbal impression. The fruits seem rounder than 2008, with a softer finish giving tobacco-like impressions on top of an underlying structure of precise tannins. The characteristic impression of precision is countered only by a touch of heat on the finish. The superficial softness at the outset is deceptive, as the graphite minerality becomes more evident on the finish and the wine becomes tauter than the 2008. Overall, this seems just a touch more refined, but it's a fine line and could reflect the stage of development. *93* Drink 2015-2028.

IGT Toscana, Gabbro, 2008
This vintage is a half and half blend from the forty year old vines in the original Montepeloso vineyard and the newer six year old plantings at the Fontanella vineyard. Initially a restrained impression with just a suggestion of spices and brooding black fruits. Intense, rich, and ripe, every drop a pure Cabernet, but just look at the sheer density. It's unready now, although it has such fruit density that some people will feel it's appropriate to drink. Tannins are almost subsumed by the ripe fruits, with just a faint mineral edge and balsamic touch to cut the fruits. At first you are blown away by the palate, then you see the structure revealed as a mineral, graphite, stony edge on the aftertaste, where there is a touch of heat. It's still holding back, although a nutty element develops on the finish in the glass. 15.0% *92* Drink 2015-2028.

IGT Toscana, Gabbro, 2001
My goodness, what a mouthful of flavor! First impressions identify deep black fruits tending to cherries with some aromatic hints of piquant blackcurrants. The rich and full palate retains enough freshness to avoid jammy overtones. The richness, together with some heat on the finish, conveys an immediate sense of high alcohol. So ripe that it gives almost an impression of sweetness on the finish. The palate seems hardly any less intense than the current vintage. With slightly calmer aromatics, this would be a better match with food. I imagine most tasters would place this blind in the New World, perhaps hesitating between Napa and Barossa. Fantastic if you like unthrottled Cabernet; more difficult if you prefer to wait for savory development. (May 2012) 14.5% *92* Drink to 2027.

Montepeloso, 2011, old vines barrel sample
The ripeness of the fruits comes right up at you with rich, dense, chocolaty aromatics. The sheer intensity on the palate is overwhelming, yet there is good acidity. The profound density of the old vines is evident, with a rich finish of tobacco. You certainly get the impression this might make a complete wine.

Fontanella 2011, barrel sample
Sterner on the nose, tighter, more suggestive of the austerity of Cabernet Sauvignon. Ripe and round with a touch of blackcurrant aromatics. Not so well integrated as the Montepeloso. You might not bottle this by itself, but it brings evident freshness and structure to the blend.

Brancaia (Maremma)

Brancaia is an unusual operation spanning Chianti to Maremma under one label. It started when Barbara Widmer's parents visited the Chianti region on holiday from Switzerland. They bought the Brancaia estate in 1980, and started to replant its 7 ha of vineyards. A couple of years later they bought the estate that is now their headquarters, at Poppi, and the grapes from the Brancaia and Poppi estates go into the same wine. Today there are 25 ha altogether in the Chianti region and since 1998 they have had an estate in Maremma with 48 ha. Vineyards are not dedicated to any particular wine; lots are assigned to wines depending on quality. The entry-level wine, Tre, is a blend from Maremma and the Chianti region, Il Blu is a Merlot-Sangiovese blend from the Chianti region, and Illatria comes from Maremma. Illatria's first vintage was 2002, with a blend of 60% Cabernet Sauvignon, 30% Sangiovese, and 10% Petit Verdot. The blend changed dramatically in 2009 to 40% Cabernet Sauvignon, 40% Petit Verdot, and 20% Cabernet Franc. Production is 30,000 cases of Tre, 5-6,000 of Chianti Classico, 4,000 of Il Blu and 3-4,000 of Illatria. Wines were tasted at Brancaia in April 2012.

IGT Toscana, Illatria, 2010
(Barrel sample.) Very stern nose dominated by wood spices. Black fruits come out on the palate, showing more as cherries than plums, quite spicy as you might expect from the high proportion of Petit Verdot. In fact, Petit Verdot seems almost to be dominating the wine at this point. Tannins are firm and powerful, some years will be needed to let them resolve. Certainly this will calm down and show its fruits more clearly as the tannins resolve, but will the massive structure allow flavor variety to develop? 14.5% *89* Drink 2017-2025.

IGT Toscana, Illatria, 2009
Perhaps partly because of its youth, but more due to the replacement of Sangiovese by Petit Verdot, the first impression is much sterner than the 2008, with underlying black fruits somewhat hidden. Full, rich, and ripe, the fruits of black cherries, plums, blackcurrants, are presently subservient to the firm tannins, although there is a touch of softening glycerin on the finish: the Cabernet Sauvignon and Petit Verdot have created an intense structure. It will take a few years for the tannins to resolve, and the question is whether and when flavor variety will develop. This new blend gives a wine that is perhaps more typical of Maremma than the old blend of 2008; is it a wine for New World devotées? 14.5% *89* Drink 2015-2024.

IGT Toscana, Illatria, 2008
This last year of the old blend gave a lighter wine than you usually find in Maremma. There's an impression of warm black fruits with hints of spices. Smooth and opulent on the palate, soft on the finish, definitely a warm climate impression with a touch of heat on the finish. This certainly feels like a Cabernet-driven wine; the Sangiovese is not really evident unless by implication, because of the lighter overall impression. Although the tannic structure can be seen on the finish, and should support maturation for several years, evolution away from the youthful state hasn't really started yet. 14.0% *89* Drink to 2019.

Cabernet Sauvignon 2010
(Barrel sample blend for Illatria.) The initial impression is not nearly so massive as the final wine. This is quite elegant and smooth, somewhat denying the reputation of Maremma for massive, jammy, wine; black fruits are well rounded and balanced between power and elegance, with an impression of precision. In fact, I like it somewhat better than the blend.

Super-Tuscans in Chianti

So far as Cabernet Sauvignon is concerned, it's somewhat a matter of odd years versus even years in the Chianti region. The 2009 and 2007 vintages tended to freshness (but with good ripeness in 2007), and 2005 had problems with rain and tended to give lighter wines; the 2010, 2008, 2006, and 2004 vintages tended to roundness. Before that 2003 was too hot (as everywhere in Europe) and 2002 had problems with ripeness. Cabernet Sauvignon ripens after Sangiovese, so conditions at the very end of the season are more important, but generally a good year for Chianti will be a good year for its super-Tuscans also. Looking at the best years in recent vintages, 2006 was better in the Chianti region than 2007 (which was the best vintage elsewhere in Tuscany), and 2004 was very good.

Tenuta Nozzole

Nozzole has a slightly chequered history. Located in the southern part of the Chianti area, there have been vineyards here for several hundred years. The Folonaris, who moved into Chianti to make a transition to quality wine at the start of the twentieth century, purchased the estate in 1971. (They owned Ruffino, and introduced the famous Chianti straw flasks). In 2000, the company was divided, and Ambrogio Folonari and his son Giovanni kept Nozzole and Cabreo, which is farther north, near Greve in Chianti. They also started Campo al Mare in Bolgheri, as well as wineries in Montalcino and Maremma. Altogether there are seven estates in their portfolio. Nozzole produces Chianti Classico, Le Bruniche Chardonnay, and the Il Pareto monovarietal Cabernet Sauvignon. From the Cabreo vineyards there are La Pietra Chardonnay and Il Borgo, a blend of 30% Cabernet Sauvignon with 70% Sangiovese. The varietal composition is more determinative of style here than the vineyard characters, since Il Pareto is sandier and lower, while Cabreo has rocky soil at higher altitude; but with 100% Cabernet, Il Pareto is a bigger wine than Cabreo. Wines were tasted at Nozzole in April 2012.

IGT Toscana, Il Pareto, 2009
A strong herbal impression with a faint touch of mint. On the palate there are smooth, precise, fruits, and those herbal touches comes back attractively on the finish. This is elegant. The herbal notes turn to perfume of violets in the glass but then come back retronasally. Fine tannins dry the finish. High alcohol is not obtrusive. 15.0% *90* Drink 2015-2025.

IGT Toscana, Il Pareto, 2008
The initial impression is savory and almost barnyard, suggesting some development already. The palate is elegant and silky, with rounded fruits. Faint savory hints provide a counterpoise to the fragrant black fruits, giving an impression of layers of flavor and variety across the palate. Youthfulness shows in a more direct impression than 2006 or 2004, but I see this as following the same general pattern of development, although more rapidly. 14.5% *89* Drink 2014-2021.

IGT Toscana, Il Pareto, 2007
Savory first impression with layers of gunflint gives way to more overt black fruits with hints of piquancy. This vintage seems a little monolithic on the palate, with black cherry fruits supported by smooth tannins and balanced acidity, but that elegant savory character does not shine through for me like it does in 2006 and 2004. Tannins are quite drying on the finish. This has more the typicity of Cabernet Sauvignon, less the typicity of Chianti, but perhaps will become less one dimensional with time. 14.5% *88* Drink 2013-2021.

IGT Toscana, Il Pareto, 2006
The initial impression is savory and mineral, smooth and silky on the palate, but not quite as round or concentrated as 2004. The first burst of black fruits turns more to red fruits in the glass and become more perfumed. Tannins still dry the finish. Overall a very fine impression. 14.5% *90* Drink to 2020.

IGT Toscana, Il Pareto, 2004
This seems to be a more restrained version of the younger vintages, especially 2006 and 2008. An initial savory impression gives way to a touch of cereal and nuts. Soft tannins enhance the smoothness of the palate and give a furry impression to the finish. The palate is supported by a touch of uplifting acidity and there is the faintest rasp of Cabernet. Very nice balance here, all coming together for a silky elegance. 14.5% *91* Drink to 2019.

IGT Toscana, Il Borgo, Tenuta del Cabreo, 2008
The savage notes of Sangiovese show at first, but then leading into smooth, black, very ripe fruits on the palate with a touch of raisins coming through. There's a fairly massive impression on the finish, which is quite opulent. Tannins dry the finish, and this really needs some time. It's a bit too forceful. 14.0% *88* Drink 2014-2021.

IGT Toscana, Il Borgo, Tenuta del Cabreo, 2006
This gives a softer, nuttier, more Cabernet-dominated impression than the 2008, with some pungent savory notes following later. Smooth on the palate, obviously ripe fruits, but a fresher impression than 2008. Firm tannins dry the finish. There's a sense that flavor variety will begin to develop in the next year or so. *89* Drink 2013-2020.

Castello di Querceto

The sixteenth century castle of Querceto dominates a small valley of 500 ha where vineyards were first planted in 1897 by Alessandro François's grandfather. Alessandro was an engineer in Milan and moved to run the vineyards in 1983. Today, Querceto has about 250 ha of vineyards, at elevations of 400-500 m; in this slightly cooler climate, harvest is generally a couple of weeks after others in the region. "We have three different areas in the valley, with very different soil types, this is why we decided to produce single vineyard wines," says Alessandro. La Corte is a single vineyard Sangiovese. "It started as an experiment. One hundred years ago my grandfather planted the first vineyard of 100% Sangiovese. This was the first single vineyard wine—our first super-Tuscan in 1904," says Alessandro. There are three other super-Tuscans. Il Querciolaia is Sangiovese-based, Cignale is a Cabernet Sauvignon with just a softening of 10% Merlot, and Il Sole di Alessandro is a monovarietal Cabernet Sauvignon. There is also, of course, a Chianti Classico. Wines were tasted at Querceto in April 2012.

IGT Toscana, Il Sole di Alessandro, 2007
There is a riper, rounder, impression from this 100% Cabernet Sauvignon than from the Cignale with its 10% Merlot. Slightly nutty, black fruit spectrum has retained good freshness. Tannins aren't immediately evident but dry the finish, showing more structure than Cignale. This is too young now, tight and closed, but has the potential to show a smooth, opulent style highlighting precision of fruits as the tannins resolve over the next few years. 13.5% *90* Drink 2016-2026.

IGT Toscana, Cignale, 2006
Although there is 10% Merlot here to cut the dominant Cabernet Sauvignon, the wine is reserved and stern; although the fruits are ripe they are holding back. Initially faintly nutty and spicy, this certainly needs two or three years to soften. It's denser and tighter than Querciolaia, but not as packed as Il Sole di Alessandro. The style here definitely tends to precision and elegance, and as the wine softens in the glass it begins to seem quite left bank-ish. 13.5% *89* Drink 2015-2024.

IGT Toscana, Il Querciolaia, 2007
As you might expect from a two thirds Sangiovese to one third Cabernet Sauvignon blend, the impression lies somewhere between fruity and savory. It's fairly restrained, with the palate driven by black fruits taking the form of black cherries with hints of blackberries. In spite of the moderate alcohol, there is a touch of heat on the finish. There's an impression of a strong black variety on the palate, with the Sangiovese initially receding into the background. Slowly some savory overtones show as the Sangiovese begins to emerge. This gives a much lighter impression than either of the Cabernet-dominated wines. 13.5% *88* Drink 2014-2020.

Querciabella

Querciabella started as a hobby in 1974 but rapidly became a fully professional producer. Located up a dirt track on a mountainside just outside of Greve-in-Chianti, the estate became organic in 1988, and biodynamic in 2000. There are 80 ha of vineyards, with more than 90% of the plantings being Sangiovese; there is also an estate of 35 ha in Maremma. The last few years have seen intensive modernization, with new facilities constructed to allow more precise control of production, including vinification plot by plot. The estate presently produces four wines: Chianti Classico (presently 100% Sangiovese: "In 2010 we did not feel the need to add the 5% of Cabernet to the Sangiovese for Chianti Classico"); the Batàr blend of Pinot Blanc and Chardonnay (named to indicate its intended relationship with great Burgundy); the Palafreno monovarietal Merlot (made only in the best vintages, which are not necessarily the warmest); and Camartina, a blend of 70% Cabernet Sauvignon and 30% Sangiovese. Mongrana, a blend of Sangiovese, Merlot, and Cabernet Sauvignon, comes from the estate at Maremma. There is increasing emphasis here on terroir, with plans to introduce single vineyard wines. Wines were tasted at Querciabella in April 2012.

IGT Toscana, Camartina, 2007
Restrained nose slowly releases some savory aromas showing more Sangiovese than Cabernet. Elegant on the palate in the red spectrum, with red cherries showing hints of black and a touch of earthiness. Ripe fruits are balanced by a definite savory component with good freshness (more evident than in the 2004): this is the Chianti expression of Cabernet typicity. Altogether a much lighter impression than the high alcohol would suggest, although there is some heat on the finish; the superficial lightness (unusual for Camartina) may be deceptive as the tannins are quite taut and should have the structure for longevity. The overall impression is quite polished and my sense is that this will develop along similar lines to the 1999, although perhaps a little faster. 14.0% *91* Drink to 2022.

IGT Toscana, Camartina, 2004
More weight than 2007 with black fruits rather than red, turning to a slightly nutty, cereal-like impression. The palate remains elegant rather than powerful, with an impression of precision, and once again the tannic structure is deceptively hidden. The Cabernet is more in evidence in this vintage and there is a faint chocolaty hint to the finish. This rich, round, vintage is only just about to start development. More the archetypical Camartina, this is firmer but less refined than 2007, with the tannins coming out on the finish, and the structure suggesting that development will be slow. 14.0% *90* Drink to 2022.

IGT Toscana, Camartina, 1999
Complex nose of spices and herbs gives an impression of the start of development. The palate is at a perfect point of balance: developing red fruits show a barely perceptible touch of sous bois with hints of gunflint developing in the glass—not quite at the tipping point but getting there. The palate turns to mineral red fruits, poised with savory flavors. This is the peak moment. But although tannins are obviously resolving, there's enough structure to support development for a few years yet. 13.5% *92* Drink to 2018.

Rocca di Castagnoli

Located in a medieval village near Gaiole-in-Chianti, in the southern part of the Chianti region, Rocca di Castagnoli occupies vineyards that have been cultivated since the Middle Ages. The estate consists of 850 ha, with 72 ha planted to vineyards. The present ownership dates from 1981. The Chianti Classico has a traditional constitution: 90% Sangiovese with 5% each of Colorino and Canaiolo. There is a varietal Merlot (Le Pratola) and a Chardonnay (Molino delle Balze). Stielle was a Sangiovese-Cabernet blend from its inception in 1985, but switched to 100% Sangiovese in 2007. This released the grapes from 2 ha of Cabernet Sauvignon to be included in the Il Buriano Cabernet Sauvignon (previously it came exclusively from the 4 ha Il Buriano vineyard). Dating from 1985, Il Buriano has always been a 100% Cabernet Sauvignon representing a selection of the best grapes. Wines were tasted at Castagnoli in April 2012.

IGT Toscana, Il Buriano, 2006
Restrained black fruit impression with some stern overtones showing the structure of the Cabernet Sauvignon clearly in this monovarietal. Fruits show as cherries and plums, black and dense but with good freshness and minerality, just short of a savory tang, followed by a nice uplift of acidity on the finish. "The freshness is the characteristic of the terroir," says director Rolando Bernacchini. Tannins are firm, just showing some dryness on the finish, but the wine is about ready to start drinking. The structure should hold for some years. There's a touch of heat on the finish. This should become more refined and elegant as the tannins resolve and the fruits lighten up. 14.5% *91* Drink to 2024.

IGT Toscana, Il Buriano, 2004
Restrained impression of black fruits with the first signs of development showing as a touch of gunflint. Age or the vintage has resulted in a softer and noticeably rounder impression than the more angular 2006. Most people would regard this as ready now, but fruits are beginning to turn red in the sour cherry spectrum, and another couple of years should allow this to show its savory development more clearly. The balance is more elegant than powerful with fine tannins

in support. 14.0% *92* Drink to 2021.

IGT Toscana, Il Buriano, 1999
Some developed notes on the nose show a savory tendency. This doesn't have the freshness of the more recent vintages, but it's nicely rounded on the palate with soft red cherries, followed by a slightly glyceriny impression on the finish. The savory impressions of the nose do not show on the palate, where the fruits are more direct. Although the wine has softened with age, it still shows those refined tannins with a smooth, silky texture. This will probably now start to decline gently. 13.5% *89* Drink to 2017.

Castello dei Rampolla

This thirteenth century estate has been owned by the Di Napoli family since 1739. During the 1960s the Rampolla estate was mostly olive trees, and Alceo di Napoli sold grapes to Antinori. Today the estate, just below the town of Panzano-in-Chianti, is mostly covered in vineyards. Basically four wines are made here, two based on Sangiovese and two based on Cabernet Sauvignon The Chianti Classico includes 5% each of Cabernet Sauvignon and Merlot, and a 100% Sangiovese IGT Toscana, matured in terracotta amphorae without any sulfur was introduced in 2010. The blend for Sammarco is the opposite of the Chianti, with 80% Cabernet Sauvignon to the minority of Merlot and Sangiovese. Vigna d'Alceo is a blend of 85% Cabernet Sauvignon with 15% Petit Verdot. The two wines are somewhat representative of two styles of super-Tuscan: the first tending towards elegance and almost savory; the second showing more direct fruits and power in a more international style. Wines were tasted at Rampolla in April 2012 unless otherwise noted.

Sammarco 2007
First impression is poised between fruity and savory, with red and black fruits just pushing back the savory notes. The palate is quite deep, with suggestions of chocolate coming up on the finish of ripe, furry, tannins. There's an altogether ripe impression of round fruits, but good acidity keeps the wine refreshing. Nice balance, perhaps three years away from reaching its peak. The savory elements should strengthen over the next few years. 14.5% (May 2012) *92* Drink to 2020.

IGT Toscana, Sammarco, 2005
In this rainy vintage there was no Vigna d'Alceo, so the latter's Petit Verdot was included in the Sammarco, which has 85% Cabernet Sauvignon, and 5% each of Sangiovese, Merlot, and Petit Verdot. The savory nose has some faint overtones of spices. Perhaps it is true that the variety takes on the character of the soil, because at least in this vintage there's a resemblance to Rampolla's Sangiovese-based wines, with red fruits and savory overtones, and then the Bordeaux varieties add touches of spice and chocolate. 13.5% *88* Drink to 2015.

IGT Toscana, Sammarco 2004
First impression is surprisingly more fruit-driven than the younger vintage of 2007, but a characteristic savory element shows as the palate develops. This is a tighter, less rounded wine than the 2007, more evidently in the tradition of the Chianti region. Tannins are quite taut underneath the fruits and there's a faintly mineral suggestion to the finish. Very nicely balanced, you can see the freshness brought by the Sangiovese (indeed, you might think there was significantly more than the stated 5%). 13.5% (May 2012) *91* Drink to 2017.

IGT Toscana, Vigna d'Alceo 2004
The color is darker, the fruits are blacker, and the general impression is more fruit-driven than the Sammarco. The palate is about black fruits, spice, and chocolate, very dense and ripe, with soft, ripe tannins showing a furry edge. Turning almost nutty on the finish, its softness places this more in the tradition of the super-Tuscans from Bolgheri, but is deceptive in that there is a strong underlying structure that will allow this wine to mature for another decade. (May 2012) 14.5% *92* Drink to 2022.

IGT Toscana, Vigna d'Alceo, 2003
The black fruit nose has almost piquant overtones. Here you see the Cabernet more clearly than in the Sammarco, with overtones of spice and chocolate coming from the Petit Verdot. There's a deep impression, with this playing the heavyweight role of a super-Tuscan more ob-

viously than the lighter impression made by Sammarco. It's impressive that the wine has retained freshness in this very hot vintage. 14.5% *90* Drink to 2017.

Villa Cafaggio

Located below the town of Panzano-in-Chianti, Villa Cafaggio was a Benedictine monastery making wine in the Middle Ages. By the 1960s, when the Farkas family purchased it, the property had fallen into decay. It was restored and replanted, largely with Sangiovese, and in 1986 the first Cabernet vineyard was planted (by field grafting Cabernet over Canaiolo). The estate was purchased in 2005 by a cooperative from northern Italy (Cantina La-Vis e Valle di Cembra), but continues to function independently. Today the principal wines are the Chianti Classico and the Riserva (amounting to around 25,000 cases annually) and two IGT wines, the 100% Sangiovese, San Martino and the 100% Cabernet, Il Cortaccio (each produced at 800-1,000 cases annually). The vineyards for San Martino and Il Cortaccio are adjacent, and the wines show a surprising similarity of house style. At Villa Cafaggio they see the wines as developing in parallel, but say that the Sangiovese is a little more delicate, so may age faster if it is not a top year. Wines were tasted at Villa Cafaggio in April 2012.

IGT Toscana, Il Cortaccio, 2006
(Not yet released.) The first impression here is made by the obvious oak. Then the fruits show as blacker than 2005, cherries and blackberries, with more overt impressions of Cabernet. The tannins are ripe and not immediately evident until you sense the dryness on the finish, where oak makes its presence felt further by some bitter nuts. At the moment the structure is clearly in front of the fruits, which is perhaps why release has been delayed. But as the tannins soften, the fruits should show as precise yet rounded in an elegant style. 14.5% *91* Drink 2015-2025.

IGT Toscana, Il Cortaccio, 2005
The initially restrained, nutty notes give an impression of oak, then the palate shows an elegant expression of Cabernet, with red and black cherry fruits, smooth and opulent with a glycerinic edge to the finish that is cut by an acidic uplift. There is certainly a modern house style at Villa Cafaggio, and the biggest obvious difference from their monovarietal Sangiovese (San Martino) is the tannic structure that dries the finish, but the palate gives a surprisingly similar impression with that sense of round fruits cut by an acid edge. This vintage hasn't really started to develop flavor interest, but it should become quite refined as it evolves. 14.5% *90* Drink to 2022

Bordeaux versus Napa: Forty Year Perspective

This tasting compared Bordeaux 1970 with California Cabernet mostly from 1974, but with one or two vintage changes. Wine were tasted blind in one flight by a panel including Joel Butler MW, Bill Blatch (Bordeaux negociant), Peter Sichel (former château owner), and Josh Greene (Editor, *Wine & Spirits* magazine) in September 2012. Wines are in order of rating.

Château Pichon Lalande, Pauillac, 1970
Slightly cedary, spicy nose, a touch of Brett lending a leathery complexity. Sturdy on the palate, giving a rather St Estèphe-like impression. Classic herb-driven flavors with almost medicinal after finish. Absolutely classic traditional Bordeaux with that delicious mingling of fruits and herbaceous influences. If there was a wine in the tasting that typifies Bordeaux of the sixties and seventies, this was it. *91* Drink to 2017.

Mount Eden, Santa Cruz Cabernet Sauvignon, 1974
Spicy with faint suggestions of cereal, then warm intimations of sweet, ripe fruits suggesting California. Still lovely and ripe on the palate, the generosity of the warm fruits is evident, but there's relatively slight savory development. Alcohol is a little higher than average. Complex array of flavors on the palate, albeit a touch rustic, with a faint impression of herbaceousness coming through. Delicious balance. 13.9% *91* Drink to 2018.

Heitz Martha's Vineyard, Napa Cabernet Sauvignon, 1974
Faintly savory intimations of roasted meats, then reverting to a faint spiciness, even a hint of perfume. Sweet and ripe on the palate although there is a touch of volatile acidity. Warm impression with nice flavor variety. There's a touch of iron that resembles Pauillac. 13.0% *90* Drink to 2017.

Freemark Abbey, Bosché Vineyard Cabernet Sauvignon, Napa, 1971
Quite youthful on the nose with slightly floral perfume mixing with impressions of spices. Palate follows the nose, nice balance, elegant and floral; a touch of that sweet strawberry impression identifies the origin with California. There seems to be very little development in a savory direction, but good acidity pushes this a little towards a Bordeaux spectrum. 12.4% *90* Drink to 2018.

Château Giscours, Margaux, 1970
Fresh, intriguing nose, hints of spices, a touch of perfume, hints of fruits, quite complex. Elegant and ripe on the palate, refined red fruits, but lacking a touch in the complexity you expect at this age. Very good, but a little rustic. This fooled almost everyone into thinking it came from Napa; it's definitely much fuller than you usually find from Margaux, but that's Giscours. *89* Drink to 2017.

Mayacamas, Napa Cabernet Sauvignon, 1974
One of the legends of 1974, this wine is now perfumed and floral with suggestions of roses and violets on the nose. A lovely balance on the palate here, firm ripe fruits yet with an impression of delicacy, and just a faint herbal underlying hint. But oxidation is beginning to creep in. A touch of Brett adds complexity. 13.0% *89* Drink to 2018.

Ridge, Montebello Cabernet Sauvignon, Santa Cruz, 1974
Initially youthful impression develops savory overtones of roasted meats in the glass. If you ignore the increasing acidity on the palate, there's an impression of ripe, sweet, warm fruits from California, but developing in a savory direction, even a hint of herbaceousness (more Bordelais than most California wines in this tasting). Like Cleopatra (age shall not wither her), although I have an impression that the fruits are beginning to dry out by comparison with a bottle three years ago, which attracted a higher rating and may have been in better condition. Lovely albeit now past its peak. 12.9% *89* Drink to 2016.

Château Mouton Rothschild, Pauillac, 1970
A very faint leathery suggestion of Brett on the nose, turning a little flat, but the palate is still lively. Solid fruits, firm, but subject to attack by the acidity. This is a very solid wine, developing some flavor complexity, with a warm impression reminiscent of California (not seen on previous bottles, which were more clearly in the herbaceous spectrum). *89* Drink to 2017.

Château Brane Cantenac, Margaux, 1970
Controversial between those who loved it and those who thought it had dried out. Classic Bordeaux nose of cedar, spices, and leather, identifying some Brett (more distinct than on the Pichon Lalande). Although acidity is threatening to take over the palate, there is still complexity to the savory fruits counterpoised against the leathery overtones, still delicious. 12.0% *89* Drink to 2016.

Diamond Creek, Volcanic Hill Cabernet Sauvignon, Diamond Mountain, 1975
Amazingly dark, youthful color. Fragrant, perfumed impression on the nose, a really clean impression compared with the other wines. The only wine not to have some Brett, said Joel Butler. Ripe, sweet, warm, acidity is showing through, but nice fruits underneath, with a touch of tobacco. The initial soft warmth of the fruits identifies California, but in the glass they become more evidently taut, reflecting the mountain site. 12.0% *89* Drink to 2018.

Château Léoville Lascases, St. Julien, 1970
Restrained nose, in fact completely closed. Piercing acidity on the palate as the fruits dry out. May have been elegant, but too old now. Slowly picks up a bit in the glass to reveal some flavor complexity in a savory Bordelais style, and then (after a couple of hours!) reverts to a warmer, softer, richer impression, although the finish remains dry and a little tart. 12.0% *87* Drink up.

Château Pontet Canet, Pauillac, 1970
Herbal and savory intimations, barely perceptible hints of raisins, a little tired on the nose, faintly musty. Tight fruits on the palate, originally elegant, but the acidity is beginning to take over, disguising its origins. Elegant fruits but tiring now. *86* Drink up.

Château Grand Puy Lacoste, Pauillac, 1970
Slightly acid nose, some herbaceous intimations, but seems old. Nice fruits on the palate, elegant style, but a touch of volatile acidity. Fruits are lightening and drying out but have not become savory. *86* Drink up

Beaulieu Private Reserve, Napa Cabernet Sauvignon, 1974
You never know what you are getting with this wine, because there were two bottlings, one of which was evidently much better than the other. In this bottle, you can see the original spices and fruits, but some oxidized notes are becoming noticeable: the general warmth of the impression identifies California as the origin. Volatile acidity is taking over, turning to raisins in the glass. 13.5% *85* Drink up.

Mondavi, Napa Cabernet Sauvignon Reserve, 1974
This was a great bottle in its time, and one of the wines that put the 1974 vintage on the map, but this example did not seem to be in the best condition. Mature nose with mixture of acid, fruits that aren't quite tertiary, but giving an impression that they are drying out. Palate shows better than nose although spoiled by a musty, moldy impression. This was delicious before the spoilage took it over. Possibly corked at sub threshold. 13.0% *85* Drink up.

First Growths versus Cults: Twenty Year Perspective

This tasting compared the Bordeaux first growths (including St. Emilion as well as the left bank) with cult wines of Napa, all from 1995. The cult wines included the new wave that had been recently established, and also the longer established Ridge Montebello; there was no Heitz Martha's Vineyard in 1995 because the vineyard was being replanted. Wine were tasted blind in one flight by the same panel as the previous tasting, in September 2012, and are in order of rating.

Château Lafite Rothschild, Pauillac
This was the wine that clearly developed to show its breed over a longer period of time. It did not place top in the tasting, but afterwards there was agreement that it had advanced to first place. "I love this wine, it's really beautiful," said Josh Greene. Slightly acrid, acid initial impression ahead of the underlying red fruits, but the palate shows much better than expected, with elegant, ripe, firm black fruits. The acrid impression of the nose becomes something more akin to herbaceousness on the palate, suggesting that this will develop along the lines of classic Bordeaux to become savory in the direction of sous bois—if the fruits hold out. Concerns raised by the initial dryness of the finish were set to rest as the wine developed over several hours, becoming smooth, elegant, and the very model of a modern Pauillac. 13.0% *92* Drink to 2024.

Screaming Eagle, Oakville Cabernet Sauvignon
Although this placed well into the top five due to two first place votes, it was one of the more controversial wines. Everyone agreed it was sweet and ripe, but after that opinions differed. "It has zero complexity," said Bill Blatch. "It's yummy," said Peter Sichel. "This is the problem with California wines, they don't age," said Josh Greene, "it's a shallow wine." Closed on the nose with a faintly acid suggestion of savory red fruits, turning to more of a cereal impression. Sweet, ripe, black fruits, touches of blackberries and blackcurrants with a slightly piquant edge, almost exotic but nicely balanced in a more refined New World style, with a touch of sweetness coming back on the finish. You have to accept a richer style, but it's very well done. After a while it seemed to simplify in the glass with not quite enough acidity to counter the softness. "The price is grotesque," was the most common comment after its identify was revealed. *91* 13.1% Drink to 2022.

Harlan Estate, Napa Valley Red Wine
This was a confusing wine to me, because only a few months ago it seemed more developed, savory, and elegant (in fact, the most elegant wine of a vertical at the winery). This bottle was youthful and less complex. "A Californian l'Angélus," said Bill Blatch, "it's in my top five, although I had to change my tasting register; it's stuck and won't age." "This to me is the problem with California," said Joel Butler, "it's powerful, lacks finesse, and too much alcohol." There's a faint impression of sweet ripe red fruits, strawberries and cherries, still apparently youthful, Napa in a more elegant style. Sweeter and riper on the palate than the nose would suggest, with ripe fruits of cherries and strawberries, full of flavor. Certainly this is an overtly riper style, but it manages to retain a sense of finesse. There's a touch of heat on the finish, which still shows a touch of dryness from the tannins, rich but almost a touch herbaceous, and later a touch of tobacco. Allowing for the differing stages of development of individual bottles, a promising future. 14.5% *91* Drink to 2021.

Château Latour, Pauillac

Although it made the top five, this was one of the wines on which opinion was divided. "I lean towards California on this because of the alcohol and sweet ripe finish," said Josh Greene. "This has a great rectilinear style, it's one of my top wines," said Bill Blatch. "Good wine but shows weakness on the finish," said Joel Butler. A reserved nose with only some very faint suggestions of savory red fruits. Strong acidity all but hides the underlying red fruit. Behind the acidity is an elegant impression of slowly developing fruits, with a refined, elegant texture, becoming more elegant in the glass, but remaining tight and just a touch short. Perhaps it just needs more time. 12.5% *89* Drink to 2019.

Château Cheval Blanc, St. Emilion

Opinions differed quite a bit here. Those who identified it as one of the St. Emilions liked it better than the others. "It's Bordeaux, it has that straightness," said Bill Blatch. "Too simple," said Peter Sichel. Reserved nose with some faint notes of cereal, and some hints of underlying red fruits. Sweet, ripe, elegant, refined, almost nutty, a very fine structure retaining some dryness on the finish, a touch of tobacco suggesting Cabernet Franc. Although it started well, it seemed to simplify in the glass, and to become a little thin, but its freshness gave it the edge over Ausone. 12.8% *90* Drink to 2020.

Château Mouton Rothschild, Pauillac

This was a perfect illustration of the perils of sub threshold TCA. A slightly musty impression, almost medicinal, left people wondering if there might be a very faint touch of TCA. Perhaps fruits are a fraction suppressed on the palate, but they seem elegant, black with refined texture; good supporting acidity is perhaps a fraction obtrusive. But then the mustiness clears, it becomes tight and acid. All the same "Short and nasty," said Bill Blatch, "it's not going anywhere, there's no richness. It's not really very ripe." But after the tasting, when it had been identified, we tried a second bottle, which was quite fresh with a touch of cereal, hiding the underlying black fruits. This has a classic cedary impression on the aftertaste. Sweet, ripe on the palate, but retaining freshness and a very faint suggestion of an underlying herbaceousness that may develop more in the future. Although remaining reserved and a fraction austere, it's still not forcefully Mouton-ish—none of us would have pegged it as Mouton, but it's unmistakably a classic left bank Médoc of high caliber as opposed to the somewhat characterless quality of the first bottle. 12.5% *89* Drink to 2020.

Abreu, Madrona Ranch, Napa Cabernet Sauvignon

"California in a Bordeaux style," said Bill Blatch. Slightly acrid, slightly acid first impression, almost medicinal, obscuring the fruits, moving towards a mix of coffee and medicinal character. Sweeter, riper, more elegant on the palate than the nose would predict, some intimations of developing complexity, a very nice balance. Certainly the palate shows better than the nose. Some new oak shows on the finish, in a nice ripe balance with the fruits, but turns a little raisiny in the glass. 13.4% *89* Drink to 2020.

Château Haut Brion, Pessac-Léognan

"A little common at the start, then turns long, a big wine," said Peter Sichel. A faintly musty impression with reserved black fruits underneath. A touch of piquancy on the palate gives an exotic impression and the mustiness turns more to a faintly herbaceous almost medicinal impression of traditional Bordeaux about to develop in the direction of sous bois. Fruits turn sweet and elegant in the glass, so perhaps there is greater potential longevity than first seemed evident, although at present it seems just a bit too lean. This was not nearly as delicate and elegant as a recent tasting at the château, so perhaps is underestimating the wine. 13.0% *89* Drink to 2019.

Bryant Family, Napa Cabernet Sauvignon

"It's not my style but it's well done, and I think it will stay that way for a while," said Bill Blatch. Lots of wood still here, a very herbal impression at first, almost medicinal then turning to cedar and eucalyptus, and then the underlying piquant black fruits poke through. Sweet and ripe on the palate, dense black fruits, but balanced acidity stops this falling off the edge into jamminess. Unmistakably Californian, true, but lots of character in an overtly New World style. Spicy, cedary, finish supported by smooth tannins: at first seems impressive, but in the glass it becomes sweeter, simpler, and the spice becomes too cloying on the finish. 13.9% *89* Drink to 2020.

Château Ausone, St. Emilion

"Stylish but a little thin," said Joel Butler. A very faintly acid impression with more red fruits than black, with a very slight leathery impression suggesting a faint touch of Brett, giving over to more of a warm, nutty, impression, suggesting a fair amount of Merlot, which strengthens in the glass (threatening to unbalance the wine). Crisp acidity supports the black fruits with a dry finish. Refined tannins and texture identify Cabernet Franc. Becoming a little earthy, this seems to lose character and to simplify in the glass. With less refinement than Cheval Blanc, this has a slightly undecided sense of style, perhaps reflecting the fact that this was the start of a new era as it was Michel Rolland's first year at Ausone. 12.5% *88* Drink to 2020.

Araujo, Eisele Napa Cabernet Sauvignon
Initial black fruit impression is slightly reserved and stern, but evidently lots of dense fruits, turning in the glass to a fugitive whiff of coffee on the nose, and then back to a slightly spicy impression. Crisp, almost tart acidity, makes the first impression on the palate, with a contradictory touch of raisins showing faintly through on the finish, punched out by high alcohol, giving some heat on the finish. Tannins are now resolving, and without the structural support, this gives the impression of being a slightly over-ripe Napa that might have been over acidified. 13.5% *88* Drink to 2016.

Ridge, Montebello, Santa Cruz Mountains
"California-like power but left bank structure," said Joel Butler. Some developed notes on the nose with a mix of red and black fruits, showing as raspberries and cherries with savory intimations, turning more to cereal impressions in the glass, generally an elegant overall impression. Acidity is just a touch too high to let the fruits show through clearly and comes close to unbalancing the wine. This would be a really elegant wine if acidity were a bit lower. Seems a little over-sweet and ripe, with a hint of coconut, but the main problem remains the pressing acidity. This bottle may simply have been out of condition. 12.5% *88* Drink to 2018.

Sassicaia, Bolgheri
This was the wine that changed most dramatically in the course of the tasting. Bursting with black fruits and a touch of piquancy at the outset, this was completely different. "Is this Châteauneuf du Pâpe?" asked Bill Blatch, as much because of the texture as the flavor. Thick, ripe and rich on the palate, distinct blackcurrants, that touch of piquancy showing through. Allowing for almost twenty years of age, you wonder what it was like on first release. But it calms down a great deal in the glass, holding up well, and reaching a point at which Bill could say, "Strong middle, but alcoholic with good texture." "The mixed ripeness troubles me," said Josh Greene, "but it has complex length." As it developed, however, it seemed to lose character. 12.0% *88* Drink to 2018.

Château Margaux, Margaux
"Unripe and not enough cover," said Peter Sichel. "It's got something," said Bill Blatch. "Tell me what," said Josh Greene, "the fruits are not pleasant." Closed on the nose, very stern and reserved. In spite of that reserve, initially there seem to be lovely fruits on the palate, more red than black, with crisp acidity, but then the fruits seem to fade in the glass, with the acidity overtaking them. 12.5% *88* Drink to 2018.

Colgin, Herb Lamb Vineyard, Napa Cabernet Sauvignon
Everyone agreed this came from California, but only Joel Butler defended it. "It's the sort of wine I run away from," said Josh Greene, "it's extremely flashy, all glitzy jewelry." "Clumsy and thick, California," said Bill Blatch, "and fading." A bit too aromatic, the nose is slightly minty, verging on eucalyptus, with cedary overtones somewhat obscuring the underlying black fruits. Sweet and ripe, but with a tendency to piquancy, the palate doesn't really live up to the exotic interest of the nose. Overall the wine seems just a little over the top in terms of fruit character without however quite having the density to back it up. Retronasal impression of earthy warm strawberries backs up the exotic sensation, becoming raisiny in the glass. 13.8% *88* Drink to 2017.

Penfolds, Bin 707 Cabernet Sauvignon, South Australia, 1994
Everyone agreed that this was a standout in its total difference from all the other wines. "Interesting nose," politely said Joel Butler. "Impressive but absolutely disgusting," said Bill Blatch. "We won't talk about this," said Peter Sichel. Josh Greene defended it. "It's savory, the tannins are ripe." Spicy, almost an impression of cinnamon, with hints of black fruits and hints of piquancy, turning thicker in the glass. For me the palate seemed to have quite a nice balance of ripe, dense fruits, supported by ripe tannins, but there's a wodge of coconut coming out on the finish retronasally that unbalances the wine, and the intensity of the aromatics would make it difficult to appreciate with food. Will it calm down in the next decade? 13.5% *87* Drink to 2016.

California

Every year is certainly not a top vintage year in California. Any warming trend was reversed in 2011, with a cold year ending in rain during the late harvest in October. This created a rare situation when ripeness was problematic. In 2010, the season was cooler and later than usual; the euphemism is to say that the wines are more European in style. With the preceding vintages, 2009 was generally less intense than 2008, which was less intense than 2007, which stands out as the most recent vintage to conform to the stereotype of Napa for lush, rich, wines. The 2009-2007 vintages share a tendency to hollowness on the mid palate, especially with 100% Cabernet Sauvignons, but also even with wines that were also blended with some Merlot. Many of the wines cry out for some (or for some more) Merlot to fill out the mid palate. Often the lighter fruits of 2008 and 2009 let the tannic structure show through more clearly, making the wine a little spartan. Perceptible alcohol is rarely a problem, although the level is often higher than would leave me comfortable after splitting a bottle at dinner. Overall, if I were to choose a wine to drink from these three vintages, 2007 would almost always be my preference. The 2006 vintage was also rich, but cool, dry conditions made most wines more tannic, sometimes verging on clumsy. Going back was a run of good vintages to 2001, which is generally regarded as a classic for Cabernet Sauvignon, but some wines are drying out now. Vintages 2000-1998 are not well regarded, with 1998 standing out for cool, wet conditions, and some of the wines now on the sour side, equivalent perhaps only to 2011. The vintage that pushed the modern trend towards richness and alcohol was 1997, a very warm year, now regarded as a classic for Cabernet. In older vintages, 1985 is my favorite for capturing Napa's character before the modern move to super ripeness.

Amapola Creek

I was extremely careful not to arrive too early when I visited Richard Arrowood at his new winery, Amapola Creek, just below the Monte Rosso vineyard. During a visit to Monte Rosso earlier, the crew had mentioned that Richard was a well known gun collector, and I was anxious not to be treated as a trespasser. I arrived to be greeted by Richard with his arm in a sling; he had had an accident when requalifying for his concealed gun permit. Richard Arrowood is a legendary winemaker. He started at Chateau St. Jean, where he stayed from 1974 to 1990, when he left to run his own winery, the eponymous Arrowood, which he had started in 1986. After Arrowood was sold to Mondavi, and then changed hands multiple times following Constellation's purchase of Mondavi, Richard moved on to another winery, Amapola Creek. He had bought the site and planted a vineyard in 2000, with the intention of selling grapes, but decided when he left Arrowood to make the wine himself. With the same red volcanic soils as the Monte Rosso Vineyard, Amapola Creek is a 40 ha ranch on the western slopes of the mountain; the 8 ha of vineyards are planted with French clones of Cabernet Sauvignon and a little Petit Verdot, Syrah, and Grenache. Around 85-90% of production is red. The first Cabernet Sauvignon vintage in 2005 was 100% varietal; in 2006 and 2007, a little Petit Verdot was included. The Cabernet is a blend of four different vineyard plots. Total production so far has reached a maximum of 2,500 cases. The most promising vintage in my tasting was the 2006. Wines were tasted at Amapola Creek in February 2012.

Sonoma Valley, Cabernet Sauvignon, 2008
Black fruit nose with blueberry and blackcurrant fruits. Sweet ripe fruits on the palate, smooth and precisely delineated; high alcohol is well integrated, with a sweet ripe kick to the finish, and some chocolate overtones, although there is a touch of heat. The youngest of the flight, this is still quite tight and hard edged. As the tannins resolve, this will become looser knit and softer, and is for the medium term. 14.9% *91* 2014-2024.

Sonoma Valley, Cabernet Sauvignon, 2007
Fresh nose of restrained black fruits. Soft black fruits of blackcurrants and plums on the palate, with a touch of coffee and chocolate on the finish, more loose knit than 2008. This is the softest and most approachable of the four vintages. A ripe vintage produced a wine for mid term drinking, which can already be started. 15.0% *91* Drink to 2022.

Sonoma Valley, Cabernet Sauvignon, 2006
Fresh nose of black fruits is faintly austere. Tight, precisely delineated black fruits show on the palate, with fine-grained tannins giving a refined texture, and showing just by some dryness on the finish. Alcohol is perfectly integrated here. There's a nicely defined edge to the fruits with a filigree of tannic support. Very fine indeed, with the promise of real longevity. 14.7% *92* Drink 2014-2026.

Sonoma Valley, Cabernet Sauvignon, 2005
Black fruit nose shows blueberries and blackcurrants with mineral overtones. Fruits have lightened up just a touch, with red cherries as well as black fruits evident on the palate, and hints of chocolate and tobacco coming up on the finish. It does not now show as much concentration as the subsequent three vintages, but although it is less forceful (perhaps because the vines were younger), it is refined with an elegant balance. 15.5% *90* Drink 2013-2023.

Araujo Estate & Eisele Vineyard

Within a protected canyon east of Calistoga, the Eisele Vineyard has been owned by the Araujos since 1990. Until 1991, the grapes were sold to Joseph Phelps; since then there has only been the Araujo bottling. The vineyard was heavily virused so the Araujos started an extensive replanting program, but the virusing prevented using selection massale. However, some years earlier, Shafer's home vineyard had been planted with cuttings from Eisele, and Shafer returned the favor with cuttings that were propagated to make the "young" Eisele selection. Cuttings from Eisele were later cured of viruses, and became the "old" Eisele selection. It tends to grow in a long loose cluster with small wings. After twenty years, the original vines are now being replanted. The property has 70 ha, and 15 ha are planted out of 16 plantable hectares. Most is Cabernet Sauvignon, but there are blocks of Merlot, Petit Verdot, Cabernet Franc, Syrah, Sauvignon Blanc, and Viognier. The estate is run on biodynamic principles, including respecting phases of the moon, and there are cows and chickens on the hill behind the vineyards; olive oil and honey are produced in addition to wine. The Eisele Vineyard bottling is a blend heavily dominated by Cabernet Sauvignon, but since 1999 there has been a second wine, Altagracia, also based on a Bordeaux blend, but which fluctuates more widely in varietal composition, from 58% to 100% Cabernet Sauvignon. As true with second wines elsewhere, some blocks usually go into Eisele or into Altagracia, but "You can never tell," says winemaker Nigel Kinsman, "in the unusually wet vintage of 2011, some blocks that usually under perform gave the best results." Vinification is conventional, with relatively extended maceration times, about 35-50 days maceration in total. "I believe in getting everything from the skins that they have to offer," says Nigel. Michel Rolland is consulting winemaker and visits regularly to advise on blending. Wines were tasted at Araujo in December 2011.

Napa Valley, Altagracia, Araujo, 2008
Slightly spicier and more forthcoming on the nose than Eisele. Less concentration and structure makes the wine softer and more immediately approachable. The intensely chocolaty finish probably reflects the high (20%) proportion of Petit Verdot. 14.8% *89* Drink to 2021.

Napa Valley, Eisele Vineyard Cabernet Sauvignon, 2008
Faintly spicy and cedary black fruit nose with hints of perfume. Smooth, velvety textured palate shows black fruits of plums and cherries with balanced acidity. Chocolaty tannins on a furry finish are subsumed by the ripe fruits. 14.8% *92* Drink to 2026.

Napa Valley, Eisele Vineyard Cabernet Sauvignon, 2007
Menthol and eucalyptus on the nose; chocolate coating on palate. Retronasal coconut and vanillin imply lots of new oak. Dense black fruits subsume the tannins that dry the finish. Classic Napa spectrum. Really needs some time. 14.8% *90* Drink 2014-2020.

Napa Valley, Eisele Vineyard Cabernet Sauvignon, 2005
The nose gives a suggestion of balanced restraint, with a mix of red and black fruits and a touch of coconut and vanillin, turning to coffee in the glass. The palate shows the coconut and vanillin more distinctly than the nose, with the overt black fruits cut by a faintly austere herbal note of anise. This gives a fine-grained textured impression, with those coconut and vanillin overtones coming back on the finish. The whopping alcohol of 14.8% is so well integrated that it is not obtrusive. This is still too young, but the herbal touch that takes the edge off the exuberance of the fruits promises that this will become a finely balanced wine in a more savory spectrum over the next decade. 14.8% *91* Drink to 2021.

Napa Valley, Eisele Vineyard Cabernet Sauvignon, 2002
The first impression is very reserved. The nose gives up little beyond a dusty impression of black fruits. This rather severe impression carries over to the palate; the fruits are quite backward and the tannic structure gives a texture resembling old style Bordeaux. It seems to need several more years. This is a food wine: it doesn't really show well on tasting alone, but opens up against food, which allows the fruits to show free of the tannins. Very slowly, black cherry, blueberry, and blackcurrant fruits release in the glass, becoming sweet and ripe. Certainly it's developing slowly, with the aromatics reluctant to reveal themselves, although as they come out the wine shows more of its New World origins. 14.6% *91* Drink 2016-2026.

Napa Valley, Eisele Vineyard Cabernet Sauvignon, Araujo, 1991
Appearance shows a slightly more mature color than the Phelps with just a touch more garnet. The bouquet is faintly savory and faintly aromatic with impressions of thyme and tarragon, becoming somewhat reminiscent of the garrigue as it develops in the glass. That garrigue-like note sits faintly on the palate of sweet, soft, ripe, open-knit fruits, with a touch of black tea and tobacco developing on the finish, and giving a refined impression. This gives a more complex impression than the Phelps. 13.0% (November 2012) *92* Drink to 2017.

Napa Valley, Eisele Vineyard Cabernet Sauvignon, Joseph Phelps, 1991
More direct fruit expression on the nose than the Araujo, but a slightly weaker impression of those garrigue-like aromas. On the palate, however, there's a less open, slightly hard edge to the brambly fruits, which becomes more evident on the finish. That sense of toughness is in line with other vintages of Phelps. Ultimately the wine becomes a little rustic. 13.5% (November 2012) *88* Drink up.

Napa Valley, Eisele Vineyard Cabernet Sauvignon, Joseph Phelps, 1985
Tasting this wine, you can see how close Napa came in the eighties to rivaling Bordeaux. Developing black fruits, in the herbaceous rather than savory spectrum, are cut by a medicinal touch of Brett showing as leather and tar. Perhaps because of the Brett the Cabernet isn't so directly forceful as it is with Insignia of this year—that is more primary, this is more developed— but maybe for that very reason Eisele is the more interesting wine. Tannins are resolved and it's definitely time to drink as the wine slowly loses fruit expression and becomes more austere in the glass. 13.3% (December 2012) *91* Drink to 2016.

Arrowood

Richard Arrowood bought land in 1986 and built his winery in 1987, focusing on varietal wines coming from various sites in Sonoma, sourced from a variety of growers; the vineyards surrounding the winery were known as Richard's spice box, and consist of just 3.6 ha of Bordeaux varieties that are used for blending with Cabernet Sauvignon. In 2000, Richard Arrowood sold the winery to Mondavi, but stayed on as winemaker. After Constellation Brands purchased Mondavi, they sold off Arrowood at the end of 2004. A troubled period followed as the winery changed hands until it ended up as part of Jackson Family Vineyards in 2010. The original facility remains in Sonoma Valley, but wine production has been shifted to Jackson's central facility at Cardinale in Oakville in Napa Valley. Richard Arrowood moved on to found a new winery, and Heidi von der Mehden took over winemaking. The top wines here, which share the same price point, are the Monte Rosso single vineyard designate and the Réserve Spéciale, a blend made most years from sources that change depending on the vintage. The Reserve was a blend until 1994, and then became a hundred percent Cabernet Sauvignon. Most of the wines in this tasting were made by Richard Arrowood before he left, and were tasted at Arrowood in February 2012.

Sonoma Valley, Smothers-Remick Vineyards, Cabernet Sauvignon, 2007
This is the structural backbone of the reserve, seen here by itself. Restrained black fruit nose conveys a light floral impression. As the nose forecasts, the palate makes a delicate impression, with nicely delineated, rather taut, fruits of black cherries and plums. Fine-grained tannins dry the finish. This is finer in texture than the Réserve Spéciale, less rounded and more austere. 15.5% *89* Drink 2014-2024.

Sonoma Valley, Réserve Spéciale, Cabernet Sauvignon, 2007
Black fruits with blackcurrant aromatics and some cherries on the nose. Soft and elegant with taut tannins showing on the finish; this needs time for a touch of bitterness to subside. This is the most elegant of the flight of Réserve Spéciale, with precisely delineated black cherry fruits. Very fine. 15.5% *91* Drink 2014-2022.

Sonoma County, Réserve Spéciale, Cabernet Sauvignon, 2002
Black fruits give way to cedary aromas on the nose, which conveys a nice sense of balance. As the nose predicts, this is the most complex of the flight of Reserve Spéciale. It doesn't seem absolutely ready yet as the black fruits are still offset by some austere notes of Cabernet Sauvignon. Very much a monovarietal, the tannins remain tight, but this seems the most complete wine of the flight, and perhaps the only one, after the switch to 100% Cabernet Sauvignon, that really seems not to need the other varieties. 14.8% *91* Drink to 2022.

Sonoma County, Réserve Spéciale, Cabernet Sauvignon, 1997
Restrained nose does not give up much fruit; there are some weakly developed vegetal overtones. The palate has a flatter profile than 1993, more monolithic in its impression; this 100% Cabernet Sauvignon seems to lack the roundness on the mid palate that other varieties brought to the blend. In the glass it develops elegance and more precision than 1993, but has less overall flavor variety, and a touch of tannic bitterness on the finish. 13.8% *89* Drink to 2019.

Sonoma County, Réserve Spéciale, Cabernet Sauvignon, 1993
Cedary black fruit nose has hints of coffee. A vegetal impression develops in the glass with a touch of bell peppers; animal overtones evolve later. But fruits are ripe and rich and no herbaceousness is evident at first on the palate, which is smooth and nicely rounded with good flavor variety; a touch of herbaceousness comes back later with some chocolate overtones on the finish, which has a touch of heat. This is a good state of maturity for a twenty year old wine. 13.9% *90* Drink to 2018.

Sonoma Valley, Monte Rosso, Cabernet Sauvignon, 2006
Smoky nose with some animal overtones that blow off to become more anise-like. Sweet and ripe, but elegant rather than opulent on the palate. Tannins are quite tight on the finish, giving an impression of precisely delineated black cherry fruits with balanced supporting acidity. The most precise of the flight of Monte Rosso vintages. 15.2% *93* Drink 2013-2025.

Sonoma Valley, Monte Rosso, Cabernet Sauvignon, 2004
Black fruit nose with some vegetal overtones and hints of bell peppers. Rich and full blackcurrant fruits on the palate have chocolate overtones. Just a hint of black fruit aromatics comes through the soft, chocolaty tannins of the finish. Slightly lower acidity emphasizes the plushness of the fruits. This is the fullest, the most lush of the Monte Rosso vintages: less precise, more rounded, more sense of higher toned aromatics. 15.8% *91* Drink 2013-2024.

Sonoma Valley, Monte Rosso, Cabernet Sauvignon, 2001
Rich black fruit nose is cut by some cedary herbal notes. Smooth black fruits give elegant impression on palate, and following the nose are cut by an austere cedary note. There's a slight impression of heat on the finish. Good acidity contributes to the impression of restraint. The taut impression makes this the tightest of the Monte Rosso vintages. 14.4% *90* Drink to 2022.

Bell Wine Cellars

After spending the 1980s at Beaulieu Vineyards, Anthony Bell started his own winery in 1991 by producing Cabernet Sauvignon from clone 6 in borrowed facilities, moving into his own winery in Yountville in 1998. His style is to make wines with a European sensibility. Today he produces monovarietal Cabernet Sauvignons from several different clones, as well as a blend with the classic Bordeaux varieties, and a "claret" that also includes some Syrah and Petite Syrah. Three barrels for each individual clone give around 900 bottles for each of clones 7, 4, 6, and 337. The wines from clone 7 and clone 4 have similar profiles, but on clone 7 you see the fruits first, and this reverses on clone 4 where you see the herbal influence first. All the wines show an impressive sense of the tradition of Cabernet Sauvignon, but the most striking difference is between clone 337, which shows the most lush character—the Dijon clone of Cabernet Sauvignon, you might say—and clone 6, which has the most traditional austerity. Wines were tasted at Bell Cellars in December 2011.

Clone 7, Napa 2008
First impressions show black fruits, followed by a subtle touch of herbs and cereal. The palate shows black fruits of damsons and bitter cherries, with tight, elegant lines. Some fine tannins are present on the finish with a faint touch of heat. 13.9% *90* Drink 2013-2023.

Clone 4, Napa, 2008
A herbal touch of tarragon shows on the nose, just ahead of the black fruits of plums and cherries. This has similar components on the nose to clone 7, but they appear in reverse order. The black fruit palate shows more cherries than plums, with very fine-grained tannins, and is more chocolaty than clone 7. Just a touch more flavor interest and length on the finish here. 14.0% *91* Drink 2013-2024.

Clone 337, Napa, 2008
Slightly austere, cedary impression to a black fruit nose, leading into a touch of chocolate. Fruits are soft and round on the palate, a touch aromatic, showing more as plums than cherries. Smooth, fine-grained tannins coat the palate, where the more opulent character of this clone really comes out, reducing the impression of Cabernet typicity. 13.8% *90* Drink 2013-2020.

Clone 6, Rutherford, 2008
A herbal impression on the nose is more evident here, just short of showing as bell peppers, with black cherries underneath. Black fruits on the palate are more cherries than plums, a little more loose knit on the palate, with quite soft, ripe, tannins. The impression of Cabernet typicity in the form of those herbal notes is really clear on the nose, but a bit more subdued on the palate, which hasn't really opened out yet. 13.2% *91* Drink 2013-2020.

Cabernet Sauvignon, Napa, 2008
This is 83% Cabernet Sauvignon from all 4 clones, 8% Petit Verdot, 4% Cabernet Franc, 3% Malbec, 2% Merlot. Just a slight herbal touch comes through the black fruits on the nose. There's definitely a softening effect here compared to the pure clonal Cabernets, with elegant fruits supported by fine-grained tannins, more obviously integrated than in the clones. Herbal notes are more subdued and a chocolate edge shows on the finish. 13.8% *88* Drink to 2018.

Claret 2008, Napa
This is produced from all four Cabernet clones with 3% Cabernet Franc, 3% Merlot, 5% Malbec, 5% Petit Verdot, 8% Syrah, and 2% Petit Syrah. A soft, nutty nose offers hints of perfume. This is altogether softer on the palate than the Cabernet clones, but the fruit profile is a little flatter, with a mix of red and black cherries, and light tannins on the finish. 13.6% *87* Drink to 2018.

Bryant

Don Bryant purchased the land for his vineyards in a striking spot on Pritchard Hill overlooking Lake Hennessy. "I bought the top of a mountain for a home site and decided it would be fun to start a vineyard. I looked for the best vineyard within 10-15 miles of the house. There was a vineyard close by, planted with Cabernet Sauvignon and Chardonnay, and run down. All the old winemakers said it was the best vineyard around. Grapes had previously been sold to Caymus and others. I made an unsolicited bid in 1986 for 12 acres, and closed the deal within 24 hours," he recollects. The first vintage was in 1992, with Helen Turley as the winemaker. Early vintages were propelled into instant success. Since then, there have been several winemakers, with changes in style depending on using techniques from barrel fermentation to greater maceration and extraction. "Helen's wines were very reflective of vintage, perfumed and delicate in 1996, massive in 1997," says a later winemaker, Helen Keplinger. The vineyard is divided into 22 blocks spread out over 5 ha, and is planted exclusively with Cabernet Sauvignon (a mixture of Spottswoode clone and 337). The vineyards are on west-facing volcanic soils, with a cooling influence from the lake just below. The character of Bryant is maintained by declassifying lots into a second wine, called DB4. "Wines that are declassified to DB4 are less concentrated, and the tannins are less refined. DB4 is not necessarily shorter lived than Bryant," says Helen Keplinger. Both Bryant and DB4 are 100% Cabernet Sauvignon, and the latest development is an extension into a Bordeaux blend, called Bettina after Don's wife, coming from David Abreu's vineyards at Madrona Ranch, Thorevilos, and Lucia Howell Mountain; the inaugural vintage is 2009. Ultimately there will be 1,500 cases of Bettina to match the 1,500 cases of Bryant. Wines were tasted at Bryant in November 2012.

Napa Valley, Bettina, 2009

Stern nose with black plums and cherries barely poking through, revealing some faintly aromatic overtones. The palate has a refined texture without going over the edge into plushness; it is smooth, ripe, and firm, with a chocolaty edge. The tannic structure comes through after several seconds to dry the finish. Although this is a blend, and Bryant is solely Cabernet Sauvignon, this seems the sterner wine, much in the tradition of the purity of Cabernet fruits, the structure distinctly dominated by Cabernet Sauvignon, although with that extra refinement coming from Cabernet Franc. It could be drunk relatively soon, but I would be more inclined to wait for the fruits to come through more clearly 15.0% *93* Drink 2015-2035.

Napa Valley, Cabernet Sauvignon, 2008

The edge is just coming off the sternness of the nose, with aromatic black fruits of plums, cherries, and mulberries just visible through the general impression of austerity. Sweet and ripe on the palate, this seems plumper in style than Bettina, with slightly brighter and more aromatic fruits, but perhaps that's the vintage speaking. The black fruits are precise yet supple, leaving a lingering impression of black strawberries, pure and almost perfumed. High alcohol and tannins are already well integrated. Certainly this gives a strong impression that Cabernet Sauvignon can make a complete wine here. 15.0% *93* Drink to 2027.

Napa Valley, Cabernet Sauvignon, 2004

The first impression here is somewhere between fruity and spicy with some savory overtones, almost a touch of the garrigue, giving a feeling that this is coming together to start its development at this point. The palate shows very ripe fruits, with aromatics verging on high toned; tannins are subsumed by the fruits, but there is still some dryness on the finish. Purity of well-delineated fruits comes through the palate, black cherries and plums, ripe, supple, and pure. This vintage really brings home the character of the Bryant style, which in a word you might describe as suppleness. 14.8% *92* Drink to 2025.

Napa Valley, Cabernet Sauvignon, 1996

Aromatics have now calmed down significantly and the first impression shows red as well as black fruits with suspicions of savory elements. There's a lovely balance of fruits against herbs, spices, and peppers; more overt than 2004, but the complex array of influences is quite hard to pin down. The fruits are less overt and that touch of the garrigue comes through, but the driving force remains the spectrum of primary fruits, clearer than in the younger vintages and with slightly brighter acidity. Tannic structure is still there in the background. The character of Bryant is that the fruits become progressively clearer as the structure resolves with age, and eventually this vintage will incline to delicacy. Already it gives a more refined impression than the preceding 1995 vintage. 14.5% *93* Drink to 2025.

Caymus

The Wagners have been involved in growing grapes in Napa for a long time. "Napa was a different place when we started in the 1880s, then we had phylloxera and Prohibition, and that put the family out of the business. They planted a litany of crops, the best was prunes, so I grew up around prunes and prune dehydration. In 1966 my father pulled up the prunes and planted grapes," recalls Chuck Wagner. Caymus Vineyards started in 1972 with a release of 240 cases of Cabernet Sauvignon. Today Wagner has expanded into a group of family businesses, with wineries all over Napa Valley. At Caymus there are two Cabernets: the Napa Valley bottling and Special Selection, which has been made most years since 1975 by selecting about a quarter of the best lots. Special Selection can come from any of the eight AVAs in which Caymus own or lease vineyards. It's usually 25% from mountain areas and 75% from the valley, but there's wide variation in sources depending on annual conditions. The style changed in the late nineties to become riper and richer, and since 2008 has included about 15% Merlot. Unlike some of the prominent Napa Valley Cabernets, Special Selection is made in good quantities, typically around 15,000 cases. Wines were tasted at Caymus in November 2012.

Napa Valley, Special Selection Cabernet Sauvignon, 2010
Deepening, soft, furry impression on the nose with a touch of chocolate and hints of blackcurrants underneath. Sweet, round and ripe, and quite nutty on the finish. "This is the top mark for me, it expresses just what I like," says Chuck Wagner. "Fruit quality is intense, flavors are ripe." The risk that the wine is so ripe it will become cloying with age is probably avoided by the good acidity. It's quite thick on the palate, but chocolaty rather than viscous. This really marks a distinct change of style from the older vintages. 15.0% *90* Drink to 2024.

Napa Valley, Special Selection Cabernet Sauvignon, 2005
The warm nutty nose is reminiscent of 1997. The palate is noticeably softer and nuttier than older vintages. Tannins are not so evident, or to be more precise, the tannins are riper, softer, and furrier, with hints of chocolate on the finish. There's just a hint of the old acid edge on the finish. Lots of density, with a sturdy structure underneath. Definitely a more modern impression but without going over the top. 15.2% *90* Drink to 2022.

Napa Valley, Special Selection Cabernet Sauvignon, 1999
This vintage was a transition between the old style (tighter) and the new style (riper). It opens a little thick and one dimensional, but expands to become a nicely aged wine. A mixture of nutty and herbal influences show on the nose with a hint of tobacco. The textural quality is more obvious here than in older vintages, very finely granular, with good acidity supporting black cherry fruits, with a faint hint of aromatic blackcurrants underneath. 14.4% *91* Drink to 2027.

Napa Valley, Special Selection Cabernet Sauvignon, 1997
There's a much warmer impression to the nose than 1990 with nutty black fruits, but again there's a fairly precise edge delineating the fruits, giving a somewhat Cabernet Franc-ish impression. Acidity is just above balanced, that faint herbal edge comes through the wine, and there's a touch of heat on the finish. 14.4% *91* Drink to 2024.

Napa Valley, Special Selection Cabernet Sauvignon, 1990
There's an elegant impression to the black fruit nose but a distinct tannic edge to the fruits, almost sharp, relieved by a fugitive whiff of tobacco. There's that tight definition of black Cabernet fruits, but the acidity is a little pressing, with some noticeable heat on the finish. A faint herbal edge lends complexity. The impression of herbs and tobacco intensifies in the glass. 13.0% *90* Drink to 2017.

Napa Valley, Special Selection Cabernet Sauvignon, 1985
A wedge of dry earth on opening, clearing to reveal earthy, smoky, aromas that hide the fruits and convey an impression of minerality. Smooth on the palate, with fruits of red cherries and redcurrants supported by a faintly piquant acidity. Very nice flavor variety cut by a touch of gunflint that brings freshness. The palate has developed complexity although without very much evident tertiary development. (February 2012) *92* Drink to 2017.

Chalk Hill

The Chalk Hill Estate shows in microcosm the diversity of terroirs in this sub-AVA within Russian River Valley, going from warm, south-facing areas resembling Bordeaux to cool north-facing areas that resemble Alsace. "Bordeaux varieties only really ripen here in just the right sites, it's much cooler than Napa," says vineyard manager Mark Lingenfelder. Chalk Hill Estate was 50% Pinot Noir in the mid eighties, but the sites that are suitable for black grapes are really too warm for Pinot. The estate today is a mix of white varieties (mostly Chardonnay with a little Sauvignon Blanc) and Bordeaux varieties. The Cabernet is planted on the tops of warm south-facing slopes where the soil is based on red volcanic rocks. There is an unusually high concentration of the old varieties, mostly Malbec (9 ha), with a little Carmenère (1 ha). This has led to the production of some unusual blends, Cabernet/Malbec, Cabernet/Carmenère, Merlot/Malbec, and a Cabernet/Petit Verdot named for the new proprietor, W. P Foley, who purchased Chalk Hill in 2010. The estate wine used to be labeled as Cabernet Sauvignon, but lost the varietal label when the proportion of Cabernet fell below 75% as the result of planting more Malbec. Judging from the massive character and very high alcohol levels of the wines, you would never guess that this was a relatively cool climate for Cabernet. It wasn't really clear to me whether the difference between the relatively open Cabernet/Carmenère and the somewhat closed Cabernet/Malbec was due to the minor variety (20% Carmenère or 10% Malbec) or the source of the Cabernet Sauvignon, as I had not expected the Malbec to bring so much more structure than the Carmenère. Wines were tasted at Chalk Hill in February 2012.

Chalk Hill, Estate Red, 2008
Ripe black fruit nose with just a hint of spice and some blackcurrant aromatics slowly emerging. The first impression is the richness of the wine, stopping just short of jammy aromatics. Spicy and intense, with good acidity and ripe tannins in the background, the wine slowly becomes more aromatic in the glass. Alcohol shows as a touch of heat on the finish. A crowd pleaser. 15.6% *89* Drink to 2019.

Chalk Hill, Cabernet/Carmenère, 2009
Black fruits with cinnamon on the nose, but quite fresh. This vintage shows as tighter, less open, than the 2008. Fine-grained, but ripe, tannins are massive in the background, and very drying on the finish. This is really very undeveloped; the structure is standing in the way of seeing the fruits. 15.5% *90* Drink 2016-2024.

Chalk Hill, Cabernet/Carmenère, 2008
Black fruit with some all spice, then cedar breaking through with fresh herbaceous overtones. Smoother on the palate than the estate blend with dense black fruits of blackcurrants and cherries. The herbaceous impression of the nose is not evident on the palate, which is fully ripe. There's a slight impression of spice, followed by opulent ripe tannins on the finish, which shows some hints of jam. This is very approachable. 15.5% *90* Drink 2014-2022.

Chalk Hill, Cabernet/Malbec, 2008
Black fruits with cinnamon spice and chocolate overtones. More restrained on the palate than the Cabernet/Carmenère. Opulence is cut by a firm structure, tannins are more obvious, black fruits of cherries and plums are brooding behind the tannins; the wine becomes more overtly aromatic in the glass. This is a lot more obviously structured than the Cabernet/Carmenère. There's a touch of heat on the finish. This needs time. 15.5% *91* Drink 2016-2024.

Chalk Hill, W P Foley II, 2009
This blend of Cabernet Sauvignon and Petit Verdot has produced a massive wine. The nose gives an impression of intense black fruits. The palate is smooth and opulent, but with good supporting acidity. Powerful tannins dry the finish. The Petit Verdot is really packing a punch and emphasizing the sheer density. There's loads of fruit here, deep and black, with blueberries and blackcurrants, but suppressed by the structure. This is too much at present; it needs at least a year or two to calm down. 15.9% *91* Drink 2016-2024.

Chappellet

Chappellet is pretty venerable as one of the first wineries to be built in Napa after Pro-hibition, in 1967 (one year after Mondavi). Driving up the narrow access road from Lake Hennessy, deep into the woods, it feels quite inaccessible. Vineyards aren't visible until you go around to the back of the winery (which is built like a pyramid). The estate has about 280 ha, with 40 ha planted. Grapes are also purchased from some neighbor-ing vineyards. There were already vines on the property when it was purchased, but they were mostly Chenin Blanc. Following a replanting program in the nineties, most of the vineyard today is Cabernet Sauvignon. There are two distinct Cabernet Sauvignon wines: Signature and Pritchard Hill. "The style has evolved but the goal has always been to make bold, fruity, wine. Signature was really designed to be ready; it has as much structure as any Cabernet to age, but we do try to reign in the tannins rather than have a heavy brooding style," says Ry Richards. "Pritchard Hill has a different stylistic objective: more extract, bigger tannins, pure black fruit, boysenberries, espresso coffee, a higher density overall." Signature comes from the estate and east-facing hillsides in the vicinity; the Pritchard Hill bottling is based on selection, and will be an estate wine from 2012. Signature uses 50-60% new oak, and Pritchard Hill has 100%. Both wines are blends with just over 75% Cabernet Sauvignon; both also have Petit Verdot and Malbec but there is Merlot only in Signature. There are 7,000 cases of Signature and 1,500 cases of Pritchard Hill. Wines were tasted at Chappellet in November 2012.

Napa Valley, Signature Cabernet Sauvignon, 2010
Black fruit nose has nicely rounded aromatics with a slightly tarry touch. There's deep black fruit expression, showing as plums and cherries with hints of blackcurrants, a smooth, firm texture with ripe tannins, and a touch of heat on the finish. Tannins are not aggressive but they are noticeable, and personally I'd wait another year or so, but by comparison with the Pritchard Hill bottling, this is quite approachable. 14.9% *90* Drink 2014-2022.

Napa Valley, Pritchard Hill Cabernet Sauvignon, 2009
Curiously the nose has a fresh impression with strong black fruits. Dense black fruits on the palate are less obvious than those of Signature; there's enough glycerin to give some plush-ness to the palate, but the fruits are brooding in the background. Tannins are certainly firm, already integrating, furry and coffee-ish on the finish, but it will be a few years before they really let the fruits show through. There's less obvious aromatic uplift than Signature; this needs more time. 15.1% *92* Drink 2015-2027.

Napa Valley, Pritchard Hill Cabernet Sauvignon, 2005
Aromatics are more evident on the nose than in 2009, with hints of piquant plums. The fruits are coming out now, with deep black plums and mulberries: you can see the Petit Verdot here. Tannins in the background are still firm and drying the finish. In fact, in some ways the strength of the structure is more evident here than in 2009, where the sheer density of the fruits hides the tannins more effectively. This is a muscular wine intended for aging. "The 2005 is calming down now and picking up a California syrupy quality which I find really attractive," says chief winemaker Phillip Titus. 14.9% *92* Drink to 2027.

Napa Valley, Signature Cabernet Sauvignon, 2001
Restrained nose, taut on the palate, there is no mistaking the intensity and ripeness of the fruits. but the tight tannins of the vintage stop them from showing through. It will take some time for the tannins to let the fruits release, again the question being whether the fruits will last long enough. There is some appreciable heat on the finish. (February 2012) *89* Drink 2014-2022.

Chateau Montelena

Although Chateau Montelena won the Judgment of Paris for its Chardonnay, its Caber-net Sauvignon was one of the trendsetters through the 1970s. This has now become the Montelena Estate bottling, sourced from the vineyards around the winery at the very northern limit of Napa Valley. The elevation is around 120 m, which no doubt compensates for the increase in temperature that's usually found going up the valley. The wine is a blend from several sites that ripen over a 4-6 week period, increasing complexity. It has a long and distinguished reputation for elegance. But there is also another, completely different, Cabernet Sauvignon, also under the Napa Valley appellation, which comes from other vineyards and is made in a much simpler style. The only distinction between them on the bottle is a gold band stating "The Montelena Estate" on the original bottling. It would be easy to become confused. Woe betides the diner in a restaurant who sees Chateau Montelena Cabernet Sauvignon at a reasonable price on the list and decides this is a good opportunity to experience the style of the winery without noticing that it is not the Estate bottling. Personally, I like the older vintages better than the more powerful recent vintages; the 1985 was still going strong in 2012. Wines were tasted at Chateau Montelena in December 2011.

Napa Valley, Cabernet Sauvignon, 2008
"This is the only wine we make where we deliberately set out to make a New World style with upfront fruits," says Bo Barrett. The wine is intended to be affordable in restaurants. There's a fruit-driven nose but it's surprisingly restrained, given the direct fruits that follow on the palate. Lack of tannins emphasizes a distinct softness on the palate. This is well made, and fits the purpose of immediate drinkability, but does not show much Cabernet typicity; it's more like a somewhat calmer version of the Zinfandel. 14.2% *86* Drink now.

Napa Valley, Montelena Estate, 2007
The restrained nose of black fruits seems on the fresh side. There is a fine, soft, gravelly texture on the palate of black cherry and blackberry fruits. The overall style is restrained for Napa. 14.3% *91* Drink to 2021.

Napa Valley, Montelena Estate, 2005
Some austerity is suggested by the black fruit nose. The palate of fresh, precise black fruits with a touch of blackcurrants offers a very fine, less textured, impression than 2007 with a herbal touch showing retronasally on the finish. 14.2% *90* Drink to 2021.

Napa Valley, Montelena Estate, 2004
Hints of perfume and spice show on the black fruit nose, Sweet, ripe, black cherry fruits make an intense impression on the palate, with taut, firm tannins on the finish. Still youthful and closed, this has really hardly started to develop. This powerful wine has a touch of heat on the finish, and needs time. 14.1% *92* Drink to 2023.

Napa Valley, Montelena, 1985
The first impression is fruity, more red than black cherries with a touch of piquancy. The palate still shows lovely smooth fruits of red cherries and redcurrants, supported by good acidity, with tannins mostly resolved. The flavor variety gives somewhat of a left bank impression, although the wine is richer than its equivalent from Bordeaux would be, with an impression of layers of flavor, although tertiary development is scarcely noticeable. Very fine indeed: I wish today's vintages were this elegant. 13.5% *91* Drink to 2017.

Chateau St. Jean

Founded in 1973, Chateau St. Jean was a pioneer for producing single vineyard designate wines. "The owners of Chateau St. Jean asked me to do vineyard designates like the Burgundians do," says Richard Arrowood, Chateau St. Jean's legendary first winemaker (who left in 1990). Chateau St. Jean was best known for its single vineyard Chardonnays, at one time as many as nine, although red wine was a major focus, with emphasis on Cabernet Sauvignon, until 1980. There was a pause in red wine production in the early eighties, and then it resumed with a blended wine based on Cabernet Sauvignon. When phylloxera forced replanting, the estate was about 80 ha, with about half planted, mostly with white varieties, but replanting focused on black varieties. "We were set on producing a blended wine, using all five Bordeaux varieties, which was close to impossible at the time," says current winemaker Margo Van Staaveren, who has been at Chateau St. Jean for thirty years, and saw the ownership change when it was sold to Beringer in 1996. 1990 was the first vintage of Cinq Cepages. "Cabernet Sauvignon has varied from 75-83%; the next most frequent variety is usually Merlot today, although previously it was Cabernet Franc. Malbec and Petit Verdot are used in small amounts because they have such varietal expression that otherwise they would dominate the blend," she says. About half of the grapes comes from vineyards owned by Chateau St. Jean, but outside the home estate, so sources may include Sonoma Valley, Alexander Valley, Knights Valley, Dry Creek Valley, and Russian River Valley, depending on the year. Until 2007, the wine carried a varietal label as Cabernet Sauvignon, but that was removed as of 2008. "This had been the intent from the beginning. We put Cabernet Sauvignon on the label at the beginning because we were so closely identified with white wine," Margo says. Wines were tasted at Chateau St. Jean in February 2012.

Sonoma County, Cinq Cepages, 2008
Black fruit nose with blackcurrants predominating. Fruits of black cherries and plums on the palate, together with red cherries, with fine tannins on the finish, together with hints of tobacco and chocolate, which intensify on the finish. This vintage achieves the stylistic objective of approachability, with a refined and elegant impression, but it's difficult to see the basis for any extended longevity. 14.4% *89* Drink to 2020.

Sonoma County, Cinq Cepages, Cabernet Sauvignon, 2007
Restrained black fruit nose with hints of black cherry aromatics. Bright and clean with linear black cherry fruits, Taut, fine, tannins on the finish give more sense of Cabernet typicity than in the 2003, and dry the finish. Overall a generally light impression. 14.4% *88* Drink to 2019.

Sonoma County, Cinq Cepages, Cabernet Sauvignon, 2003
Cherry fruit nose is more red than black. The palate has sweet ripe fruits with those red cherries mingling with black, making a clean, linear impression, bright and tight. There's not much development here compared with current releases; it might be difficult to place these wines in order of vintage if tasted blind. This vintage is a bit lacking in character and is surviving rather than developing. 14.4% *87* Drink to 2020.

Colgin

One of the estates that created the cult wine movement, Colgin started with the 1992 vintage of Cabernet Sauvignon from the Herb Lamb vineyard (on the outskirts of Howell Mountain), when Helen Turley sourced the grapes from 14 rows in the most exposed position at the top. Herb Lamb continued to be a signature wine until the vineyard had to be replanted in 2008. Two other wines come from vineyards around St. Helena. Ann Colgin purchased the Tychson Hill vineyard in 1995, and the first vintage was 2000; located at the north end of St. Helena, it was part of Freemark Abbey (but had collapsed during Prohibition and never been replanted). This is also pure Cabernet Sauvignon. There's also the Cariad Bordeaux Blend, produced since 1999 from a blend between David Abreu's Madrona Ranch and Thorevilos vineyard. The IX Estate on Pritchard Hill, where all wine is now made, was purchased in 1998; it takes its name from the fact that it was lot #9 on Long Ranch Road. It was planted with a traditional Bordeaux mix of varieties; the estate of 80 ha has 8 ha of vineyards, planted on east-facing slopes to catch the morning sun. The first vintage was 2002. In addition to the IX Estate Bordeaux blend, there's a small amount of Syrah. Production of all wines is small: 1,200-1,500 cases of IX Estate, 250 cases of Tychson Hill, 500 cases of Cariad, and (previously) 500 cases of Herb Lamb. Some change of style is evident over the years in the direction of greater refinement. Winemaker Allison Tauziet says any difference is due less to changes of vineyard source than to technical advances. "The biggest difference is the increased precision in viticulture. In the early years when we were making wine from Herb Lamb it was very rudimentary in the vineyard and vinification was in a custom crush," she points out. Current vintages are developing slowly: my concern is the pace with which flavor variety will develop. Wines were tasted at Colgin in November 2012.

Napa Valley, IX Estate, 2008
Perfume filled the room as the wine was poured, with black fruits of plums and cherries showing delicate aromatics with a faint whiff of minerality. There's a precisely defined edge to the fruits, which are partly hidden by tight tannins. This is nicely balanced but still a little one dimensional, with a tightly coiled impression of waiting to release the fruits. A harbinger of things to come is how the wine slowly softens and broadens in the glass. Alcohol is a touch evident. 15.6% *91* Drink to 2024.

Napa Valley, IX Estate, 2005
The nose shows a pungent mineral character, almost gamey. Very slowly the nose begins to show a touch of the perfume of the 2008. The fruits are more interesting aromatically on the nose than on the palate, where the initial exuberance has calmed down. In spite of the promise of the nose, the primary fruits have not been replaced or complemented by savory influences. The palate is taut, precise, and elegant, but development feels some years behind the nose; it should catch up over the next few years as flavor variety develops. 15.6% *92* Drink to 2025.

Corison

Cathy Corison has been fascinated with wine ever since she took a wine appreciation course in college; based on French wine, the course defined her reference point as European. She came to Napa in the early seventies and made wine at Chappellet through the eighties. She first made her own wine from purchased grapes, and continued to make wine for other producers until 2003. The story behind the creation of her winery in Rutherford is that she was determined to find gravelly terroir for her Cabernet Sauvignon, and this turned up in the form of a neglected vineyard in Rutherford, with Bale gravelly loam. There had been plans to develop the site but they had fallen through. This is the basis for her Kronos Cabernet Sauvignon, with vines (most likely clone 7) that were planted on St. George rootstock about forty years ago. Yields are punishingly low, as not only are the vines old, but the vineyard is infected with leaf roll virus. The extra concentration makes the Kronos Cabernet full and plush. The Corison Cabernet Sauvignon is a monovarietal bottling, blended from three vineyards in the Rutherford-St. Helena area. Corison Cabernet tends to come out around 14% alcohol, Kronos is usually closer to 13%. New oak is about 50%. Graceful aging is a major stylistic objective. "Aging is very important to me. It's almost a moral imperative to make wines that will have a life," Cathy says. Indeed, the wines age slowly; my favorite was the oldest in the tasting, the 2001. Production is about 400 cases of Kronos, and about 2,000 cases of Corison Cabernet. Wines were tasted at Corison in December 2011.

Kronos 2006
More evident aromatics than Corison Cabernet with an immediate impression of black plums and blackcurrants. The palate follows right on, with more forward, plush fruits, showing the intensity of the old vines; there are velvety tannins on the finish. 13.6% *92* Drink to 2024.

Napa Cabernet Sauvignon, 2006
Fruits initially appear a little spicy and then develop some notes of coffee. Nicely rounded black fruits show on the palate, with a kick of ripe plums and blackcurrants on the finish. That touch of spice comes out again with a soft velvety texture on the palate. The small crop of this year gives the wine an impression of concentration, softer and more overtly fruity than the preceding vintage, and perhaps less typical of the usual Corison style. Tight and closed only a few months ago, this wine has suddenly begun to open out. 13.8% *91* Drink to 2021.

Napa Cabernet Sauvignon, 2005
More black fruits than red on the nose. Nicely textured density with a soft impression on the finish, and an elegant impression overall. The mix of red and black fruits tending to cherries on the palate gives a fresh impression. There's a slight retronasal nuttiness. Sandwiched between two softer vintages (2004 and 2006) this year gives a very fine-grained impression from what was a relatively large crop. 13.6% *89* Drink to 2021.

Napa Cabernet Sauvignon, 2004
Restrained nose is developing some suggestions of coffee. Reflecting the warmer vintage, the wine is softer than usual, with more broadly diffuse black fruits, and a soft, gravelly texture to the finish. 13.8% *89* Drink to 2020.

Napa Cabernet Sauvignon, 2003
There's a fairly spicy red and black fruit nose. Fruits are quite restrained on the palate at the moment and seem to be developing very slowly; perhaps the wine is passing through a dumb phase, with a certain lack of presence on the mid palate. 13.6% *88* Drink to 2019.

Napa Cabernet Sauvignon, 2002
Restrained nose has suggestions of spices and pepper, with black fruits turning more red in the glass. Good acidity lends precision to the fruits, but with less presence on the mid palate than was evident in the 2001. This mid bodied wine is developing slowly. 13.6% *90* Drink to 2021.

Napa Cabernet Sauvignon, 2001
A touch of red fruits on the nose has some suggestions of underlying austerity with a hint of acidity. On the palate the fruits make an elegant impression, showing as precise black cherries, plums, and blackcurrants, with a lacy acidity. This shows the most precise fruits of the vertical, with a soft, gravelly texture just beginning to develop underneath. 13.6% *91* Drink to 2022.

Dehlinger

Tom Dehlinger studied winemaking and viticulture at Davis in 1970; he thought he would make wine as a hobby, but it took over. The vineyard was a pioneering effort. "I bought this parcel in 1973 and planted the first 14 acres in 1975 with the best varieties of the time, Pinot Noir, Chardonnay, Gewürztraminer, Riesling. The Riesling was re-grafted to Chardonnay a year later. Two acres of Cabernet were planted using a virus free clone in 1975, on AxR1 like all the others," he recollects. "We started our second planting with 3.5 acres of Cabernet Franc, we planted 5 more acres of Cabernet Sauvignon, and in 1988 we planted 3 acres of Merlot. The experiment was partly successful and partly unsuccessful. The Cabernet Franc and Merlot were planted adjacent to the Cabernet Sauvignon in slightly lower areas; the problem was that the areas were not optimally drained, so I don't think we have given Cabernet Franc and Merlot the best shot that they could have in this area." At first the Cabernet Sauvignon was vinified as a monovarietal wine, there were Cabernet Sauvignon-Merlot blends between 1992 and 1997 (the Cabernet Franc was too herbal to be included), and since 1998 the Cabernet Sauvignon has been a monovarietal. Today there are two bottlings of Cabernet Sauvignon; varietal-labeled from the best areas, and since 2002 a Claret from the lesser areas. My favorite was the Bordeaux blend from 1995. Wines were tasted at Dehlinger in February 2012.

Russian River Valley, Cabernet Sauvignon, 2008
Intense spicy black fruit nose. Softer on the palate than you might expect from the nose, with rounded, spicy, brooding blackcurrant fruits. Too young now, with ripe, firm tannins evident. Clean Cabernet style with a touch of nuts on the finish. 14.5% *91* Drink 2014-2024.

Russian River Valley, Cabernet Sauvignon, 2005
Black fruit nose shows wood spices. Precise blackcurrant fruits show on the palate, cleanly delineated and fine-grained, with aromatic hints. Very precise, linear Cabernet Sauvignon fruits, just a bit tight for comfort at the moment. Tannins dry the finish. 14.9% *90* Drink 2014-2022.

Russian River Valley, Bordeaux Blend, 1995
This vintage was 70% Cabernet Sauvignon and 30% Merlot. Dark garnet color with impression

still of some ruby hues. Interesting nose shows some minerality followed by developing black fruits with a savory edge of sous bois. This is just at that delicious turning point when the fruits are mingling with savory elements and the balance seems to oscillate, with sous bois evident at one moment, and the black fruits coming back a moment later. Tom Dehlinger thinks this peaked five years ago, but it was the perfect moment for me. 14.5% *91* Drink up.

Russian River Valley, Bordeaux Blend, 1993
This vintage was 60% Merlot and 40% Cabernet Sauvignon. It's a mature garnet color. There's a faintly oxidized hint of raisins on the nose. The palate makes a soft impression with a sense of the sous bois that develops with Merlot. It is well developed on the palate with a distinctly savory character, more reminiscent of Bordeaux's right bank than left bank, although the structure of Cabernet Sauvignon is evident. A delicious faintly piquant savory note catches you on the finish. 13.5% *88* Drink up.

Russian River Valley, Cabernet Sauvignon, 1986
Developed garnet color. There are some vegetal, almost musty, notes of green bean on the nose. Sweet ripe fruits on the palate are supported by a faintly piquant acidity, not quite savory. There's a definite cool climate impression. A touch of raisins and sous bois develops in the glass. 13.0% *86* Drink up.

Russian River Valley, Cabernet Sauvignon, 1982
Medium garnet color. A little musty on the nose at first, then some faint hints of sous bois develop. The mustiness clears in the glass to release fruits with a slightly acid tinge. You can still see the original sweet ripe fruits that were generated by an Indian summer that year. Good acidity and classic balance, a touch vegetal but not really herbaceous. You might mistake this for a Bordeaux of the 1970s. It is a little sweeter and riper than the 1986. 13.3% *87* Drink up.

Diamond Creek

No one had planted vineyards this far north in the mountains when Al Brounstein purchased forested land on Diamond Mountain to create a vineyard in 1968, following a visit to the property with André Tchelistcheff and Louis Martini. Al was not happy with the quality of the Cabernet material that was available in California, but three of the first growths in Bordeaux sold him cuttings, which he then smuggled in by flying privately through Mexico. He was under pressure to plant on AxR1 but stuck to the St George rootstock because it had had a good record in the mountains. He intended to emulate Bordeaux, and also planted Cabernet Franc, Merlot, and Malbec for the blend. There are three individual vineyards, all with roughly the same blend of Cabernet Sauvignon, Merlot, and Cabernet Franc; Petit Verdot comes from a separate plot nearby. Gravelly Meadow is dry farmed, and the other vineyards have irrigation supplied by wells on the property, which has a small lake and a series of waterfalls. All the vineyards were planted at the same time, but Red Rock and Volcanic Hill started producing in 1972, whereas Gravelly Meadow did not produce until 1974. The oldest vines today date from 1988; Red Rock and Gravelly Meadow have more younger vines from a replanting program in the nineties. All vines have been propagated from the original selection, using a nursery on the property. "Al thought Volcanic Hill would be the longest lived wine, but actually they all age equally well. But Volcanic always comes around last, there is no doubt about that," says Phil Ross. Production is small, around 500 cases each, except for only 100 cases of Lake when it is made. I could not say I have a favorite: in some vintages I preferred Volcanic Hill, and in others Gravelly Meadow. Wines were tasted at Diamond Creek in February 2012 unless otherwise noted.

Diamond Mountain District, Red Rock Terrace, 2008
Ripe Cabernet nose has bright cherry fruits; the most forward and open of the trio. Bright fruits on the palate with hints of blackcurrants are nicely delineated; fine, smooth tannins give a fine-grained texture. The finish is slightly hot. This comes over as the most elegant, but also the most approachable, of the trio at the present stage, with the fine tannic structure hiding behind the fruits. 14.1% *91* Drink 2014-2025.

Diamond Mountain District, Gravelly Meadow, 2008
More subdued on the nose than the others, more of a mineral impression. The mineral edge carries over to the black and red cherry fruits, which are supported by good acidity and supple tannins. This is the softest of the trio, with a characteristic earthy touch cutting the fruits and giving a nice texture. 14.1% *92* Drink 2014-2025.

Diamond Mountain District, Volcanic Hill, 2008
Mineral nose with hints of gunflint, some fugitive hints of blackcurrants breaking through and strengthening in the glass. As always, the cleanest cut of the single vineyards, an almost taut impression, more backwards than the others, although the finish already shows a delicious nutty edge. This promises to be the longest lived with a very fine underlying filigree of tannins that will bring precision to the palate. 14.1% *93* Drink 2015-2026.

Diamond Mountain District, Volcanic Hill, 2004
Fugitive piquant notes on the nose give over to blackcurrants and hints of cassis. Softer than the 2001, with bright red and black cherry fruits, leading into blackcurrants with a suspicion of cassis, taut rather than full (very much the style of the vineyard), giving a lovely, almost delicate impression with floral overtones. In terms of Bordeaux, this might make you think of Margaux. 14.1% *93* Drink to 2024.

Diamond Mountain District, Volcanic Hill, 2001
Perfumed nose shows roses and violets. Taut, precise, black cherry fruits have a perfumed edge with good acidity and refined tannins, giving above all a sense of refinement with a graceful underlying power. There is no mistaking the dominant influence of Cabernet Sauvignon in the precise linearity of the fruit; slowly some minerality emerges on the finish, although the wine lightens up somewhat in the glass. This vintage is aging very slowly. 13.5% *90* Drink to 2027.

Diamond Mountain District, Volcanic Hill, 2000
Restrained nose shows just a touch of herbaceousness. Restraint follows through to the palate, where the black fruits are somewhat closed at the moment. The tannins show a gravelly texture with almost a touch of tobacco on the finish. I see a similarity with the wines of Graves. Definitely a food wine. 12.5% (December 2011) *88* Drink to 2021.

Napa Valley, Red Rock Terrace, 1994
Fragrant nose, black fruits merging into red, aromatics of red and black plums, turning to cedar and spice in the glass. The palate shows blackcurrant fruits still with a faint tannic rasp, with those aromatic plums coming back faintly on the finish. Very nice sense of underlying structure, in fact this gives the most sense of structure of the three vineyards in this vintage; it softens in the glass as the tannins seem to become rounder. It ends up with the most grip and impression of potential longevity. Definitely a food wine in its balance. 12.5% (May 2012) *90* Drink to 2018.

Napa Valley, Gravelly Meadow, 1994
The nose shows a similar fragrancy to Red Rock, with aromatics of plums, strawberries, and raspberries. At first it seems less distinct, but then strengthens in the glass with the strawberry and raspberry fruits coming to dominate. The fruits seem sweeter and more elegant than Red Rock; the tannins are just a touch more precise and finer grained, giving this the most refined impression of the vintage. But then it seems to simplify a bit, remaining attractive, but more superficial, with a less structured impression. 12.5% (May 2012) *89* Drink to 2019.

Napa Valley, Volcanic Hill, 1994
Here is a slightly more mature impression than Red Rock or Gravelly Meadow with some hints of piquant development leading into more distinct red fruit aromatics. There's a very slight savory touch on the palate and the primary fruits seem less distinct. Tannins are slightly tauter, but there's an impression that this wine is reaching maturity with the fruits offering less generosity than the other two vineyards. 12.5% (May 2012) *89* Drink to 2017.

Napa Valley, Volcanic Hill, 1992
A clear impression of mountain Cabernet shows stern black fruits with a vegetal edge. The nose is biased slightly towards the vegetal side, but the palate gives a more direct impression of fruits. Tannins are still firm, with a granular sense of texture. The palate is poised on a delicate balance of fruits, acidity, and tannins. There's no impression that the wine will tire any time soon, but nor can I see any intimations of savory development, which would be needed to take it to the next stage of complexity. 12.5% (March 2012) *91* Drink to 2020.

Napa Valley, Gravelly Meadow, 1985
Initially very slightly sweaty on the nose, showing some signs of development, but rather reserved; then some smoky minerality develops and some faintly herbaceous notes of Cabernet come through. The fruits are beginning to dry out, along the lines of old Bordeaux, showing a

touch of dilution and reduced concentration now; this was probably at its peak five years ago. (February 2010) 12.5% *88* Drink up.

Dominus

In 1982, Christian Moueix, owner of Château Pétrus in Pomerol, entered into a partnership to produce wine from the part of the Napanook vineyard that was owned by John Daniel's daughter. Since then Moueix has been trying to reconstruct the vineyard in its entirety, and has almost succeeded—there's just a small strip at the top that is still owned by Domaine Chandon. The first release of Dominus, under the aegis of the John Daniel Society, was in 1983. In 1995, Christian Moueix became sole owner of the vineyard, and in 1996 the winery was constructed under the principle that it should blend invisibly into the landscape. It has an unusual double skin, with an outer construction of stones packed into netting hiding the construction inside—in the valley, it's sometimes called the stealth winery. In 1996, Moueix introduced a second wine, called Napanook after the vineyard, which is produced by declassification. "At this point Dominus became more refined. But Napanook has experienced the same transition over the years towards greater refinement. Napanook is the same wine Dominus was ten years ago, we say among ourselves," says winemaker Tod Mostero. There's no discrimination between the lots up to the point when the wines go into barriques, with the best lots going into new wood; assemblage is nine months later, and Dominus typically gets 40% new oak and Napanook gets 20%. Grapes from a single plot may go into both wines, sometimes coming from opposite sides of the row (harvested separately); Napanook usually comes from the sunny side, Dominus comes from the more restrained shady side. Dominus usually gives a polished, restrained, impression; Napanook is simpler, more approachable, more obvious. There are 6-7,000 cases of Dominus and 4-5,000 cases of Napanook. Wines were tasted at Dominus in November 2012.

Napa Valley, 2009
The initial impression is of faintly aromatic yet fresh black fruits. The palate is smooth and round, with a very fine granular texture, and the fruits have that characteristic sense of holding back, not exactly linear or lean, but restrained compared to the more usual exuberance of Napa. Fine-grained, tea-like tannins bring real elegance and finesse. Relative to 2001, the overall flavor profile is remarkably similar: there's just a touch more glycerin on the finish here, making the wine more approachable. 14.5% *91* Drink to 2027.

Napa Valley, 2001
The first impression is the dryness of the wine—not at all herbal or herbaceous, simply dry. Very slowly some faintly aromatic black fruits become apparent on the nose. Their depth becomes evident on the palate where the reserved black fruits show overtones of blackcurrants, but they remain taut and seem to be holding back. Reflecting a lack of the usual glyceriny overtones of Napa Cabernet, that dryness superficially gives a more European impression, but the sheer power of the fruits marks the wine as New World. The fruits have certainly lightened up since the initial burst of youthful enthusiasm at the vintage, but there is little evolution of flavor variety. This is very much a Cabernet-dominated blend; it would be easy to take this for a pure Cabernet Sauvignon given its linear purity. There is no bitterness or excess tannin influence on the finish, but the wine is quite backward; there is a touch more gravelly texture and grip than in 2009. The overall impression is that it may be another decade before this opens up, when it should reveal a taut, elegant, style. 14.1% *89* Drink to 2027.

Napa Valley, 1996
The immediate impression here puts minerality first with some of the same perfume as 1995 showing faintly behind. That sense of minerality carries through to taut black fruits on the palate, which are fuller than 1995 but also more refined. The style here is more in line with recent vintages, with more sense of structure. 14.1% (November 2012) *91* Drink to 2018.

Napa Valley, 1995
An immediate impression of more perfume and less minerality than 1996. Initially fairly hard on

the palate but then broadens out to show soft, ripe, red fruits in a gentle style, with tannins apparently resolved. Although the fruits are more obviously appealing, there does not seem to be the same sense of character as in 1996. 14.1% (November 2012) *88* Drink to 2015.

Dunn

One of the pioneers of Howell Mountain, Randy Dunn identified his vineyard in 1972 when he was winemaker at Caymus. Today it has expanded from the couple of original hectares to about 14 ha planted in a much larger estate. The winery is a practical construction with some equipment outside, and the barrel room tunneled into the mountain. The original vineyard remains the core source for the Howell Mountain grapes, but is due for replanting soon, as yields have dropped significantly. Wine making is traditional; there's very little manipulation, no sorting of the grapes, stems are retained, and pumpovers are vigorous: "We do what we can to extract as much as possible," says Mike Dunn. The only exception is alcohol: Randy Dunn remains adamant that it must be less than 14%. A program to eliminate Brett, in conjunction with a move to more new oak, lightened the style slightly in 2002. "Before 2002 the optimum age was more than twenty years: now?—give me ten years and we'll see," says Mike Dunn, adding, "I feel the need to repeat that the 'style' hasn't changed except for Brett management, barrel selection, and percent of new barrels." There are two Cabernet Sauvignons: Howell Mountain and Napa Valley. Since 2009, all the estate wine has gone into the Howell Mountain bottling. The Napa Valley bottling previously included wine from other sources on Howell Mountain as well as from elsewhere in the valley, but since 2009 has been all Howell Mountain, so it has become something of a second wine for declassified lots. In fact, my favorite was the Napa 1990. Production is around 3,000 cases of Howell Mountain and 1,200 cases of Napa Valley. Wines were tasted at Dunn in November 2012.

Howell Mountain, Cabernet Sauvignon, 2007
A faint impression of piquancy shows on the black fruit nose. Sweet ripe fruits of black plums and cherries come up on the palate. Tannins are smoother than older vintages, but there is still that clearly structured impression of Howell Mountain. There's an impression of a more modern style, but: "You asked me if the 2007 was as far down the path as we were going to go in the new style. My answer was that it was the vintage characteristic," says Mike Dunn. That said, there is still a sense that the fruits are holding back, and the wine needs more time for full flavor variety to develop, although it certainly sweetens up in the glass. 13.9% *90* Drink to 2027.

Howell Mountain, Cabernet Sauvignon, 2006
The wine seems a little subdued at first, then a more perfumed quality appears as it begins to open out. Smooth at first on the palate, then a slight tannic rasp shows on the finish. It's still relatively closed, with a touch of austerity lending a slightly flat impression. The overall impression is delicate rather than powerful, but time is needed for more flavor variety to develop. 13.8% *89* Drink to 2025.

Napa Valley, Cabernet Sauvignon, 2005
This shows a fresher, fruitier, character than the Howell Mountain, but remains quite edgy in Dunn's usual style, still fairly tight, reflecting Cabernet's traditional austerity. Although the overall impression is lighter, the Howell Mountain core shows through, maintaining consistency of house style. (In this year there was actually enough fruit from the Napa Valley floor to make the wine, but Randy Dunn insisted on keeping the Howell Mountain fruit in it to maintain its usual character.) 13.8% *88* Drink to 2024.

Howell Mountain, Cabernet Sauvignon, 2003
This vintage offers a surprisingly delicate impression on the nose, almost perfumed. It's surprisingly approachable, a Cabernet with softened edges, but the flavor profile is just a bit lacking in liveliness. There's a slight touch of heat on the finish. 13.8% *89* Drink to 2022.

Howell Mountain, Cabernet Sauvignon, 1998
This is an especially interesting wine on two counts. It comes from a very cool year in which

many Napa Cabernets have strong vegetal flavors; that was avoided here by dropping a major part of the crop. And there was a problem with Brett, developing some time after the vintage, which threatened to overwhelm the wine; but there is scarcely a trace in this bottle. The nose shows more of a herbal impression, slowly turning a little more herbaceous, but staying well clear of vegetal, and only a faint gamey touch reflecting the Brett. The palate has partly come around but is still rather reserved, with fugitive impressions of elegant fruits; flavor variety is just beginning to evolve. This wine is an education in the unexpected. 13.3% *90* Drink to 2020.

Howell Mountain, Cabernet Sauvignon, 1993
A bit flat on the palate, fruits seem a little muted by the usual intensely tannic structure. The overall impression is that the wine has never come around and the fruits will go before the tannins. (February 2012) *88* Drink 2014-2020.

Howell Mountain, Cabernet Sauvignon, 1991
Still a deep ruby with purple hues. This always takes a long time to come around: the risk is that it may dry out first. Here the nose shows black fruits overlaid with a smoky minerality. It is rather linear on the palate in the style of a monovarietal Cabernet. Fine-grained tannins reinforce the impression of precision for the black cherry fruits on the palate. But there is no savory development yet, the wine seems almost to be standing still except for some lightening of the fruits and softening of the tannins. The dryness of the finish brings a certain austerity to the palate; it seems somewhat monolithic and just unready. If this were five or even ten years old, there'd be a basis for predicting development over the next decade, but after two decades it is hard to be certain if and when the wine will start developing. (February 2012) *89* Drink to 2019.

Napa Valley, Cabernet Sauvignon, 1990
The nose shows influences ranging from herbal to spicy, with notes of thyme, later developing into almost medicinal overtones that carry through to the palate. The elegant palate shows red fruits as well as black, with a faint sheen of glycerin offsetting the austerity for which Dunn is noted. Moving from the initial impression of light fruits, the palate closes up somewhat in the glass, moving in the direction of herbal overtones, somewhat the opposite of the direction you might expect the wine to take as it becomes exposed to oxygen. Then the fruits come back on nose and palate, round, ripe, and red. Overall a very nice result, just a fraction less in intensity relative to the Howell Mountain bottlings, but in a similar style. 13.0% *89* Drink to 2020.

Robert Foley

Bob Foley started working for Heitz in the 1970s, moved to Markham, and then to Pride, and altogether has made 35 vintages in Napa. He started Robert Foley in 1998, with a single wine called Claret. He gained more access to vineyards over the following years, planted his own vineyard, and Claret graduated into a 100% Cabernet because they started bottling the Merlot separately. Until 2003 the wine was a blend, from 2004 to 2005 it had 7% Merlot, since 2006 it has been 100% Cabernet Sauvignon. Production was 500 cases when he started, today it is 8,000 altogether, but it's still a two person company. With 2010 he has gone back to a Bordeaux blend for Claret and will have a separate Cabernet bottling. He is fussy about clones: "Clones of Cabernet are very important. I work with three main clones: the two old clones 4 and 7 are my favorites for masculinity. The newest clone I work with (since 1992) is 337 for its femininity," he says. Wine was tasted at Foley in February 2012.

Napa Valley, Claret, 2008
This is a hundred percent Cabernet. Strong nose with piquant blackcurrants, smoky minerality, and ripe fruits. A reserved texture of firm, dusty tannins cuts the fruits on the palate, leading into a finish with a chocolate and tobacco overlay. This certainly needs time. *90* Drink 2017-2027.

Harlan

Harlan's hundred hectare estate, with 16 ha of vineyards, is a beautiful property in the hills above Oakville, overlooking Martha's Vineyard, To Kalon, and Napanook. After several years searching for land in Napa, Bill Harlan bought the land in tranches, starting in 1984, and planted the vineyards between 1985 and the early 1990s. The estate rises from 60 m to 350 m, with the vineyards planted between 50 m and 160 m. About three quarters of the terroir is volcanic, and one quarter sedimentary. The original vineyards were planted at 1,800 vines/ha, which was considered a relatively high density at the time, but subsequent plantings have moved up to 5,400 vines/ha, and even 7,500 (positively Bordeaux-like). The plantings are a classic Médoc mix, about 70% Cabernet Sauvignon, the rest Merlot, Cabernet Franc, and Petit Verdot. The soils vary from volcanic to sedimentary; Merlot is grown on the sedimentary soils that have better water retention. None of the first three vintages (1987-1989) were sold commercially; the first commercial vintage, 1990, was released in 1996. Michel Rolland is the consulting winemaker. Total production of the estate wine is about 2,000 cases; there are also 600 cases of a second wine, The Maiden. My favorite vintage oscillated between the 1991 and the 1995 (⊤ page 374). Wines were tasted at Harlan in December 2011.

Harlan Estate, Napa, 2007
Spicy nose shows cedary black fruits with a touch of cinnamon. General impression on the palate is somewhat closed at the moment. Slowly some fruits open out in the glass to reveal blackcurrants and blackberries, with a touch of aromatic plums, sweet, ripe, and complete, supported by firm tannins on the finish. Too youthful now but the structure promises good longevity. *91* Drink 2014-2027.

Harlan Estate, Napa, 2004
Some developed vegetal notes and hints of sous bois show on the nose. This follows through to a delicate balance on the palate between red/black fruits and sous bois, although there's just a touch of heat on the finish. Initially this seems to be developing more quickly than usual (perhaps reflecting the hot vintage), but after a while in the glass it reverts to a more youthful impression, with the fruits coming back out and the savory impressions receding, suggesting more potential longevity than had initially been apparent. 14.5% *93* Drink to 2020.

Harlan Estate, Napa, 1998
Slightly vegetal notes to the nose, varying in intensity between two bottles. There's a fair amount of oxidized notes showing here on the nose, with evident sous bois, high acidity, generally a clear cool climate impression. Fruits are more youthful on the palate than they seemed on the nose, with some black plums coming out, and then the sous bois takes over on the finish. *88* Drink to 2014.

Harlan Estate, Napa, 1992
Mineral and savory on the nose. Light and elegant, this has been quite slow to develop those savory notes, but now it is sweet and ripe on the palate with savory intimations, nicely balanced for a food match. Tannins are largely resolved to leave just a touch of dryness on the finish. This vintage may now be fading ever so gently. (February 2012) *92* Drink to 2015.

Harlan Estate, Napa, 1991
(This was the fifth vintage vinified, the second to be released commercially.) Still a medium to deep garnet color. Development shows on the nose, which has a cedary austerity with some sous bois just showing. Sweet ripe black fruits have a savory density on the palate with a herbal impression that drives the finish. Tannins are resolving. This was the most gracefully aging wine of the vertical, with the palate showing that perfect balance of old Cabernet between red and black cherry fruits, savory development, and an underlying texture of fine, elegant tannins. 13.5% *93* Drink to 2018.

The Maiden, Napa, 2005
Here the fruits are less obvious and the sense of minerality in the form of gunflint is more obvious than on the 2002. The smooth, ripe, opulent palate has aromatic overtones. This is more obviously in the new style of the Cabernet cult than Harlan Estate itself. *90* Drink to 2019.

The Maiden, Napa, 2002
Fruity nose is more overt than Harlan, and shows some pungent overtones. Sweet ripe fruits are more evident, showing as blackcurrants with aromatic overtones. Very ripe aromatics become a bit obvious. Less restrained than the 2005. *90* Drink to 2019.

Heitz Wine Cellars

Dating from the 1960s, Heitz is now regarded as one of the venerable old Napa producers. From its first vintage in 1968, Heitz Martha's Vineyard was regarded as a benchmark for Napa Cabernet; the 1974 is still regarded as one of the best wines ever made in California. However, an infection in the winery with TCA made the vintages from 1985 questionable (the 1987 was the worst affected), and it took several years for the problem to be recognized; only from 1992 have the wines been completely free of cork taint. And then the vineyard had to be replanted because of phylloxera, so there was no vintage in 1995; the wine came from relatively young vines for the rest of the decade. Has Martha's Vineyard ever fully recovered its reputation? Some recent vintages suggest a road to recovery; others seem to have lost their way entirely. In addition to its most famous wine, there are two other single vineyard Cabernets, Bella Oaks (in Rutherford) and Trailside (on the other side of the valley by the Silverado Trail). Heitz also produces Napa Valley Cabernet, Zinfandel, Chardonnay, and some other single varietal wines, but none has achieved the acclaim of their Cabernet Sauvignons. Altogether Heitz owns or farms 150 ha in Napa. The style with the single vineyard Cabernets is for quite extended oak aging, with one year in the fermentation cuves of American oak followed by thirty months in French barriques. Certainly there is a similarity of style, especially between Bella Oaks and Martha's Vineyard, although Martha's Vineyard is always the most intense, and needs the most time to come around. I still don't think any subsequent vintage has equaled the 1974 (Ɏ page 372).

Martha's Vineyard, 2006
Black undeveloped appearance. Stern herbal nose has an impression of tarragon hiding the underlying black fruits. Tight on the palate, more restrained than usual for Martha's Vineyard, with a herbal, almost minty impression. Extremely restrained fruits are nowhere near opening out. This may make an elegant wine, but will take time. 14.5% (June 2011) *89* Drink to 2023.

Martha's Vineyard, 2005
Slightly aromatic nose with touch of menthol on the restrained black fruits. Smooth palate with lively black fruits, nice balance on the finish, follows the classic tradition of the vineyard. 14.5% (January 2011) *92* Drink to 2021.

Martha's Vineyard, 2004
Tight on the nose but perhaps just a touch herbal, approaching the famous eucalyptus. Restrained elegant impression. Sweet ripe fruits on the palate are dense and concentrated, pushing the ripeness more than you would expect from the nose. Yet there's a clear structure here, with fine, firm tannins in support. A slightly more aromatic impression than you usually get from Martha's Vineyard. 14.5% (June 2011) *91* Drink to 2021.

Martha's Vineyard, 2003
O tempora, O mores! What a change from 2001. The dark inky color raises forebodings. The powerful nose still shows the influence of new oak, overshadowing the hints of aromatic blackcurrants with that slightly musty, slightly piquant quality you get close to over-ripeness. Is this more in the modern tradition of the Napa cult wine than the historical more European aesthetic of Martha's Vineyard? This will remain an intense wine for a long time, but when will it calm down enough to let its fruits be appreciated? This overly assertive, one might almost say brutal, wine makes it hard to recognize the Martha's Vineyard of the past that could be confused with Bordeaux: has it lost its way? 14.5% (October 2012) *90* Drink 2013-2030.

Martha's Vineyard, 2001
At a tasting of Napa Valley Cabernets, the Heitz Martha's vineyard stood out for tasting like wine not a fruit bomb. At a tasting of the vintage that compared left bank Bordeaux and Napa Cabernets, its affinity seemed as much with Bordeaux as Napa. The restrained black fruits convey a herbal, almost spicy, first impression. Some savory notes are just beginning to join the smooth fruits on the palate, giving a very refined, elegant impression. A touch of tobacco on the fine-grained finish might fool you into thinking there was some Cabernet Franc here. This is aging very well, with the only overt indication of its New World origins being a slightly glyceriny touch to the finish. 14.2% (September 2012) *90* Drink to 2019.

Martha's Vineyard, 1985
Mature garnet color, with a very faint impression of sous bois on the nose reinforcing the sense of development. Except for a touch of alcohol, the overall impression is European. There's that slight impression of mustiness you sometimes get with old Cabernet, and a dry finish. Tannins are resolved, fruits are mature and savory, but not tertiary. There's unlikely to be much future interesting development. 13.5% (September 2012) *90* Drink up.

Jordan

Jordan has followed an unusual course of development, moving from 100% Estate wine in 1990 to 2% today. "Tom Jordan wanted to make wine in the style of Bordeaux. He thought that what separated the first growths was that they owned their own vineyards, but the tenor of the time was that soil wasn't important, you just put in the right cultivar for the degree days," says winemaker Rob Davis, who has been in charge of every vintage since the inaugural 1976. Phylloxera forced replanting after 1990, but many of the vineyard blocks have been abandoned or the grapes sold off. Today most of the fruit for Jordan's wines comes from around twenty growers, many located in Geyserville. The Jordan Cabernet Sauvignon is usually at the limit for varietal labeling (75% Cabernet Sauvignon), with Merlot as the second component, and then about 4-7% Petit Verdot and 1% Malbec. A mixture of French and American oak is used for maturation. The wines are intended to be drinkable on release—an important aspect being that Jordan has a major presence in restaurants—and the style is best described by Rob Davis: "I like fruit," but these tend to elegance rather than power, and there's a firm policy of keeping to moderate alcohol levels (recent vintages are all stated at 13.5%). The wines seem to alternate between richer, heavier vintages in New World style (2008, 2006, 2003) and more elegant vintages in more European style (2007, 2004, 1990), and were tasted in April 2012.

Alexander Valley, Cabernet Sauvignon, 2008
Ripe black fruit nose, just a hint of spice, with some black aromatics slowly emerging. First impression is the richness on the palate, stopping just short of jammy aromatics. Intense fruits are supported by good acidity and ripe tannins in the background. The alcohol shows as a touch of heat on the finish. The wine slowly becomes more aromatic in the glass, turning nutty on the finish. There is a slightly heavy impression to this vintage; although delicious now, this should be enjoyed in the short to mid term. 13.5% *88* Drink to 2019.

Alexander Valley, Cabernet Sauvignon, 2007
Fragrant impression shows perfumed aromatics with notes of blueberries and hints of cinnamon. The palate makes a fairly elegant impression, with medium fruit density, and the tannins show some dryness on the finish. The fragrant, almost delicate, impression persists across the palate, making this a more subtle wine than 2008; my only concern is whether the intention of making the wine approachable has lightened the structure so that there will not be quite enough concentration to support longevity. Yet in contrast with the evident New World style of 2008 and 2006, this vintage has more of an Old World feel. 13.5% *89* Drink to 2016.

Alexander Valley, Cabernet Sauvignon, 2006
The style is between the elegance of 2007 and the heaviness of 2008, but with more structure and less fruit than the latter. There's a sense of structure right from the immediate impression, with black fruits tending to blackberries and blackcurrants, showing a slightly sharp edge with more of a tannic bite than you usually see with Jordan. The evident tannins give the wine a more youthful impression than either 2007 or 2008, and it remains just a touch harsh on the finish. 13.5% *88* Drink to 2018.

Alexander Valley, Cabernet Sauvignon, 2004
Bright youthful appearance, but a more developed impression on nose and palate than the 2003, with gunflint turning to a fugitive touch of sous bois, before the wine reverts to a more youthful spicy impression. Offering a more delicate impression altogether than the 2003, the palate shows a mélange of red and black fruits, with layers of flavor giving a subtle impression of fruits tinged with minerality. 13.5% *90* Drink to 2018.

Alexander Valley, Cabernet Sauvignon, 2003
A sense of nutmeg and other spices joins the first impression of black fruits, following through to an overall youthful impression resembling the 1999, but with more direct fruits and none of the bitterness. Fruits seem tight and sharp edged, with an impression of alcohol coming out on a warm finish. This seems far less well integrated than the 2004. 13.5% *88* Drink to 2017.

Alexander Valley, Cabernet Sauvignon, 1999
Relatively youthful, bright appearance for age, with as much ruby as garnet in the color. There's a mineral impression with flinty overtones and just a very faint impression of sous bois breaking through the steely fruits, with a faint touch of bitterness on the finish. That touch of bitterness gives a slightly disjointed impression to the wine. 12.8% *88* Drink now.

Alexander Valley, Cabernet Sauvignon, 1990
The nose has a lovely complexity with layers of minerality, vegetal impressions of spicy celery, and underlying red fruits. Soft and ripe at first on the palate, then very slowly some pyrazines come through to add a herbaceous note to the finish. The general aroma and flavor spectrum is quite classic, with an overall subtle impression resembling old Bordeaux. Just a touch of dilution suggests it is time to drink up. 13.0% *90* Drink now.

Alexander Valley, Cabernet Sauvignon, 1981
This wine is in beautiful shape, still lively after twenty years. The developed garnet appearance is slightly cloudy, with lots of orange at the rim. Vegetal and mineral elements show a fugitive whiff of gunflint, pushed by the high acidity, but there is a delicious counterpoise with the sweetness of the red fruits offsetting the sense of decay. This remains in balance, although it will not hold much longer. 12.8% *90* Drink up.

Louis Martini and Monte Rosso Vineyard

One of the oldest established wine producers in California, Louis Martini had its origins when the first Louis started making wine at the beginning of the twentieth century, and somewhat unusually formed his own company during Prohibition to produce sacramental wine and kits for home winemaking. At the end of Prohibition he built a winery in St. Helena. In 1938 he expanded into Sonoma by purchasing the Goldstein Ranch (originally planted in the 1880s), which he renamed Monte Rosso. In 1951 his son, also Louis Martini, took over winemaking, and in 1977 the third generation, Michael Martini, took over. The winery and vineyards were sold to Gallo in 2002. The best known vineyard in Sonoma, Monte Rosso is renowned for both its old Zinfandel and Cabernet Sauvignon. Today there are 25 ha of Zinfandel, 40 ha of Cabernet Sauvignon, and 6 ha of Petite Syrah or other varieties. There are two blocks of white grapes. Martini produces several wines from Monte Rosso. The most famous is probably the gnarly vine Zinfandel, which comes from some of the oldest plantings, followed by the (100%) Cabernet Sauvignon. A special blend called Los Ninos was produced from 1979, initially as a Cabernet, then becoming a Meritage after 1985; the blend included Petit Verdot for the first few years and from 2001 had Cabernet Franc as the other variety. In 2008 Martini introduced a Proprietary Red, which is more than half Petit Verdot with one third Cabernet Sauvignon. An intense structured style shows through all the wines, which should not be opened for at least a decade, irrespective of variety. Wines were tasted at Monte Rosso in February 2012.

Sonoma Valley, Monte Rosso, Zinfandel, 2007
Just a hint of jammy aromatics on the nose. The wine is dominated by soft black fruits, with nutty, piquant, aromas and flavors. Delicious, lots of flavor here, but with some structure. Here you see clearly the potential of Zinfandel to make a wine of complexity. 15.9% *91* Drink to 2022.

Sonoma Valley, Monte Rosso, Cabernet Franc, 2007
The Cabernet Franc was planted in the 1980s, and there's also a little (15%) Malbec. Fresh black fruits show an almost tart acidity on a powerful palate, with a tight tannic structure, and tobacco and chocolate slowly coming back on the finish. This ripe style of Cabernet Franc certainly needs more time to mature. 14.7% *91* Drink 2017-2027.

Sonoma Valley, Monte Rosso, Cabernet Sauvignon, 2006
Acidity shows on the nose of black and red cherry fruits, accompanied by faint nutty notes. There's good acid support for the black cherry fruits on the palate, with soft ripe tannins subsumed by the brooding black fruits. A layer of chocolate and tobacco develops on the finish. The present structure of ripe chocolaty tannins gives the wine great density, and needs to resolve to let the fruits show through. This was the most obviously structured wine of the flight. 14.8% *92* Drink 2015-2026.

Sonoma Valley, Monte Rosso, Cabernet Sauvignon, 2005
Black fruits have hints of red cherries on the nose. Delicate and softer on the palate than 2003 or 2004, with plums and blueberries joining the black cherries. Some perfumed aromatics lend complexity. Just about to start developing. Ripe tannins are subsumed by the fruits. This is the most subtle of the flight of Monte Rosso and has promising complexity for future development. 14.8% *93* Drink 2013-2024.

Sonoma Valley, Monte Rosso, Cabernet Sauvignon, 2004
Tart black fruit nose with a touch of cinnamon and other spices, some hints of nuts and chocolate. Less obvious acid on the palate than 2003, fruits of black cherries and plums rounding out, with tobacco, coffee, and nuts softening the finish. Taut tannic structure is just beginning to open out. 14.6% *91* Drink 2014-2024.

Sonoma Valley, Monte Rosso, Cabernet Sauvignon, 2003
This is basically a 100% Cabernet Sauvignon (it contains 1% Pinot Noir from topping up). It's a dusky purple color. A tart nose leads into dusty black fruits. The black cherry fruits are fresh on the palate, with chocolate overtones and hints of tobacco. Complexity is developing on the palate with layers of flavor slowly coming through. Fine tannins give a tight structure. Another couple of years is still needed. 14.5% *92* Drink 2014-2024.

Sonoma Valley, Monte Rosso, Cabernet Sauvignon, 1985
This is a perfect illustration of the change in style in Sonoma over the past twenty years: with a fresh nose, light palate with fresh fruits, and notes of bell peppers on the finish, this could easily be Bordeaux of the early eighties. They would never make a wine like this in Sonoma today. It's a mixed bag. On the one hand, this is a refreshing match to food: on the other hand, greater generosity of fruits would probably have enabled the wine to develop more flavor interest with age. The fruits have thinned out somewhat at this point, but have not become savory, so the counterpoise is the developing herbaceousness. The intriguing mix of fruits and herbaceous aromas remains more interesting on the nose than the palate, and at the end of the day, the wine falls short of generosity. Anyone accustomed to the wines of Sonoma today might find it hard to recognize the origins of this wine; but you might say the same about Bordeaux. 13.1% *88* Drink to 2016.

Robert Mondavi

Mondavi scarcely needs any introduction as an icon of Napa Valley. The winery was built in 1966 and the first vintage of Cabernet Sauvignon was released in 1968. A bottling originally called the Unfiltered Cabernet Sauvignon was renamed as the Reserve from 1971; the 1974 Reserve was one of the wines that put Napa Valley Cabernet on the map. The company broadened out with the introduction of the cheaper Woodbridge brand in 1979 from wine made in Lodi. Mondavi continued to be run by the Mondavi family, with Robert's son Tim as winemaker, although it became a publicly quoted company, until it was sold to the conglomerate Constellation for $1.36 billion in 2004. Today Mondavi produces three Cabernet Sauvignons. The Napa Valley bottling is dominated by grapes from To Kalon and Stags Leap District (typically around a third each); Cabernet Sauvignon is 75-85% with Cabernet Franc and Merlot as second in importance, and small amounts of Malbec, Petit Verdot, and Syrah. The Oakville bottling is dominated by To Kalon (typically more than three quarters): it has slightly more Cabernet Sauvignon, with Cabernet Franc as the second variety, and small amounts of Merlot, Malbec, and Petit Verdot. The flagship Napa Valley Reserve comes largely (sometimes almost exclusively) from To Kalon. It's usually more than 85% Cabernet Sauvignon; Merlot tended to be the second variety in the early years, but since the mid nineties Cabernet Franc has been second. Petit Verdot made its first appearance in the blend in 1997. In addition, in occasional vintages there is a bottling of a To Kalon Cabernet Sauvignon (from a block of old vines) or a Stags Leap District Cabernet Sauvignon, both 100% varietal. Wines were tasted at Mondavi in November 2012.

Napa Valley, Cabernet Sauvignon, 2010
The main sources for this wine are the bottom of the To Kalon vineyard and the Stags Leap area. A slight tarriness obscures the fruits on the nose. The palate offers a fresh impression of black fruits overlaid by a touch of chocolate on the finish. A mainstream, relatively forward wine, this needs another year. 14.5% *87* Drink 2013-2022.

Oakville, Cabernet Sauvignon, 2009
Less obvious on the nose than the Napa Valley bottling, but rounder and richer on the palate, with some faint herbal touches coming through to the dry finish, where structure is evident. A consistent house style runs through the bottlings from Oakville to the Reserve, but this does not have the silky overtones or the presence of the Reserve. 14.1% *88* Drink to 2023.

Napa Valley, Cabernet Sauvignon Reserve, 2009
This has come around quite a bit in the past year and is now showing more character than when it was released. The first impression shows very ripe fruits with a touch of tar representing the underlying structure, turning to tobacco and sage. The palate shows more restraint than would be predicted from the nose, with a nice taut edge to the black fruits. A touch of heat reinforces the aromatics of black fruits on the finish. The smooth character of the To Kalon fruits shows through. 15.0% *90* Drink 2013-2027.

Napa Valley, Cabernet Sauvignon Reserve, 2008
A ripe nose shows blackcurrant fruits cut by a savory touch of sage. Fruits are round, but there is a more obvious tannic edge than 2009; the harder tannins need more time for the structure to integrate. This is less obviously appealing than 2009 or 2007. 15.5% *89* Drink 2014-2022.

Napa Valley, Cabernet Sauvignon Reserve, 2007
There's some restraint to the nose of plums and blackcurrants. The palate shows nicely delineated black fruits with a touch of glycerin on the finish. Alcohol is bringing out the tannic structure and emphasizing Cabernet character, but that characteristic smoothness of To Kalon shows through. In some ways this is the clearest expression of the tradition of balancing the intrinsic austerity of Cabernet Sauvignon with the ripeness of Napa Valley fruit. 16.0% *90* Drink to 2023.

Napa Valley, Cabernet Sauvignon Reserve, 2006
There's a touch of piquant aromatic blackcurrants, making this more obviously New World in its origins than subsequent vintages. A touch of vanillin emphasizes the softness of the black fruits. That hint of piquancy comes back on the finish, before closing up to give a drier impression driven by the underlying tannic structure. This vintage gives the impression it can't quite make up its mind which way to go. 15.5% *89* Drink to 2022.

Napa Valley, Cabernet Sauvignon Reserve, 2005
A rather similar initial impression to the 2006 vintage with slightly piquant black fruit aromatics. Age has brought softness to the fruits, showing as cherries and plums on the palate, with a counterpoise of herbal influences such as sage. Fruit concentration is less obvious than the younger vintages. With some faint touches of bell peppers beginning to show on the finish, this gives the impression of representing a cooler vintage. 15.1% *90* Drink to 2021.

Napa Valley, Cabernet Sauvignon Reserve, 2003
The general impression here is fresher than the more recent vintages, with some herbal intimations cutting the black fruits. Nicely rounded, with a smoother balance than the younger vintages, less obvious texture on the palate, and a little less flavor variety. Cabernet character develops slowly in the glass, ending up with some classic notes of bell peppers on the finish. 14.5% *88* Drink to 2020.

Napa Valley, Cabernet Sauvignon Reserve, 2001
This was the first wine made after the Cabernet cellar came into operation, and perhaps reflecting the greater opportunities for precision in vinification, this gives a more modern impression than the vintages of the nineties. There's a lovely smooth palate with the first savory signs of development just showing. This is right on the cusp of switching from fruity to savory influences, with a silkier, more elegant, impression than the immediately preceding vintages. This impression is relatively recent, since only four years ago the wine seemed youthful and somewhat lacking in generosity, which all goes to show that Napa wines should not simply be judged on their upfront fruit properties when young. 14.6% *92* Drink to 2025.

Napa Valley, Cabernet Sauvignon Reserve, 1998
Reflecting the coolest vintage of the nineties, the nose shows a tendency to green olives, more savory than vegetal. Nicely balanced, there is only a hint of the vegetal notes that taint many wines of this vintage. There's good depth to the fruits, but this doesn't have the pizzazz or fruit-forwardness of other vintages. There's still some dryness on the finish from the tannins. At Mondavi, contrary to popular wisdom about the vintage, they feel this 1998 is just coming together. 14.1% *88* Drink to 2019.

Napa Valley, Cabernet Sauvignon Reserve, 1994
Development shows on the nose in an evolution from black to red fruits, with hints of savory overtones. Round fruits on the palate are supported by silky tannins, now resolving. The savory elements develop in the glass in the direction of sage, with a counterbalancing note of chocolate on the finish, then revert to green olives. Now beginning its development away from a fruit-driven spectrum toward savory, this is at a delicious tipping point. 13.4% *92* Drink to 2020.

Napa Valley, Cabernet Sauvignon Reserve, 1986
A slightly medicinal impression on the nose is a reminiscent of Bordeaux 1996. Napa origins show through in a greater viscosity on the palate. The To Kalon heritage shows through in that soft, silky, sheen to the fruits. The glyceriny red fruits are counterpoised by a faint return of those medicinal notes on the finish. A sense of completeness marks the wine. *92* Drink to 2020.

Napa Valley, Cabernet Sauvignon Reserve, 1985
Savory notes turn towards medicinal on the nose. Now a fully mature wine, with wide flavor variety, the medicinal notes of the nose seem scarcely evident on the palate. Quite dry on the finish, this has distinctly less glycerin than the other vintages. Mature fruits come right at you. This presents a good example of the interesting development a great vintage can bring when the wine is fully mature, but it should be drunk fairly soon. 12.1% *91* Drink to 2017.

Napa Valley, Cabernet Sauvignon Reserve, 1979
There's a savory impression to the restrained nose, but this is less obvious on the palate, which shows soft red fruits heading towards strawberries. This has a subtle palate with the red fruits cut by those savory overtones tending to sage. With the tannins resolved, the long seamless finish has layers of flavor. It is time to drink up. 12.6% *92* Drink to 2016.

Napa Valley, Cabernet Sauvignon, 1974
My recent efforts to assess the 1974 Reserve have been thwarted by bottles in poor condition, but this example of the regular bottling was quite impressive. Although it shows some mushrooms on the nose, and a touch comes through at first to the palate, the mushrooms slowly disappear to leave mature savory fruits, showing a complex array of flavors, with a faint medicinal hint on the finish. There's a delicious sweet/sour counterpoise on the finish. *90* Drink up.

Oakville, To Kalon Cabernet Sauvignon, 2005
This 100% Cabernet Sauvignon is made from the oldest vines at To Kalon, only in some years, and in very small amounts (250 cases). The ripe nose is very dark with hints of piquant cassis, rich and deep, but quite reserved. The palate shows a touch of the traditional austerity of Cabernet Sauvignon with the fruits displaying real purity of line, taut and precisely delineated. Not at all massive, however, this is true to the clean lines of the house style, with flow through the palate, as Mark de Vere of Mondavi puts it, and a sense still of holding back. *93* Drink to 2032.

Mount Eden

Driving up a precipitous dirt track on the edge of the Santa Cruz Mountains to the Mount Eden Winery with a solid sheet of water descending from the sky, I began to wonder whether current owner and winemaker Jeffrey Patterson had been euphemistic when he warned me the track was 2.2 miles long. But the drive was worth it. The Mount Eden Winery was originally the Martin Ray winery, created in the 1940s after Martin Ray had bought and then later sold the nearby Paul Masson winery. After Martin Ray left in 1970, this became the Mount Eden winery in 1972. There were several rapid changes in winemaker, until Jeffrey Patterson started making the wine in 1981. The winery is perched at a height of about 700 m, overlooking Santa Clara Valley; on a clear day you can see to the Pacific, 14 miles away. Mount Eden produces Cabernet Sauvignon, Pinot Noir, and Chardonnay, a clear indication that this is cool climate for

Cabernet Sauvignon. The Estate Cabernet Sauvignon is a Bordeaux-like blend, usually with about 75% Cabernet Sauvignon. Until 2000, when the vines had to be replanted because they had finally stopped producing, there was also a bottling of an Old Vines Cabernet Sauvignon, a 100% selection of a plot of Cabernet planted on its own roots by Martin Ray in the 1950s. Wines were tasted at Mount Eden in February 2012.

Santa Cruz Mountains, Cabernet Sauvignon, 1994
This wine is approximately 85% Cabernet Sauvignon. Appearance is garnet with some ruby hues still evident. There are restrained black fruits on the nose. On the palate the fruits are more rounded and a little more generous than the monovarietal. There's no trace of herbaceousness; there's a faint chocolate edge to the tannins showing on the finish. More sense of development, with a very faint trace of sous bois, but less precision than the monovarietal. About to enter its peak phase of maturation. 13.2% *91* Drink to 2020.

Santa Cruz Mountains, Cabernet Sauvignon Old Vine Reserve, 1994
Very faintly spicy on the nose with perhaps just a touch of cinnamon. Intense ripe black fruits on the palate have a fine-grained texture of supporting tannins. There's that taut precision of a 100% Cabernet Sauvignon. A touch of black aromatics is cut by a suspicion of herbaceousness. Restrained and taut compared to the greater generosity of the blend. 13.2% *90* Drink to 2018.

Opus One

Across route 29 from Mondavi, the Opus One winery is a somewhat bunker-like building nestled into the hillside. Over the years the vineyards have been steadily replanted at higher vine density with lower-yielding clones, and they now appear more European. After Constellation Brands acquired Mondavi, Opus One became completely independent. "The dissolution of the partnership (between the owners of Opus One) was a catalyst for change," says Michael Silacci. "This is more of an independent operation now." There is now also a second wine, Ouverture, available at the winery, produced from lots that are declassified from Opus One; it is described as "less structured than Opus One and more approachable in its youth." Production is less than 12%, and it is not vintage-dated. Always strongly dominated by Cabernet Sauvignon, Opus One started as a blend with Cabernet Franc and Merlot; Malbec was added to the blend in 1994 and Petit Verdot was added in 1997. My current favorite is the 2005. Wines were tasted at Opus One in December 2011 or as otherwise noted.

2009
This was bottled over the summer but has not yet been released. The black fruit nose of cherries and plums has some faint suggestions of piquant aromatics turning more to nuts and cereal in the glass and showing only traces of vanillin and overt new oak. The palate shows sweet, ripe, aromatic black fruits. Ripe tannins are subsumed by the fruits. Very undeveloped, still showing the primary fat of youth, but lots of fruit concentration for interesting future development. 14.5% *91* Drink 2013-2024.

2008
Austere black fruit nose of blackberries with cedary overtones. Much more restrained on the palate than the 2009, distinctly backward at the moment, a bit dumb and monotonic in the fruit spectrum. Overall impression is stern and Cabernet-driven. Opens out a little in the glass, but the black fruits seem brooding, albeit lightened by a slight touch of aromatic piquancy. Hard to judge until it comes out of this closed phase. 14.5% *91* Drink 2013-2027.

2006
Deep purple with black hues. Deep black fruit nose, some nutty aromas coming to the fore in the glass. Not as dense and rich as the 2005 (in spite of lower Cabernet Sauvignon it shows more austerity). A bit briary and closed, falls just a bit short in flavor interest at the moment. 14.4% (November 2010) *89* Drink to 2020.

2005
This wine seems to have developed significantly in the past year. Development now shows in

the savory impression of the nose, where truffles and green olives mingle with cassis. The black fruits of the palate are now more savory than overtly fruity, with a smooth, fine-grained texture, and that savory bite coming back on the finish. With its subtle aroma and flavor spectrum, this is the most elegant, complete, and complex of the vertical tasting. Winemaker Michael Silacci describes this as a classic vintage for Opus One, very central in terms of the wines produced over the past two decades. 14.0% *93* Drink to 2019.

2003
A touch of gunflint shows minerality on the nose with hints of truffles, turning a little nutty in the glass. The palate has black fruits of cherries and plums with hints of blackcurrants. The sweetness of the fruits is matched by the minerality, but there's less presence on the mid palate here, with the fruits seeming more superficial, and perhaps not the structure to support significant further aging (very common in this vintage). 14.0% *90* Drink to 2016.

2001
Faintly austere black fruit nose with stern blackberry fruits and just a savory hint of truffles. Sweet ripe black fruits dominate the palate, more blackcurrants than cherries, nice balance with quite bright fruits showing a touch of liquorice retronasally on the finish. In the past year, the aromatics have become less overtly fruity. With the sweetness of the fruits coming out on the finish now cut by those faintly savory overtones, the wine is showing signs of just beginning to develop. 14.2% *92* Drink to 2020.

1997
Undeveloped appearance is more ruby than garnet. A fugitive whiff of sharp flinty minerality shows on the nose. There are spicy red and black fruits on the palate (perhaps owing to the inclusion of Petit Verdot from this vintage). The Merlot and Malbec contribute some fleshiness to the mid palate, relieving the austerity of Cabernet Sauvignon on the finish. But in the glass the generosity disappears and the wine goes a little flat. 13.5% (November 2010) *88* Drink to 2015.

1995
A decade ago this was showing as the best vintage of the second half of the nineties, and that still holds true. The restrained nose now shows some hints of development. The palate has rich, ripe, red and black fruits, with some musty vanillin on the finish showing the high Cabernet content. Even though there's only a touch of Merlot, it offers a relief on the mid palate that is missing from some other vintages. The overall impression is correspondingly more generous. Fine wine, but when is it really going to develop? 13.5% (November 2010) *91* Drink to 2020.

1993
A cedary nose of black fruits is quite austere. Minerality and notes of cedar cut the black fruits on the palate, with that austerity of Cabernet Sauvignon driving the finish. Rather restrained on the palate with a distinctly dry finish that stops just short of vegetal influence (in which it seems a little like the 2011 vintage that's now in barrel). Possibly the fruits are now beginning to dry out. 13.5% *90* Drink to 2017.

1991
Medium garnet color. Flinty mineral nose with hints of eucalyptus and black fruits. Spices show on the palate with notes of musty vanillin coming through retronasally. However, the tannins are beginning to outlast the fruits. Very dry impression from the 99% Cabernet (almost all Sauvignon). Again you miss the fleshiness of the mid palate that comes from Merlot. Even though there is a barely perceptible touch of sous bois, the flavor spectrum is a little lacking in variety and goes a little flat on the palate. 13.5% (November 2010) *88* Drink to 2015.

1987
Still a medium garnet color. Developed nose shows steely minerality with an edge of sous bois. Slightly spicy black fruit palate with a mineral edge, just a touch of sous bois showing, a little heat on the finish, which is still quite dry. Less obvious fruit than in the 1979 in spite of the decade's difference in age. Here you see the austerity that comes from an (almost) monovarietal Cabernet Sauvignon—not enough mid palate generosity for my palate, a little too dry and monotonic. 12.5% (November 2010) *90* Drink to 2017.

1979
The lightening garnet color is good for the age. Development shows on the nose, with notes of sous bois supported by mineral overtones with a flinty edge. The palate is nicely developed, although the fruit is now lightening up a bit; the sous bois with its flinty edge follows through. Sweet ripe fruits still show on the finish, which however is a little hot. Remarkably vibrant for its age. 12.9% (November 2010) *92* Drink to 2016.

Phelps Insignia

Insignia is one of California's most genuine cult wines, meaning that it is produced in appreciable quantities (up to 20,000 cases), roughly comparable to a Bordeaux château. As a selection of the best cuvées, it should represent the best of the vintage, but at these quantities should still be strongly influenced by general vintage character. It has been a Cabernet-dominated blend since the 1980s, averaging around 80% Cabernet Sauvignon, with the remainder coming from all the other Bordeaux varieties in varying proportions. The grapes originate in about six vineyard plots, in various parts of Napa Valley. Vintage 2003 was the last year in which any grapes came from growers: today the wine is entirely an estate production. The wine is not easy to judge when young, given the powerful fruits, which take ten years or more, depending on vintage, to resolve enough to allow complexity to show. I am inclined to divide the Insignias into two series. There's a lineage of vintages 1997, 2001, 2007, which seems more European in balance and restraint; there's an alternative lineage from 1999, 2002, 2008, which shows more overt fruit and aromatics in the New World style. The differences are evident in pairwise comparisons: 1997 versus 1999, 2001 versus 2002, 2007 versus 2008. I could not see any direct correlation with varietal composition, which changes in order to maintain consistency of style, and it therefore seems that the differences reflect vintage character, which is as it should be. Wines were tasted in November 2011.

2008
A relatively stern nose for California, faintly nutty, and generally restrained. On the palate the fruits are more powerful and the aromatics more evident than 2007, with some noticeable vanillin. This is a little too powerful to enjoy right now, but should calm down over the next couple of years. 14.5% *92* Drink 2014-2023.

2007
Warm nose shows cereal notes of semolina. Full fruits of youth on the palate, but aromatics are pleasingly restrained. Blackcurrants and black plums show on the palate, with nicely restrained tannins. This shows better balance than the 2008, where the aromatics are still more evidently powerful. Good balance of fruits, acidity, tannins, promises interesting future development. 14.5% *93* Drink 2013-2020.

2006
Restrained black fruit nose with some influence of butter and vanillin. Smooth full black fruits on palate, some vanillin on the finish showing retronasally. Powerful wine in the Napa cult tradition. 14.5% (January 2011) *91* Drink to 2020.

2003
Black to purple color, no development apparent. Deep black fruit aromatics dominate nose and palate, with blackcurrants and plums to the fore. Very primary and intense on the palate, but aromatics are not oppressive. Tannic support is evident with a touch of bitterness on the finish, which is a fraction hot. 14.4% *91* Drink to 2019.

2002
Still a dark ruby color, with some purple hues. Lots of primary fruits remain on the nose, with aromatics of black plums and hints of blackcurrants. It's all upfront California. Forceful primary fruits of blackcurrants supported by vanillin dominate the youthful palate. The vanillin carries right through to the finish. Tannic structure should support this for years to come, but at present it's really still too powerful to enjoy except in small tastes. 14.4% *90* Drink to 2022.

2001
Dark ruby color still with purple hues. Black primary fruits on the nose are cut by a herbal touch of tarragon. The palate shows less complexity than might be expected from the variety of aromas on the nose. Fruity aromatics come out on the palate, but better balanced than in the rather simple style of the 2000. Overall the impression is that this wine is still too young for its full measure to be taken, but the savory notes intensify slowly on the palate, suggesting that it will mature to an interesting complexity along the lines of 1997. 13.9% *92* Drink to 2021.

2000
Deep color is just beginning to lighten to show some garnet. It's more restrained on the nose

than the vintages immediately before or after, but with hints of savory development cutting the fruits. Some vanillin shows and the wine seems about ready to start development. At the moment the fruit and aromatic notes seem a bit obvious; slowly more herbal and savory notes should begin to take over. This was a lighter year in California, and some tasters felt that the wine was too soft to show Cabernet typicity. 13.9% *90* Drink to 2018.

1999
Dark color with some garnet hues. The nose is driven by black fruit aromatics although there are hints of savory notes beginning to develop. Dense black fruits on the palate are accompanied by strong aromatics and a touch of vanillin. This is a fruit-driven palate in the New World style. It's impressive that the fruits are still primary, but with acidity just a touch on the low side, it's not evident that the wine will develop as well as the 1997 before it. 14.1% *88* Drink to 2019.

1997
Dark color with garnet hues, showing just a touch more development in its appearance than the 1999. A faint touch of gunflint on the nose leads into a palate that is more savory than fruit-driven. The overall impression is that the wine is at that delicious point where it is just beginning to turn from fruity to savory. Tannic support is in the background. The general style is Bordelais, although there is just a touch of vanillin on the finish. 13.9% *92* Drink to 2021.

1991
Restrained black fruit nose with savory intimations of black olives. The palate has a smooth texture with fine-grained tannins in the background. The main impression is the youthful character of the fruits; there is surprisingly little development. The structure of the Cabernet Sauvignon shows in a certain leanness, almost you might say austerity. My concern here is that the wine will become dilute before it turns to savory development. The lack of more varied evolution is in some ways a reflection of the old view that California Cabernets survive rather than developing. It's hard to quarrel with the interest of a wine that's more than twenty years old from a good vintage, but a certain lack of pizzazz leaves you wishing for more; it's still seemingly youthful and undeveloped, and the question is if rather than when it will mature. (November 2012) *90* Drink to 2020.

1985
Still a dark color. Not very strong but definitely a Cabernet nose, leading into an unmistakable Cabernet palate with black fruits offset by hints of woody herbaceousness. Very long finish lasts almost a minute. The first impression on the palate is the very high acidity; it takes a while, but slowly the fruits emerge as ripe and sweet with overtones of blackcurrants. Not showing a lot of development, the fruits are bright rather than tertiary, and overall the impression is more youthful than the 1991. Distinctly a food wine. 13.5% (November 2012) *89* Drink to 2017.

Pride Mountain

Pride is located right at the peak of Spring Mountain. In fact, the vineyards straddle the line between Napa and Sonoma (one inconvenient consequence being that regulations require two bonded wineries, one for handling Napa wines, the other for Sonoma). The origin of every lot has to be tracked. If a wine has more than 75% of grapes from Napa, it can be labeled with the Napa AVA, but most wines carry complicated accounts of the percent coming from Napa County versus Sonoma County. Vineyards are around 700 m, above the fog line, with 60% on the Sonoma side. Plantings are mostly Bordeaux varieties, with a little Syrah and small amounts of Chardonnay and Viognier. There are three different Cabernet Sauvignons and also a "Claret." The largest production, around 5,000 cases, is the Estate Cabernet Sauvignon, which usually has a bit more fruit from Napa than Sonoma. Winemaker Sally Johnson says this is at its peak for drinking about one year after release, although personally I'd prefer to wait another year. The two higher tiers are Vintner Select (500-600 cases) and the Reserve Cabernet Sauvignon (1,200 cases). "Vintner Select is the epitome of the California style, flashy and showy, it's 100% Napa," says Sally. It's a 100% Cabernet Sauvignon exclusively from clone 337. The Reserve is a more masculine wine intended for longer aging. "Not many people are making wines like the Reserve," she says. This sometimes has a couple of percent Petit Verdot, and is dominated by Pride's own Rock Arch clone of Cabernet Sauvignon. There's also the Reserve Claret, which is a Merlot-Cabernet Sauvignon blend. Wines were tasted at Pride in November 2012.

53% Napa 47% Sonoma, Estate Cabernet Sauvignon, 2010
This shows classic black Cabernet fruits on the palate with faint hints of cassis in the background, overall giving a pleasing, forward, approachable impression. Not as much character as other recent vintages, but perhaps that's because it's the youngest. 14.5% *88* Drink to 2019.

67% Napa 33% Sonoma, Estate Cabernet Sauvignon, 2009
Soft black fruit spectrum with blackcurrants to the fore. Supple tannins are almost chocolaty, giving a soft structure in the background. Intended for short to mid term drinking, this wine does not have quite as much concentration as other recent vintages, and is just a touch flatter in its flavor profile. 14.5% *87* Drink to 2017.

53% Napa 47% Sonoma, Estate Cabernet Sauvignon, 2008
A little reserve shows on the black fruit nose. Sweet, round black fruits show on the palate, the most well rounded and complete of the flight. A nice acid uplift on the finish keeps the wine refreshing, with just a touch of tannic dryness on the finish. 14.6% *89* Drink to 2018.

50% Napa 50% Sonoma, Estate Cabernet Sauvignon, 2007
Soft black fruit-driven nose develops some faint herbal influences. That softness continues on the palate, where structure is just evident, but this vintage will be one of the longer-lived of recent years. This also has the best balance of recent vintages, with some faint savory notes taking off the fruity edge. 14.6% *89* Drink to 2018.

Napa Valley, Vintner Select Cabernet Sauvignon, 2009
A sense of toughness on the nose initially hides the black fruits, but this is deliciously ripe on the palate, with black fruits turning to aromatic blackcurrants with a touch of cassis. Very much a modern Napa Cabernet, this has distinctly broader flavors than 2008 or 2007. Fruits are intense, but good acidity just stops the palate from becoming jammy. You feel you can see California sunshine in the fruits, but there's enough structure to hold for the mid term. This is a perfect example of the lushness that clone 337 can achieve in Napa. 14.8% *91* Drink to 2022.

Napa Valley, Vintner Select Cabernet Sauvignon, 2008
The nose is relatively closed with blackcurrant fruits struggling to show through; the impression is almost smoky. This shares with 2007 that reserve on the palate, although as the fruits come out they are quite bright, showing more as cherries than blackcurrants. Nicely balanced structure gives this vintage an elegant, fine, impression. 15.0% *92* Drink to 2024.

Napa Valley, Vintner Select Cabernet Sauvignon, 2007
There's a definite sense of the asperity of Cabernet Sauvignon black fruits, with a taut palate showing more black cherries than blackcurrants. Perhaps closing up a bit, this is less obvious than the 2008, although both show that classic linear purity of fruits of a 100% Cabernet Sauvignon. These vintages provide a clear demonstration of the interaction of clone 337 with the mountain environment. The overall style is elegant and should age well. 14.8% *91* Drink to 2023.

71% Napa 29% Sonoma, Reserve Cabernet Sauvignon, 2009
Fresh black fruits on the nose mingle with faint herbal influences, turning chocolaty in the glass. The ripe palate of black cherry and black plum fruits has a finish of furry chocolaty tannins with a gravelly texture. This is broader and softer, but not as bright and overtly fruit-driven, as the Vintner Select. This vies with the 2008 Reserve for the most deliciously youthful expression of fruits. 14.9% *91* Drink to 2025.

78% Napa 22% Sonoma, Reserve Cabernet Sauvignon, 2008
Black fruits just edge out herbal influences on the nose, but fruits are more overt than in 2009, with the furry, chocolaty tannins pushed into the background. This is a broad shouldered, more masculine style that makes a tighter impression than 2007 or 2003, with the sweet, ripe, fruits kept nicely under control. There's some heat on the finish. 15.2% *91* Drink to 2024.

68% Napa 32% Sonoma, Reserve Cabernet Sauvignon, 2007
Black fruits make a chocolaty impression on the nose, but the palate shows a broad range of fruit flavors with the chocolate less evident. Tannins remain supple on the finish. There's lots of flavor here in the modern style, supple yet with enough support for future development, although at present this seems less interesting than 2008 or 2009. 15.0% *90* Drink to 2022.

50% Napa 50% Sonoma, Reserve Cabernet Sauvignon, 2003
Chocolate and coffee notes hide the fruits on the nose. The palate has reached a lovely point of balance with the fruits counterpoised by soft ripe tannins (which however still dry the finish). Underlying structure is deceptive, appearing only with that dryness on the finish. There's an impression of soft black fruits evolving towards red fruits rather than going savory, with a delicious, almost piquant, sense of fruits coming out on the finish. This was by far the most lush and opulent of the flight. 14.7% *90* Drink to 2020.

Napa Valley, Reserve Cabernet Sauvignon, 1999
This is the most developed wine of the flight (more developed than 1994). The nose shows herbaceous overtones, becoming mineral, and developing into tertiary notes that stop just short of sous bois. This is reaching a tipping point with savory notes coming up as the fruits lighten, and a barely detectable touch of bell peppers coming through to the finish. The lovely balance of savory to fruity is right on the edge, with herbal influences strengthening in the glass. There's still some tannic support, so the wine should continue to develop in the direction of refinement and delicacy for another few years. 14.7% *92* Drink to 2018.

Napa Valley Reserve Cabernet Sauvignon, 1994
Restrained nose has faint mineral overtones but is less overtly developed than 1999. By contrast with 1999, the fruits are lightening, but savory notes have not come up; there's just a very faint whiff of herbaceousness. This is a subtle wine, and it needs a little time to come around, so its qualities might be overlooked at first blush. It's less developed than the Merlot-dominated 1994 Reserve Claret, and at its best, conveys quite a delicate impression. 13.0% *90* Drink to 2016.

Napa Valley, Reserve Claret, 2002
An intriguing mix of chocolate, herbs, and spices altogether gives quite a perfumed impression. This is one of the ripest wines made here, rich on the palate with chocolate verging into hints of raisins, and a touch of high toned aromatics. Delicious, but very ripe and a bit obvious. 14.4% *89* Drink to 2017.

Napa Valley, Reserve Claret, 1995
This has not developed the interest of the 1994. There is the austere nose of varietal Cabernet, although it is not herbaceous. Following through to the palate, the fruits continue to show that austere edge, with a certain lack of roundness on the mid palate. This is a wine that is holding up well with age, still tastes fresh, has not deteriorated, but nor does it seem to have developed savory complexity: there is little tertiary development. It is getting older, but not maturing, with that retarded development of pure Cabernet. 13.0% (February 2012) *88* Drink up.

Napa Valley, Reserve Claret, 1994
Development shows with a touch of sous bois, giving a lovely balance with the fruits, which are red more than black, supported by balanced acidity. This shows more obvious development than the 1994 Reserve Cabernet Sauvignon, an interesting demonstration that Merlot brings more rapid evolution than Cabernet Sauvignon, but it's reached its peak now and is unlikely to go anywhere more interesting. 13.0% *89* Drink to 2015.

Ridge Vineyards

The first vineyards and original Monte Bello Winery in the Santa Cruz mountains date from 1885. From this estate, since extended along the ridge, come the famous Monte Bello Cabernet Sauvignon and Chardonnay. Ridge is also famous for its single vineyard series of Zinfandels, which come from a wide range of locations, extending from Lytton Springs, Geyserville, and other vineyards in Sonoma, to a ranch in Paso Robles. At the Monte Bello estate, 24 parcels are usually used for producing the Monte Bello Cabernet, and another 21 for the Estate Cabernet. There are about 42 ha of vineyards for the black varieties altogether. The Estate Cabernet is essentially a second wine, although each parcel—or sometimes half parcel—is assessed separately. Decisions are made on most parcels before an initial assemblage, but some are left to be reassessed later, and one or two parcels change destination each year. Wines are tasted blind in flights of four, each flight containing a mix of varieties; the objective is to maintain the typicity of

Monte Bello, with a Bordelais approach of viewing lots as more important than varieties. Wines were tasted at Ridge in February 2012 or as otherwise noted.

Monte Bello, 2011
(Barrel sample: preliminary assemblage) Just a touch of spice starts out on the nose followed by a faintly nutty vegetal hint, which evolves further in the glass. The developing vegetal overtones carry on to the palate, which is quite tight at this time, with fruits slowly releasing in the glass. There's a clear impression here of a cool climate wine. It's a good result for a vintage that was generally difficult in California (although conditions were not so divergent from normal in the Santa Cruz Mountains as in the North Coast), but it may not achieve the elegance and longevity of the classic vintages. *88* Drink 2017-2023.

Monte Bello, 2010
(Barrel sample) Restrained nose with a faint cinnamon spiciness. Slowly developing, elegant black fruits are quite tight and precise on the palate. By far the finest grained of the past three vintages, this achieves a taut elegance that should develop nicely over the decade. The closest parallel in terms of Bordeaux would be with Margaux. *91* Drink 2016-2025.

Monte Bello, 2009
Restrained nose with faintly nutty notes slowly coming through, showing a touch of spice. Soft and round on the palate, the most generous of the three recent vintages, a touch obvious with some soft vanillin and oak showing on the palate. Black fruits showing as sweet ripe cherries emerge on the palate. Already quite approachable. *90* Drink 2015-2024.

Monte Bello, 2005
American oak in the form of coconut, dill, and vanilla bean leaps out of the glass to accompany deep, aromatic, black fruits. The black plums continue through to the palate where the sense of American oak intensifies. There is certainly enough fruit to stand up to the strong oak—but you need a lot. Ripe tannins give a nice balance to the finish, although I find the oak just a bit too obvious at the moment. Underneath the fruits are refined and fine-grained. 13.4% (December 2011) *92* Drink to 2026.

Monte Bello, 2003
Slightly spicy black fruit nose with overtones of vanillin and coconut. Smooth and elegant, with something of the refreshing character of Bordeaux, although overlayed by that dill and coconut. There is that lack of presence on the mid palate that seems to characterize the vintage, which also shows in the finish. The fruits seem sweet and ripe as they develop in the glass, still youthful, with a nice balance but not quite enough intensity. 13.2% (December 2011) *89* Drink to 2020.

Monte Bello, 2002
Primary black fruits show on the nose with some aromatic hints and just a suspicion of the mineral notes that will develop in the future. Nicely balanced on the palate, with fresh acidity supporting fruits that are a bit more developed than the nose would suggest. Elegant fruits are still quite tight in a manner resembling St. Julien, and in a blind tasting you might well think about European origins, although just a hint of vanillin from American oak shows on the back palate. This promises well in a lean and austere style. 13.0% (June 2009) *91* Drink 2013-2022.

Monte Bello, 1996
It's those slightly plush aromatics of blackcurrants slowly releasing more plummy overtones that tell you this wine comes from California. Fruits are sweet and ripe with just a faint telltale touch of vanillin and coconut from the American oak. Still full of flavor after close to two decades, without any trace of tertiary development, this gives an overall impression of refinement and elegance rather than power, with very fine-grained tannins providing supporting texture. As it develops in the glass, the aromatics subside slightly and there is a faint suspicion of a herbal touch and some smoke, making the wine seem more European. In a blind tasting this might be a confusing wine: the aromatic pointers to California usually go with a more massive construction, but if the roundness of the fruits suggested Pauillac or the refinement led you to St. Julien, you would be thinking more of a wine from 2004 or perhaps 2001 than the previous decade. There's no doubt about the fine quality of the texture, the roundness of the fruits, the smoothness of the tannins, the overall balance, but I'm surprised by the difference with, for example, the 1992, which feels more like a decade older. Surely the 1996 must be one of the most slowly developing vintages of Monte Bello? 13.2% (August 2012) *92* Drink to 2027.

Monte Bello, 1992
Dark garnet color. Very developed nose with some barnyard notes is quite aromatic. Nice balance although rather dry on the finish; not quite the roundness to carry the age, with some

vegetal notes coming through. The lushness of the early years seems to be dissipating quite fast. 13.5% *89* Drink to 2019.

Monte Bello, 1990

Lightening in color, the dusky appearance having turned to translucence. Mineral notes with a fairly pungent nose, some gunflint, quite developed with the original black fruits just poking through and just a faint hint of nuts. The palate follows the nose, much more developed than the 1992 or 1994, complex flavor spectrum with tertiary fruits now showing, balanced acidity supporting those seamless layers of flavor that you cannot deconstruct; alcohol although high is barely perceptible and well integrated. Faint notes of eucalyptus and menthol on the finish, still a brilliant future ahead. 13.5% (June 2009) *95* Drink to 2019.

Monte Bello, 1985

Dark garnet color shows development. Vegetal notes on the nose give an impression of forest floor. The sense of sous bois develops on the nose. Elegant balance here, caught at the turning point from fruity to savory. Fruits are ripe and smooth on the palate, with a delicious herbaceous touch coming in at the finish. Looser knit than the 1984, just a bit broader on the palate. Lovely right now. *93* Drink to 2017.

Monte Bello, 1984

Lightly developed aromatics are more restrained on the nose than the 1985. Smooth and classic on the palate with a touch of sous bois. Precise fruits show a restrained elegance and lovely balance with supporting acidity and fine-grained tannins. A nutty, herbaceous note just comes through to the finish. Noticeably more tightly knit and apparently less developed than the 1985. 12.9% *92* Drink to 2018.

Monte Bello, 1981

Translucent garnet color with broad rim. Pungent, faintly mineral impression on the nose, becoming more tertiary in the glass. Sous bois and tertiary on the palate, faint medicinal hints of eucalyptus with menthol notes on the aftertaste, layers of flavors beautifully integrated, very long finish and complex aromatically. At a point of perfection now, with the ripeness of the fruits showing on the finish. An earthy impression led some tasters to identify Brett, but the flavors are harmonious, well integrated, and complex, with that sweatiness just part of the complex flavor spectrum. 12.0% (June 2009) *94* Drink to 2019.

Monte Bello, 1978

Mature aromatics show sweet ripe fruits on nose and palate, elegant rather than rambunctious, still slightly nutty, but overlaid by some barnyard notes. That touch of bitterness on the finish has become a little more pronounced over the past three years and is accompanied by a classic but faint herbaceousness. The wine will hold for some time yet, but the bitterness is going to overtake the fruits and it would be best enjoyed soon. (Three years ago this showed the first signs of beginning to dry out, so like Bordeaux, it is declining ever so gently.) 13.6% *91* Drink to 2015.

Monte Bello, 1971

Mature appearance, garnet with some mahogany hues. Restrained nose with hints of sous bois, a generally developed and tertiary impression. Sweet ripe fruits on the palate, actually seems more youthful than the 1974 or 1978. Nice balance in restrained style, palate following the nose, just drying out a fraction on the finish to show the remaining tannic structure. 12.2% (June 2009) *90* Drink up.

Monte Bello, 1964

Lightening mature garnet color with some mahogany hues. Quite dumb nose, hints, but only hints, of tertiary aromas and nuts with some very slight indications of oxidation, although still at the stage of adding complexity. Quite tertiary on the palate, fruits drying out a bit, but acidity still fresh enough to keep it going. A slight sense of roasted meats and bitterness on the finish. 12.0% (June 2009) *89* Drink up.

Sbragia

Ed Sbragia grew up in Dry Creek Valley—"basically my heritage is Zinfandel and French Colombard," he says—got a chemistry degree from Davis, worked for Gallo, discovered wine, went back to school, worked for Foppiano for a year, and then went to Beringer for 32 years. He started his own production in 2001, while still at Beringer. His first release was in 2004. He purchased his present property in 2006. His own grapes are Sauvignon Blanc, Zinfandel, Chardonnay, Merlot; purchased grapes come from growers in Dry Creek and in Mayacamas mountains, and from two vineyards on Howell Mountain. All the Cabernets are single vineyard designates, with about 10 tons of grapes making 250 cases each. His son is the winemaker. The Sbragia winery is located in Sonoma, but most of his Cabernets come from Napa. This was an especially interesting tasting as the wines were all distinct, and it did not seem to me that there was any consistent difference between those from the Napa side and those from the Sonoma side of the Mayacamas mountains. Wines were tasted at Sbragia in February 2012.

Dry Creek Valley, Andolsen Vineyard, Cabernet Sauvignon, 2009
The vineyard is close to the base of Dry Creek Valley at an elevation of about 240 m. It is blended with (less than) 5% of Cabernet Franc from Mount Veeder to add a little extra freshness and complexity. It was matured in 60% new oak. The dusty nose is more black plums than blackcurrants with some faint overtones of tobacco. The cool climate impression comes more from the restraint of the fruits than from the acidity, which is balanced. Elegant fruits are supported by a structure of fine tannins, in a lighter style for mid term drinking. A sense of linearity identifies the almost pure Cabernet. A touch of heat on the finish marks this down a point or so. Still needs a little time. 13.7% *88* Drink 2014-2020.

Sonoma Valley, Monte Rosso, Cabernet Sauvignon, 2007
This is one of the last vintages where the Cabernet Sauvignon included some of the older vines of Monte Rosso, planted in the 1950s, as that particular block has now been pulled out. The wine also includes 4.2% of Cabernet Franc. At first the wine seems a little restrained on the nose, then the black fruits show a touch of savory development with a faint impression of gunflint, promising some complexity. The balance seems European, on a savory cusp with an intriguing mix of spices and a faintly nutty edge in the background. Although there is a touch of heat on the finish, overall the impression is of an elegant balance. My only reservation is whether this is aging too quickly; delicious now, but will it stay the course for another decade? 14.2% *92* Drink to 2024.

Howell Mountain, Rancho del Oso, Cabernet Sauvignon, 2007
This is one of two adjacent vineyards from which Sbragia makes Howell Mountain Cabernet. It's at about 650 m with some clay in the soil. The vines are clones 337 and 8, planted in 1989-1990. A perfumed nose has floral overtones of violets and roses. Generally elegant, sweet ripe fruits on the palate, with those floral overtones giving a softer and more supple impression than Monte Rosso. A sweet, nutty touch with chocolate overtones marks the finish, with a touch of heat. This is the most approachable of Sbragia's Cabernets. 14.8% *89* Drink to 2022.

Howell Mountain, Cimarosa, Cabernet Sauvignon, 2007
Here the red soils are more volcanic, bringing minerality to the wine. The vines are clones 7 and 8, and were planted in 1999. There's a slightly savory impression to the nose at first, then reverting to some floral notes with a touch of cinnamon, but less evident than from the adjacent Rancho del Oso. Soft and supple on the palate, with a mixture of savory and spicy influences following the nose. Fine tannins show on the finish, giving a nice sense of structure. 14.6% *91* Drink to 2023.

Mount Veeder, Wall Vineyard, Cabernet Sauvignon, 2006
This wine is a field blend with 10% Cabernet Franc. There are more overt fruits on the nose than from Sbragia's other vineyards, with faintly piquant fruits of red and black cherries. This is a more classic Napa style. The fruits are clear, bright, and forward, with cherries predominant, and less evolved than the other wines. There are no more than bare hints of savory development. The tight structure makes this the most closed of the flight (but of course this is also a less opulent vintage). 14.6% *90* Drink to 2023.

Schrader Cellars

Fred Schrader cofounded Colgin-Schrader Cellars in 1992, and then moved to found Schrader Cellars with his wife Carol in 1998. The present portfolio concentrates on single vineyard bottlings from To Kalon and George III. The To Kalon bottlings emphasize small plots within the vineyard, mostly planted with individual clones. The first year of production from To Kalon was 2000, but 2001 was the year when the Schraders moved to an acreage contract, giving them control over issues such as harvesting, which is late, usually at the start of October. Total production is about 1,800 cases. The style has always been towards powerful cult wines, ripe, rich, and full, but the massive underlying structure takes them far away from fruit bombs. The characters of the individual bottlings demonstrate the relative differences between the clones at a high level of concentration and ripeness, with clone 6 the most structured, 337 the most opulent, and clone 4 the most loose knit. Wines were tasted at Schrader Cellars in December 2011.

Napa, Beckstoffer George III, 2009
The George III vineyard is based on the old Beaulieu #3 vineyard at Rutherford, with the addition of three adjacent properties. Although the vines are only ten years old, yields are really low (1.5 tons/acre or 20 hl/ha). The plot for this wine is planted entirely with clone 337. The refined black fruit nose of deep cherries and plums develops a touch of chocolate in the glass. Rich chocolate-coated black plum fruits show on the palate, very dense, with coffee notes on the finish. The overall impression is powerful yet refined, with the precision of the fruits coming through. The opulent nature of the clone no doubt contributes to the impression. 14.4% *92* Drink 2013-2030.

Napa, Beckstoffer To Kalon RBS, 2009
The plot for this wine is planted exclusively with clone 337, and harvests at yields of 3.5 tons/acre (45 hl/ha). One again the opulent character of the clone comes through. There's a perfumed black fruit nose with the perfume intensifying in the glass. More restrained than George III, you can see the dense black cherry fruits holding back on the palate. Yet this is the most approachable on the palate of the Beckstoffer To Kalon bottlings. Ripe rounded tannins show more than a touch of chocolate on the finish. Powerful, with an overall chocolaty impression. 14.5% *94* Drink 2014-2031.

Napa, Beckstoffer To Kalon T6, 2009
This wine comes from a plot of clone 6 that gives only 2 tons/acre (25 hl/ha). A touch of perfume on the nose is just a bit less intense than the RBS. Restrained black fruits dominate the palate, showing as chocolate-coated cherries. Ripe tannins are subsumed by the fruits, and are evident only by dryness on the finish. The character of the clone shows in the immense underlying structure. This brooding monster will open slowly and live for ever. It's nowhere near releasing its full potential yet. 14.6% *95* Drink 2016-2033.

Napa, Beckstoffer To Kalon CCS, 2009
This wine comes from a plot of clone 4 harvested at 3-4 tons/acre (40-55 hl/ha).There's an impression of nuts and cereals as well as black fruits on the nose. The black fruits of the palate are quite restrained, held back by the firm, fine-grained tannins. Very long term aging potential, yet less evident structure than the other clones. 14.4% *95* Drink 2015-2033.

Napa, Beckstoffer To Kalon Schrader, 2009
This is a blend of clones 337 and 4 and 6 (using different plots from those where the single clonal wines originate). Average yields here are 3-4 tons/acre (40-55 hl/ha). Initial impression on the nose is a chocolate coating to black cherries, and then a faint herbal note develops in the glass. This is more open than CCS but less than RBS, chocolaty on the palate with firm tannins drying the finish. Clearly needs a lot more time. 14.6% *93* Drink 2015-2031.

Screaming Eagle

Screaming Eagle scarcely needs any introduction: it is by far California's most famous cult wine. The winery was created when Jean Phillips bought 23 ha of land just off the Silverado trail, in the Oakville area, for an unusually high price in 1986. The area was known to the neighbors as providing high quality grapes; largely Riesling, it was replanted to Cabernet Sauvignon in 1987 with small amounts of Merlot and Cabernet Franc. Heidi Barrett was engaged as winemaker. Since then, further replanting, managed by David Abreu, has brought the vineyard into a Bordeaux-like balance of Cabernet Sauvignon, Cabernet Franc, and Merlot. The slight depression in the land creates a small frost problem from time to time, which is handled by overhead sprinklers fed by a lake. Drainage has been installed under the new plantings to recapture water. They expect to dry farm more or less around two thirds of the ranch, especially where there's more clay (to the west). This is an early ripening site, but even so, they are early pickers here, usually a week to ten days ahead of everyone else. The Cabernet has historically been clones 7 and See, but in the last couple of years some clones 6, 169, and 337 have crept in. The winery was sold in 2006 to two partners, one of whom has since left. A new winery was constructed for the 2010 vintage; it's not exactly utilitarian, but certainly focuses directly on winemaking. There's an open barn covering the crush pad, with hatches to allow the grapes to go straight into the fermenters below, where there is an underground facility including all sorts of fermentation tanks. Grapes are usually picked at 24-25 Brix with a pH around 3.5; there is no acidification. There is a total of about 4 weeks on the skins, starting with cold maceration for about 5 days, yeast are added to start fermentation, which lasts 7-10 days, and then there are 2 weeks or more on the skins. Malolactic fermentation is performed in barrel. A little press wine is used most years. They worry a lot about air exposure and try to minimize handling; racking is done under argon. The wine spends about 18 months in French oak. "New oak is about 75%: 100% would be too much," says winemaker Nick Gislason, who is aided by consultant Michel Rolland. Annual production is generally less than 750 cases, and the wine is available only to a member list (with a limit of three bottles per member); the waiting list is several years long. Wines were tasted at Screaming Eagle in February 2012.

Oakville, Cabernet Sauvignon, 2010
(Barrel sample of the base blend.) The blend could yet change slightly, but this gives a good idea of style and quality. Reserved nose has black cherry and plum fruits poking through a veneer of minerality. A sheen of elegant, precisely delineated black cherries cut by redcurrants slowly develops aromatic complexity in the glass, with that mineral edge showing on the finish. Of course, the tannins are quite mouth drying at this stage, but they display a very fine texture. It's evident that this will develop slowly, but as the tannins drop out over the next five years, you can see that wine will eventually resolve to a delicate structure in a typically refined style. Some hints of tobacco and chocolate join the minerality on the finish as the tannins recede. *93* Drink 2016-2027.

Oakville, Cabernet Sauvignon, 2009
Reserved on the nose with hints more of red cherries and redcurrants than black fruits, then some nutty overtones. Nice balance already showing on the palate, that paradoxical combination of smooth suppleness on the palate and tautness on the finish, now showing more black fruits than red. The palate impression is refined with a very fine-grained filigree of tannic support, the tannins subsumed by the fruits and showing just a touch of bitterness and dryness on the finish against the touch of chocolate and tobacco. What comes across most of all is the sheen of refinement. 14.8% *94* Drink 2015-2027.

Shafer

John Shafer left a career in corporate publishing to move to Napa Valley, where he purchased 210 acres and planted vineyards in 1972 in what became the Stags Leap District in 1989. The first vintage in 1978 used Cabernet Sauvignon from the Sunspot vineyard that rises up immediately above the winery. Hillside Select started in 1983, when Doug Shafer became winemaker. "I was tasting lots and the Sunspot was head and shoulders above everything else. I thought we should bottle it separately—this became the 1982 Reserve. That started the program. I got tired of explaining what Reserve was, because everyone had a reserve, and in 1983 we called it Hillside Select. The fruits are so good you can keep your hands off it—Hillside Select is the easiest wine to make," Doug says. There are about 20 ha on the hillside block, and the best lots are selected each year for

Hillside Select, of which there are usually 2,000-2,500 cases. It's 100% Cabernet Sauvignon. There are also about 8,000 cases of the One Point Five Cabernet Sauvignon, which comes from the hillside estate vineyard and the Borderline vineyard two miles south of Shafer at the edge of the Stags Leap District. Other wines include Chardonnay, Merlot, and Syrah, bringing total production to 32,000 cases from vineyards now totaling 90 ha. Wines were tasted at Shafer in November 2012 except as otherwise noted.

Stags Leap District, One Point Five Cabernet Sauvignon, 2009
This shows Shafer's typical style of sweet black fruits with evident aromatics. There's less fruit density than with Hillside Select, so the aromatics aren't so overwhelming, and the ripe tannins show more clearly. This has the mid level concentration that is typical of the vintage. 15.3% (February 2012) *88* Drink 2013-2019.

Stags Leap District, Hillside Select Cabernet Sauvignon, 2008
Fresh nose offers an almost perfumed impression, quite delicate even though alcohol is very high. Fruits are tightly defined by an acid surround but there's still that characteristic warm, furry, impression on the finish. The solid, firm impression seems to be clearly in the modern style of Napa, with a chocolate coating on the finish. Overall the style is midway between the leaner 2000 and the distinctly opulent 2004. 15.5% *91* Drink to 2024.

Stags Leap District, Hillside Select Cabernet Sauvignon, 2006
Tight black completely undeveloped appearance. Restrained almost herbal nose with black fruits somewhere behind. But sweet ripe fruits on the palate initially seem more open knit than you expect, but then the tannins come into evidence giving an almost brutal drying impression on the finish. Constantly changing in the glass, this wine is a conundrum. 14.9% (June 2011) *89* Drink to 2021.

Stags Leap District, Hillside Select Cabernet Sauvignon, 2005
The first impression is very Californian, in the form of strong notes of coconut and vanillin on the nose, turning to coffee and chocolate, but then accompanying notes of development, with a faint tinge of barnyard, suggest there may be some evolution. The palate, however, reflects more the initial impression than the follow up, with a rather aromatic impression of black fruits, blackcurrants with overtones of cassis, and then those notes of coconut and vanillin coming back. It's intense and chewy on the finish, colored by those strong aromatics. No one could quarrel with the quality and intensity, but sometimes I think this style is more food in itself than wine to accompany food. The label claims that the Hillside Select is typical of the Stags Leap District, but I think it is more typical of itself. The big question in my mind is how long it will take for those aromatics to come into a calmer balance, and whether that will be paralleled by an extension of those faint suggestions of development to the palate. My guess is that it will take at least a decade before the wine will cease to be so assertive that it overpowers any accompaniment. 14.0% (December 2011) *90* Drink to 2021.

Stags Leap District, Hillside Select Cabernet Sauvignon, 2004
Rich chocolaty nose with hints of coffee and almost a suggestion of raisins predicts an opulent style reflecting the warm vintage. The palate is more restrained than you would expect from the nose, with fruits nicely balanced by a firm tannic structure. Those chocolate and coffee notes come back on the finish. This vintage gives the thickest impression on the palate and is really furry on the finish. This is definitely a strong representation of the vintage, and Doug Shafer says that even for him, it is almost too much. 14.9% *90* Drink to 2021.

Stags Leap District, Hillside Select Cabernet Sauvignon, 2003
Slightly nutty nose with red and black cherry fruits. Aromatic on the palate with lots of black plums and blackcurrants, ripe and rich, with a sweet kick that makes you wonder about residual sugar (no, of course there can't really be any). I'm left wondering how this level of aromaticity expresses the terroir. It's a tribute to the wine that it is interesting at this point, but it leaves you wondering when the fruits will calm down enough for this really to be a good food match. 14.9% (February 2012) *90* Drink to 2020.

Stags Leap District, Hillside Select Cabernet Sauvignon, 2001
Sweet ripe notes open the nose. Soft and supple fruits on the palate make more of a valley than mountain impression. Well rounded red black cherries slowly release aromatics in the glass. Tannins are less noticeable than on other wines of this vintage; they are now resolving but there is still a slight bitterness on the finish. This is a wine to drink now. 14.9% (February 2012) *91* Drink 2014-2021.

Stags Leap District, Hillside Select Cabernet Sauvignon, 2000
Faintly chocolaty nose is followed by some fresher overtones. It's rich and opulent on the palate, but the fruits are still restrained by a backbone of firm, chocolaty tannins with a granular texture. This has the finest structure of the decade, perhaps reflecting the refinement of age, with the most precisely delineated fruits. Lean is not a word I would use in conjunction with Hillside Select, but relatively speaking, reflecting the cooler year, this has the leanest style. 14.8% *92* Drink to 2024.

Stags Leap District, Hillside Select Cabernet Sauvignon, 1992
This wine is constantly confusing, with an unpredictable evolution in the glass that was hard to pin down. The appearance is quite youthful. The initial impression on the nose is really restrained, just some hints of red cherries and a fugitive whiff of raspberries. The palate is initially driven by red and black cherries with some hints of almonds on the finish. With just a faint impression of Cabernet-like austerity on the finish, and without great intensity of fruit, you wonder whether this is a case of retarded development, where the fruits might already be drying out without ever developing any savory, tertiary character. Then after a significant period in the glass, another wine appears. The aromatics that were so forceful when young have certainly calmed down, but ripe, round aromas still appear to have their original character with little development. The wine puts on weight in the glass, loses its original austerity, and shows more rounded fruits, with the palate turning to a mixture of sweet, ripe red and black cherries, smooth and supple, although still without any savory development. New World origin is betrayed by a touch of heat on the finish. If this wine were 10 years old, I'd know where I was and would expect it to start developing soon, but after 18 years it is not at all obvious that it is going to show any tertiary development at all. The wine is probably at its peak now; given its history, it seems doubtful that it will develop in an interesting way rather than decline. (February 2012) 89 Drink to 2015.

Spottswoode

Driving along Madrona Avenue in downtown St. Helena through suburban housing, you wonder where the Spottswoode winery can be, and then suddenly you come out into 15 hectares of vineyards that stretch from the edge of the town up to the mountains. Jack and Mary Novak purchased the property in 1972, and were refused a permit to make wine because the neighborhood was residential. The later purchase (in 1990) of a winery across the road allowed the wine to be made in the vicinity. The Cabernet Sauvignon is a blend, although there is no Merlot. "We don't have any Merlot growing here, I'm not a fan of Merlot in this area. There was some Merlot at Spottswoode long ago, but it was removed," says winemaker Aron Weinkauf. In addition to 12.5 ha of Cabernet Sauvignon, there are 1.25 ha of Cabernet Franc and 0.4 ha of Petit Verdot for the blend, and also a hectare of Sauvignon Blanc. A second wine, called Lyndenhurst, is made in a more approachable fruit-forward, less ageworthy style (using 60% new oak compared to Spottswoode's 68%). Production is usually about 3,000 cases of Spottswoode and 700 cases of Lyndenhurst. My favorite vintage of Spottswoode is the 1992. Wines were tasted at Spottswoode in December 2011 unless otherwise noted.

Napa Cabernet Sauvignon, 2008
Restrained nose suggestive of black fruits with herbal overtones. Smooth elegant fruits of blackcurrents and blackberries show in a light style on the palate; not a blockbuster. Slowly a faint impression of chocolate, vanillin, and coconut develops on the finish. Rather taut, with fine-grained tannins, this really needs another couple of years to open out. 14.5% *89* Drink 2013-2023.

Napa Cabernet Sauvignon, 2005
The initial impression is that this has a European nose but an American palate. There's a hint of development in a faint touch of barnyard on the nose as it opens, then later this clears to show aromatic black fruits, before returning again. The palate is distinctly Napa, with bursting fruits overlaid by notes of vanillin and coconut. Some intense blackcurrant aromatics stop just short of cassis and make a forceful impression on the palate and finish. This vintage seems less restrained than others from Spottswoode. The underlying tannins take a while to show directly,

but finally appear in the form of some bitterness on the finish. It's not so much the power as the strength of the aromatics that make the wine too forceful; perhaps another couple of years will make a difference. (January 2012) 14.1% *89* Drink 2013-2019.

Napa Cabernet Sauvignon, 2001
Spicy black fruit nose shows a touch of cinnamon and a suggestion of smoky minerality. Elegant black fruits are precisely delineated on the palate in a restrained style. Fruits have lost their primary fat but not yet developed savory notes. The wine still seems quite youthful, perhaps at the end of its adolescence, just about to develop. 14.2% *90* Drink to 2023.

Napa Cabernet Sauvignon, 1998
Strongly developed barnyard nose is quite pungent. The palate shows a more subtle balance than is suggested by the nose, although savory notes of sous bois are clearly dominant. Fruits are still quite concentrated, although some bitterness is creeping on to the finish. Then the barnyard blows off somewhat to reveal some tobacco notes. Delicious, but will it be too developed for some palates? A good result for this unusually cool vintage. 14.0% *87* Drink to 2014.

Napa Cabernet Sauvignon, 1992
Mature nose is intriguingly balanced between perfume and sous bois, giving an impression of delicacy, with a developing touch of minerality and smoke. The balance on the palate makes it hard to decide whether savory or fruit is the driving force. The light elegance of the palate perhaps doesn't quite deliver the full complexity promised by the nose, but right at this moment it's caught at that delicious turning point. This may be the most subtle wine Spottswoode made in the past two decades, but drink soon before the fruits begin to decline. 13.8% *92* Drink to 2015.

Stonestreet

Stonestreet was created by Jesse Jackson, who started in wine by purchasing an orchard of pear and walnut trees in Lakeport (in the Central Valley) and converting it to a vineyard for Chardonnay production. He purchased a mountain estate in Sonoma's Alexander Valley in 1995 and turned it into a brand for Cabernet Sauvignon and Chardonnay. (Stonestreet was his middle name.) Stonestreet has 3,200 ha with 350 ha planted, including 200 ha of Cabernet Sauvignon. The vineyards are largely on the mountain slopes, where 80 ha had been planted in 1982, another 80 ha in 1991, more by Jackson after the acquisition in 1995, and then again in 2005. The overall balance of production is 80% red. Stonestreet is part of Jackson Family Vineyards, and while some of the grapes are used for its own bottlings, some are used by other vineyards in the group. The Stonestreet facility is also used to make wine for other properties in the group. Cabernet tends to be grown on higher plots on the mountains, because an inversion layer of cold air lower down makes ripening difficult. A series of monovarietal Cabernet Sauvignons come from single vineyards, Bear Point (below the fog line at 400 m), West Ledge (within the fog line at 550 m), and Monolith and Christopher (above the fog line at 700 m and 800 m). Monument Ridge is a bottling from sites all across the property. Legacy is an Alexander Valley blend that includes lots from the valley floor. "Mountain sites give far more variability in growth and ripening than on the flat. New plantings of Merlot, Petit Verdot, and Malbec are going very well; but blending them in would cause loss of site specificity," says winemaker Graham Weerts. The Stonestreet wines are not wines for immediate gratification, which has been a marketing problem in the past. They have been trying to make the wines a little rounder and more opulent. Wines were tasted at Stonestreet in February 2012.

Alexander Valley, Legacy, Cabernet Sauvignon, 2007
This is Stonestreet's Bordeaux blend, usually around 85% Cabernet Sauvignon, with Cabernet Franc, Merlot, and Petit Verdot. This vintage shows a very faintly piquant touch of blackcurrants on the nose. The fruits on the palate are less precise but more rounded than the single vineyard (100%) Cabernets, but the wine is still definitely Cabernet-dominated. There's a sense of black fruit pressure on palate and finish, with less intensity than the monovarietal wines, but even so, this needs more time to release its flavors. 14.8% *90* Drink 2014-2022.

Alexander Valley, Monument Ridge, Cabernet Sauvignon, 2007
This is Stonestreet's largest bottling, representing a blend from sites across the property. The nose shows blackcurrants with hints of cassis, a touch of vanillin, and some nuttiness, but the overall impression remains fresh. Ripe black fruits on the palate have an overlay of vanilla bean. The fruits are taut in that linear style of pure Cabernet Sauvignon. The palate impression is just a fraction superficial, and in a direct comparison you see that the wine does not have the intensity of the single vineyard designates. 14.5% *89* Drink 2013-2022.

Alexander Valley, Bear Point, Cabernet Sauvignon, 2007
Faintly nutty black fruit nose, a hint of black fruits, just a touch cedary. Sweet fruits are more elegant than the general bottling of Monument Ridge, taut and linear. This is the most elegant of the single vineyard offerings, the tannins are the best integrated, and the wine has a nice taut edge. It is drinking well already. 14.5% *92* Drink to 2022.

Alexander Valley, West Ledge, Cabernet Sauvignon, 2007
A slightly softer impression on the nose than Bear Point, with a faintly vegetal nuttiness. This is looser knit than the other single vineyards, making it more approachable, although very much in the linear style that is characteristic of pure Cabernet Sauvignon. Precisely delineated black fruits of cherries and blackcurrants are tight and restrained on the palate. Still needs more time. 14.5% *91* Drink 2014-2022.

Alexander Valley, Monolith, Cabernet Sauvignon, 2007
Hints of black fruits, nutty notes with cereal overtones, but generally a fresh impression on the nose. The fruit profile is less lively than Bear Point or West Ledge, but there is more direct sense of underlying structure. Black fruits show as blackcurrants and plums, but the aromatics are less distinct than the other single vineyard bottlings. Living up to its name, the wine presently is somewhat monolithic, not really releasing its fruit flavors yet. There's quite a tannic bite to the finish, which needs time to be tamed. 13.9% *90* Drink 2015-2024

Alexander Valley, Christopher, Cabernet Sauvignon, 2007
Fresh black fruits with a touch of cereal on the nose. This is the softest on the palate of the single vineyard bottlings, with more rounded fruits, and fine tannins on the underlying structure. Elegant, well delineated black fruits show more as cherries than blackcurrants. Another year or two is needed for the tannins to soften, and then this will show as a precise, elegant Cabernet. A touch of austerity marks the finish. This promises well for future development. 15.0% *92* Drink 2013-2022.

Philip Togni

Philip Togni was first involved in planting Cabernet Sauvignon in 1959, and worked in a variety of countries before coming to Cuvaison in Napa. He was involved with several mountain vineyards, including Pride and Chappellet, before he started to clear the land for his own vineyard in 1975, when he planted the first 3 acres of Sauvignon Blanc, followed by 1.5 acres of Cabernet Franc in 1981, all on AxR1. By 1985 everything had been replanted on 110 rootstock. His estate has 10.5 acres of vineyards at the top of Spring Mountain, close to the border between Napa and Sonoma. There are three lines of wines: Togni estate, Tanbark (a second label, introduced pretty much right at the beginning, in 1986), and Ca'Togni (only for sweet wine made from Black Hamburg). "We started off saying we wanted to make a Médoc wine," he says, and his Cabernet Sauvignon is typically about 86% Cabernet Sauvignon, with the rest from the other three Bordeaux varieties. Merlot is a little under represented in the wine (6%) compared to plantings (15%) because its yields are lower than the other varieties. Production has generally been about 2,000 cases per year; the current vintage, together with ten year old wines from a library, is offered to subscribers in the Fall. Wines were tasted at Philip Togni in February 2012 unless otherwise noted.

Spring Mountain District, Cabernet Sauvignon, 2009
Restrained black fruit nose with hints of cinnamon and chocolate. Sturdy black fruits on the palate are supported by tight, strongly structured, tannins. A fair tannic bite still grips the finish. 13.8% *88* Drink 2018-2028.

Spring Mountain District, Cabernet Sauvignon, 2007
Restrained black fruit nose. A restrained style follows on the palate, with austere black fruits supported by crisp acidity. Tannins are subsumed by the fruits. Some eucalyptus strengthens in the glass. 13.8% (December 2010) *90* Drink 2014-2012.

Napa Valley, Cabernet Sauvignon, 2005
Black fruit nose of cherries with a whiff of raspberries; already the aromatics are becoming more complex. Soft black fruit palate is slowly rounding out. Overall the approach is a little stern, and seems to be lacking in generosity. When will it start to develop? 13.8% *87* Drink 2017-2024.

Napa Valley, Cabernet Sauvignon, 1998
Medium garnet color suggests some development. Savory development shows on the nose, but remains relatively faint. The palate is tight in a northern European style, with good acidity, almost piquant, emphasizing the taut black fruits. Tannins are quite fine considering the difficulties of the vintage. A touch of sous bois, with hints of minerality, just appears on the finish. Overall this is a bit hard edged, but it is a very good result for the vintage, and achieves Togni's aim of a moderate style. 13.8% *87* Drink to 2018.

Napa Valley, Cabernet Sauvignon, 1995
Restrained nose has a Bordeaux-like austerity. The dry palate is reminiscent of a cooler Bordeaux vintage. I might be fooled about the origin of this wine in a blind tasting. This is definitely a food wine: not intended for tasting by itself, it came to life against food, becoming softer and more rounded. It remains somewhat linear; you feel that more Merlot might have rounded it out. This comes into the category of surviving rather than maturing, as it doesn't seem yet to have undergone much tertiary development. 13.8% *88* Drink up.

Napa Valley, Cabernet Sauvignon, 1991
Sous bois mingles with redcurrant and red cherry fruits on the nose; some complexity is developing here. Ripe, well rounded fruits on the palate emphasize red cherries and redcurrants against a mineral background. The sous bois comes back on the finish with a touch of gunflint. This is at the turning point for savory development, with a touch of sparseness on the finish cut by notes of chocolate and tobacco. 13.8% *90* Drink to 2017.

Viader

Viader Vineyards occupies a steep slope on Howell Mountain that runs down into Bell Canyon. It's at an elevation of 400 m, just below the Howell Mountain AVA. Purchased and then cleared in 1981, the land was planted with Cabernet Sauvignon, Cabernet Franc, and Petit Verdot. There's no Merlot or Malbec because they do not do well in the mountain environment. "I planted Petit Verdot thinking it would go into the Proprietary Red but it just didn't fit," says Delia Viader, explaining why Viader's blend is solely Cabernet Sauvignon and Cabernet Franc. "Differences between the wines are more vintage driven than by variety per se because I change the blend with the vintage," she says. Cabernet Sauvignon is always a majority, varying from 51-75% over the past decade. The Petit Verdot goes into a monovarietal wine, as does any Cabernet Franc that isn't used for the Proprietary Red; there's also a blended wine that is largely Cabernet Sauvignon and Syrah. Other wines are made from purchased fruit. A change in style may occur as Alex Viader takes over, as he prefers more intensity and extraction. Total production is 5,000 cases. Wines were tasted at Viader in December 2011.

Napa, 2008
The aromatics and perfume of Cabernet Franc seem to dominate the nose, with tobacco giving way to more austere aromas. The elegant palate shows tight, precise fruits, with a chocolate coating on the finish. Once again Cabernet Franc seems more in evidence than Sauvignon. Overall impression is quite perfumed and elegant. 15.1% *91* Drink to 2022.

Napa, 2002
Development on the nose shows as savory, barnyard notes, which change to nuts and cereal in the glass. The palate is more herbal than savory, with a touch of spice to the red fruits. Tannins have resolved, there is a nice balance, and the wine is at its peak. 14.0% *89* Drink to 2016.

Napa, 2001
Characteristic Napa fruit comes right up in the glass, showing as aromatic, piquant, black plums on the nose. Very fine and tight on the palate, with a refinement brought by the Cabernet Franc. The overall balance of the palate is taut rather than fleshy. The nose promises a finely delineated elegance, which the palate delivers, although it is a touch linear, making somewhat of a contrast with the aromatics of the nose. The fine granular texture is very Cabernet Franc-ish; in fact, the overall impression is as much Cabernet Franc as Sauvignon. 14.0% *89* Drink to 2019.

Washington State

Over the past decade, vintage variation has been driven by temperature. 2011 and 2010 were cooler years. "The beauty of 2010 and 2011 is that you didn't get the convergence of ripeness in the vineyard you get in warm years. Indeed, I think you see more flavor variety in the cooler years," says Bob Betz MW. Conditions in 2009 were warm: this is a distinctly riper year than either the previous or succeeding vintages; some vintage charts rate it highly, but the character is atypically ripe. "The hot vintages bring too much ripeness which obscures the purity of line and typicity," says winemaker Jean-François Pellet. "2011 was the coolest year since 93, but fantastic in the way it ended. In 2011, 2010, 2009 for various reasons you'll see huge variation between the top and bottom wines, but in 2008 and 2007 everyone could make good wine," says Chris Figgins of Leonetti. Although 2008 is considered only an average vintage, it's easier to see the distinctions between subregions than in the riper 2009 vintage. Before that, 2007 and 2005 were warmer years that are generally considered the most successful of the decade. "These are the sweet spot vintages," says Joel Butler MW. Years 2004 and 2003 are considered to have been average. 2002 was a cooler vintage.

Betz Family Winery

Betz sources grapes from a variety of sites, including Horse Heaven Hills, Red Mountain, Snipes Mountain, and Yakima Valley. "We claim our blending starts in the vineyard by site selection. We do not own any vineyards but have detailed control of growing in all the blocks," says Bob Betz. Bob feels that blending makes more interesting wine than making many single vineyard wines. There's a range based on Rhône varieties, and two wines from Bordeaux varieties, the Clos de Betz Merlot-based blend, and the Père de Famille Cabernet Sauvignon (which contains about 10% Petit Verdot and 8% Merlot). "My goal would be to have a 100% Cabernet Sauvignon and we try every year, but we never produce it. In our blending trials, some of the lots, for example from Kiona, are very compelling but we find that something else really adds something," Bob says. From the first vintage of 150 cases in 1997 (while Bob was still at Chateau St. Michelle), Betz Family Winery has grown to become one of the most respected producers in the state. The winery was sold to Steve and Bridgit Griessel in 2012, but Bob is staying on for five years as winemaker. Wines were tasted at Betz in Woodinville in September 2012. It was hard to decide between 2001 and 2000 as favorites.

Columbia Valley, Père de Famille Cabernet Sauvignon, 2010
First impressions suggest a youthful black fruit spiciness. Aromatic sweet peppers and a suggestion of anise show on the palate with a sense of restraint. Tannins are hidden by the fruit density, but show in dryness on the finish. It's delicious already, but it would be vinicide to drink now. Generally this is less open than the 2009, and needs more time, but it should mature to a refined elegance. 14.1% *91* Drink 2014-2028.

Columbia Valley, Père de Famille Cabernet Sauvignon, 2009
Inky purple color with a distinctly aromatic initial impression. Sweet, ripe, rounded, black plum fruits, dense across the palate and into the finish. It's the aromatics more than the intensity or alcohol that give a New World impression. There's already more flavor variety evident than on the more massively structured and reserved 2007. There's an openly delicious quality of sweet peppers, perhaps a little obvious at the moment, and needing time for the aromatics to calm down. 14.6% *89* Drink to 2025.

Columbia Valley, Père de Famille Cabernet Sauvignon, 2007
Slightly nutty first impression with hints of spices. Sweet, round black fruits on the palate have stern undertones; you can see the density and spiciness of the Petit Verdot that was introduced this year. Tannins are subsumed by fruits but show in a dry finish with a smoky effect of sweet peppers. This requires time not because you can't enjoy the wine now, but because it is still a little dumb, tending towards the one dimensional, and needs time to release a wider variety of flavors and develop complexity. 14.7% *91* Drink to 2024.

Columbia Valley, Père de Famille Cabernet Sauvignon, 2002
Two year's difference in age means there's more roundness and evident fruit here than in the 2000. Fruit from Red Mountain became dominant this year (compared with Horse Heaven Hills in 2000). Although the nose suggests a savory touch, the palate tends more to spice with faintly herbal overtones. Very nice balance with the roundness of the fruits cut by a herbal touch on a chocolaty finish. This is more open than the 2000, although it develops cedary overtones on the finish. 14.4% *90* Drink to 2022.

Columbia Valley, Père de Famille Cabernet Sauvignon, 2001
Spicy black fruits notes at the first impression. Nice balance with a touch of tobacco; fruits are savory but not yet showing any sous bois. Lovely cigar box impression makes this the spitting image of a Pessac. Smooth tannins have resolved to let the complexity of the palate show through. 14.2% *90* Drink to 2018.

Columbia Valley, Père de Famille Cabernet Sauvignon, 2000
Restrained first impression suggests the border between savory and fruity with intriguing notes of herbs and spices. The palate is less savory than suggested by the nose, with fruits of black-berries, cherries, and plums, just faintly aromatic. Quite a dry impression on the finish allows the sense of spices to show through. I judge it at its peak for midlife development, although winemaker Bob Betz feels it's a fraction past the peak and will go for another five years. 14.2% *91* Drink to 2020.

Chateau Rollat

Named in honor of his great grandfather, Edouard Rollat, an authority on wine in the first half of the twentieth century in New York, Chateau Rollat was started by Bowin Lindgren. The winemaker is Christian LeSommer, formerly of Château Latour. There are three wines. Sophie is a Merlot-based wine intended to be immediately approachable. Rollat and the flagship Edouard are Cabernet-based with a typical Bordeaux blend (usually 75-80% Cabernet Sauvignon, with 15-20% Merlot and 5% Cabernet Franc). Bowin is committed to Walla Walla as the source of grapes for the style he wants to achieve. "Our wines are quite different in style; I always like to say our wines are an Old World style for expressing New World fruit. Our techniques are absolutely classic. We use specific yeast, we don't do anything with natural yeast, we don't believe in that, the yeast has quite an impact on style, on the balance and mouthfeel. How we approach the blends is classic, we are looking for a full mouth feel. It's the ripeness of the tannins that determines when you pick and it's the expression of the tannins that determines when you press." The grapes come exclusively from Pepper Bridge and Seven Hills in Walla Walla. Overall these wines are more European than most Wash-ington wines, but they still have greater softness and (except in the coolest vintages) lack the refreshing uplift on the finish. Alcohol is moderate for Washington. Wines were tasted at the tasting room in Walla Walla in September 2012.

Columbia Valley, Sophie, 2008
In spite of the appellation description, this is actually all Walla Walla fruit except for some Petit Verdot. "This wine is designed to be very approachable at a young age, so the tannins are lighter than the other wines," says Bowin Lindgren. A refined impression of tobacco on the nose continues through the palate, precise and elegant. Very fine tannins support a taut structure showcasing precisely delineated black cherry and blackcurrant fruits, with some chocolate on the finish. 14.1% *90* Drink to 2020.

Walla Walla, Rollat Cabernet Sauvignon, 2008
Refined black fruit nose. This is definitely the softest of the four vintages of Rollat, with sweet ripe black cherry fruits coming right out on the palate, but displaying a contradictory sense of precision. Tannins are remarkably soft for this cooler vintage, making this the most approachable of the recent vintages, even though it is the youngest. All this contributes to a more New World impression. 14.3% *88* Drink to 2020.

Walla Walla, Rollat Cabernet Sauvignon, 2007
Restrained black fruit nose shows faintly savory overtones. There's a sweeter, riper, richer impression than 2008 on the palate, dominated by black cherries, with chocolate-coated cherries on the finish. Refreshing acidity is more evident here than in 2008 or 2006, making this the most European in style of the three vintages. 14.1% *88* Drink to 2020.

Walla Walla, Rollat Cabernet Sauvignon, 2006
Some tertiary development is already showing on the nose, but is less obvious on the palate, where black cherry and blackberry fruits are matched by some savory notes. Firm tannins are resolving nicely, leaving the finish to the ripe fruits, with just a touch of dryness left on the finish with some cedary notes. There are still some of the more pungent aromatics of the New World, but the savory development brings a European sensibility to the wine. 13.9% *90* Drink to 2019.

Walla Walla, Rollat Cabernet Sauvignon, 2005
Mineral, cedary, pencil lead nose with a savory touch provides an interesting contradiction with the soft ripe fruits of black cherries and plums. Signs of development are more mineral than savory, making this seem less developed than the 2006. 14.1% *89* Drink to 2018.

Walla Walla, Edouard Cabernet Sauvignon, 2007
Reserved nose shows ripe black cherry and blackcurrant fruits. On the palate this is perhaps the densest of all the wines—the impression of density is clear even on the nose. Fine tannins are subsumed by the fruits but show as dryness on the finish. The combination of fruit density and firm structure promises longevity, but it's going to take several years for the wine to emerge from its presently closed state and show some complexity. 14.2% *91* Drink to 2024.

Walla Walla, Edouard Cabernet Sauvignon, 2006
Black fruit nose shows faint herbal and vegetal notes. A more open structure than 2007 has refined tannins giving a fine, graphite-like texture. Purity of fruit expression is more obvious in this vintage with a precise impression of Cabernet Sauvignon coming through the fine structure. 14.4% *90* Drink to 2023.

Walla Walla, Edouard Cabernet Sauvignon, 2005
The first impression identifies herbal overtones on top of black fruits. Sweet, ripe, black cherry fruits dominate the palate, with cedary and mineral notes coming in on the finish. Acidity keeps the wine refreshing. Development seems to be following a direction of minerality as much as savory, with flavor variety just beginning to evolve. There's a dense, chocolaty, impression of structure on the finish. 14.2% *92* Drink to 2022.

Chateau Ste. Michelle

As the largest winery and owner of vineyards in Washington State, Chateau Ste. Michelle produces a wide range of Cabernet Sauvignons. The entry-level wines here are excellent value, but the main interest comes from the contrast between the estate bottlings of Canoe Ridge and Cold Creek compared to the barrel selections of the Ethos or Artist Labels, which illustrates Washington's range. Canoe Ridge and Cold Creek are both pure Cabernet Sauvignon or close to it. "I see Cold Creek as more hedonistic, New World, than Canoe Ridge. American oak suits it," says winemaker Bob Bertheau. "I see bigger vintage variations in Canoe Ridge than I do in Cold Creek, which tends to express itself (rather than vintage)." Ethos is a reserve Cabernet Sauvignon; the Artist Series is a Meritage. "From the wines of place we move to wines of vision, I want Ethos to be a 40-50 year wine," said Bob Bertheau as we made the transition. The Artist series is very much the wine that Bob Bertheau wants to make, and it comes mostly from Canoe Ridge, compared with the Ethos, which comes mostly from Cold Creek. It's not exactly beauty and the beast, but it's a contrast between power and elegance as the primary criteria. Wines were tasted at Chateau Ste. Michelle in September 2012.

Columbia Valley, Cabernet Sauvignon, 2009
Fruity but relatively restrained for an entry-level wine. Indeed, there is a sense of reserve on the palate before the black cherry fruits come in with some light tannins on the finish. Just a touch of bitterness cuts the appealing fruits. "The objective is that the wine is immediately approachable, but yet serious enough not to be rejected by a connoisseur," says winemaker Bob Bertheau. It's a very well achieved combination for the price (you wouldn't get this out of Napa!) 13.5% *88* Drink to 2017.

Columbia Valley, Indian Wells Cabernet Sauvignon, 2010
More overt fruits at the first impression than the regular Columbia Valley bottling, following on the palate with more evident aromatics showing red cherries and plums. The wine has maintained good freshness, but there's just an impression of bitterness and alcohol on the finish. 14.5% *88* Drink to 2017.

Columbia Valley, Canoe Ridge Cabernet Sauvignon, 2009
Canoe Ridge is an almost pure varietal, with under 5% of a second variety to partner the Cabernet Sauvignon. Spicy and cedary aromas showcase black fruits on the nose. On the palate, sweet ripe black fruits show a fine-grained but firm texture, with that signature touch of Washington on the finish in the form of an aromatic, alcoholic, bitterness, relieved by a faint chocolate coating. Fleshy and immediately appealing, this is ready now. By flavor you would think the aromatic notes of plums might come from Syrah, but actually Merlot was the minor component, to calm this exotic wine down. 15.0% *89* Drink to 2022.

Columbia Valley, Canoe Ridge Cabernet Sauvignon, 2008
Black fruits, spices, and cedar show on the nose. There's a more restrained impression overall than the 2009, less aromatic, and perhaps denser on the palate. Sturdy black cherry fruits have a firm structure making a silky impression. Good balance shows already, but this needs a little time. 14.5% *90* Drink 2013-2025.

Columbia Valley, Canoe Ridge Cabernet Sauvignon, 1998
Mature appearance, garnet in hue. The nose shows touches of tertiary aromas under a mineral influence that carries over to the palate, which is herbal rather than savory. Black fruits are mature but show classic notes of blackcurrants with retronasal influences of cedar, herbs, and spices. Complex layers of flavor develop slowly in the glass. Expect this to turn quite savory over the next five years. 14.0% *91* Drink to 2018.

Columbia Valley, Cold Creek Cabernet Sauvignon, 2009
Some coconut and dill on the nose reflect the use of American oak (usually about one quarter), turning to a more savory impression in the glass. The palate shows forceful black fruits with some aromatic black plums. There's a gritty, gravelly, texture, with a fairly tight tannic structure underneath. The very high alcohol is not really noticeable. This is virtually ready to drink. 15.5% *90* Drink to 2022.

Columbia Valley, Cold Creek Cabernet Sauvignon, 2008
Again 2008 seems more restrained than 2009 with more of a herbal impression to the blackcurrant fruits and perhaps some savory undertones. The aromatics are more restrained—black cherries here versus the plums of 2009—making a rich wine, but with a firm, smooth, texture. Flavor variety is beginning to develop, and this should be a long lived, slowly evolving wine that will obtain complexity over the next decade. The high alcohol is not obtrusive on the palate. 15.0% *90* Drink to 2024.

Columbia Valley, Cold Creek Cabernet Sauvignon, 1998
A strongly mineral nose is savory and a touch gamey. The lovely palate is right at the tipping point, with savory herbal notes mingling with mature fruits. Tannins are much resolved, leaving a smooth palate. At almost fifteen years of age, the difference between Cold Creek and Canoe Ridge shows clearly, with Cold Creek emphasizing intensity and the Canoe Ridge retaining more of a refreshing brightness. 14.0% *91* Drink to 2020.

Columbia Valley, Ethos Cabernet Sauvignon Reserve, 2009
Chocolate-coated black cherry fruits share the nose with hints of alcohol. The palate is intense, rich, and ripe: there's lots of tannic structure here, but already the tannins are almost subservient to the fruits, which show just a touch of overt aromatics. Deep fruits and chocolate really coat the palate. 15.5% *91* Drink 2014-2026.

Columbia Valley, Ethos Cabernet Sauvignon Reserve, 2008
Black fruit impression has hints of chocolate and coffee. There's already a lovely balance here, as usual more restraint showing in 2008 versus 2009 (and the same difference as the Canoe Ridge with Merlot used in 2009 and Syrah used in 2008 to ameliorate vintage character). This vintage is less aromatic and therefore more classic than 2009. The dense, chocolate-coated, black cherries of the palate have hardly started to develop yet, and there's such fruit density, it may well take another decade to develop. 15.0% *91* Drink 2015-2030.

Columbia Valley, Meritage Artist Series, 2009
The Artist Series was one of the rare cases where I actually preferred the 2009 to the 2008. It's more restrained on the nose than the Ethos and shows a slightly spicy black fruit impression. It's a more elegant impression, refined and precise, compared with Ethos, reflecting the vineyard sources and winemaking intentions. For a plump year, this is a nicely fleshed out wine without becoming too heavy. Tannins recede into the background against the fine-grained gravelly texture. Some hints of chocolate round out the finish. Unmistakably a Cabernet in its lineage, with real finesse. 15.0% *92* Drink to 2027.

Columbia Valley, Meritage Artist Series, 2008
Restrained nose with very faint savory herbal notes. The palate gives a slightly sturdier impression than the 2009. More of a herbal sense here, a stronger underlying structure, and perhaps more longevity, although less precision of fruit. My sense is that the 2009 will have an advantage for the next five years or so, but that possibly the 2008 will then pull ahead as its structure resolves and the complexity of the dense fruits can show through. 14.5% *91* Drink to 2032.

Washington State, Cabernet Sauvignon, 1976
A surprisingly deep color. An impression of lively fruit on opening, deep and black, following to a fugitive whiff of raisins (not surprising as the cork was quite wet). Good acidity keeps the wine refreshing (quite a contrast with the softer character of Napa Cabernets as they mature). The overall flavor spectrum is quite youthful, with blackcurrants and blackberries still evident, and no savory development, but there is good flavor variety across the palate. Tannins are all but resolved; aside from this marker, the wine could well be a mere decade or so in age. It has very much the sturdy style of the later vintages from Cold Creek. It is sweet, ripe, and surprisingly complete; although it fades in the glass, it has held up better than many Napa Cabernets of the period, and is an extraordinary effort considering that the first vinifera vines in Washington were planted only a few years earlier. 12.0% *89* Drink up.

Col Solare

Created as a partnership between Chateau Ste. Michelle and Tuscany's Antinori, Col Solare's inaugural vintage was 1995. Grapes were sourced from a variety of vineyards for the first few years; the estate on Red Mountain was purchased in 2005, the winery (with its now-famous bell tower) was constructed in 2006, and the vineyard was planted in 2007. From 2009 the 12 ha vineyard has been an increasing part of the Col Solare Cabernet. It is planted with five clones of Cabernet Sauvignon, the other Bordeaux varieties, and some Syrah. Recent vintages have been around three quarters or a little less Cabernet Sauvignon, with 15-20% Merlot, up to 10% Cabernet Franc, and sometimes a small touch of Syrah. The 2010 is almost 50% estate fruit. In 2011, 85% of the wine will come from the Estate, Klipsun, and Kiona (all on Red Mountain). "Now I use only one of the original vineyards. Col Solare is moving towards becoming an estate wine from Red Mountain," says winemaker Marcus Notaro. In addition to Col Solare itself, there is also a second wine, called Shining Hill, from declassified lots. Wines were tasted at Col Solare in September 2012.

Red Mountain, Cabernet Sauvignon, 2009
Made in only 200 cases, this limited release, coming one third each from the estate vineyard, Kiona, and Klipsun, previews the future nature of Col Solare as an estate-driven wine from Red Mountain. (It's also 98% Cabernet Sauvignon compared with 73% for the Columbia Valley.) A restrained nose of red and black fruits slowly develops nutty overtones that strengthen in the glass. Pure black fruits show as cherries and blackberries, very fine and precisely delineated—very tight by comparison with Col Solare's Columbia Valley bottling—conveying a direct, linear expression of Cabernet Sauvignon. Finer and more elegant than the regular bottling, but will it develop as much flavor variety and age as well? 14.5% *90* Drink 2013-2023.

Columbia Valley, 2009
Red Mountain fruit is about 40% of the 2009 release, which shows a restrained black fruit nose with a broader impression than the Red Mountain Cabernet Sauvignon. There are more forceful black fruit aromatics of cherries, blackcurrants, and plums. Blending has achieved a broader impression with more flavor variety, and possibly longer aging potential for development in a savory direction, making this a more obvious match for food. The 2009 vintage, as so often the case, is softer and richer than 2008 or 2007. 14.5% *89* Drink to 2022.

Columbia Valley, 2008
About one third of this bottling comes from Red Mountain. Ripe, aromatic black fruits show as blackcurrants and plums, with a faintly nutty impression retronasally. Fine tannins give a silky texture; alcohol is integrated. The overall impression is smooth and silky, with a faint touch of bitter chocolate on the finish. Fruits are a bit brighter and a touch more youthful than the 2007. This has really scarcely started to develop. 14.5% *90* Drink to 2021.

Columbia Valley, 2007
The nose shows a mixture of fruits, nuts, and herbal influences, indicating that some complexity is beginning to develop. Then in the glass the wine reverts to more of a raspberry nose impression. Its more youthful edges have smoothed off, the wine is softening, but it retains suggestions of bitter chocolate on the finish. A little finer and rounder than the 2008, with some faint herbal notes, it seems as though it's ready to start its savory development. 14.5% *91* Drink to 2022.

Columbia Valley, 1998
This vintage predated Col Solare's interest in Red Mountain, which is not included at all in the blend. The nose is evolved, but more in the direction of intense minerality and pencil lead than tertiary development, although there's a fugitive whiff of sous bois. The palate is less developed than the nose would predict, smooth and fine, with the faintest of savory intimations. This is the perfect moment to catch the wine at mid term development, showing elegance rather than power, and a beautiful mix of fruits, herbal influences, and tobacco. It will no doubt become more overtly savory over the next few years. 13.1% *92* Drink to 2018.

Corliss

Corliss is located in a former bakery in Walla Walla; the tasting room is a lovely hundred year old building, and the winery is located in a concrete structure behind that was built in the 1930s and recently renovated and extended. Most of the Corliss Estate consists of a 33 ha vineyard planted on Red Mountain in 1992. They have just acquired the Blackwood Canyon property on Red Mountain, which adds another 45 ha, most of which will be replanted. Michael Corliss is committed to Red Mountain: "If you own a vineyard in Washington, your chance of getting fruit every year is much higher in Red Mountain; we always lose some crop in Walla Walla. One of the advantages of Red Mountain is that the fruits always get ripe." They also own the separate label of Tranche Estate, which takes most of the fruit from 17 ha in Walla Walla. "When we bought Tranche, we tried to blend Red Mountain fruit with Walla Walla, but it didn't add anything, so we decided to keep them separate", says Michael. Corliss is 90% Bordeaux varieties and 10% Rhône, Tranche is 60% Rhône and 40% Bordeaux. A Bordeaux blend (just labeled Red Wine) is priced just below the Cabernet Sauvignon. Wines were tasted at Corliss in September 2012.

Columbia Valley, Red Wine, 2007
Broader and softer than the varietal Cabernet Sauvignon, a sense of nuts on the palate. The style is opulent but still fresh, with some impressions of glycerin on the finish, generally showing more open structure with less precision but more flavor variety. Fruits extend from cherries to raspberries. Whereas the Cabernet Sauvignon of this vintage needs more time, this blend is ready to drink and perhaps at its peak for mid term development. This is a wine to drink now for sheer enjoyment. 15.3% *90* Drink to 2020.

Columbia Valley, Cabernet Sauvignon, 2007
This varietal label is 98-99% Cabernet Sauvignon, with 60% of the fruit from Red Mountain, and 40% from the Bacchus vineyard in Columbia Valley. The reserved first impression shows more red fruits than black, following to a rich palate dominated by fruits of red and black cherries, with firm tannins drying the finish, and the structural backbone restraining the overt fruits of the palate. There's still a touch of bitterness and some heat on the finish. This hasn't quite come around yet, raising the question of whether the tannins may outlast the fruit. 14.9% *89* Drink 2013-2022.

Columbia Valley, Cabernet Sauvignon, 2005
Some orange splaying out on the rim is followed by the first impressions of tertiary development on the nose, but development is less evident on the palate, although the wine has certainly opened out and broadened. The softening and broadening flavors are more the marker of age than a change to tertiary flavors. With a sweet, ripe style developing complexity, this shows more affinity with the Bordeaux blend of 2007 than with the varietal Cabernet of that year. 14.9% *91* Drink to 2020.

Columbia Valley, Cabernet Sauvignon 2003
The dusky garnet color offers a less mature appearance than the 2005. First impressions are savory with suggestions of minerality. Sweet ripe fruits of blackberries seem relatively dumb on the palate and don't quite fulfill the promise of complexity from the nose; they are dense and black with just a hint of tertiary development. This vintage is evolving slowly, more slowly in fact than the 2005. 14.7% *90* Drink to 2019.

Walla Walla, Cabernet Sauvignon, Tranche Estate, 2008
The color here is distinctly more youthful than the 2007 vintage. There's a faintly mineral impression to the black fruit nose. Relatively open blackcurrant fruits dominate the palate, sweet, ripe, and very approachable without going over the edge into jamminess. Nice freshness restrains the fruits, with a touch of cedar on the finish. 14.8% *88* Drink to 2020.

Walla Walla, Cabernet Sauvignon, Tranche Estate, 2007
This 100% Cabernet Sauvignon comes from vines planted in 2002 and already shows some orange hues on the rim. Red and black fruits show against a backdrop of savory notes. Dense fruits seem restrained on the palate, supported by firm tannins that subside into the background. Although there's a faint touch of cedar, the overall impression remains somewhat dumb. 14.5% *87* Drink to 2018.

Côte Bonneville

Côte Bonneville is all but synonymous with the famous DuBrul vineyard in Rattlesnake Hills, known for its finesse. The winery is located in Yakima Valley just below the long range of the low Rattlesnake Hills. Côte Bonneville's bottlings from the DuBrul vineyard are labeled as Yakima rather than Rattlesnake Hills because the rules say that for an estate bottling, the winery must be located in the same AVA as the grapes. The 18 ha of DuBrul were an apple orchard until Hugh and Kathy Shiels purchased it and converted it to a vineyard in 1992. "We have such different soil types within the vineyard that we blend by soil types rather than variety," says current winemaker Kerry Shiels. "We broke the rock drill when we planted—the driller never came back and the last third of the vineyard was planted by hand." Plantings are Cabernet Sauvignon, Merlot, Cabernet Franc, Syrah and Chardonnay. Most of the grapes are sold, and the first vineyard-designated wine from DuBrul was 1998. The first commercial release from Côte Bonneville was the Carriage House bottling in 2001, which comes from the lower slopes of the vineyard. The bottling from the higher slopes, simply described as DuBrul vineyard, started in 2002. The main difference between the wines is concentration: yields are about 3.5 tons/acre lower down, but fall to 2 tons/acre on the hillside. Wines were tasted at Côte Bonneville in September 2012.

Yakima Valley, Carriage House, 2008
The terroir consists of cobblestones in the lower part of the DuBrul Vineyard where this wine comes from. It is two thirds Cabernet Sauvignon and a quarter Merlot, with Cabernet Franc making up the rest. The nose tends towards gamey notes but the palate shows more of a mineral impression, with hints of tobacco, making you feel that Cabernet Franc is showing through, even though it's only a small proportion of the blend. There's a gravelly texture with firm tannins. A touch of bitterness is pushed by alcohol on the finish. 14.7% *89* Drink to 2020.

Yakima Valley, DuBrul vineyard, 2007
The vineyard is steep and there are heterogeneous rocks on the basalt base from the upper slopes where the Estate bottling originates. The fruit spectrum is similar to the Carriage House bottling, but gives a broader impression. In this blend of 57% Cabernet Sauvignon and 43% Merlot, the main difference with Carriage House seems to be the absence of Cabernet Franc, making the profile not quite as bright. However, the deeper density is likely to make this wine longer lived. The gravelly texture comes through to a long finish. Alcohol is not so evident in this vintage except for a slight flush of heat on the finish. 14.2% *89* Drink to 2022.

Yakima Valley, DuBrul vineyard, 2002
The inaugural vintage of Côte Bonneville's DuBrul Vineyard estate wine shows just a faint touch of development on the nose, and is scarcely developed on the palate; in fact, the fruit seems if anything brighter than the 2007, with more flavor variety. There is a classic gravelly, almost mineral, texture, with a slightly nutty aftertaste to the long finish. A slight touch of remaining bitterness on the finish attests to the good tannic structure. Perhaps in another five years there will be some savory development. 14.5% *90* Drink to 2022.

Efeste

Efeste (F-S-T) is an acronym for the surnames of the three founding families. The winery is located in a utilitarian warehouse in a semi-industrial estate in Woodinville known as the North Ghetto. Vineyards are located all over Columbia Valley, including Red Mountain, Wahluke Slope, and Yakima Valley. Plantings include both the Bordeaux and Rhône varieties; in addition to the Cabernets and Syrahs, there are also Chardonnay, Sauvignon Blanc, and Riesling. Winemaker Brannan Leighton says that, "For me, I really like the purity of varieties, and I also like the purity of the vineyard, so I tend to make single varietals from single vineyards. Big Papa is a 100% varietal Cabernet Sauvignon that comes from a variety of sources, but all are vineyards older than 30 years—it comes from various areas as it's too difficult to find enough old vines in one AVA." There is also a right bank blend that is more Merlot-Cabernet Franc oriented. There are several single vineyard Syrahs. The Final Final is a second wine made from declassified lots of Cabernet Sauvignon and Syrah. Wines were tasted at Efeste in September 2012.

Columbia Valley, Final Final, 2009
There's a restrained, earthy impression on the nose, but the warm vintage is reflected in a rich, ripe, palate offering somewhat of an impression of aromatic Syrah, showing plums and blackcurrants. There's some tannic bitterness on the finish. Overall there's a fairly pronounced impression of a New World wine. 14.7% *88* Drink to 2018.

Columbia Valley, Final Final, 2008
More restrained than the 2009, this offers a stony impression with overtones of tobacco, balanced between the richness of Syrah and the structure of Cabernet Sauvignon. This makes a more complete impression than either 2009 or 2007, perhaps because the Cabernet Sauvignon shows through more clearly to give a better sense of structure. There's some heat on the finish. 14.4% *88* Drink to 2018.

Columbia Valley, Final Final, 2007
Although the wine is a blend of Cabernet Sauvignon and Syrah, aromatics from black plums of Syrah create an initial impression of ripeness jumping out of the glass. The palate is rich and

ripe, quite aromatic, with a touch of tannic bitterness on the finish, which shows some heat. The overall impression is of a slightly unstructured rich New World Syrah. 14.3% *87* Drink to 2017.

Columbia Valley, Big Papa Cabernet Sauvignon, 2011
(Barrel sample.) Herbal nose with notes of tobacco. Sweet ripe fruits, very soft for this early stage of development, spice and nuts showing on the palate, round fruits but with nice taut edges, and the sense of tobacco returning on the finish. *91* Drink 2015-2027.

Columbia Valley, Big Papa Cabernet Sauvignon, 2010
The nose is dominated by nuts and vanillin. It's fresh on the palate, with a tighter, leaner impression overall than 2009 (an accurate reflection of the two vintages), with a touch of tobacco on the finish. Very tight now, this needs time to open up. 14.5% *90* Drink 2015-2028.

Columbia Valley, Big Papa Cabernet Sauvignon, 2009
Undeveloped nose shows spices, nuts, and vanillin. The palate is smooth with a touch of glycerin; it's rounder and more open knit, more approachable than 2008 or 2010. 14.6% *90* Drink to 2019.

Columbia Valley, Big Papa Cabernet Sauvignon, 2008
This cooler vintage has produced a smoky impression with herbaceous notes showing through. There's some restraint, with an earthy undertone to the deep black fruits. Tannins are firm on the finish, with a touch of bitterness. This still needs time to resolve but promises some elegance. 14.5% *91* Drink 2014-2026.

Columbia Valley, Big Papa Cabernet Sauvignon, 2007
The aromatic first impression presages a forceful New World wine. Ripeness jumps out of the glass, with rich, aromatic, black plums that dominate the finish retronasally. Tannins are subsumed by the fruits but evident by dryness and some bitterness on the finish. 14.5% *90* Drink to 2020.

Fidelitas

Fidelitas is a boutique winery on Red Mountain focusing on Cabernet Sauvignon and Bordeaux blends from single vineyards. Cabernet Sauvignon comes from the Ciel du Cheval and Champoux vineyards, Merlot comes from Champoux, and there's also a Merlot-dominated blend from Boushey vineyard. Some blends come from broader sources. Wines were tasted at Fidelitas in September 2012.

Red Mountain, Red Wine, 2009
Aromatic red and black fruit nose suggests a bold wine, which carries through to the palate. But this is not one of those heavily extracted New World wines; the texture is quite fine, and the overall impression is graceful, but the heat of the alcohol comes through on the finish and detracts from typicity. 14.5% *87* Drink 2014-2021.

Columbia Valley, Optu, 2009
This was originally described as a Meritage, but now is identified by a proprietary name. A light red fruit nose of cherries and raspberries leads into faintly earthy notes on the palate with black cherry fruits coming in, almost nutty, but with a touch of bitterness that needs another year to resolve. This has a darker spectrum than the Red Mountain wine. Some heat shows on the finish. 14.8% *88* Drink 2014-2022.

Red Mountain, Ciel du Cheval Cabernet Sauvignon, 2009
Dark cherry fruit nose leads to sweet, ripe fruits on the palate, with a dark background of firm tannins, almost integrated already, but with a touch of heat on the finish. There's a more open impression compared to the reserve of the Champoux vineyard bottling, with brighter fruits; you might possibly say it's a bit more aggressive. 14.8% *89* Drink 2014-2023.

Horse Heaven Hills, Champoux Vineyard Cabernet Sauvignon, 2009
Slightly darker and more purple in hue than the Ciel du Cheval. More reserved on the nose, with intimations of black fruits. There are earthy notes, nuts, and vanillin on the palate, and influences verging on savory. There's high alcohol, and some of the accompanying aromatics, but the overall impression is more classic for Cabernet Sauvignon, with a sense of reserve. 14.6% *90* Drink 2014-2024.

Horse Heaven Hills, Champoux Vineyard Cabernet Sauvignon, 2007
The initial reserve of the black fruit nose has evolved into savory and herbal intimations. With two years' extra age, the black fruit aromatics are less overt than in the 2009. Herbal and cedary notes are now complementing the blackcurrant and blackberry fruits, and become more distinct on the finish. Cabernet typicity becomes more evident as the underlying structure reveals itself in a drying influence on the finish, and there is some promise with regards to longevity. 14.9% *91* Drink to 2022.

Columbia Valley, Meritage, 2000
This was the first vintage of this wine (later renamed as Optu). Some maturity shows in the garnet hues. Evolution shows at once in tertiary aromas with a touch of sous bois. The palate still has sweet, ripe fruits, but now cut by savory notes, with a cedary touch on the finish that becomes almost herbaceous or medicinal, cutting the glyceriny impression of the palate. This is maturing along the classic lines of Bordeaux, but retains that thicker impression of the New World on the palate. 14.2% *90* Drink to 2017.

Gramercy Cellars

Gramercy Cellars is the project of Greg Harrington MS to make wines in a classical style. The focus is on Walla Walla but there are also other grape sources. "With Walla Walla I noticed that whatever the ripeness there was an earthiness and consistency and I thought we could make European style wines. The key to Washington is that you really have to stay with cooler sites where the grapes will ripen," Greg says. The focus is mostly on Rhône varieties, ranging from individual varietal wines to blends. There are two Cabernet Sauvignons, one under the general Columbia Valley label, one specifically Walla Walla. The two main sources are Pepper Bridge (which goes into the Walla Walla bottling) and Phinney (across from Champoux in Horse Heaven Hills). Gramercy shares a winery with Waters and produces one wine as a joint project. Wines were tasted at Gramercy in September 2012.

Columbia Valley, Cabernet Sauvignon, 2010
Fresh, faintly appley nose. Very fine, precise black fruits, with tight cherries, very much a pure Cabernet Sauvignon (this vintage was 99% Cabernet Sauvignon; the 2009 and 2008 were both just under 80%). A distinctly tighter wine than the 2009, as you might expect from the difference between the vintages, this shows all the pure refinement of Cabernet Sauvignon now, but will its fruit spectrum be too narrow to show complexity as it ages? 14.2% *90* Drink to 2020.

Walla Walla Valley, Cabernet Sauvignon, 2010
Broader nose than Columbia Valley with more suggestions of black fruits. Softer than Columbia Valley in this vintage, still a suggestion of precision, but accompanied by a slightly furry impression on the finish. Tannins are firm but not as tight as Columbia Valley, although there is a more obvious sense of structure. 14.2% *91* Drink to 2022.

Columbia Valley, Cabernet Sauvignon, 2009
This wine comes mostly from the Phinney Hills Vineyard and could be labeled under the Horse Heaven Hills AVA. It shows a fresh nose with impressions more of red than black fruits. Although it's soft and round, even this warmer year retains freshness, with fruits precisely delineated on the palate and a faint suggestion of blackcurrants. The purity of line of Cabernet Sauvignon shows through clearly. 14.2% *90* Drink to 2021.

Walla Walla Valley, Cabernet Sauvignon, 2009
Restrained black fruit nose, sterner and denser than the Columbia Valley bottling (very much the difference between Walla Walla and Horse Heaven Hills). There are darker fruits here. Very good acidity almost leaves an impression of apples, with a refined, precise, texture to the palate. 14.2% *91* Drink to 2021.

Columbia Valley, Cabernet Sauvignon, 2008
Fresh nose with impressions of nutty black fruits. The palate offers a complex mélange of red cherries, raspberries, and blackberry fruits with some faint chocolate overtones. The overall impression is fairly linear and precise. Tannins and alcohol are nicely integrated. There's a characteristic uplift of freshness on the finish 13.9% *89* Drink to 2020.

Kiona

The Kiona Vineyard was one of the pioneers on Red Mountain. Scott Williams recalls, "When we started we had no idea what varieties would do well. We knew we needed an east-west slope and we could grow grapes here, but it was pure serendipity this terroir turned out to be one of the best places in the world. The original block in 1975 was 20 acres, with equal parts of Cabernet, Chardonnay, and Riesling. The next year another 10 acres was planted with Cabernet Sauvignon, Chenin Blanc, and Lemberger. The original plan was to plant 10 acres a year, but we ran out of money. At this point we have a couple of hundred acres and it's predominantly Cabernet Sauvignon." Today about half of the grapes from Kiona are sold and half used for production. The Reserve comes from the original block of old vines. Wines were tasted at Kiona in September 2012.

Washington State, Cabernet-Merlot, 2010
The name of this entry-level wine is quite misleading, as Cabernet Sauvignon is a third, Merlot another 7%, and Cabernet Franc just 4%, so "Cabernet-Merlot" is under half the blend. With almost a quarter Sangiovese, and a healthy dollop of Carmenère, not to mention small amounts of other varieties, it's not at all obvious what to expect by way of typicity. In fact, the wine tastes more like a Zinfandel or Grenache than a Bordeaux blend. There's a warm, aromatic, red fruit nose showing raspberries, forward aromatic red and black fruits on the palate, and a warm nutty impression on the finish. It's delicious, but it ain't Cabernet. 13.7% *85* Drink to 2015.

Red Mountain, Cabernet Sauvignon Estate Reserve, 2005
Smoky nose with herbal overtones and then a whiff of red fruits coming out. More black cherries than red on the palate, with a touch of blackcurrants. A little darker in flavor spectrum than you sometimes find on Red Mountain, but with relatively bright fruits. In spite of the moderate stated alcohol, there is distinct heat on the finish. 13.5% *88* Drink to 2018.

Washington State, Cabernet Sauvignon, 2004
The nose shows light red cherries, following to a palate of more red cherries than black, with some light tannins on the finish. Pleasant but rather unresolved for eight years of age. Some heat on the finish seems likely to take over as the somewhat one dimensional fruits begin to fade. 13.8% *87* Drink to 2016.

Leonetti

Gary Figgins fell in love with California Cabernets of the old school, began growing grapes and making wine in his backyard in Walla Walla, and then started Leonetti as a commercial business in 1978. The initial plantings were Cabernet and Riesling; in 1980 a Merlot was added; and from 1981 some Merlot was being blended with the Cabernet. A new facility was constructed in 2007 at the home vineyard, which now stands in a splendid park. Today Leonetti has three estate vineyards: Seven Hills, Upland, and the home estate (Loess). There's about three weeks difference in harvest dates across the vineyards. When Chris Figgins took over as winemaker, the style changed. "My Dad started making wine, pitching back 25-50% of stems, fermenting dry. In the early nineties he started using more oak, including American oak, with hot fermentation. These were very style-driven wines, people freaked out about them. When I came in 1996, my personal palate preferences were more European; I wanted to change the style dramatically and did so very suddenly, with the 2000 vintage. We went from 50% to 5% American oak, and now we are at zero. We went from 100% new oak to 70% new oak," Chris says. The model is to make varietal wines at Leonetti, but the new project of Figgins Estate has a single vineyard focus where the composition of the blend varies significantly from year to year. "I would like over time to get to where we have Leonetti single vineyard wines instead of varietals. I always think in Bordeaux people get too hung up on the varieties—why do you care?—it's where it comes from that matters." Wines were tasted at Leonetti in September 2012.

Walla Walla Valley, Merlot, 2010
Round, rich impression, soft and opulent, but with structure underneath: textbook Merlot for Washington. Tannins kick in to dry the finish. A nice chocolate impression develops in the glass, cut by good acidity. A light touch with the winemaking. 14.3% *90* Drink 2013-2023.

Walla Walla Valley, Cabernet Sauvignon, 2009
Rather closed on the nose. Herbal overtones with notes of tarragon on top of the chocolaty black fruit impression on the palate, with tannins subsumed by the fruits, but drying the finish. Not exactly savory but perhaps a touch of black olives to cut the fruits. 14.6% *89* Drink 2013-2021.

Walla Walla Valley, Reserve, 2009
The Reserve is a barrel selection that is usually dominated by Cabernet Sauvignon (although in some early years the Cabernet was less than 50%). It often has a significant amount of Petit Verdot, although in the hot 2009 vintage it reached a record 92% Cabernet Sauvignon, with the rest Merlot. The relatively faint nose shows some black fruits. It is riper and deeper than the varietal Cabernet Sauvignon on the palate, and the dark fruits show chocolate on the finish. Although this is a more structured wine, the tannins (perhaps a little riper here) are less evident because the fruits are deeper. A very fine result. 14.7% *91* Drink to 2024.

Columbia Valley, Cabernet Sauvignon, 1998
This was one of the last vintages of the old style Leonetti, which employed a heavy usage of new American oak, giving the young wines those intense oaky aromas (very popular at the time). The current style, focusing on less new and more French oak, is certainly more elegant and gives the impression it will age well. The question is how the older wines have developed. This vintage now gives a strongly developed impression with tertiary aromas, and a touch of herbaceousness on the nose tending to the medicinal, which carries over to the palate. Tannins still dry the finish; in fact I have the impression that the tannins are likely to outlive the fruits, even though the fruits are still deep and black. There's fairly pungent acidity. At its best, you might call this cedary, but it tips over the edge into herbaceousness on the nose, although it seems younger on the palate. Perhaps I am underestimating longevity because the liveliness of the fruits does revive in the glass. The overall impression is old fashioned, verging on rustic. 13.9% *87* Drink up.

Walla Walla Valley, Cabernet Sauvignon, Figgins Estate, 2009
The initial impression offers floral aromatics with a touch of violets. The palate is round and ripe and chocolaty, with a glyceriny sweetness to the finish. In fact, the blend seems more like the right bank than the left bank, although it's two thirds Cabernet Sauvignon. The fruits come out well ahead of the structure, making this instantly approachable. 14.4% *88* Drink to 2020.

Long Shadows

Long Shadows is a consortium of seven wines, with winemakers who come in and make "their" wine. It started in 2003, and the first crush was in 2006. The winery is a purpose built facility designed to satisfy their various needs. Michel Rolland has wood tanks, whereas others have stainless steel. Armin Diehl likes whole cluster pressing for Riesling in a pneumatic press; others have vertical presses. Each winemaker decides on a cooper. Each winemaker chooses his source of grapes. The search for sources to satisfy the winemakers is illustrative. "To get the source material they need to go to a variety of vineyards. To choose one source would link the winemaker to one vineyard, to make their stamp, they need a diversity of sources," says resident winemaker Gilles Nicault. The wines don't always come out as prejudice would predict. Michel Rolland's Merlot (Pedestal) is tightly structured; Philippe Melka and Agustin Huneeus' Cabernet Sauvignon-based blend (Pirouette) tastes more right bank than left bank; and they expected Randy Dunn to source the 100% Cabernet Sauvignon (Feather) from Red Mountain, but he found that it wasn't sufficiently savory and sourced the grapes from

Wahluke Slope and Horse Heaven Hills. Production is 1,000-1,500 cases of each wine, and there is a second label with 3,000 cases for the lots that aren't included in any of the winemaker wines. Wines were tasted at Long Shadows in September 2012.

Columbia Valley, Feather Cabernet Sauvignon, 2008
Nutty vanillin influences are more dominant on the initial impression of the nose than on the palate; then comes a smooth, finely textured, impression with the structure of Cabernet showing clearly, although subservient to the fruits as it should be. The fruits are sweet and ripe, but youthfulness shows in some dryness on the finish. 14.2% *90* Drink 2013-2023.

Columbia Valley, Feather Cabernet Sauvignon, 2004
First you see aromatic notes of the New World, then some herbal impressions kick in. The palate shows a lovely balance of fruits, showing more as red cherries than black, with silky tannins that are very finely textured on the finish. The overall impression is very elegant, almost floral. This has not really started its savory development yet; the herbal impressions of the nose don't carry over to the palate, except in a certain sense of reserve on the finish. This should show a classic development towards a savory spectrum over the next decade. 14.2% *91* Drink to 2024.

Columbia Valley, Pirouette, 2009
This is a classic Bordeaux blend with just over half Cabernet Sauvignon, made by winemakers Philippe Melka and Agustin Huneeus. It uses an unusual technique of fermentation in 400 liter barrels on a spinning system. A slightly aromatic, slightly chocolaty, first impression leads into a spicy palate; from the density and spiciness you would think there's some Petit Verdot, but there isn't. The distinctly black fruit palate has aromatic overtones of blackcurrants and plums, with a soft, rich impression in which the structure is partly hidden by the fruits. The overall impression is more right bank than left bank. 14.9% *89* Drink to 2021.

Columbia Valley, Pirouette, 2004
A faintly savory and herbal first impression leads into aromatic red fruits, showing as cherries and raspberries on the palate. This is an elegant rather than blockbuster style, although the aromatics point more to the New World in a lighter style than to Europe. There's some heat on the finish. 14.6% *89* Drink to 2020.

Columbia Valley, Pedestal Merlot, 2008
This wine is Michel Rolland's take on Merlot from Washington (including a small proportion of Cabernet Sauvignon and a touch of Cabernet Franc and Petit Verdot). The black fruit nose suggests a reserved richness. That sense of reserve carries through the palate, with chocolate-coated tannins conveying a dense, rich, impression, quite structured. At first the fruits seem quite expressive, then they close up, and it becomes apparent that the wine needs more time to let the tannins resolve and the fruits come out. 14.7% *90* Drink 2014-2024.

Columbia Valley, Pedestal Merlot, 2004
"Pedestal's 2004 vineyard sources were selected to produce a rich, jammy, fruit-forward wine," says Long Shadows' description of the wine. Curiously the nose is more overtly savory than the Feather (Long Shadows' one hundred percent Cabernet), with the red fruits hidden behind. Evidently round and rich on the palate, but well structured, demonstrating the particular character of Washington Merlot. The structure is if anything more evident than in Feather; the Pedestal has a lovely balance built for aging. It wouldn't be difficult to mistake this for an elegant Cabernet-driven blend in the modern idiom. 14.7% *92* Drink to 2027.

Columbia Valley, Chester-Kidder, 2007
Described as a "New World blend" this is fairly unusual for Washington in blending Cabernet Sauvignon (60%) with Syrah (25%): there's also some Petit Verdot. Matured for 30 months in oak, this is released a year after the other blends. This current release shows a floral red fruit nose with aromatics than resemble Syrah more than the majority Cabernet Sauvignon; the dominant impression is the sweet ripeness of the fruits. 14.9% *89* Drink to 2019.

Columbia Valley, Chester-Kidder, 2004
Pungent New World aromatics at the first impression: Syrah seems dominant although it is the minor component. Aromatic and floral on the palate, almost perfumed, with a touch of bitterness pushed by the alcohol on the finish. I'm inclined to view this as a relatively elegant Syrah, although it does have the structural attributes of the Cabernet Sauvignon. 14.7% *88* Drink to 2019.

Pepper Bridge Winery

Pepper Bridge owns two of the best known vineyards in Walla Walla: Pepper Bridge itself, and Seven Hills (ten miles south). Pepper Bridge started with 4 ha of Cabernet Sauvignon and Merlot in 1991; today it is 70 ha. Seven Hills started planting in 1981 and is now up to 85 ha. Seven Hills is one of the driest spots in the AVA, and harvests about two weeks later than Pepper Bridge. Production is about 5,500 cases, with 2,500 Cabernet Sauvignon, 1,000-1,500 Merlot, and 300 cases of Trine (a Bordeaux blend with roughly equal amounts of Cabernet Sauvignon and Merlot). There is also a Seven Hills bottling (400 cases, available only to the wine club). Amavi Cellars is a separate label intended for lower end, more approachable, wines. All the wines are made by Jean-François Pellet, known to everyone as J-F. Wines were tasted at Pepper Bridge in September 2012.

Walla Walla, Seven Hills Vineyard, 2010
With 69% Cabernet Sauvignon this could almost qualify for a varietal label (the rest is 25% Merlot with some Cabernet Franc). The nose is reserved, but the red and black cherry fruits are quite forward on the palate. There's more evident freshness on the finish than in the riper 2009, and the structure offers a sense of openness. With a mineral sense of precision in the fruits, this gives a more European impression than the 2009 vintage. 14.5% *90* Drink 2014-2024.

Walla Walla, Merlot, 2009
Dumb first impression with a suggestion of reserved, structured, black fruits. Initially seems quite soft on the palate, with fruits of black cherries and blackberries, but then the structure kicks in and the fruits seem more reserved. There's a fair tannic backbone with some bite to the finish pushed by the alcohol. Definitely a strongly structured impression for Merlot, and needs at least another year for the tannins to calm down. 14.8% *88* Drink 2014-2022.

Walla Walla, Seven Hills Vineyard, 2009
This Bordeaux blend (roughly 60% Cabernet Sauvignon and 40% Merlot) gives an initial impression of reserved black fruits. There's a smooth, elegant, impression on the palate with slightly dusty black fruits and a definite sense of structure. Blackcurrant fruits slowly emerge on the palate; tannins are firm in support, with just a touch of bitterness on the finish driven by the heat of the alcohol. Needs another year. 15.0% *89* Drink 2013-2022.

Walla Walla, Cabernet Sauvignon, 2009
This is really a Cabernet-dominated Bordeaux blend, with 79% Cabernet Sauvignon blended with Merlot, Cabernet Franc, Malbec, and Petit Verdot. There are more overt black fruits on the nose than for Seven Hills, although the fruits are more reserved and less openly delicious on the palate. Tannins are smoother and finer grained, giving an elegant impression of dark fruits, with a dry finish. The elegance of the style should show through more clearly as the tannins begin to be resolved over the next year or so. 14.8% *90* Drink 2013-2023.

Walla Walla, Trine, 2008
This vintage offers a constantly changing impression from black cherry fruits to smoke to herbal notes with a savory undertone. There's a soft, not quite aromatic impression of red and black fruits on the palate, with some complexity beginning to show in developing flavor variety. The fruits are nicely cut by herbal impressions, and "this is typical Walla Walla," says winemaker Jean-François Pellet. There's actually a more direct impression of Cabernet here than in the 2009 Cabernet Sauvignon, with notes of Franc as well as Sauvignon bringing impressions of tobacco notes and some earthiness to the savory finish. The combination of this vintage with the selection of reserve barrels has produced a subtle wine with refined tannins fading into the finely-textured background. 14.5% *91* Drink to 2022.

Walla Walla, Cabernet Sauvignon, 2002
This 95% Cabernet Sauvignon was sourced equally from Pepper Bridge and Seven Hills. A cooler vintage, this took time to develop, and now shows a mixture of fruity and savory aromatics, with herbal overtones verging on the medicinal. Smooth and refined, the palate offers a mixture of spices and herbal influences, with leathery, cedary, overtones making the finish almost gamey. Now evolving well, this should become steadily more savory over the next few years. Tannins are not obvious except in some dryness on the finish. 14.2% *92* Drink to 2018.

Walla Walla, Cabernet Sauvignon, Amavi 2009
Owned by Pepper Bridge, and made by winemaker Jean-François Pellet, Amavi is a value line. The wine still has a dark, almost purple, color. First impressions show blackcurrant fruits combined with freshness. This is sweet, ripe, approachable, forward, and very ripe, with some black plum aromatics on the palate. This gives a good impression for a New World entry-level wine, delicious but not overly structured or showing much Cabernet typicity. There's a touch of heat on the finish. 14.7% *87* Drink to 2017.

Quilceda Creek

Devoted exclusively to Cabernet Sauvignon, Quilceda Creek is beyond question Washington's quality leader. Quilceda Creek was started by Alex Golitzin in Snohomish (just north of Seattle) in 1978; he wanted to get out of corporate America and the vision was to have a small business making wine. The impetus came from his uncle, Napa's famous winemaker André Tchelistcheff. Alex decided he wanted to make Cabernet Sauvignon as there was no good wine in Washington at the time. Why Cabernet? He was not interested in whites; Syrah wasn't known at the time, and it was too hot for Pinot Noir. It was really controversial to plant Cabernet then, he recollects. Initially the grapes came from Otis vineyard in Yakima Valley, then they started taking grapes from Kiona on Red Mountain, which was the sole source from 1983 to 1985. This was a change of flavor profile, from the green olives of Otis to the very ripe grapes of Kiona. From 1986 the major source of grapes was Champoux vineyard, in Horse Heaven Hills, together with the Tapteil and Klipsun vineyards on Red Mountain. When a new vineyard, Galitzine, was planted on Red Mountain, the original intention was to use it in the Quilceda Creek bottling, but it overwhelmed the Champoux character, so instead became the source of a single vineyard Cabernet Sauvignon. In addition to the two Cabernets, Palengat is a Bordeaux blend, coming from a vineyard just below Champoux; varieties vary from year to year, with Cabernet Sauvignon dominating in 2009, but Merlot in 2010 and 2011. The Columbia Valley Red Wine is in effect a second wine for the third of the crop that is declassified (since 1997). A new winery was built in 2003 and another production facility in 2007. Total production is 9,000-10,000 cases, and 90% of the wine is sold directly from a mailing list via two releases per year. Wines were tasted at Quilceda Creek in September 2012.

Horse Heaven Hills, Palengat, 2009
Initially stern, faintly herbal with hints of spices. The spicy impression continues on to the palate and finish, with a firm tannic structure pushed a bit by the high alcohol. The overall impression is the typical precision of Quilceda Creek, with tightly defined black cherry fruits, but significant heat on the finish. In spite of the alcohol, there's good freshness, indeed the wine is tart around the edges on the finish and needs a couple of years to soften. It would hard to deny this is a well balanced wine, but you do see the alcohol. 15.2% *90* Drink 2015-2030.

Columbia Valley, Cabernet Sauvignon, 2009
This almost pure Cabernet Sauvignon comes largely from the Champoux vineyard in Horse Heaven Hills, with small contributions from the Klipsun and Tapteil vineyards; the 3% Merlot comes from the Palengat vineyard just below Champoux. There's a characteristic black fruit nose with spices of cinnamon and nutmeg from the new oak. The very ripe vintage has produced some fine black cherry aromatics. It's smooth, elegant, and refined on the palate with a softly tannic aftertaste. Precisely delineated black fruits show as cherries and blackcurrants, with fine-grained tannins giving a silky structure. The overall impression is taut, with lots of tension in the wine, relieved by some faintly nutty notes on the finish. The high alcohol is well integrated except for showing a touch of heat on the finish. 15.2% *92* Drink 2014-2029.

Red Mountain, Galitzine Vineyard Cabernet Sauvignon, 2009
Less obvious on the nose than Quilceda Creek or Palengat. Smooth and ripe on the palate, with fruits of red and black cherries and plums, and a slightly glyceriny, more open, impression

than the Quilceda Creek. Round but fine textured tannins are in the background. The roundness gives an impression of being opulent while maintaining freshness. Although this is almost
pure Cabernet Sauvignon from Red Mountain, the overall impression is that the mid palate has
softened and fleshed out in a way that elsewhere requires Merlot. 15.2% *91* Drink 2013-2025.

Washington, Cabernet Sauvignon, 2001
This is a Scarborough Fair wine: first comes the rosemary, then the sage and thyme. Although
the herbal elements develop steadily in the glass, this is less obviously from Washington than
younger vintages of Quilceda Creek. It has those deep, dark fruits, with overtones of musty
vanillin that are common from Napa Valley. It would be a very fine taster who could reliably
distinguish this vine from a Cabernet from one of the Napa mountain AVAs of the same vintage.
The finish is pretty tarry, with taut tannins, which if not aggressive are certainly evident, seeming reminiscent of (say) Howell Mountain. The alcohol and acidity are both a touch higher than
you would be likely to find in Napa. The flavor spectrum seems broad compared to that crystalline precision showing in the most recent vintages of Quilceda Creek. For enjoyment with a
meal, this still needs more time to calm down 14.9% *88* Drink to 2027.

Robert Ramsey Cellars

Coming from software, winemaker Bob Harris is self-educated in wine, and started
Robert Ramsey (named after a family relative) in 2005. Robert Ramsey's motto is "Old
World character, New World wine." Varietal wines include Cabernet Sauvignon, Syrah,
and Mourvèdre; there's also a lower level blended red wine. The focus is on the Rhône
varieties, and the entry into Cabernet Sauvignon was the availability of grapes from
Upland Vineyard. Bob sometimes blends a little other varieties into the Cabernet. In
2007 and 2008 there was 2% Mourvèdre, but "All the wines from 2009 are 100% Cabernet. I sat around and tried to tweak it, but I just couldn't get it no matter how many
varieties I tried," he says. Wines were tasted in Woodinville in September 2012.

Phinney Hills, Horse Heaven Hill, Cabernet Sauvignon, 2009
Spicy black fruit impression showing cinnamon spice with herbal overtones of anise. Sweet,
ripe, and round, with dense black cherry fruits on the palate, showing a glyceriny impression on
the finish. The darker character of Horse Heaven Hill shows through. Anise comes back on the
finish with some dark fruit aromatics. Tannins dry the finish and leave a touch of bitterness with
some heat showing. (Only 31 cases produced.) 14.3% *90* Drink 2013-2023.

Snipes Mountain, Uplands Vineyard Dump Block Cabernet Sauvignon, 2009
Spicy black fruit impression with nuts, cinnamon, and semolina. Distinctly sterner than the Uplands Vineyard bottling; a real sense of restraint runs across the palate to a long cedary finish.
This wine offers a darker, more muscular, impression, more herbal and less precisely defined,
with a strong underlying structure. A touch of chocolate marks the finish. (Only 63 cases produced.) 14.1% 89 Drink 2013-2023.

Yakima Valley, Uplands Vineyard Cabernet Sauvignon, 2009
Spicy impression of red and black cherries with overtones of cinnamon and tobacco. There's a
richer, rounder, impression than the previous vintages with a touch of glycerin on the finish
rounding out the finely textured impression. Tannins are quite unobtrusive at first and then kick
in to dry the finish. 14.0% *90* Drink to 2022.

Yakima Valley, Uplands Vineyard Cabernet Sauvignon, 2008
Initial impression is somewhat reminiscent of Cabernet Franc, spicy on the palate, with the typical restraint of the 2008 vintage in the background. There are elegant, pure, fruit lines, with very
fine supporting tannins giving an impression of tension and restraint. Purity of line runs through
the vintages, with freshness standing out in this vintage. 14.0% *91* Drink to 2022.

Yakima Valley, Uplands Vineyard Cabernet Sauvignon, 2007
There's a savory impression with hints of tobacco and a touch of sous bois. The palate has a
mix of red and black fruits with cherries prominent, and spice and tobacco on the finish. Overall
this shows as elegant with a refined texture, although there is a touch of heat on the finish. It's
not the weight as this is a relatively light-bodied wine, but the aromatics, that place this in the
New World. (Only 119 cases produced.) 13.9% *90* Drink to 2021.

Waters

"We only make a 100% Cabernet Sauvignon, we made that commitment right from the start," says Jamie Brown of Waters. "We don't make an über-ripe wine, if you want to make the ripe style you might need to mix in other varieties like Merlot. The common concern here is to keep natural acidity, I just can't drink flabby wines." He believes that the key to great Cabernet is blending from different sites, and his main sources are Chateau Ste. Michelle's Cold Creek vineyard (the reverse of its name as it is actually rather a hot site), Pepper Bridge, and Windrow. By contrast, for Syrah there are some single vineyard wines. The first vintage was 2003, and total production has varied between 4,500 and 7,000 cases recently, split between the varietal Cabernet Sauvignons and Syrahs. Wines were tasted at Waters in September 2012.

Washington State, Cabernet Sauvignon Reserve, 2010
The identification as Washington State does not reflect any change of sources, but the view that Columbia Valley is no longer a useful description. This was the first year a Reserve was made; it has 75% Cabernet Sauvignon (from Cold Creek) and 25% Malbec (from the Stonestreet vineyard). There's a faintly aromatic, but reserved, black fruit nose. The refinement of the Malbec tannins gives this a distinctly smoother impression than the other Cabernets. The palate of black cherry and blackcurrant fruits is supported by fine-grained tannins giving a fine, elegant, smooth texture, beautifully integrated with the ripe fruits. 14.6% *90* Drink to 2022.

Columbia Valley, Cabernet Sauvignon, 2008
The major source for this wine is Chateau Ste. Michelle's Cold Creek vineyard. The light, black fruit nose leads into an elegant palate of black cherries and blackberries with hints of blackcurrants; the mid weight body has a refreshing uplift on the finish from good acidity that exposes the fruit structure. This can be enjoyed now, but a touch of bitterness on the finish should resolve over the next year. 14.5% *88* Drink 2013-2021.

Columbia Valley, Interlude, 2009
This blend of slightly more Merlot than Cabernet Sauvignon offers a light red fruit nose leading into an elegant palate, but with a touch of bitterness and alcohol showing on the finish. There's the underlying sense of structure you get with most Washington Merlot. This really needs another year to show its potential elegance. There's the nicely balanced fresh acidity that is the mark of the house. 14.5% *87* Drink 2013-2019.

Columbia Valley, 21 Grams, 2009
A selection of the best lots in a collaboration between Waters and Gramercy Cellars, the 21 Grams bottling has varied from 76% Cabernet Sauvignon to the 100% used in this very hot vintage. "This has a touch more ripeness than I really like," says winemaker Jamie Brown. There's a sturdy impression to the nose with black fruits set against a faintly herbal background. The solid, firm, body has blackberry fruits supported by refreshing acidity—an accomplishment in the context of the vintage—with tannins drying the finish, but not otherwise obtrusive. This will benefit from some aging. 14.5% *88* Drink 2013-2021.

Woodward Canyon

Dating from 1976 when the first vines were planted, with its first release in 1981, Woodward Canyon is one of the pioneers in Walla Walla. However, grapes are sourced from a variety of locations in addition to the home estate, including Champoux in Horse Heaven Hills, and DuBrul in Rattlesnake Hills. The focus is on Cabernet and Merlot (although there are also some whites from the usual suspects). In Cabernet Sauvignon there is the Walla Walla bottling, the Artist Series, and the Old Vines (which comes from Champoux). Unusually for Washington, Woodward Canyon has been experimenting with clones. "We usually find the blend of three clones is more interesting than the linear line of a single clone," says winemaker Rick Small. Wines were tasted at Woodward Canyon in September 2012.

Walla Walla, Cabernet Sauvignon, 2009
At first a wodge of fruit, then the more reserved character of Walla Walla takes over the nose, but the palate shows full, ripe fruits of black cherries and plums, aromatic and almost piquant. A slightly rustic tannic structure gives some bitterness on the finish. Alcohol is only just perceptible. The wine needs a year or two for the evident supporting structure to soften and for the aromatics to calm down. 14.5% *88* Drink 2014-2024.

Washington State, Artist Series Cabernet Sauvignon, 2009
A more European impression on the nose than the regular bottling, with a balance of savory and nutty undertones to the reserved fruits, becoming a little nutty in the glass. Smooth on the palate, with refined tannins—does that come from Champoux, which provides almost half the grapes?—and a seamless texture, although a touch of alcohol shows on the finish (surprising that it's only a touch given the very high level). Another year should allow this to display its full elegance. 15.8% *90* Drink 2013-2025.

Walla Walla, Estate Reserve, 2009
This wine is more a right bank blend, almost a half Merlot and a quarter Cabernet Franc, with the rest split between Petit Verdot and Cabernet Sauvignon. Slightly nutty and herbal, this gives a more complex impression than the Artist series. Black fruits mingle with herbal notes and lead pencil with a touch of tobacco. Although this is a Merlot-dominated blend, if you wanted to draw parallels with Bordeaux, they would be as close to the left bank as to the right, a tribute to the structure that Merlot develops in Washington. It's amazing that the high alcohol doesn't unbalance the wine. 16.0% *91* Drink 2013-2025.

Washington State, Old Vines Cabernet Sauvignon, 2009
The grapes are sourced from several vineyards that were planted in the 1970s (Champoux, Sagemoor, and Woodward Canyon itself). There's a rather restrained first impression with some faint herbal suggestions. You can see the influence of the old vines in the very dense, ripe, palate. Fruits tend to blackberries and blackcurrants, with chocolaty tannins and a spicy impression on the finish. Fruit density largely hides the tannins, but although the alcohol does not unbalance the taste it does push some bitterness from tannins on to the finish. The wine turns to notes of nuts and vanillin in the glass, probably a harbinger of things to come, and together with the density, this gives the wine a bit more of a New World impression than the other wines. 16.7% *91* Drink 2014-2024.

Columbia Valley, Old Vines Cabernet Sauvignon, 1999
An expressive nose shows aromatic, almost piquant, forceful fruits. There's a faint whiff of herbal notes with some pencil lead and tobacco coming in on the aftertaste. The richness gives more of a right bank than left bank impression. As the wine opens out in the glass, those cedary, tobacco notes become more evident. The wine remains fresh, and even after a decade, there isn't much tertiary development. "This still seems like a baby," says Joel Butler. This should continue to evolve for the next decade or so, when I would expect to see some more development. You can see the lineage from 2009 to 1999, with density, texture, and richness, but the increase in alcohol says it all about the decade; indeed, although the 2009 is impressively massive now, it may not survive as long as the 1999. 13.9% *92* Drink to 2024.

Chile

The recent vintages of 2011 and 2010 in Maipo Valley were cool and late, with harvests running into May. 2011 may be a bit better than 2010, which can be rustic and is usually referred to simply as the year of the earthquake, which often disrupted the harvest. 2009 is considered to have been a good, warm, year giving ripe wines; and 2008 is generally regarded as slightly better. The 2008s have more evident tannins than 2007, which has a softer, riper character. 2006 was dry and cooler on average by 2 °C, leading to wines with good acidity. 2005 was also a cooler vintage with a long growing season giving good ripeness. The problem in 2004 was early ripening driving a high level of tannins; 2003 was an average year for Cabernet; 2002 was difficult. The vintage that started the trend to ripeness was 2001, a very good, dry, warmer year that gave concentrated wines. The most recent vintages (2011-2008) are generally regarded as a bit below average, 2007 and 2005 as above average, and before that 2001 stands out.

Almaviva

At one end of the old Tocornal vineyard, Almaviva is (literally) a stone's throw away from Chadwick. It consists of 40 ha provided by Concha y Toro to be the basis of a joint venture with Château Mouton Rothschild. The original intention was to have a blend that resembled Mouton, but the "Merlot" turned out to be Carmenère. The blend was successful, and has stayed around three quarters Cabernet Sauvignon to one quarter Carmenère, with a little Cabernet Franc, since the first vintage in 1999. "The wines of Mouton, Opus One, Almaviva all taste completely different. Almaviva is round and opulent, it's very different from Opus One; the fact that Chile has very cold nights gives us a certain freshness that's not evident in Opus. What's very specific up here is to get the quality of ripe fruit, lots of red and black fruits, we are looking for finesse, elegance, quality of the tannins. Maybe the first vintages were more French," says winemaker Michel Friou. There is a lot of selection: a second wine, called Epu, resulting from declassification, is sold mainly in Brazil and the domestic market, and about a third of production is sold off in bulk. Wines were tasted at Almaviva in March 2012.

Puente Alto, Almaviva, 2009
A restrained mix of influences: black fruits, savory, herbaceous, chocolate. Then opening out to show plums, prunes, cinnamon, and nutmeg, overlaying suggestions of complex spicy black fruits. This is awfully approachable for such a young wine, with very well rounded fruits supported by silky tannins, which show only as a dryness on the finish counterpoising the kick of sweetness. Perhaps just a fraction lacking in freshness. 14.5% *90* Drink 2013-2026.

Puente Alto, Almaviva, 2006
Some pungent mineral notes almost suggestive of gunflint clear to a suggestion of fine, elegant fruits. The flavor spectrum is similar to other vintages, but with the lesser concentration that characterizes this vintage. A smooth impression of silky opulence becomes quite soft on the finish, but there's less focus than usual. *88* Drink to 2019.

Puente Alto, Almaviva, 2001
A more intense initial impression of Cabernet Sauvignon than the other vintages, with a mix of spicy black fruits and vegetal overtones. The ripe fruits are elegant and nicely rounded, with black cherries on the palate marked by spicy overtones of nutmeg. Refined tannins give a nice edge to the finish, and very slowly show some dryness, indicating underlying structure for further aging. The extra smoothness and elegance compared to 1996 demonstrate the improvements in winemaking. However, at this stage, I'd like to see some tertiary development, although there's a very faint herbaceous touch cutting the finish and adding character; freshness should support some reasonable longevity. 14.2% *91* Drink to 2020.

Puente Alto, Almaviva, 1996
Mature but not yet savory, with vegetal rather than herbaceous overtones to the fruits, still with some spicy character. Still ripe and round, the fruits remain quite youthful. Winemaker Michel Friou thinks this is evolving faster than current wines. Some lightening with age means there's less presence on the palate, and as there is so little tertiary development so far, this will probably tend to become a little medicinal as the fruits mature further. 13.7% *88* Drink to 2017.

Altaïr

It is a comment on the Chilean wine industry that Altaïr, which has 72 ha of vineyards, sees itself as a small estate. It is located at the end of a small valley in Cachapoal Alta, just at the pre-Andes. Altaïr started in 2000 as a collaboration between Château Dassault (of St. Emilion) and San Pedro (one of the largest wineries in Chile). The winery was built in 2001, and the first vintage was 2002. Since then, San Pedro has taken complete control, but Altaïr continues to be run as an independent operation. In addition to Altaïr itself, there is a second wine, called Sideral. Both are blends based on Cabernet Sauvignon, typically 60-80%, with the rest from Syrah, Carmenère, Petit Verdot (started in 2009), and Cabernet Franc. There are about 3,000 cases of Altaïr and 10,000 cases of Sideral. "People think of Sideral as a second wine but it's not. It comes from different vineyards. Altaïr uses wood fermenters, Sideral uses stainless steel. There is 80% new oak in Altaïr and 20% in Sideral. Sideral is a fruitier wine that is easier to drink. It has similar varieties but different proportions. We want the fruit of the New World. There is more extraction with Altaïr. The difference isn't due to Cabernet Sauvignon, which is about the same proportion in each," says Claudia Gomez Martinez. Wines were tasted at Altaïr in March 2012.

Rapel Valley, Viña Altaïr, 2007
The youngest of the flight of Altaïr has the least developed nose (and is evidently much less developed than its sibling Sideral from the same vintage). The sweet ripe fruits tend more to red cherries than black; there are some faint intimations of the start of savory development. Tannins are supple; there are touches of nuts and tar on the finish. At this moment it seems a little one dimensional, but if it follows the path of previous vintages, it will become interesting in the next year. 14.7% *89* Drink to 2018.

Rapel Valley, Viña Altaïr, 2006
Savory development at first seems more advanced than 2005, with notes of sous bois and gunflint coming in ahead of the fruits on the nose, but then this reverses on the palate, which seems more youthful, fruits showing against a savory background. This seems a touch less concentrated than the 2005. It's already quite open and ready to drink and seems likely to develop quite quickly. 14.9% *89* Drink to 2017.

Rapel Valley, Viña Altaïr, 2005
This gives a more subtle impression than the later vintages, with red fruits melding with savory notes showing as a touch of sous bois. The savory impression strengthens in the glass. Sweet ripe fruits are more red than black, and just coming up to the tipping point from fruity to savory. A touch of heat shows on the finish. That touch of gunflint comes back to cut the roundness of the fruits, bringing character to the finish. 15.1% *90* Drink to 2018.

Rapel Valley, Sideral, Viña Altaïr, 2008
A subdued black fruit impression compared to the red fruits of the 2007. Fruits are overt but restrained, with tarry overtones. A touch of vanillin makes the round, smooth, palate seem very New World-ish, with supple tannins very much in the style for immediate enjoyment. There's not much evident structure. Will it age as quickly as the 2007? 14.7% *87* Drink to 2017.

Rapel Valley, Sideral, Viña Altaïr, 2007
Restrained fruity impression but with distinct savory elements and even a whiff of gunflint, leading into a mature impression of red and black fruits, with a slightly gritty texture, but carrying its tannins lightly. For all the New World aspirations, this seems a typical half way house, with more fruit and body than the Old World, but something of the savory development (albeit on a more rapid timescale) of Europe. There's some distinct heat on the finish. The apparently rapid development of this bottle may not be typical because a second bottle was more restrained, nutty rather than savory, seeming a year behind the first bottle in its pace of development. 14.8% *88* Drink to 2015.

Antiyal

Antiyal is that rare endeavor in Chile: a boutique winery. It is the brainchild of Alvaro Espinoza, who was winemaker at the large producer Carmen (now part of Santa Rita) in the nineties. After spending two years in Bordeaux, and a sabbatical year in Napa, he was the first in Chile to create a start-up: from an initial single hectare, he expanded to 8 ha, and recently purchased two further parcels totaling 13 ha close by. The original vineyard used to be an almond orchard, and there are still almond trees interspersed with the vines every few rows; in fact, the almond harvest was in full swing when I visited, just before the grape harvest. Alvaro is a fervent believer in biodynamics, extending to self sufficiency of the farm (with a cow, three horses, and three alpacas), including operating by phases of the moon; Antiyal is certified by Demeter. One of his wines is labeled as the "egg tank" Carmenère, because it is vinified in an egg-shaped fermenter, which is believed to mix the contents by natural fluid motion, therefore requiring less intervention by stirring or pumping over. Alvaro believes in blending, and the vineyard is largely planted to Carmenère, Cabernet Sauvignon, and Syrah, with Antiyal itself dominated by Carmenère, and the entry-level wine Kuyen dominated by Syrah. All wines are intended to be ready when they are released. "I like to make wines that are soft from the beginning so people can drink them if they want. I don't like those tight wines that are acid that you cannot drink for five years," says Alvaro. Wines were tasted at Antiyal in March 2012.

Maipo, Antiyal, 2010
Antiyal's eponymous wine is usually about half Carmenère with a quarter each of Cabernet Sauvignon and Syrah. Development in a savory direction for this vintage is suggested by a touch of gunflint; underneath are fruits of black plums, more restrained than the Kuyen entry-level wine, with firm black fruits and tannins, Some time is needed for that firm impression on the palate to soften and to allow the fruits to express themselves. Here the smoothness of the Carmenère is definitely subservient to the structural tannins of Cabernet Sauvignon and Syrah. 14.5% *88* Drink 2014-2021.

Maipo, Antiyal, 2007
There's a faintly pungent impression of gunflint with chocolate overtones, which carry over to the restrained palate; certainly there's a more restrained impression than the youthful 2010, showing that the aromatics have calmed down with age. Perhaps because of age, perhaps because of the character of this vintage, the smoothness of ripe Carmenère dominates over the structure of Cabernet Sauvignon and Syrah, although a tannic dryness on the aftertaste attests to the underlying structure. Alvaro thinks this vintage is now at its peak. "I like fruity wines, my wines are for 4-6 years, but people can love them at 10 years." 14.6% *89* Drink to 2018.

Maipo, Egg Tank Carmenère, 2010
There's a freshness to the wine that melds into just a touch of the minty overtones for which Maipo Valley is known. The smooth palate has chocolate overtones and a tannic backbone that ends up in a soft, furry finish. Not ready yet, this needs another year to release its fruits. 14.2% *90* Drink 2013-2022.

Maipo, Viñedo Escorial Carmenère, Antiyal, 2007
This is a 100% single vineyard Carmenère. Its nose is quite austere for the variety, giving more the impression you usually get from Cabernet Sauvignon, with a stern, tarry quality overlaying the black fruits, but then some nuts and cereal come up. It's softer on the palate than you expect from the nose, and the fruits are quite bright, especially on the mid palate. This is a most interesting expression of ripe Carmenère, very smooth, just nicely cut by the structure, with real character. 14.8% *91* Drink to 2020.

Casa Lapostolle

Casa Lapostolle started in 1994 as a joint venture between the owners of the Clos Apalta estate in the Apalta Valley, with its old vines, and the Marnier-Lapostolle family who own Grand Marnier and wineries in France. Today the Lapostolle family are exclusive owners. A striking new winery was constructed, going several stories underground to allow gravity-fed operation, for producing the top wines; others are handled at a large facility not far away. Michel Rolland is their exclusive (within Chile) consultant. Holdings total 370 ha, including Clos Apalta, another vineyard farther south in Colchagua, and one in cool climate Casablanca Valley. The top wine, Clos Apalta, is typically about 60-70% Carmenère and 15-20% Cabernet Sauvignon; there may be Merlot or Petit Verdot depending on the year. Clos Apalta is the only wine not labeled as a varietal. The second line in the brand lineup is Cuvée Alexandre, which may come from the estates in Apalta Valley, Colchagua, or Casablanca, depending on the variety.

The Cuvée Alexandre Cabernet Sauvignon comes from a block of old vines planted in 1920 at the Apalta estate. Some grapes are purchased for the entry-level Casa line. "We look for a ripe style with Cuvée, but with Casa we look for freshness," says winemaker Andrea Leon. Production is 4,000-6,000 cases of Clos Apalta, 23,000 cases of Cuvée, and 120,000 cases of Casa. Wines were tasted at Casa Lapostolle in March 2012.

Colchagua Valley, Clos Apalta, 2010
(Barrel sample.) Spicy, almost stern, black fruits with good attack and freshness pushing the fruits back. Lots of structure, should resolve to elegance with time, although a little hot on the finish. *90* Drink 2014-2022.

Colchagua Valley, Clos Apalta, 2009
There's a perfumed almost spicy impression at the start, with suggestions of layers of aromas and flavors. The palate makes a very classy impression, refined, elegant, perfumed, with a fine-grained texture. A faintly nutty impression on the finish cuts the purity of fruits. Hints of dark chocolate reinforce the smooth impression of the finish. This needs another couple of years but will be very fine indeed. 15.0% *92* Drink 2014-2024.

Colchagua Valley, Clos Apalta, 2001
This is a very Carmenère-ish vintage (although it's unclear what proportion of the 80% Carmenère-Merlot was actually Carmenère) with a herbal impression coming to the fore as the fruits mature. The finish is dry and herbal with little in the way of savory development yet; the fruits seem to be softening without becoming tertiary. The characteristic elegant rather than powerful style displays itself well, although the lightening fruit density does allow a faint touch of bitterness to poke through the finish. Ideally I would like to see just a touch of tertiary development by this time. 14.0% *88* Drink to 2017.

Colchagua Valley, Cuvée Alexandre, Apalta Vineyard Cabernet Sauvignon, 2009
An almost perfumed nose turns towards nuts and cereal. There's a smooth, subtle impression on the palate, with fine-grained tannins drying the finish. Showing a similar winemaking style to the Clos Apalta, this reflects the greater austerity of Cabernet Sauvignon (which at 85% to the 15% of Carmenère more or less reverses the proportions of Clos Apalta). Really closed now, it's going to take a while for this to come out of its shell. 14.1% *90* Drink 2016 to 2024.

Colchagua Valley, Cuvée Alexandre, Apalta Vineyard Cabernet Sauvignon, 2005
An interesting mix of influences shows here, with subtle savory notes offsetting the red and black fruits. There's a fugitive whiff of gunflint. This is just before the tipping point from fruity to savory, with fruits more evident on the palate than savory elements; tannins are still quite drying. There's a subtle herbal touch on the finish, nicely complementing the fruits. This is quite a classic Cabernet profile, just a touch short of generosity, as it can be. 14.5% *89* Drink to 2019.

Colchagua Valley, Cuvée Alexandre, Cabernet Sauvignon, 1999
Showing age in its garnet color, this has a nicely developed savory impression with some sharp gunflint, later showing a subtle touch of sous bois on the finish. Development is a little less obvious on the palate than the nose. The fruits still seem black, but savory development cuts their evident ripeness. Perhaps there is not quite enough fruit concentration to hold out much further against the savory development. The austerity may reflect the fact that this vintage was exclusively Cabernet Sauvignon. The wine was probably at its absolute peak about two years ago. 14.3% *89* Drink to 2015.

Rapel Valley, Casa Cabernet Sauvignon, 2011
Muted nose offers black fruits, faint herbaceous suggestions, and chocolate. Smooth and ripe, but restrained, nice balance for an entry-level wine, but inevitably lacking real character. Tannins seem rather light, not much sense of structure. I'd like a bit more concentration on the mid palate. 13.0% *86* Drink to 2016.

Rapel Valley, Casa Cabernet Sauvignon, 2010
This vintage was bottled both under cork and screwcap. In a comparison of the two wines, I preferred the screwcap (which has been adopted since this vintage).
Cork: Tight on nose, slowly releasing black fruits with herbaceous overtones. Fruits show a faint granular texture, with hints of tobacco and chocolate and a touch of perfume. Fruit quality is slow to emerge and the overall spectrum seems a bit one dimensional. *86* Drink to 2015.
Screwcap: Really closed nose, just faint hints of black fruits. Tight, more precise impression, more linear black fruits on palate, but elegant for entry-level. Greater purity of fruits shows through, needs more time, but will be more elegant. 13.0% *87* Drink to 2017.

Chadwick

Viñedo Chadwick is located at the site of the old family home in Maipo Alta. In 1945, Don Alfonso Chadwick Errázuriz purchased the 300 ha Tocornal vineyard. As a result of the problems in the 1960s, he sold it to Concha y Toro, keeping back just 25 ha around the house. Don Alfonso was one of Chile's leading polo players, and there was a polo field just behind the house. The soils are part of the Antumapa series—shallow clay loam over an alluvial stony subsoil—which are considered to be the best soils in Maipo Alta, and in 1992 the polo field was planted with Cabernet Sauvignon and Merlot, although the Merlot turned out to be Carmenère. The Carmenère did not do very well, and was taken out. Almost all vintages have been 100% Cabernet Sauvignon, although there are small amounts of Cabernet Franc and Merlot in the vineyard that may sometimes find their way into the wine. The wine shows classic purity of Cabernet Sauvignon. Wines were tasted at Chadwick in March 2012.

Maipo, Viñedo Chadwick, 2009
The initial impression shows a wine of character, with red and black fruits, and some spicy, almost cedary notes turning to tobacco. There's a nice balance, with dense, smooth, chocolaty fruits already becoming approachable, although flavor variety has not really started to develop yet. The impression of sweet ripeness is nicely restrained. Supple tannins allow the wine to become softer in the glass, reflecting the warm conditions this year. 14.5% *90* Drink to 2020.

Maipo, Viñedo Chadwick, 2001
Initially a restrained impression with freshness bordering on a herbaceous touch, then hints of ripe fruits and even a suspicion of raisins, and a subtle touch of chocolate. This is a classical palate, by which I mean clean pure fruits with no jammy overtones, lively and fresh, a refined elegance circumscribed at the edge by hints, but only hints, of herbaceousness and chocolate. Part of the elegance may be due to the moderate level of alcohol, reflecting a vintage that was cooler than average. Tannins are fine and firm, and there is an attractive touch of tobacco and chocolate on the finish. Evolving slowly, very attractive now, although it has not yet reached a savory turning point. 13.0% *91* Drink to 2022.

Concha y Toro

Founded in 1883, Concha y Toro is today one of the largest producers in Chile; its annual production of 11.5 million cases accounts for almost ten percent of the country's production. Although they own vineyards all over Chile, the focus here is on brand identification: "Concha y Toro aims to be a leading global branded wine company," says the company website. "In each case we look for the top area for each variety," says winemaker Marcelo Papa. So each brand sources its wines as appropriate, using (for example) Casablanca for cool climate varieties such as Chardonnay, or Maipo for varieties such as Cabernet Sauvignon. Most wines are varietal-labeled, including the Gran Reserva, Marques de Casa Concha, Terrunyo, and Don Melchor, one of the first icon wines. All of the Cabernet Sauvignon wines are more than 95% of the variety. Don Melchor comes from the major part of the old Tocornal vineyard in Puente Alto, which is considered cool climate for Maipo, at an elevation of about 650 m. Vines go back to very old stock, propagated by selection massale on their own roots. About 80% of production from Tocornal is used for Don Melchor. Wines were tasted at Concha y Toro in March 2012.

Puente Alto, Don Melchor Cabernet Sauvignon, Concha y Toro, 2011
(Barrel sample.) This is surprisingly approachable for a barrel sample, with just some dryness from the tannins showing on the finish, and perhaps a touch of heat. The palate of black fruits tends mostly to cherries with soft yet elegant tannins. This is distinctly more complex than any of the individual parcels from which it was assembled. Slowly the sense of underlying structure

develops in the glass. There's an attractive combination of elegance and softness, with chocolate and tobacco notes coming out faintly in the background. 14.5% *91* Drink 2016-2027.

Puente Alto, Don Melchor Cabernet Sauvignon, Concha y Toro, 2008
Already some interesting savory development shows suggestions of barnyard and gunflint, more overt on the nose than palate, where it forms a backdrop to elegant red and black fruits. The elegance of the fruits makes a strong impression, backed by refined tannins, with a touch of heat on the finish. A very faint herbaceous touch develops slowly in the glass to add complexity. The tannic backbone in the background is more evident than on 2007, but that initial savory burst suggests this may be a more rapidly maturing vintage. 14.8% *91* Drink 2014-2023.

Puente Alto, Don Melchor Cabernet Sauvignon, Concha y Toro, 2007
The initial impression is more restrained than the 2008, with black fruits showing hints of chocolate and tobacco. The well balanced palate has a delicate, almost floral, impression, with a touch of violets, and interesting aromatic development just beginning. Fine-grained tannins lurking in the background give a very fine texture. This should make a refined and elegant, even delicate, wine. 14.5% *93* Drink to 2025.

Puente Alto, Don Melchor Cabernet Sauvignon, Concha y Toro, 2003
Some subtle savory development shows on top of red and black fruits, and is consistent across nose and palate, with a fine, elegant impression foreshadowing future savory development that will bring increasing complexity. Savory notes close up in the glass, so development may be slower than suggested by the first impression, but should lead to a nicely balanced mingling of savory and fruity elements. The softness of the palate is quite striking, perhaps accompanied by a faint dilution in the glass that may limit longevity. 14.5% *92* Drink to 2022.

Puente Alto, Marques de Casa Cabernet Sauvignon, Concha y Toro, 2009
Initially there's a smoky impression of black fruits, leading into a smooth, but restrained palate. Tannins are evidenced by dryness on the finish. Superficially this gives a somewhat characteristic impression of those dense fruits in the Chilean style, perhaps reflecting the clay in the soil, but there's a lack of concentration and focus on the mid palate. 14.5% *87* Drink to 2017.

Pirque, Block Las Terrazas, Terrunyo Cabernet Sauvignon, Concha y Toro, 2009
A nutty, cereal, impression leads into sweet rounded black fruits, with plums and blackcurrants coming through. Quite an elegant style, reflecting the sandy terroir, not at all the in-your-face style of the New World, although there is some heat on the finish. 14.0% *88* Drink to 2019.

Errázuriz

One of the oldest producers in Chile, founded in 1870 in Aconcagua, Errázuriz remains one of the driving forces. Like many others who started wineries in the period, Don Maximiano Errázuriz made his fortune in copper mining. The vineyard started as a large endeavor, with several hundred hectares. The old house that still stands at the center of its operations was built in 1906, following the earthquake. The vineyards were essentially expropriated during the bad period following the 1960 land "reform," and the new Errázuriz reopened in 1982 with 10 ha of vineyards, to be run by Eduardo Chadwick, the fifth generation. Since then, Errázuriz have been buying land, and now have around 150 ha in vineyards Max I-VII in the vicinity (mostly planted with Bordeaux varieties), with further vineyards at Aconcagua Coasta and in Casablanca Valley (another 150 ha for cooler climate varieties). There is a striking new purpose built winery, referred to as the "icon winery." Under the Errázuriz label there are the Estate wines, the Max Reserva, and the Specialties, almost all single varieties. The leading icon wines are La Cumbre (Syrah), Kai (Carmenère), and Don Maximiano (Cabernet Sauvignon), the flagship wine whose first vintage was 1989. (The Don Maximiano Founder's Reserve should not be confused with the Single Vineyard Cabernet Sauvignon from the Don Maximiano estate, which is more of an entry-level wine.) Don Maximiano was exclusively or almost exclusively Cabernet Sauvignon until 2002; since then the blend has been broadened to include, according to the vintage, Cabernet Franc, Carmenère, Syrah, and Petit Verdot, with Cabernet Sauvignon staying around

95%. The first vintage is still going strong, so this is clearly a long lived wine. Wines were tasted at Errázuriz in March 2012.

Aconcagua, Don Maximiano Founder's Reserve, Errázuriz, 2008
Youthful purple appearance, but a more restrained style in this vintage, with a subtle nose offering some suggestions of perfume, and the palate following with a classy impression of fruits having a sweet, ripe edge, but generally subdued. There's just a touch of tarry tannins, and the vanillin that is more evident in the 2006 is only just poking out here. This is a classic impression, showing Chile's relationship to European tradition. It needs time not so much for the tannins to resolve as for the fruit flavors to develop. Slowly more complexity develops in the glass, a promising sign of longevity. 14.5% *91* Drink to 2024.

Aconcagua, Don Maximiano Founder's Reserve, Errázuriz, 2006
Some garnet shows in the appearance, but this is a deceptive guide to development. Black fruits show an overlay of vanillin, and at first blush you expect a full blown New World wine. The palate is quite supple, the vanillin turns to nuts on the finish, quite noticeable retronasally, giving a warm impression that is reinforced by a touch of heat. Although 2006 was a cool vintage, with a relatively late harvest, this wine gives a much riper impression than 2008, and seems far and away the most overtly New World in style. With tarry tannins in support of the fruits, this still needs to calm down a bit. It should show a solid palate in another year or so, but will not be as long lived as 2008. 14.5% *89* Drink to 2020.

Aconcagua, Don Maximiano Founder's Reserve, Errázuriz, 1989
Medium garnet color indicates some development. Initial impressions are muted, but the wine seems fresh with only faint notes of development. Fruits are beginning to fade but still show good balance, with some lively acidity picking up in the glass; slowly more fruits emerge and revert to a sweeter character with a delicious touch of bell peppers coming out on the finish, suggesting there may be more longevity than was initially apparent. 12.5% *90* Drink to 2016.

Los Vascos

A sizeable operation occupying its own valley of 4,000 ha, Los Vascos is Château Lafite's affair in Chile. The first 120 ha were planted after the Rothschilds acquired the property in 1986 (there were already some old vines present), and plantings today have reached 600 ha, mostly of Cabernet Sauvignon. Los Vascos farm 60 ha organically, but they do not see any difference in the grapes. There are also corn, olives, and wheat on the property, and there is a nursery for vines. There are three red wines, and the age of the vines is the main distinction between sources for each wine, with the plots farmed to purpose, and yields declining as you go up the hierarchy. The varietal Cabernet Sauvignon Los Vascos is harvested at 10 tons/ha from 20-30 yr old vines (400,000 cases), the Gran Reserva (70% Cabernet Sauvignon) is harvested at 8 tons/ha from 40 year old vines (100,000 cases), and Le Dix (90% Cabernet Sauvignon) is harvested at 5 tons/ha from 60 year old vines (10,000 cases). Le Dix and the Gran Reserva are harvested by hand, but the entry-level Cabernet Sauvignon has moved to 60% machine harvesting. General manager Claudio Naranjo defines the styles of the wines: "The first is an expression of terroir by Cabernet Sauvignon. Not too much extract, soft vinification, no green notes, maintain alcohol and acid balance by not picking too late, no oak. It's important that someone who buys it can drink it straight away. It's a classic Cabernet Sauvignon, so no blending. Gran Reserva maintains the style of the classic with the fruit, but the idea is to give more structure to the wine with the possibility of aging. Keeping the fruit and not too much oak is important. Le Dix comes from some of the old vines and spends 18 months in all new French oak." Wines were tasted at Los Vascos in March 2012.

Colchagua, Le Dix, Los Vascos, 2009
The initial impression is of quite closed black fruits with faint spicy overtones. Slowly opening out in the glass, the black fruits are fresh and refined, and a touch livelier than the 2008. The

characteristically supple tannins give structure to a fine-grained, smooth, almost glyceriny, finish, with a touch of tobacco adding character. A very nice effort in a refined style. 14.0% *90* Drink to 2020.

Colchagua, Le Dix, Los Vascos, 2008
Attractive nose makes an initial impression of black fruits with subtle spices and hints of cereal. There's an evident increase in concentration over the Gran Reserva, but in the same generally refined style. Nutty finish strengthens retronasally. Nice balance of elegant fruits and supple tannins, with some aromatics at the end with overtones of chocolate and coffee. 14.0% *89* Drink to 2020.

Colchagua, Gran Reserva, Los Vascos, 2010
More restrained impression than the 2009; the black fruits with spicy hints have not opened out yet. The restraint runs through the palate. This does not need time so much for the tannins to resolve, as they are already quite supple, but more to let the fruits develop more flavor variety. 14.0% *88* Drink to 2019.

Colchagua, Gran Reserva, Los Vascos, 2009
Spicy character with nutmeg on top of elegant black fruits makes an attractive initial impression. Smooth, nicely rounded black fruits on the palate, a touch of glycerin on the finish, where there are supple tannins, Nicely integrated to give an overall refined impression. Some flavor variety is beginning to develop; this should do well in the mid term. 14.0% *89* Drink to 2018.

Colchagua, Cabernet Sauvignon, Los Vascos, 2011
Here the nose shows a mix of redcurrant and black fruits, with red cherries coming up on the palate, which seems just a fraction lighter than the 2010 and 2009 vintages. Nicely balanced acidity, but not much structure. A touch of red fruit aromatics comes back on the finish. 14.0% *85* Drink to 2014.

Colchagua, Cabernet Sauvignon, Los Vascos, 2010
Fresh black fruit impression with faint touch of tea. Smooth palate with hints of chocolate, elegant, in some ways quite a European impression except for the touch of heat on the finish. Refined for entry-level wine. 14.0% *86* Drink to 2015.

Colchagua, Cabernet Sauvignon, Los Vascos, 2009
Fresh, forward, black fruits with a touch of raspberries coming up. Soft and fruity, attractive, light, and elegant, touch of heat on a slightly flat finish. Well made, balanced, entry-level wine—but where's the typicity of Cabernet Sauvignon? 14.0% *86* Drink to 2014.

Colchagua, Cabernet Sauvignon, Los Vascos, 2007
Restrained black fruits have more evident varietal character than later vintages in the form of a herbal edge to the palate, even a slight impression of austerity, although some heat comes through the finish. 13.5% *86* Drink to 2014.

Montes

Originally put together on a shoestring by a group of four (Aurelio Montes, Douglas Murray, Alfredo Vidaurre, and Pedro Grand), who were connected through the giant winery San Pedro during its period of near-bankruptcy in the difficult 1980s, Viña Montes is often given the credit for defining Apalta Valley as a top area for quality wine production. Production started in 1987 with grapes from an old vineyard in Curicó, farther south, but the company's first own vineyard was planted in the Apalta Valley, where land was more affordable. When the land was purchased in the early 1990s, there were some old Malbec vines growing on the flat part of the property near the road, but going up the slopes, the land was virgin and had to be cleared. Altogether there are more than 700 ha, with more than 135 ha planted. The elevation at the entrance is 200 m, and the highest plantings are at 650 m. As plantings extended from the roadside to the slopes, yields dropped from about 8 tons/ha to 1.5 tons/ha, and quality increased. At the very top is a vineyard with very high density planting, containing 16,600 vines/ha growing as tight vertical bushes. The inaugural vintage of what remains the top wine, Montes Alpha "M" was 1996; it is a Cabernet-dominated (80%) blend from the Apalta Vineyard. Expansion has been rapid and considerable. A new winery was constructed on Feng-Shui principles in 2004, and is used exclusively for icon wines including "M;" there's another winery not far away with a ten-fold greater capacity that is used for other brands, and there are five wine estates in Chile, as well as subsidiaries in Argentina and Napa. Wines were tasted at Viña Montes in March 2012.

Santa Cruz, Apalta Vineyard Cabernet Sauvignon, Montes Alpha "M", 2009
Montes's top wine is a classic Cabernet-dominated blend (80% Cabernet Sauvignon with Cabernet Franc, Merlot, and Petit Verdot), matured entirely in new French oak. A restrained nose offers subtle aromas of red and black fruits mingling with coffee and savory elements extending to a fugitive whiff of gunflint. Soft and almost opulent on the palate, there is a ripe, sweet, impression, smooth until the tannins kick in on the finish, with some dryness indicating the underlying structure. The contrast between the sweetness of the palate and dryness of the finish promises some longevity and elegance as the tannins resolve over the next few years. 14.8% *90* Drink 2014-2022.

Colchagua Valley, Montes Alpha Cabernet Sauvignon, 2009
A very faint vegetal impression with light red more than black fruits, a touch dry on the finish, but not displaying much evident varietal typicity. Certainly this avoids over-ripe or jammy fruit, but I'd like to see a bit more mid palate presence (even though it is in fact a blend containing 10% Merlot). 14.4% *87* Drink to 2016.

Mendoza, Ultra Cabernet Sauvignon, Kaiken, 2009
This Cabernet Sauvignon (it contains 4% Malbec) is equivalent to the Montes Alpha range, but represents application of the Montes style of winemaking to their subsidiary winery in Mendoza. It comes from 50 year old vines at the Vistalba vineyard. It is matured 60% in oak with one third new. In an interesting contrast with the Montes Alpha Cabernet, soft perfumed impressions of violets lead into those characteristically more opulent notes of Mendoza, with the floral notes coming back clearly on the finish. Immediately attractive, this should drink well in the mid term, but does not have the structure for longevity. 14.5% *87* Drink to 2017.

Napa Valley, Aurelio's Selection Cabernet Sauvignon, Napa Angel, 2007
This is Montes's wine from Napa, sourced from sites in Coombsville, Yountville, and Oakville, pricing more or less the same as the top Montes Alpha "M". An attractive perfumed nose melds violets and other floral notes with hints of coffee. The lush fruits of Napa are soft and almost opulent, with tannins evident only by some dryness on the finish. A very faint herbal note turns nutty in the glass. There's more backbone than you find in Mendoza. 15.1% *87* Drink to 2016.

Colchagua Valley, Twins, Montes, 2010
This is the first release of a blend of equal proportions of Cabernet Sauvignon and Malbec, with the Cabernet Sauvignon coming from the Apalta Vineyard, and the Malbec coming from the more powerful site of Marchigue. There's an initial impression of milk chocolate, almost coffee, soft and supple with the Malbec dominating. The Cabernet Sauvignon isn't really obvious and I'd like to see a touch more presence on the mid palate. 14.5% *85* Drink to 2015.

Colchagua Valley, Limited Selection Cabernet /Carmenère, Montes, 2010
This wine is a blend of 70% Cabernet Sauvignon to 30% Carmenère and spends nine months in French oak. The muted nose gives a faint sense of red fruits and chocolate. The Carmenère has added character (compared to the Limited Selection varietal Cabernet Sauvignon) with some faint vegetal overtones, but the flavor spectrum remains a bit limited. 14.1% *87* Drink to 2016.

Colchagua Valley, Limited Selection Cabernet Sauvignon, Montes, 2010
"The Colchagua area tends to make powerful tannins, but we are trying to get more fruit and elegance," says Dennis Murray. Some of the wine (40%) spends six months in 2-year and 3-year oak barrels. This has given a muted but classic impression on the nose, leading into a palate that balances light fruits with some tannic bitterness. This is a nice enough entry-level wine but doesn't offer a great deal of varietal typicity. 14.1% *86* Drink to 2015.

Neyen de Apalta

Neyen de Apalta is within a small sub valley at the eastern end of Apalta Valley, close to Viña Montes and Casa Lapostolle, and Apalta's rise in fame prompted a move from grape growing to wine production. In 2003, Patrick Valette was brought in as wine-maker, the old winery (originally built in 1890) was refurbished to be used as a barrel room, and a new winery was constructed. Then Neyen merged with larger producer Veramonte in 2010. Today about 20% of the grapes go into a single wine, a blend typically of two thirds Carmenère and one third Cabernet Sauvignon (although Carmenère has been as low as 55% and as high as 80%); some of the rest is used by Veramonte for its Colchagua brand, Primus, and some is sold. Soils vary from sandy on the flat to more clay on the slopes, and barrel samples show the Cabernet varying from a light elegant impression of red fruits to rounder black fruits tinged with chocolate, according to location. The Neyen wine has an annual production of about 4,500 cases, with the intention of building up to 9,000 cases. Wines were tasted at Neyen in March 2012.

Colchagua Valley, Neyen de Apalta, 2009
An initial impression of earthy black fruits is succeeded by an elegant balance, with quite precise, almost linear black fruits; the Cabernet Sauvignon (45% this vintage) dominates the fine-grained texture. This is the most elegant wine of the vertical, and in spite of the high Cabernet, will be ready before the 2008. Another year is needed to free the fruits of the tannins to allow their elegance and precision to come through. 14.0% *90* Drink 2013-2022.

Colchagua Valley, Neyen de Apalta, 2008
Youthful black fruits make the primary impression with some tarry aromas suggesting the need for time. Aromatics turn from black fruits to cereal. There is lots of extract and concentration, indeed this is the most concentrated of the vertical. Fruits are nicely in balance with tannins, which need a couple of years to resolve. The overall impression presently seems a little rustic, but this is the most powerful wine Neyen has produced to date. 14.5% *88* Drink 2014-2022.

Colchagua Valley, Neyen de Apalta, 2007
More earthy impression than most, black fruits with spicy hints underneath, and a hint of barnyard. Smooth but seems less concentrated on the palate than the other vintages. Firm tannins dry the finish. This will be the most rapidly developing of the flight, as already there is a faint savory development evident on nose and palate. 14.0% *88* Drink to 2020.

Colchagua Valley, Neyen de Apalta, 2006
Still a youthful ruby color with some purple hues. Slightly earthy, black fruit impression at the outset. Smooth and black, initially more impression of Carmenère than Cabernet, although it's a 50:50 blend, then a tannic bite comes through the finish and you see the underlying structure. There's a touch of heat. This blend is presently poised between the influence of its two constituent varieties, but really needs some further time. Perhaps it is the most mainstream and classical of the flight. 14.0% *89* Drink to 2021.

Pérez Cruz

This expansive estate and sparkling new winery built out of local wood are signs of the increasing interest in wine in Chile. The Pérez family have owned this estate of 580 ha since 1964, and in 1994 decided to plant vineyards; the winery was constructed in 2001. About three quarters of the terroir is alluvial, extending from a river at the edge of the property, and quarter at the eastern edge is colluvial, resulting from the collapse of a hill. There's a small transitional area between the alluvial and colluvial terroirs. Clay content decreases approaching the river and that's where the Cabernet Sauvignon is concentrated. The vineyards are so stony that mechanical control of weeds is impossible, but cover crops can be a problem because the soils are so poor. Pérez Cruz is making a transition towards more premium or icon wines that are based on blends, contrasted with the Reserva line that is labeled as Cabernet Sauvignon. They've also been making parcel selections over the past five years, although they have not yet decided whether to introduce a top-end single parcel Cabernet. Wines were tasted at Pérez Cruz in March 2012.

Maipo Valley, Quelen, Pérez Cruz, 2008
One of Pérez Cruz's two lead wines, Quelen has traditional Bordeaux varieties, but not Cabernet Sauvignon. The focus of this blend is on the forgotten varieties: 43% Petit Verdot, 32% Carmenère, and 25% Malbec. Here the impression is classically Old World, with restrained if not stern black fruits, not quite herbaceous, but certainly fresh on the finish. Generally Bordelais in character, but a little fuller on the palate, with a touch of heat on the finish. 14.5% *90* Drink to 2022.

Maipo Valley, Cabernet Sauvignon Reserva, Pérez Cruz, 2010
A touch of Syrah is used in cooler years or Carmenère in warmer years; this vintage includes 5% Syrah and 1% Carmenère. It's a bright purple color with a fresh, fruity initial impression, giving way to a slightly tarry, hot note on the finish. Black fruits are balanced by acidity and some tannic support, but the overall impression is a little rustic. Well made for its entry-level role in the marketplace, if somewhat generic. 13.8% *86* Drink to 2016.

Maipo Valley, Cabernet Sauvignon Reserva, Pérez Cruz, 2007
In this warmer year there was 1% Syrah and 5% Carmenère. There's a surprising touch of development in the initial impression, with savory barnyard and stewed fruit notes that become more muted in the glass. As the wine calms down, the fruits seem more in balance, with the savory development forming more of a backdrop. This is at its peak now. 14.7% *86* Drink to 2014.

Maipo Valley, Cabernet Sauvignon Reserva, Pérez Cruz, 2004
In this fresh and wet vintage, there was 3% Syrah and 2% Carmenère. Some savory development shows as a subtle contrast to the black fruits, with over-ripe overtones just showing retronasally. Well balanced with the fruits showing as ripe and fresh, high alcohol not noticeable, and the savory development nicely counterpoised. 14.4% *87* Drink to 2014.

Santa Rita

One of the oldest existing wineries in Chile, Santa Rita was founded in 1880, and stayed under the same family ownership until the late twentieth century. In 1980 it was acquired by the Claro telecommunications group. In the late eighties it acquired the Carmen winery, which has contiguous vineyards, and continued to expand by further vineyard purchases. Today it owns 4,000 ha in a variety of locations from cool climate Casablanca to Maipo, Colchagua, and Apalta Valleys, and then down to Curicó in the south; together with grapes purchased under contract from growers, Santa Rita produces 4.2 million cases per year, just under 4% of the country's production. There are five modern wineries, as well as the original facility in a historic park in Maipo. The major Santa Rita brands are the entry-level line called 120, The Reserva, Medalla Real, and, at the top, the icon Casa Real which is Cabernet Sauvignon only (and is not produced every year); the wine comes from 30-40 year old vines, and spends 18 months in new oak. Casa Real comes from the best blocks, but there is also some selection, so there may be some declassification from Casa Real to Medalla Real. The focus is on varietal-labeled wines, although Triple C is a blend of Bordeaux varieties. Wines were tasted at Santa Rita in March 2012.

Maipo, Casa Real Cabernet Sauvignon, Santa Rita, 2008
Youthful deep purple color. Brooding black fruits give an impression of a minty overlay. Sweet ripe fruits are accompanied by chocolaty tannins on the finish, but this is a touch lacking in concentration on the mid palate, a consequence of the conditions this year. Tannins are a little rustic, and there is some heat on the finish. There's not quite enough grip for longevity. 14.7% *88* Drink to 2019.

Maipo, Casa Real Cabernet Sauvignon, Santa Rita, 2007
Medium garnet color suggests fairly rapid development. An interesting array of aromas here, with nuts mingling with celery and hints of other vegetables. The characteristic sweet ripe fruits of Maipo Cabernet are evident, distinctly better rounded and smoother than the 2008, but cut by a herbaceous edge that develops on the finish. Tannins are quite fine. This is about three years from peaking. 14.5% *88* Drink to 2019.

Maipo, Casa Real Cabernet Sauvignon, Santa Rita, 2002
Developed garnet appearance leads into a mature vegetal impression with medicinal overtones (resembling a Bordeaux a decade or so older). But the palate is not at all tired, although it is mature; the fruits are lightening up and allowing the herbaceous overtones to come through more clearly, a trend that will intensify with time, although the ripeness of the fruits carries you past the herbaceousness. Development of a touch of sous bois reinforces the impression that this is now around its peak, or perhaps just past it, right at the tipping point, with the balance poised between fruity and herbaceous. 14.4% *89* Drink to 2016.

Maipo, Medalla Real Gran Reserva Cabernet Sauvignon, Santa Rita, 2008
There's a characteristic herbaceous note with bell peppers, becoming just a little more perfumed in the glass, but the sweet, ripe fruits are nicely restrained by the herbaceous edge. The wine contains 5% Cabernet Franc. Perhaps there is a very faint medicinal note of eucalyptus, but the sweetness of the fruits carries you past. Nice balance although not a great deal of flavor variety. 14.5% *88* Drink to 2019.

Maipo, Winemaker's Reserve Cabernet Sauvignon Blend, 2008
Some asperity here with a tarry impression hiding the black fruits. Sweet, ripe, softer than you expect from the nose, with refined, nutty overtones on the finish and a touch of aromatic black plums, in fact more evident aromatics than the Casa Real Cabernet. A chocolaty smoothness runs across the palate, perhaps reflecting the 1% Petit Verdot and Syrah. Refined tannins support the impression of precision. 14.2% *88* Drink to 2020.

Maipo, Gold Reserve Cabernet Sauvignon, Carmen 2009
The restrained fruits show faintly herbaceous overtones. Lovely sweet fruit on the palate is not in your face. The smooth black fruits are elegant rather than powerful, although a little monotonic at the moment, and it may take time to develop some flavor variety. Supple chocolaty tannins show on the finish. This has hardly started to develop, but the smooth structure conveys a sense of some potential longevity. 14.2% *89* Drink to 2022.

Maipo, Gold Reserve Cabernet Sauvignon, Carmen 2007
This comes from fifty year old vines. The first intimations of savory development are showing here. The palate shows a smooth balance of elegant red and black fruits with herbaceous overtones becoming faintly evident. Good freshness gives a sense of Old World style. Some flavor variety is developing, but this is a wine for the next few years rather than long aging. 14.3% *90* Drink to 2019.

Maipo, Triple C, Santa Rita, 2007
Triple C is a blend with two thirds Cabernet Franc to one third Cabernet Sauvignon, with just a touch (5%) of Carmenère. Whereas the 2006 is clearly dominated by Cabernet Franc, this vintage offers more of a blended feel, with some fresh, leafy notes just poking through the fruits. There's a tinge of tobacco, and tannins dry the finish. This is pretty tight and closed at the moment, but the structure is quite promising for opening up to become fine and elegant. 14.8% *89* Drink 2013-2021.

Maipo, Triple C, Santa Rita, 2006
There's that leafy, tobacco impression with some herbaceous overtones, immediately pointing to Cabernet Franc. In fact, this feels like a Cabernet Franc varietal wine. The smooth palate offers almost delicate fruits with a characteristic perfume of tobacco. There's a strong sense of tobacco and chocolate on the finish, but less impression of concentration and structure compared to 2007. 14.5% *88* Drink to 2020.

Seña

Seña started as a joint venture between Eduardo Chadwick and Robert Mondavi in 1995, but has been under the sole ownership of Errázuriz since 2004. The first vintages were a blend of Cabernet Sauvignon and Carmenère or Merlot sourced from Errázuriz vineyards; Cabernet Franc was added later, and more recently there has also been some Petit Verdot and Syrah. The Seña Estate was 350 ha of virgin land and crops such as herbs, corn, or potatoes before the 42 ha of vineyards were planted starting in 2000. Some of the original virgin land has been maintained in the form of "biological corridors" between the vineyards. Managed biodynamically, the estate extends from a plateau at 180 m where most of the vineyards are located, up the surrounding hills to a height of 450 m. As the Seña vineyards have slowly come on line, they have come to provide the major source of the grapes (now about 80% of total, planned to increase to 100%). Until 2002 the wine was heavily dominated by Cabernet Sauvignon (70-95%), but from 2003 the proportion was reduced to 50-65%. Production is around 800-1,200 cases. The wine seems to peak between five and ten years of age, although the inaugural 1995 vintage is still lively. Wines were tasted at Errázuriz in March 2012.

Aconcagua, Seña, 2008
Altogether a youthful impression, with a ruby to purple color and black fruits overlaid by nuts and vanillin. This has now come off its initial burst of primary fruits to give a more restrained or subdued impression, and the flavor spectrum hasn't really started to develop. It's a little dumb at the moment, making it difficult to get a good feel for its potential, but in a couple of years those faintly spicy, dumb black fruits should begin to turn savory. There's a faint suspicion of heat on the finish. A second bottle was livelier, showing a fresher quality, and a more direct impression of Cabernet Sauvignon, and might justify a higher score. 14.5% *89* Drink to 2021.

Aconcagua, Seña, 2005
A little development shows in some garnet hues, but there's a black fruit nose where the evident ripeness is accompanied by faint notes of vanillin, giving over to vegetal notes to provide a nice contrast. There's a lovely balance on the palate between developing fruits and savory elements, before the nuts and vanillin come back. This is about to turn to savory development, so there is an intriguing counterpoise between youthful and developing fruits; this may now be at its most delicious point. It's close to the turning point, as it switches in the glass from youthful to developed impressions, very hard to pin down, all of which argues that it's now at its peak. 14.3% *92* Drink to 2019.

Aconcagua, Seña, 1995
This is quite impressive for an inaugural vintage. Now showing a developed garnet color, there are subtle developed notes with suggestions of red more than black fruits underneath. Sweet ripe fruits show just a bare touch of savory development, about to reach the cusp of turning from fruity to savory. The finish shows a nice blend of savory notes and some nuts, becoming more savory on a long aftertaste, with fugitive notes of sous bois. The fruits seem still to have enough residual sweetness and ripeness to support a good balance with future savory development, although there isn't quite Bordeaux's sense of freshness. 13.0% *90* Drink to 2016.

Vik

Norwegian billionaire Alex Vik has undertaken the largest new viticultural development in Chile in decades, by purchasing 4,200 hectares, occupying twelve small valleys, and planting up to 480 hectares of Cabernet Sauvignon and Carmenère, with small amounts of Cabernet Franc, Syrah, and Merlot. The aim is to start at the top. "We are not looking at Vik to make a typical Chilean Cabernet Sauvignon, we are looking for more elegance and less alcohol. If it's not very good, there is no point to create a new wine," says winemaker Patrick Valette. The vineyards have been divided into 54 parcels based on varying soil types and climatic exposures; for the first two vintages, 32-40 of the parcels were used for the wine, which is called simply Vik. There are striking differences in the varietal composition of the first two vintages, but this will settle down as they work up to the intended average around 60% Cabernet Sauvignon, very much on the Bordeaux model. Production in 2009 was only 850 cases, but is expected to reach 5,000-6,000 for 2011. Wines were tasted at Vik in March 2012.

Colchagua, Vik, 2010
Dominated by Cabernet, this vintage (almost 50% Cabernet Sauvignon plus 10% Cabernet Franc) gives an initially muted impression. More aromatic than 2009, there are hints of black cherries and blackcurrants. There's a more obvious sense of structure as might be expected from the greater content of Cabernet Sauvignon. The overall impression shows a fine, granular texture, smooth on the finish, which should age well. 14.0% *91* Drink 2015-2025.

Colchagua, Vik, 2009
Dominated by Carmenère (two thirds), this vintage has a suggestion of spice with faint aromatic uplift. There's a smooth impression with a sort of silky opulence showing faintly glycerinic overtones. A touch of aromatics goes with the opulence, leading into tobacco and chocolate on the finish. This is almost ready, but needs to develop some more flavor variety. Supported by firm but fine tannins, this should mature in an elegant style. 14.0% *90* Drink 2014-2024.

Argentina: Mendoza

Vintages are not to be ignored in Mendoza, although variation tends to be less than elsewhere. Recently 2011 was a cool, late vintage sometimes spoiled by rain, 2010 was a slightly cooler year which increased the length of the growing season, 2009 was very warm with a dry end to an early season giving low yields and a rich (sometimes over-ripe) style of wines, 2008 was a cooler vintage, 2007 had some problems due to dilution from rain in March, 2006 is considered to be very good with concentrated Cabernet Sauvignon, 2005 required an extended season to get to phenolic maturity and the wines have less alcohol than usual (producers feel it was the best vintage since 2002), 2004 was a warm vintage giving aromatic wines but perhaps not so successful for Cabernet, 2003 had alternating temperatures and was very dry, 2002 is regarded as perfect in the region, and 1999 was warm. The last vintage that was regarded as bad in the region was 1998, when rainfall was catastrophic. The general view is that 2002 was the best vintage of the decade, followed by 2005 and 2006.

Catena Zapata

Catena Zapata is one of the most important wineries in Argentina, perhaps the most important in terms of driving quality. Nicola Catena planted his first vineyard of Malbec in Mendoza in 1902. Ups and downs over the century culminated in the decision by his grandson, Nicolás, to move into quality production. An extensive range of wines is now produced at their dramatic new winery, constructed to resemble a Mayan pyramid, including Catena Zapata (which includes the Nicolás Catena Zapata Cabernet/Malbec blend and several single vineyard Malbecs), Catena Alta (single varietal Malbec, Cabernet Sauvignon, and Chardonnay from vineyards at various elevations in the Andes), and Catena (single varietals sourced from estate vineyards in the foothills). Within Argentina, they also have Angélica Zapata, D. V. Catena, and Saint Felicien, all of which focus on varietal-labeled wines. Altogether, there are 500 ha of vineyards at various locations. In addition, Bodegas Caro is a joint venture between Catena and Lafite Rothschild, with its own vineyards; the eponymous wine is a blend dominated by Cabernet Sauvignon, with Malbec as the second partner; its first vintage was 2000. There is also a blend with reverse proportions, dominated by Malbec, called Amancaya Gran Reserva. Wines were tasted at Bodega Catena in March 2012.

Mendoza, Nicolás Catena Zapata, 2003
This vintage had a more or less average varietal composition for the blend, with 72% Cabernet Sauvignon to 28% Malbec. It shows the superficial smoothness of Malbec, that somewhat glossy surface, which at the moment is the dominant influence. The firm underlying structure shows the presence of Cabernet Sauvignon, and with time the Cabernet will no doubt emerge more clearly to strengthen the black fruit impression. Slightly nutty on the finish with tertiary development not yet in sight. 13.9% *90* Drink to 2022.

Mendoza, Cabernet Sauvignon, Catena Alta, 2003
Here you see the classic elegance of pure Cabernet Sauvignon. with a nutty background to the black fruits, and a touch of heat on a finish with some bite. The ripeness of the region makes

this wine readily approachable at this age, but reflecting the character of the variety, it is more linear than the Nicolás Catena Zapata blend of the same vintage. 14.2% *89* Drink to 2020.

Mendoza, Cabernet Sauvignon, Catena, 1996
Medium garnet color shows the age. Fruits are now restrained with a savory edge, supported by high acidity, and surprisingly like a Médoc of the same vintage; it's a little sparse on the palate, very much like one imagines pure Cabernet Sauvignon might have been from this vintage in Bordeaux. Savory notes strengthen in the glass, and the fruits take on a little more weight, countering the impression that the wine has reached its natural lifespan, and suggesting that it may age longer than first appeared. 14.0% *88* Drink to 2015.

Mendoza, Bodegas Caro, 2005
This vintage still seems very unevolved, more muted than the 2002, although showing a similar style. The palate is elegant and refined, with a silky, fine-grained texture. A slight increase in the proportion of Malbec in this vintage shows itself with an impression of infinite smoothness, the tannins quite subsumed by the fruits. A slowly developing gritty touch on the finish promises longevity. 14.0% *90* 2024.

Mendoza, Bodegas Caro, 2002
Smooth black fruits are cut by subtle savory and even vaguely animal overtones. There's a lovely balance, in terms of maturity perhaps equivalent to a fifteen year old Bordeaux. Smooth tannins give ripe, firm support to the fruits with a touch of nuts developing on the finish. You can see—if this is not too imaginative—the influence of Lafite. 13.8% *91* Drink to 2023.

Terrazas de Los Andes

The winery here was the first to be built in the middle of vineyards, in 1898, by one of the founders of winemaking in Argentina, but it went bankrupt (like almost all) in the bust of the 1960s. It was purchased by Domecq, who intended to use it as a distillery, but when they in turn sold it, Chandon purchased it with the intention of using the house for entertainment. When Chandon decided to move into production of dry wines in Mendoza, this became their headquarters and winery. Terrazas's first vintage was made at Chandon in 1992, and its own winery was refurbished and used from 1998. Some of the original Chandon vineyards were transferred to Terrazas, and when the trend to making varietal wines intensified in the late nineties, they purchased more land. Today Terrazas has vineyards at various altitudes into the Andes, with 500 ha of black vineyards, which include 270 ha Malbec, 180 ha Cabernet Sauvignon, 50 ha Petit Verdot, and some Merlot and Syrah; there are also 52 ha of white. Among the vineyards were 110 ha of Malbec that had been planted around 1930 at an elevation of 1070 m; some was pulled out to plant Pinot Noir and Chardonnay, but 60 ha remain. The top wines are the Afincado (single vineyard) Malbec and Cabernet Sauvignon varietals, followed by the Reserva range (which also includes Merlot, Syrah, Torrontés, and Chardonnay), and the entry-level Terrazas range. Terrazas also has a joint venture with Château Cheval Blanc, which produces the Cheval des Andes blend of Cabernet Sauvignon, Malbec, and Petit Verdot. Cheval des Andes has its own vineyards with 16 ha of old Malbec, 20 ha of Cabernet Sauvignon, and 2 ha of Petit Verdot. Wines were tasted at Terrazas in March 2012.

Mendoza, Terrazas Cabernet Sauvignon Reserva, 2010
There's more impression of character here than the preceding vintage, with a savory edge to the fruits, and a better balance on the palate, with fresh acidity pointing more in the direction of cooler climates and nicely lifting up the fruits. Tannins are more refined. Comparison of the 2010 and 2009 is a good indication of the range of vintage variation. 14.2% *88* Drink to 2021.

Mendoza, Terrazas Cabernet Sauvignon Reserva, 2009
There's an immediate fruity impression of smooth black fruits with the tannins giving a slight edge to a warm finish. This is very much in the New World approach of fruit-driven wine, easily approachable, with just a touch of high toned aromatics. It's soft and furry and the structure isn't really evident (although 30% new oak was used). 14.4% *87* Drink to 2018.

Mendoza, Afincado Los Aromos Cabernet Sauvignon, 2007
The vineyard is in Perdriel, but the appellation name has been trademarked and so cannot be used on the label. Its character shows immediately with a savory impression initially extending almost to barnyard and then clearing more towards a spicy and vegetal spectrum. Smooth on the palate, an elegant, refined impression, with a fine texture from the tannins; a touch of black-currants and cassis emerges on the finish. It's just a touch linear, with precisely delineated fruits in the style of pure Cabernet Sauvignon, somewhat reminiscent of samples of pure Cabernet from Bordeaux. The wine was matured in 100% new oak. 13.6% *91* Drink to 2022.

Mendoza, Afincado Los Aromos Cabernet Sauvignon, 2002
This vintage has developed a nutty, spicy character, going into a palate of smooth, ripe, black fruits, tending to elegance more than power. This particular vintage seems to be developing more slowly than average, with hints of nuts and even vanillin rather than savory elements. The sweet ripe fruits, broader than those of the 2007 vintage, come back on the finish, where the tannins are quite soft and furry. *91* Drink to 2022.

Mendoza, Afincado Los Aromos Cabernet Sauvignon, 1999
"In its time this wine was a monster," says Hervé Birnie-Scott. Some development is immedi-ately evident in the form of sous bois and a pungent, fugitive whiff of gunflint, but the ripeness of the black fruits remains obvious, and a touch of blackcurrants and cassis comes up on the palate. With a lovely balance, this is right at the tipping point from fruity to savory. Perhaps one would have liked to see just a touch more acid uplift. It feels much more than three years older than the 2002, an interesting demonstration of the different rate at which each vintage devel-ops. 13.6% *90* Drink to 2019.

Mendoza, Cheval des Andes, 2007
A warm nutty quality on opening makes you think about very ripe Cabernet Franc, a reasonable thought given the antecedents of this wine in a collaboration between Terrazas de los Andes and Cheval Blanc, although in fact it is a blend of Cabernet Sauvignon and Malbec. Smooth on the palate to the point of obscuring the tannins, some wood spices showing, but after the initial burst of generous fruit, a more sober palate shows a somewhat monolithic black fruit character with a dense structure that will take some time to resolve. It's quite elegant and well balanced, but lacks the sense of uplifting acidity that characterizes the left bank in Bordeaux. "It lacks subtlety," said my constant companion, the Anima Figure. 14.5% *88* Drink to 2020.

Weinert

Bodega Weinert has a chequered history. Built by the Spanish in 1890, it was taken over in the 1920s, subsequently went derelict, and was purchased by Weinert in 1975. The first vintage was 1977. Weinert has no vineyards, and they have relations, not con-tracts, with growers, but sources are mostly the same each year. Wines are matured in 2,000 liter casks of old oak, somewhat on the Gran Reserva model of Spain. "We are the only winery that ages the wine in classic style in cask," says winemaker Hubert Weber, citing as his winemaking influences Lopez de Heredia, Vega Sicilia, and Gia-coma Conterno. The period in cask was three years until 2003 when it was lengthened; as the result of some changes in the cleaning process to eliminate Brett from the casks, the wines started to develop more slowly. The top wine is Estrella, an icon range, con-centrating on single varieties and made only occasionally. Cavas de Weinert is a blend of Cabernet Sauvignon, Malbec, Merlot, but is consistent from year to year, and is not used to compensate for vintage variation as it would be in Bordeaux, so it was not made in 1995 (when the Cabernet was not satisfactory) or in 1998, 2001, and 2005 (because of problems with the Merlot). There is also an entry-level wine, Carrascal. Hubert also makes wines under his own name, with the production varying from year to year depending on the available supplies of grapes. Here he uses some barrels in more conventional fashion. Wines were tasted at Weinert in March 2012.

Mendoza, Weinert Estrella Cabernet Sauvignon, 1994
The immediate impression is savory and developed, with notes of barnyard and gunflint, all

integrated with the underlying sweet ripe fruits. There's still a lot of intensity. This is a powerful wine with an interesting blend of savory and fruity elements, supported by balanced acidity and smooth, firm tannins. Notes of gunflint on the finish really bring the wine to life, with the savory to fruit balance at its peak, almost salty in its overall impression. Only at the very end do you see the austerity of pure Cabernet Sauvignon beginning to take over. No one could call this wine elegant—it has too much intensity for that—but the balance should allow it to continue to age for another decade at least. 14.5% *92* Drink to 2024.

Mendoza, Weinert Estrella Merlot, 1999
This Merlot bucks the trend for clay terroir by coming from relatively sandier soils. It spent three years in cask and ten years in concrete before bottling. Initially this seems full and ripe, showing Merlot's characteristic presence on the mid palate, with the typical barnyard notes of development, and just a touch of pungent gunflint. But there's a finer impression than comes from Merlot grown on its more traditional clay, with an impression of refinement that's unusual for the variety, and there isn't much impression this will be much shorter lived than the Estrella Cabernet. *91* Drink to 2027.

Mendoza, Cavas de Weinert 2004
(This is the current release.) The immediate impression is of those characteristic savory, almost pungent, almost piquant, notes. Smooth and ripe on the palate, there's a sensation of coated black fruits. Tannins underneath the fruits dry the finish, but overall the impression is quite glyceriny. There's an openly delicious quality. 14.5% *89* Drink to 2022.

Mendoza, Cavas de Weinert 1994
Development has taken a slightly different path here, in fact the nearest parallel would be the 1977 Cabernet Sauvignon, as there are only some hints of savory notes, and more of a delicate, almost perfumed impression. Apparently this wine has gone up and down, and appeared oxidized a year or so ago, when it was taken off the market for a while, but then it recovered. There's a slight sense that the smooth fruits are beginning to dry out, allowing the tannins to show more as a dryness on the slightly nutty finish. 14.5% *88* Drink to 2016.

Mendoza, Cavas de Weinert 1983
Savory and animal with pungent overtones of gunflint, overall contributing to a slightly sweaty impression (perhaps a touch of Brett). The smooth palate tends to opulence, but is beautifully cut by the savory overtones. This is at a perfect tipping point from fruity to savory (although it's probably been here for a while). Hubert sees this wine as having become more dominated by Malbec over the past five years; indeed, it shows more Malbec as it develops in the glass, becoming smoother, more elegant, more perfumed, less animal. *93* Drink to 2019.

Mendoza, Cavas de Weinert 1977
We compared two bottles. Around 2004 one lot of wines was recorked for an importer who insisted on having fresh corks. The rest remain under original corks. The difference was like night and day. The wine under new corks showed slightly oxidized fruits with hints of raisins; otherwise the wine remains youthful, with the evident fruits lacking savory overtones, and a little restricted in flavor variety. By contrast the wine with the original corks has more of that classic savory impression, with rather restrained fruits, kept lively by an acidic uplift. Matching the greater tertiary development, the color is also a little more garnet. Compared with the varietal Cabernet Sauvignon of the same year, the wine is a little more developed and a little less obvious. *92* Drink to 2019.

Mendoza, Weinert Cabernet Sauvignon 2005
This wine spent four years in cask after the vintage, and then a further year in concrete. It has a relatively restrained character, showing smooth, black fruits with a faint tannic rasp and only some hints of the savory, animal notes of older vintages. Carrying its structure lightly, it should age for the mid term. 14.5% *87* Drink to 2018.

Mendoza, Weinert Cabernet Sauvignon 1997
There's an immediately powerful suggestion of savory, animal character, with sweet ripe fruits of black cherries, melding into an elegant impression with fine-grained tannins on the palate, and then black fruit aromatics coming out on the finish. This should continue to develop interestingly for another decade. 14.0% *91* Drink to 2026.

Mendoza, Weinert Cabernet Sauvignon 1977
This vintage is now quite delicate and refined with those savory overtones taking on more of a perfumed air. The elegant impression persists on the finish, with a glyceriny character to the finely grained texture. This is very fine indeed. 13.5% *92* Drink to 2019.

Mendoza, Weinert Carrascal 2007
This is matured for two years in large oak casks, and then for six months or more in concrete. It shows the faintly animal notes of cask aging, and quite nice complexity for an entry-level wine. Fruits on the palate are more straightforward than the varietal Cabernet Sauvignon, but the nose retrieves the situation, although the wine simplifies a bit in the glass. 14% *87* Drink to 2017.

Mendoza, Hubert Weber Cabernet Sauvignon 2007
This wine spent two years in barrels of half French and half American oak. Here you see the effects of the (more conventional) élevage. By comparison with the 2006, the wine is softer and more rounded, with those savory, animal overtones much less in evidence. The structure is less obvious, although tannins dry the finish, with a touch of bitterness, and some heat on the finish. 14.5% *87* Drink to 2018.

Mendoza, Hubert Weber Cabernet Sauvignon 2006
This wine comes from a single vineyard in Lujan de Cuyo. It was matured 10% in barrels (half French and half American), the rest in concrete, and then spent two years in bottle before release. It starts out with a characteristic savory, animal character overlaying sweet, ripe fruits, with just a touch of primary blackcurrants still showing. This clears in the glass to give a more perfumed impression, perhaps an indication of the path of future development. There's some tannic bitterness and heat on the finish. 14.5% *88* Drink to 2020.

Mendoza, Hubert Weber 2007
This blended wine has adopted a different philosophy from Weinert's blended wine, and here the blend is made according to what is available. Initially there is a savory, slightly animal impression, and then the smooth opulent black fruits take over, leading into a slightly nutty impression on a chocolaty finish. This is refined and elegant rather than powerful. 14.7% *89* Drink to 2022.

South Africa

Vintages in Stellenbosch can be variable. 2011 was problematic because of variable conditions. Reduced yields in 2010 led to concentrated red wines. In spite of early difficulties, subsequent good conditions have caused 2009 to be regarded locally as the vintage of the decade. Before that, 2008 was below average, 2007 was average, 2006 is well regarded, and 2005 is below average. Wines were tasted in June 2012 except as otherwise noted.

Graham Beck, Cabernet Sauvignon, Western Cape, 2010
A fairly classic first impression with some herbal overtones to the black fruits. Sweet, ripe fruits dominate on the palate, but there is a slightly jammy edge, and a rather straightforward flavor spectrum. The slight tannic bite should wear off in the next year, but there isn't any evidence for a structure that might support interesting aging. This is a well made wine at the entry-level. 14.5% *86* Drink to 2015.

Glenelly, Cabernet Sauvignon, Stellenbosch, 2010
A herbal nose gives a surprising impression of unripe fruits, but the palate follows with pleasant, if not very characterful, black fruits, with a herbaceous touch to the finish. There's a rustic quality to this entry-level wine, which is quite the antithesis of the smooth elegance of the top line Lady May bottling. 14.5% *86* Drink to 2016.

Glenelly Lady May Cabernet Sauvignon, Stellenbosch, 2010
Having sold Pichon Lalande, May de Lencquesaing is now making Cabernet Sauvignon in South Africa. Lady May, the flagship wine, spends a full two years in barriques. The style here is distinctly more restrained than most South African Cabernets, although it betrays the oak regime with those nutty overtones of vanillin. The palate shows smooth, black fruits, more plums than blackcurrants; the underlying structure shows itself as a trace of bitterness on the finish. It doesn't show immediately, but the New World origins make themselves felt by some overt aromatics that develop in the glass. There's some potential here for interesting development, although I'd place it more at the level of Cru Bourgeois than Grand Cru Classé. 14.5% *88* Drink to 2017.

Warwick Estate, Cabernet Sauvignon The First Lady, Stellenbosch, 2010
Restrained nose with impression of black fruits hidden by the nutty vanillin from the oak. The impression of oak follows through to the distinctly nutty palate, where the black cherry fruits are supple and soft. Overall the impression is as nutty as fruity, becoming more overtly aromatic in the glass. 14.0% *86* Drink to 2016.

Cederberg Private Cellars, Cabernet Sauvignon, Cederberg, 2009
The vineyards for this wine are unusual on several counts. They are in the Cederberg Ward, about 250 km north of Cape Town, and are not part of any District. One reason they stand alone is their location in the mountains; at elevations of around 1,000 m, they are among the highest locations where Cabernet Sauvignon is grown anywhere in the world. The first impression identifies tight black fruits with herbal overtones; a faint touch of bell peppers develops later. The palate has the typical tightness of mountain tannins, with a definite taut grip on the finish. Fruits show good concentration, with the structure of Cabernet Sauvignon showing through. There's just a touch of heat on the finish. This may be a little tight for some palates; a touch of Merlot would have rounded it out, but it's quite a classic representation of mountain Cabernet. 14.0% *88* Drink to 2017.

Edgebaston, Cabernet Sauvignon, Stellenbosch, 2009
The nose is restrained but offers an impression of ripe aromatics, an accurate prediction of the palate, where black cherry fruits dominate with some distinct aromatic overtones. In a rich, ripe, extracted, style, this flirts with jamminess in an overtly New World style. The high alcohol emphasizes its richness. 15.0% *87* Drink to 2016.

Jordan, Cabernet Sauvignon, Stellenbosch, 2009
Restrained nose has some faint suggestions of nuts with black fruits following. Smooth, soft, pleasant, nutty black fruits on the palate make this an undemanding entry-level wine, with just enough structure in the background to justify the varietal label. A little too nutty retronasally, there's a risk it will become cloying as the structure resolves. 14.0% *85* Drink to 2015.

Land of Hope, Cabernet Sauvignon Reserve, Stellenbosch, 2009
Restrained nose leads into soft black fruit palate, but then a surprising herbaceous quality shows on the finish, definitely identifying Cabernet. In contrast with the initial impression, the final impression is that some Merlot would have helped to round out the fruits. Somehow the superficial softness on the palate and the herbaceous finish do not come together; perhaps another year will help. 14.0% *86* Drink to 2015.

Le Riche Wines, Cabernet Sauvignon Reserve, Stellenbosch, 2009
Restrained nose with intimations of black fruits leads into palate of blackcurrants with nutty overtones. There's a good structure underneath the fruits, with enough tannin to identify the Cabernet, although the finish becomes increasingly aromatically nutty in the glass, leaving some faintly jammy overtones. 14.5% *87* Drink to 2016.

Rustenberg, John X Merriman, Stellenbosch, 2009
A dry first impression is succeeded by fugitive notes of black fruits, followed by some round fruits of redcurrants and red cherries. Palate is quite soft and round, again more red than black fruits. Flavor profile is a little lacking in variety. Tannins are quite light. Overall impression is a little soft and I'd like to see a little more Cabernet character coming out. 14.6% 87 Drink to 2016.

Waterford Vineyards, Cabernet Sauvignon, Stellenbosch, 2009
Restrained on the nose, so the sweet ripeness of the fruits on the palate comes as a surprise. This seems a typical entry-level wine, soft and supple, with fruits of blackcurrants and plums, but then a tannic bite on the finish shows a surprising level of underlying structure, and the finish is quite dry. That dry finish makes it very much a 100% Cabernet Sauvignon. As the tannins resolve, the fruits may come to seem a little straightforward. 14.3% *87* Drink to 2016.

Glen Carlou, Gravel Quarry Cabernet Sauvignon, Paarl, 2008
The initial impression shows some nutty overtones suggesting the wine will have full, generous fruits. Following through, the palate is quite soft and spicy, with the blackcurrant fruits obscured by waxy, almost soapy, notes. Distinctly aromatic retronasally, the wine has overtones that are more Syrah-like than typical of Cabernet's usual restraint. There's a risk this will become more cloying as it develops. 14.5% *86* Drink to 2015.

Hartenberg Estate, Cabernet Sauvignon, Stellenbosch, 2008
The nose gives quite an intense impression of ripe, almost over-ripe, fruits, so the sweet, ripe, rich fruits of the palate, showing blackcurrants and plums, do not come as a surprise. Very much in the mode of an interdenominational entry-level wine, this is perfectly well made, but it's

hard to get much sense of place or variety from its soft, supple, impression. 14.5% *85* Drink to 2015.

Starke-Condé, Cabernet Sauvignon Oude Nektar, Jonkershoek Valley (Stellenbosch), 2008
This wine comes from a high elevation (600 m) vineyard at the top of Oude Nektar farm in Jonkershoek, in Stellenbosch. Unfortunately, the vineyard burned down during the mountain fires of 2009, so this is the first and only vintage. The first impression is of deep black fruits with spicy, peppery, overtones. Good acidity gives a fresh impression to the palate, with a faintly herbaceous impression in the background that strengthens in the glass, with tight mountain tannins defining the finish. Elegant rather than powerful, this wine carries the high alcohol well, but it's awfully tight and structured, and I have the impression that a little Merlot would have brought some helpful generosity to the fruits. A typical mountain Cabernet, it poses the classic question: will the tannins soften sufficiently before the fruits dry out? 14.0% *88* Drink to 2016.

Thelema, The Mint Cabernet Sauvignon, Stellenbosch, 2008
The famous mintiness is not especially in evidence, but there is something of a savory, herbal impression, perhaps more akin to tarragon, with a suggestion of menthol only showing very faintly on the finish. Mid weight fruits are weighted towards blackberries, nicely rounded, with cedary, herbaceous, menthol notes coming back on an elegant finish with a hint of dark chocolate to give an impression of complexity. 14.5% 90 Drink to 2018.

De Trafford Wines, Cabernet Sauvignon, Stellenbosch, 2008
A restrained black fruit nose leads into a palate with ripe fruits, just cut by a touch of firm tannins on the finish. The high alcohol indicates a ripe style, but the palate manages sufficient restraint to carry it off. There's even a faint herbal touch on the finish before it's obscured by the nutty vanillin of the new oak. This is a bit too obvious for my palate, but it's certainly a well-made wine that captures what Cabernet can give in Stellenbosch. 15.0% *88* Drink to 2017.

Meerlust, Rubicon, Stellenbosch, 2007
Powerful cedar and cigar box create the first impression of a wine more in a European than New World style. Then come overtones that are more herbal than herbaceous. Black fruits show the classic bell peppers, especially on the finish and retronasally, with blackcurrants kicking in on the aftertaste. The overall impression is more of Graves than of the New World; indeed, this is a wine that might well appeal to traditional Bordeaux drinkers. 14.1% *91* Drink to 2019.

Simonsig Estate, Labyrinth Cabernet Sauvignon, Stellenbosch, 2007
Restrained black fruit nose with nutty overtones. Pleasant if not especially characterful black fruits on the palate, with a tannic tang to the finish, then becoming just a touch aromatic in the glass. This shows signs of over-ripeness that may intensify with age. 14.0% *85* Drink to 2015.

Vergelegen Labyrinth Cabernet Sauvignon, Stellenbosch, 2006
First impression here is classic Cabernet Sauvignon with the herbaceous elements of the nose taking the form of bell peppers. The dry palate shows fruits of blackcurrants and black cherries, with a distinctly herbaceous touch to the finish, followed by those typical notes of nutty vanillin from new oak still evident. This clearly distinguishes itself from the run of the mill Cabernet from Stellenbosch in its more classical flavor spectrum, as opposed to the predominant soft international style. It would be possible to confuse this with a Cru Bourgeois from Bordeaux from, say, 2004. 14.0% *88* Drink to 2017.

Vergelegen Red, Stellenbosch, 2005
First impressions are distinctly Cabernet-ish, with faintly herbaceous notes and cedary overtones rising out of the glass. Then come fugitive notes of chocolaty black fruits. Cedar certainly follows through to the palate and quite dominates the finish. Fruits tend to herbaceous, and the tannins are quite stern. The impression here, from a finish that dries the mouth and still seems bitter, is that even after several years, the wine needs more time. 14.5% *88* Drink to 2018.

Morgenhof Estate, Stellenbosch, 2004
The initial impression is restrained and herbal, then somewhat dry and restrained. Mid weight body shows a mix of red and black fruits, tending towards redcurrants, just a touch of bitterness from the tannins; the finish is soft and rounded but a little short. 14.2% *88* Drink to 2016.

Waterford Estate, Bordeaux Blend, Stellenbosch, 2004
The initial rich chocolaty impression is succeeded by cedary overtones, and these two countervailing notes continue to alternate as the wine develops in the glass. Fruits are quite elegant; a slight sense of tobacco suggests that some of the refinement is due to the high proportion of Cabernet Franc. Certainly this is one of the most refined of South Africa's Bordeaux blends. 13.8% *89* Drink to 2017.

South Australia

The warm climates of Barossa Valley, McLaren Vale, and Langhorne Creek in South Australia mean that achieving ripeness with Cabernet Sauvignon is rarely a problem: the difficulty is more in preventing the grapes from becoming too ripe. So general assessments for vintage quality based on success with Shiraz (the predominant variety) will not necessarily provide good predictions for Cabernet Sauvignon. That said, 2011 is regarded as problematic, 2010 as good, 2009 not quite as good, 2008 average, 2007 below average, 2006 only average, 2005 above average, and 2004 was good. Obviously there are also differences between the subregions.

Barossa Valley: Charles Melton

A boutique winery in Tanunda, Charles Melton focuses on old vines of Shiraz and Grenache, with the southern Rhône valley as the model. Aside from a rosé and sparkling wine, the Cabernet Sauvignon is the only exception. Two blocks of Cabernet at Lyndoch in the southern part of Barossa Valley, 1.5 ha (20-28 years old) and under 1 ha (19 years old), are blended to make the single Cabernet. It is matured in new French oak for 20-24 months, with soft tannins emphasized by pressing off into barriques before fermentation is completed. It shows a typical Barossa style focusing on intense fruit concentration. Production is between 300 and 500 cases. Wines were tasted in Barossa in October 2012.

Barossa Valley, Cabernet Sauvignon, 2009
Black fruit nose with a slightly gamey, almost over-ripe impression, gives way to a finer, more mineral impression. Good fruit concentration tends to blackberries. Fine tannins show a touch of asperity on the finish. This needs another year or so to come together, when it should become quite elegant. It's certainly not a big, brawny style, although there is a touch of heat on the finish. 14.5% *90* Drink 2014-2029.

Barossa Valley, Cabernet Sauvignon, 2005
A little reduced on the nose, slightly gamey with a mineral sensation. Comparison with the 2001 (which was bottled under cork) raises the question of whether the aromatics will always stay more forceful under screwcap. Crisp, almost piquant, acidity showcases blackcurrant fruits with a touch of cassis; although the fruits are concentrated, the overall impression is surprisingly lean. The fine tannins still really need a little more time to resolve and meld with the fruits. This does not really seem as much as four years more evolved than the 2001 (perhaps reflecting the difference in closures). But this wine was an education in the perils of tasting: an hour or so later with food, it seemed too aromatic and sweet to match a meal. 14.5% *90* Drink to 2024.

Barossa Valley, Cabernet Sauvignon, 2001
A more restrained nose than the younger vintages, although conveying the same generally tense impression of blackcurrant and blackberry fruits. A softer impression on the palate has come with age, but the tight, concentrated, fruits still show a touch of asperity. This is certainly evolving very slowly, and I would like to see a little more flavor variety develop. 14.5% *91* Drink to 2024.

Elderton

At Nuriootpa in the heart of Barossa Valley, the Elderton vineyard was purchased by the Ashmead family in the late seventies, and is run today by Cameron and Allister Ashmead. The top plots in the vineyard have very old Shiraz vines (planted in 1894) and old Cabernet Sauvignon (planted in 1944). This is the source for the Command Shiraz, Cabernet Sauvignon, and 'Ode to Lorraine' Cabernet Sauvignon-Shiraz-Merlot. Other vineyards purchased later are located elsewhere in Barossa. Viticulture is moving towards biodynamics. The winery itself is close to downtown Nuriootpa and is a former fruit-processing plant. The style here has been changing. "We are trying to get more finesse into the wines," says Cameron. Winemaker Richard Langford adds, "The style in the nineties was 'get it really quite ripe'. We are trying to get as far away from that as we can. These days we pick as early as we can." Even so, there is no mistaking the richness of Barossa in the wines, but there does seem to be more elegance on comparing today's vintages with those earlier in the decade. Wines were tasted at Elderton in October 2012.

South Australia, Ode to Lorraine Cabernet-Shiraz-Merlot, 2009
A faintly chocolate impression to the nose. Ripe on the palate but with a bite on the finish bringing character. Full rich fruits, but certainly in a cleaner, more directed, style than the vintages a few years earlier. The style is fruit-driven but the Cabernet character shows over the Shiraz fruit and aromatics. Can drink now but the fruits will show more clearly when the tannins calm down over the next year or so. 14.5% *89* Drink 2014-2022.

South Australia, Ode to Lorraine Cabernet-Shiraz-Merlot, 2002
A slightly reduced expression on the nose quickly blows off. Very rich on the palate, quite robust, but with a very dry finish. Here is a demonstration of the tight structure of Cabernet and the superficial richness of Syrah in a blend in which neither clearly dominates. I would like to see a little more flavor variety developing, however. 14.5% *88* Drink to 2018.

Barossa Valley, Ashmead Single Vineyard, 2010
(Not yet released) There are 300-500 cases of this 100% Cabernet Sauvignon, which is matured in hogsheads (300 liter barrels), with 80-100% new oak. Interestingly, although this is younger, the aromatics are more restrained than the 2004, and there's more sense of refinement. (2004 and 2010 were very comparable vintages, says Cameron Ashmead.) This vintage exhibits a nicely delineated purity of line for the black cherry Cabernet fruits, with hints of blackcurrant marking the finish. A touch of tannin is evident on the finish (but no more than the 2004); overall impression shows some finesse although there is a touch of heat on the finish. 14.5% *91* Drink to 2024.

Barossa Valley, Ashmead Single Vineyard 2004
This was the first vintage under screwcap. There's a savory, almost piquant, blackberry fruit nose; a touch of blackcurrant aromatics comes out on the palate. Definitely a fruity Barossa edge on the palate, with a tight tannic expression on the finish. This is a wine in the powerful Barossa style, but displaying quite a tight edge to the fruits. 14.5% *90* Drink to 2022.

Barossa Valley, Cabernet Sauvignon, 1992
Preceding the Ashmead Single Vineyard, this was the only varietal Cabernet made at the time (it probably included some other varieties). The mature nose shows some tertiary aromatics. The palate is less developed than the nose suggests, with ripe, rich fruits giving an impression of sweetness. Savory notes are still subservient to the fruits; tertiary sensations are just detectable retronasally. Initially this seems on the rustic side, but then it freshens up in the glass. 14.5% *89* Drink to 2016.

Greenock Creek

As I approached Greenock Creek through a long row of palm trees along Seppeltsfield Road, I found myself wondering what sort of climate could be suitable for both tropical vegetation and Cabernet Sauvignon. Greenock's home vineyard at Seppeltsfield Road has been extended and steadily planted since the initial purchase in 1975; and the property just across the way at Roennfeldt Road was purchased in 1994. The estate Cabernet comes from 1.5 ha of plantings at the home vineyard, and a separate bottling comes from a half hectare plot of 80 year old vines at Roennfeldt Road. This is red wine country: a plot of Chardonnay has just been grafted over to Shiraz, as the Chardonnay wasn't successful because it's just too hot. Winemaker Michael Waugh is self-trained, and has a great reputation for his Shiraz, made in a typically opulent Barossa style. The Cabernets are matured in hogsheads (300 liter) of French wood, with 27 months in shaved seasoned wood for the estate wine, and 36 months in all new wood for the Ro-ennfeldt Road. Production levels are tiny. A mini vertical tasting of Cabernet Sauvignon certainly gave a dramatic impression of vintage variation in recent years. The 2010 Cabernet seemed mainstream (for Barossa), but the 2009 couldn't decide whether to be over-ripe or herbaceous, and the 2008 was grotesquely ripe. I was left wondering whether this was the right spot for Cabernet if it oscillates so violently. By contrast, Ro-ennfeldt Road seems to have more varietal character, although in a very ripe, alcoholic, style. Wines were tasted at Greenock Creek in October 2012.

Barossa Valley, Cabernet Sauvignon, 2010
This has the best balance of the past three vintages, with a more restrained fruit impression on the nose, and a slightly leafy impression of black fruits on the palate, turning to tobacco on the finish. Acidity stops just short of piquant, and tannins are firm but not obtrusive, allowing the fruits to come to the fore. Alcohol is unusually moderate for the house and region. 13.5% *90* Drink 2013-2023.

Barossa Valley, Cabernet Sauvignon, 2009
The nose shows over-ripe, slightly stewed fruits, following through to a slightly stewed impres-sion on the palate, yet with a fugitive whiff of vegetal aromas changing to a touch of tobacco. This wine can't make up its mind whether it wants to be herbaceous or super ripe. Piquant acid-ity is pressing on the finish. Perhaps there is too much oak for the fruits, as the wine seems to be somewhat disjointed. 12.5% *87* Drink to 2020.

Barossa Valley, Cabernet Sauvignon, 2008
This was a hot year, with 14 days over 42 degrees, and the initial impression is that this is not a wine, it's a fruit bomb. Although the grapes were picked just before the final heat wave, this is a full throttle New World style with massive black fruits on nose and palate. Alcohol is at a record level for Cabernet Sauvignon. There are rich, ripe, black fruits of cherries and plums, with hints of blackcurrants; pungent aromatics come through the distinct heat on the finish. Tannins need to resolve, but there are always going to be massively extracted fruits, making this altogether overwhelming. 16.0% *89* Drink 2014-2026.

Barossa Valley, Roennfeldt Road Cabernet Sauvignon, 2006
There's a restrained first impression of black fruits of chocolate-coated cherries with perfumed, almost floral, overtones of violets. The palate does not show the delicacy of the nose, but has black fruits beginning to show nuances of flavor, with a fugitive whiff of cedar. Tannins are mostly pushed into the background, but there's some heat and alcohol-derived sweetness on the finish. 16.0% *92* Drink to 2024.

Penfolds

One of the oldest names in Australian wine production, and now part of Treasury Wine Estates, Penfolds has a historic winery at Magill (just east of Adelaide) and a huge plant just off the highway south of Nuriootpa. The top wines follow a Penfolds tradition in keeping to a template established many years ago by legendary winemaker Max Schu-bert. During red wine fermentation the caps are kept submerged by header boards, they are pressed off into wood at about 2% potential alcohol, and there is racking in barrels to get some oxygen exposure and to soften the tannins. "The Penfolds style for all wines is a bigger, richer, style made in the cellar," says winemaker Steve Lienert. Wines were tasted at the Kalimna Vineyard in October 2012 or at the Penfolds Recorking Clinic in New York in September 2012.

Barossa Valley, Block 42 Cabernet Sauvignon, 2012
(Barrel sample.) The wine is presently earmarked for Bin 707, but no final decision has yet been taken on whether it will all be included in Bin 707 or whether there will be a separate re-lease of Block 42 or a Cellar Reserve. The fresh nose offers a floral, perfumed, impression, overlaid by some barrel aromatics of pears and apples, with a savory touch of sage. For Barossa this has a lot of precision: the fruits are well delineated, yet offer an intense, generous, impression. The concentration of the fruits hides the oak (by contrast with the overall balance of

707 where oak is usually more in evidence). You don't often see this combination of elegance, precision, and intensity. Tannins dry the finish, of course. This is very promising.

Coonawarra, Bin 169 Cabernet Sauvignon, 2010
Restrained nose shows a touch of roasted meats with black fruits. Very pure line shows precisely defined black cherry fruits, quite tight: "that's Coonawarra," says winemaker Steve Lienert. There are beautiful, elegant, fruits, with just a barely perceptible touch of new oak showing retronasally as vanillin. Reflecting the 100% Cabernet fruit from Coonawarra, this is tighter than Bin 407. The core of youthfulness brings a strong fruit impression, but the sheer refinement argues that this will mature to an elegant style. This needs time not so much for the fine-grained tannins to resolve—they are quite subdued in the background—but to allow flavor variety to develop. 14.5% *92* Drink to 2027.

South Australia, Bin 407 Cabernet Sauvignon, 2010
This vintage came about half from Coonawarra. "For the Penfolds style, we are not looking for leafiness or herbaceousness, we are looking for dark fruits," says winemaker Steve Lienert. The reserved black fruit nose shows strong purity of fruits with finely delineated edges supported by almost crisp acidity. Fruits of blackcurrants and cherries stop just short of outright aromatics. A straight, almost linear, impression is supported by fine-grained tannins bringing elegance and finesse to the finish. The tannins are elegant enough to allow the wine to be enjoyed now, but there is potential for aging, although possibly the style may become more linear with age. You can certainly see the Coonawarra origins in that characteristic linearity. 14.5% *90* Drink 2014-2024.

South Australia, Bin 707 Cabernet Sauvignon, 2010
Immediately different from Bin 169, the nose is more forthcoming, with lots of spice, cinnamon, and vanillin: a very forceful impression. Broader on the palate, there are notes of coffee and chocolate opening out into a touch of coconut. Fruits show as blackcurrants with an aromatic edge, lifted by the vanillin and coconut: it's really more Bin 707 than Cabernet. "It's a big style of Cabernet, this one," says winemaker Steve Lienert. Firm tannins show as dryness on the finish. This is for people who like a really powerful, exotic, style, and it may not calm down for years. *90* Drink 2014-2032.

Barossa Valley, Cellar Reserve Cabernet Sauvignon, 2010
Broad nose offers ripe, very close to over-ripe, black fruits, with hints of piquant blackcurrants and cassis. There's a wide flavor spectrum on the palate showing blackcurrants and blueberries, with oak showing as vanillin and coconut; that over-ripe sensation comes back retronasally. The tannins are scarcely noticeable against the strong fruit impression, with some alcohol-derived sweetness driving the finish. *89* Drink to 2030.

South Australia, Bin 707 Cabernet Sauvignon, 2009
The nose is less flamboyant than usual, and the wine is also a little more restrained on the palate, but it makes a similar fruit impression. Piquant blackcurrants mingle with aromatic black cherries on the palate. The combination of piquancy and fruit gives an almost jammy impression. Smooth tannins are quite subsumed by the fruits. This is not a wine for the fainthearted. 14.5% *90* Drink to 2027.

Coonawarra, Bin 169 Cabernet Sauvignon, 2008
Very ripe nose with piquant, almost jammy, fruits, pungent aromatics on the palate, sharp acidity, and a contradictory touch of raisins. The sweet impression on the finish is very forceful, almost as powerful as a Shiraz. Although this offers the unthrottled Australian style, it manages to retain well delineated fruits: but I might find a bottle too much to handle at dinner. 14.5% *89* Drink to 2022.

South Australia, Bin 389 Cabernet-Shiraz, 2009
Curiously the nose of this 75% Cabernet to 25% Shiraz is more restrained than the varietal Cabernet Sauvignon, as is the palate, although it follows the general stylistic spectrum of intense black fruits tending to piquancy. There's less depth and structure than in the Cabernet, so the fruit shows clearly through the structure that is only just discernible in the background. 14.5% *88* Drink to 2022.

Barossa Valley, Block 42 Cabernet Sauvignon, 1996
Development shows in an earthy, almost gamey, nose. The palate follows the usual Penfolds style but there's more reserve to the piquant black fruits. Although this wine usually goes into the openly flamboyant flagship Bin 707 Cabernet, as a representation of the individual block with some age, this has now developed a light, almost elegant and lacy impression, with complexity just beginning to show. *92* Drink to 2020.

South Australia, Bin 98 Cabernet-Shiraz, 1990
This comes from a mix of Cabernet Sauvignon from cooler areas with Shiraz from Barossa. Age has brought some restraint, and there's a more complex, mellow impression compared to the younger wines. While this is developing complexity, it is not at all tertiary. There's a slightly nutty, slightly piquant, retronasal impression on the long finish. *92* Drink to 2022.

Rusden

Rusden's 16 ha of vineyards are mostly Shiraz, with small plots of other warm-climate varieties, with the exception of the Cabernet Sauvignon and Malbec. Malbec is an enthusiasm of owner Denis Canute, who has been persuading his winemaker son of its virtues. "As far as Rusden is concerned, if it has a variety on the label, it is 100%, there are no little bits and pieces. It's a philosophy, we are very much into showing varieties, the only decision should be is it new oak or old, is it French or American," Denis says. These wines were by far the most exotic of any Cabernets I encountered in the region and for that reason are hard to rate. Viscous and chewy, they were almost a meal in themselves, but with strong savory and herbal influences rather than the usual directly intense fruits of Barossa. Given that maturation is largely in neutral oak, and that there is reported to be no extraneous vegetation that could account for these influences, although they seem to extend well beyond the usual varietal character of Cabernet, I am at a loss to explain the effect. Wines were tasted at Rusden in October 2012.

Barossa Valley, Good Shepherd Cabernet-Malbec, 2010
This 60:40 Cabernet-Malbec blend offers a gamey, leathery, impression on the nose—perhaps representing a faint touch of Brett—but the fruits on the palate are more mainstream than the Boundaries Cabernet Sauvignon. There are those typically smooth, velvety, tannins of Malbec, followed by a rich, glyceriny, impression on the palate, more viscous than the varietal Cabernet Sauvignon, although lower in alcohol. The variety of fruit flavors is a bit hidden at the moment; in spite of the blend, this is a little one dimensional right now. 13.0% *88* Drink to 2019.

Barossa Valley, Boundaries Cabernet Sauvignon, 2009
Powerful, spicy nose shows bay leaf, sage, roasted meats, and capers with a touch of evergreen, before developing in the direction of minty tobacco with an exotic touch of soy. This is somewhat the same impression as the garrigue in southern France, but more intense. Denis Canute says that there is no extraneous vegetation that could account for these influences, which are intrinsic to the berries. Although the nose gives a cool climate impression, the palate is pure Barossa fruit, ripe and sweet, but cut by a distinctly herbal savory set of flavors that reprise the nose. The ripeness is balanced by an almost piquant acidity on the finish, but turning sweeter in the glass, and running a risk it will topple over the edge. This is sui generis, and hard to relate to other Cabernets in Barossa. 14.0% *88* Drink to 2018.

Barossa Valley, Boundaries Cabernet Sauvignon, 2003
The savory aromatics of the nose are similar to the 2009, with capers and herbal notes of sage, and age has brought the savory influences closer to a tertiary impression. Overall the impression is close to over-ripe, with the rich, ripe, fruits becoming more obviously herbal retronasally. It might seem that the tertiary evolution indicates limited longevity, but there is in fact relatively little development in character compared to 2009; basically the 2003 is a version of the 2009 in which the balance has shifted just a bit. 14.0% *88* Drink to 2016.

Yalumba

Yalumba bills itself as Australia's oldest family-owned winery. The original vineyard was established on 30 acres at Angaston on the edge of Barossa Valley in 1849, and a retail nursery was also established (the core stock being vines collected in Europe by James Busby). The first wine was produced in 1854. Today the winery is a vast operation, still on the original site. The nursery is located a few miles away in Barossa Valley proper. More than a century later, Yalumba extended its operations to Coonawarra (Y page 475). Wines were tasted in Barossa in October 2012.

Barossa, The Signature Cabernet-Shiraz, 2005
Unusually for a Cabernet-Shiraz blend, especially considering that Cabernet is only just over half the blend (56%) this year, the dominant expression here is a savory Cabernet character, towards roasted meats, almost gamey, ahead of the tense impression of blackberry fruits on the palate, followed by some aromatics from the Shiraz, and finishing with a crisp impression of tannins. 14.0% *91* Drink to 2027.

South Australia, The Reserve Cabernet-Shiraz, 1992
This was the first release of The Reserve, originally made as a selection of the best twenty barrels, although since then it has moved towards coming from specific parcels (but is made only some years). Barossa was the predominant influence (70%) in the inaugural vintage, but with a 15% contribution each from Langhorne Creek and Coonawarra. A complex nose ranges from savory influences to blackberry fruits. The precisely defined black fruits show some real finesse, more sense of freshness than seen with a 100% Barossa Cabernet. A touch of cedar on the finish leads into the first tertiary notes that are just beginning to show against the ripe fruits of the palate. This has at least another decade ahead of it. 14.0% *92* Drink to 2022.

Barossa, The Signature Cabernet-Shiraz, 1987
This vintage had a tiny contribution of fruit from Langhorne Creek and Coonawarra. "This was a different era, a leaner era," says winemaker Kevin Glastonbury, "you wouldn't get this out of Barossa now, people pick for more generosity, they picked earlier then at higher yields." The first impression here is Bordelais, showing a herbaceous nose with a touch of leather (suggestive of Brett, but the consensus among winemakers present was that this was the expression of the grape and there was in fact no Brett), but the fruits are rich, ripe, and sweet—yet at the same time showing a delicious herbaceous to savory balance. The intensity of those New World fruits shows even though they have dried out a bit. However, in an interesting reversal, over the next hour or so, the 1987 became a little tired, whereas the 1970 revived and sparkled against food. 12.0% *92* Drink to 2017.

Barossa, Galway Vintage Reserve Claret, 1970
This was the wine that evolved into The Signature. In this vintage it was 90% Cabernet to 10% Shiraz, with the Cabernet basically coming from Barossa and the Shiraz from McLaren Vale. "This is classic Barossa claret," says winemaker Kevin Glastonbury. It's a mature color with a broad rim. The nose is restrained but seems a little tired at first. Good acidity shows on the palate but the fruits are drying out a bit, with some loss of flavor variety, although the body still gives a ripe impression reflecting what was presumably a great initial fruit concentration. It's lovely but the acidity is going to take over and it's time to drink up. But this was an education in the perils of tasting, as with dinner the 1970 revived completely and sparkled, whereas the 1987 reverted to a dry impression. This would compare favorably with most Bordeaux from 1970, which is a stunning achievement for the period. *92* Drink up.

McLaren Vale: D'Arenberg

D'Arenberg was founded as part of the expansion in the 1880s when McLaren Vale was converted from wheat growing as viticulture moved south from the areas where the first vineyards were established in the 1830s close to Adelaide. Most estate fruit from d'Arenberg comes from the home vineyard, called Beautiful View; altogether, d'Arenberg owns 180 ha and buys fruit from another 600 ha. Several generations on, current winemaker Chester Osborn is conscious of tradition, and wine is made by similar techniques to a hundred years ago, using 5 ton fermenters with submerged caps, and basket-pressing the wine into oak. With 10 single vineyard bottlings of Shiraz, and 3 single vineyard Grenache wines, d'Arenberg are certainly into terroir: unfortunately this has not yet extended to Cabernet. "I would love to do single vineyard Cabernets as well, but I can't do everything at once," says Chester. Wines were tasted at d'Arenberg in October 2012.

462   Claret & Cabs

McLaren Vale, High Trellis Cabernet Sauvignon, 2009
Some gamey hints on the nose with a touch of minerality. There's some restraint to the sweet, ripe, black fruits of the palate, with a mineral impression on the finish. Tight black cherry fruits create a sense of tension. There's just a touch of Merlot and Petit Verdot (5% of each) in addition to the Cabernet Sauvignon. 14.5% *88* Drink to 2019.

McLaren Vale, Coppermine Road Cabernet Sauvignon, 2008
This was introduced as d'Arenberg's top Cabernet cuvee in 1995. Early vintages were very aromatic when young. This vintage shows a more subtle mineral nose with almost gamey overtones. There are some similarities of style with The Galvo Garage, but there's greater purity of fruit in this 100% Cabernet Sauvignon, showing as blueberries and blackcurrants. The palate is more youthful and more intense, with precisely delineated fruits showing real purity of line, and refined tannins providing support in the background to bring tautness to the finish. The style of this wine has certainly become more refined over the past decade. 14.5% *91* Drink to 2024.

McLaren Vale, The Galvo Garage, 2007
This Cabernet-dominated blend (almost 50% Cabernet Sauvignon) is named after the garagistes in Bordeaux, and is made with minimalist treatment: no pumping or filtering, just extended time on the lees. There's a faintly pungent mineral expression on the nose. Full and ripe, the palate has an edge of aromatic black plums. There are nicely rounded, full flavors across the palate, with the one quarter Merlot bringing a soft, almost gamey, impression, together with a sort of dense spiciness from the Petit Verdot (almost another quarter). The overall impression is that this is on the verge of starting savory development. 14.5% *89* Drink to 2021.

Shirvington

Paul Shirvington picked McLaren Vale as the site for his vineyard because he wanted to make both Shiraz and Cabernet Sauvignon. The Shirvingtons started with a 16 ha almond grove; the original plan was to replace one half and later replant the other half, but the price of almonds collapsed, so they planted the whole plot. Out of the present total of 24 ha, half are Shiraz, with just a little less Cabernet Sauvignon; the minor varieties are Mourvèdre and Grenache. The wines are all varietals. "We only make single varieties. If we can grow the fruit and it is good enough, we think it should stand alone," is Paul's philosophy. Up to now there has been a single Cabernet Sauvignon, but a reserve made from a barrel selection is about to be introduced; with more skin contact, this will less approachable than the estate bottling and should age longer. Wines were tasted at Shirvington in October 2012.

McLaren Vale, Cabernet Sauvignon Reserve, 2011
(Barrel sample.) There's a certain reserved asperity to the nose. More roundness shows in the fruits on the palate, more black than red, with cherries prominent, and a touch of plums: altogether a darker impression than the regular bottling. There's fine, unobtrusive, tannic support in the background, and a general sense of finesse. A touch of heat shows on the finish (although alcohol is lower than the regular bottling). *90* Drink to 2021.

McLaren Vale, Cabernet Sauvignon, 2011
(Barrel sample.) There's a nutty, red fruit impression on the nose, with a touch of vanillin. The palate offers a fairly lean impression of pure red fruits, tending to cherries, with quite light tannic support. This is a wine that will mature to elegance over the next few years, but should not be held too long. *88* Drink to 2020.

McLaren Vale, Cabernet Sauvignon, 2010
Initial impressions show red cherries and raspberries as well as black fruits. The palate is sweet, ripe, and round, with balanced acidity, a soft, plush, character cut by just a touch of tannin on the finish, with a hint of chocolate that strengthens in the glass. This is a very approachable style. 14.0% *89* Drink to 2019.

McLaren Vale, Cabernet Sauvignon, 2009
Richer, plusher, and darker than 2010, with nicely delineated black fruits stopping just short of aromaticity to give a pure expression of Cabernet. Ripe, chocolaty, tannins are subsumed by the fruits with a very faint touch of bitterness on an alcoholic finish. Elegance of style shows through with some finesse, although there is a touch of heat on the finish. 14.5% *90* Drink to 2023.

McLaren Vale, Cabernet Sauvignon, 2005
Some garnet in the appearance shows the start of development. Cedar shows on the nose in front of the black fruits. Sweet and ripe on the palate, with a soft impression as the tannins resolve, and a fugitive whiff of tertiary flavors developing, although there's still a touch of vanillin retronasally. The ripeness of the fruits hides the underlying structure. There's an openly delicious character here that makes you reluctant to spit when tasting. 15.0% *91* Drink to 2020.

McLaren Vale, Cabernet Sauvignon, 2002
More developed in color than 2001 (reflecting a cool vintage versus a hot one), there's certainly more of a leafy, herbaceous impression on the nose. The cool climate background is not so obvious on the palate, but overall the impression is drier and less opulent than 2001, with savory notes coming up to match the fruits in a more generally linear style. 15.0% *88* Drink to 2016.

McLaren Vale, Cabernet Sauvignon, 2001
Age has brought some quasi-leathery overtones, possibly representing a touch of Brett (there was some dissent about this), but certainly adding complexity. Very soft and plush on the palate, flavor variety is developing as red fruits add to the black fruits, with cedary overtones coming in retronasally. Really at its peak now, this shows a beautiful balance of fruits to developing savory notes. 14.0% *91* Drink to 2015.

Langhorne Creek: Brothers in Arms

Wine production at Brothers in Arms goes back a long way, with the name of the latest line, Sixth Generation, referring to the children of Guy Adams, the present winemaker. Brothers in Arms is the flagship label of the Adams family, but they also make wine (at lower price points) under the Formby & Adams and the Killibinin labels. The property has 1,000 ha, with 320 ha of vineyards, including roughly equal proportions of Cabernet Sauvignon and Shiraz. About a third of the grapes are used for their own production; a majority of the crop is sold. The leading wines are the Bothers in Arms estate bottlings of Cabernet Sauvignon (which usually includes some Malbec and Petit Verdot) and Shiraz. The heart of these wines comes from the old vines at the Metala vineyard across the road from the winery (planted in 1891). The Brothers in Arms Cabernet Sauvignon is released relatively late, when it is considered ready to drink, with 2007 being the current release in 2012. (There was no release in 2006 or 2008.) Wines were tasted at Brothers in Arms in October 2012.

Langhorne Creek, Leading Horse Cabernet Sauvignon, Formby & Adams, 2010
This 100% Cabernet Sauvignon used no new oak. A barrel sample immediately after the final blend had been made showed a very ripe, piquant, black fruit nose, following through to aromatic blackcurrants and plums on the palate. The rich black fruits convey a powerful, very approachable, New World style. This is very much a wine for immediate gratification. Marketing manager James Hall says, "This should be a wine that people can enjoy without being gripped by tannin." Yes indeed, but the price is that the fruits are a bit one dimensional at the outset. 14.5% *89* Drink to 2019.

Langhorne Creek, Cabernet Sauvignon, Killibinin 2010
More sense of austerity on the nose, and a cooler impression on the palate, less aromatic than the Sixth Generation with more sense of structure and less overt fruit. Smooth, fine, tannins on the structure allow more sense to come through of the flavor variety that will develop with time. There are some herbal notes with a faint impression of tannins drying the finish. This wine is intended to appeal to the consumer, but this vintage seems relatively austere; by contrast, the previous vintage of 2009 is more openly approachable and New World in its impression. *89* Drink to 2022.

Langhorne Creek, Scaredy Cat Cabernet-Shiraz, Killibinin 2009
Although Cabernet is the majority grape here, aromas and flavors are driven by the aromatics of Shiraz. This is a big wine, with aromatic black plums evident on nose and palate, and it's hard to see the Cabernet through the aggressive fruits of the Shiraz; perhaps the Cabernet structure is holding the fruits back just a bit. But view this more as a Shiraz whatever the numbers. 14.5% *86* Drink to 2016.

Langhorne Creek, Sixth Generation Cabernet Sauvignon, Brothers in Arms, 2010
A fresher impression to the nose than the Leading Horse Cabernet, with ripe, soft chocolaty fruits of black cherries and blackcurrants in a forward style. What impresses here is the sheer richness, a very direct expression of fruit purity, with soft, supple, tannins subsumed by the fruits. Not surprisingly, the wine is a bit one dimensional at this point, but more complexity should develop as the fruits calm down. Only 10% new oak was used here. *89* Drink to 2020.

Langhorne Creek, Cabernet Sauvignon, Brothers in Arms, 2010
Slight nutty, initial impression of deep black fruits. Smooth, refined fruits of blackcurrants and black cherries are concentrated on the palate with chocolaty overtones and notes of coffee; tannins are subsumed by the fruits and evident only by some dryness on the palate. The style is refined but there is no mistaking the intensity. Of course the fruit flavors are still direct but there's a sense of herbal underlay to the supple structure, with a characteristic overall furry impression and a slight nuttiness counterpoising the tannins. *92* Drink 2015-2026.

Langhorne Creek, Cabernet Sauvignon, Brothers in Arms, 2009
Restrained black fruit nose shows some faintly chocolaty aromatics. Smooth and elegant, this makes a finer, tighter, impression, although slightly more aromatic, than the 2010. Pure black Cabernet fruits are precisely delineated on the palate, if a touch linear at the moment. Fine-grained tannins give a silky texture, compared to the broader, softer, more velvety impression of 2010. *91* Drink 2014-2025.

Langhorne Creek, Cabernet Sauvignon, Brothers in Arms, 2007
Closed and tight on the nose, but sweet, ripe, and concentrated on the palate; the style falls between 2005 and 2009. A slight spiciness comes from the 3% Petit Verdot, with smooth, refined tannins reinforced by the 8% Malbec. The fine-grained texture brings elegance to the presently taut structure, which is relieved by some nutty influences. 15.0% *91* Drink to 2024.

Langhorne Creek, Cabernet Sauvignon, Brothers in Arms, 2005
Restrained nose with some youthful aromatics and a touch of savory herbal influences suggests elegant fruits. Finely delineated black cherry fruits on the palate are supported by smooth tannins with a touch of heat on the finish. Slowly the aromatics give way in the glass to a more herbal impression. Not as generous as the 2009, there is more sense of tension in the tannins; the tight impression overall suggests that more time is needed to fully release fruit flavors, although a nutty mintiness slowly develops in the glass. The elegance of this vintage is reinforced by its 15% Malbec. 14.5% *91* Drink to 2021.

Noon Winery

Drew Noon MW and his wife Raegan took over the winery from Drew's father in 1996, and it remains a boutique operation in McLaren Vale producing only red wine. The winery is surrounded by very old bush vines of Grenache planted in 1934 (which go into the highly regarded Eclipse bottling), but the Cabernet has been sourced since its first vintage in 1996 from the 1.2 ha Fruit Trees block planted in Langhorne Creek in 1972. Although the Cabernet is labeled as South Australia, it is basically a single vineyard wine, usually but not always 100% varietal; in 2009 a little Grenache was used to soften the wine. The vineyard is dry farmed: it lies in the flood plain, and essentially is flooded each winter to provide enough water to get through the following summer. The wine is not produced every year. There are some eucalyptus trees around the block, and in warm seasons there can be a touch of mint on the wine. Very intense, this wine scarcely develops during its first decade. Wines were tasted at Noon in October 2012.

South Australia, Cabernet Sauvignon Reserve, 2009
Dark purple color immediately suggests a highly extracted wine. Stern Cabernet fruits dominate the nose with blackberries, hints of blackcurrants, and a touch of spicy black plum aromatics. Very rich and ripe, very concentrated, with an immediate impression of tiny berries representing the drought conditions of the year—it was extremely hot just before picking. But there is good supporting tannic structure, firm and chocolaty, but pushed into the background by the plush fruits. The high alcohol is not directly evident. The purity of fruits develops into cassis, cut by the dense chocolate finish. This will take a very long time to develop. It could be drunk now but it would be vinicide. 15.5% *92* Drink to 2027.

South Australia, Cabernet Sauvignon Reserve, 2005
There's a touch of asperity on the nose of spicy black fruits. Intensely ripe black fruits are re-strained by the strong underlying structure with firm tannins. High alcohol shows indirectly in enhancing the forceful expression of the fruits, and there's a touch of alcohol-derived sweet-ness hiding the dryness of the finish. Powerful aromatics of black plums are more evident than cassis, more overtly aromatic than the 2009 vintage, and very long on the finish. The aromatics do not seem to have calmed down at all. The fruit lines are pure, without going over the edge into jamminess, and the tannins are quite hidden by the concentrated fruits. This is about as intense as Cabernet gets. 17.0% *92* Drink to 2027.

South Australia, Cabernet Sauvignon Reserve, 1999
This shows remarkably little development compared with the 2009. "Customers want an old wine that tastes young," says Rae Noon. The main evolution is a lightening of intensity allowing the fruits to show more clearly through the tannins that have partly resolved to leave a fine structure supported by a touch of acidity on the finish. After a relatively restrained nose come blackcurrant and black plum fruits, with just a touch of aromatics, and a sensation that the wine would like to display a herbal touch but can't quite get there. As the wine develops wider flavor variety with age, the primary black fruits are joined by some red fruits. 14.6% *91* Drink to 2022.

Coonawarra

"They used to say the even vintages were good," says James Freckleton of Ya-lumba. That's still not a bad guide. Recent vintage variation in Coonawarra has been due to two effects: summer temperatures and winter freezes. In terms of best vintages, 2012 is expected to be very good, comparable to the very good 2006. The 2011 vintage was cool and the wettest ever. It was warmer than usual in 2010, but without any real heat spikes; "we didn't realize how warm until the end," says Sue Hodder of Wynns. Conditions in 2009 were close to historical averages: very good if not great. There were heat spikes in 2008, with 12 days over 40 °C, so there is some unevenness in results. A savage winter frost in 2007 meant that some producers did not make their top wines. The vintage was dry with just a touch of rain in 2006; "it stands out as one of the iconic years for Coonawarra," says James Freckleton. Overall the results were average in the warmer vintage of 2005, but it was unusual in that vineyards in the south gave better results than those in the north. 2004 was a late vintage of high quality.

Balnaves

Starting as a grower, the Balnaves farm was planted in 1971, and grapes were sold until winemaking started in 1995. The size of the estate has expanded from the initial 5 ha to 58 ha today; 70% of plantings are Cabernet Sauvignon, mostly the Reynella selection. Wines are produced exclusively from the estate. There's a big jump from the lower level wines (Chardonnay, Shiraz, Cabernet-Merlot, Cabernet Sauvignon) to the top wine, The Tally, which is usually a 100% Cabernet Sauvignon blended from the Dead Morris, Quarry, and Walker vineyards. The best six cuves are selected for longer mac-eration, and then the best two are selected for The Tally. It's recognized as one of Australia's leading Cabernets in the Langton's Classification. My favorite is the 2000. Production is 350-1,200 cases. Wines were tasted at Balnaves in October 2012.

Coonawarra, The Tally Cabernet Sauvignon Reserve, 2010
This vintage was basically a single vineyard wine from Dead Morris (which is usually the struc-tural backbone of a blend of three vineyards). Ripe black fruits show an austere edge on the palate, with a touch of vanillin and coconut on a rich chocolaty finish. Fine-grained tannins give a smooth structural impression. The finish is a bit hot. The fruits are exuberant enough to hide the tannins and to allow consumption now. 14.5% *91* Drink to 2022.

Coonawarra, The Tally Cabernet Sauvignon Reserve, 2009
First impressions show fruits of black cherries and plums with hints of blackcurrants, making a softer, finer impression than the 2010. Elegant tannins show just a touch of bitter chocolate on the finish. The Dead Morris vineyard makes its presence felt in a really strong tannic backbone. Another year or so should see the structure resolve to let the fruits show more clearly. 14.5% *90* Drink 2014-2024.

Coonawarra, The Tally Cabernet Sauvignon Reserve, 2008
Here a touch of blackcurrant aromatics shows on the nose, leading into lovely well-rounded fruits on the palate of blackcurrants and plums, with a characteristic touch of acidity showing on the finish. Although not as taut as the 2009 vintage, this still shows those tight, precisely confined, fruits that mark the height of the Coonawarra style. The fine tannic backbone still requires some time to resolve. 14.5% *90* Drink 2013-2027.

Coonawarra, The Tally Cabernet Sauvignon Reserve, 2007
The initially restrained impression begins to open out a little on the palate until tannins seize you on the finish. Black fruits of plums and cherries show a distinct tannic edge with a dry finish. The concentrated fruits require some time to let the tannins resolve. This is still a bit hard and tight, but perhaps another year will see it ready to start. 15.0% *89* Drink 2013-2026.

Coonawarra, The Tally Cabernet Sauvignon Reserve, 2006
Rounded black fruits are supported by crisp acidity. Purity of line shows with blackcurrant and cassis coming through on the palate. I'm afraid the acidity gives a slightly disjointed impression. Blackberry fruits display some aromatics on the finish. (January 2011) 15.0% *88* Drink to 2021.

Coonawarra, The Tally Cabernet Sauvignon Reserve, 2005
Faint hints of nuts, cereal, and savory influences open out into a palate of black plums and cherries, with a touch of vanillin on the finish. The ripe tannins, with chocolate-coated bitter cherries on the finish, are now softening just enough to let the wine become approachable. This classic Cabernet with purity of fruits has lots of concentration, and should develop for years. 14.5% *92* Drink to 2027.

Coonawarra, The Tally Cabernet Sauvignon Reserve, 2004
Herbal black fruits show a fugitive whiff of more aromatic blackcurrants. Softer on the palate than the 2005, flavor variety is beginning to develop, showcased by a characteristic acid lift on the finish. Tannins are still very tense. This is very much a pure Cabernet in the tradition of austere black fruits needing time to come around. 14.5% *92* Drink to 2027.

Coonawarra, The Tally Cabernet Sauvignon Reserve, 2001
First impressions show soft, almost nutty, black fruits. Age has brought a gentle touch to the palate, but the black fruits are still quite primary, and that sense of tension continues to run through the wine. Development so far has taken the form of relaxing the tannins, but it is going to take a while before full flavor variety develops. 14.0% *91* Drink to 2027.

Coonawarra, The Tally Cabernet Sauvignon Reserve, 2000
This vintage offers a fuller, riper, impression of black fruits on the nose, with a mix of fruity and savory aromatics. Coming through the characteristic lift of acidity on the finish, the palate is distinctly softer than more recent vintages. The ripe fruits turn towards blackcurrants and plums. Tannins remain firm but are slowly becoming more supple, and that tannic edge of the younger vintages is dissipating. Flavor variety is beginning to develop. Altogether, a fine, firm, impression with the best yet to come. 13.5% *92* Drink 2025.

Coonawarra, The Tally Cabernet Sauvignon Reserve, 1998
Complex savory elements on the nose mingle with fruits and nuts. Soft, black, and chocolaty on the palate, with hints of vanillin retronasally, an acidic edge, and firm, ripe, tannins. The palate is less advanced than the nose would suggest, with the primary edge just coming off the fruits. A touch of cedar brings complexity to the finish. This is just starting the mid term phase of its development. 13.5% *92* Drink to 2024.

Katnook

Katnook Estate is the historical site of the old Riddoch homestead, and includes the building that was the original woolshed. Replanting started in 1971, but fruit was sold until wine production started in 1980. Today there are 135 ha of vineyards, reduced from 165 ha at the peak of plantings. Wayne Stehbens has been the winemaker since the very first vintage. There are four ranges of Cabernet: Founder's Block is the entry-level wine; the Estate wine is a signature series for single varieties (the Cabernet Sauvignon is usually close to 100%); there are single vineyard wines; and the top wine is Odyssey (rated in the second tier of Langton's classification of top Australian wines). This is a powerful Cabernet Sauvignon, carrying lots of new oak, and matured for up to three years in barrique. Katnook is part of the Wingara Wine group, which is Freixenet's holding corporation in Australia. Wines were tasted at Katnook in October 2012.

Coonawarra, Founder's Block Cabernet Sauvignon, 2010
This wine is intended for immediate consumption and Wayne Stehbens says, "I have erred a little bit towards the more aromatic soils." Direct black fruit nose shows blackcurrants and plums. Delicious black fruits mingle plums, mulberries, and cherries in a very approachable style, although faintly acid on the finish, which has a slight chocolate edge. A lovely wine at its level, but without much of the varietal typicity of Cabernet. *87* Drink to 2017.

Coonawarra, Amara Vineyard Cabernet Sauvignon, 2010
This is the first single vineyard wine produced at Katnook. It's quite restrained on the nose with some faint savory hints. There are the usual clean fruit lines of the house style, very fine, with round, deep fruits showing the purity of Cabernet Sauvignon. Finely grained tannins, already well integrated, give a refined texture. Already this is ready to drink. 14.0% *89* Drink to 2023.

Coonawarra, Estate Cabernet Sauvignon, 2010
Rather closed on the nose with just a suggestion of acidic red fruits. More weight on the palate here than in 2009, with black fruits showing as cherries, blackcurrants, and blackberries. The clear lines of acidity give a tight impression to the fine tannins. Some minty overtones develop on the finish. 13.5% *89* Drink to 2021.

Coonawarra, Estate Cabernet Sauvignon, 2009
Slightly spicy, aromatic, black fruit nose with savory overtones. Smooth and elegant on the palate, with impressions of black fruits supported by finely textured tannins. Perhaps a little one dimensional at this stage, but shows nice finesse. 13.5% *88* Drink to 2019.

Coonawarra, Odyssey Cabernet Sauvignon, 2009
(About to be bottled.) Very savory nose with some hints of acidity. Sweet and ripe on the palate, broader in its flavors than 2008, although showing its youth more overtly at this stage with quite a bit of vanillin and some coffee evident. The blackcurrant fruits are positively exuberant at the moment; this certainly needs to calm down. *89* Drink 2015-2025.

Coonawarra, Odyssey Cabernet Sauvignon, 2008
Katnook's top Cabernet comes from a couple of specific vineyard blocks: it gets the full treatment, including close to three years in almost all new oak. There's more character to the nose of black fruits with savory overtones. Lots of fruit density, with an Amarone-like richness on the palate. Oak shows as vanillin and roasted coffee, with smoky notes on the finish, dried by some tannins; the structure is quite in evidence, and its richness makes this drinkable now, but it will really take another year or so for the oak to integrate. There's certainly a more overt New World style here. 14.5% *90* Drink 2013-2023.

Coonawarra, Estate Cabernet Sauvignon, 2002
"This is probably as Bordeaux-like as Coonawarra has got in the last twenty years," says Wayne Stehbens. Savory aromatics are quite tertiary on the nose. Fruits are sweeter, riper, and more vibrant than would be predicted by the developed character of the nose. There's a touch of pungency, with sous bois developing in the glass. This vintage is developing more rapidly than most; but as a result of the cool conditions, the wine has always had those sweet but vegetal flavors. The sous bois is at the stage of adding delicious complexity, but in combination with the vegetal ripeness of the fruits gives a slightly rustic impression. *88* Drink to 2016.

Coonawarra, Estate Cabernet Sauvignon, 1994
Still a dark color. A slightly stern, slightly aromatic, black fruit impression on the nose leads into a palate of black cherries with smooth tannins now resolving but showing fine gravelly texture. Aside from the softening brought by the resolution of the tannins, and a very faint touch of sous bois, there isn't a great deal of evidence of aging. There's still a relatively tight impression of a cooler vintage, with the fruits conveying more a slightly perfumed than savory impression, but at almost twenty years of age, this certainly demonstrates the potential of Coonawarra for aging. It's probably time to drink up. *89*

Leconfield

Leconfield is a dual operation in Coonawarra and McLaren Vale. It was established in Coonawarra in 1974 by Sydney Hamilton, an admirer of Bordeaux, who planted all the Bordeaux varieties. The McLaren Vale estate was established by Richard Hamilton in 1972, and he acquired Leconfield in 1981. There are 38 ha at the estate in Coonawarra, and another 70 ha at the McLaren Vale estate. All the wines are made at the winery in Coonawarra. "In the past ten or twelve years we have gone away from the typical Bordeaux blend. About ten years ago we saw that the strength in the wines was coming from the Cabernet Sauvignon and Cabernet Franc, and we didn't think the Merlot and Petit Verdot contributed enough to the blend," says winemaker Tim Bailey. Wines were tasted at Leconfield in October 2012.

Coonawarra, Cabernet-Merlot, Leconfield, 2010
After the fresh nose, the palate seems a little rounder and softer than Cabernet alone, with an impression of the sweetness of the black fruits supported by a crisp finish of nice cherry fruits. 14.0% *87* Drink to 2017.

Coonawarra, Cabernet Sauvignon, Leconfield, 2010
This is a more linear wine than the Cabernet-Merlot blend, with very straight black cherry fruits highlighted by crisp acidity. With less generosity, this is rather tight and you wonder where the fruits will come from to round up the flavors in the future. 14.5% *86* Drink to 2017.

Coonawarra, Cabernet Sauvignon, Leconfield, 2001
(This was one of the last bottles under cork before the switch to screwcap. It was also the last year of including all the stems in the ferments.) Very mature appearance is garnet with some orange/brown hues. The original ripeness of the fruits keeps this sweet and lively on the palate, with some hints of perfume and also a touch of piquant acidity. A rustic impression suggests that the tertiary influence is in danger of outbalancing the fruits, and a faint developing touch of raisins suggests it is time to drink up.14.0% *87*.

McLaren Vale, Hut Block Cabernet Sauvignon, Richard Hamilton Wines, 2010
The nose is fresh in the characteristic house style. Black cherry fruits on the palate offer suggestions of piquancy. There's just a faint impression of the austerity of Cabernet Sauvignon on the dry aftertaste, but I'm not seeing a forceful expression of Cabernet typicity in this lighter-styled wine. *86* Drink to 2017.

Lindemans

Lindemans was founded in 1843 by Henry Lindeman who planted vines in the Hunter Valley region of New South Wales. It grew into a large-scale producer, and today is owned by Treasury Wine Estates. In the early stages of the renaissance of Coonawarra, Lindemans purchased the Rouge Homme winery and vineyards from the Redman family. Their three Cabernet-based wines from Coonawarra are known as the Coonawarra Trio: the St George Vineyard Cabernet Sauvignon, Limestone Ridge Vineyard Cabernet Sauvignon-Shiraz, and Pyrus Cabernet Sauvignon-Merlot-Malbec. These remain quality wines, but have somewhat lost their luster against the overtly commercial operation of Lindemans as a whole. All these wines are made by barrel selection, but stylistic objectives are different. "The wine styles for Limestone Ridge and St. George are determined by vintage (and single vineyard site for the latter), but Pyrus tries to minimize vintage variation by blending," says winemaker Brett Sharpe. Wines were tasted at Lindemans in October 2012.

Coonawarra, Pyrus, 2010
This blend has 79% Cabernet Sauvignon, 16% Merlot, and 5% Cabernet Franc. There's more evident fruit and oak (showing as vanillin) in a more overtly New World style than the St. George Cabernet Sauvignon. The palate is distinctly softer than St. George, with broader flavors but less fruit purity, more approachable than the pure Cabernet, as you might expect, but

with the same elegant acidity showcasing the fruits. This was the first year when the new Merlot clones were included. *88* Drink to 2020.

Coonawarra, St. George Cabernet Sauvignon, 2012
(Barrel sample.) The nose is quite fresh rather than aromatic (perhaps due to recent sulfuring). Lots of fruit concentration. Good acidity makes a slightly malic impression at the moment, reinforcing the sense of freshness. The wine follows the usual elegant style. *91* Drink 2015-2027.

Coonawarra, St. George Cabernet Sauvignon, 2010
At this point the wine shows a youthful purple appearance. This hot year gives a much riper impression than the older vintages, with a noticeable softness on the palate of black cherry and blackcurrant fruits. There's a deceptively soft overlay of vanillin, making this already approachable, with ripe, furry, tannins in the background. It's deceptive because slowly the lacy acidity of older vintages emerges, but it's too early to tell whether aging will follow the same path or be overtaken by the greater ripeness. 14.3% *90* Drink 2013-2023.

Coonawarra, St. George Cabernet Sauvignon, 2009
The wine shows a dusky ruby color. Some of the austerity of Cabernet Sauvignon is evident on the nose of red and black cherry fruits, but then the palate shows soft, black fruits with a touch of new oak evident in some vanillin. Even in this recent vintage, the elegance of style shows through, with fruits showcased by an acid surround and firm, chalky, tannins. The elegance of the fruits and the good acid support make this very much a wine to match with food. Alcohol is barely noticeable on the finish. This is already ready to start. 14.3% *90* Drink to 2024.

Coonawarra, St. George Cabernet Sauvignon, 2005
Some garnet is already evident in the appearance. There's a touch of cereal on the red fruit nose, which has suggestions of asperity. Fruits are balanced by crisp acidity, giving a cool climate impression, with a hint of earthy strawberries and just a very faint touch of vanillin evident retronasally. This wine makes a very fine impression that is absolutely the antithesis of the Australian blockbuster style. An obvious lineage back to 1996 and 1976 would predict that the wine will turn delicate and lacy in a few years. 12.9% *89* Drink to 2022.

Coonawarra, St. George Cabernet Sauvignon, 2001
Deep color with garnet hue. Restrained on the nose. Somewhat tight and not very giving on the palate, very much a pure Cabernet in the intimations of austerity. Fruits have narrowed down—I was left with the feeling that some Merlot might really have rounded out this 100% Cabernet. A touch of acidity on the finish threatens to take over. This is in much the same style as 1996 but without as much fruit concentration to carry it forward. This vintage spent 15 months in a mixture of hogsheads and barriques (all new), as an intermediate step en route to complete maturation in barriques. 13.8% *87* Drink to 2015.

Coonawarra, St. George Cabernet Sauvignon, 1996
A relatively cool growing season led to a long hang time and this is considered a great vintage. Certainly this vintage has a more youthful appearance than the 1995, still showing some red hues. The red and black cherries of the nose show a touch of spice; sweet, mature fruits on the palate are supported by good acidity, with a touch of cereal on the finish, tending towards the fragrance and perfume of 1976 rather than the savory quality of 1995. The fruits are now drying out a bit, allowing an austere structure to show on the finish, but the overall impression is in the direction of delicacy: it is time to drink up. 12.9% *88*.

Coonawarra, St. George Cabernet Sauvignon, 1995
This was one of the coldest and wettest vintages on record, and not much fun to make, says Brett Sharpe. Age shows in a medium garnet color and expression of sous bois on the nose, very much a cool climate impression, with a somewhat spicy, vegetal, earthiness; a tartness pulling at the finish reprises the sous bois of the nose. Still holding up; and it's a tribute to longevity that a relatively poor vintage should make it through almost two decades, but it's time to drink up as there's nowhere to go. 12.7% *87*.

Coonawarra, St. George Cabernet Sauvignon, 1976
This was only the second vintage of the St. George single vineyard bottling (the first was 1973). It shows a lightening mature garnet color. Maturity has taken this wine in the direction of fragrance and perfume on the nose, followed by some subtle notes of sous bois. Good acidity supports an elegant, lacy style, with a finesse resembling mature Bordeaux. Becoming sweeter and riper in the glass, the wine obviously came from very ripe fruits; in fact, this vintage was riper than usual, because picking was delayed by space constraints for fermentation at the winery. It then spent 10 months in oak (somewhat shorter than the 21 months that became the standard in nineties). Overall impression is fine and elegant, but it is time to drink up. 13.0% *93*.

Majella

A family-owned winery, Majella regards itself as quite small, with 55 ha of vineyards, including 35 ha of Cabernet Sauvignon. Planting started in 1974 with Shiraz, and continued until 1998. "At first everyone wanted Shiraz, and there was more Shiraz than Cabernet, but the balance shifted in the late nineties," says winemaker Bruce Gregory. The Musician is an entry-level Cabernet-Shiraz blend. The Cabernet Sauvignon is a mid-tier pure varietal, and the top wine here is The Malleea, a Shiraz-Cabernet blend. All the wines have a fruit-driven style, becoming increasingly more forceful as you move up the hierarchy. Wines were tasted at Majella in October 2012.

Coonawarra, Musician Cabernet-Shiraz, 2011
Intended for immediate consumption, this wine sees little oak. There's a restrained nose with some hints of perfumed aromatics; fruity and approachable, the palate shows red cherry and raspberry fruits with a touch of piquant acidity. The combination of aromatics and piquancy gives the wine a New World feel. 13.5% *86* Drink to 2015.

Coonawarra, Musician Cabernet-Shiraz, 2010
Restrained nose with faint impression of piquant black fruit aromatics. Round, almost piquant, black fruits on the palate show a slightly nutty aftertaste lending more character than 2011. There's a touch of chocolate on the finish. This is really quite impressive for the price point, albeit strictly for current consumption. It's delicious and very quaffable. 14.5% *87* Drink to 2013.

Coonawarra, Cabernet Sauvignon, 2010
Initially reserved on the nose, with hints of black fruits. Ripe fruits on the palate have quite an acid bite, and then piercing blackcurrant aromatics come out. The combination of ripe fruits, aromatics, acidity, and firm tannins seems typically Australian. 14.5% *88* Drink to 2019.

Coonawarra, Cabernet Sauvignon, 2009
There's a touch of blackcurrants evident on the faintly aromatic black fruit nose. Sweet, riper and softer than 2010, with flavors of blackcurrants extending to cassis on the palate; the aromatics come back on the finish to create an intensely ripe impression. 14.5% *88* Drink to 2018.

Coonawarra, Cabernet Sauvignon, 2008
This has an inky, black color. Pungent aromatics on the nose show blackcurrants almost giving a savory tertiary impression. There's a powerful palate in full throttle New World style, with the pungency of cassis coming out on the finish, which is sweet, ripe, and jammy. You might well think there was a dollop of Shiraz in here. *87* Drink to 2017.

Coonawarra, Cabernet Sauvignon, 2007
Slightly aromatic black fruit nose shows blackcurrants. The palate is sweet, ripe, and aromatic, and does not yet show much evidence of aging. This is delicious, but more in the direct flavor profile of Shiraz than what you expect from Cabernet; those aromatics linger on the finish to leave a long impression of cassis. 14.5% *87* Drink to 2017.

Coonawarra, Cabernet Sauvignon, 2006
Relatively restrained on the nose compared to other vintages, with just a hint of savory herbal undertones. Going back, this is the first vintage to give a relatively calm impression. Black fruits still have a touch of those pungent blackcurrant aromatics, with an acid edge to the finish, but cut by some savory hints and a touch of tannic bitterness emphasized by some heat on the finish. 14.5% *88* Drink to 2018.

Coonawarra, Cabernet Sauvignon, 2005
Almost pungent nose of aromatic blackcurrants. Sweet and ripe with that pungent edge of blackcurrants continuing on the palate, with an accompanying piquant touch of acidity, but followed by a distinct touch of bitterness on the finish. Not much sign of flavor evolution yet, although the sweetness of the fruits on the palate offsets the dryness of the tannins on the finish. 14.5% *87* Drink to 2018.

Coonawarra, The Malleea Shiraz-Cabernet, 2010
(Not yet released.) Restrained nose offers just a faint impression of black fruit aromatics with some savory hints. The palate has a chocolaty impression of black fruits, firm and solid with a good sense of structure. This is more aromatic and less piquant than the Cabernet Sauvignon alone. The firmness of structure should carry this wine into a ripe old age. In a blind tasting, superficially you might think Cabernet was more important than Shiraz in this blend (the Shiraz

is actually about 55%) given the depth, concentration, and balance. Yet the overall impression is quite refined. 14.5% *91* Drink to 2023.

Coonawarra, The Malleea Shiraz-Cabernet, 2009
More aromatic than the varietal Cabernet Sauvignon, with black fruits of cherries, plums, and blackcurrants offering some piquant aromatics that linger on the finish. Ripe, sweet blackcurrants dominate the finish. This is the most overtly New World in style of the three vintages of The Malleea. 14.5% *89* Drink to 2019.

Coonawarra, The Malleea Shiraz-Cabernet, 2008
A restrained nose shows aromatic black fruits cut by a faintly savory herbal touch; altogether more restrained than the pungent aromatics of the varietal Cabernet Sauvignon. The palate shows ripe black fruits, somewhat more aromatic and piquant than the nose suggests. Ripe, sweet, and long on the palate, cut by a touch of tannic bitterness on the finish, in an overtly fruit-driven style. 14.5% *90* Drink to 2022.

Parker Coonawarra

The estate was established in 1985 by John Parker, a Bordeaux lover who wanted to have a Bordeaux château in Coonawarra. The flagship wine is the Terra Rossa First Growth; matured for 20 months in French oak, it is released only if it is felt to have the structure for long aging. Six vintages have been declassified. Initially the wine was a blend of Cabernet Sauvignon with Merlot and Cabernet Franc. When Peter Bissell took over as winemaker in 1996, he took out the Cabernet Franc; Petit Verdot was included for the first time in 2008. But the wine is usually more than 95% Cabernet Sauvignon, coming principally from the Reynella selection. It can be a little stern when young, and reaches a perfect balance after a decade. My favorite is the 2000. The second wines are the Terra Rossa Cabernet Sauvignon and Merlot. In 2004, Parker Coonawarra was purchased by the Rathbone family, who own Yering Station in Yarra Valley. Wines were tasted at Balnaves in October 2012.

Coonawarra, Terra Rossa First Growth, 2010
(Not yet released.) Restrained nose but with impression of intense, deep, black fruits, then rich and dense on the palate; taut, fine, tannins dry the finish with some heat evident. Brooding blackberries give a pretty stern overall impression. This is so young it tastes more like a barrel sample (it is still maturing in the bottle and will be released in 2014). *90* Drink 2017-2029.

Coonawarra, Terra Rossa First Growth, 2009
More of an impression of blackcurrants here compared with the blackberries of 2010, with a slightly more lifted aromatic impression. Sweet, ripe, intensely black fruits show great purity of line, supported by fine-grained, taut, tannins that dry the finish. The Cabernet fruit really comes straight at you. Alcohol is well integrated. This is an unusually forward vintage for Parker Coonawarra, with some nuts and vanillin adding to the relatively open fruits. *92* Drink 2015-2030.

Coonawarra, Terra Rossa First Growth, 2008
Restrained nose offers faint suggestions of cereal and black fruits. A less aromatic profile than 2009 gives a slightly flatter impression of slowly releasing blackberry fruits. This is a classic Cabernet with the typical austerity of the variety showing a strong underlying tannic structure. Yet this needs time not so much to let the tannins resolve as to allow fruit flavor variety to develop. There's no mistaking the sheer density and quality of the fruits, but my goodness, this needs time. 14.5% *91* Drink 2017-2032.

Coonawarra, Terra Rossa First Growth, 2006
Savory hints show on a restrained nose leading into a slightly piquant acidity on the palate, giving a fresher impression to the wine than more recent vintages. Underneath the acidic shell are blackberry fruits, very reserved and tight. It's hard to say when this will come out of its tight structural shell. 15.0% *89* Drink 2013-2025.

Coonawarra, Terra Rossa First Growth, 2005
Initial impression shows smooth black fruits, with blackberries showcased by crisp acidity. Although the wine is quite closed now, fugitive whiffs of blackcurrants promise some interesting future development. Tight tannins dry the finish, reinforcing that closed impression. *89* Drink 2016-2030.

Coonawarra, Terra Rossa First Growth, 2004
The nose is distinctly more open than the 2005 and shows a touch of development, with influences of cedar and cigar box showcasing black fruits. Superficially there is less development on the palate, where the fruits seem more primary. Black cherries and blackcurrants are poking out of the dark fruits on the palate, with just a touch of black aromatics coming out on the finish, and notes of cedar coming back retronasally, with a variety of influences identifying the first signs of development. Fine-grained tannins bring a sense of finesse to the structure. This is almost ready to drink. 14.5% *93* Drink 2013-2029.

Coonawarra, Terra Rossa First Growth, 2001
Development is evident in the form of some faintly savory notes on the nose, but is less evident on the palate, which shows great purity of line, with pure Cabernet fruits showing as precisely delineated black cherries with hints of blackcurrants. A touch of nuts shows retronasally. Hints of tarragon on the finish show that development is just starting. 14.0% *92* Drink to 2027.

Coonawarra, Terra Rossa First Growth, 2000
The tertiary hints on the nose make this seem more than a year older than the 2001. There's an absolutely delicious counterpoise of subtle savory elements with the faintest hints of sous bois, showing against clear, pure, Cabernet fruits with a touch of cedar on the finish. This vintage has it all, and is at a powerful point at the end of youthful development, where ripeness of fruits is still dominant, but beautifully cut by those developing savory influences. Tannins are fine-grained, very smooth and round, bringing great finesse to the texture. Over the next few years, savory flavor variety should develop further. 14.0% *93* Drink to 2025.

Coonawarra, Terra Rossa First Growth, 1999
Closed on the nose and less overtly developed on the palate than the 2000. There are ripe, sweet, black fruits on the palate, showing as blackcurrants and cherries, and some cedar on the finish. Elegant, well-rounded, tannins are firm on the finish, and not as fine-grained as usual. This is about to start its savory development, but it feels younger, not older, than the 2000. 14.0% *91* Drink to 2024.

Coonawarra, Terra Rossa First Growth, 1998
A touch of cereal on the nose leads into a less aromatic, slightly flatter, profile than the 1999 or 2000. Not quite as concentrated, the palate shows blackberry and plum fruits in the background, with a smooth, glyceriny impression, and a supporting structure of firm, round tannins. As always, a convincing expression of Cabernet, but less concentration and finesse than some vintages. 13.5% *89* Drink to 2022.

Coonawarra, Terra Rossa First Growth, 1996
Savory, herbal impression with a touch of tobacco. Elegant, fine-grained texture with some savory elements, and a touch of sous bois developing in the glass. Fruits recede a little in the glass as the sous bois comes up. This seems a little out of balance and may not be a good bottle. 13.5% Drink up.

Penley Estate

The estate was purchased in 1987 and the first vines were planted in 1988; planting continued until 2006. The estate has 166 ha with 111 ha planted to a variety of grape types; two thirds is Cabernet Sauvignon, and another fifth is Shiraz. The mid tier Cabernet Sauvignon, Phoenix, was started in 1997; after that the former regular bottling became the Reserve. Phoenix may have small amounts of Cabernet Franc and Merlot, but the Cabernet Reserve is usually 100% Cabernet Sauvignon; it comes mostly from the three oldest blocks. Until 2008, the wine used to be pressed off the skins at about 1% remaining potential alcohol, and fermentation was finished in barrel, but since then there has been a move towards fermenting to dryness and allowing more extended skin contact. The move to more maceration was extended into the new Tolmer cuvée in 2009. Out of total production of 35-40,000 cases, Phoenix accounts for 16,000, the Reserve 2,000-2,500, and Tolmer about 1,000. Wines were tasted at Penley Estate in October 2012.

Coonawarra, Tolmer Cabernet Sauvignon, 2009
This is the inaugural vintage of this special cuvée, which is an attempt to make a more tradi-

tional wine by allowing more continued skin contact to give more structure. It certainly shows a tighter structure than the Reserve, with a stern nose that has intimations of deep black fruits. Here the blackcurrants, cherries, and plums are at the fore, and tannins are finer, giving a tighter and more elegant overall impression. There's more purity of fruit, but perhaps less flavor variety, than the Reserve. *88* Drink to 2020.

Coonawarra, Cabernet Sauvignon, 2006
Restrained nose of blackberries with hints of plums leads into a black fruit palate where tannins are mostly resolved although there is still a touch of dryness on the finish. There's just a faint touch of the savory influence that characteristically takes over the Cabernet relatively rapidly. Although the high use of new oak is not manifested overtly by vanillin or wood spices, still the oak dominates the wine. 15.0% *88* Drink to 2018.

Coonawarra, Cabernet Sauvignon Reserve, 2004
The nose shows just hints of the savory influences that show strongly on the older wines. On the palate, ripe black fruits display a savory edge with just a touch of sous bois already becoming evident. You can certainly see the sheer ripeness of the fruits in this wine that is now at its peak. The high alcohol is not noticeable. There is a touch of acidity on the finish. The overall impression is just a touch rustic, perhaps reflecting the extensive use of new oak. 15.0% *89* Drink to 2016.

Coonawarra, Cabernet Sauvignon Reserve, 2002
This has the same impression of pungency on the nose as the older vintages, but much less developed, and more of a counterpoise to fruits that are lively and ripe enough to hold the sous bois at bay. The very ripe, mature, fruits show as blackberries with just a hint of plums. Just on the verge of taking over, the sous bois is developing quite rapidly, bringing a slightly rustic impression to the wine. 14.5% *89* Drink to 2014.

Coonawarra, Cabernet Sauvignon, 1996
A pungent mineral impression of old Cabernet on the nose shows a mixture of oxidized and savory influences. Here you see the same influences that have taken over the 1992, but not so developed; although this is past its peak, there's still enough fruit to be interesting. Crisp acidity gives an almost tart impression to the finish. The overall impression is a little tired, although delicious remnants of the original fruits show on the aftertaste. 13.0% *87* Drink up.

Coonawarra, Cabernet Sauvignon, 1992
Mature garnet appearance with broad orange rim and some brown. Very mature nose with some impressions of oxidation, although turning a little spicy. Highly developed on the palate: although fruits are still quite lively, they will be too tertiary for most tastes, more in an oxidized than savory direction. Although the wine is past its peak and the fruits are drying out somewhat, it is still interesting, but drink up. 13.5% *86*.

Rymill

Grapevine plantings started here as a small patch on the farm, and then the property on Terra Rossa soil was purchased in the seventies; from selling the grapes, the Rymills have now moved into bottling all the estate production. The range extends from an entry-level Yearling Cabernet Sauvignon, the MC^2 blend of Cabernet Sauvignon, Merlot, and Cabernet Franc at a slightly higher price point, and the estate Cabernet Sauvignon (also seen as a re-release a few years later). These are workmanlike wines, intended for the current market. "I'm not impressed with aging, I prefer wines where you can still recognize the fruit, say under ten years," says Peter Rymill. "Blending and aging are compensations for poor winemaking." What they care about here is the purity of fruit in the first decade. Wines were tasted at Rymill in October 2012.

Coonawarra, MC^2, 2010
This is approximately an equal blend of Cabernet Sauvignon and Merlot with a little Cabernet Franc holding the ring. The objective is to make a wine that is more immediately approachable and should be consumed in a couple of years. There's an impression of soft black fruits on the nose, following to a slightly nutty, very soft palate, with a ripe, sweet, touch to the finish. This is well made and fulfills its objective, but it seems uncertain to what extent it represents the typicity of Cabernet. 14.0% *87* Drink to 2015.

Coonawarra, Cabernet Sauvignon, 2008
Faint herbal touch of tarragon on the nose with a hint of spice. Nice acidity showcases the blackberry fruits, with just a touch of cedar on the finish, strengthening in the glass. A sweetness to the finish slowly emerges, nicely balanced by notes of cigar box. Very much a pure Cabernet in its overall flavor spectrum. 14.0% *90* Drink to 2022.

Coonawarra, Cabernet Sauvignon, 2010
Restrained nose offers spicy black fruit impressions. Smooth black fruits of pure Cabernet dominate the palate, with a touch of blackcurrants evident on the finish with notes of cedar. Somewhat linear and direct in the style of pure Cabernet. 14.5% *89* Drink to 2023.

Coonawarra, Cabernet Sauvignon, 2004
Dusky ruby with garnet hues. Restrained nose has some savory intimations. Good acidity with that characteristic edge on the finish. A faint cedary influence melds into hints of savory and herbal notes, with blackberry fruits receding into the background. There's the fairly tight flavor spectrum you often see with varietal Cabernet Sauvignon. The style is elegant rather than blockbuster and gives the impression that the wine wants to become savory but can't quite get there. 14.0% *89* Drink to 2018.

Coonawarra, Cabernet Sauvignon, 1998
Dark garnet color shows some age. Maturity shows in the tertiary aromas of the nose, giving the impression the wine might be a little tired, but this blows off on the palate, which still has sweet, ripe, round fruits, black with herbal overtones. There are hints of cedar and a touch of leather. There might be a faint touch of Brett, but it adds complexity to what remains a vibrant wine. Now that Brett has all but been eliminated, you would not see this type of wine made today. 14.3% *91* Drink to 2018.

Wynns Coonawarra

By far the largest wine producer in Coonawarra, Wynns owns almost 20% of the area's vineyards (900 ha comprising 60 different vineyards, varying from 1 ha to 40 ha). After several changes at the top levels of corporate ownership, Wynns is now owned by Treasury Wine Estates, which also owns Penfolds, Lindemans, and Wolf Blass. Total production is 150-250,000 cases; Cabernet (including blends) is about 60%, and Shiraz is 25%. The best known Cabernet is the Black Label, which goes back to the start in 1954, and is a selection of the best lots. At the top level, produced in less than 1,000 cases each, are the V & A Cabernet-Shiraz (a blend coming from around the V & A Lane), the John Riddoch Cabernet Sauvignon (a reserve wine first made in 1982), and single vineyard wines. Wynns now make a single vineyard Cabernet each year, but it's a different vineyard each time. The first single vineyard wine was Harold in 2001. "Today there are about 20 vineyards that are potentially suitable for a single vineyard label: each should have an important Coonawarra story, have a quality track record, and give a distinctive reflection of vineyard and vintage, and be different from the regular wine and the reserve," says winemaker Sue Hodder. Wines were tasted at Wynns in October 2012.

Coonawarra, V & A Lane Cabernet-Shiraz, 2010
This blend of 75% Cabernet to 25% Shiraz has a faintly blackcurrant first impression with plummy overtones and crisp, almost tart, acidity. It carries its structure lightly as seen in a relatively delicate mid palate. Tannins are quite light and elegant; some chocolate overtones develop in the glass. The austerity of Cabernet is more in evidence than the fleshiness of Shiraz, but the fruit is more overt than seen in the single vineyard Cabernets 13.5% *87* Drink to 2018.

Coonawarra, Glengyle Vineyard Cabernet Sauvignon, 2009
The vines at Glengyle are among the oldest in Coonawarra as the vineyard was planted in 1969 in an early ripening spot. The initial impression is mineral, almost gamey. A crisp impression of tight fruits on the palate belies the high alcohol. The flavor spectrum is not quite minty but is certainly towards the savory rather than overtly fruity. The herbaceous origins of the variety show in that impression of savory reserve rather than any direct herbaceousness. 14.0% *88* Drink to 2022.

Coonawarra, Davis Vineyard Cabernet Sauvignon, 2008
Just a touch of garnet shows in the appearance. The restrained nose is savory with some herbal intimations. There's a richer, more chocolaty, impression here, with a savory background of tarragon to the palate of blackcurrants and plums. At the present, the fruits just outweigh the savory influences, and the overall impression is a touch rustic. Crisp acidity gives an appropriate balance to match food. *89* Drink to 2022.

Coonawarra, Alex Vineyard Cabernet Sauvignon, 2006
A little development shows here in the garnet color and some savory suggestions on the nose. Fruits are round and chocolaty with a touch of sternness showing in the aftertaste. The savory palate with chocolate overtones makes a medium bodied food wine rather than a powerhouse to blow you away. The nice balance gives the impression that the savory character is built in from the start, as it were, rather than something that will come only with age. Becoming cedary on the finish as it ages, this is perhaps the most subtle of the single vineyard wines. 14.0% *88* Drink to 2022.

Coonawarra, Messenger Vineyard Cabernet Sauvignon, 2005
This comes from a cooler vineyard in the southern area, balancing the warm vintage. There's a distinctive garrigue-like character to the nose, savory and herbal, with a touch of sage. The impression on the palate is soft and elegant, somehow appearing more European in style, although there are lighter, more lifted, aromatics. With a touch of cedar strengthening on the finish, the overall impression shows much finesse. 13.5% *90* Drink to 2022.

Coonawarra, Johnson's Block Shiraz-Cabernet, 2004
This three quarter Shiraz to one quarter Cabernet has developed a mature garnet color. There's a dusty red fruit nose of plums and cherries. It's quite round on the palate, with those aromatic plums of Shiraz showing more obviously on the aftertaste. The palate shows the usual clear acidity of the house, with Cabernet perhaps showing as a touch of cedar on the finish. 13.0% *89* Drink to 2020.

Coonawarra, Harold Vineyard Cabernet Sauvignon, 2001
The inaugural single vineyard wine, this now shows a mature garnet color. There's a fine chocolaty impression at first blush, then some herbal notes develop; the complex impression of the nose follows through to the palate, where there is a lovely intermingling of fruits of blackcurrants and plums with savory and chocolate influences. At a lovely point of balance, this is at its peak for mid-term drinking. 13.5% *91* Drink to 2021.

Coonawarra, John Riddoch Cabernet Sauvignon, 1991
From the first vintage in 1982 through the early nineties, the Childs vineyard at the V & A line was a major source; since then the sources have been moving progressively farther north. The mature garnet appearance shows a touch of orange. The restrained nose makes a mature impression, followed by sweet, ripe fruits that are still lively on the palate. Savory elements cut the fruits in a classic style reminiscent of Bordeaux; only the weight and richness of the fruits betray the wine's origins; there's the faintest touch of sous bois. It's surprising how restrained the nose is relative to the palate, but slowly the savory notes of sous bois strengthen on the nose. The sweet, ripe, fruits of the palate are cut by dry cedary notes on the finish. 13.5% *91* Drink to 2020.

Yalumba

Producing only estate wine from its 45 ha, the Yalumba estate in Coonawarra is much smaller than its headquarters in Barossa Valley. The Menzies has been Yalumba's estate Cabernet Sauvignon since 1987; since 2006 another varietal Cabernet Sauvignon, The Cigar (named for the so-called cigar-like shape of the Terra Rossa strip) is effectively a second wine from the same estate, tending to come from the younger vines. "For Menzies and Cigar everything is made in small (8 ton) fermenters. Those lots that are bold with more ageability are picked for Menzies, but they tend to come from the older (1975) planting. Menzies is 100% Cabernet but Cigar has a bit of Merlot blended in to make it more presentable early," says Dan Newson. Wines were tasted at Yalumba in Coonawarra in October 2012.

Coonawarra, Cigar Cabernet Sauvignon, 2010
The restrained nose conveys an impression of stern, black, Cabernet fruits, turning to slightly aromatic notes of blackcurrants in the glass. Acidity verges on crisp, reinforcing the sense of purity on the palate, and giving a cool climate, edgy, impression. 13.5% *89* Drink to 2021.

Coonawarra, Cigar Cabernet Sauvignon, 2009
This vintage shows just a touch more development than the preceding or succeeding vintages in the form of a slightly gamey impression on the nose. Overall it is softer, but more refined, smooth, and elegant. Nicely delineated black fruits add to the sense of tautness, and show a touch of piquancy on the finish. 14.0% *89* Drink to 2022.

Coonawarra, Cigar Cabernet Sauvignon, 2008
The initial impression of black fruits is not so overtly driven by Cabernet Sauvignon as the 2006 vintage, showing black plums, cherries, and blackcurrants with just a touch more evident aromatics than 2006 (perhaps reflecting the 8% Shiraz), and a hint of piquancy on the finish. Is there a faint suggestion of menthol? The blackcurrant aromatics come out more obviously on the finish, where there is just a touch of heat. Tannins are ripe but just faintly rustic compared with the purity of expression of 2006 and the finesse of 2009. 13.5% *88* Drink to 2021.

Coonawarra, Cigar Cabernet Sauvignon, 2006
This was the first year of Cigar, and the wine, which is usually a blend of 95% or so Cabernet Sauvignon with a little Merlot (or occasionally Shiraz) was 100% Cabernet this year for an unusual reason. The Cabernet cuvée won an award; and in order to label the wine with the award, only the Cabernet could be used. It's still a purple color. The black fruit nose has a touch of cedar, with Cabernet revealed by a stern impression. There's a classic black fruit profile on the palate, a touch of tobacco, and faint bitterness still present on the finish. Overall, a very direct, pure, impression of Cabernet. 14.5% *89* Drink to 2022.

Coonawarra, The Menzies Cabernet Sauvignon, 2008
A touch of tobacco and cigar box identifies a classic nose. The palate is marked by taut, precisely delineated, linear black fruits showing the purity of Cabernet, very clean and fine. Refined tannins are evident only by their dryness on the finish. Very tight now, this needs time to develop more flavor variety. 14.0% *89* Drink to 2023.

Coonawarra, The Menzies Cabernet Sauvignon, 2006
This seems to be a much gentler vintage; first impressions show soft black fruits with a touch of vanillin that blows off. Slowly the underlying structure of Cabernet Sauvignon shows itself, but tannins are quite furry on the finish with only a faint touch of the asperity of other vintages. This slightly less structured vintage should mature nicely but more rapidly. *88* Drink to 2020.

Coonawarra, The Menzies Cabernet Sauvignon, 2005
The taut black fruit nose offers a hint of piquancy, but the palate offers a more rounded impression than the Cigar cuvées, even though this is 100% Cabernet. Smooth, fine, tannins leave an impression of chocolate on the edge. Fruits show more as black cherries than blackcurrants, finely delineated, and there isn't much development yet, but the taut structure promises good longevity. 14.5% *91* Drink to 2024.

Margaret River

"We had a series of dream vintages," says winemaker Glen Goodall of Xanadu Wines, referring to the past few years. "2010 was one of the easiest viticultural seasons," says winemaker Travis Lemm at Voyager, "but 2009 makes a prettier wine." The mark of 2010 was the long growing season; the results are considered similar to 2005. 2009 was characterized by an Indian summer that allowed the reds to ripen well. 2008 was a classic year, a touch on the warm side, but generally moderate with no heat spikes, and long hang times like 2004 and 2001. 2007 was one of the hottest vintages ever (the earliest on record), but although the producers are very pleased with the results and there are many generous wines, I mostly did not like them as well as 2008, which I felt brought out the typicity of Margaret River very well. The real exception in the decade is 2006, the coolest vintage on record, which produced few good red wines (to the point at which it's rarely included in

vertical tastings. 2005 is widely regarded as one of the most balanced and successful vintages of the decade. All wines are labeled under the Margaret River GI
(occasionally with an additional subregional origin indicated on the label).

2007 Horizontal Tasting

This horizontal tasting was an insight into the warm 2007 vintage, which is generally
regarded as a real crowd-pleaser. Styles ranged from reserved, driven by black fruits
(Ashbrook, Juniper, Leeuwin, Vasse Felix, Voyager), more open black fruits (Cullen,
Fraser Gallop, Stella Bella, Woodlands, and Xanadu), and more driven by red fruits
(Cape Mentelle, Lenton Brae, Moss Wood, Thompson). This did not correlate in any
clear way with geographic origins, perhaps because the warm vintage lifted ripeness all
round. Wines were tasted blind, and it's a measure of the coherence of Margaret River
Cabernet that none of the producers claimed to be able to identify their own wines. The
producers' own order of preference was Xanadu, Fraser Gallop, Woodlands, Juniper,
Leeuwin, Voyager, Cape Mentelle. The tasting was in Margaret River in October 2012.
Wines are presented in my order of rating.

Fraser Gallop Estate
Slightly piquant black fruit nose changing in the glass to more herbal overtones. Fine, elegant
black fruits, real finesse here, black cherries and plums with subtle aromatic overtones, silky
tannins giving a fine-grained texture. This gives a classic impression of pure Cabernet fruits
poised on the perfection of ripeness. The very faint herbal overtones on the finish should develop in the next few years to bring complexity to the finish. 14.5% *91* Drink to 2022.

Juniper Estate, Cabernet Sauvignon
A slightly austere black fruit nose tends to savory herbal impressions of sage. Precisely delineated black cherry fruits dominate the palate, round and elegant, very much the pure varietal
character of Cabernet Sauvignon. Firm tannins dry the finish where there is a very faint sensation of herbaceousness. A classic example of the firm style of Wilyabrup. More approachable
than usual from this estate, although still needs some time, not so much for tannins to resolve—
they are quite held back by the fruits although detectable as dryness on the finish—as to let
flavor variety develop from the presently somewhat monolithic fruits. Should age well for a decade. 14.0% *90* Drink 2013-2022.

Voyager Estate, Cabernet-Merlot
Herbaceous opening to the nose with black fruits hiding behind, giving a cool climate impression. Classic impression on palate of black fruits, softer than the nose would suggest, with soft,
ripe chocolaty tannins, those notes of pyrazines coming back on the finish, which shows a
touch of heat, but overall a fine elegant impression. 14.2% *90* Drink to 2020.

Cullen, Diana Madeline
Nose of fresh red and black berries, opening out into fragrant, perfumed impressions with hints
of roses and violets. Sweet, ripe, elegant, well rounded fruits of black cherries and black plums,
with reserved tannins holding back the fruits on the finish. Flavor variety is developing in an
elegant style reminiscent of Margaux, but another year is required to let the tannins resolve.
There's some heat on the finish. 14.0% *89* Drink 2013-2020.

Leeuwin Estate, Art Series Cabernet Sauvignon
Warm nose with vanillin and nuts hiding black fruit character and giving an impression of new
oak; then some herbaceous notes of pyrazines develop and strength in the glass. Sweet, ripe,
rounded, firm style on palate, with ripeness of fruits evident, but cut by a herbaceous touch
coming back on finish, accompanied by nutty notes from new oak. Impression at this point is a
little rustic from the new oak. Surprisingly (given the hot character of the vintage) this wine
gives a less exuberant impression than the 2008; certainly fuller, it's rich and round, and quite
glyceriny on the palate, but has less flavor variety than 2008. Although this is a bit one dimensional at the moment, the richness on the palate speaks more directly to its New World origins
than other vintages. "The punters love it," they say at Leeuwin. 14.0% *89* Drink 2013-2021.

Woodlands Wines, Nicolas Cabernet Sauvignon

Slightly austere nose with impressions of cherries. Fine, elegant palate of red and black cherry fruits with refined impression from silky, fine-grained tannins. Just a touch of nuts on the finish. Nice balance, needs another year to let the tannins resolve and fruit flavor emerge to show a wine with some real finesse in a lighter style. 13.5% *89* Drink 2013-2020.

Cape Mentelle, Cabernet Sauvignon

Fresh nose holding back the red fruits, with some sweet herbal elements, including thyme developing in the glass, giving a rather surprising cool climate impression for the year. This shows nice flavor variety on the palate with strawberry and cherry fruits coming out, against a light tannic support. Give this another year to let the dryness of the tannins on the finish resolve, and it should begin to develop a nice savory balance to the red and black fruits. Some heat shows on the finish. 14.0% *89* Drink to 2020.

Moss Wood, Cabernet Sauvignon

Light elegant fresh nose of red fruits, opening out to become spicy and floral, showing cinnamon and nutmeg. The height of elegance on the palate, but with a flavor profile more like Pinot Noir than Cabernet Sauvignon, with fragrant red fruits pointing towards raspberries and strawberries. The elegance and warmth remind me of Sassicaia in a lighter vintage. This is ready to drink but I suspect that may be deceptive and it will last longer than might be evident at first blush. 14.5% *89* Drink to 2020.

Lenton Brae, Wilyabrup Cabernet Sauvignon

Slightly piquant red fruit impression on the nose, leading into a soft palate of ripe red fruits of raspberries and cherries. Tannins are fine and silky, bringing an elegant impression of fine texture to the finish. As the tannins resolve this will become soft and elegant in a style driven by red fruits. 14.5% *89* Drink to 2019.

Stella Bella, Serie Luminosa Cabernet Sauvignon

Stewed fruit character on nose suggests ripeness, and then pyrazines develop in the glass. More classical on the palate than might be suggested by the nose, with smooth, ripe, elegant black fruits cut by that touch of herbaceousness typical of Wallcliffe (which accounts for a major part of the wine). Light tannins dry the finish, which shows some heat. This is a light, elegant style, but does it have the stuffing for longevity? 14.0% *88* Drink to 2018.

Ashbrook Estate, Cabernet Merlot

Fresh nose with underlying black fruits and slightly nutty cereal overtones (reflecting new oak). Sturdy, ripe, well rounded impression of Wilyabrup, blackberry fruits cut on finish by drying effect of tannins, with some faintly herbal impressions. Not a wine for instant gratification, but should develop in an elegant style over next five years, although there is a slight impression of hollowness on mid palate. 14.0% *88* Drink 2013-2020.

Vasse Felix, Cabernet Sauvignon

Ripe vegetal impression, with mix of ripe stewed fruits and green overtones, leading into a palate mixing ripe and green impressions. Fruits tend to blackberries and blackcurrants, tannins are firm; there is a fairly robust impression on the palate, but some flavor variety is developing. 14.5% *88* Drink to 2019.

Xanadu, Cabernet Sauvignon

Black fruit nose with some faintly over-ripe impressions clears in the glass to a faintly herbal expression. Elegant balance on the palate, with blackberry fruits showing a touch of reserve as the tight tannins of the finish cut in, showing a touch of tobacco and some leafiness and hints of sage. The usual tightness of Xanadu's style is softened only a little by the heat of the vintage, and the risk here is that the favor profile may become narrower with age. 14.0% *88* Drink 2013-2020.

Thompson Estate, Cabernet Sauvignon

The character of the vintage speaks directly in this wine, which is fatter than usual. Soft black fruit nose, with some cereal impressions, turning to riper stewed fruits in the glass giving a warmer climate impression. Warm, sweet, ripe red cherry and strawberry impression on palate, with a lingering sweetness on the finish, and slightly nutty notes coming back. Some heat on the finish. A warm, forward, delicious style—already approachable—with some savory hints that should strengthen in the next year or so, making this a wine to drink in the immediate future. 14.5% *87* Drink to 2018.

Brookland Valley

Located in the Wilyabrup subregion, Brookland Valley was established in 1984 with plantings of Cabernet Sauvignon, Chardonnay, Sémillon and Sauvignon Blanc. There are three ranges of wine: the Verse 1 entry-level includes a Cabernet-Merlot; the Estate wines include a Cabernet Sauvignon-Merlot; and the Reserve wines carry single varietal labels. The approach is fairly classic for Margaret River, with the top lots going into the varietal reserve, and others being blended. "In each of these vintages (2010-2008), the Cabernet for the Cabernet-Merlot had that linear nature before we added the Merlot, which filled in the classic doughnut," says winemaker Pete Dillon. On top of the Reserve, there is now the Houghton Gladstones, which is a single vineyard, pure Cabernet Sauvignon. Wines were tasted at Brookland Valley in October 2012.

Cabernet-Merlot, 2010
Slightly perfumed nose leads into tarry black fruits, showing blackcurrants and red and black cherries. A bit light on the palate, where acidity gives a fresh impression, and tannins show as dryness on the finish. Less opulent in style than 2009 or 2008. 14.2% *88* Drink to 2019.

Cabernet-Merlot, 2009
Nose shows black fruits with touch of asperity, leading into a palate of blackberries. Nice acid balance. Not quite as rich or fine as 2008, but firm, sturdy tannins give good structure, with a slight note of herbaceousness cutting the fruits. 14.2% *88* Drink to 2020.

Cabernet-Merlot, 2008
There's a rich chocolaty impression of black fruits, tending to blackcurrants, cut by faint herbal notes. The tannic structure cuts the richness with a touch of bitterness on the finish, which is a little hot. Certainly the structure of the Cabernet is driving the wine. This can be enjoyed now but should develop more flavor variety over the next few years. 14.4% *89* Drink to 2020.

Reserve Cabernet Sauvignon, 2011
(Not yet released.) The chocolaty black fruit nose shows just a touch of asperity. Very rich blackcurrant fruits, bordering on cassis, cut by some fresh red cherry fruits, dominate the palate. Acidity is noticeable. Although this is beginning to show a mix of fruits flavors, it will need time for flavors to release fully. It will probably lighten up and turn from black to red fruit flavors by the time it is released. *89* Drink 2015-2025.

Reserve Cabernet Sauvignon, 2004
Not made every year, this is the current release of the Reserve Cabernet, coming from a vineyard in Wilyabrup. A classic nose shows black fruits with touches of herbaceousness and some coffee following on. Fine and lively on the palate, with lovely elegant, taut, black fruits balanced by that subtle touch of herbaceousness. Fine-grained texture reflects silky tannins. You definitely know you are in Cabernet country. This is now at a perfect point of balance, but I would expect it to hold for several years yet. 13.5% *92* Drink to 2024.

Houghton Gladstones Cabernet Sauvignon, 2010
This wine comes from a single vineyard in Wilyabrup. "This is a completely different style. Because the vineyard is dry farmed we see a completely different evolution of flavor and tannins," says Pete Dillon. The vines were planted in 1988, more or less at the same time as those used for the Reserve. This is definitely a far more masculine wine, as seen immediately by the inky color and the aromatic black fruits on the rich, chocolaty, nose. There's great concentration, black plums and blackcurrants showing aromatic overtones of cassis, with a taut underlying structure almost hidden by the fruits. This is so concentrated and rich it could be enjoyed already, but that would be vinicide. 14.0% *92* Drink 2014-2029.

Cape Mentelle

One of the first wineries to be established in the Wallcliffe area, Cape Mentelle started with 16 ha in 1971. Today it has 180 ha spread among several vineyards. The focus on red wines was emphasized when Cape Mentelle won the prestigious Jimmy Watson trophy in 1983 and 1984; the wine was then called Cabernet Dry Red Claret. A move into white wines was reinforced when Cape Mentelle established Cloudy Bay in New Zealand in 1985. Cape Mentelle (together with Cloudy Bay) was purchased by LVMH in 2003. The resources this has brought to bear are evident in the form (for example) of an optical sorting line—something that is extremely unusual in a region where there is usually no sorting at all at the winery. It's also one of the few wineries in the region to have its own bottling line. Half of production is white, a Sauvignon Blanc-Sémillon blend, followed by the 30,000 cases of the Cabernet-Merlot regional blend, which comes mostly from Wilyabrup and Wallcliffe. A higher-flying Cabernet-Merlot blend is merely labeled Wilyabrup, with its 400 cases intended for the restaurant trade; it is matched by a Graves-style white wine called Wallcliffe. Made since 1974, the most expensive of the Cabernets is the varietal-labeled Cabernet Sauvignon, 98% pure varietal in 2010, produced in about 1,200 cases, always coming principally from the home estate vineyard, with up to about 5% of other sources. "We want this to be the best expression of the vineyard, and ultimately it may morph into a Cabernet blend," says winemaker Rob Mann. Wines were tasted at Cape Mentelle in October 2012.

Cabernet-Merlot, 2010
Soft, fruity, and forward, with soft tannins, but not a lot of structure. Nice enough balance. The Merlot is not very fleshy so the overall balance is soft rather than generous. Acidity is crisp on the finish. This is a regional blend, the predominant sources being Wilyabrup and Wallcliffe. 13.5% *87* Drink to 2016.

Wilyabrup, 2010
This is a roughly equal blend of Cabernet Sauvignon and Merlot with the balance made up by Cabernet Franc. It has more of a black fruit nose than the Cabernet-Merlot blend, but is quite restrained, although an aromatic lift develops in the glass. The palate offers a refined impression, with sweet, ripe, tannins in a fine-grained texture, leading to a touch of chocolate on the finish. It's unusual to have such refinement with a high content of Merlot. Acidity is a touch noticeable on the finish, where tannins show only by a touch of dryness. 13.5% *89* Drink to 2020.

Cabernet Sauvignon, 2010
The initial impression of chocolate-coated black cherries is countered by faintly savory influences. The elegant impression carries over to the fruits on the palate, supported by balanced acidity and quite fine tannins on the finish, where some expression of tobacco and coffee develops, turning quite nutty, with vanillin from new oak coming out. Becoming more youthful in the glass, this can be enjoyed now, but should benefit from aging. 13.4% *90* Drink to 2020.

Cabernet Sauvignon, 2001
An initial mineral impression with some overtones of tobacco and cedar turns to savory and cereal notes. Complex, sweet, ripe fruits dominate the palate, with a touch of glycerin sweetening the finish, where those savory cereal notes return. Overall a rich, soft, impression, although some dryness still shows on the finish, leading into a touch of herbaceousness. This is not as lively as the 1993, and the fruits may be beginning to dry out. This was probably around the peak year for alcohol, and this has not helped graceful aging. 15.0% *90* Drink to 2022.

Cabernet Sauvignon, 1993
A strongly developed nose shows tertiary aromas extending to sous bois, a little mint, and some mineral impressions. This has now reached a perfect tipping point where savory notes with herbal touches balance the developed ripe black fruits. Some bell peppers come out in a classic expression of Cabernet on the finish, but are cut by a touch of glycerin to offer a countering sweetness. This could easily be mistaken for a Bordeaux from the late eighties, with something resembling that characteristic acidic uplift of Bordeaux at the end. Perhaps a touch of heat on the finish betrays the New World origins. 13.5% *93* Drink to 2020.

Cabernet Sauvignon, 1983
The impression is only a little more tertiary than the 1993 with savory mineral notes and some sous bois. There's still a full, ripe, fruit impression, although more balanced towards dry, savory, notes than the sweeter fruits of 1993. Although this is beginning to dry out, it remains lively on the palate. The target in this period was to make a wine resembling Bordeaux of the late seventies, and the result is pretty classic. "This vintage literally took 25 years to be drinkable," says winemaker Rob Mann. 12.7% *91* Drink to 2017.

Cabernet Sauvignon, 1979
Sweet, ripe impression, at first clouded by a touch of oxidation with some herbal overtones, which however seemed to dissipate in the glass. The palate opens with a faint impression of mint cutting the sweet finish. As the impression of oxidation recedes, the palate shows increasing complexity, with notes of coffee developing together with some pyrazines on the finish. The initial impression of rusticity is replaced by a complex granular texture, which becomes steadily more refined in the glass, and the flavors become more subtly varied, with mature fruits in the spectrum of blackcurrants and plums. (This bottle was recorked at a month earlier: at that time, 40% of the remaining bottles of this vintage were rejected.) *91* Drink to 2016.

Credaro

Credaro divides its wines into the estate wines under its own name and the entry-level wines under the Beach Head label. The Beach Head wines are intended to be immediately approachable, the wines under the Credaro label to be a better food match. The Cabernet-Merlot blends come largely from Carbunup; the Cabernet Sauvignons tend to be blends from Carbunup and Treeton. The Cabernet Sauvignon is fermented in hand-plunged bins, compared with the static fermenters used for the Cabernet-Merlot. 2009 was the first year a varietal Cabernet Sauvignon was produced. There are plans to introduce a higher tier level Cabernet for 2012 as a barrel selection. Wines were tasted at Credaro in October 2012.

Cabernet-Merlot, Beach Head, 2011
Quite tarry on the nose, more distinct evidence of Cabernet structure on the palate than seen in the Beach Head wine, showing black cherry fruits with some tight tannins on the finish cut by a touch of glycerin. Needing time, this gives more of a classic impression than you would expect at this level. 13.5% *87* Drink 2014-2020.

Cabernet-Merlot, Beach Head, 2010
There's a light cherry fruit nose with chocolate overtones, and a soft impression on the palate with Merlot certainly fleshing out and rounding up the tighter fruits of the Cabernet, which just show as some tannic notes on the finish. 13.5% *87* Drink 2013-2019.

Cabernet-Merlot, 2011
The greater proportion of Merlot in this vintage (almost half the blend) really shows in the softer, rounder, impression of black fruits. Quite firm supporting tannins show on a nutty finish, with dryness cut by some glycerin. This is probably the direction the blend will take in the future (previous years were largely Cabernet Sauvignon). 14.0% *88* Drink 2013-2022.

Cabernet-Merlot, 2010
Slightly tarry nose leads into palate of soft black fruits, but tannic structure is in evidence on the finish. There's more depth and flavor variety than in the Beach Head line, and this is very much a Cabernet-dominated blend, with black cherry fruits supported by taut tannins. This really requires another year or so. 14.0% *88* Drink 2014-2023.

Cabernet Sauvignon, 2011
A fragrant impression on the nose is followed by softer, rounder, fruits on the palate than 2010, with those perfumed, floral, impressions of Carbunup (which dominates the sources of grapes this year). Fine-grained tannins bring an elegant style, with a touch of glycerin moving the palate towards opulence. This is likely to be ready to drink sooner than the 2010, and may not last as long. 14.0% *89* Drink 2013-2023.

Cabernet Sauvignon, 2010
Sterner, tighter, impression, more reserved than 2009 or 2011. Fruits are really holding back here, with a taut structure gripping the finish. Very much a Cabernet in the classic tradition of austerity when young. However, this should have the structure to age to elegance. 14.0% *89* Drink 2015-2025.

Cabernet Sauvignon, 2009
Restrained nose with a touch of spice and faintly tarry overtones to the black fruits. Perfume of violets develops in the glass. Quite round and firm on the palate, with supple tannins bringing a nice balance to the fruits. The fine structure would benefit from another year of aging. 14.0% *89* Drink 2014-2024.

Cullen Wines

One of the founding group of wineries, Cullen has stayed relatively small with about 29 ha of vineyards, roughly one third Cabernet Sauvignon, but they also operate the adjacent Mangan vineyard owned by Vanya Cullen's brother. The focus is on the various Bordeaux varieties (both black and white) and Chardonnay. There is a complete commitment to biodynamic viticulture here—Cullen has been organic since 2000, biodynamic since 2003, and was certified in 2005—extending to trying to follow the lunar cycle for all stages of viticulture and vinification. The philosophy here is that blending makes a better wine. A Cabernet-Merlot blend was the predecessor to the Diana Madeline, which took its present name in 2001. For the last few years, it has effectively been a single vineyard wine. Annual production is about 4,000 cases. There is also a (lower priced) Cabernet Sauvignon-Merlot blend, introduced in 2007, to replace the varietal-labeled Cabernet Sauvignon; production is 1,500 to 2,000 cases. Wines were tasted at Cullen in October 2012.

Cabernet Sauvignon-Merlot, 2010
Light red cherry nose follows through to a crisp palate of red fruits. A light style, which doesn't become overtly fruity, and is not very structured. Well made enough, but needs to be consumed in the near future as there is little potential for significant longevity. 12.5% *88* Drink to 2017.

Diana Madeline, 2010
Here is a stern nose with some spicy notes in front of restrained black fruits. Rounded black fruits on the palate are supported by fine, supple, tannins, with hints of a chocolate edge. The fine-grained texture goes into a nice sweet ripeness on the finish that maintains elegance by not becoming too glyceriny. Balanced acidity showcases a somewhat linear purity of fruits; when will flavor variety develop? 13.0% *92* Drink to 2024.

Diana Madeline, 2004
Warm nose is more aromatic than usual, with suggestions of spice against a blackcurrant background. Sweet, riper than the 2010, with a faint glyceriny richness to the finish, and that evident touch of aromatics, but balanced acidity prevents the opulence from getting out of hand. Good fruit concentration, hints of tobacco, coffee, and chocolate on the finish, although still relatively primary. The richness of the fruit makes the structure less evident in this vintage. 14.0% *91* Drink to 2022.

Cabernet-Merlot, 1996
This was the predecessor to the Diana Madeline. Restrained nose, but the rich palate deepens slowly with some herbal influences cutting the fruits. In terms of modern vintages, the style falls between 2004 and 2010. Fruits are superficially rich but there is a touch of herbal restraint, with a faint suspicion of tobacco on the finish. This is fine and elegant, but still youthful, with a lovely contrast between the richness and the herbal restraint, with the faintest touch of pyrazines developing to add complexity. 13.5% *92* Drink to 2020.

Fraser Gallop Estate

Fraser Gallop is a beautifully manicured estate hidden behind high walls. Relatively small, its 20 ha include 8.5 ha of Cabernet Sauvignon, 7 ha of Chardonnay, and small plots of Merlot, Cabernet Franc, and Petit Verdot. There are about 5,000 cases combined of the (lower level) Cabernet-Merlot and the varietal Cabernet Sauvignon. "Bordeaux is very much a reference point for me—they are still the benchmark to look at in judging where we are—but remember I'm not trying to make Bordeaux. I'm heavily committed to the estate wine," says Nigel Fraser. There is almost always the same percent of Cabernet Sauvignon, but proportions of the other varieties vary from year to year. Usually Petit Verdot and Malbec are small components, but Cabernet Franc rarely makes it. Merlot has made it in the past couple of years. Wines were tasted at Fraser Gallop in October 2012.

Cabernet Sauvignon, 2011
Some residual barrel aromatics show in this wine, which has just been bottled. Rich on the palate, deep black cherry fruits are matched by an impression of vanillin from new oak, with coffee, nuts, and chocolate evident on the finish. By the time this is released in another year, it should all come together. A lighter style than the 2010 suggests that maturation will follow the path of elegance. 14.5% *89* Drink 2013-2022.

Cabernet Sauvignon, 2010
(This is the current release.) A slightly acid red fruit impression on the nose turns towards chocolate in the glass. Lively black fruits with hints of red cherries are supported by chocolaty tannins on the finish. A touch of new oak shows as vanillin and coffee but is beginning to subside. This offers a firm, sturdy, style with solid fruit flavors across the palate. *89* Drink to 2021.

Cabernet Sauvignon, 2009
Ripe nose with some blackcurrant aromatics and a touch of cedar. Sweet, ripe, and lively on the palate, with smooth, refined fruits showing some finesse in the tannins. Finely textured, and maturing towards elegance, in fact the most elegant of recent vintages. Tannins still dry the finish, showing an edge of tobacco and chocolate. 14.5% *89* Drink to 2019.

Cabernet Sauvignon, 2004
A slightly developed acrid impression at first. Lively fruits of red and black cherries show a smooth palate with an edge of mocha and more floral undertones. Almost delicate in style as it matures, this has a nice balance of acidity to fruits and resolving tannins. 14.0% *90* Drink to 2019.

Cabernet Sauvignon, 2002
This was the first vintage, actually made at Moss Wood. There were some oxidation problems with one bottle, but a second bottle was much livelier. (This wine would certainly have done better under screwcap). Developed aromas are clearer on the nose than palate, which still has lively fruits showing as black cherries. Overall a more robust expression than the subsequent vintages, with a slightly rustic impression to the tannins. Acidity is just a touch pressing. 12.8% *87* Drink to 2018.

Happs

About as far north as you can go in the Margaret River area, seemingly cut off in the woods, Happs is an idiosyncratic operation. Erl Happ rejects conventional wisdom and grows 33 different grape varieties on his 6 ha home estate and another, larger, estate of 32 ha that he purchased more recently in Karridale to the south. Here the conventional relationship between the varietal wine and the blend is reversed; the Cabernet Sauvignon is the estate wine, and the higher-flying Charles Andreas is a blend that varies from year to year—the 2002 was mostly Cabernet Sauvignon, the 1999 was mostly Malbec. "We like to use whichever of the Bordeaux varieties makes the best wine," says Erl. Wines were tasted at Happs in October 2012.

Cabernet-Merlot, 2010
This is a roughly equal blend of Cabernet Sauvignon and Merlot. There's a soft impression with more rounded fruits, distinctly more approachable than the straight Cabernet. The black fruits are generally supple, making this ready to drink now; there isn't much stuffing for longevity. 14.0% *88* Drink to 2018.

Cabernet Sauvignon, 2010
Sharp black fruits on the nose with a tendency to blackcurrants strengthening on the palate; some tannic bite to the finish. Tightness is emphasized by high acidity. Angular tannins give an aggressive impression, but sweet fruits come out after a while to show a more rounded impression with an almost spicy finish. Erl Happ says that since the transition to screwcap, it's been the case that the wines often need a few hours to open up. 13.5% *87* Drink 2014-2022.

Cabernet Sauvignon, 2009
A piquant black fruit nose leads into a slightly sharp palate of black fruits, tending to blackcurrants with overtones of cassis. Tight tannins show with some heat on the finish, which is a bit sharp and aggressive: this calms down a bit in the glass—will it resolve further with time? 14.0% *87* Drink 2013-2021.

Cabernet Sauvignon, 2006
A slight impression of truffles on the nose, leading into a classic representation of Cabernet Sauvignon on the palate, with taut black fruits cut by bell peppers and tobacco. The herbaceous element strengthens on the finish, emphasizing the cool climate impression. 13.5% *86* Drink to 2018.

Charles Andreas, Three Hills Vineyard, 2002
We tried two bottles of this wine as the first was spoiled by a combination of TCA and oxidation due to failure of the cork. Illustrating the perils of corks in older wines from Australia, the second bottle was much fresher, showing just a touch of tertiary development with some impressions of minerality. Sweet, ripe, fruits on the palate are cut by just a touch of pyrazines coming out on the finish, but the overall impression is relatively soft on the palate, yet with a sensation of austerity from some tannins on the finish. Altogether quite a classic impression of Cabernet Sauvignon (which was 90% of the blend in this vintage). 14.0% *88* Drink to 2020.

Juniper Estate

Juniper is two operations: Juniper Estate was part of the first wave of plantings in Wilyabrup in 1973; and the Higher Plane vineyard 15 km to the south of the town of Margaret River in the Forest Grove area in Wallcliffe was purchased in 2006. Juniper's top tier of wines are single varieties carrying the Estate description; the Crossing wines are a lower level, including single varieties and blends. Higher Plane produces both single varieties and blends under its own name. In terms of a hierarchy, Crossing wines are intended to be the most approachable, and Higher Plane fits somewhere between them and the more ageworthy Juniper Estate wines. All are made by winemaker Mark Messenger at the Juniper winery. There's a masculine character here, with firm tannins that require time to resolve, running through both Higher Plane and Juniper Estate, giving the wines a distinctive style. Wines were tasted at Juniper Estate in October 2012.

Cabernet Sauvignon, Higher Plane Wines, 2010
Fruity nose shows red and black cherries. The open impression is less evident on the palate, where some stern tannins support darker fruits and there is a touch of heat on the finish. The style is light but the black fruits are tightly defined. This needs another year or two for the tannins to resolve, and then should show quite an elegant, almost floral or feminine style. 14.5% *87* Drink 2014-2022.

Cabernet Sauvignon, Higher Plane Wines, 2009
More of a black cherry impression on the nose than 2010. A taut black fruit expression on the palate gives the impression the wine will soften in the next year; black cherry and plum fruits are just beginning to emerge. Fine tannins dry the finish but should recede into the background within the year. There's a touch of heat on the finish. 14.5% *88* Drink 2013-2022.

Cabernet Sauvignon, Higher Plane Wines, 2008
Almost spicy red and black fruit nose. Soft red and black cherries on the palate, some complexity developing in the range of berry flavors, supported by fine tannins with edges defined by the supporting acidity. Quite a light, almost fragrant, impression, with faintly nutty overtones on the finish. This vintage shows the femininity of Higher Plane contrasted with the masculinity of Juniper Estate. 14.5% *89* Drink to 2017.

Cabernet Sauvignon, Higher Plane Wines, 2007
An open expression of red fruits on the nose with faintly savory or mineral undertones. A more rounded fruit impression is beginning to appear, turning from the red fruits of the nose more to black fruits on the palate. The sweetness of the fruits is just beginning to show through the structure, which is still a little tight, with tannins drying the finish. 14.0% *89* Drink to 2021.

Cabernet Sauvignon, Juniper Estate, 2010
A little more restrained on the nose than Higher Plane. Good black fruit density with cherries and plums evident, more of a direct impression of berries than Higher Plane. Fruits are nicely delineated and the firm tannins in the background need another year to resolve; the wine should then show some finesse. 14.5% *88* Drink 2013-2022.

Cabernet Sauvignon, Juniper Estate, 2009
The stern nose is not very forthcoming. This is clearly more masculine than the Higher Plane, with dense black fruits on the palate and a tannic edge still just evident on the finish. A fugitive whiff of perfumed aromatics gives an impression of elegance. This still needs another year to soften and integrate completely. 14.5% *89* Drink 2013-2023.

Cabernet Sauvignon, Juniper Estate, 2008
Stern nose with hints of spicy black fruits. A classic Margaret River expression of black fruits showcased by the acidity, with firm tannins in the background. Most people would think this was ready to drink, although I would prefer to wait another year until the tannic dryness on the finish dissipates. 14.5% *90* Drink to 2023.

Cabernet Sauvignon, Juniper Estate, 2005
A classic impression of Cabernet with faint herbaceous notes in the background of the black fruits, showing the cool end to the vintage. That mingling of herbaceousness and black cherries has reached a delicious point, turning slightly nutty retronasally. Reaching the end of its primary phase of development, this wine should now mature in a savory direction. In some ways, this seems the most developed, softest, and most ready to drink of the older vintages. Perhaps this is the trade-off—this vintage includes other varieties, whereas the previous vintages were 100% Cabernet Sauvignon. 13.5% *90* Drink to 2017.

Cabernet Sauvignon, Juniper Estate, 2004
Not very forthcoming on the nose. A mix of red and black cherry fruits shows on the palate, with the tannic structure offset by a slight touch of glycerin, but tannins are still fairly tight and dry the finish. This is a robust wine in Juniper's typical masculine style—"it was a brute when it was young," says Mark Messenger—and it hasn't completely come around yet, with the flavor spectrum still giving a monolithic impression. 14.0% *89* Drink to 2020.

Cabernet Sauvignon, Juniper Estate, 2001
This was the only wine of the flight under cork, and the only one to show any suspicion of development, in the form of a faintly mineral, savory, quality. The palate seems more primary than the nose had suggested, focusing on black cherry fruits, but there's just enough softening and movement towards savory elements to make this now the right moment to drink, although the black fruits are still supported by furry tannins drying the finish. 14.5% *90* Drink to 2021.

Leeuwin

Originally a cattle farm, Leeuwin Estate was one of the first vineyards to be established in the Wallcliffe area (just south of the town of Margaret River). Robert Mondavi was a consultant when the vineyards were planted, and the winery was constructed in 1978. Today there are 120 ha planted, including 25 ha Cabernet Sauvignon, 30 ha Riesling, 42 ha Chardonnay, and 12 ha Sauvignon Blanc (making Leeuwin an unusual producer for whom Cabernet is not the most important variety). Cabernet has in fact been cut back a little. "We used to have more Cabernet and we have kept the blocks that we know work," says vineyard manager David Winstanley. Leeuwin's flagship wines are the Art Series Cabernet Sauvignon and Chardonnay. The Art Series Cabernet usually contains about 6% Malbec. The wines are released relatively late when they are ready to drink; 2008 was the current release in 2012. Production of the Cabernet is 2,000-3,500 cases. Wines were tasted at Leeuwin in October 2012.

Art Series Cabernet Sauvignon, 2010
(Not yet released.) Restrained nose suggests a touch of asperity. Smooth elegant balance on the palate has refined tannins bringing a sense of finesse to the structure. The wine is a little tight at the moment, especially on the mid palate, but expect it to fill out in the next couple of years, to give an elegant style. 14.0% *89* Drink 2016-2030.

Art Series Cabernet Sauvignon, 2009
(Not yet released). More rounded impression than the 2010 vintage. Softer, richer, and more aromatic on the palate, with black plums and cherries, supported by soft tannins giving a supple yet fine impression on the finish. Even allowing for the year's extra age, this seems likely to remain a prettier wine than the 2010. Overall the impression is elegant, although flavor variety has yet to develop. 14.0% *91* Drink 2015-2029.

Art Series Cabernet Sauvignon, 2008
Strong nose of blackcurrants with some piquant overtones turns chocolaty. Overall there is a generous yet well structured impression, tannins showing as dryness on the finish, but cut by a glyceriny impression on the palate. This is not as fine, but is broader, with more flavor variety, than the 2009. I would expect some convergence with age, but the 2008 vintage is likely to retain breadth, and the 2009 more purity. 13.0% *91* Drink to 2025.

Art Series Cabernet Sauvignon, 2006
"This is probably stylistically what Margaret River was like in the 1990s, but less green," comments Leeuwin's viticulturalist, David Winstanley. Cabernet Sauvignon is immediately identified by a classic touch of pyrazines on the nose. A refined palate has elegant, precisely delineated fruits tending to black cherries, with those herbal notes less evident on palate than nose, but lending a subtle complexity. This vintage got a bad reputation from the outset, but my initial impression of this wine was quite classical. However, it proved an education in the underlying character, as what seems to be an intriguing combination of ripeness and pyrazines when first tasted, turned overly herbaceous when subjected to the reality check of being carried through to dinner a few hours later. This is a vintage to enjoy in the short term for those who like a more classical character to Cabernet Sauvignon, but it's not one to hold. 13.0% *88* Drink to 2017.

Art Series Cabernet Sauvignon, 2005
Widely regarded as one of the most successful vintages of the decade, this has an elegant but slightly glyceriny impression on the finish. Fruits show as red and black cherries with a typically tight Cabernet structure. The overall impression is quite tight and restrained, and the wine will benefit from further time. 13.5% *90* Drink to 2026.

Art Series Cabernet Sauvignon, 2004
Distinctly rich and ripe impression, with generous fruits but good underlying structure. There's a touch of piquant blackcurrants on the palate, counteracted by firm tannins that dry the finish and promise longevity. The overall impression is youthful and lively. 14.5% *91* Drink to 2024.

Art Series Cabernet Sauvignon, 2002
Restrained nose shows a fugitive touch of pyrazines. The palate shows elegant but tight fruits, with that touch of herbaceousness more distinct on the finish. This is a classic representation of cool climate Cabernet, but I would like to see just a little more fruit flavor variety on the mid palate, even though there is a touch of glycerin on the finish. 13.5% *88* Drink to 2019.

Art Series Cabernet Sauvignon, 2001
The smooth impression of sweet, ripe fruits is cut by a touch of barely detectable herbaceousness. This is a classic representation of Wallcliffe, still making quite a stern impression. Tannic structure remains evident on the finish. Showing clearly the character of Cabernet Sauvignon, there's a sense of austerity restraining the fruits. Overall a very nice balance, true to the grape and region. 14.0% (November 2012) *90* Drink to 2022.

Art Series Cabernet Sauvignon, 1982
Before this vintage Leeuwin produced a Reserve, but this was the first year that was named as the Art Series. Some savory development now shows in the form of tertiary aromas mingling with herbaceous influences on the nose. The palate is rich and ripe, less tertiary than the nose would suggest, with the fruits showing an edge of glycerin but cut by a touch of pyrazine on the finish, giving a very nice balance. The effect of tannins drying the finish strengthens in the glass. This vintage was probably 100% Cabernet Sauvignon. The flavor spectrum is very Left Bank, but there's more body than you would see in Bordeaux of the period. 12.5% *89* Drink to 2017.

Moss Wood

This was one of the pioneer vineyards in Wilyabrup, and the winery, built in 1973, still expresses that spirit: utilitarian, it is the antithesis of the sleek tasting rooms that are sprouting up elsewhere. Half of the 20 ha estate vineyard, in a sheltered northeast-facing locale, is Cabernet Sauvignon. Across the way is the 13 ha Ribbon Vale vineyard, planted in 1977, which Moss Wood purchased in 2000. There are some interesting differences between the two vineyards. Moss Wood was planted with Houghton selection, and Ribbon Vale with the SA126 clone. Ribbon Vale is on top of a hill with more wind, and the Cabernet needs to be blended with Merlot to get more roundness. Winemaker Keith Mugford is happy to say that, "The Penning-Rowsell twenty year benchmark applies to Moss Wood, which needs ten years' minimum cellaring to shows the beginning of its bottle-age characters, and twenty years' cellaring to show a predominance." I would say that's more or less on target, as the 2003 (nine years old) showed the first intimations of tertiary development and the 1995 (eighteen years) showed more progress, although we had to go back to 1986 to get the full impression of tertiary development. Wines were tasted at Moss Wood in October 2012 except as noted.

Cabernet Sauvignon, 2010
(About to be bottled.) Black cherry nose with chocolate overtones. Rather spicy at the moment, partly from the new oak, perhaps partly from the Petit Verdot. The oak stands out rather obviously, but that's typical at this stage, and should come into balance by the time the wine is released. Balanced acidity outlines the edges of the fruits. Tannins are smooth and elegant and there are perfumed impressions on the finish. This will be a wine with real finesse once the new oak blows off. 14.0% *92* Drink 2015-2030.

Cabernet Sauvignon, 2009
(This is the current release.) "This has the prettiness associated with the vintage, which makes it attractive when young, but I expect it to mature very slowly," says Keith Mugford. A spicy nose of black cherry fruits with hints of blackcurrants and plums offers complex aromatics for such a young wine. There's a soft impression on the palate, with smooth, opulent, black fruits going into furry tannins with a chocolaty edge, but lively acidity ensures freshness. Very refined and elegant, indeed this is a pretty wine with a sense of finesse limited only by a touch of heat on the finish. 14.5% *91* Drink to 2027.

Cabernet Sauvignon, 2006
Restrained nose with some austere cedary notes. Very slowly some blackcurrant fruits poke through. And then comes a fugitive but intense note of cedar, making you think of Graves. Crisp acidity on the palate leads into pure black fruits with an austere finish of blackcurrants, cedar and cigars. 14.0% (January 2011) *88* Drink to 2021.

Cabernet Sauvignon, 2003
There's just a touch of development on the nose which takes the form more of minerality than overt savory influence: the initial aromatics have died down but savory development has not yet started. Fruits are black and still deep, but have flattened a bit. Tannins are not directly evident but certainly the wine retains enough structure for aging. Now we need to see some savory development start. 14.0% *90* Drink to 2022.

Cabernet Sauvignon, 1995
Some tar and tertiary aromas, but judgment complicated by a touch of oxidation. Even so, you can see the ripeness, depth, and concentration of the fruits. There's not a whole lot more development than 2003. Smooth, ripe, tannins give a supple, opulent, finish. I would recommend this bottle if I were sure of finding one without a flaw in the cork. 14.5%.

Cabernet Sauvignon, 1986
Mature appearance with broadening garnet rim. Notes of tar and leather add complexity to the maturing nose. Ripe and sweet, the fruits on the palate seem less advanced than the nose. "This is a Margaret River thing. One of the reasons we put in Cabernet Franc in the early years was that Cabernet Sauvignon tended to be a bit restricted in its aromas," says Keith Mugford. Deep, black, and lively on the palate, the fruits go into a long, tarry finish. This wine now makes quite a Bordelais impression, but with the slightly more viscous palate reflecting the New World, and not quite the same acid uplift. It's very good for the age, and would no doubt be even more formidable had it been bottled under screwcap instead of cork. It is, incidentally, an education in relying on the label, because the wine seems awfully rich for its stated 12.5% alcohol; in fact, the alcohol is 13.8%. *92* Drink to 2022.

Stella Bella

The Stella Bella winery is located way out in the woods, to the south of Margaret River, but has sources of grapes from vineyards in the Wallcliffe area resulting from its merger with Rosabrook wines, more or less doubling the vineyard area. It has the distinction of owning the Suckfizzle vineyard which is the farthest south in Margaret River. The total vineyard area is now 90 ha. The wines seem generally to have a southern influence, with a slightly lean impression for Margaret River, showing as a dry finish leading into a herbaceous edge that seems reminiscent of Bordeaux, with a touch of hardness that reminds one of St Estèphe. The overall impression is that the Cabernets might benefit from a touch of Merlot; even the Cabernet-Merlot seems a little tight. The flagship series is the Luminosa, based on a barrel selection; the Luminosa Cabernet Sauvignon is mostly sourced from vineyards in Wallcliffe. Wines were tasted at Stella Bella in October 2012.

Cabernet-Merlot, 2008
A piquant blackcurrant fruit nose calms down somewhat in the glass. A soft initial impression of black fruits tending to blackcurrants is followed by a touch of herbaceousness on the dry finish. This gives a classic impression in which Cabernet is certainly more evident than Merlot; you feel it might actually benefit from a little more Merlot. Give it another year for everything to come together. 14.0% *89* Drink 2013-2023.

Cabernet-Merlot, 2004
Distinctly more restrained on the nose than the 2008 vintage with just a touch of those piquant blackcurrant fruits evident. The restrained palate shows an initial softness to the fruits, with balanced acidity, but is a little lean on the finish, so the overall impression is still quite tight. 14.5% *89* Drink to 2020.

Serie Luminosa Cabernet Sauvignon, 2009
Restrained nose with hints of cedar leads into a faint touch of herbaceousness. The initial soft impression on the palate has a touch of cereal and becomes nutty on the finish. The Cabernet fruits seem relatively generous, although there is a characteristic touch of leanness on the long, nutty, finish. The overall impression is rounder than 2008. 14.0% *89* Drink to 2021.

Serie Luminosa Cabernet Sauvignon, 2008
Moderately aromatic nose shows hints of piquant blackcurrants. The palate has a softer and rounder expression than the 2009 vintage, with aromatics dissipating in the glass to leave a fairly classic black fruit impression with a sense of restraint that's almost herbaceous on the finish. Aside from that fugitive touch of piquancy on the nose, the overall impression seems quite Bordelais. 14.0% *88* Drink 2013-2022.

Suckfizzle Vineyard Cabernet Sauvignon, 2008
There's a distinct touch of pyrazine herbaceousness on the nose, coming back on the finish to cut the sweet, round, fruits of the palate. Generally this vintage gives a more herbal impression of a cool climate. 14.5% *89* Drink to 2021.

Suckfizzle Vineyard Cabernet Sauvignon, 2001
A touch of tertiary development shows against a faintly herbaceous background (possibly more developed than you might expect relative to recent vintages, as they are under screwcap and this was under cork). Still sweet and ripe, with the faintly herbaceous impression of the nose becoming more overtly savory on the palate, where the impression of pyrazines strengthens. Are the fruits beginning to dry out? 14.5% *88* Drink to 2016.

Thompson Estate

Following the tradition of physicians starting wineries in Margaret River, Peter Thompson, a cardiologist in Perth, established Thompson Estate in Wilyabrup in 1994. The emphasis here is on varietal wine, but the Cabernet-Merlot (an 80:20 blend) started in 2005. "We put some surplus wine into barrels, and it came out so well they were bottled. Now this is our right bank blend, based on a barrel selection," says owner Peter Thompson. In fact, the Cabernet-Merlot is in such demand that it now prices above the varietal Cabernet Sauvignon. The Cabernet Sauvignon shows an abrupt change in style from 2006, with the wines of earlier vintages showing distinctly more maturity than the wines of later vintages. This is most likely due to the transition from cork to screwcap (although there was also a change of winemaker, when Bob Cartwright took over during the 2005 season). Vintages from 2010 back to 2008 show a tight elegance of primary black fruits, 2007 shows the fatness of the warmer year, and then vintages from 2005 to 2003 show a distinct edge of developing savory influences. When we got back to the older vintages, problems with the corks—either as TCA or oxidation—were too common for comfort, but the quality of the wines shone through all the same. Wines were tasted at Thompson Estate in October 2012.

Cabernet Sauvignon, 2010
Dusty ruby hue. Light red cherry fruit nose has tarry overtones, leading into some spice notes. Elegant red cherry fruit nose has hints of blackcurrants, sweet and ripe with fairly tight tannins on the finish. The general style tends towards elegance, and this is the lightest vintage since 2006. 14.0% *88* Drink to 2020.

Cabernet Sauvignon, 2009
Dusty purple color. Tight and closed at first impression, slowly releasing black cherry fruits with tarry overtones. Sweet and ripe, darker fruits than 2010, with firm tannins showing a touch of dryness on the finish, cut by hints of glycerin on the palate. Overall a supple impression, yet with backbone. This shows the most finesse of recent vintages. 14.0% *90* Drink to 2022.

Cabernet Sauvignon, 2008
Dusty purple with first development showing in some garnet at rim. Savory hints of sage restrain the black fruit nose, which reverts to chocolate in the glass. There's a broader, more glyceriny impression on the palate than the tighter 2010 or 2009 vintages, but with faintly herbal hints in the background. Firm tannins give good support but are subsumed by the fruits. Fine overall impression with silky finish. 13.5% *89* Drink to 2019.

Cabernet Sauvignon, 2006
This was the last year under cork, and accordingly two bottles had to be tasted. The first did not seem to be overtly corked, but certainly had a problem that suppressed fruits and brought out vegetal impressions. The second showed more subtle herbaceous impressions (a characteristic of this cool year), with some classic bell peppers highlighting the tightness of the fruits on the palate. Overall a good representation of Cabernet Sauvignon, but the fruits may not have enough stuffing to withstand the herbaceousness in the future. *86* Drink to 2017.

Cabernet Sauvignon, 2005
The maturing nose shows a mix of red fruit elements and savory influences with hints of tarragon. Sweet and ripe on the palate, the black cherry and blackcurrant fruits are nicely restrained by a faint herbal influence. Possibly the fruits are beginning to dry out as a slightly bitter note reveals itself on the finish, perhaps pushed by the alcohol. Yet the overall impression is quite fresh compared with 2004 and 2003. 14.5% *90* Drink to 2018.

Cabernet Sauvignon, 2003
One bottle was slightly corked, but a second was much better, although showing a faint touch of oxidation (due to the cork). The faint but savory nose shows sous bois in the background. The palate has lovely ripe black fruits, oxidation is much less evident than it was on the nose, and lively acidity is keeping the wine fresh. The way the oxidation problem resolved itself in the glass suggests that this wine may in fact have the resilience to have a very good future when in top condition. 14.0% *89* Drink to 2017.

Andrea Reserve Cabernet-Merlot, 2008
Spicy, herbal, cereal notes on the nose. Very fruity on the palate and glyceriny on the finish; this is all about red and black cherries and strawberries. The sweetness of the finish pushes the structure into the background. A nice wine, but somewhat obvious, and more evidently New World than the varietal Cabernet Sauvignon, this feels more like a Merlot-dominated wine than the reverse. 13.5% *87* Drink to 2016.

Andrea Reserve Cabernet-Merlot, 2007
This wine really reflects the hot vintage, with a pungent whiff of development, calming down in the glass. Bright acidity supports ripe, round, fruits, very warm and nutty in a distinctly Merlotish style, cut by that touch of sous bois on the finish. There's some alcohol-derived sweetness on the finish. Once again, in spite of the proportions this seems more like a Merlot-dominated blend in its stylistic spectrum. 14.0% *86* Drink to 2015.

Andrea Reserve Cabernet-Merlot, 2005
More overt red fruit expression here, pointing to strawberries and going slightly nutty in the

glass. This is the lightest and most elegant of the Cabernet-Merlot vintages. Earthy strawberries on the finish are quite glyceriny, but there are clearer intimations of structure in the background than shown by more recent vintages. Tannins are not directly evident but do dry the finish. 14.5% *87* Drink to 2015.

Vasse Felix

The first commercial winery in Margaret River, Vasse Felix was founded by Perth cardiologist Tom Cullity in 1967, starting with 8 acres (at a cost of $75 per acre). In 1984, Vasse Felix was sold to its vineyard manager, David Gregg, who in turn sold it to the Holmes à Court family in 1987. Bruce Pearse, a viticulturalist whose family vineyard was also sold to Holmes à Court, came to Vasse Felix and recollects that, "When the Holmes à Court family bought Vasse Felix, we were included with the art gallery and collectibles. It was moved into the farm section with Directors who talked about grape trees. Around 2001 it became its own entity." Production expanded from 10,000 to 150,000 cases, but has cut back a bit now. Today Vasse Felix owns vineyards in Wilyabrup, Karridale, and Carbunup, and purchases fruit from Yallingup. There's a wide range of wines from entry-level to the Heytesbury barrel selection. The Cabernet-Merlot blend mostly comes from the Carbunup vineyard. The varietal Cabernet Sauvignon comes mostly from Wilyabrup (where the winery is located), with a smaller component from Yallingup, and always contains a little (up to 10%) Malbec; sometimes there are smaller quantities of the other Bordeaux varieties. Heytesbury is the top wine, consisting of a barrel selection of around three quarters Cabernet Sauvignon, with the rest made up of Petit Verdot and Malbec, in that order. The varietal Cabernet and Heytesbury are both sturdy wines needing time to develop, especially Heytesbury, and I'm impressed that it's possible in the New World to make a wine so clearly intended for aging against a trend to demand that everything is instantly drinkable. Wines were tasted at Vasse Felix in October 2012.

Cabernet-Merlot, 2010
Nose shows some pungent aromatics with hints of tertiary aromas. Ripe fruits are soft and succulent on palate, with furry tannins in the background, and those tertiary notes extending almost to sous bois on the finish. This gives a surprisingly developed impression for such a young vintage. 14.5% *89* Drink to 2019.

Cabernet Sauvignon, 2010
Closed nose with some hints of cereal, slowly releasing vanillin and nuts to show the influence of new oak. The sense of reserve carries through the black fruits on the palate, with the fruits remaining subservient to the new oak and tannins. Slowly a faint piquancy brings some variety to the fruit flavors. Firm tannins dry the finish, and this needs time both to resolve the tannins and to let flavor variety develop. 14.6% *91* Drink 2014-2026.

Cabernet Sauvignon, 2009
Fresh nose makes a somewhat mineral impression. Ripe but reserved black fruits show on the palate. Some classic, almost piquant, blackcurrants come out on the palate with flavor variety beginning to develop. There's a spectrum of strong black fruits with impressions of herbs, and tannins drying the finish. This will evolve to an elegant style with nicely defined fruits and firm tannins. 14.8% *91* Drink 2013-2023.

Cabernet Sauvignon, 2008
Fresh nose with mineral hints leads into savory overtones with a fugitive touch of bell peppers. Warm, ripe, fruits show on the palate, with those savory notes coming back on the finish. This is a classic representation of the black fruits of Cabernet in an elegant style where the fruitiness is just cut by that faint note of herbaceousness. Of course, this is still young, but already it is beginning to develop that delicious counterbalance of savory to fruity against the background of Vasse Felix's characteristically elegant style. 14.4% *92* Drink to 2024.

Cabernet Sauvignon, 1978
The restrained nose shows hints of black fruits with a faint suspicion of pyrazines. Perhaps just

a touch of oxidation has now developed on the lovely palate of ripe black fruits (no doubt the fault of the inferior corks available at the time). The overall impression is dark and black, faintly herbaceous, with age bringing complexity, but not yet any savory development. The faintly herbaceous touch on the finish brings a lovely contrast to the ripe fruits of the palate. All of the elements you see here are classic for Cabernet Sauvignon, but would not be likely to be combined in quite this way in a European wine. 12.6% *90* Drink to 2017.

Heytesbury, 2010
(Not yet released.) Closed on the nose and tight on the palate. Fruits are really holding back; blackcurrants are in the background, with smooth, silky, tannins driving the finish. Very slowly more aromatic impressions come out retronasally, suggesting that behind the tight tannins and new oak, there are black fruits waiting to emerge—but they're going to be in attendance for several years. Too monolithic to drink now, but I expect this to become round and complex, yet always to show its backbone, perhaps following the tradition of Pauillac. 14.5% *91* Drink 2016-2028.

Heytesbury, 2009
Fresh nose with restrained impression of black fruits. Rather closed at the moment, with the succulence of the fruits hidden by the tannins. Deep and black with a faint hint of menthol. Big tannins on the finish, but more to the point, the fruits need to emerge and develop flavor variety. Hints of vanillin and nuts on the aftertaste show the new oak, which is about to integrate. Wait at least another couple of years before starting, but to get the full potential, wait several years. 14.1% *92* Drink 2015-2029.

Heytesbury, 2008
Faintly herbal impressions of tea and sage on the nose show this vintage is starting to come off its primary fruit spectrum. It's sweet, round, and black on the palate, with a faint whiff of herbaceousness bringing a classic impression to the finish. The texture is very fine and gravelly, the aftertaste is long, and as soon as the tannins resolve a little more, the full range of fruits and savory flavor variety should become apparent. A very fine effort, on the verge of coming out. 14.5% *92* Drink 2014-2028.

Voyager

Just south of the town of Margaret River, Voyager has a 300 ha estate with 108 ha of vineyards, including 25 ha each of Cabernet Sauvignon and Chardonnay. There is both a Cabernet-Merlot blend and a varietal Cabernet Sauvignon. Historically the blend used to have about 70% Cabernet Sauvignon, but since 2008 it has had more than 85% (and therefore could now be given a varietal label), usually with 6-14% Merlot and 1-2% Petit Verdot. It comes each year from the three core vineyard blocks. Made in very small quantities, only about 100 cases each, two varietal Cabernet Sauvignons represent different blocks: the 5 ha North Block planted in 1995 and the 2 ha Old Block planted in 1978. A third, Tom Price, is a blend between the two blocks. All three use about 50% new oak. Wines were tasted at Voyager in October 2012.

North Block Cabernet Sauvignon, 2010
Restrained nose offers impressions of chocolaty black fruits. Sweet, ripe, fruits are supported on the palate by fine, taut, tannins. This has the finest and most precisely delineated impression of the single vineyard bottlings, with a nice sweetness on the finish. *90* Drink 2014-2024.

Old Block Cabernet Sauvignon, 2010
This is a touch more aromatic on the nose and denser on the palate than the North Block. Firm tannins are almost subsumed by the fruits. A chocolaty impression develops on the finish. This is broader than North Block, but less refined. *90* Drink 2014-2024.

Tom Price Cabernet Sauvignon, 2010
Denser and more chocolaty than either of the single vineyards alone, with a rounder, deeply textured, impression on the palate. Very slowly a touch of herbaceousness develops to add complexity in the glass. Overall, there's more flavor variety than in the individual wines from these vineyards, and also an impression of potentially greater longevity. A very fine effort. *91* Drink 2014-2025.

Cabernet-Merlot, 2010
Fresh impression followed by sweet, ripe, aromatics, with a touch of piquant blackcurrants. Precisely delineated black fruits lead into a taut finish with some heat. With a nicely rounded balance, this makes the finest impression of the past three vintages. *90* Drink to 2021.

Cabernet-Merlot, 2009
Contradictory impressions here at first between the softness of the black fruits and the tightness of the palate. Smooth and elegant, with fine tannins bringing a little asperity and dryness to the finish. A touch of chocolate develops, but it's still quite tight on the finish. Perhaps another year will see this become more generous. *89* Drink 2013-2021.

Cabernet-Merlot, 2008
This vintage is quite restrained, with first impressions of herbal blackcurrants, then softer on the palate than the nose suggests. There's a flatter fruit profile, especially on the mid palate, compared with 2009 or 2010. Sturdy tannins aren't really obvious on the finish. Somehow the fruit profile is just a bit lacking compared with the subsequent vintages. *88* Drink to 2020.

Cabernet-Merlot, 2005
There's a curious mix of richness on the palate cut by herbaceousness to give a ripe vegetal impression. The fruits seem ripe, yet show some pyrazine flavors, turning more towards coffee in the glass. Perhaps the Merlot was much riper than the Cabernet. This wine has a hard time deciding on its identity. 14.0% *87* Drink to 2016.

Woodlands

Established in 1973 in Wilyabrup by David and Heather Watson, Woodlands was one of the first five wineries in Margaret River. Wine production was halted between 1992 and 1999, when grapes were sold off, but after it resumed Stuart Watson took over as winemaker in 2002, joined by Andrew Watson in 2005. They expanded in 2007 by purchasing the nearby Woodlands Brook vineyard. Total production is now 9,000 cases; only 20% is white (as seen in the Chloe Chardonnay). "We are red-centric here," says Andrew Watson. The Cabernet Franc-Merlot blend comes from the Woodlands Brook vineyard, Margaret is a Cabernet Sauvignon-Merlot blend also including some Malbec, and the Cabernet Sauvignon changes its name every year, that is, it has been variously named Rachel, Heather Jean etc. It seems confusing, but aficionados know the name indicates the top wine. There's an effort here to produce wine in a moderate style. "We pick early, but we're not the leading example. We don't necessarily want to accentuate fruit in our wines—our wines have enough fruit anyway. Ours will be 13.5%, but unfortunately others will be 14% or more," says Andrew Watson. Wines were tasted at Woodlands in October 2012.

Margaret Reserve Cabernet-Merlot, 2011
A perfumed nose leads into dark fruits on the palate, with lively acidity bringing elegance. One dimensional youthfulness dominates at the moment, but there's a silky impression to the smooth palate, and this should begin to broaden out in a couple of years. *88* Drink 2014-2022.

Margaret Reserve Cabernet-Merlot, 2010
This wine is a blend of two thirds Cabernet Sauvignon with equal smaller amounts of Merlot and Malbec. The wine seems curiously fresh on the nose compared with the pure Cabernet but has a similar sense of well delineated black fruits; the smoothness of the Malbec is more in evidence than the fleshiness of Merlot. Perhaps this does need a bit more presence on the mid palate as it is less generous and more linear than the Heather Jean. 13.5% *88* Drink to 2019.

Heather Jean Cabernet Sauvignon, 2010
(Not yet released.) 1,000 cases were produced of this wine, matured in 100% new oak. There's a touch of mint and herbs on top of taut black fruits, which give a more distinct impression of varietal purity than the Cabernet-Merlot blend. A lean touch cuts the ripe fruit impression on the finish. There's good fruit concentration, balanced acidity, and nicely balanced alcohol, giving a smooth and refined, yet generous, impression, with tobacco and vanillin coming back on the finish. This is promising, but needs time for the new oak to integrate. *90* Drink 2013-2022.

Alma May Cabernet Sauvignon, 2009
Initially closed, opening out slowly to show herbal impressions of black tea. Smooth in the typical style of the house, not as full an impression on the palate as 2010, with tannins flattening the finish. 14.5% *88* Drink to 2022.

Wilyabrup Cabernet-Merlot, 2005
There's an austere impression on the nose with black fruits showing a herbal impression and a touch of herbaceousness; this suggests a European aesthetic except for the more evident richness of the palate. Although herbaceous notes strengthen on the finish, they are held in a subtle balance with the superficial richness of the fruits, and that impression of subtlety strengthens in the glass. 13.5% *89* Drink to 2020.

Rachel Cabernet Sauvignon, 2004
Two bottles at first seemed quite different, and then after being opened for an hour converged in aroma and flavor.
Under screwcap: Translucent appearance, garnet in color, with some orange at the rim. An intensely pyrazined nose, yet showing an underlying expression of ripe fruits. The classic old style impression of Cabernet Sauvignon on the nose is countered by the evident ripeness of the palate. You might say that the nose was Bordelais but the palate shows New World richness. An intriguing wine, making a fine impression.
Under cork: Initially only a slight impression of herbaceousness on the nose, showing also on the palate but not nearly as intensely as the wine under screwcap. The touch of herbaceousness blends more naturally into the black fruits that are evident on the palate. Fruits seem more generous, with pyrazines coming out more slowly on the finish. After an hour, the two wines tasted quite similar. *91* Drink to 2025.

Margaret Reserve Cabernet-Merlot, 2001
Mature nose conveys a ripe impression with blueberry aromatics emerging in the glass. Some over-ripe notes, not quite balanced by the structure, give a slightly rustic impression. There's some bite to the finish, where the tannins are pushed by the alcohol. 14.5% *88* Drink to 2017.

Colin Cabernet Sauvignon, 1985
This was the first wine at Woodlands that went into new oak (for two years). The nose conveys an impression of elegance with a slight touch of herbaceousness. The palate has fine black fruits with smooth, elegant, tannins, and a classic touch of pyrazine on the finish, making a pure, but relatively austere impression. There's no savory development yet, but the wine is holding up very well for its age and should develop for many years yet. 12.0% *90* Drink to 2020.

Xanadu

The Cabernet Sauvignon is a classic Bordeaux blend, with Cabernet Sauvignon usually just over 85%, and the other varieties always including Petit Verdot, with the levels of Malbec, Merlot, and Cabernet Franc varying according to the vintage. Usually around half of the grapes come from the home estate in Wallcliffe (accounting for the slightly severe character of the wine), with the rest coming from vineyards in Wilyabrup and Yallingup. Production is usually about 4,000 cases. The special cuvée was introduced under the name of Limited Release in 2007, changed to Reserve from 2008. It is a barrel selection based on a blend of around 90% Cabernet Sauvignon with 10% Petit Verdot. Only around 100 cases are produced. Sources have alternated between Wilyabrup (96% in 2010, 100% in 2009 from the Timber Lake vineyard, and 65% in 2007) and Wallcliffe (85% in 2008). In addition, 100 cases of a 100% Cabernet Sauvignon single vineyard wine are produced from the Stevens Road vineyard, near the winery in Wallcliffe. However, "the Reserve should be the best wine we can produce in any year," says winemaker Glen Goodall, and it usually prices above the single vineyard wine. Personally, however, I saw more fruit concentration and structure in the Stevens Road than in the Reserve in both 2010 and 2009. Wines were tasted at Xanadu in October 2012.

Cabernet Sauvignon, 2010
Chocolaty black fruit nose with savory impressions of sage. Crisp acidity highlights tight lines of fruit, rather closed at the moment, with a hot finish. Fruits are faintly herbal, with overtones of tobacco hidden by the acidity. This should begin to release its flavors in another year. 14.0% *88* Drink 2013-2021.

Cabernet Sauvignon, 2009
Fresh nose with hints of black fruits turns towards herbal in the glass. Crisp acidity emphasizes the tightness of the fruits. There's a tightly coiled, somewhat linear, impression on the palate. Tannins are light and quite refined. Acidity is standing a bit in the way of the fruits: when will this wine release its flavors? 14.0% *87* Drink 2014-2024.

Cabernet Sauvignon, 2008
Mélange of red and black fruits shows on nose. Crisp acidity supports tight, linear, fruits. Although there is almost 10% Merlot, the wine shows the taut style of pure Cabernet Sauvignon, but the fruits do soften and open out just a little in the glass. Although the reputation of the vintages is the reverse, the 2008 seems overall a little more generous than the 2007, with more flavor variety developing. 14.3% *89* Drink to 2021.

Reserve Cabernet Sauvignon, 2010
Herbs on the nose show bay leaf and sage with a touch of tar. Ripe and sweet on the palate, pure black and spicy, more complete than the regular bottling, with deep blackcurrants showing on the finish. This is relatively open for a young vintage at Xanadu, although still well structured. 14.0% *91* Drink to 2022.

Reserve Cabernet Sauvignon, 2009
Cabernet nose of black fruits with hints of blackcurrant aromatics reverting more to tarry overtones in the glass. Tighter on the palate than 2010, less approachable with more evident structure. This seems to be on the verge of releasing its fruit flavors, and a little glycerinic softness shows in the glass. Nicely balanced with overall a ripe impression. 14.6% *91* Drink to 2021.

Reserve Cabernet Sauvignon, 2008
Tight, restrained, nose with just some intimations of black fruits. Taut impression of tight black fruits on the palate. The classic austerity reflects the origins of the grapes in Wallcliffe (mostly from the Stevens Road vineyard). Beginning to open out just a little in the glass, this should release good flavor variety in an elegant style over the next few years. 14.5% *89* Drink to 2023.

Limited Release Cabernet Sauvignon, 2007
The nose is beginning to open out to show ripe black fruits with a fugitive whiff of more savory or tertiary aromas. This still shows the typically tight style of young wine from Xanadu, with tobacco-like tannins drying the finish, where acidity is just a touch evident. With structure showing ahead of the fruits, this is not really ready yet. 14.0% *89* Drink 2013-2024.

Stevens Road Cabernet Sauvignon, 2010
This is more restrained in style than the Stevens Road 2009, making a more classic representation of Cabernet Sauvignon. Tight black fruits are supported by a taut tannic structure with overtones of cedar and tobacco showing on the finish. The fruit concentration carries this past the youthful tightness and I expect a long flavor variety to develop across the palate as this opens up over the next few years. 13.7% *92* Drink 2014-2027.

Stevens Road Cabernet Sauvignon, 2009
The tight nose offers only a fugitive whiff of tobacco and cedar. This is a rich, deep, wine, with hints of glycerin bringing opulence to the finish, in fact making a riper impression than the Reserve. This is more overtly fruity than the Stevens Road 2010, but is also very well structured. This should become a generous wine as it matures. 13.7% *91* Drink 2013-2025.

New Zealand

The wines were independently selected to represent Gimblett Gravels in promotions during 2011. They come from the 2009 vintage, which is regarded locally as one of the best. Some older vintages and Merlot-dominated blends are also included to indicate the range of the region. Wines were tasted in November 2012 except where otherwise noted.

Babich Wines, The Patriarch, Hawkes Bay, 2009
A perfumed nose with the classic tobacco notes of Cabernet Franc makes the first impression. Smooth and refined on the palate, with those perfumed notes of the nose coming back on the finish. Structure comes from Cabernet Sauvignon, perfume and freshness from Cabernet Franc, and refinement from Malbec. There's an argument here for believing that Bordeaux lost something when the left bank abandoned Malbec for Merlot. Tannic support is fine-grained but unobtrusive in the background; the sense of dryness on the finish should soften over the next year. A very fine effort for enjoying over the next decade as it matures in an elegant style. The closest parallel in Bordeaux might be Margaux. 13.5% *88* Drink to 2018.

Mills Reef Winery, Elspeth Cabernet Sauvignon, Gimblett Gravels, 2009
It's hard to pin down the conflicting notes of the nose—savory, perfumed, floral—there seems to be a lot going on here. The palate has ripe black fruits reprising the elements of the nose, and leading into a finish with an impression of sweetness from the rich fruits. My concern here is that relatively low acidity will allow some over-ripe elements in the fruits to become cloying as the wine develops. 13.5% *86* Drink to 2018.

Mission Estate Winery, Jewelstone Cabernet-Merlot, Hawkes Bay, 2009
Rich chocolaty nose with some suggestions of raisins raising the question of over-ripeness. Palate is rich, round, and ripe, but not in fact over-ripe, although on the verge. Tannins are ripe and supple, this feels like quite a Merlot-ish wine, quasi-competitive with the right bank rather than the left bank, with a glyceriny finish. This gives the impression of representing a warmer climate than the other wines in the tasting. 14.4% *88* Drink to 2020.

Newton Forrest, Cornerstone, Hawkes Bay, 2009
There's no Cabernet Franc in this wine but there's a rather Franc-ish impression of tobacco on the nose. The palate is smooth and refined, a glyceriny impression to the palate hiding a touch of youthful tannic bitterness on the finish, where there's a savory impression, almost sage-like. There's just a touch of hardness off-setting the fruits in a manner reminiscent of St. Estèphe. This can be enjoyed now, but will be better given another year. Comparison with the 2006 suggests it may become elegant as it softens. 14.2% *87* Drink to 2020.

Sacred Hill Wines, Helmsman, Hawkes Bay, 2009
Black fruits seem to be competing with more acrid notes on the nose, but the palate is quite smooth, although taut. The fruits are tight with youth, but there is good concentration here. The tannins are firm but quite fine, and in another couple of years this should all come together to release the fruits in an elegant framework with some potential for aging. This is very much a Cabernet wine, with the structure of Sauvignon and the refinement of Franc. 14.0% *88* Drink 2015-2022.

Te Awa Farm Winery, Cabernet-Merlot, Hawkes Bay, 2009
Restrained black fruit impression, smooth on the palate, firm, sturdy tannins holding back the fruits, and the structural support just showing in a very faint touch of bitterness on the finish. There's a slightly sharp impression to the acidity, but this keeps the fruits lively on the palate. Slowly the structure pushes the fruits more into the background, indicating that this really needs another year. Tight now but should become better rounded over the next year. 13.5% *87* Drink 2013-2020.

Trinity Hill, The Gimblett, Hawkes Bay, 2009
Quite a fruity nose, definitely dominated by black fruits, turning more clearly to blackcurrants on the palate, but with quite a tannic rasp to the finish. The combination of fresh acidity and tannic structure certainly places this in a cool climate, although there's a distinct touch of heat on the finish. The overall impression just lacks a little refinement, with some slightly rough edges to the rustic tannins, and the strength of the structure suggests more Cabernet Sauvignon than is in fact the case. Those edges should smooth down with another year in the bottle and the wine should then drink well in a sturdy style for a few years. 14.0% *86* Drink 2013-2019.

Vidal, Reserve Series Cabernet Merlot, Gimblett Gravels, 2009
Black fruit impressions more of cherries than blackcurrants, a little monotonic in its flavor impression, somehow just a bit flat on the palate, although some hints of blackcurrants emerge on the finish. Tannins are ripe and supple; in fact, this would perhaps benefit from a little more evident structural support and brighter acidity. However, it's a well made wine that should drink well in the immediate future. 13.5% *86* Drink to 2018.

Villa Maria, Private Bin Merlot Cabernet Sauvignon, Hawkes Bay, 2009
An initial impression of smooth black fruits with hints of black cherries follows through to the palate, but there's a touch of acidity evident and the fruits don't seem to have a lot of depth.

You don't get much impression of the fleshiness of Merlot. It's a nice enough entry-level wine (matured in old oak), more delicate than a typical New World, but somewhat lacking character. (May 2012) 13.5% *86* Drink to 2015.

Villa Maria, Cabernet Sauvignon Merlot Reserve, Gimblett Gravels, 2009
Black fruit impression with hints of cherries leads into a touch of piquant aromatics with some earthiness developing in the glass. Somewhat reserved in an elegant style, this is fresh and smooth on the palate. But there isn't a great deal of flavor variety; it's a bit one dimensional and flat on the finish. Although perfectly ripe with no herbaceousness, it's rather light for Cabernet Sauvignon and it's not evident that it has the structure to support longevity. (May 2012) 13.5% *87* Drink to 2017.

Villa Maria, Reserve Cabernet Sauvignon-Merlot, Hawkes Bay, 2007
Black fruit nose with very faint suggestions of some savory development. Sweet and ripe on the palate, with some raisiny elements verging on over-ripe, but cut by the bitterness of the tannins on the finish. Palate impressions vary from fruit to nuts. This seems just a touch out of balance. 14.5% *86* Drink to 2015.

Newton Forrest, Cornerstone, Hawkes Bay, 2006
Restrained nose of black fruits with some spices in the background turning to savory herbal notes of sage and tarragon. Nicely developing impression on the palate of black cherry fruits, tobacco spices and herbs, still cut by the dry finish from the tannic structure. The structure of the Cabernet Sauvignon and refinement of the Malbec show more evidently than the fleshiness of the Merlot at the present, but this is a very nicely balanced wine, maturing in classic fashion. 14.0% *88* Drink to 2019.

Gimblett Gravels, Sophia, Craggy Range Winery, 2008
One of the top wines from Craggy Range, this is a Merlot (60%-90%)-driven blend, with Cabernet Franc usually as the second variety. There's an immediate cool climate impression, with fruits of blackcurrants showing crisp overtones. Nuts and vanillin from new oak gives way to more savory impressions of tarragon and thyme; a mixture of herbs and spices gives an impression that is more European than New World, turning towards tobacco in the glass. The high alcohol is not immediately obvious; although the palate is rich, it is not lush or overbearing. Good acidity outlines the herbal overtones of the fruits. The only giveaway for the high level of extraction is that a certain fatigue begins to settle in halfway through the bottle. It's an interesting demonstration of the ability of Merlot to produce structure in this climate, and therefore an interesting contrast with Cabernet Sauvignon. 14.5% (August 2012) *90* Drink to 2022.

Gimblett Gravels, Sophia, Craggy Range Winery, 2005
Distinctive nose is spicy and nutty. Full and fruity on the palate, but with a fairly stern reserve from the structure of ripe tannins. Less forthcoming than the 2008 vintage, this hasn't really rounded out yet. Although this is Merlot based, it seems to have more structure than many of the Cabernet-based blends of Gimblett Gravels. The issue here is simply if and when the structure will resolve enough to let the fruits show through; this may turn out to be a long lived wine for those who have the patience to sit it out. 14.1% *89* Drink to 2022.

Gimblett Gravels, Quarry Cabernet Sauvignon, Craggy Range, 2001
Deep purple color with black hues. Slightly gamey nose with animal overtones seems more European than New World. Some violets develop in the glass. The flavor profile is a little flatter than you would expect from the nose (perhaps the wine could use some Merlot) Good acidity supports austere black fruits, which are slightly spicy but a little monotonic. A touch bitter on the back palate. 14.0% (March 2011) *88* Drink to 2019.

Bibliography

Gerard Aubin, Sandrine Lavaud, and Philip Roudié, *Bordeaux, Vignoble Millénaire* (L'Horizon Chimérique, Bordeaux, 1996).

Eric Bernardin & Pierre Le Hong, *Crus Classés du Médoc* (Editions Sud Ouest, Bordeaux, 2010).

Stephen Brook, *The Complete Bordeaux* (2nd edition, Mitchell Beazley, London, 2012).

Charles Cocks & Édouard Féret. *Bordeaux Et Ses Vins Classés Par Ordre De Mérite* (Editions Féret, Bordeaux, 1868, 1908, 1929, 1949, 1969, 1982, 2001, 2004, 2007).

Roger Dion, *La Création du Vignoble Bordelais* (Editions de l'Ouest, Angers, 1952).

Roger Dion, *Histoire de la Vigne et du Vin en France. Des Origines aux XIX Siècle* (Imprimerie Cevin et cie, Paris, 1959).

William Franck, *Traité Sur Les Vins Du Médoc Et Les Autres Vins Rouges Et Blancs Du Département De La Gironde* (Chaumas, Bordeaux, 1864).

Paul Gregutt, *Washington Wines and Wineries, 2nd edition* (University of California Press, Berkeley, 2010).

Germain Lafforgue, *Le Vignoble Girondin* (Louis Larmat, Paris, 1947).

James T. Lapsley, *Bottled Poetry: Napa Winemaking from Prohibition to the Modern Era* (University of California Press, Berkeley, 1997).

Sandrine Lavaud, *Bordeaux Et Le Vin Au Moyen Age* (Editions Sud Ouest, Bordeaux, 2003).

Benjamin Lewin, *What Price Bordeaux?* (Vendange Press, Dover, 2009).

Benjamin Lewin, *Wine Myths and Reality* (Vendange Press, Dover, 2010).

Dewey Markham, *A History of the Bordeaux Classification* (John Wiley & Sons, New York, 1997).

Edmund Penning-Rowsell, *The Wines of Bordeaux* (Wine Appreciation Guild, San Francisco, 1985, 1989).

David Peppercorn, *Bordeaux,* (Faber & Faber, London, 1982, 1991).

Peter Richards, *The Wines of Chile* (Mitchell Beazley, London, 2006).

René Pijassou, *Le Médoc: Un Grand Vignoble De Qualité: Tomes I & II* (Tallandier, Paris, 1978).

Philippe Roudié, *Vignobles et Vignerons du Bordelais 1850-1980, 2nd edition* (Presses Universitaires, Bordeaux, 1994).

Charles L. Sullivan, *Napa wine: a history from mission days to present* (Wine Appreciation Guild, San Francisco, 1995).

Charles L. Sullivan, *A Companion to California Wine: An Encyclopedia of Wine and Winemaking from the Mission Period to the Present* (University of California Press, Berkeley, 1998).

Jonathan Swinchatt & David G. Howell, *The Winemaker's Dance. Exploring Terroir in the Napa Valley* (University of California Press, Berkeley, 2004).

Marie-José Thiney, *Fascinant Médoc* (Editions Sud Ouest, Bordeaux, 2003).

Larry Walker, *The Wines of the Napa Valley* (Mitchell Beazley, London, 2005).

Notes

Chapter 1: Incestuous Relationships

[1] Established by DNA mapping (John Bowers & Carole Meredith, *The parentage of a classic wine grape, Cabernet Sauvignon,* Nature Genetics, 16, 84, 1997).

[2] Jacques Peuchet, *Statistique générale et particulière de la France et de ses colonies,* F. Buisson, Lyon, 1803, p. 389.

[3] It was named after its rediscovery in an abandoned vineyard in Charente (north of Bordeaux).

[4] A few châteaux have tiny amounts, less than 1% (Brane Cantenac, Clerc Milon, de Fonbel).

[5] Txakoli is more commonly used as the name of a lightly sparkling white wine made in the region (largely from a variety called Hondarribi Zuria).

[6] J.-M. Boursiquot et al., *Parentage of Merlot and related winegrape cultivars of southwestern France: discovery of the missing link* (Australian J. Grape and Wine Research, 15, 144-155, 2008).

[7] The archives of the *Real Chancillería* of Valladolid (in Rioja) in 1520 mention the purchase of three and a half casks of chacolín. The Archives of Arespalditza in the town of Ayala (in the province of Álava, Spain) refer to chacolín in November 1, 1623 (Juanjo Hidalgo, Accessed August 10, 2011: http://revuesshs.u-bourgogne.fr/territoiresduvin/document.php?id=811 ISSN 1760-5296).

[8] Boursiquot et al., *Parentage of Merlot,* op cit.

[9] Louis Bordenave, *Origine Historique et génétique des cépages Bordelais* (L'Union Girondine 1060, 44-49, Bordeaux, 2009).

[10] Comte Odart, *Ampélographie universelle ou Traité des cépages les plus estimés dans tous les vignobles de quelque renom, 6th edition* (Tours, 1824), p. 118.

[11] The variety was identified as Bidure, the traditional variety of Bordeaux from the Middle Ages (Jean Barennes, *Viticulture et vinification en Bordelais au moyen-age,* Marcel Mounestre-Picamilh, Bordeaux, 1912, p. 60; Germain Lafforgue, *Le Vignoble Girondin,* p. 156).

[12] Guy Lavignac, *Les cépages du sud-ouest, 2000 ans d'histoire* (Editions du Rouergue, Arles, 2001), p. 24.

[13] France includes 26,790 ha in Bordeaux and 18,722 ha in the Languedoc; the United States includes 31,417 ha in California.

[14] Penning-Rowsell, *The Wines of Bordeaux,* p. 192.

[15] Contrary to press reports that these are ungrafted vines, they are in fact grafted, following the first wave of replanting after phylloxera.

[16] Jane Anson, *Cabernet Sauvignon,* Wine Business International, April 2008.

[17] Statistics are often somewhat out of date and reliability varies by country, but best estimates (in hectares) from figures available in 2011 are:

Country	Cabernet	Merlot
France	56,386	115,746
Chile	40,727	10,040
United States	36,595	23,964
Australia	25,967	10,028
China	20,675	2,386
Spain	19,430	13,325
Argentina	17,738	6,985
Bulgaria	16,600	15, 200
South Africa	12,469	6,588
Romania	12,000	6,700
Moldova	9,360	10,530
Italy	7,682	21,898
New Zealand	516	1,363
Portugal	317	
Austria	312	112
Germany	253	370
Canada	140	320
Greece		183
Switzerland		876
Total	274,696	244, 194

Principal data sources: ONIVINS (Les Principaux Cépages De Cuve / Départements Principaux : Blancs, Noirs); California Department of Food and Agriculture, Sacramento (California Grape Acreage Reports); Australian Bureau of Statistics (Annual Reports 1329.0); Argentine Instituto Nacional de Vitivinicultura (Registro de Vinedos y Superficie), Catastro Viticola Nacional, Chile; SAWIS-Statistics of Wine Grapes; Superficie De Viñedos En España Por Variedades, Observatorio Español Del Mercado Del Vino, 2007; Walker & Ragg, *Tong,* 10, 39, 2011.

[18] Jane Anson, *Cabernet Sauvignon,* Wine Business International, April 2008.

[19] As a very rough measure, average growing season temperatures in the past twenty years have been: Bordeaux, 17.6 °C; Napa, 18.5 °C; Aconcagua (Chile), 18.2 °C; Mendoza (Argentina), 21.8 °C; Montpellier (Provence/Languedoc), 19.8 °C.

[20] Average temperature for growing season of seven months, based on weather station reports from NASA Goddard Institute and Australia Bureau of Meteorology.

[21] Although the 2010 and 2011 vintages reversed the trend dramatically.

[22] Temperature data for Napa and for Merignac from the NASA Goddard Weather Center. Preferred range for Cabernet Sauvignon taken from Gregory Jones, *Climate and Terroir: impacts of cli-*

mate variability and change on wine, in *fine wine and terroir - the geoscience perspective,* Macqueen, R.W., and Meinert, L.D., (eds.), Geoscience Canada Reprint Series Number 9, Geological Association of Canada, St. John's, Newfoundland, 2006.)

[23] IBMP levels were measured in Cabernet Sauvignon grown in Tarragona by Christina Sala et al., *Contents of 3-alkyl-2-methoxypyrazines in musts and wines from Vitis vinifera variety Cabernet Sauvignon: influence of irrigation and plantation density* (J. Science Food Agric., 85, 1131-1136, 2005).

[24] The detection threshold is 2 ppm; levels in Sauvignon Blanc vary from 2 ppm to 40 ppm (Jan H. Swiegers et al., *Meeting consumer expectations through management in vineyard and winery,* AWRI Report, 2005).

[25] The compounds responsible for black fruit aromas and flavors in Cabernet Sauvignon are not so well defined. Some that have been implicated are DMS, ethyl acetate, mercaptohexanol, but they are also found in other varieties, such as Merlot, Syrah, Grenache. The combination that uniquely differentiates Cabernet Sauvignon has yet to be determined.

[26] When the so-called Dijon clones of Pinot Noir became available for planting in Oregon in the 1990s, quality improved enormously because they ripened two weeks earlier than the clones that had been previously available. (Benjamin Lewin, *In Search of Pinot Noir,* Vendange Press, Dover, 2011, pp. 12-18, 218).

[27] ENTAV, *Catalog des variétés et clones de vigne cultivés en France, 2nd edition* (Viniflhor, Montpellier, 2007), p. 383.

[28] Origins are not exact, but appear to be Bordeaux AOC (#15, #169), St. Emilion (#338, #341), Côtes de Blaye (#337), Loire (#170), and Southwest (#685). Clones in order of popularity in Bordeaux are #169 (27%), #15 (22%), #337 (16%), #685 (11%), #191 (8%), #338 (6%), #341 (5%), #170 (3%) (Christophe Sereno, *Variety Focus: Cabernet Sauvignon,* University of California Davis, 2008).

[29] Château Haut Brion cannot confirm this but point out that they did not commercialize their vines (Turid Alcaras, November 2011); certainly the vines no doubt originated on the left bank some time before the second world war.

[30] Marie-Catherine Dufour, *Huit clones de Cabernet Sauvignon en comparaison* (Service Vigne et Vin, Bordeaux, 2008).

[31] Actual results were measured in tons/acre, with 3.28 for the lowest yielding clone and 6.90 for the highest. For red wine, 1 ton/acre corresponds approximately to 13 hl/ha. For full results of the trial, see Anthony Bell, *The Story of Clone 6 and Bell Wine Cellars,* www.bellwine.com.

[32] Louis Liger, *La Nouvelle Maison Rustique,* Tome 2, 3rd ed., Claude Prudhomme, Paris, 1721, p. 407.

[33] The difference in production, compared with planted hectares (see footnote 17), is that much of the Cabernet Sauvignon in Bordeaux goes into blends in which it is only a minor component, and very little of the Cabernet Sauvignon planted in Spain makes varietal-dominated wines. Production in equivalent cases of (pure) Cabernet Sauvignon is:

France	21 million
United States	38 million
Chile	32 million
Australia	18 million
Argentina	11 million
South Africa	8 million
Bulgaria	3 million

Data sources: Argentina - Instituto Nacional de Vitivinicultura, Cosecha y Elboracion, 2010; Australia - Australian Bureau of Statistics, report 1329.0, 2010; Chile - División de Protección Agrícola, Subdepartamento de Viñas y Vinos, Sistema de Declaración de Cosecha Vinos 2011; California Crush Report 2010; France - CIVB annual report; OIV; South African Wine Industry Statistics, 2010.

Chapter 2: European Classicism

[1] Bas-Médoc (or lower Médoc) takes its name from its location closer to the sea; Haut-Médoc (or upper Médoc) reflects its position farther up the river.

[2] Bernardin & Le Hong, *Crus Classés du Médoc,* p. 13.

[3] Narbonne, close to the Pyrenees, was the major source of wine, imported to Bordeaux via Toulouse.

[4] Pijassou, *Le Médoc,* pp. 290-293; Dion, *Histoire de la Vigne,* pp. 121-126.

[5] One of the first mentions of vines in the Bordeaux region was by Pliny, in 71 C.E.

[6] Salut, o ma patrie, célèbre par tes vins, tes fleuves, tes grands hommes, les traditions et le caractère de tes habitants.

[7] Gerard Aubin, *La seigneurie en Bordelais au 18e siècle d'après la pratique notariale, 1715-1789* (Université de Rouen, Rouen, 1989), p. 15.

[8] Guy Lavignac, *Les Cépages du Sud-Ouest, 2000 ans d'histoire* (Editions du Rouergue, Arles, 2001), p. 26.

[9] Dion, *Histoire de la Vigne,* p. 384.

[10] Lavaud, *Bordeaux et le Vin,* p. 171

[11] René Pijassou, *Le Médoc,* p. 308.

[12] Thiney, *Fascinant Médoc,* p. 159.

[13] Dion, *Histoire de la Vigne,* p. 396.

[14] Aubin, *La seigneurie en Bordelais,* op. cit., p. 18.

[15] "Thin and infertile countryside" was a description used in 1416 and repeated in 1524 by the local authorities (Pijassou, *Le Médoc,* p. 314).

[16] Pijassou, *Le Médoc,* p. 304; Thiney, *Fascinant Médoc,* pp. 166-168.

17 Pijassou, *Le Médoc*, p. 477.

18 Paul Massé, *Le dessèchement des marais du Bas-Médoc*. In Revue historique de Bordeaux et du Département de la Gironde (No. 1 pp. 1-44, 1957); Henri Enjalbert, *Les Pays Aquitains*. (Bordeaux: Biere, Bordeaux, Tome I, 1960, p. 171).

19 Biturica was described by Columella (DA 3.2.28) and Pliny (NH 14.27) as robust and high in yield.

20 Aubin et al, *Bordeaux, Vignoble Millénaire*, p. 9.

21 An idea advocated by Auguste Petit-Lafitte, *La Vigne dans le Bordelais* (J. Rothschild, Paris, 1868), pp. 146, 148. He also suggested that Vidure was a contraction of vigne dur, and that Bidure was local patois for Vidure.

22 see Chapter 1.

23 Jean Merlet, *L'abrégé des bons fruits*, 3rd edition, Charles de Sercy, 1690, p. 147. Nothing had changed by 1721 when the same entry was copied word for word into Louis Liger, *La nouvelle maison rustique or economie générale de tous les biens de campagne, 2nd edition* (Claude Prudhomme, Paris, 1721).

24 The black Sauvignon could have been Cabernet Sauvignon, but could also have been Carmenère, which was known as Sauvignon in the Médoc and as Carbenet in the Graves (Franck, *Traité sur les vins du Médoc*, p. 32).

25 Henri-Alexandre Tessier et al., *Encyclopédie méthodique. Agriculture* (Panckoucke, Paris, 1787), pp. 804-805.

26 The varieties planted at the time were: L'Amaroy (or Morillon Noir), equivalent to Pinot Noir; Le Masoutet or Massoutet, a variety of Pinot; Le Tarney, equivalent to Manseng rouge; Le Luquin (or Noir de Pessac), which is Malbec; La Grande Vidure or Carmenet (Cabernet Franc or its ancestor), L'Alicante (related to Grenache). Cabernet Sauvignon may not have been introduced until a major replanting after an oïdium epidemic in 1851-1853 (Turid Alcaras, Château Haut Brion, November 2011).

27 Franck, *Traité sur les vins du Médoc*, p. 32.

28 At Château Latour in 1845, Malbec was included in the list of best varieties, and Merlot was in the list of second-best varieties (Charles Higounet, *La Seigneurie et le Vignoble de Château Latour*, Federation Historique de Sud Ouest, Bordeaux, 1974, p. 395). Malbec was considered best on the right bank (Edouard Féret, *Statistique générale topographique, scientifique, administrative, industrielle, commerciale, agricole, historique, archéologique et biographique du département de la Gironde*, Éditions Féret, Bordeaux, 1874).

29 In 1843 the proprietor of Domaine de Carbonnieux in the Graves listed the major varieties in order of merit as Carmenère, Carmenet-Sauvignon, Verdot, Merlot, and Malbec (Georges Bord, *Essai sur les variations*, p. 8).

30 Armand d'Armailhacq, *De la culture des vignes, de la vinification et des vins dans le Médoc*, Chaumas, Bordeaux, 1867), pp. 37-38.

31 Édouard Féret, *Statistique générale topographique*, op. cit.

32 See Chapter 7.

33 The wine used to be known as the "black wine of Cahors."

34 Lafforgue, *Le Vignoble Girondin*, p. 150.

35 Aubin et al., *Bordeaux, Vignoble Millénaire*, p. 150.

36 For blacks restricted to Cabernet Sauvignon, Cabernet Franc, Merlot, and Malbec, and in addition, the local varieties Fer Servadou and Mérille. The proportion of Cabernet Sauvignon is generally low, more like the right bank than the left bank of Bordeaux. The wines are lighter and less structured than Bordeaux, generally intended for consumption in the first three years after the vintage.

37 "Clairet" remains an official description for wine style in Bordeaux, in addition to red, white, and rosé. AOC Bordeaux Clairet is like a much darker rosé or a very lightly colored red. It may be quite like "claret" of the 18th century. Clairet and rosé together account for about 1% of Bordeaux production, with clairet about one third of this. Specifications for clairet production are at www.inao.gouv.fr; statistics for production are from the CIVB for the 2006 vintage.

38 From 1435 (Aubin et al, *Bordeaux, Vignoble Millénaire*, p. 43.)

39 Aubin et al, *Bordeaux, Vignoble Millénaire*, p. 47.

40 The leading French medieval historian Jean Froissart said, "Wine that is neither red nor white is called clairet" (*Les chroniques de Sire Jean Froissart*, vol. 3, 1389, p. 4). He also drew an interesting distinction in recommending that to sleep better, you should take "spices, clairet, or La Rochelle," presumably referring to clairet wine or wine from La Rochelle (the port to the north of Bordeaux). English translations often substitute claret for clairet, and this might have been an early reference associating it specifically with Bordeaux, but it's not clear that Froissart was referring to the origin of the wine as opposed merely to its color (Œuvres de Froissart, *Poésies*, vol. 2).

41 "New French Claret" accounted for 70% of French wines sold in London during this period. There's some controversy as to whether "New French Claret" actually referred to wines in a new style of higher quality (specifically Haut Brion, Margaux, Lafite, and Latour) or to the most recent vintage (Pijassou, *Le Médoc*, pp. 373, 377-378; Nicholas Faith, *The Winemasters of Bordeaux, 2nd ed*. Prion Books, London, 1999, p. 26).

42 The concept of "grand vins" first developed around 1690; they were distinguished by a higher quality that deserved higher prices relative to other wines. grand vins were first mentioned in

official documents in 1730 (Henri Enjalbert, *La naissance des grands vins et la formation du vignoble moderne de Bordeaux*: 1647-1767, in *Géographie historique des vignobles*, (Ed.) Huetz de Lemps [Paris: Actes du Colloque de Bordeaux, CNRS, 1978. p. 81]. Also see Pijassou, *Le Médoc*, p. 345).

43 The producers were well aware of the need for blending. Lamothe, the régisseur (manager) at Château Latour, noted in 1810 that the vintage was ordinary but the wine was "agreeable and the help from old Hermitage that we propose to give it should compensate for the small deficiency in body" (Quoted by Pijassou, *Le Médoc*, p. 591).

44 During the nineteenth century, Bordeaux shippers purchased vineyards in Hermitage in order to assure their supply, and as much as 80% of the production of Hermitage was shipped to Bordeaux (J. A. Cavoleau, *Oenologie Française, ou statistique de tous les vignobles et de toutes les boissons vineuses et spiriteuses de la France*, Paris, 1827).

45 By the end of the century, there was demand for wines with origins in specific places, especially from English merchants (Pijassou, *Le Médoc*. p. 328).

46 "Châteaux" multiplied quickly. There were about fifty in 1850; in the 1868 edition of Cocks and Féret there were just over 300; by the 1908 edition there were 1600.

47 Lewin, *What Price Bordeaux?*, p. 217.

48 Pijassou, *Le Médoc*, p. 323.

49 Lewin, *In Search of Pinot Noir*, op. cit., pp. 32, 53, 83-86.

50 Aubin et al, *Bordeaux, Vignoble Millénaire*, p. 31.

51 Aubin et al, *Bordeaux, Vignoble Millénaire*, pp. 79-80.

52 Pijassou, *Le Médoc*, p. 371.

53 Pijassou, *Le Médoc*, p. 397.

54 Guildhall Library, *A descriptive catalogue of the London traders, tavern, and coffee-house tokens current in the 17th century* (London: Corporation of the City of London, 1855).

55 Aubin et al, *Bordeaux, Vignoble Millénaire*, p. 81.

56 Aubin, *La seigneurie en Bordelais,* op. cit., p. 275.

57 The seigneuries accounted for about 15% of total wine production, but obtained the highest prices for their wine because their level of investment achieved better quality than could be produced by the bourgeoisie or peasants (Robert Forster, *The noble wine producers of the bordelais in the eighteenth century*, The Economic History Review, New Series, 14, 18-33, 1961, p. 29).

58 One indication of the continuing difference in level of investment, which directly affected quality, is that châteaux on the left bank, led by Latour in the Médoc and by d'Yquem in Sauternes, started to install drainage systems in the early 19th century, but châteaux on the right bank usually did not have resources for this until after 1945 (Lewin, *What Price Bordeaux?*, p. 74).

59 The only area of generic Bordeaux AOC on the left bank is immediately south of Graves.

60 "Claret" probably originated as a description during the English ownership of Bordeaux (1152-1453). It is mentioned in Shakespeare, and became a commonplace description in England for dry red wine from Bordeaux. "Let him be roasted very leisurely and often basted with Claret wine and anchovis" (*The Complete Angler: Or, The Contemplative Man's Recreation*, Izaak Walton, 1653).

61 Lewin, *What Price Bordeaux?*, p. 5.

62 Lewin, *What Price Bordeaux?*, p. 229-252.

63 In addition to the châteaux of the Médoc, the producers of sweet white wines in Sauternes were also classified. Dry white wine did not attract any attention.

64 The châteaux of the Graves were classified in 1953; all the classified châteaux are in the part of the Graves that separated as Pessac-Léognan in 1987. The final classification, as ratified in 1959, lists 13 châteaux for red wine production; 6 of them, plus another 3 châteaux, are classified for white wine production. In 1954 St Emilion classified its leading châteaux on the basis of price, reputation, and terroir. St. Emilion uses the terms Premier Grand Cru Classés (but this has very different significance from the same term used in the Médoc) and Grand Cru Classés. Pomerol has never been classified.

65 The original classification in 1932 divided 447 châteaux into three levels of Cru Bourgeois. An attempt at reclassification in 2003 reduced the overall number to 247, but was overthrown by a court order. A single-level classification of 243 Cru Bourgeois was introduced in 2010 (Lewin, *What Price Bordeaux?*, p. 48).

66 In 1953 varieties were divided into "recommended," "authorized," and "tolerated." Recommended varieties could be freely planted, authorized varieties could be planted only in smaller amounts, and tolerated varieties could not be replaced when vineyards required replanting. Even so there was a tendency to concentrate on plantings that would rapidly give high yields; when the regulations were further strengthened in 1964, almost 20% of plantings still consisted of old varieties rather than those being encouraged by the authorities (Roudié, *Vignobles et vignerons du Bordelais* p. 329).

67 Lafforgue, *Le Vignoble Girondin*; Philippe Roudié, *Vignobles et vignerons du Bordelais*, p. 349; CIVB.

68 INAO lists Cabernet Sauvignon, Cabernet Franc, Merlot, Malbec, Carmenère, and Petit Verdot as the only permitted black varieties. Sémillon, Sauvignon Blanc, Sauvignon Gris, and Muscadelle are listed as "principal" white varieties, with the lower quality varieties Colombard, Merlot Blanc, and Ugni Blanc listed as "acces-

sory" varieties.(CDC Bordeaux Homologation, June 11, 2008.)

[69] Lewin, *What Price Bordeaux?*, p. 180.

[70] White wine has been produced at Château Margaux since the 19th century, when it was sold as "vin blanc de Sauvignon." The name Pavillon Blanc de Margaux was introduced in 1920.

[71] The Médoc and Pessac-Léognan together account for about 9 million cases of wine out of Bordeaux's total of 65 million (CIVB).

[72] The figures for the Cabernets for 1958 are only approximate, because about a third was classified only as "Cabernet" (Pierre Galet, *Cépages et vignobles de France : Tome 3, Les vignobles de France, II, 2nd edition,* Tec & Doc Lavoisier, 2005; CIVB census, 1968, 1979, 1988, 2000; FranceAgriMer Stats 2009).

Chapter 3: The Bordeaux Blend

[1] Estimated proportions of Cabernet Sauvignon are; Pauillac 65%; St. Julien 64%; Margaux 54%; St. Estèphe 53%; Pessac-Léognan 53%; Haut-Médoc and Médoc (excluding communes) 48%; Graves (excluding Pessac-Léognan) 37% (from a survey by the author in 2011).

[2] Approximate distribution of Cabernet Sauvignon is: 8,500 ha in Médoc and Haut-Médoc, 1,500 ha in Graves, 750 ha in St. Emilion and its satellites, 15,000 elsewhere, making a total in all Bordeaux of 26,746 ha (CIVB and ONIVINS).

[3] Henri-Alexandre Tessier et al., *Encyclopédie méthodique,* op. cit., pp. 804-805.

[4] Proportion of the major three black varieties in major areas are:

	Cabernet Sauvignon	Merlot	Cabernet Franc
Haut Médoc & Médoc	48%	47%	1%
Graves & Pessac-Léognan	39%	54%	7%
Premières Côtes de Bordeaux	29%	56%	14%
Bourg/Blaye	21%	74%	5%
Entre-deux-Mers	26%	55%	17%
Bordeaux AOC	17%	71%	13%
St. Emilion	8%	74%	17%
Pomerol/ Fronsac	8%	77%	14%

Data from Mairie Catherine Dufour, *Les travaux du selection du Cabernet Franc en Gironde* (L'Union Girondine 1060, 44-49., Bordeaux, 2008) based on CIVB census 2000.

[5] Data source: Château Palmer.

[6] 52% Merlot, 30% Cabernet Sauvignon, 13% Petit Verdot, 5% Cabernet Franc.

[7] Under the local name of Cot, Malbec remains one of the major grape varieties in Cahors, to the southeast of Bordeaux.

[8] At source. By the time the wine reached an export market such as London, it might be significantly stronger.

[9] This was an expensive option, but oak from Stettin was considered the best (Pijassou, *Le Médoc*, p. 572). The cost of the oak amounted to almost 20% of the total cost of production (Aubin et al, *Bordeaux, Vignoble Millénaire,* p. 103).

[10] Lewin, *What Price Bordeaux?*, p. 60.

[11] At Château Latour, always one of the wines most dominated by Cabernet Sauvignon, the blend in 1855 was about two thirds Cabernet Sauvignon, 15% each of Malbec and Cabernet Franc, and about 5% Merlot (Charles Higounet, *La seigneurie et le vignoble de Château Latour,* Bordeaux: Federation Historique de Sud Ouest, 1974, p. 397).

[12] Technical analyses of Château Lafite for vintages from 1865 to 1905 showed a small range of variation in alcohol around an average of 11%, and equally low variation in acidity or solid extract (Encyclopedia Britannica, 11th edition, *Wine*, 1911, p. 722). Bordeaux wines were described in the early 19th century as having 10.5% alcohol and 0.175% tannin, not very different from those of 1855 (New International Encyclopedia, Dodd Mead, 23, 1907, p. 697).

[13] "The highest grades of claret will keep for from fifteen to eighteen years, constantly improving in delicacy. After that time they rapidly deteriorate." (Henry Wolsmar Ruaff, *The century book of facts*, The King-Richardson Company, p. 425, 1900).

[14] Lewin, *What Price Bordeaux?*, p. 176.

[15] Alexis Lichine, *Alexis Lichine's new encyclopedia of wines and spirits* (Knopf, New York, 1977), p. 115.

[16] The reason was to improve hygiene by eliminating poor barrels.

[17] Emile Peynaud pointed out that the 1982s actually had more tannin than the 1978s or 1975s but the tannins were less evident because they were hidden by fruit (Alexis Bespaloff, *Waiting for Bordeaux*, New York Magazine, October 3, 1983).

[18] IPT increased from 62 to 78 (*Lewin, What Price Bordeaux?*, p. 188).

[19] Destemming (removing the stems from the berries before fermentation) is a contributory factor, because the stalks contain harsher tannins than the skin. Because the stalks contain water, but not sugar, and absorb alcohol, this change also increased alcoholic strength by up to 0.5%. It was advocated by Emile Peynaud in his book of 1970 (translated as *Knowing and Making Wine.* New York: Wiley-Interscience, 1984, p. 146).

[20] Sugar levels estimated as potential alcohol before chaptalization: pyrazine levels estimated on basis of ripeness indicated by sugar.

[21] Jean-Bernard Delmas, *Le collection ampelographique du Château Haut Brion* (Château Haut Brion, Bordeaux, 1989), p. 22.

[22] Cocks & Féret, *Bordeaux*, 1985, 1991, 2004,

2007; Hubrecht Duijker, *The Bordeaux Atlas and Encyclopedia of Château* (London: Ebury Press, 1997); survey by the author, 2011.

[23] James Wilson, *Terroir* (Wine Appreciation Guild, San Francisco, 1998), pp. 187-191.

[24] Bernardin & Le Hong, *Crus Classés du Médoc* (Editions Sud Ouest, Bordeaux, 2010), p. 12.

[25] Lewin, *What Price Bordeaux?*, p. 78.

[26] Wilson, *Terroir*, op. cit., pp. 194-198.

[27] Wilson, *Terroir*, op. cit., p. 197.

[28] Wilson, *Terroir*, op. cit., pp. 198-199.

[29] Gérard Seguin, *Influence des facteurs naturels sur les caractères des vins*. In Traité d'ampélologie (Sciences et Technique de la vigne, Bordas, Paris, 1980); James Wilson, *Terroir* (Wine Appreciation Guild, San Francisco, 1998), p. 188.

[30] The first growths have an average of 88% in the most recent vintages; the super-seconds average around 69%. Below the super-seconds, there's a wide spread of Cabernet Sauvignon proportions, with an average at 64%. But in each group there's a prominent exception to show that there are other paths to greatness. Château Haut Brion, the only first growth outside the Médoc, has about 50% Cabernet Sauvignon; and at the top of the super-seconds in the Médoc, Château Palmer in Margaux has even less.

[31] Actually the name of Clos du Marquis originated with the Petit Clos, a separate vineyard to the south of the Grand Clos. This was presumably the source for the wine at the start of the twentieth century.

[32] Ronald Barton, *How the clarets were classified*. In The Compleat Imbiber, ed. Cyril Ray. Eriksson, New York, pp. 113-124, 1973.

[33] The vineyard has 35% Cabernet Sauvignon, 35% Cabernet Franc, and 30% Merlot, but the wine usually has one third of each variety, because Merlot is more productive (Eric d'Aramon, Château Figeac, June 2012).

[34] Ian D'Agata, *Petit Village*, Stephen Tanzer's International Wine Cellar, April 2012.

[35] "I abandoned to the second wine some cuvées that were intended for the first wines, but which did not please me… The second wines benefited from 10 tonneaux of first wines that I sacrificed because they did not reach my standard," according to Lamothe, régisseur at Château Latour in 1810 (quoted in Pijassou, *Le Médoc*, p.

[36] Second wines would use less expensive oak, have a lower proportion of Cabernet Sauvignon, and sometimes represent inferior plots of land (Pijassou, *Le Médoc*, pp. 551, 572).

[37] Paul Butel, *Grands propriétaires et production des vins du Médoc au XVIIIe siècle* (Revue historique de Bordeaux et du Département de la Gironde 12, p. 129-141, 1963).

[38] Lewin, *What Price Bordeaux?*, pp. 195-199.

[39] Michel Rolland, *Le gourou du vin* (Glénat, Grenoble, 2012), p. 154.

[40] The grand vins of the left bank on average have 52% Cabernet Sauvignon, but second wines have 44% (based on the author's survey of the 2006 vintage).

[41] Lewin, *What Price Bordeaux?*, pp. 204-205.

[42] Data based on survey of the grand cru classés.

[43] Lewin, *What Price Bordeaux?*, pp. 200-202.

Chapter 4: American Renaissance

[1] The first recorded import was in 1852. It was planted in Santa Clara Valley by the end of the decade, and in Sonoma and Napa by the 1880s. It was usually bottled under a generic name as part of a Médoc blend. A research study in 1907 concluded that California's best wines were based on Cabernet Sauvignon, but commented that growers were reluctant to plant it because of low yields (Nancy Sweet, *Cabernet Sauvignon at FPS*, FPS Grape Program Newsletter, October, 2008; Charles Sullivan, *Napa Wine*, p. 102).

[2] Inglenook started bottling varietal-labeled Cabernet immediately after Repeal, in 1933, but it is not clear if any others followed suit during the period. There was a category for "Cabernet" at wine fairs in the 1930s, but the wines were not necessarily labeled with the varietal name (Lapsley, *Bottled Poetry*, p. 17.

[3] Charles L. Sullivan, *Zinfandel : a history of a grape and its wine* (University of California Press, Berkeley, 2003), p. 41.

[4] This was not generally acknowledged (Sullivan, *Zinfandel*, op. cit., pp, 76, 79).

[5] The Santa Clara Island Wine Company labeled a wine as Zinfandel in the 1880s (Thomas Pinney, *A history of wine in America from the beginnings to prohibition*, University of California Press, Berkeley, 1992, p. 314).

[6] Used for producing a fairly rough red wine, this is still grown in South America under the name of País.

[7] Half was produced from table grapes, and of wine grapes, Zinfandel was 30%, Alicante 22%, and Carignan 15% (Pinney, *A history of wine*, op. cit., p. 63).

[8] At Repeal, the "big four" of Napa were Inglenook, Beaulieu, Beringer, and Larkmead, but although Larkmead was known for quality, it did not produce much varietal wine. Inglenook was committed to estate bottling of varietal wines; Beaulieu and Beringer produced relatively smaller proportions; Martini abandoned sweet wine production and became the largest producer of varietal-labeled wine in 1940 (Lapsley, *Bottled Poetry*, pp. 14-18, 22, 131).

[9] Cabernet Sauvignon had been planted previously, but Niebaum introduced the small-berried clone 29 (which subsequently was lost from Bordeaux), according to Larry Stone MS.

[10] The profitable year was actually the last one before it was sold (Larry Stone MS).

[11] The winery was sold to United Vintners in 1964, and then became part of Heublein when United Vintners was itself sold in 1969. In 1975, Francis Ford Coppola purchased Niebaum's former home together with 49 hectares of surrounding vineyards, and then in 1995 Heublein tired of the business and sold him the property of the Inglenook winery together with the rest of the vineyards.

[12] André Tchelistcheff, *Grapes, Wine, and Ecology* an oral history conducted 1979 by Ruth Teiser and Catherine Harroun, Regional Oral History Office, The Bancroft Library, University of California, 1983, p. 112.

[13] Alexis Lichine, Frank Schoonmaker, Maxwell Kriendler, Charles Codman, San Aron, and Ella Brennan.

[14] Stony Hill, built in 1951, was actually the first. Mondavi's was therefore really second, and Chappellet, a year later, was third. Louis Martini's winery, built in 1933, was constructed just before the end of Prohibition.

[15] Napa Valley Vintners Association.

[16] Lapsley, *Bottled Poetry*, p. 170.

[17] The major areas for Cabernet production are:

	hectares	cases of wine
Napa	7,725 (25%)	4.4 million (12%)
Sonoma	4,420 (14%)	2.75 million (3%)
San Luis Obispo	3,860 (12%)	4.4 million (14%)
Monterey	1,775 (6%)	2.4 million (7%)
Central Valley	6,400 (20%)	11 million (32%)

Percent figures are relative to all Cabernet Sauvignon in California. Production is estimated from tons of grapes produced. Data source: California Acreage and Crush reports, 2010.

[18] Data for Napa are estimated from production in tons given in California Crush Reports. Data for the Haut Médoc are taken from CIVB data for 1990-2007; estimated from overall production figures for Bordeaux for other years.

[19] A difference is that most of the white in Napa is Chardonnay, which has almost the same high reputation as its Cabernet, whereas in Bordeaux the whites are struggling.

[20] Donald G. Janelle, *Geographical Snapshots of North America*, 27th Congress of the International Geographical Union and Assembly, Guilford Press, 1992, p. 389.

[21] The starting point for calculations is a base of 50 °F (10 °C), the temperature at which the vine comes out of dormancy and begins to grow. Each region is characterized by its number of *degree days*—the sum of the average daily temperatures in excess of the base temperature.

Regions were divided into five zones from zone I (below 2,500 degree days), through zones II-IV at 500 degree day intervals, up to the top category (zone V, over 4,000 degree days) (Albert Julius Winkler et al., *General Viticulture*, University of California Press, 1962, p. 61).

[22] Lapsley, *Bottled Poetry*, pp. 47-51.

[23] A.J. Winkler et al., *General Viticulture, 2nd edition* (University of California Press, Berkeley, 1974), pp. 62-66.

[24] Winkler's data showed 2,880 degree days for Napa, 3,100 for Oakville, 3,150 for Calistoga, and 3,170 for St. Helena (A.J. Winkler et al., *General Viticulture, 2nd edition*, University of California Press, Berkeley, 1974, pop. 64-65). Weather station data for the past two decades show average growing season temperatures (in °C) of 17.7 for Napa, 18.2 for Yountville, 18.5 for St. Helena, and 19.3 for Calistoga, which would correspond to °F degree days of 2,910 for Napa, 3,100 for Yountville, 3,213 for St. Helena, and 3,515 for Calistoga (Data from Goddard Weather Center).

[25] Peter Fimrite, *Restoring Napa River to benefit both the fish and the vineyards*, San Francisco Chronicle, December 10, 2011.

[26] Lapsley, *Bottled Poetry*, pp. 206-209.

[27]

AVA	ha Planted	Wineries & Growers
Atlas Peak	600	16
Calistoga	1,000	44
Chiles Valley	400	7
Coombsville	1,360	39
Diamond Mountain	200	11
Howell Mountain	240	45
Mount Veeder	160	33
Oak Knoll	1,400	54
Oakville	2,025	71
Rutherford	1,625	86
Spring Mountain	400	25
St. Helena	400	52
Stags Leap	485	29
Wild Horse	30	1
Yountville	1,620	41

Data source: producers associations in the individual AVAs.

[28] Excluding Carneros.

[29] Doug Shafer, *A vineyard in Napa* (University of California Press, Berkeley, 2012), pp. 136-157.

[30] Swinchatt and Howell, *The Winemaker's Dance*, pp. 112-114.

[31] Degree days are calculated by summing the (average temperature –50) °F for every day in the growing season (April - October), but the exact

number depends on whether daily, weekly, or monthly averages are used.

32 Doug Shafer, *A vineyard in Napa*, op. cit., p. 69.

33 See note 27.

34 André Tchelistcheff, *Grapes, Wine, and Ecology* an oral history conducted 1979 by Ruth Teiser and Catherine Harroun, Regional Oral History Office, The Bancroft Library, University of California, 1983, p. 193.

35 The shortsightedness of the industry is indicated by the violent opposition in this period to proposals to introduce a more stringently regulated category with 85% of the named variety and 95% from the named area (Lapsley, *Bottled Poetry*, p. 205).

36 The definition is that a red Meritage must be made from a blend of at least two or more of the traditional Bordeaux varieties, with no variety comprising more than 90%. There are 250 members worldwide of the Meritage Alliance, which established "Meritage" as a trademark.

37 Bell, Foley, Newton, Pride, Ramey, Stelzner, White Rock.

38 Quoted in David Darlington, *An Ideal Wine* (Harper, New York, 2011), p. 2.

39 A cultivar of Vitis vinifera grown in the south of France.

40 A report issued by the University of California commented that AxR1 had "only moderate phylloxera resistance," but nonetheless recommended it as "the nearest approach to an all-purpose stock" (Lloyd A. Lider, *Phylloxera-resistant grape rootstocks for the Coastal Valleys of California*, Hillgardia, 27, 287-318, 1958).

41 Jeffrey Granett et al., *Biology and management of grape phylloxera* (Annual Reviews Entomology, 46, 387-412, San Francisco, 2001), p. 401.

42 According to Phil Ross at Diamond Creek, December 2011.

43 Charles Sullivan, *Napa Wine*, p. 362.

44 Some important second wines are Altagracia (Araujo), DB4 (Bryant), Napanook (Dominus), Napa Valley (Dunn's Howell Mountain),. The Maiden (Harlan), Ouverture (Opus One). Grand cuvées, that is, wines produced as the peak selection from a larger general bottling are Caymus Special Selection, Joseph Phelps Insignia, Shafer Hillside Select. Wines for which there has been no identified second label include Abreu Madrona Ranch, Schrader To-Kalon, and Screaming Eagle (but Screaming Eagle is introducing one called Second Flight from 2012).

45 It's unclear whether the Wine Institute actually coined this phrase in the 1950s-1960s or simply adapted a well known saying. It was also used on Charles Krug wine.

46 However, it was explicitly dismissed as erroneous by Albert Winkler of the University of California Davis (A.J. Winkler et al., *General Viticulture, 2nd edition*, University of California

Press, Berkeley, 1974, pp. 70-71).

47 Mick Winter, *Who owns Napa valley's vineyards?* (Wine Business Monthly, May 23, 2001).

48 Roughly 50% of the harvest in 2007 was available for purchase, compared with the one third that would be available according to the wineries' claim (USDA NASS California Crush Report). Larger discrepancies have been noted for earlier years (Sullivan, *Zinfandel*, p. 365).

49 Charles Sullivan, *Napa wine*, p. 87.

50 Eugene W. Hilgard, *Report of the agricultural work during the seasons 1883-4 and 1884-5*, University of California, Sacramento, 1886, p. 57.

51 Mondavi initially purchased 4.7 ha to construct the winery, and then obtained further plots as the result of his lawsuit with Charles Krug (which was owned by other members of his family); together with other purchases this brought his total to around 100 ha.

52 There's a certain amount of creep in use of the name To Kalon, from Crabb's original 145 ha to Mondavi's 220 ha. The vineyard is primarily planted with Cabernet Sauvignon, but in addition there are other Bordeaux varieties and the Sauvignon Blanc that forms the basis for Mondavi's Fumé Blanc white wine.

53 Including Schrader Cellars Napa Valley Beckstoffer To Kalon, Paul Hobbs Beckstoffer Oakville Vineyard, Provenance Beckstoffer To Kalon, Carter Oakville Beckstoffer To Kalon Vineyard, Realm Napa Valley Beckstoffer To Kalon Vineyard, Tor Oakville To Kalon Clone 6, Janzen Napa Valley Beckstoffer To Kalon, Atalon Oakville Beckstoffer To Kalon, Max Beckstoffer To Kalon Vineyard.

54 Beckstoffer prices the grapes in relation to the retail price of the wine, the formula being that the price per ton equals 100 times the retail bottle price. The most expensive wines from the vineyard sell for around $250 per bottle, which places the grape price at around $25,000 per ton, compared with the Napa Valley average of $4,500 per ton in 2010 (see Lettie Teague, *The most powerful grower in Napa*, Wall Street Journal, March 19, 2011).

55 Quoted in James Conway, *Napa. The story of an American Eden* (Houghton Mifflin, New York, 2002), p. 363.

56 www.winespectator.com/Wine/Daily/News /0, 1145, 1664,00.html

57 According to Phil Ross at Diamond Creek, December 2011.

58 In 2009, there were 1,812 ha in Napa versus 2,226 ha in Sonoma. Production was 138,000 tons in Napa versus 190,000 tons in Sonoma. Total value of the crop (for 2008) was approx. $400 million in Napa and $381 million in Sonoma. (California Acre and Crush Reports).

59 In 2009, Napa produced 27,000 tons of Chardonnay and 55,000 tons of Cabernet Sauvignon;

Sonoma produced 73,000 tons of Chardonnay and 41,000 tons of Cabernet Sauvignon (California Crush Report, 2009).

[60] Average growing season temperature since 1990 is 18.5 °C in Napa and 17.8 °C in Santa Rosa (data from Goddard Weather Center).

[61] There is no significant difference in the wines since year 2000 (based on a survey conducted by the author). However, California Crush Reports show that the sugar levels at harvest vary from a fraction lower to as much as 1% lower in potential alcohol in Sonoma over the past decade, possibly an indication that more alcohol reduction is practiced in Napa.

[62] In addition to Louis Martini's own production, Cabernet Sauvignon from Monte Rosso is made by M Squared (Michael Martini's own winery), Sbragia (an old friend of Michael Martini who plays with him in a rock band), Arrowood, August Briggs, Paradise Ridge, and T-vine.

[63] The favored technique was "high fermentation," in which large amounts of sugar were used to increase alcohol up to the legal limit of 17% (Gregutt, *Washington Wines and Wineries*, p. 4).

[64] Lewin, *Wine Myths and Reality*, p. 270.

[65] Stonebridge Research, *Economic Impact of Washington State Wine and Grapes*, St. Helena, CA, April 2012.

[66] *Wine Grape Release*, USDA National Agricultural Statistics Service, Washington Office, 2012.

[67] Washington gets 17.4 hours of sunshine /day during the growing season, compared with 15.4 hr in Napa Valley (Alan Busacca et al., *Geologic Guide to the Yakima Valley*, Washington Division of Geology and Earth Resources, June 2008).

[68] Lake Missoula covered 7,800 km^2 (ibid).

[69] Floods occurred roughly every 30 years over a period from 18,000 to 13,000 years ago (ibid).

[70] Most vineyards in Columbia Valley are planted in soils derived directly or indirectly from silt and sand deposited by the floods (Kevin Pogue, *Folds, floods, and fine wine: geological influences on the terroir of the Columbia Basin*, Geological Society of America, Field Guide 15, 2009).

[71]

AVA	Hectares
Columbia Valley	(excluding sub-AVAs) 3,023
Columbia Gorge	160
Yakima Valley	5,446
Walla Walla	730
Red Mountain	513
Horse Heaven	4,285
Wahluke Slope	2,680
Rattlesnake Hills	647
Snipes Mountain	285
Lake Chelan	100
Naches Heights	15
Puget Sound	72
Total	14,918

Hectares are currently planted vineyards.

[72] The AVA that covers the area (Puget Sound) has a risible 75 ha of vineyards.

[73] Region 2 in terms of degree days as opposed to region 3.

[74] Locations and establishment of vineyards:

Vineyard	AVA	Date
Red Willow	Yakima	1973
Champoux	Horse Heaven Hills	1979
Klipsun	Red Mountain	1984
Kiona	Red Mountain	1975
Ciel du Cheval	Red Mountain	1975
Pepper Bridge	Walla Walla	1991
Seven Hills	Walla Walla	1981
Sagemore	Columbia Valley	1972
DuBrul	Rattlesnake Hills	1992

[75] Based on a survey by the author in September 2012.

[76] Chateau Ste. Michelle, *Experiences with Clones*, 2006.

[77] Clone 15 from California is the same as clone 181 from France.

Chapter 5: The Pursuit of Ripeness

[1] George M. Taber, *Judgment of Paris: California vs. France and the historic 1976 Paris tasting that revolutionized wine* (Scribner, New York, 2006).

[2] Freemark Abbey was the longest established but had actually closed for some years before reopening in 1967; Heitz was founded in 1961, Spring Mountain in 1968, Chateau Montelena in 1969, Stags Leap and Veedercrest (closed in 1982) in 1972, and Clos du Val in 1973.

[3] Until 1990, Pinot Noir production was about half of Cabernet Sauvignon production. It declined to about a quarter relative to Cabernet in the nineties, and then declined again over the past decade to its present level of about 15%. In absolute terms, Pinot Noir production has been steady in Napa Valley since the mid seventies, but Cabernet production has increased about three fold. Data from California Crush Reports.

[4] Stereoscopic Views, *The vineyards and prune orchards of the Napa Valley, Cal.*, H.C. White Co., 1909.

[5] Percent is tons of Cabernet Sauvignon as proportion of all black grapes harvested in Napa Valley. Data from California Crush Reports.

[6] *The Wine Advocate*, issue 33, June 14, 1984, p. 2.

[7] *The Wine Advocate*, issue 45, June 7, 1986, p. 2.

[8] *The Wine Advocate*, issue 49, Feb 23, 1987, p. 12.

[9] *The Wine Advocate*, issue 186, Dec 23, 2009.

[10] *The Wine Advocate*, issue 194, May 2, 2011.

[11] James Laube, *A question of style at Mondavi*. Wine Spectator, July 31, 2001.

[12] Tim Mondavi, *The Mondavi controversy*, Wine Spectator, September 15, 2001.

[13] Based on the author's survey of Bordeaux 2009 vintage and of Napa Cabernet (and other reds) in September 2011. Data are plotted by tenth percentiles, i.e. the proportion at 50% Cabernet is the percent of wines with 40-49% Cabernet.

[14] California Crush Reports.

[15] Within 1.5% in the United States and Australia, but reduced to within 1% when the level is over 14% in the U.S. Within 0.5% in Europe. Within 0.3% in Argentina.

[16] Underestimation is typically about 0.5% (Julian Alston et al., *Spendide Mendaz: false label claims about high and rising alcohol content of wine*, AAEW Working Paper 82, 2011).

[17] Based on Brix levels at harvest according to California Crush Reports.

[18] Watering back is not always as bad as it seems. One producer uses a saignée (bleeding off liquid) very early, when it contains only water and sugar. "Then it's replaced with water, so all you lose is the sugar," he says.

[19] Addition of water is legal in order to allow fermentation to proceed when Brix is too high, but this effectively provides a loophole that is used to dilute the must.

[20] Vinovation, a company in Sonoma that specializes in alcohol adjustment, claims that it removes up to 1% of alcohol from California wines on average.

[21] Based on a survey by the author of Cabernet Sauvignon from the 2005 vintage and later.

[22] Based on the author's survey of wines from the left bank.

[23] Data for Napa Cabernet from Brix at harvest as stated in California Crush Reports. Data for wines of the Médoc from author's survey of alcohol levels in wines of the Grand Cru Classés. Estimate for potential alcohol before chaptalization based on historical data for use of sugar in Bordeaux (Pierre Galet, *Cépages et vignobles de France : Tome 3, Les vignobles de France, II, 2nd edition*, Tec & Doc Lavoisier, 2005, p. 713).

[24] Official figures for the extent of chaptalization show that it continued through the 1996-1999 vintages, with the extent varying from an average increase of 0.9-1.3% (Pierre Galet, *Cépages et vignobles de France : Tome 3, Les vignobles de France, II, 2nd edition*, Tec & Doc Lavoisier, 2005, p. 713). But the figures are for Bordeaux as a whole and probably apply more to Bordeaux AOC than to the Médoc or Pessac.

[25] Pierre Galet, *Cépages et vignobles de France : Tome 3, Les vignobles de France, II, 2nd edition* (Tec & Doc Lavoisier, 2005).

[26] Results obtained at the University of Bordeaux from a test plot harvested in the Médoc. Potential alcohol is calculated by assuming that 17 g/l sugar in grapes gives 1% alcohol in wine.

[27] When alcohol was stated during this period, often enough it was on a back label that said Table Wine, 11-14% alcohol.

[28] Quoted in Jordan Ross, *Balancing Quality & Yield: Impact Of Vine Age, Clone, And Vine Density*, Practical Winery and Vineyard, November, 1999.

[29] I have heard this story several times in Bordeaux. As I have been unable to confirm it directly, it may well be apocryphal, but it does capture the spirit of the era.

[30] Michel Rolland, *Le gourou du vin* (Glénat, Grenoble, 2012), p. 151.

[31] Benjamin Lewin, *The Role of Second Wines in Bordeaux*, Institute of Masters of Wine, London, 2008.

[32] Benjamin Lewin, *The Spirit of Alcohol*, World of Fine Wine, 32, 60-63, 2011.

[33] Bordeaux data are based on weighted averages of en primeur prices on the Place de Bordeaux for 175 châteaux of the Médoc communes and Pessac-Léognan. Napa data are based on weighted averages of prices for Cabernet Sauvignon grapes according to California Crush Reports. The curves are aligned on the basis of the traditional relationship that price for grapes/ton is 100 times the price of wine/ bottle.

[34] Lewin, *What Price Bordeaux?*, pp. 113-139.

[35] MKF *Wine Industry Update*, December 1989.

[36] See page 54.

Chapter 6: Mediterranean Cabernet

[1] Cabardès requires half Atlantic varieties and half Mediterranean varieties. Malepère allows eight varieties, of which Merlot is usually half in the blend.

[2] Data from FranceAgriMer Stats 2009.

[3] The inspiration for a blend of Cabernet Sauvignon and Syrah came from the belief that Jules Guyot had commented in his authoritative work on the vines of France that this was successful in Provence in the 19th century. However, I have been unable to find any reference to such a blend. Guyot extols "Carbenet-Sauvignon" in the Médoc (p. 455), remarks on the success of experiments with Carbenet and with Syra (sic) in the Var (to the east of Trévallon) (pp. 89-90), comments that both succeed in the Vaucluse (p. 213), recommends them for Tarn-et-Garonne (p. 417), but says of Bouches-du-Rhône that it was probably the Département with the greatest number of cépages, amongst which he mentions Mourvèdre, Brun Fourca, Bouteillan, Monestel, Ugni Noir, and Grenache—but neither Cabernet nor Syrah (p. 192). It is clear from his encyclopedic tome that Cabernet Sauvignon and Syrah were both grown widely over the south, but there is no specific discussion of a blend or for their planting specifically in Bouches-du-Rhône (Jules Guyot, *Etude des Vignobles de France pour servir a l'enseignement mutual de la viticulture et de la*

vinification Françaises, tome I, 2nd edition, Georges Masson, Paris, 1868).

[4] Since the average permitted yield in Bordeaux is 50 hl/ha, and the limit in a Vin de Pays is 85 hl/ha, both Bordeaux and the Languedoc could in theory produce about 15 million cases of pure Cabernet Sauvignon.

[5] Yassen Borislavov, *Bulgarian Wine Book* (Trud, Bulgaria, 2004), p. 101.

[6] Salvatore Mondini, *I vitigni stranieri da vino coltivati in Italia (Foreign wine grapes grown in Italy)*, published in Florence in 1903.

[7] Around 1600 there were vineyards in two areas: San Guido (the site of Sassicaia today) and Belvedere (farther south and closer to the coast, now part of Guado al Tasso).

[8] Colorino and Canaiolo are the other black varieties; until 1996, the white varieties Malvasia and Trebbiano were also blended in.

[9] The vines came from the Salviati estate in Migliarino, near Pisa.

[10] Marco Fini, *Sassicaia* (Centro Di della Edifimi, Firenze, 2000), pp. 42-44.

[11] Based on temperatures for July-October at the Guado al Tasso and Tignanello estates over the past twenty years (personal communication, Marco Ferrarese).

[12] Bolgheri Superiore is distinguished from Bolgheri Rosso by requiring greater maturation time in oak. The rules introduced in 1994 required 10-80% Cabernet Sauvignon, and 0-70% Merlot or Sangiovese. They changed in 2011 to allow 100% Cabernet Sauvignon, Cabernet Franc, or Merlot; Syrah is allowed up to 50%. There is a separate DOC, Bolgheri Sassicaia, just for the Sassicaia estate.

[13] Summary of super-Tuscans tasted from the coastal areas:

Producer - Wine	Varieties
Batzella - Tam	60% Cabernet Sauvignon 40% Merlot
Brancaia – Illatria	40% Cabernet Sauvignon 40% Petit Verdot 20% Cabernet Franc
Ca'Marcanda - Camarcanda	50% Merlot 40% Cabernet Sauvignon 10% Cabernet Franc
Guado al Tasso	60% Cabernet Sauvignon 30% Merlot 10% Cabernet Franc
San Guido - Sassicaia	85% Cabernet Sauvignon 15% Cabernet Franc
Michele Satta - I Castagni	70% Cabernet Sauvignon 20% Syrah 10% Teroldego

Montepeloso - Gabbro	100% Cabernet Sauvignon
Tenuta Ornellaia	55% Cabernet Sauvignon 25% Merlot 15% Cabernet Franc

[14] http://www.bolgheridoc.com.

[15] Summary of super-Tuscans tasted from the Chianti region:

Producer - Wine	Varieties
Nozzole – Il Pareto	100% Cabernet Sauvignon
Querceto - Il Sole d'Alessandro Cignale	100% Cabernet Sauvignon 90% Cabernet Sauvignon 10% Merlot
Querciabella - Camartina	70% Cabernet Sauvignon 30% Sangiovese
Rampolla - Vigna d'Alceo - Sammarco	85% Cabernet Sauvignon 15% Petit Verdot 85% Cabernet Sauvignon 15% Sangiovese
Rocca di Castagnoli - Il Buriano	100% Cabernet Sauvignon
Villa Cafaggio - Cortaccio	100% Cabernet Sauvignon

Chapter 7: Southern Challenge

[1] Lewin, *Wine Myths and Reality*, pp. 322, 327.

[2] Data sources: Instituto Nacional de Vitivinicultura, Argentina, Registro de Vinedos y Superficie; Australian Bureau of Statistics, report 1329.0; Catastro Viticola Nacional, Chile; SAWIS Statistics of Wine Grape Vines.

[3] The first grapevines have been traced back to Father Francisco de Carabantes, who brought them from Peru in 1548.

[4] There were 15,000 ha of vines at the end of the 18th century, 30,000 ha in mid 19th century, increasing sharply in the second half of the century. Production doubled between 1875 and 1884, from 5.6 million cases to 12.2 million cases (Rodrigo Alvarado, *Chilean Wine. The Heritage*, Wine Appreciation Guild, San Francisco, 2005, pp. 79, 117).

[5] San Pedro, Santa Rita (now also including Carmen), Concha y Toro, Errazuriz.

[6] French viticulturalist Claudio Gay established a research station in Santiago in 1830.

[7] Usually without detailed knowledge of the actual blend (Rafael Guilisasti, *The Carmenère Wines of Chile*, Concha y Toro, Santiago, 2007).

[8] Sauvignon Blanc is in second place, and Merlot close behind in third place (División de Protección Agrícola, Subdepart. de Viñas y Vinos,

Sistema de Declaración de Cosecha Vinos 2011.)

9 Preponderant varieties in the Cabernet-based icon wines with tasting notes in this book are:

Name	Varieties
Almaviva	Cabernet Sauvignon 70%, Carmenère 25%
Alpha M (Montes)	Cabernet Sauvignon 80% Cabernet Franc 10%
Altaïr	Cabernet Sauvignon 75% Syrah 20%
Antiyal	Carmenère 50% Cabernet Sauvignon 25% Syrah 25%
Casa Real (Concha y Toro)	Cabernet Sauvignon
Chadwick	Cabernet Sauvignon
Clos Apalta (Casa Lapostolle)	Carmenère 70% Cabernet Sauvignon 20%
Don Maximiano (Errazuriz)	Cabernet Sauvignon
Don Melchor (Concha y Toro)	Cabernet Sauvignon
Le Dix (Los Vascos)	Cabernet Sauvignon 85%
Liguai (Pérez Cruz)	Syrah 40% Carmenère 30% Cabernet Sauvignon 30%
Neyen de Apalta	Cabernet Sauvignon 60% Carmenère 40%
Seña	Cabernet Sauvignon 60% Merlot 25% Carmenère 15%
Vik	Cabernet Sauvignon 45% Carmenère 45%

10 Data sources: Instituto Nacional de Vitivinicultura, Argentina, Registro de Vinedos y Superficie, 2010; Catastro Viticola Nacional, Chile, 2009.

11 Juan Ricardo Couyoumdjian, *Vinos en Chile desde la independencia hasta el fin de la belle époque* (Historia, Santiago, 39, 23-64, 2006).

12 Patricio Tapia, *Almaviva and Don Melchor 1987-2009* (World of Fine Wine, 34, 64-66, 2011).

13 The Rappel river is where the rivers from Cachapoal and Colchagua join together to run down to the coast.

14 In the early years, while they were still sorting out the vineyard, the predominant portion was just described as Carmenère-Merlot; from the change in descriptions in later years, it seems that most of the Carmenère-Merlot, perhaps two thirds or three quarters, was actually Carmenère.

15 Quoted in Richards, *The Wines of Chile*, p. 74.

16 There's much more diurnal variation at the higher elevations and also an increase in solar radiation. Terrazas de los Andes say that at 800 meters the thermal amplitude (difference between day and night temperatures) is 13 °C, but at 1200 meters it is 16 °C.

17 This was based on a study with Malbec, but there is no reason to suppose that Cabernet Sauvignon would behave in a different way (Madeleine Stenwreth, *The effect of altitude on Malbec in Mendoza, Argentina,* Institute of Masters of Wine, Dissertation, 2008.)

18 With 17,000 ha, Stellenbosch has 17% of South Africa's vineyards. Cabernet Sauvignon is 12% of plantings in South Africa overall; it is 21% of plantings in Stellenbosch. Merlot is another 12% of Stellenbosch, so varieties for the Bordeaux blend are more than a third of plantings (SAWIS statistics, 2011).

Chapter 8: Antipodean Range

1 Black and white grape plantings are about equal in Australia.

2 They account for a smaller proportion of production because of the higher yields obtained elsewhere. Plantings and production of Cabernet Sauvignon are approximately:

	hectares	cases
Coonawarra	3,439	2.2 million
Barossa	1,462	0.6 million
Margaret River	1,050	0.7 million
Australia total	26,400	10.6 million

Data from South Australia Regional Summary reports for Coonawarra and Barossa (2012) and from Margaret River Wine for 2012 (including estimated Cabernet-Merlot blends).

3 As early as the 1950s and 1960s, Cabernet was regarded as the ultimate black grape. One indication of attitudes is that Max Schubert's intention when he set out to create Grange was to use Cabernet, but he was diverted to Shiraz by the lack of a suitable supply of high quality grapes.

4 Plantings of Cabernet and Shiraz were roughly equal as about 10% of all plantings in Australia until 1996, but since then Shiraz has increased to 25% and Cabernet Sauvignon has increased to 16% (Australian Bureau of Statistics, 1329.0 Reports, 1992-2011).

5 Produced in 2005, 2006, 2008, and 2010.

6 Recently produced in 1996 and 2004.

7 The only official weather station in McLaren Vale is at the coast where there are no vines. But data collected from private weather stations across the region by Chester Osborn of d'Arenberg show a range from very close to Barossa to a degree or more cooler (Fay Woodhouse, *The Story Behind the Stripe: A 100-year history of d'Arenberg,* John Wiley, Melbourne, 2012, p. 196).

8 Coonawarra Wine Region: regional summary report 2012, Phylloxera and Grape Industry Board of SA; http://www.margaretriverwine.org.au/aboutregion.php accessed October 2012.

9 Ratios of Cabernet to Shiraz are more or less reversed between Barossa and Coonawarra.

10 Jake Hancock and Jennifer Huggett, *The geologi-*

cal controls in Coonawarra (J. Wine Res., 15, 115-122, 2004).

[11] Mardi Longbottom et al., *Unearthing Viticulture in the Limestone Coast*, Limestone Coast Grape and Wine Industry Council, 2011.

[12] 89 ha of the allotments were planted, and Riddoch planted another 52 ha.

[13] Longbottom et al., *Unearthing Viticulture in the Limestone Coast*, op. cit., p. 159.

[14] At the time working on lupins at the University of Western Australia.

[15] There's a popular myth that Gladstones identified the soils and climate of the right bank of Bordeaux as specifically comparable (some accounts even pinpoint St. Emilion and Pomerol). In fact, he was far more circumspect in analyzing areas of Southwestern Australia in a technical paper in 1965 and then following up with reports of soil types in 1966 (John Gladstones, *The climate and soils of south-western Australia in relation to vine growing*, J. Aus. Inst. Ag. Sci., 31, 275-288, 1965; John Gladstones, *Soils and climate of the Margaret River-Busselton area: their suitability for wine grape production*, Department of Agronomy, The University of Western Australia, mimeo, 1966).

[16] By 1971, Vasse Felix, Moss Wood, and Cullen were established in the area of Wilyabrup, and Leeuwin and Cape Mentelle in Wallcliffe just south of the town of Margaret River.

[17] John Gladstones, *History of the Margaret River Viticulture region - a personal perspective*, Wine Industry Journal, November/December, 2005.

[18] Margaret River Wine Industry Association, *A vision of fine wine : stories from 30 years of Margaret River Winemaking* (1997).

[19] When Cape Mentelle recently recorked all the old wines, 40% had to be discarded.

[20] Unpublished Research Paper of the WA Dept. of Agriculture, *History of Cabernet Sauvignon*, 2012.

[21] The rule for blends is that varieties must be stated in order of their proportions in the blend, and there must be more than 5% to be included on the label. The average for a Cabernet-Merlot blend is about 70% Cabernet Sauvignon to 20% Merlot, with small amounts of other varieties (based on analysis of entries to the 2012 Margaret River Wine Show).

[22] Sensitivity to Brett depends on pH but the perceived level of acidity depends on TA (titratable acidity). pH is a logarithmic scale that measures the concentration of hydrogen ions in solution on a scale from 0 (highest acidity) to 14 (lowest acidity). A pH of 7 is neutral (pH <7 is acid, pH >7 is alkaline). Titratable acidity is the number of hydrogen ions that the acid can release into solution, which includes *both* the free hydrogen ions and the undissociated hydrogen ions. Two acids can have the same titratable acidity (that is, the same *total* number of hydrogen ions), but a strong acid will release more hydrogen ions, and therefore generate a lower pH. This means that the titratable acidity of two wines that have the same pH will not necessarily be the same, but will depend on the balance of the exact acids that are present. As a result, if the pH values of wines are adjusted to a specific, constant level, then the titratable acidity (and the perception of acidity when you taste) will not necessarily be consistent.

[23] During the 1970s some Chenin Blanc and Müller Thurgau had been planted.

[24] There are more than twenty wine producers and also some growers.

[25] 44% Merlot, 14% Cabernet Sauvignon, 7% Syrah, 6% Malbec, 5% Cabernet Franc; most of the 20% whites are Chardonnay or Sauvignon Blanc.

[26] A Gimblett Gravels wine must be 95% from the region in totality, but to carry a varietal label needs to be only 85% of that variety.

[27] Technically, Gimblett Gravels is a brand owned by an association of New Zealand wineries and winegrowers in the Hawkes Bay region of the eastern North Island.

[28] Silt content varies from 0-20% and clay content from 0-9%.

[29] Based on a survey by the author.

Chapter 9: Cults and Icons

[1] Maria Rosa Guasch-Jane et al., *The origin of the ancient Egyptian drink Shedeh revealed using LC/MS/MS* (J. Arch. Sci, 33, 98-101, 2006).

[2] Pliny the Elder, Natural History 14.6, 77 C.E.

[3] Aided by the fact they had the same proprietor (Pijassou, *Le Médoc*, p. 398).

[4] Lewin, *What Price Bordeaux?*, pp. 40-45.

[5] Setting the average price of first growths for the period 1840-1854 at 100%, Mouton was at 67%, the other second growths ranged from 65-54%, the third growths at 49-38%, the fourth growths from 45-34%, and the fifth growths from 35 to 28% (Lewin, *What Price Bordeaux?*, p. 44).

[6] Lewin, *What Price Bordeaux?*, pp. 238-241.

[7] Philippe de Rothschild, *Vive La Vigne* (Press de la Cité, Paris, 1981), p. 27.

[8] Lewin, *What Price Bordeaux?*, p. 237.

[9] Baron Philippe's influence extended far beyond elevating Mouton, and had a lasting effect when he led the first growths into bottling their own wines from 1923, which further reinforced their unique position.

[10] Some of the wines that have risen into the top 25 in the past few years are second wines, where the grand vin is already on the list, so there is even less change in terms of producers.

[11] Dewey Markham, *A history of the Bordeaux Classification*, p. 5.

[12] Diary of Samuel Pepys (London: Bell Publisher, 1900), p. 83.

[13] Pontack's stayed in business until the building

was demolished in 1780. Some consider it to have been London's first restaurant. Prices were extremely high, with Haut Brion at 7 shillings/bottle compared to 2 shillings/bottle for other quality wines.

[14] *Alexis Lichine's New Encyclopedia of Wines and Spirits* (Knopf, New York, 1977), p. 255.

[15] John Locke, *The Works of John Locke*, (Letters and Misc. Works, 1685), vol. 9, paragraph 1073.

[16] Detailed information on the price of Haut Brion before the classification is missing, but in the first half of the nineteenth century, prices were generally quoted for the four first growths (Lafite, Latour, Margaux, and Haut Brion) as a group (Dewey Markham, *A history of the Bordeaux Classification*).

[17] The most likely cause of lack of interest in the Graves was due to increased prices resulting from the English focus on the Médoc during the craze in England for "New French Clarets;" Haut Brion was immune because of the individual reputation it had already established (Dewey Markham, January 2012).

[18] Personal communication, Mission Haut Brion, February 2012.

[19] *Claret and Sauternes* (Wine and Spirits Society, London, 1920), p. 198.

[20] Quoted in Nicholas Faith, *Château Margaux* (Mitchell Beazley, London, 1991), p. 11.

[21] Quoted in Pijassou, *Le Médoc*, p. 653.

[22] Charles Cocks & Édouard Féret, *Bordeaux et ses vins classés par ordre de mérite, 1st edition* (Editions Féret, Bordeaux, 1868).

[23] Over eighteen months from February 2011 to July 2012, the Shanghai index fell to 65% of the starting value, while Lafite fell to 57%, based on prices for a bundle of vintages.

[24] Jane Anson, *The Rise and Rise of Carruades de Lafite*, Wine Business International, May 2010.

[25] 1997 was a relatively poor vintage with unreasonably high prices. Léoville Las Cases opened on the Place de Bordeaux at 68.60 compared with 76.22 for the Médoc first growths. Its second wine, Clos du Marquis, was quoted at 18.29, in the middle of the prices for second wines of the first growths (Forts de Latour 22.87, Pavillon Rouge de Margaux 19.51, Carruades de Lafite 16.01 €/bottle.) Fluctuations in prices during the en primeur campaign might explain reports that Léoville Las Cases equaled first growth prices that year, and that its second wine placed higher than the second wines of the first growths.

[26] Eric Conan, *Tempête sur les grands crus* (l'Express, November, 2005).

[27] René Pijassou, *Château Palmer. Noblesse Oblige* (Editions Stock, Paris, 1997).

[28] Pijassou, *Château Palmer*. op. cit., p. 99.

[29] Pijassou, *Château Palmer*. op. cit., p. 112.

[30] Lewin, *What Price Bordeaux?*, pp. 150-152.

[31] Decanter, July 2012, p. 15.

[32] Lewin, *What Price Bordeaux?*, p. 244.

[33]

1987	Present
Beaulieu Private Reserve	Abreu
Carmenet (Sonoma)	Anderson Conn
Caymus Special Selection	Bevan
Château Montelena	Bond Estate
Conn Creek	Cade
Diamond Creek	Colgin
Dominus	Continuum
Dunn Howell Mountain	Dana Estates
Foreman	Dominus
Groth	Harlan
Heitz Martha's Vineyard	Hundred Acre
Lyeth	Kapcsandy Family
Mayacamas	Lokoya
Mondavi Reserve	Maybach
Monticello	Outpost
Opus One	Paul Hobbs
Phelps Insignia	Phelps Insignia
Ridge Monte Bello	Plumpjack
Rubicon	Rudd
Silver Oak	Schrader Cellars
Spottswoode	Screaming Eagle
Stag's Leap Cask 23	Shafer
William Hill Gold Label	Sloan

Top Cabernet wines for mid eighties as listed in the *Wine Advocate*, issue 49, February 1987, p. 13; top producers today from average scores for wines from vintages 2004-2008 where at least three vintages are scored.

[34] It is thought that the wines were identical and that only the labels were different. Bellows had the exclusive rights to distribution on the East Coast and presumably used their own label (left); the winery label (right) essentially never changed.

[35] Walker, *Wines of Napa Valley*.

[36] The owners also produced Cabernet under the name of HL vineyards from 2001.

[37] If planting density was 2,500 vines/hectare, and yields were 40 hl/ha, 80 vines would give 1.3 hl = 14 cases. So the old vines would account for about 8% of the 1992 vintage if total production was 175 cases, which was the level reported at the time.

[38] Frank Prial, *Joseph Heitz, 81, a Standout In California Winemaking*, New York Times, December 23, 2000.

[39] Raimond Boireau, *Culture de la Vigne*, Paul Chaumas, Bordeaux, 3rd edition, 1887; Emmet H. Rixford, *The wine press and the cellar*, Payot, Upham & Co, San Francisco, 1883.

[40] Marco Fini, *Sassicaia* (Centro Di della Edifimi, Firenze, 2000).

Index